Law and the Physician:
A Practical Guide

Law and the Physician: A Practical Guide

Edward P. Richards III, J.D., M.P.H.
Associate Professor, University of Missouri-Kansas City, School of Law, Kansas City, Missouri

Katharine C. Rathbun, M.D., M.P.H.
Director and Health Officer, Topeka/Shawnee County Health Agency, Topeka, Kansas

Little, Brown and Company
Boston/Toronto/London

Copyright © 1993 by Edward P. Richards III and Katharine C. Rathbun

First Edition

All rights reserved. No part of this book may be reproduced in any form or by any electronic or mechanical means, including information storage and retrieval systems, without permission in writing from the publisher, except by a reviewer who may quote brief passages in a review.

Library of Congress Cataloging-in-Publication Data

Richards, Edward P.
    Law and the physician : a practical guide / Edward P. Richards, Katharine C. Rathbun.
      p. cm.
    Includes bibliographical references and index.
    ISBN 0-316-74417-4
    1. Medical laws and legislation—United States. I. Rathbun, Katharine C. II. Title.
    KF3821.R53 1993
    344.73′041—dc20
    [347.30441]   92-32594
                                                                               CIP

Printed in the United States of America

RRD-VA

Contents

Preface   vii

Acknowledgments   xi

I Physicians and Lawyers
1 The Legal System   3
2 Civil Litigation   15
3 Discovery   29
4 Damages   40
5 Dealing with Attorneys   50
6 Legal Standards   64
7 The Malpractice Insurance Crisis   79
8 Management of Medical Information   95

II Physicians and Patients
9 Physician-Patient Relationship   113
10 Conflicts of Interest   128
11 Consent to Medical Treatment   145
12 Special Consent   162
13 Substituted Consent and Terminal Illness   174
14 Medical Research   189

III Physicians and Other Medical Personnel
15 Delegation of Authority   215
16 Referral and Consultation   232
17 Teaching   249

- 18 Peer Review 259
- 19 The Federal Peer Review Law 271

IV Physicians and Public Health
- 20 General Public Health 287
- 21 Disease Control 301
- 22 AIDS 315
- 23 Communicable Diseases in the Workplace 332

V Physicians and the Family
- 24 Legal Aspects of Parental Rights 349
- 25 Contraception, Sterilization, and Abortion 368
- 26 Genetic Counseling and Fertility Treatment 390
- 27 Delivering Babies 412
- 28 Taking Care of Children 432

VI Physicians and Special Practice Areas
- 29 Institutional Practice: Teams, Schools, and Prisons 451
- 30 General Occupational Medicine Practice 467
- 31 Occupational Safety and Health Administration Rules on Occupational Medicine Practice 484
- 32 Access to Emergency Care 496
- 33 High-Technology Medicine and Critical Care 507
- 34 Surgery and Anesthesia 522

Glossary 535

Index 551

Preface

Over the last 30 years it has become impossible to practice medicine without conscious attention to the law. It is difficult for most physicians to see this change in terms other than increased interference with their practices. Yet in many areas of practice, the intrusion of the courts has increased physicians' freedom to treat and advise their patients. *Law and the Physician: A Practical Guide* will help physicians better understand the relationship between law and medicine. Through greater understanding it is hoped that physicians will be able to practice in greater harmony with the law. This is critical to short-term objectives such as avoiding medical malpractice lawsuits. It is also vital to the long-term goal of reducing the conflicts between law and medicine.

The objective of this book is to help practicing physicians avoid legal conflicts. Most physicians find winning a lawsuit a Pyrrhic victory. The toll in legal fees, time, and anxiety is seldom worth the satisfaction of a successful defense. This is not to say that all lawsuits can, or should, be avoided. There are times when ethical or professional principles must be defended. Unfortunately, few medical lawsuits involve a conscious choice to defend principle. Even when an important professional value is at issue, it is often compromised through the routinization of the litigation.

Most guides to law are written from the lawyer's perspective. Unfortunately, profound differences in medical and legal professional paradigms make lawyer-oriented materials of little value to physicians. No one is surprised that most attorneys are unable to understand the medical literature. Conversely, it should not be surprising that legal articles have limited utility for physicians. They may have less Latin and fewer equations, but they are no more accessible to outsiders than are medical references. The problem is most acute for the practicing physician who needs practical advice. While this book contains essential general information, it also contains chapters that are specific to different areas of medical practice. These sections should help practitioners triage their problems into those that require specific legal advice, those that are only phantom problems, and those that may be solved through common sense leavened with a little general knowledge of the law.

Medical practice is governed by personal ethics, professional standards, and legal rules. Each sets certain limits on a physician's allowable behavior. Each is confining in certain spheres and liberating in others. This book is concerned with the constraints imposed by the law. Legal conflicts arise when the law constrains behavior that is either permitted or mandated by personal or professional ideals. These conflicts may involve moral issues (such as opposition to certain types of human experimentation), economic issues (such as who should pay to care for a patient injured by medical treatment), or criminal issues (such as narcotic law violations).

There are situations where the law permits conduct that is in violation of either ethical or professional standards. We have attempted to highlight these conflicts, but this book is not an ethics text. Readers who wish to know more about these ethical dilemmas are directed to the many excellent books and articles on the subject. In general, this book is concerned with the situations in which the law is more restrictive than ethical or professional conduct. In particular, we have attempted to make this more than a book about malpractice. Medical malpractice was the issue of the 1980s, but we believe that conflicts of interest and medical business law will be the critical issues of the 1990s.

Laws exist to stabilize society. The criminal laws punish and deter those who would engage in violence or other socially disruptive conduct. The civil laws provide an alternative to violence for the resolution of personal and societal conflicts. The laws of a society are a reflection of the values of that society. The United States Constitution is a statement of the core values of our society. The United States Supreme Court tries to ensure that the actions of the legislatures and the executive officers of government conform to these core values. The legislatures must balance the wants of vocal segments of society against the greater good of the society. Both civil and criminal laws reflect this balancing. The executive branch must endeavor to carry out what are sometimes vague and frequently conflicting laws, while being responsive to its political survival. As members of the courts, legislatures, and executive offices, lawyers shape these laws. Yet it is wrong to assume that laws are the creation of lawyers. Law is a service profession, much more so than medicine. Physicians are taught to do what is good for their clients. Lawyers are taught to do what their clients want. As attorneys quickly learn, a client's wants are often different from his needs.

Since the middle of the 1970s, many physicians have viewed the law with fear and loathing. Lawyers question the medical judgment of physicians through medical malpractice litigation, accuse them of improper motives when they attempt to remove incompetent physicians from hospital medical staffs, and call them common criminals when they submit improper Medicaid or Medicare bills because of inadequate understanding of the government regulations. Legal conflict has become inseparable from medical practice. Yet it is the evolution of medicine, more than of law, that has caused this change.

Medical practice has become more technological, less personal, more a business than the traditional notion of a profession. Medicine is not alone in this metamorphosis. In many ways law has been as dramatically transformed, with perhaps a greater loss of traditional professionalism. Many of the legal problems discussed in this book arise from business arrangements or technologies that were unknown 30 years ago. More critically, they stem from practices that have evolved so quickly as to have outpaced the development of accompanying ethical and professional norms. Unfortunately, our ability to drive technological and social change has not been accompanied with an increase in moral and legal wisdom.

Most litigation involves the inadvertent violation of legal rules, violations that could have been avoided through advance legal planning. The avoidance of legal conflicts through education and planning is called preventive law. This book is a preventive law approach to medical practice, written from a medical, rather than a legal, frame of reference.

Preventive law is the legal equivalent of preventive medicine. The basic premise of both disciplines is that it is desirable to prevent problems rather than to treat them. Just as a physician interested in the health of children must be concerned with "nonmedical" problems such as wearing seat belts, a lawyer interested in reducing medical legal conflicts must be concerned with "nonlegal" problems, such as the communication between physicians sharing call. When either profession seeks to prevent future problems, it must deal with its clients in the larger context of society, rather than as isolated individuals.

Preventive law does not accept case precedents and statutes as the only source of legal knowledge. While these are valuable guides for litigation, most medical law involves legal conflicts that may be avoided through advance planning. This planning must include an understanding of both medical practice and the legal and societal expectations for medical practice.

As discussed in the chapter on Dealing with Attorneys, law and medicine have different professional paradigms. They also have extensive knowledge bases that must be integrated into preventive legal planning. Lawyers must be better informed of the realities of medical practice, but physicians must become informed about the law. Neither profession is so simple that one person can effectively practice both. A physician client can be a valuable source of expertise. Tapping this expertise requires a change in the way attorneys work with physicians and a commitment by physician clients to work with their attorneys.

Most important, this book is based on the preventive law premise that physicians, with their detailed knowledge of medical practice, can learn enough law to recognize and avoid many legal conflicts without requiring the advice of a lawyer. Physicians cannot practice medicine while looking over their shoulders for lawsuits. The goal of this book is to help physicians make law a natural part of their practice.

While we have endeavored to cover most areas of medical law, we acknowledge that some important areas, such as mental health law, have been excluded. This reflects the wish to keep the book a manageable length. The exclusion of a given topic does not reflect a value judgment about the importance of the topic. This book is divided into six parts, each with several chapters. To some extent, this division is arbitrary and there are extensive cross-references. *Law and the Physician: A Practical Guide* can be used as a reference, but it is intended to be read as a whole. Most of the chapters have bibliographies to guide the reader to more detailed materials or materials written from a different perspective from ours. Chapters that deal with controversial topics or topics that are not usually discussed in medical legal materials have specific references to supporting materials.

There are areas in which this book differs from the conventional medical legal wisdom. We have endeavored to identify these areas and explain why their analysis differs from the accepted dogma. In some cases the difference is due to our own research. In others, such as the application of business law principles to medical practice, we are drawing on statutes and cases that are not generally known in the health law community.

E. P. R.
K. C. R.

(Comments can be sent to E.P.R. via Internet at "erichards@vax1.umkc.edu")

Bibliography

Annas GJ: *Judging Medicine*. 1988.
Bloch S; Chodoff P eds.: *Psychiatric Ethics*. 2nd ed. 1991.
Brody BA; Engelhardt T eds.: *Bioethics: Readings and Cases*. 1987.
Callahan D: *What Kind of Life: The Limits of Medical Progress*. 1990.
Culver CM ed.: *Ethics at the Bedside*. 1990.
Jonsen AR: *The New Medicine and the Old Ethics*. 1990.
Kapp M; Bigot A: *Geriatrics and the Law*. 1985.
Levine RJ: *Ethics and Regulation of Clinical Research*. 2nd ed. 1988.
Macklin R: *Mortal Choices: Ethical Dilemmas in Modern Medicine*. 1987.
Pellegrino ED; Thomasma DC: *For the Patient's Good: The Restoration of Beneficence in Health Care*. 1988.
Reiser S; Dyck A; Curran W eds.: *Ethics in Medicine: Historical Perspectives and Contemporary Concerns*. 1977.
Rosner F: *Modern Medicine and Jewish Ethics*. 1986.
Veatch RM: The patient as partner: A theory of human-experimentation ethics. In *Medical Ethics Series*. Edited by D. H. Smith and R. M. Veatch. 1987.

Acknowledgments

We first thank Paul Tuller and Meg Morey for reading and critiquing the materials that eventually became the Physicians and the Family section. Their advice and counsel were invaluable. We also thank Jeff Roberts, Marc Markel, and Alan Folger, with whom E.P.R. practiced law for several years, and Dr. Charles Walter, with whom E.P.R. has written many articles.

This book greatly benefitted from the research support provided by COPIC Insurance, Inc., of Denver, Colorado. Special thanks go to Dr. K. Mason Howard, Larry Thrower, and Dr. Jerome Buckley, whose belief in the importance of risk management led to the support of the medical malpractice research project at the National Center for Preventive Law. We thank Dr. George Thomasson for the many months we spent together working on real problems in medical risk management. We especially thank Dr. Thomas M. Vernon, then Director of the Colorado Department of Health, for his leadership in managing HIV infection and his support of research into birth injuries. We also thank Dr. Richard Hoffman, Fred Wolf, and Dr. Carol Garrett, of the Colorado Department of Health.

Dr. Arnold Miller, the co-investigator on the risk management and birth injury studies, is both a friend and a valued colleague. Professor Donald C. Bross, of the C. Henry Kempe National Center for Child Abuse and Neglect, provided intellectual and moral support in working through the difficult problems caused by sexually transmitted diseases. We thank Professor Richard Grimes for contributing his eminent good sense on the politics and epidemiology of HIV and Professors Lawrence Tiffany and Donald Brodie and Doctors Jay Gold, John A. Sbarbaro, and Justus Baird for their insight into public health practice. E.P.R. particularly thanks Professor Angela Holder for her thoughtful perspective on presenting legal information to physicians and medical students.

We thank Louis Brown and Edward Dauer for establishing the National Center for Preventive Law, where the empirical research underlying much of this book was conducted. We thank Dean Robert Popper and the faculty of the University of Missouri-Kansas City, School of Law for the support that allowed the completion of this book. E.P.R. was ably assisted by Barry Bounds, Timothy Moreland, George Donovan, and Allen DeCamp.

I Physicians and Lawyers

1

The Legal System

CRITICAL POINTS
- Physicians have many different types of legal relationships.
- The laws governing medical practice vary by state.
- Legal decisions often fail to resolve the underlying controversy.
- The legal system stresses litigation rather than problem solving.

Law and medicine are based on different professional paradigms. Medicine is a science-based profession. Since knowledge of medical science is both vast and imperfect, most medical decisions are based on experiential information combined with nondeterministic rational analysis (the art of medicine). Although all physicians recognize the importance of art in medicine, most also appreciate the scientific advances that reduce the necessity of art-based practice. Art is overemphasized because we ignore how much is predetermined by science and thus taken for granted in decision making.

Law is not based on a scientific paradigm. There have been efforts to bring social science and economic analysis techniques to bear on legal problems, but these have been of limited utility. The evolution of legal theory is a nonrational social process that most resembles religious disputation. One accepts a premise and then develops an intricate set of rules and theories based on that premise. We see Marxist-based legal systems, democratic-based legal systems, and legal systems such as Islamic law that are openly derived from religious beliefs. Understanding law and lawyers requires an appreciation of legal belief systems, as well as rules.

This chapter is a brief introduction to the U.S. legal system, one characterized by a complexity stemming from the high value Americans place on pluralism and the difficulties of maintaining an eighteenth-century system of government in the late twentieth century. For nonlawyers, the most perplexing aspect of the U.S. legal system is that it is not unified. There are two primary divisions: federal law and the laws of the fifty states. These systems are divided still further into civil, criminal, and administrative divisions. This chapter also reviews the problem of the cost of legal services and the uniquely American practice of contingent fees.

LEGAL RELATIONSHIPS

The law is concerned primarily with relationships between individuals and between individuals and the state. Some legal rules apply equally to all relationships; others depend on the particulars of the relationship. The rules that apply equally to all persons—business law, constitutional rights, criminal law, and family law—define the civic role of citizens of society.

Medical practice involves several types of legal relationships. The legal rules that are unique to these relationships define the professional role of the physician in society. For example, physicians may prescribe drugs and carry out procedures that are forbidden to nonphysicians. A physician who wishes to avoid legal conflicts in a particular relationship must be aware of the legal rules governing that relationship. The first step, however, is understanding the classes of relationships that a physician may be involved in.

The State

The fundamental legal relationship is between the physician and the state and federal governments. In the United States, most of the law governing medical practice, exclusive of payment issues, is state law. The legal status of physicians is created by state law. (In contrast, the licensing of pilots is a creature of federal law.) It is the state laws that allow the practice of medicine and restrict it to physicians. While this monopoly is frequently taken for granted, there is no legal principle that would prevent a state from allowing a nurse or a layperson to practice medicine.

The physician owes the state certain duties in return for the right to practice medicine: the duty to protect the public health, the duty to practice competently, the duty to practice within the constraints established by the state laws, and the duty to help ensure that other physicians maintain proper standards of medical practice.

Patients

The physician-patient relationship arises from state statutes and common law rules. The special rights attendant to the medical license, combined with the physician's superior knowledge and access to medical care facilities, underpin the physician-patient relationship. In the past, physician paternalism and failure to give patients adequate information left the patient little power. Through informed consent doctrine and the patient's rights movement, patients have gained substantial autonomy in relation to physicians. This patient empowerment has been greatly constrained by the increasing power of third-party payers over both physicians and patients. Informed choice means little if insurers will not pay for alternative care or limit the patient's right to choose a physician.

Employees

Physicians employ personnel to aid in the practice of medicine. These persons are protected by the usual business laws governing the employer-employee relationship. In addition, the law restricts the extent to which the physician can substitute the judgment or actions of these nonphysicians for his or her own.

Paramedical Personnel

Physicians work with various nonphysician medical personnel: nurses, laboratory technicians, physician's assistants, respiratory therapists, and many others.

The law must balance the restrictions on the delegation of medical decision making to nonphysicians against the special skills that these paramedical personnel possess. While a physician's license includes the right to perform all paramedical acts, the physician often is not as skilled as the paramedical personnel in carrying out these acts.

Other Physicians
Physicians work with other physicians in three roles: as colleagues, supervisors, and competitors. Physicians have a duty to consult with other physicians when it is necessary for a patient's welfare. They must also ensure that other physicians they work with deliver good medical care. Finally, physicians must compete fairly with other physicians, resisting the temptation to use quality-of-care issues as a cover for anticompetitive activities. This has become a major area of legal conflict as medical practice has become more competitive. The United States has traditionally valued free enterprise and has strict laws governing attempts to restrict competition. Physicians must balance the need to preserve good-quality medical care against the policy of allowing the market to regulate business activities.

Employers
Approximately half of the physicians in the United States are employees rather than private practitioners. While most work for physician-controlled businesses, these increasingly resemble nonmedical businesses rather than medical partnerships. This is a recent shift from the historical domination of medicine by private practitioners. Physician employees must balance their duty to the company against their duties to the state and to individual patients. Medical law and professional standards based on a private practice model provide little guidance for employee physicians.

Institutions
Most physicians practice within an institutional setting—typically a hospital, but it may be a medical school, a clinic, or another type of health care institution. The physician may not be an employee of the institution but is still subject to the rules of the institution. These rules may increase the duty and the legal liability of the physician toward his or her patients. Violation of these rules may also imperil the physician's right to practice at the institution. Conversely, the institution owes the physician some duty of fairness in the application of its rules. Many physicians have challenged the prerogatives of hospital medical staff committees and institutional administrators.

ORIGINS OF LAW
Common law is law that evolves through judicial opinions interpreting statutes, treaties, and, in the United States, a written constitution. Civil law evolves through legislation rather than opinions of courts. The law of the original thirteen colonies was based on the English common law. This was modified by the Articles of Confederation and then the Constitution. As the United States expanded into regions originally controlled by the Spanish and French, this common law tradition was modified by the local civil law systems. This is most

obvious in Louisiana, which still retains a French- rather than an English-oriented legal system. The Spanish influence is pervasive in the legal systems of California, Texas, and several other southwestern states.

The English common law was the king's law, as distinguished from the Church's or ecclesiastical law. During the early evolution of the English legal system, the Church and the king were equally powerful. The two legal systems were separate, with the nature of the injury determining which system had jurisdiction. The U.S. Constitution ended the role of the church in the legal system. Some of the terminology and forms of the ecclesiastical courts persist, however, in the legal systems of the states that had strong state churches.

The Role of Judges

A current debate in our society is whether judges make law, and, if they do, whether that is their proper role. There is an underlying assumption that making law is a new role for judges and reflects a liberal bias in the judiciary. Common law judges were said to interpret law implicit in the statutes or precedent cases. In this sense, they found law rather than made it. It was this process of interpretation that gave life to the common law. Most critically, England had no equivalent to the U.S. Supreme Court. Parliament and the king had final authority and could overrule the courts. In the U.S. constitutional system, the Supreme Court can overrule both the president and Congress. Judges in the United States today make law just as surely as do legislators.

The difference between finding and making law may seem inconsequential, but it has profound implications. The Constitution prohibits ex post facto laws—laws that punish past conduct that was allowed at the time. This means that if a state passes a law making it a criminal offense to prescribe amphetamines, that law cannot be applied to allow the prosecution of physicians who wrote prescriptions for amphetamines before the effective date of the law. However, if a judge finds a common law rule, such as an obligation to obtain informed consent from patients, then, in theory, this is just a new interpretation of the existing law. A physician who fails to obtain informed consent for a surgery performed before the first court decision on informed consent in the state could still be sued.

From the defendants' perspective, there is little comfort in knowing that the judge did not make the law that they are accused of violating. Since the criminal law demands that the law be specific, most criminal law decisions are not retroactive. Some courts apply this same principle in civil law by making the new standards prospective when they dramatically increase a defendant's legal duties. They warn potential defendants of the new standard of conduct without allowing them to be sued for past conduct. This poses a policy problem because it denies compensation to persons previously injured by the now proscribed conduct.

The Appellate Process

The state and federal court systems have at least two levels of courts. At the first level are the trial courts. The higher levels review the decisions of the trial courts. Most of the written legal decisions come from these higher-level courts. The major problem is that more than 90 percent of lawsuits are settled before trial, and many of those that are tried are settled before a final verdict. Among those that are tried, only a small number are reviewed by higher courts. Cases become the subject of higher court review because they represent a departure from accepted law, they involve peculiar facts, or counsel made an error preparing or presenting the case. Even when a case is reviewed, the higher court may choose to uphold the trial court without an opinion. The tendency is for courts to write detailed legal opinions only when they are modifying the law.

Good law can be lost because it is so well accepted that no court bothers to write about it. The most striking example of this is in public health law (Richards 1989). Most of the public health precedents for quarantine and personal restrictions were set many years ago. Civil rights activists have convinced most public health officials that these precedents are no longer valid. As a result, they have not exercised their authority to restrain individual liberties to prevent the spread of disease. In some cases, carriers of diseases such as drug-resistant tuberculosis have been allowed to remain in the community. (See Chapters 20 and 21.) When health authorities do act, even long-delayed and controversial actions, such as closing gay bathhouses, are readily accepted by the courts (*City of New York v. New Saint Mark's Baths* 1986).

The appellate process is lengthy. In many urban jurisdictions, it takes years to get a case to trial and nearly as long to appeal the case to a higher court. Rarely is a legal issue reviewed by a higher court in less than five years. Eight to ten years is much more likely, with complex cases often appearing to be immortal. Cases involving the internment of the Americans of Japanese ancestry were still on appeal after forty years.

When the court rules, the opinion is often peripheral to the legal conflict that resulted in the litigation. This is especially common in medical jurisprudence. In the *Cruzan v. Director, Missouri Dept. of Health* (1990) case, which dealt with a family's right to terminate a patient's life support, the court made a narrow ruling on the right of a state to set evidentiary standards. (See Chapter 13.) Many landmark civil rights cases turn on arcane questions about the procedure of determining whether federal or state law applies in a given case.

The Litigation Bias

These problems with the selection of the cases and facts that give rise to legal opinions make it difficult to evaluate legal problems prospectively. There is often little congruence between real-world problems and the law as found in legal opinions. For example, most legal opinions discussing the duty of a physician to obtain the patient's informed consent also involve proved malpractice. The opinions do not discuss the malpractice because it does not involve any new issues. An attorney reading the opinion may not properly appreciate the importance of the underlying malpractice and attach too much significance to the technical requirement for informed consent.

Taken in the long view, the common law tradition has been critical to the development of our democratic traditions. In late-twentieth-century America, reliance on the common law tradition of deriving law from judicial opinions has given false direction to legal teaching and practice. The fundamental problem with deriving legal rules from published legal opinions is that most law practice does not involve litigation. Focusing on litigation ignores the role of lawyer as negotiator, conciliator, and counselor, and it distorts the attorney's perspective on the management of nonadversary situations: "From the point of view of the parties to a lawsuit, the costs are in vain; almost every litigated case is a mistake" (Fisher 1985, 151). It ignores the issue of prospective planning to prevent legal problems.

THE FEDERALIST SYSTEM

The United States has a federalist system: a central government that has certain powers, with the state as the basic unit of political power. The allocation of power between the state and federal government has been a point of contention from the Articles of Confederation to the present day. Historically, the states retained power over domestic matters. The federal government was given power over trade between the states and foreign policy issues. The federal government took greater power over domestic affairs with the Civil War, and this shifting of power increased during the 1930s as a result of the constitutional battles over the authority of the federal government to pass laws designed to end the depression. The civil rights acts passed in the 1960s and 1970s shifted the balance of power between the state and federal governments even further. The 1980s saw the federal government assume more power through mandating entitlement programs (such as Medicare and Medicaid) while reducing the federal support for these programs.

It is the federal government that determines the extent to which medical practice regulations will be uniform in the different states. In most areas of medical practice, the states maintain the central regulatory role. They license physicians, determine the tort rules under which physicians practice, and put additional restrictions on federal laws, such as the food and drug laws. This means that physicians practicing the same specialty in different states have to modify their practice in accordance with their state's laws.

The Federal Court System

The federal court system has three levels. The first level is the federal district courts. Most lawsuits brought in the federal system start in the district court (although some go directly from state courts to the U.S. Supreme Court). There are several hundred district courts, spread among 94 districts. In general, the case must be brought in the district court that is geographically related to the defendant or where the incident occurred. The choice of court is not a neutral decision. Districts differ in the way sitting judges apply the law and the willingness of their juries to award damages.

The second level is the federal courts of appeals. As the name suggests, those who believe that the district court has misapplied the law or abused its discretion in the handling of their case appeal to these courts. District courts are grouped together into 13 circuits, each with several judges who sit in panels to hear the cases appealed from the district courts within the circuit. The appeals courts within a circuit attempt to apply the law consistently within their circuit. Although they try to maintain consistency with the other circuits, they are bound only by the Congress and by U.S. Supreme Court, not the holding of the other circuits.

The third level is the U.S. Supreme Court. Some types of cases may be brought directly in the Supreme Court, but most travel from the federal district court through a circuit court of appeals, to the Supreme Court. The Supreme Court has four primary roles: determining if acts of the U.S. Congress are constitutional; reviewing state laws and court decisions for conflicts with the Constitution and acts of Congress; adjudicating conflicts between the states; and resolving conflicts between the federal circuit courts of appeals. The Supreme Court reviews only laws or court decisions that are contested in a court. It does not provide advisory opinions on the constitutionality of proposed state or federal laws. Even with this limited scope of review, the Supreme Court can decide only a small percentage of the cases that are presented to it each year. Its decision not to review a case, which allows the lower court's decision to stand, influences precedent nearly as much as the cases in which it issues an opinion. For this reason, the Supreme Court devotes substantial resources to sorting through the thousands of appeals cases presented each year.

Not every case may be brought in federal court. The case must involve federal statutes or regulations, constitutional rights, suits between states, or suits between citizens of different states. Medical malpractice cases are usually tried in state court unless one of the defendants is an employee of the federal government. Cases involving constitutional issues such as the right of privacy are brought in the federal courts. Cases involving antitrust law, racketeering law, and Medicare/Medicaid laws are brought in the federal courts because these are federal laws. A case originally brought in federal court may be sent back to the state court if the judge determines that it does not involve a federal issue. Alternatively, a case filed in state court may be sent to federal court if substantial federal questions arise as the case proceeds.

The State Court System

The state legal systems are quite diverse. Many predate the formation of the United States. The East Coast states derive from the English common law, many of the western states were influenced by the Spanish civil law, Louisiana follows the French civil law, and Texas entered the Union as an independent nation with a strong Mexican heritage.

Despite the diverse backgrounds, the state court systems tend to follow the three levels of the federal courts. The levels have different names, but the process of starting in a trial court, progressing to an appeals court, and ending up in a state supreme court is common to most of the states. In some cases that involve federal laws or constitutional rights, it is possible to appeal the state supreme court decision directly to the U.S. Supreme Court.

With these exceptions, most litigation is brought directly in the state courts. Even in medical cases brought in the federal courts, the federal court will apply state law unless the case involves a specific federal statute or a constitutional right. For example, if a Veterans' Administration physician working in Maryland is sued for medical malpractice, the case would be brought in federal court because the physician is an employee of the government. The federal court would then apply Maryland's law to determine if the physician was negligent.

One of the difficulties in writing a law book is that the laws vary greatly among the states. This is most pronounced in laws that govern financial matters and tax, but it extends to some of the laws that affect medical practice. For example, in some states, hypodermic syringes are a prescription item. Possessing them without the requisite prescription violates the state's drug paraphernalia law. In other states, these same syringes are legal to buy without a prescription and may be possessed without violating the law.

Determining Sovereignty

Determining whether state or federal law takes precedence in a given situation was a central debate among the drafters of the U.S. Constitution, and it continues to be a critical legal issue. Some powers are reserved to the states, in other areas the Congress can overrule state law, and in some areas neither the states nor the Congress may freely make law. The Constitution determines which sovereign, if any, may make laws on a topic.

The Constitution is a general document, drafted over 200 years ago, so there is a practical problem of resolving disputes over the meaning of the various sections. Fortunately, the Constitution created the U.S. Supreme Court as a referee between the Congress and the states. Shortly after its creation, the Supreme Court reserved to itself the right to determine the meaning of the Constitution. It is through this power of interpretation that the Court can declare that a law is unconstitutional—that is, that it violates the protections that are part of the Constitution.

TYPES OF LAW

The basic divisions in the U.S. legal system are the criminal, civil, and administrative. Criminal laws are statutes enacted to maintain order in society. Compensating individuals who have been injured physically or economically is a civil law problem. Administrative law is concerned with the promulgation and enforcement of regulations by administrative agencies.

Criminal Law

Criminal laws—those dealing with homicide, illegal drugs, theft, and other antisocial behavior—are enforced by agents of the state against specific persons or corporations. If a person is a victim of a crime, that person will be a witness in the prosecution of the criminal case. The victim does not prosecute the criminal case and does not have the right to determine if the state will prosecute the criminal. Although the state may do so, a victim cannot offer not to press charges if the perpetrator makes restitution. This is because the criminal law is designed to protect society as a whole rather than to compensate individuals who have been victims of criminal activity. This is why the cases are titled "State versus John Smith."

Special Characteristics of Criminal Law

Criminal law (rather than civil law) applies when a wrong harms society, as opposed to only individuals. Classic crimes, such as murder, certainly affect the rights of the individual victim. So why are they crimes rather than private lawsuits for personal injuries (torts)? Because they injure the state's ability to keep the peace. (They are also torts in that the victim may go to the civil justice system and sue for redress.) The state will have statutes that make committing murder a crime, that specify the penalty for the crime, and that establish the proof that must be offered to establish the crime. Perhaps the most consistent difference between civil and criminal law is the certainty of proof necessary to find a defendant guilty.

Crimes—violations of the state or federal criminal laws—must be proved *beyond a reasonable doubt*. Torts and other civil wrongs must be proved by a *preponderance of the evidence*. "Preponderance" is taken to mean a majority, 51 percent, or other equivalent measures that imply that the defendant more likely than not committed the act. "Beyond a reasonable doubt" is a more difficult standard to define. It defies statistical definition because of the problem of defining reasonable.

The standard of proof is higher in criminal cases for three reasons: (1) the state is a party and may bring unlimited resources to bear on the prosecution of the case; (2) a person's liberty, rather than just money, is at issue; and (3) an injured individual may seek redress through a civil action even if the accused is not prosecuted for a crime.

Defending a Criminal Case

The role of the defense attorney in a criminal case is to identify weaknesses in the prosecution's case and convince the jury that these raise a reasonable doubt about the defendant's guilt. This strategy is most successful in complex crimes that require proof of a guilty mind (the defendant intended to commit the crime). Most of the crimes discussed in this book are sins of omission, such as failure to report a communicable disease. The physician's intent does not matter; if it can be established that the report was not filed, a guilty verdict will follow. The only instances where we will deal with the issue of a guilty mind involve withdrawal of life support. In these cases, the state may raise the issue of whether the physician intended to commit active euthanasia.

The state has considerable discretion in deciding whether to prosecute a criminal case. This is not the discretion to decide that a given criminal will not be punished but the discretion not to file a case that the state does not believe it can prove. The victim of a crime may be able to pressure the state to prosecute through political means, such as media exposure, but it is not the victim's legal right to demand prosecution. Victims generate great sympathy, but the criminal act is against the state, not the victim. The victim's personal remedy is to file a tort claim in the civil courts. Unlike the criminal justice system, the civil courts may deny a person access only if the court finds that the person's lawsuit has no legal basis.

The Citizen's Duty

In general, a person is required to report criminal activity and to appear and testify as a witness if requested by the defendant or the state. This creates a conflict of interest with a patient's expectation that a physician will preserve the confidences of the physician-patient relationship. This conflict is most acute for psychiatrists: their physician-patient relationships are critically dependent on trust, and their patients are much more likely to discuss matters such as criminal activity with them. There are explicit protections for the psychiatrist-patient relationship, except as necessary to protect the lives of third persons (see Chapter 8). The law also ignores, without necessarily explicitly protecting, the nonpsychiatric physician-patient relationship. This means that a physician can be forced to divulge information if the police believe that it is necessary to prevent or investigate a crime. This does not happen often, but it does happen.

The Right to Counsel

Comparing access to legal and medical services illustrates the ambivalence of society toward the provision of essential services. Most persons believe that there is a basic right to medical treatment, a belief embodied in the extensive state and federal systems for providing medical services to indigents. The courts, however, have never accepted a constitutional right to medical care. Conversely, while the U.S. Supreme Court has found a constitutional right to legal services in several situations, society has provided only a rudimentary system for providing legal services to those who cannot afford them.

In the criminal justice system, it has been recognized that a poor person cannot exercise the right to effective counsel because of the expense. Lack of representation so compromises a criminal defendant's rights that the U.S Supreme Court requires all criminal defendants to have appointed counsel at government expense, if the defendant is unable to pay a lawyer. The court has not recognized a corresponding right to counsel in personal injury or business litigation. There is no provision of legal services for matters such as litigation to recover compensation for an injury. A person needing civil law services must purchase them in the marketplace. For legal problems that do not generate money, such as adoption proceedings or writing wills, a person either pays the attorney's fees or does without the service. For potentially money-generating situations, the contingent fee system has evolved (see Chapter 2).

Civil Law

A civil wrong may be defined in statute, or it may be established by previous court decisions. Civil lawsuits involve personal injuries, business disputes, land deals, libel and slander, and various other commercial interests. Civil law actions must be brought by an attorney hired by the injured party (the plaintiff) against the alleged wrongdoer (the defendant). The parties in a civil case may be individuals, corporations, or the state itself. Because medical malpractice is a civil law action, physicians are frequently preoccupied with civil law concerns. These lawsuits can be risky since the violation of many physician duties carries criminal penalties. These are infrequently prosecuted, but they can cost a physician his or her license and freedom. The violation of a law will also make it virtually impossible to defend any civil actions brought as a consequence of the violation.

The civil law is concerned with the peaceable resolution of disputes between individuals. Physicians often ignore the importance of this peacekeeping function. Being sued for medical malpractice is an unpleasant experience, but it is much preferable to being gunned down in the hospital corridor by an irate patient. This is an extreme example, but it has occurred. The civil courts are an imperfect but essential safety valve. It has even been argued that the delays and rituals of the process, which decrease its economic efficiency, increase its ability to cool passions and prevent violence.

Civil Remedies

Criminal courts can take away a person's freedom and even life. The civil courts are usually limited to taking away the defendant's money or prohibiting certain conduct. In the special case of family law jurisdiction, the courts may also determine the custody of children and use imprisonment to enforce their orders to pay money. In general, however, the civil courts are a useful recourse only if the defendant has enough money to pay a judgment. We are unwilling to incarcerate a person for being unable to pay a debt.

While the parties usually dispute the amount of money at issue, paying money is a logical way to resolve the dispute. The business deal has a certain value, as does the land. While the monetary value of a personal injury is more difficult to quantify, it is possible to assess the costs of medical care, lost wages, and so forth and arrive at an award that will compensate the plaintiff for injuries. This reduction of personal injuries to monetary damages is an emotional issue in medical malpractice litigation. In the case of severe injuries or injuries to children, money will not make the plaintiff whole. Few people would trade a child's health for a monetary award. Conversely, most physician defendants believe that it is their good name that is at issue rather than their insurance company's money. This debate is usually framed in terms of whether plaintiffs should be compensated for pain and suffering in addition to actual monetary losses. There are other economic concerns involved in this debate over the adequacy of awards in medical malpractice (see Chapter 4).

Nonmonetary Remedies
In certain situations, the court has the right to order that a person be prevented from or, more rarely, required to do something. This order is called an *injunction*. To obtain a temporary injunction, the plaintiff must show that the defendant's actions would cause irreparable harm and that the plaintiff has a substantial chance of prevailing in a trial. Temporary injunctions are frequently used in environmental law disputes, such as attempts to stop the clear-cutting of national forests. In these cases, a temporary injunction would be appropriate because the cutting of the trees would constitute irreparable harm.

When a temporary injunction is granted, the plaintiff must post a bond that is sufficient to compensate the defendant if the plaintiff does not prevail in the case. If the plaintiff does prevail, the bond is refunded, and the court may enter a permanent injunction to prevent the complained-of conduct. Violating an injunction is contempt of court and may be punished by a fine or imprisonment.

Injunctions are often requested in medical cases such as medical staff disputes, withdrawal of life support cases, and cases involving the treatment of children. In these cases, the complaining party attempts to convince the court that since human lives are at stake, the court must step in. In some cases, courts have ordered pregnant women not to have abortions or to submit to certain types of medical care ordered by their physicians. These are controversial actions and will be discussed in greater detail in subsequent chapters.

A new area of interest to physicians is the enforcement of personal service contracts, such as research contracts or employment contracts. The law has traditionally refused to order people to render personal services. As an example, assume that you sign a contract to perform a study for the Dreck drug company but never complete the study. Dreck is furious and sues to force you to complete the study. You offer to return the money you have been paid, but Dreck refuses, claiming that you must complete the study so approval of its drug will not be delayed. Since you have a detailed agreement as to how the study is to be conducted, why should the court refuse to force you to comply with the agreement?

Courts like to make rulings that end disputes. If the court orders you to complete the study, it will be faced with determining whether you are working fast enough, if your work is of acceptable quality, and other issues as to the performance of the contract. The court's ruling would only create new disputes. This pragmatism, combined with a reluctance to interfere in individual behavior, results in the policy of refusing to enforce personal services contracts. The court may award the plaintiff monetary damages for any extra costs entailed in having someone else complete the study.

Administrative Law

With the exception of the Defense Department and law enforcement agencies, the federal government carries out its activities through administrative agencies: the Internal Revenue Service (IRS), the Health Care Finance Administration (HCFA), the Social Security Administration, and many others. The states also operate through administrative agencies. Many of these, such as state equal employment opportunity commissions, parallel federal agencies. Others, such as boards of medical examiners, have no federal counterpart.

Except for criminal laws, most of the laws passed by Congress and the state legislatures are implemented through administrative law proceedings. In addition to enforcing laws passed by the legislatures, administrative agencies flesh out these laws with regulations. Some laws, such as the Americans with Disabilities Act, leave the agencies little latitude for regulation. For others, such as those creating public health agencies, the enabling legislation is vague, giving the agency the authority to determine the scope and detail of its regulations. Agencies must satisfy specific procedural requirements when promulgating regulations. Once the regulations are promulgated, they have the force of law.

Administrative regulations may be enforced by private courts presided over by administrative judges or in the state and federal civil courts. While administrative law proceedings are less formal than civil litigation, they often involve complex issues that are expensive and time-consuming. When administrative agencies bring civil litigation to enforce their regulations, these proceedings are punitive in nature and resemble criminal proceedings. If the legislature so provides, violations of administrative regulations may also be crimes, punishable by imprisonment. For example, physicians who violate certain HCFA rules are subject to prosecution for Medicare/Medicaid fraud.

BIBLIOGRAPHY

American Bar Association: *You and the Law.* 1990.
Blackstone W: *Commentaries on the Common Law of England.* 1765.
Brown L: *Preventive Law.* 1951.
Cardozo B: The paradoxes of legal science. In *Selected Writings of Benjamin Nathan Cardozo.* Edited by M. Hall. 1947.
City of New York v. New Saint Mark's Baths. 497 NYS2d 979, 983 (1986).
Fisher R: He who pays the piper. Harvard Business Review 1985 Mar–April:150.
Gilmore G: *The Death of Contract.* 1974.
Grad F: *The Public Health Manual.* 1990.
Holmes OW: *The Common Law.* 1881.
Kent J: *Commentaries on American Law.* 10th ed. 1860.
Pollock F; Maitland F: *The History of English Law.* 2d ed. 1898.
Richards EP: The jurisprudence of prevention: Society's right of self-defense against dangerous individuals. Hast Const LQ 1989; 16:329.
Story J: *Commentaries on the Constitution of the United States.* 1833.

2

Civil Litigation

CRITICAL POINTS
- Civil litigation is time-consuming, expensive, and emotionally draining.
- Juries rule for physicians in the majority of medical malpractice trials.
- Understanding the litigation process will help defuse physicians' fears.
- Physicians can gain some control over their cases by working closely with their attorneys.
- Physicians should try to avoid litigation through alternative dispute resolution.

One of the most serious problems in medical legal jurisprudence is the emotional impact of litigation on physicians. More than other businesspersons, physicians see litigation as a personal attack rather than one of the risks of doing business. The first step in defusing this emotional response is understanding the litigation process and its chronology. This understanding should help reduce the anxiety that comes from the seemingly random course of a lawsuit. More important, it will allow the physician to become an active participant in the preparation of the case, critical to ensuring that the physician's interests are properly protected. It has an added benefit of reducing the psychological burden of standing helplessly by while the lawsuit unfolds.

This chapter discusses the procedures that make up a civil lawsuit. Discovery, the court supervised investigation of the facts at issue in the lawsuit is discussed separately because of its special significance in medical litigation.

THE COST OF LITIGATION

Justice is expensive in the United States. Every citizen has the right to seek redress for his grievances in the courts. The problem is paying the bills. Lawyers' fees are typically $75 to $400 an hour, and associated costs can amount to tens of thousands of dollars.

If the lawyer works for a percentage of the plaintiff's award (a contingent fee), the fee must cover three costs of litigation. The first is the out-of-pocket costs and the salaries for the support personnel in the lawyer's office. Out-of-pocket costs include filing fees, court reporters, expert witness fees, copying charges, and payments for other goods and services necessary to prosecute a case. In a contested medical malpractice case, these costs usually run $20,000 to $40,000.

The second is the value of the attorney's time. In a contested malpractice case, the attorney may invest hundreds of hours of work that will never be paid for if the suit is unsuccessful. The third component is the uncertainty and delay in litigation. The attorney must invest time and cash in a case that might take years to resolve and result in no payment. The attorney may have $150,000 in direct and indirect costs at risk in a case. Plaintiff's litigation is a business gamble.

Contingent Fees

Except for large businesses and wealthy individuals, most potential plaintiffs do not have the money to pay the costs associated with litigation. There are third-party payers in law, but they are insurance companies, which usually limit their payments to defense lawyers. In the United States, this has led to entrepreneurial law, where plaintiffs' attorneys become their clients' partners to earn their fees. In other words, the attorney loans the client the value of his or her legal services in return for a percentage of the money obtained for the client.

Since few people have the resources to hire an attorney on an hourly basis, persons with valid personal injury claims would be denied their day in court if this were the only payment system. This would be an injustice. The solution adopted in the United States is the contingent fee contract. In this arrangement, attorneys take a percentage of the winnings as their fee. The clients make their claims, the attorneys have a chance to earn a fee, and the contingency aspect gives attorneys added incentive to work hard for their clients.

The contingent fee contract provides that the fees will be paid out of the money received from the defendant when a case is won or settled. Most contracts also provide that the attorney will loan the client the money to pay the out-of-pocket expenses of the case. Although the money for these expenses is styled as a loan, few attorneys attempt to collect them from the client if the recovery is less than the expenses in the case. The attorney's fee is based on a percentage of the gross recovery, without regard to the number of hours actually worked on the case. The fees are typically staged—perhaps 33 percent if the case is settled without filing a lawsuit, 40 percent after a lawsuit is filed, and 45 percent if the case must be defended on appeal. Most cases are settled after the filing of a lawsuit but before the rendering of a judgment by a court. Under this schedule, the attorney would receive 40 percent of the settlement and would be reimbursed for expenses out of the client's share.

Problems with Contingent Fees

Contingent fees are unfair because plaintiffs are not allowed to recover the cost of the fee from the defendant—that is, add the fee to the judgment awarded.

Plaintiffs must prove the economic worth of their injuries. (See Chapter 4.) In a simple case, this might be the extra medical bills and lost wages incurred as a result of the negligence. If these total $20,000 and there are no other alleged injuries, then the jury will be limited to awarding $20,000. Approximately half of that will go to paying the attorney and the costs of the litigation. Therefore the purpose of tort law—to make the plaintiff "whole" by compensating him or her for the losses due to the defendant's negligence—is not fulfilled. The plaintiff is able to recover 50 percent of the actual losses because the defendant does not have to pay the plaintiff's attorney's fees and costs of court. The problem of recovering litigation costs drives many of the claims for imaginative damages.

Contingent fees create an undue emphasis on the extent of the plaintiff's damages, and they encourage the filing and prosecution of cases with large damages but little negligence. Take the case of parents who come to the attorney's office with a brain-damaged child requiring custodial care. The potential recovery is so large that it is worth searching for any possible negligence to justify a lawsuit. Conversely, contingent fees deny access to the courts to plaintiffs with meritorious claims but low damages. Every plaintiff's medical malpractice lawyer has turned away cases in which the patient was injured by clear, even gross, negligence, but the potential recovery was too small to cover the cost of litigation. In general, if the provable damages are not in excess of $100,000, it does not make economic sense for an attorney to take the case.

In both law and medicine, it is ethically questionable to stop providing services to a client because the client cannot afford the fee. In criminal cases, the courts make it nearly impossible for an attorney to withdraw once representation has begun. As a result, criminal attorneys demand fees, which are nonrefundable, in advance. (There is also the problem of collecting from the incarcerated client.) In civil lawsuits, it is difficult to withdraw after the lawsuit has been filed. Ideally, every case will be investigated before a lawsuit has been filed. The problem is that the defense often refuses to cooperate in the investigation of a case. The plaintiff's attorney must decide whether to sue based on limited information. This encourages the filing of a case with large damages in the hope that liability can be found as the case proceeds. For an attorney, this is the most ethically responsible step. Refusing to represent the client because the defense makes it difficult to investigate the case would compromise the client's rights.

Many state legislatures are capping the fees of plaintiffs' attorneys (Birnholz 1990), typically in two ways: sliding scale caps and limits on the percentage that the attorney may charge. In the sliding scale system, the fees that the attorney may charge for small cases—those under $100,000—are unaffected. Using the previous example, in a case settled before trial, the attorney would get 40 percent ($40,000) and be reimbursed for expenses (perhaps $5,000). As the award increases, the allowable fee, as a percentage of the award, is diminished, falling to perhaps 10 percent of the proceeds over $1 million. This type of cap does not affect the initial decision to accept the case; rather, it encourages the attorney to settle the case at a discount. After a certain point in the history of a case, it acquires a settlement value. In the traditional contingent fee contract, the attorney is provided an incentive to continue to invest work and money to raise that settlement value. With a sliding scale cap, the reduced reward for increasing the value from, say, $900,000 to $1 million may not offset the work involved.

Limiting the percentage of an award that the attorney may claim as a fee affects the litigation process in a different way. Capping the percentage charged (perhaps at 25 percent) raises the threshold value for accepting a case. A case that was profitable at 40 percent ($100,000) would have to be worth $160,000 to yield the same fee at 25 percent. It has been argued that sliding scale caps prevent attorneys from gaining windfalls. Percentage caps, however, serve only to deny access to the courts.

Costs in Other Countries

The European countries, Canada, and the United Kingdom do not allow contingent fees. They also have almost no medical malpractice litigation and little personal injury litigation of any type. It is assumed that the limitation on contingent fees is responsible for the dearth of litigation. This underlies the call by many physicians and others to limit or abolish contingent fees in the United States. Although it is true that contingent fees are necessary to ensure that most individual plaintiffs access to the courts, the important question is why other counties have not adopted contingent fees. The answer is that there is a quid pro quo for this lawsuit-free climate.

In the medical context, other developed countries are less dependent on litigation because their citizens have some level of guaranteed access to medical care and rehabilitation services. In the United Kingdom, for example, the National Health Service provides medical services without regard to the cause of the injuries or the patient's personal financial status. Other social welfare agencies help with disability relief. Therefore there is no need for patients to sue to force negligent third parties to pay for the cost of their injuries. The disciplining of physicians is separate from compensating the plaintiff. A physician found to be incompetent is struck off the register rather than incurring a large litigation loss that will ultimately be paid by the other physicians in the same insurance pool.

In the United States, patients are responsible for their own medical bills and rehabilitation services. Many persons have medical insurance through their employers, but a substantial number do not. Moreover, this employment-based insurance is lost if the patient's injuries interfere with his or her ability to do the job. Politically, it is easier to leave compensation to an entrepreneurial law system rather than to address the problems of an incomplete medical care delivery system. (See Chapter 7.)

PREPARING FOR TRIAL

There are two basic types of legal systems—inquisitorial and adversary—each based on different theories of how best to find truth. In both systems, the opposing attorneys are charged with fighting for their clients; the difference in the systems stems from the role of the judge.

In an inquisitorial system, the judge may inquire into the presentation of the case and its underlying facts. In general, a judge allows the jury to hear all of the evidence in a case but tells the jury which evidence to ignore and which to give special credence. This gives the judge the ability to control the case and to ensure that justice (in a societal rather than a personal sense) is done. The attorneys in an inquisitorial system present the facts of a case in the light most favorable to their clients, but they are not permitted to withhold facts that are material to a case. In criminal prosecutions, where the state is both a party and the judge, inquisitorial systems may not provide a defendant with the protections that are inherent in an adversarial system. Conversely, in a civil action in which both parties are private citizens, the inquisitorial judge's prerogatives may result in a more objective trial than is possible in an adversarial system.

The United States has an adversarial system. The opposing attorneys have primary responsibility for controlling the development and presentation of the lawsuit. The judge acts as a referee, seeing that the rules of civil procedure are followed and that the jury is insulated from "improper" information. The attorneys may not lie but have no duty to volunteer facts that do not support their client's case. It is expected that each attorney, through discovery and courtroom confrontation, will flush out the facts concealed by the opposing side.

Supporters of the adversarial system argue that the competition between the opposing attorneys is a better guarantee of truth than inquiries by an impartial judge, but this ideal is seldom achieved. In many cases, particularly those that involve complex or technological or scientific issues, truth becomes *secondary* to the theater presented by an effective, well-financed advocate. The importance of an attractive presentation, combined with the reality that few cases actually go to trial, makes pretrial preparation the major activity of trial lawyers.

Preparing a lawsuit for trial involves a great deal of work. The facts in the case must be explored, experts must be engaged, the law must be researched, and the opposing counsel must be ritually bludgeoned. Lawyers are expected to prepare each case as if it will inevitably result in a trial, although most cases settle before trial. Most lawsuits are settled to avoid the risks of trial. In a settlement, the defendant's liability is fixed and cannot exceed the limits of the insurance policy; the plaintiff receives a certain award, even if it is less than might be awarded at trial.

Cases are tried only when the plaintiff's attorney and the defendant's attorney have greatly differing views on the settlement value of the case. While the purpose of pretrial preparation is ostensibly to allow the case to be tried, the actual purpose is to reduce the uncertainty over the valuation of the case so that a settlement can be reached.

Making a Claim

When an aggrieved person seeks legal counsel, the attorney first determines if there is a legally redressable harm. If there is, the attorney will usually contact the potential defendant and try to negotiate a settlement before filing a lawsuit. To encourage this informal resolution of claims, some states require that defendants be notified before a lawsuit is filed. Unfortunately, few medical malpractice claims are resolved prior to the filing of a lawsuit. Physicians contacted by a patient's attorney must refer the plaintiff's attorney to their medical malpractice insurance carrier. They should encourage their carriers to evaluate the case seriously before reflexively refusing to work out a settlement with the claimant. If a physician believes that the claim has merit, it is easier on all parties to resolve the claim before a lawsuit is filed.

One distressing part of malpractice litigation is that someone comes to the physician's office—a police officer or sheriff in uniform—and demands to hand the physician personally the documents alleging wrongdoing. This is called *service of process,* and it begins the timetable on the various parts of the lawsuit. The papers that begin the lawsuit, as well as papers that announce certain other critical events, are served personally to ensure that the party being sued is notified of the lawsuit. The ignominy of being served personally is preferable to missing a deadline that can irretrievably compromise a defendant's legal rights.

Defendants are always advised to accept service politely; process servers have no interest in the litigation, and there is no justification for vilifying them. There is also a risk to dodging service. Dodging service in the office may result in being served at church, the country club, or another acutely embarrassing situation.

A physician who is served legal papers should call his or her insurance company and attorney—*not* the plaintiff or the plaintiff's attorney. A copy of the papers should be retained, with the date and time of service carefully noted. Once the defendant's attorney has filed a reply to the plaintiff's allegations, most of the succeeding documents are sent to the defendant's attorney without the need for personal service.

Pleadings

Pleading is the general term for the papers that set out the plaintiff's allegations and the defendant's defenses. These pleadings go by different names in different courts. In some courts, the plaintiff's pleading is called the *complaint* and the defendant's is the *answer*. In others they are *original petition* and *answer*.

It is this initial pleading that the plaintiff must have served on the defendant. The defendant has a certain amount of time (frequently twenty days) to file a reply to the initial pleading. If the defendant has been properly served and fails to file the reply on time, the plaintiff may ask the court to rule in his or her favor as a matter of law. In most cases, the court will allow the defendant to file after the deadline but frequently requires the payment of a fine to cover the cost of the delay to the plaintiff. Since the court is not required to accept late filings, it is imperative that the plaintiff's allegations be answered on time.

The Plaintiff's Complaint

A plaintiff begins a lawsuit by formally alleging that the defendant violated a legal duty owed to the plaintiff. Historically, the common law rules for pleading a cause of action were very complex. These rules have been greatly simplified, but have a vestigial remnant in the form of the prima facie case that a plaintiff must plead in most states. (See Chapter 6.) A prima facie case is a formal statement of the facts that support the plaintiff's claim for compensation or other legal relief.

A medical malpractice lawsuit is a special instance of the general class of lawsuits that are based on the theory of negligence. To establish a prima facie case of negligence, the plaintiff must allege that:

1. The defendant had a duty to treat the plaintiff in a proper manner.
2. The defendant breached this duty.
3. The breach of the defendant's duty proximately caused the plaintiff's injuries.
4. A certain sum of money paid to the plaintiff will compensate for the injuries.

These allegations must be supported with a recitation of facts surrounding the plaintiff's injuries, but the plaintiff need not present expert opinion to support the prima facie case.

The Defendant's Answer

If the plaintiff's complaint is the first notice that the defendant has of the plaintiff's claim, the defendant's attorney will call the plaintiff's attorney before filing the answer. Although it is always best to discuss resolving claims before a lawsuit is filed, it is never too late to discuss the merits of the claim. After discussing the claim with the plaintiff's attorney, the defendant must file an answer to the complaint. The answer tells the court in what ways the plaintiff's prima facie case is defective and to assert any affirmative defenses. This is also the time to object if the case has been brought in the wrong court.

In some states, the defendant may file a denial of all of the plaintiff's allegations without addressing the specific issues raised by the plaintiff. This is called a *general denial*. The defendant may also deny the plaintiff's allegations specifically. The advantage of specifically addressing the plaintiff's allegations is that it personalizes the case for the judge. If the defendant is in the right, it is better for the judge to see the facts of the case. For example, assume that the defendant has been sued solely because his name appears on the plaintiff's medical records. If the defendant did not treat the patient and did not have any legal duties to the patient, then it is better to explain this than to file a general denial. It is frustrating for both the plaintiff's attorney and the defendant physician to fight a lawsuit for years, only to find at deposition that this physician was not involved in the patient's care.

Witnesses

The U.S. system of justice depends heavily on finding truth through the courtroom testimony of witnesses. The testimony is highly constrained by the rules of evidence and the lawyers' efforts to present only the material that is supportive to their cases and detrimental to that of their opposition. These constraints can be frustrating to witnesses, who often come away from a trial or deposition with the feeling that neither side wanted to hear the truth.

Witnesses are asked to present either facts or opinions. Most witnesses are fact witnesses; they have personal knowledge of either the incident that underlies the lawsuit or the persons involved. Anyone may testify as to facts; only an expert may present opinions. Fact witnesses are usually laypersons who have little experience in the courtroom. Cross-examination is more effective with these witnesses than with experienced expert witnesses.

An expert, such as a physician, may be called as a fact witness in areas that are outside his or her expertise. For example, a physician may have witnessed an automobile accident. A physician may be a fact witness when a case involves a person whom the physician has treated. The physician may be asked to testify as to the fact of the patient's injury, the treatment rendered, the cost of the treatment, and the current condition of the patient. These are matters of fact contained in the patient's medical record. Questions about the patient's prognosis, however, require an expert opinion. It is this requirement of special qualifications to render opinions that separates fact from expert testimony.

The most important fact witnesses are the parties themselves. The jurors' sympathy for the plaintiffs versus the defendants is an important determinant of their ultimate verdict. The plaintiffs in a medical malpractice case must convince the jury that they have been injured and that they are deserving of compensation. The defendants must convince the jury that they deserve to be vindicated. Trials are partly personality contests, but the best way for a defendant to be vindicated is to convince the jury that the medical decisions were correct.

Most litigation requires the testimony of expert witnesses. In a contract dispute over the sale of land, for example, there will be testimony by an appraiser as to the value of the land. In cases involving personal injuries, there will be testimony as to the seriousness of the patient's injuries and prognosis. In litigation involving the negligence of a person with special skills or training, there will be testimony as to whether these skills were properly exercised. For example, in medical malpractice litigation, the plaintiff must present the testimony of an expert who believes that the defendant did not care for the plaintiff properly and that this breach of professional conduct caused the plaintiff an injury. This testimony may come from a consulting physician engaged only to review the patient's medical care or from a physician who treated the patient. A treating physician who also renders an opinion on the quality of the patient's care would be both a fact witness and an expert witness.

THE TRIAL

Assuming that both parties are represented by competent counsel, cases are tried only when the opposing parties cannot agree on the value of the case. The value of a case depends on the damages, the proof of causation, and the robustness of the law under which the claim is made. In medical malpractice cases, the law is usually certain, so the disagreements center on damages and causation. Cases in which these disagreements are not resolved during pretrial preparation generally involve unusual facts. Trials are extraordinary events. They are expensive and time-consuming, and verdicts are subject to pressures beyond the issues in the case.

Movies and television give the impression that trials move quickly and are interesting; the testimony of witnesses is fast-paced and stimulating; most deceptively, the trial quickly follows the crime or accident precipitating it. In real life, trials are tedious, emotionally draining, and generally bewildering to plaintiffs and defendants alike. This conflict between expectation and reality aggravates the anxiety accompanying litigation.

Pretrial Delay

The legal procedures for collecting and authenticating information are complicated and time-consuming. (See Chapter 3.) In most jurisdictions, the discovery proceedings must be substantially complete before the attorneys can ask for a trial date. Once a trial date has been requested, the case is put in a queue with every other case set for trial. This queue is generally six months to a year long. In some urban courts, it may take two or more years to go to trial after discovery is complete.

It is the uncertainty of the process, not the delay itself, that is the most difficult aspect of the trial-setting queue. It is difficult to predict how long a trial will last, so to increase their efficiency, many courts schedule several cases for each trial date. This ensures that the court will have work to do, even if several of the cases settle right before trial. This also means that several of the cases that are set on a given date will not be tried as scheduled. The attorneys cannot be sure whether their case will be reached. To be prepared to try the case on the specified date, they must contact witnesses, prepare trial documents, and review the case with their client—time-consuming, and thus expensive, work. It is not unusual for a case to be set for trial and then postponed several times.

Courtroom Formalities

The legal preliminaries necessary to establish the qualifications of a witness are long and tedious. If the opposing attorney takes issue with the witness's qualifications or testimony, these objections will usually be discussed outside of the presence of the jury. First, the jury must be removed from the courtroom. Then the lawyers and judge spend several minutes discussing the legal issues involved, and finally the jury is brought back into the courtroom. The effect is to break up the flow of trial, making the proceedings confusing and frequently tense.

Testimony is drawn out over a prolonged period. The attorney who calls a witness asks the first questions. The person is then cross-examined (questioned) by the opposing counsel. If there are several opposing parties in the case, the attorney for each of these parties may examine the witness. The original attorney is then allowed to requestion the witness. The attorneys go around the circle until each is satisfied that testimony most favorable to their client has been elicited.

The procedure known as "invoking the rule"—a rule of civil procedure that allows a party to request that a witness be prevented from hearing the testimony of other witnesses in the trial—can be distressing to witnesses. The intent is to prevent witnesses from refreshing their memory or shaping their testimony to fit other testimony. The rule is particularly frustrating to physicians acting as expert witnesses. They will be asked to testify about the validity of other testimony that they are prevented from hearing. Since the attorneys are free to paraphrase the words of other witnesses, perhaps putting a different cast on them, the expert may be in the position of condemning another physician for something the physician did not say or do.

Trying the Act or the Person

Physician defendants win 60 to 80 percent of the medical malpractice cases that go to trial. Even when they lose, their insurance company nearly always pays the settlement.

Considering these odds in their favor, physicians should view a trial with equanimity. Most do not. Some have even committed suicide before their cases came to trial.

One of the roots of this fear is the belief that the physician's personal worth, rather than the quality of the medical care, is on trial. Most physicians believe that being found guilty of malpractice is a moral judgment equivalent to being found guilty of a crime. This belief partly reflects a misunderstanding of civil law. One is not found guilty of malpractice; one is only found liable to pay money for the injuries attributable to the malpractice.

More fundamentally, though, it reflects the correct perception that trials are about people, not actions. Although every case must meet technical legal requirements—otherwise the judge will not allow the case to go to the jury—the plaintiff must do more than present evidence on the technical elements of the case. The critical issue is that the jury must be persuaded to rule for the plaintiff.

Persuading the jury to agree with the client is the heart of the trial lawyer's art. Facts are sometimes persuasive on their own, but usually it is their presentation that is critical. Creating empathy for one's client is critical to successful litigation. (This is true even in business litigation, where the legal questions may be complex and the actual injured party a faceless corporation.) Lawyers want to focus on people rather than legal technicalities.

The best example of this technique is the case of *Texaco, Inc. v. Penzoil Co.* (1987), whose $10 billion verdict is the largest in U.S. history. The legal issue in this case was whether, and when, a contract to sell a company was formed. The damages were the loss of the value of the contract by Penzoil, a large corporation. The beneficiary of the contract was Texaco, another large corporation. The plaintiff's attorney (representing Penzoil) presented the necessary technical evidence on the contract questions, but he persuaded the jury to give his client money by personalizing the case. He was able to vest the corporate identity of Penzoil in its chairman, ostensibly a lovable Texas businessman. Texaco was identified with its New York investment bankers. The defense exacerbated its problems by rebutting the plaintiff's presentation of a human drama with dry financial and legal niceties. The verdict was achieved through trying the personalities in the case as much as trying their actions.

Attacking the Defendant

To prevail in a medical malpractice trial, the plaintiff's attorney must convince the jury that the plaintiff is more deserving than the defendant. Ideally, this would be done by building up the plaintiff; practically, it always involves some level of attack on the defendant. The plaintiff must provide testimony that the defendant's actions were below the acceptable standard of care. (See Chapter 6.) This in itself is a morally loaded accusation. The defendant's justification for his or her behavior affects the level of personal attack necessary for the plaintiff's case.

The most important consideration in assessing the strategy in a medical malpractice case is that physicians are held in high esteem in the community. Physicians win most malpractice cases that are tried because of this community respect. If the plaintiff maligns a physician whom the jury respects, the jury will be more difficult to persuade on the factual issues of the case. Conversely, if the plaintiff can successfully undermine the jury's confidence in the defendant, the defendant will suffer from the jury members' implicit comparison with their idealized notion of physicians.

These considerations also apply to attacks on the plaintiff. Attacks on the plaintiff's technical case can defeat the plaintiff entirely. Attacks on the plaintiff's character can reduce the potential damages in the case by lowering the value that the jury puts on the plaintiff's future earnings and so forth. Attacks on the plaintiff's character, if believed, can also reduce the credibility of the plaintiff's expert witnesses. While the testimony of witnesses should be seen as independent of the character of the plaintiff, if the plaintiff is not credible, it will be assumed that his or her witnesses are not credible either. There are plaintiffs (and defendants) whose personalities destroy their cases, irrespective of the underlying merits.

Trial Costs

A medical malpractice trial can take one to six weeks. A trial of a complex business case frequently takes months; some have gone on for more than a year. Trials cost each party $2,000 a day and up, depending on the number of attorneys representing the party. Expert witnesses' fees and expenses can add another $1,000 to $2,000 a day for every day or part of a day that the witness must be in court. For parties paying their own lawyers, a trial can be so expensive that any victory will be pyrrhic. For plaintiffs represented on contingency contracts, a trial increases the expenses that they must pay out of any money they receive, but it is their attorneys who bear the major expense of the trial. The time, expense, and uncertainty of a trial is the major justification for the 30 percent to 50 percent of the award that a contingent fee client must give up to the attorney.

Defendants represented by counsel paid by an insurance company must bear the costs of lost business. Although the insurance company pays all of the direct costs of the trial and these costs do not directly raise the defendant's insurance premium, they must be recouped from all of those insured in the defendant's insurance pool, including the defendant. Defense costs are a major factor in the decision to settle any lawsuit. An insured defendant may want to fight a case on principle, but it is usually a bad business decision to spend $150,000 to fight a case that could be settled for $25,000.

The most disturbing consequence of trial costs is that they allow a very well-funded party to punish an opponent, irrespective of the merits of the case. A wealthy surgeon can use litigation to force colleagues on a peer review panel to back down from limiting his or her privileges. A tobacco company can devote unlimited resources to fighting persons who sue for injuries caused by smoking.

Surviving a Trial

The more a party knows about what is happening at the trial, the easier it is to stay intellectually involved. An informed client, particularly a defendant in a medical malpractice case, is also an asset to the attorney. The client can assist with the review and organization of records, the evaluation of witnesses, the analysis of testimony, and other tasks that require special knowledge of medicine or the facts of the case. In addition to the advantage that this gives the physician's attorney, it reduces the anxiety associated with litigation by reducing the uncertainty.

Despite the salutary value of becoming a partner in their litigation, few physicians involve themselves in the preparation of their cases. There are several reasons for this lack of involvement. If the attorney is being paid by the insurance company, the physician has no short-term financial incentive to assist in the case. The attorney will hire the necessary personnel to prepare the case and bill the insurance carrier. Even when physicians are paying their own legal bills, it is unusual for an attorney to explain the potential savings that might accrue if the client assists in the case.

Attorneys cannot completely control the progress of a case through the courts. For example, an attorney may work diligently at setting the depositions in a case. If all the witnesses are available, the case can proceed; if a witness is not available, it may delay the case for months. Whenever an attorney files a motion with the court requesting action from opposing counsel, the opposing counsel has ten to sixty days to reply. Ideally for the client, the attorney will push the case forward at every opportunity. The reality of law practice is that attorneys work on so many cases simultaneously that they cannot push every one forward. This differential attention helps level out the work flow in the attorney's office, but it slows the resolution of each case. In the worst situation, the attorney becomes reactive, only responding to actions by the court or opposing counsel. If opposing counsel on the case is also in a reactive mode, the case can languish for years.

All attorneys share the problem of getting good expert witnesses and help with the preparation of cases. Even when experts are available, they are expensive and time-consuming to deal with. Few clients, insurance companies included, are willing to hire an expert witness to do more than testify in a case. Attorneys in medical malpractice cases often get by with the help of nurses and their own expertise. But even attorneys with medical degrees find that there is not enough time to be both a good lawyer and a good doctor.

POSTTRIAL PROCEDURES

At the conclusion of the trial, the judge or jury will render a *judgment:* a decision on whether the defendant owes the plaintiff money. In a *take nothing judgment,* the defendant owes the plaintiff no money.

For a certain period, the judgment may be appealed. If it is not appealed or if the court rejects the appeal, the judgment becomes payable. In some situations, the judgment is apportioned into periodic payments, but in most cases the full value of the judgment is due in cash.

If the defendant does not pay the judgment, the plaintiff may levy on (have the sheriff seize) such of the defendant's property as is necessary to pay the judgment. What may be seized is a matter of state law. In addition, in some states, the plaintiff may be able to attach a part of the defendant's earnings to pay the judgment. The defendant may declare bankruptcy. In this event, the bankruptcy court apportions the defendant's nonexempt assets (those subject to sale to pay creditors) as determined by state and federal law. When the bankruptcy is complete, tort judgments are usually discharged. Bankruptcy is a harsh remedy, but it provides the ultimate control over tort judgments.

The judgment entered in a case is final unless an affected party can convince the appeals court that it should be reversed or modified because of legal errors. A common request is that a large judgment be reduced (*remitted*) as being unsupported by the facts. In most states, the judge who tried the case has the right to order that the plaintiff take less money than the jury has awarded. If the plaintiff refuses, the judge can order that the case be retried.

When a case is accepted for review by a higher court, the attorneys prepare detailed legal analyses of the alleged errors in the case. They must also provide the appeals court with a transcript of some or all of the trial. This transcript can cost $10,000 or more, making an appeal an expensive proposition. Appeals also take time—usually two or more years. For these reasons, plaintiffs often agree to settle a case for less than the jury award if the case is accepted for appeal.

ALTERNATIVE DISPUTE RESOLUTION

Alternative dispute resolution (ADR) is the use of nonlitigation techniques to resolve legal disputes. While some tort reform legislation has sought to impose ADR in malpractice cases, ADR is primarily a private, contractual remedy. Unlike criminal law, which is concerned with protecting the interest of the state, plaintiffs are not required to file lawsuits if they are injured. An injured person can contract with a potential defendant to resolve the dispute privately. Private resolution is attractive because it can be faster, reduce the attorney's fees and preparation costs, and protect the parties' privacy.

ADR has several disadvantages. Once a person is injured and seeks legal counsel, the plaintiff's potential attorney may discourage agreeing to ADR because of the potentially lower awards; the decision makers in ADR are not as susceptible to jury sympathy arguments. The potential defendant's attorney may also discourage ADR because it is more difficult to use superior resources and delay to defeat the plaintiff's demands. From a societal perspective, ADR may allow important problems to be privately settled without proper review. Since publicity is a major part of the deterrent effect of litigation, ADR may limit the deterrent effect of the tort law.

ADR Techniques
Of the several ADR techniques, the best established is *arbitration,* an agreement to use a private individual to decide the dispute and determine the damages, if any. If a party refuses to comply with an arbitration order, it can be enforced as

a contract in the usual courts. The American Arbitration Association (AAA) provides a uniform set of rules for arbitration and a roster of approved arbitrators. In the usual agreement, each side chooses one arbitrator and these two arbitrators choose a third. Because there is a requirement that arbitrators have legal training, these arbitrators are often attorneys or retired judges.

The other techniques do not impose a binding settlement but are intended to help the parties resolve the dispute themselves. In *mediation*, each party agrees to share information with an impartial person who seeks to find areas of agreement that might otherwise be overlooked. In the simplest situation, the parties actually have common objectives but do not realize it. For example, a plaintiff may be willing to settle a $300,000 claim for as little as $100,000. The defendant, who has offered only $10,000 to the plaintiff, may be willing to pay as much as $110,000. In a lawsuit, these parties might expend enormous resources on pretrial preparation before reaching a settlement. The mediator can help them resolve the dispute without this prolonged warfare.

Mini-trials allow the parties to see what their cases will look like to a jury. These are used most commonly in disputes between corporations, but they can be useful in medical business disputes. In a mini-trial, each side's attorneys and experts present a brief (usually only a few hours) synopsis of their case. This is presented to the parties themselves rather than an arbitrator. The value of a mini-trial is that it allows a party to see the case through the eyes of the opposing counsel. In litigation, parties are carefully isolated from the opposing counsel until the trial itself. This makes the parties dependent on their own attorneys for information about the case. The attorneys, however, may not know the other side's strategy. More fundamentally, it is difficult for attorneys to remain objective while zealously representing their clients. The mini-trial ends this isolation and gives both parties more information about the nature of their case.

Implementing ADR

The major benefit of ADR is not as an alternative to disputes that have already ripened to the point that a lawsuit is about to be filed. ADR should been seen as part of a general strategy of avoiding disputes rather than just a more expeditious method of resolving them. ADR is most effective when it is incorporated in all business transactions. Many *Fortune* 500 companies are putting ADR provisions in their contracts with suppliers and corporate customers. In addition to requiring ADR should a formal dispute arise, the unavailability of litigation encourages the quick, informal resolution of disputes.

All states allow ADR for medical business disputes, and most allow it for medical malpractice claims but only if the choice of ADR is voluntary. For example, a health maintenance organization (HMO) might require persons who choose to subscribe to agree to the binding arbitration of potential medical malpractice claims. This would be acceptable as a condition of the HMO-patient contract. In contrast, the courts would likely reject an agreement with a private physician who allowed a patient to present in the office, but then required the patient to agree to arbitration before treatment. ADR agreements would never be allowed as a condition of emergency care.

In many cases, it is the malpractice insurance companies that resist ADR agreements because ADR has the potential to increase the overall payments to claimants. An efficient system for resolving disputes will allow patients with small claims to be compensated. Studies of the incidence of medical malpractice find that many more patients are injured by negligent medical care than file medical malpractice lawsuits (Harvard 1990). Some of these patients do not realize that they were the victims of malpractice, some intentionally choose not to sue their medical care providers, and some are unable to secure representation because their claim is too small. If the cost of these small claims exceeds the savings in limiting large claims and attorney's fees, then ADR will only increase the cost of insurance.

BIBLIOGRAPHY

Birnholz RM: The validity and propriety of contingent fee controls. 37 UCLA L Rev 949 (1990).

Brown L; Dauer E: Professional responsibility in nonadversarial lawyering: A review of the model rules. Am Bar Found Res J 1982; 519.

Bundy SM; Elhauge ER: Do lawyers improve the adversary system? A general theory of litigation advice and its regulation. Calif L Rev 1991; 79:313.

Center for Public Resources Legal Program: *ADR and the Courts: A Manual for Judges and Lawyers.* 1987.

Center for Public Resources Legal Program: *Containing Legal Costs: ADR Strategies for Corporations, Law Firms and Government.* 1988.

Fiss OM: Against settlement. Yale LJ 1984; 193:1073.

Lambros TD: The summary jury trial and other alternative methods of dispute resolution: A report to the Judicial Conference of the United States, Committee on the Operation of the Jury System. FRD 1984; 103:461, 465–67.

Miller FH: Medical malpractice litigation: Do the British have a better remedy? Am J Law Med 1986; 11(4):433–63.

Patients, Doctors, and Lawyers: Medical Injury, Malpractice Litigation, and Patient Compensation in New York. Report of the Harvard Medical Malpractice Study to the State of New York. 1990.

Posner R: The summary jury trial and other methods of alternative dispute resolution: Some cautionary observations. U Chi L Rev 1986; 53:366, 374.

Sokol DJ: The current status of medical malpractice countersuits. Am J Law Med 1985 Winter; 10(4):439–57.

Trail WR; Maney M: Jurisdiction, venue, and choice of law in medical malpractice litigation. J Leg Med (Chic) 1986 Dec; 7(4):403–40.

3

Discovery

CRITICAL POINTS	• Most of the process of litigation is pretrial discovery. • Discovery rules determine how medical records may be used as legal evidence. • The physician-patient privilege is more limited than the attorney-client privilege. • Legal privilege can be lost by careless record keeping.

Discovery is the process of finding (discovering) the relevant facts that must be presented to the court. Discovery by set rules is a modern innovation designed to further justice by giving both litigants access to the facts in the case. Discovery is termed a procedural rather than a substantive matter (an ironic use of language, since rules that affect the procedure of the law often have more profound effects than rules that affect the substance of the law). In most civil litigation, and especially in medical malpractice litigation, the majority of the time between the filing of the plaintiff's complaint and the point at which the case is ready for trial is taken up with discovery proceedings. These proceedings consume substantial resources and are quite expensive. A major argument for alternatives to litigation for resolving disputes is avoidance of the cost of discovery.

Understanding discovery will help physicians understand the legal role of medical records. Physicians are constantly told to keep good records, but this admonition has little force unless physicians know what constitutes a good record.

FORMS OF DISCOVERY

Discovery may be carried out by directly asking a person questions (*oral depositions*), by sending a person written questions (*interrogatories* and *depositions on written questions*), and by requesting that the person provide documents (*motions for production, subpoenas duces tecum*). The person answering the questions must refuse to answer the questions or swear that the answers provided are correct to the best of his or her knowledge. If it is later determined that the person was lying, he or she may be fined or prosecuted for perjury. If a party to the lawsuit lies, the court has the authority to direct a verdict for the opposing party.

Interrogatories

Interrogatories are written questions that may be sent to any person or legal entity who is a party to the lawsuit (plaintiff or defendant). They may not be sent to persons who are not parties to the litigation. The questions are directed to the party personally, but they are sent to the party's attorney and the attorneys representing all the other parties to the litigation. The attorney gives the questions to the client and either asks the client to prepare a set of draft answers or has a paralegal work with the client to prepare the draft.

Once the draft answers are prepared, the attorney edits this draft to prepare answers that are technically correct but provide as little information as possible. If the question is even slightly ambiguous, the attorney will refuse to provide an answer until the ambiguities have been resolved. This process of disputing the interrogatories can take several months and one or more hearings before the judge. Interrogatories can be a cost-effective way of collecting information, but in practice they are often abused.

Requests for Admissions

Like interrogatories, these may be directed only at parties to the litigation. Unlike interrogatories, however, the questions do not allow for narrative answers. Each question is phrased so that it must be answered as "admitted" or "denied." Requests for admissions are used to delineate which facts are not in issue and may thus be agreed to before trial. A typical question might be, "Admit or deny that you treated plaintiff on 23 October 1985."

Once an item has been admitted or denied, the court is reticent about allowing the answer to be changed. The party requesting the right to amend a request for admissions has the burden of convincing the court that there is a good reason that the original answer is incorrect. Conversely, the party requesting the admissions must ask simple and unambiguous questions if he or she wants the answers to be effective in court.

Depositions by Written Questions

These written questions resemble interrogatories, but they may be addressed to any person or entity, not just persons who are party to the litigation. Before a deposition on written questions is sent to the deponent, it must be sent to the other parties in the lawsuit. Any other party may object to a question or request that additional (cross) questions be asked, serving the purpose of cross-examination. (Interrogatories do not require cross-questions because there will be other opportunities to cross-examine the party.) In a deposition by written questions, a third party, such as a notary public or process server, presents the questions to the deponent. The questions are answered in the presence of the third party, who also attests that the answers are properly sworn.

In medical malpractice litigation, depositions by written questions usually are used to establish the authenticity of medical and other business records. Some states also allow depositions by written questions as proof that the charges to the patient were reasonable and customary. They must be answered by either the person who made the entry or by the custodian of the records. The custodian does not need to have personal knowledge of the entries in question to testify about the record-keeping protocol. However, the custodian must be able to answer certain legal questions for the medical records to be admissible in the court.

In the following example, the required set of questions is directed to a witness who is the custodian of records for Dr. Mary Jones:

Sample Affidavit
State your full name, residence, and occupation.
Has John Doe been treated or examined by Dr. Mary Jones?

Proof of Records
Has Dr. Jones made or caused to be made any notes, records, and/or reports of the examination and/or treatment of said patient?
Were the entries on these notes, records, and/or reports made at the time, or shortly after the time, of the transaction recorded by these entries?
Were these notes, records, and/or reports made or caused to be made by Dr. Jones in the regular course of business as a doctor or physician?
In the regular course of business at Dr. Jones's facility, did each of the persons who signed the reports contained in the record either have personal knowledge of the entries shown on the report or obtain information to make the entry from sources who had such personal knowledge?
Do you have such records as described above on John Doe?
Were these records kept as described above?
Please hand such records on John Doe to the notary public taking this deposition for photocopying and marking as exhibits to be attached to this deposition.
Have you done as requested in the preceding question? If not, why not?

Proof of Charges
Are you familiar with the charges usually and customarily made for the medical services reflected in the bills furnished as a part of the requested written records?
Please state the full amount of charges in the treatment of John Doe.
Please state whether such charges are reasonable and customary for like or similar services rendered in the vicinity in which they were incurred.
Were the services performed, as reflected in the records, necessary for the proper treatment of the patient in question?

Oral Depositions
A party may take the oral deposition of any person who has information relevant to the litigation. The person to be deposed may agree to appear at a certain time and place for the deposition, or the deposing party may ask the court to order the witness to appear. All of the parties to the litigation must be notified of the time and place for the deposition. Each party to the litigation has the right to be present and to question the witness, usually through attorneys.

At the beginning of the deposition, the witness must swear or affirm an oath to tell the truth. The deposition is recorded stenographically or electronically. If the witness might not be available for trial, a videotape is often prepared. After the deposition is completed, a transcript will be prepared so that the attorneys and the judge will be able to discuss the admissibility of each question and answer. This transcript can also be used at trial to question the credibility of (impeach) the witness if his or her testimony changes between the deposition and the trial.

The attorney requesting the deposition asks the first questions. When this attorney completes the questioning, the attorneys for the other parties ask their questions (cross-examination). When all the parties' attorneys have had their turn, the requesting attorney may ask additional questions (redirect), starting the round robin again. This process of cross-examination makes depositions time-consuming for the participants and expensive for the clients.

Requests for Production
These are written orders that may be directed only to persons who are parties to a lawsuit. A request for production describes certain documents or classes of documents and requests that the party either provide copies or produce the document at a convenient time for inspection by the requesting attorney.

These requests can be quite onerous. In business litigation, opposing counsel might request all of a company's business records for the last ten years. In medical litigation involving allegations of systematic fraud, the physician may be required to produce the records of all patients.

Motions for production are also used by defense attorneys to evaluate the plaintiff's case. These defense motions may inquire into past tax returns, employment records, divorce decrees and settlements, and any other documents that may illuminate the value of the plaintiff's case.

Motions for production can be a valuable way to develop evidence, or they may be used to harass and financially exhaust an opponent. Since they may be sent only to a party in a lawsuit, that party's attorney will review and contest unreasonable requests.

Once the items to be produced have been agreed upon, it is critical to comply fully with the request. Under no circumstances should records be destroyed after they have been requested. This can result in monetary fines. In extreme cases, when it is clear that the party intended to obstruct justice through the destruction of the documents, the judge may order that the opposing party wins the case.

Subpoenas
Subpoenas are written orders requiring that a person or documents be brought to a certain place at a certain time. Subpoenas are issued under the authority of the court, although in most situations they do not need to be approved by a judge. Subpoenas may be issued to any person; they are not restricted to the parties in the lawsuit. Subpoenas may be used to ensure the attendance of a person at a court hearing or a deposition. These subpoenas must specify the place the person is to appear and a time to appear. Subpoenas used at trials may require a person to appear at a set time, or they may request that the person be available to testify during the course of the trial. If the subpoena is not for a specified time, the judge usually makes arrangements to give the subpoenaed person adequate notice of the time when he or she is actually needed at the courthouse. In most cases, the judge will also accommodate the person's schedule as much as possible. The courts show particular deference to physicians who request a reasonable accommodation. Conversely, ignoring a subpoena, especially one to testify at a trial, can result in the refusing party's being taken into custody (arrested) and brought to the trial at the judge's convenience.

A physician who receives an unexpected personal subpoena should talk to the attorney who sent it to find out what he or she is being summoned to and why the testimony is necessary. He or she should discuss rescheduling the appearance if it is unduly burdensome. If agreements are made, the attorney must be asked to reissue the subpoena in accordance with the changes. The attorney may also agree to withdraw the subpoena and reach an informal agreement as to the time and place of the physician's appearance. The physician should request that this informal agreement be confirmed in writing and sent to him or her at once.

Subpoena Duces Tecum
These are subpoenas for physical objects. In the context of personal injury litigation, they typically request the production of medical records, calendars, office diaries, X rays, and any other physical record that concerns the medical care of a specified person. The records are usually those of the plaintiff, but an attorney may issue a subpoena for the records of any person whose medical condition is an issue in the lawsuit. In some situations, such as toxic exposure litigation, the records of many patients may be subpoenaed. The attorney is not allowed to keep the subpoenaed records but may inspect them and make copies.

It is unusual for an attorney to issue a subpoena for records without first attempting to obtain them through informal means. Since subpoenas may be issued without the approval of the court, physicians should ensure that they are valid before releasing records by calling the issuing attorney and determining the circumstances of the case. In states that have established procedures for the release of medical records, it is appropriate to ask for a signed release for the records. If the attorney is requesting records for persons other than his or her client, the physician may want to ask his or her own attorney to investigate the validity of the request. In cases that involve records with special legal protection (such as patients in a substance abuse treatment program) it may be necessary to request that the court deny (quash) the subpoena or restrict access to the records. The court may order that all patient identifiers be removed, or that the records be given to the judge, rather than the requesting attorney.

Contesting Discovery Orders
Physicians frequently receive questionable discovery requests. These may concern patients or the physicians' personal affairs. A physician who does not believe that the request is proper may ask his or her attorney about quashing it. The judge may quash it—rule that the request need not be complied with—or, more commonly, modify the request to limit the information that is provided.

CROSS-EXAMINATION

Once the discoverability of information has been determined, rules determine how to ensure the validity of the information. These include the form and necessary certifications of government documents, the acceptability of photocopies versus original copies, and, most important, whether the opposing counsel has proper opportunity to cross-examine the information.

Cross-examination is the process of elucidating the truth through the examination of the contested information by adversary attorneys. The best example of cross-examination is the examination of witnesses. Each attorney questions the witness in turn, and each is allowed to requestion the witness on matters brought out by subsequent questioners. This may take a few minutes or several weeks, depending on the complexity of the testimony. In theory this relentless questioning eventually flushes out the truth. This theory, however, is predicated on the assumption that the adversaries are sufficiently well versed in the technicalities of the witness's testimony as to recognize the truth when it makes an appearance. In practice, cross-examination of witnesses frequently illuminates little more than the relative acting skills of the examining attorneys and the witness.

Documents are also subject to cross-examination under the hearsay rule so familiar to everyone who has read a detective novel or watched a courtroom drama. Few other concepts in law arise so often and yet are so inadequately understood as the concept of hearsay. The hearsay rule is important in the medical setting because the admissibility of the medical record into the court as evidence is governed by the hearsay rule. A basic understanding of this rule is necessary to an understanding of the legal significance of medical record-keeping protocols.

The Hearsay Rule

The *hearsay rule* holds that one person cannot testify about the truth of what another person said. Witnesses can testify only as to what they heard the person in question say. For example, a nurse may testify that she heard Dr. Jones say, "I must have been drunk to have nicked that patient's intestine!" The jury could accept this as evidence of what Dr. Jones said but not as evidence that she was drunk or had nicked the intestine. These facts would need to be proved through the testimony of Dr. Jones herself or the testimony of appropriate expert witnesses.

The hearsay rule arises from the need for counsel to cross-examine every witness and document to determine its truthfulness. If a statement made out of court is accepted as evidence, the person making that statement cannot be questioned (cross-examined) about the truthfulness of it. The court demands that the person who actually made the statement be brought into the courtroom, placed under oath, and asked to repeat the statement.

If this rule were applied to the medical record, everyone who made an entry in the record would have to be called into the courtroom and asked which entries they made, why they made them, and what information they based these entries upon—an extremely time-consuming process and maybe even impossible. Because of these practical difficulties, the courts have created the business records exception to the hearsay rule: documents may be admitted into evidence without the requirement that the persons who made the entries be available for cross-examination.

Business Records Exception

Medical records are business records for the purpose of the hearsay rule. Medical record-keeping procedures must fulfill the legal requirements of the business records exception if a medical record is to be admissible in court. This exception to the hearsay rule requires that the record meet four basic tests:

1. The record was made in the regular course of the business.
2. The entry in the record was made by an employee or representative of that business who had personal knowledge of the act, event, or condition that is being recorded in the record.
3. The record was made at or near the time that the recorded act, event, or condition occurred or reasonably soon thereafter.
4. The records were kept in a consistent manner, according to a set procedure.

Entry in the Regular Course of Business

The first requirement is that the entry be made in the regular course of business. For a physician, the regular course of business is providing medical care, keeping medical records, and complying with state and federal health laws. The medical record will be admissible to prove the truth of activities related to the practice of medicine. Entries in the medical record that do not deal with the practice of medicine will not be considered to have been made in the regular course of business.

For example, if a patient seeks medical care after being involved in an automobile accident, the patient's physical condition, as described in the medical records, will be admissible as evidence in a legal proceeding. However, if the physician also entered the patient's description of the accident into the medical record, this would not be admissible because investigating accidents is not part of the regular course of business for a physician. Thus, the information about the accident would be excluded from the courtroom as hearsay.

In general, physicians should refrain from making entries into the medical record that are not directly concerned with the provision of medical care or with legal matters that are necessary to the rendering of medical care (for example, guardianship status or court orders bearing on the rendering of medical care).

Personal Knowledge
The requirement that the entry be made by someone who has personal knowledge of the event being recorded or that the information be transmitted directly to the person making the entry from someone who has personal knowledge allows a physician to dictate notes to be transcribed and put in the chart. The transcriptionist need not have any personal knowledge of the medical care rendered because he or she is getting the information from someone who is familiar with the care given.

The requirement of personal knowledge is a problem in teaching institutions. In some cases, a physician may write chart notes and summaries for a patient he or she has not personally cared for or discussed with the physician who did care for the patient. If the recording physician does nothing more than summarize data already in the medical record, there will be no problem with the personal knowledge requirement, because the physician, by reviewing the record, will have personal knowledge of the data in the record.

Problems arise when the physician draws conclusions about the patient's condition based on data in the record. Although these conclusions are incorporated in the medical record, they are not based on personal knowledge of the patient's condition. This failure of personal knowledge would be legal grounds for attacking the admissibility of the conclusions in court.

Timely Entry in the Usual Course of Business
The requirement of the law that is most frequently not complied with is that the entry be made at or near the time of the act, event, or condition described. The courts allow reasonable delay, given the circumstances of the business. Most hospitals use the JCAHO (Joint Commission on Accreditation of Healthcare Organizations) 30-day standard for completing the chart, with certain time-critical entries to be completed in 24 hours. (This does not mean that entries can be backdated. Progress notes and other daily memoranda must be made on the day to which they pertain.)

While the courts would generally ignore this delay, it is certainly questionable whether 30 days is a reasonable delay. Since both plaintiffs and defendants usually want the record admitted to court, there has been little litigation on whether medical records actually meet the requirements of the business records exception.

In theory, the most important requirement is that the records be kept in the usual course of business. This is a twofold requirement: the records must be kept in a standard, well-defined form, and they must be kept as part of the day-to-day activities of the business. This requirement goes to the accuracy of the records. It is assumed that the business does not have an incentive to lie in its routine business records. Once the business's activities are under question, however, it is assumed that there may be some incentive to slant the entries. Self-serving entries that do not relate to the factual basis of a patient's care could be challenged under this requirement.

THE LATITUDE FOR DISCOVERY

Attorneys do not have an obligation to develop and present fully the facts of a lawsuit. Because of this institutionalized obfuscation, there are elaborate rules that determine what facts may be presented to a jury and how these facts must be presented. Many of the facts developed in a case may not be presented to the jury because they are inadmissible. The test for whether a party must give a particular piece of information to an opponent is whether that information will be admissible itself or whether it may lead to admissible information.

The latitude for discovery is very broad. The trial judge controls the discovery in a case through the discretion granted in the rules of procedure for his or her jurisdiction. In theory the judge should be involved in discovery only in the rare situation of a request for information that is not admissible and has no chance of leading to admissible information. In practice it is not unusual for attorneys to contest every discovery order to inconvenience the opposition. This dilatory practice is commonly used by defense attorneys in medical malpractice litigation to deplete the plaintiff's resources.

In exercising discretion to control the discovery in a case, the judge looks for the relationship of the requested information to the facts that are necessary, either for the plaintiff to establish a prima facie case or for the defendant to rebut the plaintiff's allegations. Discoverable information in a medical malpractice case would include all of the plaintiff's medical records, information about the plaintiff's lost wages, the defendant's medical records if there were allegations of incapacity to practice medicine, various hospital records that would reflect on the treatment rendered the plaintiff, and so forth. Protected information would include the defendant's tax forms, peer review documents protected by statute, business records that did not bear on the issues in the case, and other matters that are not part of the plaintiff's prima facie case. Discovery might be contested in areas that are generally not relevant to a medical malpractice case but are at issue because of special questions raised by parties. For example, if the plaintiff pleads that the defendant lied about the risks of a treatment because the defendant was getting a kickback from the hospital to induce patients to have the treatment, then contracts and other information about the relationship between the defendant and the hospital might become discoverable.

Privileged Information

Historically, Anglo-American law did not recognize a physician-patient privilege. Unlike priests and attorneys, physicians could be examined in court, and their records were treated no differently from the records of other businesses. Most states, however, have passed laws that create a limited legal privilege for medical information. In general, a person's medical records may be used in court if that person's medical condition is at issue. A physician sued for medical malpractice must use the plaintiff's records to defend the care rendered the plaintiff. In this situation, the medical records will be admissible in court if they meet the test for business records.

Legal records are much more protected than medical records. If a physician is sued for civil damages or prosecuted for criminal misconduct, certain types of information can be protected from discovery by opposing counsel under the attorney-client privilege and the attorney work product doctrines. These doctrines protect what clients tell attorneys and what attorneys find out when investigating a lawsuit for the client.

Legal privilege, also known as the attorney-client privilege, is limited to communications between attorney and client made in anticipation of litigation. Both of these conditions—communication and anticipation of litigation—must be met if a document is to be privileged. While the legal basis for privilege is different in criminal law and civil law, the idea of communication is much the same.

To be legally privileged, a communication must pass directly from one party to the other, and it must pass intentionally. It may be written, spoken, signed, or otherwise communicated. It may not involve the actual witnessing of the illegal event. For example, one of the traditional privileges in criminal law is the protection of communications between husband and wife. This privilege is intended to preserve domestic relations. It prevents people from testifying about information they told to their spouse. If a husband is told by his wife that she has been filing fraudulent Medicare claims, he may not testify if she is prosecuted for criminal Medicare fraud. However, if he actually watches her filling out fraudulent forms on their home computer, he may be compelled to testify as to his observations.

The threat of litigation need be only potential, not imminent. For example, if a physician retained an attorney to determine if a joint venture was legal, the new information developed through the attorney's investigation would be privileged under the work product doctrine. The attorney's advice would be privileged under the attorney-client privilege. These protections apply only to what happens after the attorney is involved. The physician cannot make otherwise unprivileged information confidential just by telling it to an attorney. The attorney must be involved in the exercise of legal judgment for the privilege to apply. The attorney-client privilege is designed to encourage individuals to consult with attorneys to avoid breaking the law.

Losing the Privilege

Attorney work product is the legal work that an attorney performs or supervises. It does not include communications with the client because these are protected by the attorney-client privilege. An independent investigation that the attorney carries out for the client is work product. The key distinction involves whether the work in question contains information obtained from the client. The reason for making this distinction is that information protected by the attorney-client privilege is (almost) never available to discovery. Attorney work product is available, however, if the opposing party can show that justice would be denied if the work product was unavailable.

Assume that a defense attorney made detailed notes from a medical chart, and the chart later disappeared. The plaintiff's attorney could get access to the notes if the judge decided that this was necessary for a just proceeding. In contrast, if the physician defendant communicated incriminating information about Medicaid fraud in the patient's care, that information would be protected if the chart disappeared. The prosecutor could not obtain that information even if it was vital to the case against the physician. In practice, the distinction between attorney work product and attorney-client communications is seldom made; judges tend to protect both equally.

When privileged information is mixed with unprivileged information, the courts usually disallow the legal privilege for all the information. If a physician files a letter from defense counsel in the patient's medical record, this letter might lose its legal privilege when the plaintiff obtains the medical records. This conservative attitude stems from the underpinnings of legal privilege. Privilege is a statutory doctrine intended to encourage people to use legal counsel in the hope that this will increase compliance with the laws. (This applies only to civil law; privilege in criminal law is based on constitutional mandates.) Although the full extent of legal privilege is uncertain, the courts continue to clarify the extent of legal privilege.

BIBLIOGRAPHY

Appelbaum PS: Confidentiality in the forensic evaluation. Int J Law Psychiatry 1984; 7(3–4):285–300.

Ayer JL: "I persuaded a judge to protect my patient's secret." Leg Aspects Med Pract 1979 Jun; 7(6):25–26.

Cranford RE; Hester FA; Ashley BZ: Institutional ethics committees: Issues of confidentiality and immunity. Law Med Health Care 1985 Apr; 13(2):52–60.

Dickens BM: Legal protection of psychiatric confidentiality. Int J Law Psychiatry 1978; 1(3):255–82.

Fiscina S: Information about patients: How confidential? Leg Med 1980:247–60.

Hastings DA: Professional Standards Review Organizations and confidentiality: The question of public access to medical peer review data through the Freedom of Information Act. J Health Polit Policy Law 1981 Spring; 6(1):136–58.

Holder AR: The biomedical researcher and subpoenas: Judicial protection of confidential medical data. Am J Law Med 1986; 12(3–4):405–21.

Khajezadeh D: Patient confidentiality statutes in Medicare and Medicaid fraud investigations. Am J Law Med 1987; 13(1):105–37.

Lansing P: The conflict of patient privacy and the Freedom of Information Act. J Health Polit Policy Law 1984 Summer; 9(2):315–24.

Meisel A: Confidentiality and rape counseling. Hastings Cent Rep 1981 Aug; 11(4):5–7.

Rosner BL: Psychiatrists, confidentiality, and insurance claims. Hastings Cent Rep 1980 Dec; 10(6):5–7.

Shulman LJ: The Freedom of Information Act and Medicare costs reports. Am J Law Med 1981 Winter; 6(4):543–58.

Slovenko R: Accountability and abuse of confidentiality in the practice of psychiatry. Int J Law Psychiatry 1979; 2(4):431–54.

Southwick AF; Slee DA: Quality assurance in health care. Confidentiality of information and immunity for participants. J Leg Med (Chic) 1984 Sep; 5(3):343–97.

Taranto RG: The psychiatrist-patient privilege and third-party payers: *Commonwealth v. Kobrin*. Law Med Health Care 1986; 14(1):25–29.

Thorburn KM: When X rays show, must prison doctors tell? Hastings Cent Rep 1985 Jun; 15(3):17–18.

Vacco PJ: The physician-patient privilege: Should the pharmacist be included? J Leg Med (Chic) 1981 Sep; 2(3):399–414.

Veatch RM: Ethics committees. Advice and consent. Hastings Cent Rep 1989 Jan–Feb; 19(1):20–22.

Woodside FC III; Grote J: Will what you tell insurance investigators be kept secret? Leg Aspects Med Pract 1980 Jul; 8(7):32–34.

4

Damages

CRITICAL POINTS	• Tort law emphasizes damages over negligence. • Jury sympathy inflates awards for pain and suffering. • Plaintiffs are not allowed to recover the cost of litigation. • Most large settlements and verdicts represent the enormous cost of long-term medical care.

Damages, the amount of money necessary to "make the plaintiff whole," are the engine that drives civil law for injured individuals. If the plaintiff is personally wealthy or backed by a litigation advocacy group such as the American Civil Liberties Union, the decision to proceed with the case may be made on moral principle. Otherwise, without adequate damages to pay the plaintiff's attorney's contingent fee and provide reasonable compensation for the client, most plaintiffs will be unable to obtain representation. This is especially true of medical malpractice litigation, in which litigation expenses are very high and the jury is not allowed to compensate the plaintiff for the cost of bringing the lawsuit. Newspaper accounts of medical malpractice verdicts give the impression that juries are free to award the plaintiff any arbitrary amount of money. In reality, damages are determined by a detailed analysis of the plaintiff's losses, both financial and emotional.

DIRECT ECONOMIC DAMAGES

Direct damages are the money that plaintiffs will not get or will pay out as a consequence of their injuries. There are two classes of direct economic losses: those that have already matured as of the time of trial and those that will mature in the future. Although there may be disagreement over whether a past loss was proximately caused by the injury, the amount of these matured losses may be determined with reasonable certainty. Future losses are much more difficult to analyze. In addition to factors unique to each type of future loss, all financial prognostications are subject to the vagaries of the economy. Interest rates rise and fall, wages fluctuate, and, most important, future expenses such as medical care are difficult to estimate. Future losses also depend on projections of the plaintiff's future behavior. Every plaintiff's attorney will argue that the client would have had a meteoric rise in his or her chosen field. Every defense lawyer will argue that the plaintiff was on an inexorable slide to financial ruin. The truth usually lies between these extremes, giving the jury considerable latitude in arriving at an award. In medical malpractice litigation, direct damages usually consist of lost earnings, medical expenses, and rehabilitation and accommodation expenses.

Lost Earnings
Lost earnings are calculated by comparing the plaintiff's expected income with actual income. For past losses (those that occurred prior to trial), this calculation is usually based on the assumption that the plaintiff's earnings would have been in equilibrium. Plaintiff's expected income is assumed to include cost-of-living adjustments and scheduled promotions and raises but does not include factors such as claims that the plaintiff was about to change to a more lucrative occupation. This calculation is simple for employees and persons in stable businesses. It becomes more difficult when it involves a plaintiff in a transitory state. For example, assume that the plaintiff is just starting a private medical practice. He has been in business six months when he is severely injured in an automobile accident and he is unable to return to work. If it takes four years for his case to go to trial, he will be entitled to the earnings he lost during that period. His income during the first six months of practice probably will not be representative of what his earnings would have been when the practice was fully established. In this case, the plaintiff's counsel will need to present projections of his client's potential earnings capacity.

Future earning capacity is what the plaintiff might have earned had the injury not occurred. The damages would be this earning capacity minus projected earnings in the injured condition. This is not always a positive number. If because of injuries the plaintiff was retrained for a higher-paying job, he or she may have no damages attributable to lost earning capacity. If the plaintiff is well along in life in a dead-end job, then or her his future earning capacity may simply equal present wage plus cost-of-living adjustments.

The difficult cases involve plaintiffs starting their careers. These cases require a balancing of the plaintiff's goals against the probability of his or her achieving those goals.

Assume that the plaintiff has suffered a head injury that makes it impossible to do any job more demanding than manual labor. If the plaintiff is a successful surgeon, then his future earning capacity is fairly certain, as is his potential professional lifetime. Assuming a net income of $200,000 per year and 25 years until retirement, minus a potential income of $5,000 per year as a laborer, a first-level approximation of lost earning capacity would be ($200,000 − $5,000) × 25, or $4,875,000. If he is a first-year medical student, it is fairly certain that he would have become a physician, but his level of future financial success is much less certain. In this situation, the plaintiff's future earning capacity may be limited to the average income for physicians in general. If the plaintiff is a freshman in college, then the probability of his becoming a surgeon is further reduced, as is his ability to establish a high future earning capacity.

These assumptions about the uncertainty of the plaintiff's future may cause the jury to award him less money for lost future earning capacity, but they do not prevent the plaintiff from putting on evidence to reduce the assumption of uncertainty. If the college freshman is an honor student at Yale whose mother is a prominent surgeon and there is evidence that he intended to join her practice, the jury might assume that he had a high probability of achieving his goals. Information that tends to convince a jury that the plaintiff's goals were both reasonable and personally achievable is key to a successful claim for a large award for loss of future earning capacity.

Medical Expenses

Plaintiffs are entitled to be reimbursed for all of the medical expenses attributable to their injuries. They must first prove that the expenses were due to the defendant's conduct rather than a preexisting or coincidental condition. They must then prove that the expenses were reasonable and necessary. Finally, they must project the cost of future medical care necessitated by the injury. Each of these issues requires expert testimony, usually available from the plaintiff's treating physician. (This is true even in medical malpractice cases because it does not require questioning the competence of a fellow physician.) The defendant must then contest the plaintiff's need for medical care. This is complicated by the general assumption that a plaintiff has no incentive to submit to unnecessary medical care. Unfortunately for the defense, medical expenses have great strategic value.

Unlike medical malpractice litigation, most personal injury cases begin with a plaintiff who was in good health and suffered an acute injury. In an automobile accident case, the plaintiff must prove that the accident was due to the defendant's negligence. The plaintiff also must put on evidence that the accident caused the injuries in question. This is usually a perfunctory matter because the link between the accident and the plaintiff's injuries is obvious. The only question is whether some of the medical expenses are attributable to a preexisting condition and would have been incurred without the accident. Even if the plaintiff has chronic back pain, she may still claim that the accident aggravated her problems. The defendant will be liable for the additional expense of treating the now-worsened back pain. Determining the extent that a defendant's conduct aggravated a plaintiff's preexisting condition is difficult even in simple automobile accidents. It is frequently the pivotal issue in medical malpractice litigation.

Preexisting Illness

Unlike automobile accidents, most medical malpractice litigation involves plaintiffs with substantial preexisting illness. These cases require expert testimony on the issue of causation—the extent that the defendant's negligence increased the patient's medical costs. If the patient has a serious chronic disease, it may be impossible to prove that the physician's negligence increased the cost of the patient's care. This fact, combined with the patient's limited earning capacity, makes it very difficult to establish sufficient damages to justify bringing a medical malpractice lawsuit on behalf of an elderly, chronically ill patient.

There are two classes of cases in which the defendant causes an injury independent of the patient's preexisting illness or condition. A small number are pure accidents, unrelated to questions about medical judgment. Typical of these are slips and falls in the hospital, burns from improperly grounded electrosurgical devices, and the patient's receiving medications and procedures meant for a different patient. It is usually easy to separate the medical costs of these mishaps from the patient's overall medical care. The more difficult cases are those in which the patient has a self-limited or curable medical condition and suffers a severe injury from medical treatment—for example, birth trauma cases and anesthesia-related injuries in otherwise healthy persons undergoing elective procedures such as orthopedic surgery. The plaintiff may have difficulty in proving that the defendant was negligent, but once negligence has been established, the excess medical costs are obvious.

Future Medical Costs
The uncertainty of future medical expenses makes them controversial. Projecting future medical costs requires a long-term prognosis for both the plaintiff and the economy. Given the recent inflation rate for health care, any projection of the cost of care 30 years in the future will result in an astronomical number. The plaintiff's most certain evidence of future medical needs is the current cost of the needed medical care. If the plaintiff requires constant care, the jury's starting point is the current cost of these services. To attack the plaintiff's projections successfully, the defendant must convince the jury that the plaintiff's condition will improve. Conversely, the defendant's position is strongest when the plaintiff is not currently in need of medical care.

Awards for future medical expenses underlie many large jury verdicts. The largest awards are for persons who will require long-term skilled nursing case, augmented with acute medical services. Central nervous system injuries are perhaps the most expensive, especially given the legal assumption that the patient will have the same life span as an uninjured person of the same age. Although respiratory and other complications greatly decrease the average survival of severely brain-injured patients or those with high spinal cord injuries, the law is concerned with the theoretical possibility of a long life, not its statistical probability. It is the cost of future medical rehabilitative services that makes birth injury cases so expensive.

Rehabilitation and Accommodation
The plaintiff is entitled to rehabilitation and retraining expenses. These are also to the defendant's benefit if they increase the plaintiff's earning capacity or reduce his or her need for custodial care. They are detrimental to the plaintiff's case if they create the impression that the plaintiff may recover from the injuries. Plaintiff's attorneys do not stress the extent to which their clients might be rehabilitated. Insurance companies exacerbate this problem by not offering the plaintiff money for rehabilitation expenses immediately. The ideal situation for the plaintiff's attorney is to convince the jury that the client might have been rehabilitated but for the callous refusal of the defendant to pay the claim, but now it is too late.

A plaintiff who has been disabled or requires special care is entitled to the cost of any housing modifications necessary to facilitate his or her care. These may be as simple as installing wheelchair ramps or as costly as buying the plaintiff a house to ensure that his or her medical needs will be met. The plaintiff is also entitled to the value of any property damaged as a result of the defendant's conduct. This is usually an automobile, but it may be a house (plane crash cases), a horse, or any other property involved in the accident.

The Strategic Value of Medical Expenses
Medical expenses and lost wages are the most concrete elements of the plaintiff's damages. The plaintiff's personal characteristics often undermine his or her lost

wage claims, but medical expense claims do not depend on the personal worth of the plaintiff. In many medical malpractice cases, the medical expenses are the bulk of the plaintiff's damages, driving the enormous awards in cases involving brain-damaged babies. Juries are not reticent about giving the plaintiff money to pay for medical care. From their perspective, it is not a choice between the plaintiff's or the physician's bearing the costs; it is a choice between the physician and society. The jury may assume that if they do not give the plaintiff money to pay for medical care, he or she is likely to become a ward of the state.

Medical expenses provide the most psychologically convincing evidence of personal injuries. A long stay in the hospital and a projection of substantial future medical needs add credibility to all of the other elements of the plaintiff's case. There is a rule of thumb in automobile accident cases that the cases should settle for a multiple of the sum of the medical expenses and the plaintiff's lost wages (usually three to five times the sum).

INDIRECT ECONOMIC DAMAGES

Indirect economic damages are those that do not have a ready monetary equivalent. They fall into two classes: those that represent services that the injured person might have provided to his or her family, and those that represent various aspects of mental or physical suffering by the injured person or his or her family. Services include home repairs, household services, and special services that the plaintiff might have provided. The value of sexual services in a marriage are an important component in these damages, but they are lumped with loss of companionship to form consortium. This avoids the problem of presenting expert testimony on the value of sexual services.

Defending against these noneconomic claims has pitfalls. If the defense disputes the plaintiff's pain but that pain is credible to the jury, the defendant will be seen as cruel. Establishing that the plaintiff was a shiftless wife beater is unlikely to defuse the testimony of a small child that he misses his daddy. The high ground in defending these claims is to sympathize but to question the propriety of replacing daddy with money. Inevitably, the award of indirect economic damages depends on the jury's balancing their sympathy for the plaintiff with their sympathy for the defendant.

Juries may use noneconomic damages as a way of compensating plaintiffs for items that are not directly compensable. For example, juries know that attorneys do not work for free, and they also recognize that the list of compensable items that plaintiff's counsel presents does not contain an entry for legal fees. It is widely believed, but untested, that jurors put money for attorney's fees in soft categories, such as pain and emotional distress.

Pain and Emotional Distress

One of the most controversial damage elements is compensation for pain and suffering. Pain is difficult to measure, and money does not reduce the pain, so the rationale of making the plaintiff whole falls apart. Conversely, pain profoundly disrupts the plaintiff's life, and it would seem to be an injustice to deny any recovery for it. Currently, all states allow compensation for pain, although some have established monetary ceilings for allowable recoveries for pain.

Pain and suffering may be emotional or physical. Valuing these states of mind is a speculative process. The jurors are asked to determine how much money they would need to be paid to endure the suffering that the plaintiff must live with.

More specifically, they are asked to determine this sum with a short time unit, say, a few dollars an hour. The objective is to have the juror accept that the plaintiff's pain is worth a certain small amount of money per hour or per day. It is a simple exercise to multiply this small number by the number of units in the rest of the plaintiff's life and arrive at a large dollar value.

Pain is highly idiosyncratic. Some medical conditions are always associated with severe pain (burns, tic douloureux), but for most conditions, the presence and intensity of pain are a function of the individual. Experts may testify that the plaintiff's condition is not usually painful, but they cannot objectively establish that the plaintiff does not feel pain. The jurors weigh the plaintiff's credibility, the nature of the injury, and the medical testimony on the plaintiff's condition and prognosis. If the injury was not severe and there is no credible medical testimony that there is a physiologic basis for severe pain, typically they will award little or nothing for pain. In a medical malpractice case that involves the treatment of an inherently painful condition, the defendant may argue that the plaintiff is entitled to compensation only for increased pain.

As with pain, compensation for emotional distress is not readily reduced to a monetary value. The old rule for emotional distress limited recovery to plaintiffs who were personally in the zone of danger related to the accident. If a mother was in the street next to her child when the child was struck by a car, the mother could recover. If she was not threatened or injured herself, but only witnessed the accident, she could not recover. This harsh rule has been relaxed in most states to allow recovery in cases in which the plaintiff was not personally threatened. Recovery is still limited to close relatives. Friends and cohabitants cannot recover for emotional distress occasioned by injury to another. Most medical malpractice cases do not give rise to injury-related claims for emotional distress. It is an issue in cases that involve intentional actions, such as refusing treatment, or engaging in outrageous activities, such as sexually assaulting a patient.

Consortium

Consortium is a relatively new damage element that arose from the acceptance that the services performed by a homemaker have economic value. It has evolved to cover either spouse, and in some states it can include claims by children. Consortium is the economic value of the services that the injured person would have provided to the family but for the injury: cooking, cleaning, shopping, helping with school work, fixing the roof, and other domestic services that could conceivably be purchased from a third party. Consortium also includes elements that are unique to the injured individual: advice and counseling, companionship, and sexual services. These not readily reducible to a monetary value but are compensable in the same way as pain and emotional distress.

Consortium claims are important in cases in which there is no significant wage loss or when loss of sexual services includes the loss of reproductive potential. If the couple has not completed their family and the accident makes procreation impossible or improbable, they are entitled to compensation. They are not required to mitigate their damages through fertility technologies, and the courts do not regard adoption as a substitute for personally bearing children.

PUNITIVE DAMAGES

The primary role of the tort system is to compensate injured persons. A secondary role is the deterrence of socially unacceptable behavior. Making defendants pay for the harm they cause does have a deterrent effect, but in some situations the outrageous nature of a defendant's actions is out of proportion to the cost of compensating the plaintiff. In these cases, the jury is allowed to award *punitive* (also called *exemplary*) *damages* to punish the defendant:

> It is a well-established principle of the common law, that . . . a jury may inflict what are called exemplary, punitive or vindictive damages upon a defendant, having in view the enormity of his offense rather than the measure of compensation to the plaintiff. . . . By the common as well as by statute law, men are often punished for aggravated misconduct or lawless acts, by means of civil action, and the damages, inflicted by way of penalty or punishment, given to the party injured. (*Day v. Woodworth*, 1851)

Punitive damages may not be awarded for merely negligent behavior. The conduct must be intentionally harmful or grossly negligent:

> The penal aspect and public policy considerations which justify the imposition of punitive damages require that they be imposed only after a close examination of whether the defendant's conduct is "outrageous," because of "evil motive" or "reckless indifference to the rights of others." Mere inadvertence, mistake or errors of judgment which constitute mere negligence will not suffice. It is not enough that a decision be wrong. It must result from a conscious indifference to the decision's foreseeable effect. . . . We prefer the term "reckless indifference" to the term "wanton," which has statutory roots now largely extinct. Wantonness is no more a form or degree of negligence than is willfulness. Willfulness and wantonness involve an awareness, either actual or constructive, of one's conduct and a realization of its probable consequences, while negligence lacks any intent, actual or constructive. (*Jardel Co., Inc. v. Kathleen Hughes*, 1987)

Punitive damages are seldom at issue in medical malpractice litigation that arises from traditional treatment situations. In the medical treatment context, they are usually awarded when the physician engages in conduct—medical (a drunk surgeon), social (sexual abuse), or financial (fraudulently inducing the patient to undergo medically unnecessary treatment)—before a court would allow the awarding of punitive damages. They are a more significant problem for medical device manufacturers. Even in these cases, the plaintiff must usually show that the defendant knew that the product was dangerous, continued to market the product, and covered up the product defect.

THE COLLATERAL SOURCE RULE

The United States has a tradition of favoring private insurance for compensation. One strategy to encourage the purchase of private insurance is to allow plaintiffs to recover from defendants irrespective of their own insurance coverage. This is called the *collateral source rule*. The rationale for this rule is that the defendant should not benefit from the plaintiff's foresight in paying insurance premiums. This allows insured plaintiffs to get a double recovery, to the extent that their medical bills and lost wage claims have already been paid by their insurance carrier. The traditional collateral source rule also prevented the defendant from informing the jury that the plaintiff had already been compensated by private insurance.

If the insurance company wishes to be reimbursed, this may be made part of the insurance contract. This is called a *subrogation agreement*. Worker's compensation insurance usually contains a subrogation provision, and many group health insurance policies are adding subrogation clauses, which require plaintiffs to repay their own insurance company. A subrogation agreement reduces the value of a plaintiff's case, often dramatically. If the insurer insists on full reimbursement, the plaintiff will not be able to find representation. Although the subrogation agreement allows the insurance company to litigate the claim on behalf of the plaintiff, there is no incentive for plaintiffs to cooperate if they will not receive the award. Some insurers agree to a discounted reimbursement to make it attractive for the plaintiff to sue for compensation. Others refuse to compromise their claims, forcing the plaintiff to omit medical costs from the lawsuit.

Some states have moved to modify or abolish the collateral source rule. They may allow the judge to reduce the plaintiff's award by the amount of already paid expenses, allow the defense to tell the jury that the plaintiff has been compensated, or prevent the plaintiff from claiming for reimbursed injuries. It is not clear how these rules affect claims for future medical expenses since their payment is contingent on the plaintiff's maintaining his or her insurance.

STRATEGIES FOR PAYING DAMAGES

The central problem in determining the proper compensation for an injury is the speculative nature of the claimant's future medical and economic needs. Traditional insurance schemes pay medical costs as they are incurred. If the claimant requires treatment five years after the injury, that claim is paid by the insurer at the time the care is rendered. This creates an open-ended obligation, but it obviates the need to speculate on the future needs of the claimant when evaluating the claim.

Lump Sum Payments

Courts do not like open-ended obligations. When the court enters a judgment, it wants to be rid of the case. If the defendant is found not liable, the plaintiff may not bring another lawsuit on the same facts. If the defendant is found liable, he or she must pay the plaintiff a sum that will compensate the plaintiff for both existing losses and all the future losses related to the injury. The plaintiff cannot come back to the court and ask for money for unforeseen consequences of the injury, and the defendant cannot come back to court and request a refund of the money if the plaintiff does not need all of it. This finality creates an incentive on both sides to put an unrealistic value on the plaintiff's injuries: plaintiffs demand too high a figure, and defendants offer too little. If the plaintiff prevails with the high value, the defendant must pay more than is appropriate. If the defendant prevails, the plaintiff may become a ward of the state for unpaid medical expenses.

The lump sum payment in a lawsuit is intended to last for the duration of the effects of the injury. For many cases, this means the rest of the plaintiff's life. These judgments may be $1 million cash, tax free. (Personal injury settlements and court awards are tax free.) Managing a sum of this magnitude so that it provides current income and future security is a difficult task. In many, perhaps most, cases, the money will be gone in a few years, and the plaintiff is left in debt, sometimes from failed investment schemes. This is undesirable social policy because plaintiffs or their dependents often become wards of the state after the lump sum has been dissipated.

Structured Settlements

The most desirable situation is to provide a way of paying the plaintiff's expenses as they arise, with offsets for both increased and reduced needs. This is incompatible with having lawsuits result in fixed obligations.

The remaining alternative is to retain the lump sum determination but to pay out the lump sum only as it is needed by the plaintiff. This is termed a *structured settlement* and is available only in a structured manner. Structured settlements may be agreed to as part of the overall judgment in a case or required by the court if the plaintiff is a minor or the state has a specific statute requiring that certain awards be structured.

Plaintiff's attorneys have an ethical obligation to inform the client fully of the value of entering into a structured settlement. Many attorneys will even reduce their fees to provide an incentive for the client to waive a right to the lump sum.

There have been many proposals to require that all large settlements and verdicts be paid on a structured or periodic payment basis. The intent is to ensure that money is available to meet the plaintiff's needs and to allow the defendant to recoup any unused money. This can happen when a plaintiff does not live long enough to use up the projected nursing and medical care allowances. In one extreme instance, a quadriplegic plaintiff was awarded more than $1 million for future medical needs. The plaintiff died shortly after the settlement papers were signed, and the money went into the plaintiff's estate. In this case, a periodic payment law would have led to a more just result.

There are problems with structured settlements. Most periodic payment proposals are not symmetric; the defendant's contribution is reduced if the plaintiff's needs diminish, but it is not increased if the plaintiff's needs were underestimated. A second problem is that they make the calculation and awarding of attorney's fees difficult. The value of the award must be reduced to net present value and fees calculated and paid as a lump sum in addition to the periodic payments. The most serious problem is ensuring that the defendant will be solvent during the period over which the award must be paid out. The usual way to handle this is to require the defendant to buy an annuity from a third-party financial institution. The defendant will want to buy the least expensive annuity that will provide the necessary payments to the plaintiff. Since the stability of the financial institution is a factor in the pricing of annuities, the least expensive annuity may be backed by the least stable institution. If the institution fails, the plaintiff will receive no compensation.

BIBLIOGRAPHY

Breece JN: Loss of spousal consortium. Leg Aspects Med Pract 1978 Jan; 6(1):47–51.
Cahill NE: Compensation of subjects injured in experimental medicine programs: The ethical and legal considerations. J Leg Med (Chic) 1979 Apr; 1(1):110–39.
Cooper PJ: Compensation for human research subjects: Reform ahead of its time? J Leg Med (Chic) 1980 Oct; 2(1):1–13.
Day v. Woodworth, 54 US (13 How) 363, 371, 14 L ED 181 (1851).
Eisberg JF: Doctor must pay damages, child-rearing expenses for failed vasectomy. Leg Aspects Med Pract 1978 Mar; 6(3):48–49.

Gaskins R: Equity in compensation: The case of swine flu. Hastings Cent Rep 1980 Feb; 10(1):5–8.

Hurwitz WJ: Environmental health: An analysis of available and proposed remedies for victims of toxic waste contamination. Am J Law Med 1981 Spring; 7(1):61–89.

Jardel Co., Inc. v. Kathleen Hughes, 523 A2d 518, 529–30 (1987).

McClellan FM: Informed consent to medical therapy and experimentation: The case for invoking punitive damages to deter impingement of individual autonomy. J Leg Med (Chic) 1982 Mar; 3(1):81–115.

Modlin HC; Schneider-Braus K: Compensation neurosis. Bull Am Acad Psychiatry Law 1986; 14(3):263–71.

Moran PT: The New Zealand experience of "no fault" compensation. Med Leg J 1985; 53 (Pt 4):222–24.

Pennock LM: The effect of comparative fault on personal injury awards in malpractice lawsuits involving multiple tortfeasors. J Leg Med (Chic) 1985 Jun; 6(2):223–47.

Shoenberger AE: Medical malpractice injury. Causation and valuation of the loss of a chance to survive. J Leg Med (Chic) 1985 Mar; 6(1):51–83.

Steinbock B: The logical case for "wrongful life." Hastings Cent Rep 1986 Apr; 16(2):15–20.

Taub S: The current status of actions for wrongful life and wrongful birth. Leg Med 1985: 180–95.

Titus AC: Governmental responsibility for victims of atomic testing: A chronicle of the politics of compensation. J Health Polit Policy Law 1983 Summer; 8(2):277–92.

Weller MP: The timing of compensation claims in head injury cases. Med Leg J 1987; 55(Pt 3):166–69.

5

Dealing with Attorneys

| CRITICAL POINTS | • The attorney-client relationship is fundamentally different from the physician-patient relationship.
• Legal clients must request preventive law if they want more than symptomatic treatment for their legal problems.
• Legal clients take personal responsibility for their legal health.
• Physicians must cooperate with their attorneys to ensure effective representation. |
|---|---|

Physicians' views of attorneys tend to be shaped by their fears of medical malpractice litigation. Physicians dislike plaintiff's attorneys and are often none too happy with attorneys in general. The result of this uneasy relationship is that physicians do not make effective use of legal services, and they may take unnecessary legal risks. When they do consult an attorney, their attitudes toward and preconceptions about legal services reduce the effectiveness of their representation.

The objective of this chapter is to help physicians understand the difference between the attorney-client relationship and the physician-patient relationship so that they can use legal services effectively.

THE CONFLICT OF CULTURES

Law and medicine are both learned, licensed professions, practiced by demographically similar individuals. Each profession has a well-developed paradigm that governs the relationship between independent professionals and their clients. While physicians recognize that law is not science based, they may assume that the two professions deal with clients/patients in much the same way. This is not a correct assumption. The attorney-client relationship is profoundly different from the physician-patient relationship. This difference can lead to hostility and dangerous misunderstandings between physicians and attorneys.

The attorney-client relationship shares many characteristics with the physician-patient relationship: attorneys have special education and experience not possessed by clients; attorneys have a license that allow them to perform tasks that a layperson may not perform; attorneys must keep clients' matters confidential; and attorneys owe clients a special duty to put clients' interests before their own interests (a fiduciary duty). It is these shared values that lead physicians to assume that attorneys deal with clients' needs in the same way as physicians deal with patients.

Physicians and Paternalism

The physician-patient relationship is a paternalistic, beneficent relationship; that is, the physician is expected to do what is medically best for the patient. Paternalism and beneficence are important in the physician-patient relationship because of the physician's superior technical knowledge and access to pharmaceuticals and medical technology. Despite the importance of patient involvement and informed consent, physicians are expected to do what is best for their patients. Even the termination of life-support cases are predicated on the assumption that termination is in the patient's best interest. (See Chapter 13.)

The courts' skepticism in cases in which patients allegedly make an informed choice of medically improper treatment highlights the expectation that physicians will offer patients only the choice of medically proper and indicated treatments. (See Chapters 9 and 11.) This reflects a general societal consensus on what constitutes acceptable medical care. In most cases, physicians, patients, and society agree on the desired outcome and the appropriate spectrum of treatments to accomplish that outcome. While this is not meant to minimize the very real conflicts between physicians and patients, debates over contentious issues such as abortion, right to die, and entrepreneurial medical practice tend to obscure the congruence of interest that defines the vast majority of patient care.

Attorneys and Autonomy

The attorney-client relationship, in contrast, is based on autonomy rather than paternalism. Law is an adversarial process with many areas in which there is no clear societal consensus on the correct role of the attorney. Respecting a person's autonomy can mean protecting a mentally ill homeless person's right to freeze on a grate. Legal paternalism and beneficence was a rationale for the Jim Crow laws that institutionalized segregation in the United States. Short of helping clients commit crimes, attorneys are expected to advocate their clients' wishes zealously, not limit their services to those that are good for the client.

Beyond this philosophical prejudice toward client autonomy, traditional codes of legal ethics limited the attorney's obligation to do the legal equivalent of a complete history and physical. These ethical codes created the *limited engagement doctrine*. The limited engagement defined the attorney's role as providing the specific legal services sought by the client. In its strictest form, the limited engagement doctrine prohibited the attorney from asking the client about other potential legal problems. This prohibition was intended to prevent barratry, the stirring up of litigation. Such a prohibition was beneficial to attorneys because it greatly limited their liability for legal misdiagnosis. Given that it is difficult to police barratry prohibitions, the limited engagement served to limit attorneys' liability without greatly limiting their ability to stir up litigation.

If the physician-patient relationship was a limited engagement, a physician might prescribe cough medicine to a coughing patient without inquiring into the underlying cause of the cough—ethically and legally proper care under the traditional standard of the limited engagement. The physician-patient relationship is not a limited engagement, however; the physician is ethically bound to consider the patient's overall medical needs. An attorney held to the standards that govern the physician-patient relationship would be required to do a legal checkup on clients to ensure that the services requested by the client were appropriate for the client's total legal health.

The limited engagement is beginning to erode for both business and professional reasons. For example, severe tax consequences of divorce are so pervasive that it is considered unprofessional not to counsel divorce clients about tax problems. This benefits the client and generates an opportunity to deliver additional legal services. In most areas of law, however, the client cannot assume that the attorney will inquire into hidden but related legal problems. Since the law has not developed a comprehensive doctrine of informed consent, the attorney is not required to inform the client of the implications of the limited engagement. A physician seeking legal services must be sure that the attorney addresses the underlying legal disease rather than just providing symptomatic treatment.

STRUCTURE OF LEGAL SERVICES

Attorneys sell little other than their time, so the accounting for this time becomes a substantive measure of their professionalism. Understanding attorneys' billing practices is critical to an understanding of the attorney-client relationship.

Legal Bills

Physicians and attorneys provide professional services that are heavily dependent on exercising judgment. Physicians record their diagnoses and procedures in complex, standardized notations. Physicians throughout the world use the standard taxonomy for medical diagnoses, the ICD-9 (international classification of disease, revision 9). In the United States, physicians use the American Medical Association's current procedural terminology (CPT) system to classify medical procedures.

The lack of a rigorous descriptive system for legal problems and events is intimately tied to the structure of legal education and practice. The lack of formal structure makes it difficult for clients to track and manage legal services. Physicians may not understand from the notations on a bill what was done. Unlike the medical insurers, legal clients do not have any data on prevailing charges. From the client's perspective, the absence of a standard procedure code for legal procedures is more noticeable than the lack of a standard diagnostic code. While attorneys' hourly bills may be intricately detailed, they are seldom comparable among law firms or even from attorney to attorney in the same law firm. This lack of standardization prevents clients from comparing their legal services with those rendered to other clients. This lack of a consistent coding system makes it difficult to relate the billing entries to the progress of the client's case.

The Structure of Legal Work

Some legal work is simple and closed-ended: reviewing the papers for a real estate sale, drafting a will, or negotiating a settlement with a medical equipment vendor over an overcharge on office equipment. This work is frequently done for a fixed fee, sometimes with an hourly override for unexpected problems. Although the client must be careful to identify the services covered by the fixed fee, the client has fairly accurate information about the cost of the legal services and how long it will to take to complete them.

Most adversary legal work, including all but the simplest litigation, is open-ended as to both cost and duration. It tends to resemble a severe chronic illness like renal failure. The care of a patient with renal failure may cost hundreds of thousands of dollars over a ten-year period. A physician who has his or her medical staff privileges terminated improperly may spend $200,000 over several years to contest the decision. The cost of legal services becomes dramatically higher than medical services only when the services involve complex commercial litigation.

Attorneys' Product
As professionals, physicians and attorneys charge for the exercise of professional judgment. Most physicians charge based on procedures and patient encounters. These tend to be fixed charges that are independent of either the results or the time actually spent on the procedure. Some physicians, such as anesthesiologists, have charges that are related to the time spent with the patient. Physicians also charge for services performed by their staff.

Attorneys have more open-ended charge structures. Basically they sell their time and the time of their staff. Plaintiff's attorneys usually work on a contingent fee. Fixed fees are used in certain routine matters such as divorces and in most criminal defense cases. Criminal attorneys also demand the fee in advance, since unsuccessful clients have little incentive to pay the attorney's fees. Although the basic fee arrangement is the same for physicians and attorneys, there are two critical differences: except for insurance defense work, legal fees are usually paid by the client rather than by a third party, and legal fees can be much higher for individual transactions.

In most parts of the country, attorney's fees range from $75 to $400 per hour, with certain specialists charging up to $1000 an hour. Within a large law firm, the younger, less experienced attorneys are billed at a lower rate than the senior members of the firm. Nonattorney support personnel are also billed on an hourly basis. These may include nurses, physicians, engineers, certified public accountants, and other nonattorney professionals whose expertise is necessary for the proper preparation of a case. They also include law students and paralegals who work on client matters. The client is billed for every minute that law firm personnel spend on activities related to the client's case. If an attorney does the work, the client pays the attorney's hourly rate. It does not matter that the attorney is doing work that does not require the exercise of legal judgment. The rates are the same for solving a difficult analytical issue as for making telephone calls to schedule a deposition.

Business and defense attorneys pass all expenses through to the client. These range from a few dollars for photocopying and messenger charges to expert witness fees in the thousands of dollars. The client sometimes pays the bills directly, although in most cases, the law firm includes the expenses with the professional services bill. The client pays the aggregate charges, and the law firm pays the outside vendors. Expenses in a simple collection matter may be $100. Expenses in the defense of a medical malpractice case may be $30,000 or more.

The Impact of Client-Paid Legal Fees
Personal legal services are no more expensive than many medical services, yet only rich individuals and relatively large corporations use attorneys routinely. The deterrent to the use of preventive legal services is that the only third-party

system is insurance defense. The result is that individuals and small businesses generally do not see attorneys until they are in legal trouble. This increases the cost and reduces the effectiveness of legal services. While the Constitution guarantees a court-appointed attorney for persons accused of crimes, there is no provision for civil attorneys. Many persons cannot obtain civil legal services when they are in legal trouble because they must pay legal costs from their own pockets.

The state of legal services provides an interesting lesson for medicine. It is very difficult to persuade clients to pay for preventive legal services. Typically they seek legal help only in emergencies. This is the same pattern that is seen with indigent health care. Persons who have to pay a significant proportion of their disposable income for medical care seek medical care only for emergencies. They have no ability to pay for preventive treatment. Since everyone has to pay for legal services, even relatively wealthy individuals such as physicians will not seek preventive care.

Legal Billing

Open-ended work is done on an hourly basis, plus expenses. The attorney bills the client for each increment of time the attorney spends on the case. Since law does not have standardized diagnoses or procedures, the delineation of these increments may seem arbitrary, they may not appear to match the tasks that must be completed to solve the client's problem. Attorneys bill the client based on the physical task the attorney performs: charges for talking on the telephone, reading documents, traveling, reading cases, and the other physical things attorneys do. It is as if a carpenter charged by how long he pounded nails, sawed boards, climbed ladders, and so forth. If you have hired this carpenter to remodel your house, knowing how long he spends on each carpenter task does not tell you whether the stair is finished and how much work remains on the kitchen.

When a client reads an attorney's bill, he or she may not care how much time the attorney spent doing research, talking on the telephone, and so forth. The client wants to know how the course of the legal work has been furthered by the work he or she is being asked to pay for. Ideally, he would pay the attorney progress payments, in the same way that he would pay the carpenter. This analogy breaks down, however, because attorneys expect clients to pay them for learning their trade, as well as completing the client's work.

Chronological Billing

Most attorneys bill chronologically rather than aggregating the charges for a given task. As attorneys work, they fill out time slips that document the client, the task, the attorney, and the time spent on the task since the last time slip was completed. Assume that the attorney is reviewing your file:

>He looks at the correspondence (*review correspondence*—.25 hr.).
>He makes three telephone calls in response to the correspondence (*phone call, Sara Smith*—.25 hr.; *phone call, Jack Jones*—.25 hr.; *phone call—Dr. Alexander*—.25 hr.).
>He looks over the pleadings (*review pleading*—.25 hr.).
>He dictates a motion (*prepare motion*—.25 hr.).

He reads an article on the use of thermography to see if it would help in your case (*research*—.5 hr.).
He spends a few minutes rearranging the papers (*reorganize file*—.25 hr.).

This single work session generates eight billing entries, most of which are for the law firm's minimum billing increment, a quarter-hour. None of these entries is of value in determining the status of the case.

Legal bills also fail to give the client proper information on the cost of the discrete elements of the case. The information is in the bills, but it is just not aggregated in time. Assume that you want to know the cost of a deposition. The monthly charges for a deposition might resemble the following:

May
Telephone conference with an expert: 1 May—0.5 hr.
Research on the factual issues: 15 May—0.75 hr.
Research on the factual issues: 21 May—1.5 hr.
Phone calls to schedule the deposition: 30 May—.25 hr.

June
Research on the factual issues: 30 June—1.0 hr.
Phone calls to schedule the deposition: 10 June—.25 hr.

July
Research on the factual issues: 12 July—.5 hr.
Research on the factual issues: 14 July—.75 hr.
Phone calls to schedule the deposition: 13 July—.5 hr.

August
Research on the factual issues: 1 August—.5 hr.
Review the file before the deposition: 21 August.—2.5 hr.

September
Predeposition client conference: 10 September—2.0 hr.
Travel to deposition: 11 September—3.5 hr.
Take deposition: 11 September—5.5 hr.
Return from deposition: 12 September—3.5 hr.

October
Summarize deposition: 10 October—1.5 hr (paralegal).

November
Court reporter's bill: 10 November—$637.00.
Charge for airline tickets: 12 November—$560.00.
Charge for hotel room and meals: 12 November—$150.00.
Review deposition summary: 30 November—1.0 hr.

This deposition accounts for nineteen billing entries spread over seven monthly bills. If this is a typical litigation case, these seven bills may each have 150 other entries. It would easily take an hour to locate and tabulate the entries for this single deposition. It would be impossible to tabulate them in most bills because the individual entries do not reference the deposition that they are associated with. Importantly, each monthly bill has had more charges for the deposition. The client has no way to know how long these charges will go on.

The Limitations of Legal Education

Unlike the combination of medical school and residency, most law schools do not prepare graduates for the practice of law. Becoming skillful at a learned profession requires both technical knowledge and judgment, which take time and practice to develop. The problem is the short duration of law school and the absence of a legal equivalent to medical residency training. Law school training is usually three years, excluding summers. If the school offers a summer program, it is possible to finish in just over two years. Given that most medical schools are four years, including all but one summer, basic medical education is almost twice as long as legal education. Law students get the "basic sciences" and a smattering of classroom-based "clinical education." They get almost no intensive, problem-oriented clinical experience. The parallel would be licensing physicians after the basic science phase of medical school.

Not unlike medical students, law students are rewarded for spotting low-probability events. In medical education, these are referred to as zebras: if a third-year medical student hears hoofbeats, he or she looks around for a zebra. In legal education this is called issue spotting. The third and fourth years of medical school and residency training allow the student to gain perspective on low-probability events. They learn to treat patients based on the most probable diagnosis but to reevaluate that diagnosis as more information becomes available. This is a process of learning both judgment and the factual basis of medical practice.

Law schools teach students to recognize legal issues and how to find the law to address these issues. Legal academics, however, define law somewhat differently than do practitioners and their clients. As with other academic disciplines, including medicine, law professors are rewarded for research in narrow specialty areas that may have little relevance outside the academic institution. Even when law students learn "black letter" law (statutes, cases, and legal treatises), these provide little guidance without the experience of working with clients in a structured teaching environment. Even law schools with extensive clinical education programs expose law students to clients with only simple legal problems. In most schools these clinical programs occupy less than six hours of the students' academic requirements.

Client-Funded Legal Education

Both physicians and attorneys learn and polish their skills on their clients. In both cases, their clients or patients pay for this education. Physicians amortize the cost over all patients. No individual patient is charged extra because the physician spends an hour reading a journal article about his or her disease. Attorneys, however, charge each client for the time the attorney spends learning about the law governing the client's problem. A surgeon trying a new technique the first time may have an ethical duty to obtain a special informed consent from the patient. Attorneys trying a new area of law not only have no duty to warn the client; they may be paid extra for the additional time needed to research this unfamiliar area.

Attorneys working in an unfamiliar area spend time researching irrelevant issues, miss important issues, and have difficulty in translating legal research into useful legal advice. Once it is accepted that clients should pay for educating senior attorneys, then it is a logical extension to expect clients to pay for educating junior attorneys. Thus, the client's financial advantage of hiring an attorney expert in a particular problem evaporates. The client may get the advantage of the senior attorney's judgment but have to pay junior attorneys to duplicate this knowledge. In the worst case, the client pays the junior attorneys to learn judgment and the senior attorney to supervise their lessons.

Incentives against Settlement

A candid defense attorney once described a medical malpractice case as an annuity, bearing interest above the prevailing rate. The longer a file is open, the longer the law firm can draw that interest. Every few months additional court papers can be filed. Client reports need to be done on a regular basis. Each piece of paper and court appearance that the defense attorney can generate, or force the plaintiff's attorney to generate, results in substantial fees. This approach is usually described as being "tough" on the plaintiff. Being tough usually means forcing court appearances and motion practice rather than coming to agreement.

Most malpractice lawsuits settle before a final jury verdict. Unlike attorneys who defend criminals, malpractice defense attorneys have an incentive not to cooperate with the plaintiff's attorney in reaching a settlement. Cases are often settled at the courthouse door because that is the longest the defense can delay before running the risk of a trial. Defense attorneys are risk adverse; they would rather settle a case than run any substantial chance of losing the case. This is related to the public relations aspects of litigation. A successful defense of a malpractice lawsuit is not news, but a $1 million verdict will attract news coverage. A case that is settled is not lost and usually does not generate adverse publicity. From an earnings perspective, the ideal defense case is one in which the defendant was negligent enough to justify settling the case but careful enough to justify delaying that settlement to the bitter end.

Legal Practice Styles

Legal fees are determined by the amount of time spent on the client's problem. Ideally, the amount of time is a function of the complexity of the client's problem. However, an important secondary determinant, which can account for 50 percent or more of the fee in a case, is the practice style of the law firm. Law firms have a powerful incentive to generate hourly billings.

Clients should be especially wary of "wolf packing," which occurs when the law firm assigns more than one attorney to the same piece of work. This is most obvious when several attorneys attend the same meeting or court hearing. It is less obvious when the client is billed for conferencing by several different attorneys, when the conference is actually a firm meeting. The client should ask the attorney to explain which additional firm members may be involved in the case and their specific expertise. If possible, the client should be introduced to everyone who will work on the case, including the paralegals.

A more controversial practice is the padding of hours. For example, an attorney who is supposedly being paid by the hour will charge for drafting a document that is actually printed up by a secretary from a form file. He or she may charge, say, 5 hours for a piece of work that takes only 30 minutes. This practice is justified as amortizing the cost of the work over all the clients who benefit from it. Unlike traditional amortizing, the first client to request the work probably paid the full cost of drafting the document. Moreover, there is no time when the document is deemed fully amortized and becomes a free service to future clients.

"Dilatory practice" is the legal euphemism for wasting time. It occurs for a number of reasons: time may be wasted because a witness, or even the client, cannot be found, for example, or it may occur because of disorganization and a failure to do long-range planning. Plaintiffs' cases usually deteriorate with time. In the worst case, the plaintiff or a critical witness will die, making it difficult to try the case effectively. Unless there is a strategic reason for the delay, wasted time costs plaintiffs and their attorneys money.

In contrast, delay can be rewarding for defense attorneys. Defenses get stronger as time erodes the plaintiff's case. Death can transform a multimillion-dollar injured-baby case into a "loss of future services" case worth very little. Witnesses disappear, lovable children turn into surly adolescents, and grieving widows remarry. The insurance company benefits from the delay if the cost of reinsuring the risk of the unpaid claim is less than the income they can earn on the money that will be needed to pay the claim. Defense lawyers personally benefit because delayed cases require constant maintenance, with the attendant opportunities to bill the client.

CONFLICTS OF INTEREST

Exercising independent legal judgment requires an objective detachment from the client's interests. This objectivity may be compromised by financial or personal conflicts. Conflicts of interest are usually thought of as limited to situations in which an attorney attempts to represent parties with conflicting interests. Attorneys usually avoid such obvious conflicts. The more common problem is a conflict between the attorney's interests and the client's interests. This is always the case when attorneys provide legal advice to their business partners. A special problem is the lack of objectivity that arises when attorneys are patients of their physician clients.

It is not unusual for attorneys to identify with physician clients. They have common educational backgrounds, interests, and friends. Because of this identification, the attorney may not evaluate the physician's legal problems objectively. This loss of objectivity can hurt the client in many ways. The attorney may not investigate the physician's recitation of the facts diligently or appreciate how a jury will view the physician's actions. These misperceptions increase the risk of poor legal advice. Just as physicians are cautioned about treating their close friends and family members, so should physicians take care to ensure that their attorneys are objective.

Whenever a physician is in a business venture with an attorney, there is potential for confusion of roles. If the attorney acts only as a businessperson, there is no conflict of interest. However, if the attorney also provides legal services or makes legal decisions, there is a conflict with the other participants in the venture.

As long as the interests of all of the participants are the same, this conflict will not be a problem. But in most ventures, the interests of the participants are not the same. It is best if the legal work for the business is done by an attorney who has no financial or other interest in the business. If this is impractical, the nonattorney participants should have a separate attorney review the basic business documents. They should also consult with their own counsel whenever there are changes in the business organization.

CONFLICTS WITH OTHER CLIENTS

Attorneys who represent clients with adverse interests eventually will be forced to compromise the interests of at least one of the clients. This is a particular problem in legal specialty areas such as medical law. There are advantages to the client in hiring a law firm that has experience in the problems at hand. In medical law, this means a law firm with experience in representing health care providers. Now, with the competition between hospitals and between individual physicians, it is important to ask the identity of the law firm's other health care clients. (This is not privileged information.) If the law firm represents real or potential competitors, it is best to hire a different law firm. Sometimes it is impossible to find another law firm with the appropriate expertise. It is then up to the law firm and the client to discuss the potential conflicts and establish a plan for avoiding them. This is especially important in medical malpractice defense.

In most medical malpractice cases, the physician is insured. A condition of this insurance is that the insurance company pays for the defense of a case. This benefits the insurance company because it is mostly its money that is at risk. It benefits the physician because attorneys are expensive, and a principal reason for buying insurance is that it pays defense costs. The problem is that the defense attorney represents the insurance company, not the physician. This becomes obvious when the potential recovery is substantially larger than the coverage provided by the insurance policy. If the insurance company misjudges the case, the physician also pays. In these situations, physicians should retain their own attorneys to ensure that the insurance company protects their interests as well as its own.

The most important conflict is more subtle. It involves how the aggregate cost of defending many medical malpractice lawsuits drives up the cost of insurance. In any lawsuit, the physician defendant will want the insurance company to spare no expense on his or her defense. Unfortunately, every physician suffers when it is time to pay the insurance premiums attributable to the increased cost of defense. (See Chapter 7.)

BEING AN EFFECTIVE CLIENT

Legal services in the United States are used inefficiently. We tend to focus unduly on the resolution of existing disputes rather than their prevention. We treat law as a specialist concern to be left to attorneys. This parallels earlier views of medicine, before the idea of individual responsibility for medical decisions came to the fore. It is now accepted that a patient has the responsibility to make an informed decision about medical treatment; thus, patients must understand basic preventive medicine to become partners in protecting their medical health. In the same way, physicians must become sophisticated about legal services if they are to become partners in protecting their legal health. Being an effective, involved client has many advantages: it reduces the fear and uncertainty inherent in litigation; it reduces the risk of an adverse verdict; it can reduce legal costs for the physician or insurer; and it allows the physician and attorney to develop preventive law strategies to avoid future legal problems.

Choosing an Attorney

Attorneys vary in abilities just as physicians do. Personal friendships, club memberships, and financial success are no better (or worse) a measure of attorney competence than they are of physician competence. Physician clients must try to determine their attorneys' general competence, as well as their expertise in the specific legal problem at issue. Clients should inquire into the attorney's experience in the problem area. They should pay attention to how effectively the attorney questions them about their legal affairs. If the attorney does not appear knowledgeable, the client must question the attorney's experience in the area. For example, if the problem involves a medical joint venture, it is important that the attorney ask about the impact of this venture on professional decision making. If the arrangement might create a conflict of interest with certain patients, the specific constraints that the state imposes on the physician-patient relationship should be discussed in the interview.

Preventive Law

Clients must specifically discuss whether they want the attorney to review their general legal situation. This process, called a *preventive law audit*, is meant to assess the client's legal condition in the same way that a history and physical examination is meant to assess a patient's medical condition. The client may make an informed choice and decide not to remedy all of the legal problems that are detected, just as a patient may make an informed choice to forgo treatment for conditions detected in a general history and physical. A preventive law audit will cost more than symptomatic treatment, but it is cost-effective in the long run, just as treating the underlying pathology is more cost-effective than treating the symptoms of a disease.

A preventive law audit has three goals: identifying mature, previously undetected legal problems; identifying legally risky situations; and identifying potential legal risks. The audit is usually performed by an attorney, and it requires the client's cooperation and participation. The client will have to provide partnership agreements, insurance policies, leases, and all other legal agreements, answer questions, and fill out legal audit forms. The result is the legal equivalent of a complete history and physical examination.

Undetected Legal Problems

These are situations in which the legal risk has already occurred but the client is not aware of the problem. Income tax law changes are perhaps the most common source of mature but undetected legal problems. If Congress has changed the record-keeping requirements to claim a deduction and a client is unaware of the change in the law, he or she may lose the deduction for a year or forever.

Detecting problems such as this one is an unalloyed benefit because of the near certainty that the client's failure to comply will be detected and penalized. Some problems, however, may not result in legal penalties. For example, many states make it a crime for physicians to receive incentives to influence their decisions about their patients. (See Chapter 9.) Nevertheless, many physicians receive potentially illegal incentives from hospitals and managed-care plans. A preventive law audit would indicate these incentives as a potential legal problem.

Once a legal problem has been identified, it becomes more dangerous to ignore. Conduct that was negligent when done unknowingly becomes intentional or reckless once the physician is notified that the behavior is questionable. This does not mean that ignorance is defensible. Physicians who violate the law can be prosecuted irrespective of whether they know the specifics of the law that they break. The constitutional requirement is that the law be specific enough to define illegal behavior clearly, not that defendants be on notice that they are breaking the law. In this case, the physician must decide whether it is worth the risk of continuing to receive what could be characterized as an illegal bribe.

Legally Risky Situations
Some situations may result in legal problems in the future—for example, a partnership agreement that did not provide for an orderly dissolution if a partner dies. This is not a problem until the partner dies. Once the death occurs, it is difficult and expensive to remedy the problem.

When a legally risky situation is identified, the client must decide if the remedy is cost-effective. The incomplete partnership agreement would cost little to correct, and the benefit would be great. In cases in which the potential costs are both well known and small, it may be cheaper to accept the risk than to invest in a remedy. An example is the purchase of an inexpensive, easily replaced office machine. The warranty provisions of a sales contract for an adding machine may be ambiguous, but it is not worth the trouble to have an attorney redraft the contract.

Potential Future Risks
These are risks that may arise from changed circumstances. The client may get divorced, necessitating a new will. The law governing medical practice may change, necessitating changes in the office routine. It is impossible to anticipate all future problems. The objective of the legal audit is not to predict the future but to compile an inventory of the client's legal relationships. This inventory will help both the client and the attorney to recognize when they need to take action to protect the client's legal health.

Terms of the Relationship
Attorneys advise clients that contracts for services should be clear and specific about work to be done, how much it will cost, and how to resolve disputes if the client is dissatisfied with the services. Unfortunately, legal representation contracts are usually vague about charges and the work to be done. The legal client should require that the representation agreement provide the same information as any other contract for services: the work to be done and what it should cost.

An effective client must understand the dimensions of his or her legal problems and the specific tasks that must be performed. The attorney must teach the client about the legal problem just as the physician must teach patients enough about their medical problems to allow them to make informed decisions. Simple legal services do not require a lengthy explanation, but many legal services are complex, requiring months to years of work. These services may cost the client tens to hundreds of thousands of dollars. A client engaging an attorney for such a prolonged relationship is entitled to considerable detail about the strategy and progress of his case.

The client must not fall into the trap of equating cheap legal services with cost-effective legal services. A client who wants the services of an experienced attorney must be prepared to pay for them. Conversely, clients should not be expected to pay for training the law firm's personnel and should refuse to do so. This happens when the client's case is transferred to a new attorney. The new attorney will have to spend time becoming familiar with the case, and the client should not have to pay for that time.

Unlike medical services, the attorney the client talks to is frequently not the person who does the client's work. What would be ghost surgery in medicine is delegation of authority in law office practice. This problem is most troublesome in large law firms. The physician client believes that he or she is buying the expertise of a senior partner but may be paying for on-the-job training for an associate just out of law school or new to the client's problem. This client-funded education is particularly inefficient because the unskilled associate usually researches the client's problem before it is reviewed by the senior partner. This ensures that the experienced attorney's ability to focus the inquiry will not reduce the hours that the client will be billed for the legal work.

The client should ask the attorney to document the information the client is given about the case: the work to be done, who will do the work and their expertise, the billing rates for various personnel, and estimated costs of the different services to be performed. The client may want to ask the attorney to draw a diagram of all the steps in resolving the legal problem. This graphic display of the chronology is effective in eliminating uncertainty about what needs to be done. This diagram should be included in the client's documentation.

In addition to the traditional bill, the client should ask for a running total for each task outlined on the legal road map. For a deposition, each month's bill should include the total of all charges relating to the deposition that have been incurred to date. The bill should also group hourly charges for the deposition together rather than presenting all the hourly charges in chronological order. If the client's road map of the case includes the various steps in a deposition, the client can reconcile the road map with the bill each month.

Becoming a Partner in the Case

A physician must make an effort to learn about his or her case and convince the attorney that he or she wants to be involved in the case. If the case entails litigation, the physician should discuss the specific tasks that require medical expertise. The attorney may be reluctant to have the client involved in the case—and not unreasonably. Physicians are notoriously poor clients; they do not show up for appointments, they do not want to come to the attorney's office, and so forth. In general, physicians spend untold time and energy agonizing over being sued, and this anxiety is often expressed as hostility and passive aggression toward their own attorneys rather than being channeled into productive activities.

The physician must convince counsel, through words and deeds, that he or she can constructively be involved in the case—for example, by taking on a simple task such as organizing the medical records and preparing a chronological summary of the care provided and the personnel involved. If this is done quickly and impartially, it will demonstrate the physician's sincerity and value to the attorney.

BIBLIOGRAPHY

Croake JW; Myers KM; Singh A: Fears of physicians and other professionals groups. Int J Soc Psychiatry 1986 Winter; 32(4):13–18.

Danner D; Sagall EL: Medicolegal causation: A source of professional misunderstanding. Am J Law Med 1977 Fall; 3(3):303–8.

Dickens BM: Patients' interests and clients' wishes: Physicians and lawyers in discord. Law Med Health Care 1987 Fall; 15(3):110–17.

Gibson JM; Schwartz RL: Physicians and lawyers: Science, art, and conflict. Am J Law Med 1980 Summer; 6(2):173–82.

Gillette RD: Malpractice: Why physicians and lawyers differ. J Leg Med 1976 Oct; 4(9):9–11.

Healey JM: Beyond the adversarial relationship: The lawyer as physician's consultant. Conn Med 1980 Aug; 44(8):529.

Hughes RL: Principles governing physician-attorney relations. J Med Assoc Ga 1972 Nov; 61(11):384–86.

Kaul RH: Lawyers and physicians. Professional responsibility. J Kans Med Soc 1968 Aug; 69(8):371–75.

King JF: Medico-legal briefs. Viewpoint of a physician's attorney. J Miss State Med Assoc 1974 Aug; 15(8):354–55.

Krakowski AJ: Stress and the practice of medicine. III. Physicians compared with lawyers. Psychother Psychosom 1984; 42(1–4):143–51.

Mandell MS: Ten commandments for defendant-doctors: A lawyer's advice to furious, injured physicians accused of malpractice. Postgrad Med 1981 Dec; 70(6):202–3.

Meador CK: The mind of the physician, or why lawyers have trouble with doctors. Ala J Med Sci 1970 Oct; 7(4):363–67.

Moline JN: Professionals and professions: A philosophical examination of an ideal. Soc Sci Med 1986; 22(5):501–8.

Moore JL Jr: Lawyer pays for physician's malpractice. J Med Assoc Ga 1971 Apr; 60(4):126–27.

Naitove BJ: Medicolegal education and crisis in interprofessional relations. Am J Law Med 1982 Fall; 8(3):293–320.

Piccirillo M; Graf GJ: Medical malpractice: A case study in medical and legal decision making. Yale J Biol Med 1989 Jan–Feb; 62(1):23–42.

Rose EF: Lawyers' contingent fee—protection for physicians. J Iowa Med Soc 1974 Mar; 64(3):111–3.

Schwartz RL: Teaching physicians and lawyers to understand each other: The development of a law and medicine clinic. J Leg Med (Chic) 1981 Jun; 2(2):131–49.

Strodel RC: Medical-legal relationships: A physician's patient is the same person as an attorney's client. Leg Aspects Med Pract 1978 Mar; 6(3):54–61.

Young RA: Medical malpractice as seen from the perspective of the physician's defense attorney. NY State J Med 1986 Jul; 86(7):344–47.

6

Legal Standards

| CRITICAL POINTS | • Ambiguous practice standards increase medical malpractice litigation.
• The expert witness system is fundamentally flawed.
• Physicians can improve medical care and reduce litigation by setting clear standards for medical care.
• Physicians must guard against sexual assault allegations. |
|---|---|

This chapter discusses the legal standards for whether a physician has been negligent; that is, whether there has been medical malpractice. Much of the litigation over scientific and technical issues, including medical practice, is driven by a lack of accepted standards to judge the defendant's conduct. Lawyers and physicians must share the blame for this state of affairs. Physicians have been reticent to set clear standards for medical practice. As judges, lobbyists, and legislators, lawyers have made it increasingly easy for quacks and charlatans to be presented as credible experts on science and medicine (Huber 1991).

The second problem is medical faddism. Some physicians flock to new and unproved treatments or marginal therapies. The main diagnostic indication may be a patient or insurance company willing to pay for them. Physicians and medical societies who do not actively oppose this faddism are complicit in it. They are ignoring the duty of self-governance that has been given to the medical profession. (See Chapter 18.) If courts seem unable or unwilling to distinguish between true authorities and self-styled experts with dangerous and unorthodox opinions, it is partially due to the medical profession's squandering of its moral authority.

PROVING MALPRACTICE

A plaintiff initiates a lawsuit by filing papers with the court claiming that he or she was harmed by the defendant and is entitled to legal redress. These papers must set out the plaintiff's prima facie case: the statement of facts and legal theories that establish that the plaintiff has a legally enforceable claim against the defendant. There are four elements to a prima facie case of medical negligence:

1. Duty—a statement of the facts that establishes the legal relationship between the physician and the patient. (See Chapter 9.)

2. Breach—a statement of facts that illustrate that the defendant breached the legal duties implied in the physician-patient relationship or duties generally imposed on members of society.
3. Causation—that the breach of the defendant's duty caused the plaintiff's injuries.
4. Damages—the monetary value of the plaintiff's injuries. (See Chapter 4.)

Upon the filing of these claims, the defendant may ask the judge to dismiss the plaintiff's lawsuit for deficiencies in prima facie case. For the purpose of this review, the judge will assume that the facts presented by the plaintiff are correct. If, despite this assumption, the plaintiff's prima facie case is incomplete or legally unfounded, it may be dismissed, or the plaintiff may be given an opportunity to amend it to satisfy the defense's objections. During the pretrial phase of the lawsuit, the plaintiff must present legally sufficient evidence to support the allegations in the prima facie case.

Duty

A basic rule of Anglo-American law is that an individual has no duty to another person unless there is a legally recognized relationship with that person. Physicians have many legal relationships, all of which have accompanying duties that might form the basis of a lawsuit. In some cases, the defendant will deny that there was a legally recognized relationship with the plaintiff. If the plaintiff's claim is based on medical malpractice, the plaintiff must allege facts to support the existence of a physician-patient relationship. If the patient does not make the factual allegations necessary for the court to find a physician-patient relationship, the plaintiff's lawsuit will be dismissed. This often happens if a patient sues several physicians and includes one who did not treat the patient and had no legal relationships with the physicians who did treat the patient.

Standard of Care

Once the plaintiff has established that there was a legal relationship with the physician defendant, the plaintiff must establish the appropriate standard of care. In theory, establishing the standard of care and establishing the breach of that standard are legally separate. In reality, unless there is a factual question about what the defendant did, the proof of the standard of care also proves the defendant's breach. For example, assume that the defendant admits that she did not counsel the patient about prenatal testing. If the patient can establish that the standard of care was to offer this testing, the defendant breached the standard. If, however, the physician claims to have done the counseling, the patient will have to prove both that counseling was the standard of care and that the physician did not do the counseling.

The most common legal definition of standard of care is how similarly qualified practitioners would have managed the patient's care under the same or similar circumstances. This is not simply what the majority of practitioners would have done. The courts recognize the *respectable minority rule*. This rule allows the practitioner to show that although the course of therapy followed was not the same as other practitioners would have followed, it is one that is accepted by a respectable minority of practitioners. (*Respectable* is used in both senses.) The jury is not bound to accept the majority standard of care. Jurors may decide that a minority standard is the proper standard and that a physician following the majority standard was negligent.

In most medical malpractice cases, both the standard of care and its breach are established through the testimony of expert witnesses. There are situations in which the plaintiff may be able to establish the standard of care and breach without an expert witness.

Res Ipsa Loquitur

Res ipsa loquitur means, roughly, "the thing speaks for itself." Courts developed the concept of res ipsa loquitur to deal with cases in which the actual negligent act cannot be proved, but it is clear that the injury was caused by negligence. This doctrine was first recognized in the case of a man who was struck and severely injured by a barrel that rolled out of the second-story window of a warehouse. In the trial of the case, the defense attorney argued that the plaintiff did not know what events preceded the barrel rolling out of the window and thus could not prove that a warehouse employee was negligent. The plaintiff's attorney countered that barrels do not normally roll out of warehouse windows. The mere fact that a barrel fell from the window was res ipsa loquitur; "it spoke for itself," and it said that someone must have been negligent.

Most law students learn about res ipsa loquitur by reading a case about an airplane that disappears without a trace. There is no evidence of negligence, but there is a strong presumption that airplanes do not disappear without some negligence. In medical negligence cases, res ipsa loquitur can be invoked only when: (1) the patient suffers an injury that is not an expected complication of medical care; (2) the injury does not normally occur unless someone has been negligent; and (3) the defendant was responsible for the patient's well-being at the time of the injury. For example, assume that a portable X ray is ordered in an intensive care unit on a young, otherwise healthy patient recovering from peritonitis. After the technician leaves, it is found that the patient has a dislocated shoulder. This is not an expected complication of an X ray, there are no explanations for the injury other than mishandling or failing to restrain the patient properly, and the defendant was responsible for the patient's well-being at the time the injury occurred.

The strategic value of a res ipsa loquitur claim is that it does not require an expert to testify as to the proper standard of care. This has led plaintiffs to try to make res ipsa loquitur claims whenever they are unable to secure expert testimony to support their cases. Many states have limited the use of res ipsa loquitur in medical malpractice litigation, usually to claims such as a surgeon's leaving a foreign body in the patient or operating on the wrong patient. In all other cases, the plaintiff must present expert testimony as to standard of care and its breach.

Negligence Per Se

Negligence per se lawsuits are brought by private plaintiffs but are based on the defendant's violation of a law. In these cases the appropriate standard of care is defined by the law that was violated. For the court to accept a negligence per se claim, the plaintiff must show that a law was violated, that the law was intended to prevent the type of injury that occurred, and that the plaintiff was in the class of persons intended to be protected by the law. The plaintiff may claim negligence per se even if the defendant has not been convicted or administratively sanctioned under the law in question. In such cases, the plaintiff must prove that the defendant has violated the law. The plaintiff does not need to prove independently the violation if the defendant has been convicted or had pleaded guilty. (The plaintiff may not use a plea of nolo contendere, that is, not contesting the charges but not admitting guilt.)

Traffic violations are the most common instance of negligence per se. Assume that a driver hits a child while driving at night without headlights. This behavior is illegal, it is prohibited to prevent this type of accident, and the plaintiff is in the class of persons who were intended to be protected. The driver could be found negligent based on the violation of the statute. Conversely, assume that a physician injures a patient while practicing without a current medical license. This will not support a negligence per se claim because medical licensing laws are not intended to protect specific patients from medical malpractice.

The most common prosecutions of physicians for practice-related crimes involve tax and other economic fraud laws. These will not support negligence per se claims in medical malpractice cases because the laws are not intended to prevent patient injuries. (As discussed in Chapter 10, such violation can support other causes of action against the physician.) Negligence per se claims are a threat to physicians who disregard laws intended to protect patients, such as the federal provisions on patient dumping (discussed in Chapter 32) and state laws requiring physicians to provide emergency care. Since these laws make it illegal to deny a person necessary emergency medical care, a person refused emergency care suffers the injury the law was intended to prevent. Negligence per se claims also could be brought against physicians who do not obey disease control regulations and laws requiring the reporting of dangerous individuals.

Intentional Torts

Intentional torts are intentional actions that result in harm to the plaintiff. The harm need not be intended, but the act must be intentional, not merely careless or reckless. Most intentional torts are also crimes. The classic intentional tort in medical practice is forcing unwanted medical care on a patient. The care may benefit the patient, but if it was refused and the physician has no state mandate to force care on the patient, the patient may sue for the intentional tort of battery. (See Chapter 11.)

The most common intentional tort is battery. The legal standard for a battery is "an intentional, unconsented touching." (Batteries such as shootings, stabbings, and beatings are also criminal law violations.) Although battery is commonly linked with assault, an assault is the act of putting a person in fear of bodily harm. Battery occurs only if there is an actual physical contact. The law of battery has been tailored to the problems of living in a crowded society. Not every unconsented touching is a battery—only those that are intended. Even among intentional unconsented touchings, the courts will allow recovery only for those that manifest some malign intent. Thus, neither bumping into a person on a bus nor grabbing a person to prevent him or her from falling is a battery. In contrast, an unwanted kiss is a battery, though it does not cause any physical injury.

Most battery claims against health care providers are based on real attacks, not technical violations of informed consent rules. One case involved a patient who became pregnant while having an affair with her physician (*Collins v. Thakkart*, 1990). When she allowed the physician to examine her to confirm the pregnancy, he repeatedly forced a metal instrument into her uterus, triggering a miscarriage. The court found this constituted a battery, allowing the patient to claim for wrongful abortion.

Sexual Assault

One particularly troubling, and legally dangerous, class of batteries are sexual assaults. It is difficult to determine the true number of sexual assault claims against physicians. When a claim is made public, it receives extensive publicity, creating the impression that sexual assaults are a common problem. In other cases, sexual assault claims are paid off by the physician's malpractice insurance company. While all medical malpractice insurance policies exclude coverage for criminal activity, plaintiffs' attorneys include an allegation that the assault was a breach of medical standards as well as a criminal act. This creates a dilemma for the insurance company.

If the insurance company pays the claim, it forces its other insureds to subsidize illegal conduct. If it refuses to pay the claim, the plaintiff's attorney can make a deal with the defendant physician. In return for the physician's agreeing to confess to negligent (and covered) behavior, the plaintiff's attorney will agree to settle both claims for whatever can be extracted from the insurance company. If the insurance company refuses to settle the case, the plaintiff's attorney may offer to represent the physician defendant in a claim of bad faith against the insurance company. The defendant, now represented by the plaintiff's attorney, sues the insurance company on a breach of contract theory for failing to pay the claim. If the plaintiff's attorney wins the lawsuit, the defendant collects from the insurance company and then passes the money to the plaintiff.

Sexual assault claims are increasing because of the heightened societal concern with sex crimes and child sexual abuse. A sexual assault claim stigmatizes the physician and gives the plaintiff a strategic advantage in what might otherwise be a weak medical malpractice case. Ethical attorneys will not make such a claim if they know it to be false. However, if the attorney's client insists that she or he has been assaulted, the attorney can only judge the assertion based on the circumstances of the medical treatment. The legal standard of care is that male health care providers do not examine female patients without a female attendant present. This standard is frequently ignored, however. A physician who violates this norm or allows a male nurse or physician's assistant to examine a female patient unattended will find it very difficult to defend a sexual assault claim. An attorney representing such a patient will accept the patient's claims as credible because allowing an unattended examination of a female patient is concrete evidence that, at the least, the physician has bad judgment.

Establishing the Standard of Care

The courts have delegated the setting of professional standards to members of the various professions. This is in contrast to the standards for nonprofessional skills, such as driving a car. The legislature establishes the rules of the road, and a lay juror is deemed capable of determining when they have been violated. In contrast, legislatures do not adopt detailed standards for professional practice. Medical practice standards are drawn from the customs and behavior of the members of the profession. If the profession has developed documents that reflect a consensus on how the profession is to be practiced, these documents will set the standard for judging individual transgressions.

The Expert's Role

An expert witness must establish a standard for medical care and give an opinion on whether the defendant's conduct met this standard. The standard must at once be general to all practitioners and specific to the individual plaintiff's circumstances. Ideally, it should be supported by uncontroverted scholarly literature. While it need not prescribe a single course of action, it must either (for the plaintiff) proscribe the defendant's conduct or (for the defense) endorse the defendant's conduct as an acceptable alternative.

These standards ignore the conflict between actual medical practice and legal expectations. The courts expect that medicine, as a learned, science-based discipline, will have articulated standards for practice. While recognizing the art in medicine, the law assumes that the science of medicine will be sufficiently formalized that the regions of art will be readily identifiable. Rather than face the core problem of inadequately defined practice standards, the courts allow experts to step into this void with standards tailored to serve the desired ends of the lawyer engaging the expert.

Schools of Practice

Obtaining expert testimony has always been the most difficult part of medical malpractice litigation. Historically, there have been two competing interests: members of a professional group did not want to testify against their colleagues, but they did want to run their competitors out of business. Allopathic physicians were happy to label homeopathic physicians as incompetent, and any physician would dispute the competence of a chiropractor. These rivalries led the courts to use the legal doctrines of the school of practice and the locality rule as the basis for qualifying a person as an expert witness.

The school of practice distinctions also predated modern medical training and certification. At one time medical practitioners were divided into chiropractors, homeopaths, allopaths, osteopaths, and several other schools based on different philosophical and psychological beliefs. Since state legislatures did not discriminate among these different schools of healing, judges were reluctant to allow litigation to be used to attack an approved school. Except for chiropractors, allopathic practices (and osteopaths using primarily allopathic methods) have driven out the other schools of medical practice. The courts retain the traditional school of practice rule when they refuse to allow physician experts to question chiropractic care or chiropractors to testify in cases with physician defendants.

The school of practice rule is now applied to the differentiation of physicians into self-designated specialties (self-designated because few state licensing boards recognize specialties or limit physicians' right to practice the specialties in which they have been trained). The relevance of the specialty qualifications of an expert witness depend on whether the case concerns procedures and expertise that are intrinsic to the specialty or general medical knowledge and techniques that are common to all physicians. This dichotomy is reflected in strategies for expert testimony. Whether the parties to the lawsuit will stress the specialty or general knowledge depends on the qualifications of the expert that each has retained.

The Locality Rule

The locality rule is the progenitor of the debates over the proper specialty qualifications for an expert witness. The locality rule evolved before the standardization of medical training and certification. During this period, there was a tremendous gulf between the skills and abilities of university-trained physicians and the graduates of the unregulated diploma mills. In many parts of the country, parochialism and necessity combined to create the rule that a physician's competence would be determined by comparison with the other physicians in the community, or at least in similar neighboring communities. The strictest form of the locality rule required the expert to be from the same or a similar community. This made it nearly impossible for injured patients to find experts to support their cases, effectively preventing most medical malpractice litigation.

The underpinnings of the locality rule are diametrically opposed to contemporary specialty training and certification. There is no longer a justification for a rule that shelters substandard medical decision making on the sole excuse that it is the norm for a given community. Many states have explicitly abolished the locality rule for physicians who hold themselves out as certified specialists. Unfortunately, the locality rule is being reinvigorated in some states as a tort reform measure. This resurgence is driven by the problem of access to care and facilities in rural areas.

Proponents of the locality rule often confuse access to facilities with physician competence. A national standard of care implies that the rural physician will have the same training and exercise the same level of judgment and diligence as an urban practitioner. It does not require that the rural physician have the same medical facilities available. If the community does not have facilities for an emergency cesarean section, the physician cannot be found negligent for failing to do this surgery within the 15 minutes that might be the standard in a well-equipped urban hospital.

Under a national standard, however, the physician must inform the patient of the limitations of the available facilities and recommend prompt transfer if indicated. This allows patients to balance the convenience of local care against the risks of inadequate facilities. The protection of a national standard is especially important as rural hospitals attempt to market or retain lucrative medical services that their facilities are not properly equipped to handle.

Qualifying an Expert

The attorney offering the testimony of an expert witness must follow certain legal formalisms to have the expert's testimony accepted in court. The attorney must first establish that the witness has the proper medical qualifications. When the witness is presented, the opposing counsel may ask to stipulate that the witness is qualified. This is done when the witness is clearly qualified and opposing counsel would prefer that the jury not dwell on the witness's background. If the defense does not stipulate to the witness's qualifications, the expert witness must describe his or her background, practice, or academic experience and any other training or experience that is relevant to the case. Most important, the expert must assert familiarity with the treatment of patients with the plaintiff's complaint by physicians similarly situated to the defendant.

The attorney offering the expert witness will tailor the testimony to the expert's qualifications. If the expert is a general practitioner testifying against a specialist, the testimony will be heavily weighted toward establishing that any competent physician would have avoided the defendant's error. If the expert is a specialist testifying against a general practitioner, the expert will be questioned whether the general practitioner had a duty to refer the patient to a more skilled physician.

If both the expert and the defendant are specialists, the jury must be convinced that the defendant delivered substandard care, as opposed to making a well-reasoned but incorrect judgment. The plaintiff's expert will try to explain the plaintiff's medical condition and the standard of care question in simple terms. This allows the jurors to convince themselves that there was no acceptable excuse for the defendant's failure to render the care described by the plaintiff's expert.

An alternative tactic is to attack the defendant's qualifications to treat the plaintiff's condition. This may be done with either a same-specialty expert or, preferably, an expert from a different and more appropriate specialty. The best situation for this approach is when the patient's condition is usually managed by a different specialty: for example, a surgeon defending his supervision of a certified registered nurse anesthetist against damning testimony by an anesthesiologist. The hope is to force the defendant to abandon his posture of special knowledge. If the plaintiff is successful in establishing the defendant's lack of special knowledge, then the defendant must contend that the treatment of plaintiff's condition was a matter of general medical knowledge. Even if the plaintiff is not wholly successful, he will still force the defendant to expend credibility on refuting the allegation that he was unqualified to manage the patient's condition.

The Problem with Expert Witnesses
The testimony of expert witnesses is inevitably theater. Jurors have no alternative but to judge the testimony of expert witnesses on the personal credibility of the witness. Positive factors such as academic degrees, specialty board certification, and publications influence credibility. So do factors such as physical appearance, race, gender, command of English, and personality. For an expert witness, the foremost qualifications are effective presentation and teaching ability. The expert must educate the jury in the technical matter at hand, just as he or she might educate an undergraduate physiology class. The objective is to convince the jurors that they understand the technical issues. Once there is a perception of understanding, the expert can convince them that they are making an independent decision that his or her testimony is correct rather than just agreeing with him or her.

The problem is that an untutored audience may not be able to separate a well-told tale from the truth. When the testimony involves areas that do not have consensus standards of practice, it is not unusual for the jury to be told separate, mutually exclusive tales by each party in the litigation. The absence of standards also makes it difficult to identify impartial third parties to act as scientific referees. If physicians cannot agree on common standards of practice, there can be no agreement on persons to testify as to standards of practice. This is reflected in proposals by defendant groups to limit who may testify as an expert witness. These proposals all involve requiring that the expert witnesses have the same training and practice habits as the defendant. While ostensibly aimed at nonpracticing professional witnesses, they also eliminate medical school professors and persons who do not practice full-time private medicine. Since the defendant also must put on expert testimony, the impact of these proposals may be as severe on defense witnesses for physicians involved in innovative treatments as for plaintiffs' witnesses with alternative practice styles.

Causation
Merely breaching established standards is not enough to support a medical malpractice lawsuit. Once a breach of standards has been established by expert testimony, the plaintiff must establish that the breach was the proximate cause of

the injury. For example, assume that the patient is brought to the emergency room with severe injuries from a motorcycle accident. After a prolonged stay in the intensive care unit (ICU), the patient ultimately loses his leg. Upon discharge from the hospital, the patient has an attorney investigate the care he received in the ICU. The attorney finds that the patient was repeatedly given the wrong dosage of his antihypertensive medication, and, as a result, his blood pressure was out of control. Although this is a clear breach of the standard of care, the attorney also must prove, by expert testimony, that the incorrect dosage of medication caused the loss of the leg. Showing that the standard of care was breached and that the patient has an injury is not enough. The attorney must demonstrate that but for the incorrect dosage of medicine, the patient would still have his leg.

Causation is a problematic defense. Juries are not sympathetic to a physician who acts negligently and then claims that the patient's injuries are not due to the substandard care. Since there is usually an element of punishment in a verdict against a physician, juries tend to be distracted by the negligent behavior and ignore whether the negligence actually caused the injury. The physician should not escape punishment because the patient was lucky enough to escape injury. Causation defenses work best when the physician's behavior is below the acceptable standard but is not obviously dangerous. A physician who misses a shadow on a lung film may successfully argue that the tumor was too far advanced for an earlier diagnosis to matter. A physician who refuses to continue caring for a pregnant woman because her insurance lapses at 34 weeks will have difficulty convincing a jury that this was unrelated to her baby's brain injury.

Vicarious Liability

Physicians are legally responsible for the actions of nonphysician personnel acting under their supervision. This is termed *vicarious liability*. (See Chapter 15.) In general, employers are responsible for the actions of their employees. This is *respondeat superior*, or the master-servant relationship, a term that dates the origins of the concept. The employer is responsible for the actions of the employee that are in the course and scope of the employment. This rule poses two questions, Who is an employee? and What is the course and scope of employment?

While it is commonly assumed that employment status is determined by how a person is paid, this is only one of several factors that are considered. Even unpaid volunteer workers may be classified as employees for the purpose of vicarious liability. The usual focus is on payment because most disputes about employment status involve the tax laws rather than the tort laws. The whole work situation is considered when determining whether there is vicarious liability for a person's actions.

Method of Payment

Persons who are paid as employees (the employer pays federal or state withholding tax, FICA, insurance, and so on) will generally be considered employees for determining vicarious liability. If the worker is a volunteer who receives no pay but does a defined job that is usually done by paid employees, the volunteer is also treated as an employee. If FICA should be paid but is not because the employee and the employer are trying to evade their tax liabilities, the court can still find the putative employer vicariously liable for the person's actions. In addition, the employer may have both financial and criminal liability. The Internal Revenue Service has become intolerant of paying an individual as a contract worker to avoid employment taxes and FICA. If the worker is truly a contract worker, is a volunteer who is not displacing a paid worker, or is paid by someone else, then vicarious liability is determined by the extent to which the individuals control their own work.

Control

The fundamental issue that determines whether a person is legally treated as an employee is the extent to which the person hiring the work may control the details of the work. To illustrate this, consider the situation of hiring a licensed plumber to install a new sink in a physician's office. In this situation, the physician determines what type of sink to install and where to put it, but the plumber determines how to install the sink. If someone is injured because the sink is improperly installed, the physician is not vicariously liable for the plumber's work.

Conversely, assume that the physician hires an unskilled worker to install the sink. The physician tells the worker how to cut the hole for the sink, attach the pipes, and install the garbage disposal. In this situation, the physician would be vicariously liable for an injury caused by the unskilled worker's negligent installation of the sink. There will be vicarious liability when the employer directs the details of the work or has the responsibility for directing the details of the work.

Licensed Professionals

Professional licensing laws restrict the authority of nonlicensed personnel to control the work of the licensed professional. The clearest example is aviation. Only the pilot can determine whether it is safe to make a given flight. A company can hire pilots and tell them when and where to fly, but the pilot retains the responsibility for determining if a given flight is safe to make. Physicians have the same responsibilities. Nonphysician personnel cannot direct a physician's actions. If the physician gives in to the hospital's pressure to discharge a patient, the physician will be liable if that patient is injured. (See Chapter 10.)

Nurses, physician assistants, and other physician extenders are licensed professionals, but they have a limited license. The extent to which they may make medical decisions is determined by state law, but they must usually work under the supervision of a physician. The physician's license is unlimited, however, in that physicians may legally perform nursing tasks without violating nurse practice laws. (In contrast, a pilot cannot perform tasks limited to a certified aviation mechanic.) The breadth of the medical license means that physicians can be found vicariously liable for the actions of the other licensed personnel they employ or supervise.

Scope of Employment

An employee's scope of employment is the activities that the employee may properly carry out and that the employer is expected to supervise. Determining scope of employment is important because an employee can collect worker's compensation benefits only for injuries that arise within the scope of employment. It is also important if the employee injures another person. The injured person may recover from the employer only if the employee's actions were within the scope of employment. Disputes about scope of employment arise from actions, such as driving to a work site, that are not under employer supervision, or intentional actions, such as drunken driving or sexual assaults.

Intentional Acts

Intentional torts are usually not within the course and scope of employment. Employers may be vicariously liable for the intentional torts of their employees only if the employer tolerated the activities or did not properly screen the employees for dangerous tendencies. For example, assume a physician hires a physician's assistant who subsequently sexually assaults a patient. If the employee has no history of assaulting patients or other persons and the physician has not had any notice of problems, the physician will not be liable for the assault. If, however, the employee had assaulted persons in the past and the physician was negligent in discovering this, the physician could be liable under the theory of negligent hiring. The physician could be liable for negligent retention if there were complaints about the behavior of the physician's assistant and the physician failed to act on them.

Physicians must have employment criteria designed to detect employees who are a potential hazard. They must take quick action if an employee is suspected of intentionally harming patients. Intentional injuries must never be covered up. Cover-ups can result in large financial losses through the assessment of punitive damages, and they undermine public confidence in the physician or medical institution. In one example, which occurred in a San Antonio teaching hospital (*New York Times* 1984, 1985), a pediatric ICU nurse became so involved in the thrill of resuscitating patients that she began poisoning children with a muscle relaxant to create resuscitation opportunities, not all of which were successful. Rather than investigating the unexpected increase in deaths, the hospital and physician committees covered up the evidence pointing to murder and offered the nurse a good recommendation if she would resign. She continued to poison children in her subsequent job but was found out and convicted of murder. Through its participation in the cover-up, the hospital and physicians increased their liability for the nurse's actions while she was in their employ and may have assumed liability for the murders she committed later because the job was obtained with their false recommendation. They may have also committed crimes themselves by not reporting suspicious deaths and injuries under both the child abuse reporting laws and murder laws.

Hospital Employees

Physicians' liability for the actions of hospital employees is problematic because of the persistence of the *borrowed-servant* and *captain-of-the-ship doctrines.* These doctrines hold that all the actions of hospital employees are attributable to the patients' attending physicians. Under these doctrines, a physician may be found liable for the actions of a nurse whom the physician cannot hire, fire, or otherwise control. These doctrines evolved because, until recently, most hospitals were nonprofit corporations and were protected by charitable immunity. This immunity was predicated on the assumption that a nonprofit hospital provided a community service that was financed through patient revenues. The courts ruled that it would be against the public interest to allow an injured patient to recover a judgment against a charitable hospital because the judgment would drain off resources that could be used to treat many other patients.

Since the patient could not recover against the hospital, the courts created doctrines that attributed the actions of hospital employees to the attending physicians. As private practitioners independent of the hospital and the charity, these physicians were susceptible to suit. Finding that nurses were always under the control of the patient's attending physician allowed the patient to sue the physician when the hospital employee was at fault. This borrowed-servant doctrine was useful because the courts are reluctant to deny injured persons their day in court. As the courts have dismantled charitable immunity, many states have modified or abolished the borrowed-servant doctrine.

The captain-of-the-ship doctrine is a special case of the borrowed-servant doctrine that applies in operating rooms. In the operating room, the surgeon, as the captain of the ship, picks the crew and gives all the orders. The surgeon is charged with supervising all members of the operating room team. This made some sense in the early days of surgery when the surgeon was usually the only physician in the room, and the entire surgical team was a nurse to assist and a nurse to give anesthesia. In a modern operating room, with a physician giving anesthesia and a team of highly-trained nurses, the idea that the surgeon controls all the activity in the room has become untenable. This has led most courts to abandon the captain-of-the-ship doctrine in favor of determining the liability of each person caring for the patient. While this correctly reflects the shared responsibility in the operating room, it does reduce the incentive of the surgeon to ensure that all members of the team are competent.

PRODUCTS LIABILITY

Physicians become involved in products liability litigation as witnesses and defendants. When medical devices fail, injured patients usually sue the physician using or prescribing the device, as well as suing the device manufacturer. Lawsuits involving products are brought under the legal theory of strict liability because they use a less rigorous standard of proof than a negligence lawsuit. The general form of this standard is found in the Restatement of Torts, Second, section 402a. (The Restatement is a compilation of legal principles. It is not a statute and does not have legal force unless adopted by a state's courts or legislature.)

>§402A. Special Liability of Seller of Product for Physical Harm to User or Consumer
>(1) One who sells any product in a defective condition unreasonably dangerous to the user or consumer or to his property is subject to liability for physical harm thereby caused to the ultimate user or consumer, or to his property, if
>　(a) the seller is engaged in the business of selling such a product, and
>　(b) it is expected to and does reach the user or consumer without substantial change in the condition in which it is sold.
>(2) The rule stated in Subsection (1) applies although
>　(a) the seller has exercised all possible care in the preparation and sale of his product, and
>　(b) the user or consumer has not bought the product from or entered into any contractual relation with the seller.

It is section 1 that creates the strict liability. It allows the injured person to recover if the product was defective and unreasonably dangerous but does not require that the defect be caused by negligence of the defendant. Some states also reduce the plaintiff's burden of proving causation in products cases. For example, assume the respirator hose connector breaks on a patient dependent upon the respirator. An ICU nurse notices that the patient has suddenly developed an arrhythmia but does not check the patient for 20 minutes. When the nurse finally checks the patient, the broken connector is found, and so is a severely hypoxic patient.

The nurse was clearly negligent in not checking on the patient. This is the proximate cause of the injury and would support an independent negligence action against the nurse and her employer. While the respirator connector was defective, the injury would not have occurred if the nurse had attended to the patient properly. In a pure negligence case, the product manufacturer might successfully argue that the nurse's intervening negligence cut off its liability. This is a strong argument in the ICU because part of the nurse's job is to be alert to failing equipment. In most states, however, the device manufacturer will be held strictly liable for the injury, irrespective of the nurse's negligence. Both the respirator manufacturer and the nurse (hospital) would be liable for the injury.

Physicians are often drawn into products liability litigation. The plaintiff sues the physician in hopes of a potential second recovery or help in pinning the liability on the product manufacturer. The manufacturer may force the physician to be joined as a codefendant by alleging that the injury was caused by misuse of the device rather than by a defect. This is common when the alleged defect is in design, not manufacture. One series of cases involved an anesthesia machine whose connectors could be reversed, with fatal consequences. The manufacturer alleged that the machine was designed for an expert user who had the responsibility for ensuring that the device was properly assembled. The anesthesiologist claimed that the machine should have been designed to prevent misassembly. The manufacturer lost because the jury determined that the manufacturer could not rely on the anesthesiologist to know how to properly assemble the anesthesia machine (Richards and Walter 1989).

THE IMPORTANCE OF SETTING OBJECTIVE STANDARDS

There have been many suggested solutions to the expert witness problem. Most of these are defensive strategies that seek to reduce the availability of plaintiff's experts; they do not address the root problem of ambiguous medical practice standards.

The best approach is to reduce the ambiguity in practice standards. While courts will still require expert testimony, both judges and juries are very deferential toward explicit standards of practice that are promulgated by credible professional organizations. Since plaintiffs' attorneys are aware of the increased difficulty in proving a case against a physician who has followed approved standards, standards lead to reduced litigation. (See Chapter 34.)

Most important, standards allow effective quality assurance review. This reduces the legal risk to peer reviewers and improves the quality of care. Standards are also critical in medical cost containment. Most standard-setting efforts in the financial context have been directed at reducing unnecessary care. As the pressure to reduce medical care costs increases, well-articulated practice standards will be critical in ensuring that cost-containment efforts do not deny patients necessary care. Without standards to back their decisions, individual practitioners will not be able to resist third-party payer pressures to reduce medically indicated care.

There are three impediments to standard setting in medical practice. The first is the belief that setting a standard will inhibit innovation. While this may be relevant in a medical research setting, innovation is much less significant in routine medical care. Even in a research setting, rigid adherence to standard protocols is fundamental to the controlled trials that advance medical science. The second is resistance by medical malpractice defense lawyers. Defense lawyers assert, correctly, that it is much more difficult to defend a physician who violates an explicit practice standard. This ignores the reduced litigation against physicians who do comply. It also ignores the long-term reduction of negligent practice as the peer review process urges practitioners to follow appropriate practice standards.

The third, and most important, impediment to standard setting is the Federal Trade Commission (FTC). In its efforts to reduce anticompetitive practices in medical care delivery, the FTC has discouraged professional standard setting. While correctly recognizing that many professional standards are anticompetitive, the FTC does not seem to recognize that this is the price of professional self-regulation. Any rule that restricts marginal practitioners will reduce competition. The fear of FTC enforcement actions has discouraged professional societies from setting standards for practice. This has been most evident in the reluctance to address entrepreneurial practices that encourage patients to undergo unnecessary and vanity procedures. The FTC has focused on reducing prices through competition, ignoring the problem of physicians' and hospitals' using the classic advertising technique of creating a demand for unnecessary or inappropriate services.

BIBLIOGRAPHY

Expert Witnesses

Black B: Evolving legal standards for the admissibility of scientific evidence. Science 1988 Mar 25; 239(4847):1508–12.

Brent RL: Improving the quality of expert witness testimony. Pediatrics 1988 Sep; 82 (3 Pt 2):511–13.

Brent RL: The irresponsible expert witness: A failure of biomedical graduate education and professional accountability. Pediatrics 1982 Nov; 70(5):754–62.

Dash GP: The infection control practitioner as expert witness. Am J Infect Control 1987 Aug; 15(4):178–81.

Faust D; Ziskin J: The expert witness in psychology and psychiatry. Science 1988 Jul 1; 241(4861):31–35.

Ginzburg HM: Use and misuse of epidemiologic data in the courtroom: Defining the limits of inferential and particularistic evidence in mass tort litigation. Am J Law Med 1986; 12(3–4):423–39.

Goldstein RL: Psychiatrists in the hot seat: Discrediting doctors by impeachment of their credibility. Bull Am Acad Psychiatry Law 1988; 16(3):225–34.

Holder AR: Testimony of expert witness. Leading cases. JAMA 1975 Mar 17; 231(11):1177.

Holthaus D: States judge expert witnesses before they testify. Hospitals 1988 Mar 5; 62(5):60–61.

Huber PW: *Galileo's Revenge: Junk Science in the Courtroom*. 1991.

Kunin CM: The expert witness in medical malpractice litigation. Ann Intern Med 1984 Jan; 100(1):139–43.

Lunde DT; Sigal HA: Psychiatric testimony in "cult" litigation. Bull Am Acad Psychiatry Law 1987; 15(2):205–10.

Needell JE: Psychiatric expert witnesses: Proposals for change. Am J Law Med 1980 Fall; 6(3):425–49.

Piccirillo M; Graf GJ: Medical malpractice: A case study in medical and legal decision making. Yale J Biol Med 1989 Jan–Feb; 62(1):23–42.

Sadoff RL: Malpractice in psychiatry: Standards of care and the expert witness. Psychiatr Med 1984 Sep; 2(3):235–43.

Shuman DW: Testimonial compulsion. The involuntary medical expert witness. J Leg Med (Chic) 1983 Dec; 4(4):419–46.

Torrey SB; Ludwig S: The emergency physician in the courtroom: Serving as an expert witness in cases of child abuse. Pediatr Emerg Care 1987 Mar; 3(1):50–52.

General References

Altschule, MD: Bad law, bad medicine. Am J Law Med 1977 Fall; 3(3):295–301.

Cecchini RA; Ferraro PJ: The standard of care in emergency room procedure. Leg Aspects Med Pract 1977 Dec; 5(12):45–50.

Christianson JB: Long-term care standards: Enforcement and compliance. J Health Polit Policy Law 1979 Fall; 4(3):414–34.

Collins v. Thakkart, 552 NE2d 507 (1990).

Gibbs RF: The new JCAH standards: What is their legal standing? J Leg Med 1977 Feb; 5(2):9–16.

Greenlaw J: Enforcing professional standards. Nurs Law Ethics 1980 Dec; 1(10):3, 7.

Houtchens B: Initial evaluation and management of major trauma in the rural setting: An appeal for a "national standard." Leg Aspects Med Pract 1977 Dec; 5(12):38–39.

Johnson RH; Wood JJ Sr: Judicial, legislative, and administrative competence in setting institutional standards. In Kindred M et al., eds.: *The Mentally Retarded Citizen and the Law*. 1976.

Khan A; Wolfgang A: Standard of proof in medical negligence. Med Leg J 1984; 52 (Pt 2):117–22.

Mestrovic SG; Cook JA: The dangerousness standard: What is it and how is it used? Int J Law Psychiatry 1986; 8(4):443–69. [Published erratum appears in Int J Law Psychiatry 1986; 9(1):137.]

Morreim EH: Cost constraints as a malpractice defense. Hastings Cent Rep 1988 Feb–Mar; 18(1):5–10.

Nelkin D: Establishing professional standards: Ecologists and the public interest. Hastings Cent Rep 1976 Feb; 6(1):38–44.

New York Times: Federal investigators report on clusters of infant deaths. 1985, Jul 25.

New York Times: Investigators near end of inquiry into deaths of infants at hospital. 1984, Apr 11.

Norton ML: Ethics in medicine and law: Standards and conflicts. Leg Med Annu 1977:201–15.

Overcast TD; Merrikin KJ; Evans RW: Malpractice issues in heart transplantation. Am J Law Med 1985 Winter; 10(4):363–95.

Reuter SR: Why is a state court setting standards of care? Leg Aspects Med Pract 1979 Dec; 7(12):16–18.

Richards EP; Walter CW: How is an anesthesia machine like a lawnmower?—The problem of the learned intermediary. IEEE Eng Med Biol 1989; 8(2):55.

Rubenstein HS; Miller FH; Postel S; Evans HB: Standards of medical care based on consensus rather than evidence: The case of routine bedrail use for the elderly. Law Med Health Care 1983 Dec; 11(6):271–76.

Sanbar SS; Thompson CS: Developing standards of care for the diagnosis and treatment of coronary artery disease. J Leg Med (Chic) 1983 Mar; 4(1):87–108.

Schelling TC: Standards for adequate minimum personal health services. Milbank Mem Fund Q Health Soc 1979 Spring; 57(2):212–33.

7

The Malpractice Insurance Crisis

CRITICAL POINTS
- There are more myths than objective information about medical malpractice.
- Practicing defensive medicine may raise, rather than lower, the risk of litigation.
- There are conflicts of interest between physicians and malpractice insurance carriers.
- Physicians must be careful consumers of malpractice insurance.

In the mid-1970s rates for medical malpractice insurance skyrocketed. Since that time the specter of medical malpractice litigation has preoccupied physicians. In some areas of practice, such as anesthesia, this fear of litigation and the costs of malpractice insurance have led to reforms that have both improved patient safety and reduced malpractice insurance costs. In other areas, destructive patterns of defensive medicine have evolved. These have increased medical care costs and complicated patient care and have not reduced malpractice claims and the resulting insurance premiums. These inconsistent responses to a common problem result from the paucity of useful empirical data about medical malpractice litigation.

The material in this chapter reflects both the general literature and empirical research conducted by one of the authors, but it is not a review of the literature. The intent of the chapter is to help physicians separate the medical practice problems from problems that stem from the structure of the malpractice insurance business. The goal is to help physicians practice constructive preventive law rather than destructive defensive medicine.

RESEARCH PROBLEMS IN MALPRACTICE

Most of the debate about medical malpractice is permeated by unsubstantiated beliefs (Kapp 1987). We term these myths because there is little reliable quantitative or qualitative information about tort litigation in general and medical malpractice litigation in specific. There are many studies and uncounted policy articles, but very few pass even rudimentary study design criteria. The best-controlled and most comprehensive study is the Harvard Medical Practice Study. It began with hospital records rather than insurance claims. It was made possible because it was done for the state of New York under state authority (Patients, Doctors, and Lawyers 1990). The major predecessor of this study was done in California in the 1970s to determine if a no-fault malpractice system would be cost-effective (Mills 1977; Sanazaro and Mills 1991).

The most common methodological flaw in most studies is improper sample selection. This is not the fault of the researchers so much as a reflection of the disarray of the primary data sources. There are three primary sources of data about medical malpractice claims: court records, reports to third parties such as Boards of Medical Examiners (BOMEs) and insurance commissions, and insurance company data.

There are several problems with court records. Few courts have comprehensive computer access to all court documents, making it very difficult to extract data. Court records are incomplete because some claims are settled without a lawsuit being filed. They are inaccurate because many states do not require that the settlement filed with the court be the same as the agreement between the plaintiff and the defendant. It is not unusual for defendants to settle cases for substantial payments on condition that the plaintiff withdraw the lawsuit and file court papers to the effect that the defendant paid nothing and the lawsuit was just a misunderstanding. This prevents reporters and others seeking to investigate the physician from knowing that a malpractice settlement has been paid.

With the advent of the National Practitioner Databank, most states require all payments for medical malpractice claims to be reported to the BOME or the state insurance commission. In the long term, these promise to be excellent sources of financial data if obvious loopholes are closed. The most serious problem with most state reporting laws and the National Practitioner Database is that they are triggered only by payments made in the physician's name. Physicians can avoid being reported if another party, such as a hospital or health maintenance organization, is willing to pay the plaintiff to drop the physician from the lawsuit (Rushford 1991). Additional problems are that these reports usually do not contain sufficient data to evaluate the underlying medical care, requiring the researcher to obtain individual claims records from the insurer.

INSURANCE COMPANY DATA

Insurance companies have the best data on claims, but the data are not as complete or comprehensive as might be expected. Companies have extensive records on the amounts paid in individual cases, but they may not collect detailed information about the medical care leading to the claim. This information is not cost-effective to collect and analyze. Understanding claims is valuable only if it is used for individual underwriting decisions or claims prevention. Since most medical malpractice insurance is not experience rated, physicians with increased claims do not pay higher rates, obviating the need for individual underwriting decisions. Using claims data for prevention is controversial because it requires insurance companies to set standards for medical practice. Some companies have done this in limited situations, but most shy away from setting standards that might be used by plaintiff's attorneys suing their insureds. (See Chapter 6.)

Insurance company data are hard to compile because most states have several insurers at any given time, and these companies enter and leave the market over time. The most common technique is to study the claims closed during one or more years (GAO I–VII). These closed claim studies are valuable if every closed claim is available for study; unfortunately, many studies have been done on poorly defined subsets of closed claims. Even if the complete set of claims is available, most claims take several years to close. (A claim closed in 1986, for example, may have resulted from medical care rendered in 1980.) This makes closed claim studies insensitive to trends and changes in medical malpractice claims.

Like all other retrospective studies, closed claim studies are limited because important data are often missing from the files. Ideally, claims studies would be conducted on all claims—not just those that are closed—but few companies allow researchers to analyze open claims. This is partly out of concern with the loss of proprietary information that might influence the resolution of open claims. It also stems from the desire to prevent state regulatory commissions from obtaining complete information about the companies' real financial exposure.

MYTHS OF MALPRACTICE

Myth 1: Getting Sued Is a Random Event

Many physicians fatalistically believe that malpractice litigation is random and that nothing they do can reduce the chance of being sued (Sloan et al. 1989). They also overestimate their risk of being sued. The Harvard study found that physicians in New York believed that they had a 20 percent chance of being sued in a given year (Patients, Doctors, and Lawyers 1990). The real risk of being sued was closer to 6 percent. The gap between the perceived risk and the real risk was greater in areas of the state that had highly publicized medical malpractice problems.

The rate for most physicians is probably less than the average rate because there is evidence that medical malpractice claims are not evenly distributed but tend to cluster. In the extreme case of a small subspecialty, one physician with multiple claims can account for most of the litigation burden for the entire group. There is a randomness due to the low level of claims. Relatively few patients who are negligently injured by their physicians ever make a claim for compensation (Patients, Doctors, and Lawyers 1990).

Myth 2: Every Physician Is King

This is the belief that individual physicians should be allowed to perform any procedure without outside interference. Hospitals are intended to act as a brake on unnecessary or dangerous procedures, but many hospitals are in such financial trouble that they encourage any treatments that bring in paying patients. Even hospital review can be avoided by moving procedures to physician-controlled outpatient surgery centers. As a result, unnecessary and dangerous treatments are proffered with impunity. The malpractice claims that accompany these procedures raise the premium for all physicians in the same specialty. In some states, for example, the malpractice awards and settlements for radial keratotomies drastically increased the insurance costs for all physicians.

Myth 3: Patients Should Be Sophisticated Consumers

Sometimes a patient sues a physician when the bad result was not the latter's fault. But patients and their attorneys are not medical scientists and do not immediately know the difference between bad practice and bad luck. It is very difficult for a lay patient to be a knowledgeable consumer of medical care. Interestingly, it is not clear that physicians are any better at recognizing when they have negligently injured a patient. One study of a malpractice insurance plan that encouraged the early reporting of adverse incidents found that these reports appeared to be made at random (Miller and Richards 1989).

Myth 4: Breakthroughs Are Good Public Relations

Modern medical research is capital intensive. Institutions and individuals engaged in research must constantly seek new infusions of money. Some of this money comes from the federal government, but increasingly it comes from private foundations and for-profit businesses. The competition for these funds is fierce. Grant seekers must differentiate themselves from their competition. This is usually done by announcing breakthroughs.

A cynic might define a breakthrough as a dangerous, expensive, and/or extremely limited treatment offered as a general remedy for a common medical problem. Hardly a week goes by without a medical breakthrough or a miracle drug being trumpeted in the lay press. This publicity creates unreasonable expectations; patients show their physician the news clippings touting the latest cure. If the physician is unwilling to try the medication or procedure, the patient will often look for a physician who will.

The most obvious examples are AIDS treatments and cardiac drugs. Researchers create the illusion that their drug will work miracles if only the Food and Drug Administration would allow them to sell it. This has been especially cruel to HIV carriers, many of whom have become convinced that the government is suppressing effective AIDS treatments.

Myth 5: The Perfect Baby Can Be Guaranteed

Obstetrics has suffered the most from unreasonable patient expectations. Defending unfounded birth injury claims is costly. Frequently, technically unfounded claims must be settled because of the difficulty of convincing a jury that the injury was not the physician's fault. These claims usually involve some improper action by the physician but one that had no influence on the health of the baby.

Birth injury cases are difficult to manage because obstetricians and institutional obstetrical service providers base their marketing on the illusion of the perfect baby. Every soft-focus advertisement for a woman's center implies that using its facilities will guarantee a perfect baby. Every advertisement for a fertility center begins with the premise that everyone can have, and should have, a baby. Physicians in dangerous locations (high altitude, areas with poor hospital support, or areas where snow or flooding can paralyze transportation) reassure their patients that these factors do not present a significant problem. Given these marketing ploys, it should not be surprising that juries expect obstetricians to be guarantors of their work.

Myth 6: The Physician's Lot Is Not a Happy One

The average physician earns several times the mean annual income for families in the United States; aggressive practitioners can earn several hundred thousand dollars or more a year. When the equity of this compensation is questioned, the profession responds that high pay is the only way to reward physicians for the onerous burden of practicing medicine. Yet fewer and fewer physicians practice medicine in a style that earns them any sympathy from their patients.

The lovable family doctor who takes calls every night and sees his or her own patients in the emergency room has virtually disappeared. When physicians join large groups so they are only on call a few nights a month, require patients to pay up-front for care so collections stay high, practice at expensive for-profit hospitals, and then assure patients that financial considerations never color their medical decision making, the entire profession looks hypocritical.

Myth 7: You Cannot Set Standards Because Medicine Is an Art
Most medical professional societies have resisted setting rigorous professional standards. (See Chapter 6.) When a lawsuit is tried, the jury must determine the proper standard of care. The plaintiff and the defendant each has expert witnesses testify as to the proper care of the patient under the circumstances present in the case. Generally, neither side accurately presents the standard of care. The defense tries to portray the standard of care as being very low so the defendant physician's care appears proper. The plaintiff will argue that the standard of care is high—higher than the defendant provided. Depending on who the jury believes, the case will either raise or lower the legally acceptable standard of care.

Myth 8: Tort Reform Is the Solution
There are two types of tort reform. The more common variety is unilateral tort reform. These reforms make it harder for all persons to sue physicians and to recover adequate compensation when they win a lawsuit. While unilateral tort reform benefits physicians, it does so at the expense of injured persons with meritorious claims. In many cases, it shifts the cost of medical malpractice to society by making the injured person a ward of the state.

Unilateral tort reform is the process of putting obstacles in the way of persons seeking compensation for an iatrogenic injury. It is referred to as unilateral reform because the defendants do not give up any of their traditional protections. Unilateral tort reform may be substantive or procedural. Substantive reforms may limit certain causes of actions such as lawsuits for failure of informed consent, or they may cap the damages that a successful plaintiff can recover. Procedural reforms include shortened statutes of limitations, special restrictions on the qualifications of expert witnesses, and the required use of pretrial screening panels or affidavits to establish that the claim has merit.

Most unilateral tort reform has been enacted without empiric evidence of the magnitude of the problem being addressed. For example, many statutes limit a plaintiff's recovery for pain and suffering to a fixed amount, such as $250,000. This is based on the unsubstantiated belief that large awards for pain and suffering make a substantial contribution to malpractice insurance rates. The lack of proper baseline data also makes studies that purport to evaluate the effectiveness of tort reform methodologically unsound. A drop in insurance rates may be due to tort reform, but it may also be due to the cyclic nature of the insurance business.

Bilateral tort reform attempts to make the tort system more equitable and affordable for both parties. Bilateral reforms are usually based on alternative dispute resolution techniques. (See Chapter 2.) These can make it both cheaper to defend an unfounded claim and easier to prevail on a meritorious claim. Bilateral reforms best serve society's interest in justice. They can be devastating to malpractice insurance costs, however, because they reduce the opportunity cost of presenting a valid claim (Mills 1977).

The malpractice insurance carriers have been adroit in persuading general medical societies and specialty societies to lobby for tort reform. These physician organizations have viewed lobbying for tort reform as a no-cost (other than the cost of the lobbyists) benefit. While it is true that unilateral tort reform will reduce certain of the costs of medical malpractice litigation, this is at a political cost to physicians. However necessary and beneficial tort reform may be, lobbying for it puts physicians in the position of asking for a special exemption from the laws that govern other businesses. Moreover, unilateral tort reform clearly benefits the physician at the expense of the injured patient.

The cost of tort reform is that it convinces legislators that physicians are no different from other businesspersons. This reduces the credibility of physicians when they lobby for measures, such as increasing the availability of prenatal care, that benefit the public's health. It also increases the likelihood that legislators will see tort reform as a trade for other special favors that physicians enjoy. As physicians lobby for their own parochial interests, they should not be surprised to find themselves treated as just another trade group.

DEFENSIVE MEDICINE

Defensive medicine is aptly named. The term implies both actions to prevent litigation and an untrusting attitude toward patients. Defensive medicine is based on three assumptions: that making more accurate diagnoses will reduce malpractice claims; that tests and procedures improve the probability of a correct diagnosis; and that the use of more technology implies better medical care (Harris 1987). These assumptions come from a physician-oriented view of medical care. The problem is that patients, not physicians, bring malpractice lawsuits. Patients are primarily concerned with the outcome and the humanistic aspects of their treatment. It is physicians who care about diagnoses. Patients want to be treated well and successfully. Defensive medicine generates anger and expense, both of which increase the probability that an injured patient will seek legal counsel.

Defensive medicine directly increases the probability of injury when it involves dangerous tests or procedures. For example, intravenous pyelograms (IVPs) pose a significant risk of complications. If an IVP is ordered as a necessary diagnostic test, the risk of the procedure is balanced by the benefit of the diagnostic information that it produces. If an IVP is ordered as a defensive measure, there is no benefit to the patient to offset the risk. Since a defensive test or procedure is, by definition, one that does not have a favorable risk or cost-benefit ratio for the patient, the patient may be expected to sue successfully for any major complications of a defensive test or procedure.

Technology-Oriented Medicine

The last 30 years of technology-oriented medicine have shifted patients' perception of the role of the physician. Before the explosion of technological medicine, the role of the physician was to cure, if possible, and to comfort. It was accepted that in many cases the physician would not be able to cure the disease. This was not a failing of the physician but a recognition that illness and death are an integral part of life. The shift to technology-oriented medicine helped to drive the growth of procedure-oriented specialty medical practice. This view of the physician as a skilled mechanic leads to an expectation of cure and to irreconcilable conflicts.

If the technological interventions offered fail, the physician fails because the supplementary role of comforter has been lost. Defensive medicine must perceptibly improve the outcome of care if it is to be an effective strategy. If it does not improve the patient's perception of the outcome of the care, its negative impact on the humanistic aspects of care will engender patient dissatisfaction and hostility, resulting in an increase in litigation. In the worst case, it interferes with providing quality medical care: angering the patient and providing the grounds for a lawsuit.

Diagnosis and Testing

Arriving at a diagnosis is the intellectual end point of defensive medicine. Defensive medicine is directed at finding the definitive test to establish the diagnosis or doing enough tests to rule out other possible diagnoses. This ruling out is considered an important legal protection should someone later determine the patient's actual problem.

The ruling out of alternative diagnostic hypotheses is a valid strategy if the universe of possible alternatives is sufficiently large. But it is a dangerous strategy if the initial diagnostic assumptions constrain subsequent data collection and hypothesis generation. The physician must guard against ignoring the patient's stated problem in favor of a diagnostically tidier problem. For example, if the patient has trouble walking because of a plantar wart, the physician should not attempt to repair the patient's asymptomatic slipped disk as a substitute for removing the plantar wart.

This emphasis on diagnosis leads to laboratory diagnosis as the ideal of technological medicine (Fortess and Kapp 1985). Clinical laboratory tests are seen as objective, while taking a history and physical is subjective. Laboratory tests are easy to replicate, may be discussed without reference to the context of the specific patient, and, at least superficially, are easy to interpret. Tests with numerical results lend an air of science to medical practice.

Before the advent of digital electronic calculators, calculations were worked out with slide rules. When digital calculators became cheap enough for general use in the classroom, many teachers opposed their use. There was a philosophical concern with the false rigor that electronic calculators created. The slide rule was accurate to only two or three digits; thus, using a slide rule constantly reminded the student of the approximate nature of the underlying data. Digital calculators and digital reading instruments display many digits—but most medical data are approximate, usually to only two digits of accuracy and sometimes less. Manipulations of these data that do not take into account their limited accuracy lead to spurious results, but results that appear to be scientific because they are numerical.

This problem of false rigor is exacerbated by the use of multiple test panels. These panels include large numbers of tests that measure mostly unrelated parameters. The test results are expressed numerically, but the evaluation of the results depends on the comparison of these numerical values with normal values. Normal values are determined by statistical techniques. They are usually set such that 5 or 10 percent of healthy people given the test will have values outside the normal range.

When a patient is given a panel with 20 independent tests, each with a normal value defined by the ninety-fifth percentile, then the probability is high that at least one test will be falsely normal or abnormal. The noise from the false test results makes it more difficult to evaluate the diagnostic content of the test panel and increases the chance that important information will be lost in the mass of data. The tests may also document important problems that the physician missed. When an injured patient seeks the advice of an attorney, the attorney has the luxury of working backward from the injury. If the physician did not order the proper tests, then all the other tests that were ordered become irrelevant. And if the proper test was ordered but the results were overlooked or ignored, the emphasis on ordering tests accentuates the error in not acting on the relevant test results.

Specialty Blinders

Many specialists believe that the best way to avoid litigation is to ignore all problems that are not part of their specialty. But many patients have multispecialty problems that require one physician to take overall responsibility for their care. This problem is exacerbated if the specialist is at the end of a long referral chain. In this situation, the specialist is prone to assume that someone else has ruled out all diagnoses other than those that would be appropriate to his or her special field of practice.

One case that settled prior to trial involved a woman in her mid-50s who presented to her physician with abdominal pain. Initial evaluation did not uncover an explanation, and she eventually sought care at a hospital emergency room. The emergency room physician did a general evaluation and wrote a differential diagnosis that included abdominal aortic aneurysm. She was admitted to the hospital under the care of a gynecologist and given an ultrasound and a pelvic examination. A mass was noted in her abdomen, and the pelvic examination discovered cervical cancer. She was then transferred to the regional cancer center for definitive treatment. Once in the cancer center on the gynecology service, she was treated for the cancer.

Over the next couple of weeks, she continued to complain of pain that was inappropriate for the extent of her cancer. Her treating physicians assumed that this pain was partially psychogenic, and they had her evaluated by a psychiatrist. The pain suddenly became much worse, and she was given a tranquilizer for anxiety. When she was finally examined three hours later, there was no blood supply to her legs; she had clotted off an abdominal aortic aneurysm. This diagnosis had been hinted at early in her evaluation, but once she was on a subspecialty gynecology cancer service, all diagnostic considerations were limited to gynecologic cancer and its complications.

THE MALPRACTICE INSURANCE BUSINESS

The crisis over malpractice litigation has always been driven by malpractice insurance premiums, not over abstract concerns about incompetent physicians or greedy patients. Although there are a small number of physician-directed insurers that provide low-cost insurance, they are the exception. Insurance companies exist to make money, not to serve social policy by providing affordable insurance for physicians.

Malpractice insurance companies provide a necessary service. Physicians generally cannot choose to forgo insurance. There are relatively few malpractice carriers in any state. While some state laws prohibit insurers from acting collusively in setting rates and policy conditions, insurance companies are exempt from the federal antitrust laws. There is an ongoing debate over whether insurance companies use this oligopoly power to manipulate the market to optimize their profits at the expense of their physician insureds.

The basic economics of medical malpractice insurance are no different from other insurance products. But insurance is different from most other businesses in that it involves long-term relationships with its clients, and these relationships persist beyond the actual term of the policy. Malpractice insurance is also a highly regulated business, with limited competition in rate setting. Physicians must become sophisticated buyers of insurance. They must understand the principles of insurance and be prepared to resist being manipulated by short-term rate cuts. They must demand that their insurance carrier not subsidize the practices of incompetent physicians. Finally, physicians must accept that settling malpractice claims should be a business decision, not a matter of honor.

Rates

From a physician's point of view, the most contentious issue in malpractice insurance is rate setting. Physicians want affordable insurance; insurance companies want maximum income. Income is the product of the number of insureds and the premiums that each pays. As premiums increase, there are physicians who can no longer afford insurance. (Some of these leave practice, but the vast majority take a salaried job and continue to practice medicine.)

The important issue for the insurance company is not whether some physicians are now priced out of the market but whether the total dollars paid by the remaining insureds is higher at the new rate. Even if a company's nominal rates are temporarily higher than those of its competitors, the cost of tail coverage and contributions to reserves limit the ability of insureds to move to a competing insurer.

The Reserves Game

A malpractice insurance company's profits are not simply the premium income minus the administrative costs and the costs of paying and defending claims. The malpractice insurance business is not in equilibrium. There is uncertainty in evaluating claims, a long delay in closing claims, and the potential for political change during the interval between the presentation of a claim and the resolution of it. Claims-made policies were introduced to lower rates by reducing the uncertainty of future payouts. Unlike occurance policies which cover any injuries that occur during the term of the policy, claims-made policies cover claims filed during the term of the policy.

Insurance companies manage the uncertainty of future payouts through reinsurance and the accumulation of reserves. *Reinsurance* is the process of spreading the risk of loss to another insurance company. The primary insurer pays a premium to the secondary insurer that is determined by the level of risk shifted and the potential losses that are being reinsured. *Reserves* are premiums that are invested to cover future losses. They are treated as losses, and the income from reserves is not categorized as profit. The controversy over malpractice insurance profitability arises from the accounting practices for reserves.

When an insurance company wants to justify a rate increase to a state regulatory commission, it can increase its reserves, which reduces its cash on hand and its investment income. If enough capital is shifted to reserves, a prosperous company can appear to be on the edge of insolvency. The rate commission must then approve higher rates or face political blackmail as the company threatens to leave the state.

The most troubling aspect of the reserves game occurs when a company with excess reserves does leave the market because excess premiums that these reserves represent are never returned to the insureds. They eventually revert to the company as claims are paid. If the company can successfully argue that it still has outstanding claims against these reserves, it can keep them off the books for years. Malpractice insurers can enter and leave state markets so that they can continually recapture excess reserves.

The return on invested reserves depends on the world business cycle. Precipitous changes in interest rates, bond yields, and the stock market can drastically reduce the value of a poorly hedged reserve investment portfolio. These losses must be offset by increasing premium income. Since it is financially costly for a company to be underreserved, investment shortfalls must be offset very quickly. This is easiest to do in lines of insurance in which current increases in claims may be projected into huge future losses, thus justifying sudden premium increases. Shortfalls in reserve investment income have been a primary cause of the volatility of malpractice insurance rates since the early 1980s.

Underwriting Standards

In a booming financial market, an insurance company can make a high return on invested reserves. Companies lower underwriting standards to get more money to invest, but since claims are often paid years later, this amounts to borrowing against the future. When investment income declines and claims begin to come in, the companies raise rates and cancel policies, again without proper concern for underwriting standards. This manipulation of underwriting standards underlies the irrationality of medical malpractice insurance rating schemes.

Medical malpractice insurance is rated by medical specialty, the procedures performed, and geographic location. Except in rare circumstances, there is no individual rating of physicians, although a company may decline to insure a particular physician (Schwartz and Mendelson 1989). Unlike automobile insurers, malpractice insurers do not charge differential rates based on individual physician loss histories or risk factors. This lack of individual ratings puts responsible physicians at a financial disadvantage; they must cross-subsidize the legally high-risk individuals in their specialty.

For example, in most states obstetricians who limit their practices to the number of women they can personally care for and deliver pay the same rates as physicians who accept many more women than they can care for properly. The cost of malpractice insurance is much more significant for these physicians than it is for high-volume practitioners who generate much larger cash flows. Insurance companies have not chosen to determine whether high-volume practitioners pose a greater risk per woman delivered. It seems obvious that they pose at least the same risk per delivery, and thus a much higher aggregate risk than smaller practices (Miller et al. 1990).

A major political issue in underwriting is using premium differentials to subsidize certain specialties. Again, obstetrics is a common example. In many states family practitioners have lobbied the insurance commission to force insurers to give them preferential rates for delivering babies. Without any evidence that family practitioners have a lower risk of malpractice, some insurance commissions have acceded to their demands for lower insurance rates than for obstetricians.

A more subtle subsidization occurs when insurance commissions limit the rate classes that an insurance company may offer. Sometimes referred to as rate or class compression, the result is to limit the insurance companies' ability to target rates narrowly. Limiting the insurance companies' pricing options forces physicians in lower-risk categories to subsidize the practices of their higher-risk colleagues in higher-risk specialties.

Medical malpractice insurance generally extends to all legal procedures that a physician performs on patients. The carrier may sometimes have to pay for an illegal action, such as sexual assault, because the action was hidden behind legitimate procedures. The difficult rating decisions involve unnecessary procedures, vanity procedures, and unproved procedures.

Insurance companies do not like to set medical standards. If the company refuses to set standards, more conservative physicians have to bear the cost of unorthodox treatments. As a policy matter, it is not in the public interest to squander the limited resource of malpractice insurance on unorthodox treatments. The clearest example is the litigation risk of vanity procedures. Radial keratotomies have made some ophthalmologists rich, but the cost of paying the associated malpractice claims is staggering. Liposuction and cosmetic laser surgery promise the same cycle: enormous profits in the early years, followed by enormous litigation losses four to six years later. The losses are shared by the practitioners who did not provide this sort of care.

Competition

Rates and competition are inextricably linked. The insurance business in general is less competitive than other comparable businesses because insurance companies are immune from the federal antitrust laws. This insulation from market forces allows insurance companies to charge higher rates than would exist in a free market.

The limited competition between insurance companies allows companies to manipulate markets in ways that would not be tolerated by the customers of other businesses. A typical strategy is to enter a market with low rates and attractive terms on contribution to reserves. Once a group of physicians is insured with the company, the rates are quickly raised. The cost of tail coverage is kept high, trapping these physicians in several years of high premiums. Legitimate companies will be reticent to compete for these physicians if they must offer lower than break-even rates to do so. The result is that the physicians who switched companies for discount rates ultimately pay more for insurance for several years.

Because insurance companies are insulated from market forces, their competitive positions are established through governmental regulation. While insurance is an international business, it is regulated by individual states. A state's authority to control an insurance company's business practices ends at the state's borders. Less populous states do not have the resources to audit and regulate a national insurance company.

These problems are exacerbated for specialty insurance products such as malpractice insurance. These products affect relatively few persons in the state but require special expertise to evaluate. Most state insurance commissions are not capable of regulating malpractice insurance companies properly. In some cases, this results in discriminatory pricing and unreasonably high premiums. In others, the regulatory commission holds rates to artificially low levels, benefiting physicians in the short term but inevitably resulting in a crisis in the availability of coverage.

The Changing Nature of Insurance Coverage

The traditional malpractice insurance policy was an occurrence policy: it covered all incidents that occurred during the term of the policy. It did not matter if the claim was not presented until after the expiration of the policy. The claims made after the term of the policy are called the *tail* (from the tail of a normal distribution). These tails could be several years' long, which makes it difficult to do loss projections. Malpractice insurance companies began to abandon occurrence policies several years ago, and most now offer only claims-made insurance.

A *claims-made policy* covers only claims that are presented during the term of the policy. If a patient is injured while the policy is in force, a resulting claim is covered only if it is presented before the expiration of the policy. If the claim is presented after the expiration of the policy, it is not covered. Claims-made policies do not have the tail associated with occurrence policies because there is no liability beyond the policy year.

On first entering practice, a physician has no history of potentially injured patients who may make a claim against his or her insurance. Over the years, this physician's universe of potential claimants begins to increase until it begins to reach a plateau. The major determinant of the plateau is the statute of limitations for bringing a malpractice lawsuit. Secondary determinants include the probability that a patient will decide that he or she has been injured by the physician and the willingness of an attorney to represent the patient.

The risk plateau is reached within a few years of beginning practice. This is reflected in the pricing structure of claims-made policies. The first-year rate for these policies is usually much lower than the mature rate (that charged after the insured reaches the risk plateau). Physicians who have been in practice for several years before buying a claims-made policy may be asked to pay the mature rate and a substantial surcharge in their first policy year. This surcharge represents the reserves that the insurance company would have put aside during the physician's first years of the practice had the physician been insured with the company during those years.

When a claims-made policy expires, the physician is no longer insured for events that may have happened during the term of the policy but have not yet been presented as a claim. The physician must procure insurance, called *tail coverage*, for these events. Tail coverage is an occurrence policy for events that occurred during the term of the claims-made policy. This tail coverage may be bought from the same insurer that provided the primary coverage or may be obtained from a new insurer.

The cost and availability of tail coverage is a major determinant of a physician's ability to change malpractice insurance companies. The terms of availability for tail coverage are an important consideration when evaluating the cost of malpractice insurance. The cost of the tail should be predictable and its availability guaranteed.

Some companies do not require that an event be presented as a claim before it is covered by the policy. These policies provide coverage for all untoward events reported by the physician during the policy life. These early reports help the insurance company to estimate its future risks better. Theoretically, it is to the physician's benefit to have potential future claims covered. However, this benefit accrues only if the physician allows the policy to expire without obtaining tail coverage.

Conflicts of Interest

There are two conflicts of interest inherent in malpractice insurance defense. The obvious conflict is between the defendant and the insurer. At the beginning of a lawsuit, defendants are interested in preserving their honor and paying nothing to the plaintiff. They want the insurance company to spare no expense in their defense. As the trial approaches, their resolve is frequently shaken by the emotional stress of the proceedings and the potential of a verdict that will exceed the limits of their policy. At this point, they will usually pressure the insurance company to settle the case rather than risk a trial.

The second conflict is between the defendant and the universe of insureds not being sued. It is the premium dollars of these insureds that the defendant wants spent on his or her representation. This was not a problem when medical malpractice insurance was both inexpensive and available. In today's market, it increases the cost of insurance, thus reducing its availability.

The consequences of allowing individuals unfettered access to a limited resource were effectively described in an essay by Garet Hardin entitled "The Tragedy of the Commons." Hardin dealt with grazing sheep on ground held in common by a community. Each individual sheep herder can maximize his or her income by grazing as many sheep as possible. The common ground, however, has a limited carrying capacity for sheep. If too many sheep are allowed to graze on the common, the grass is destroyed and all the sheep herders starve. Individual sheep herders, if left to pursue their own interests, will eventually destroy the commons and their own livelihood.

In today's market, medical malpractice insurance is a limited resource. Each time an insurer raises its rates or restricts the availability of coverage, some physicians are driven out of independent practice. Physicians who are not priced out of private practice must modify the nature of their practice to accommodate the cost or restrictions on their insurance. Each unnecessary dollar spent on claims management has an adverse impact on every physician insured by the company.

An insured who holds up the settlement of a case increases the cost of managing that claim. Interestingly, the insured is almost never successful in forcing a trial or affecting the terms of the judgment. All he or she can do is generate substantial extra legal fees until such time as he or she is persuaded to settle. Conversely, an insured's willingness to settle a case that the insurer wants to defend may weaken the insurer's case, but it has little ultimate effect on the management of the case. In each case, the insured is expending community resources for little or no personal gain.

Independent Representation

Under a traditional insurance contract, the carrier agrees to provide the insured with independent representation. This means that the insurance company pays an attorney to represent the defendant as if the defendant had hired the attorney directly: the defense attorney must put the insured's interest before the insurance company's interest. Paying the cost of this representation is a major benefit of malpractice insurance because attorney costs account for approximately one-third of premium dollars. This duty of independent representation is taken to an extreme in medical malpractice insurance policies that allow the physician to veto a settlement.

The most pervasive problem with the duty to provide independent representation is that it puts the insurer in an adversary position with its defense attorneys. As independent counsel representing the insured, the defense attorney is ethically bound to put the insured's interests first. This conflict of interest hurts the insurer in several ways: (1) counsel may not provide the insurer adverse information learned about the insured during the investigation of the case; (2) the ethical duty to represent the insured zealously means that counsel must do everything possible to defend the case, even if these activities are not cost-effective; and (3) the insurer is prevented from presenting a unified defense when a case involves several insureds.

Putting aside the marketing value of allowing physicians to believe that they control settlements, independent representation is important to insureds to protect their reputation and their assets. An adverse settlement in a malpractice case can put a physician at a competitive disadvantage. This has become more important with the requirement in many states that settlements and judgments be reported to the state board of medical examiners.

The more significant threat to the physician is that the insurance company will fail to settle a case in which the plaintiff wins a verdict in excess of policy limits. When an excess judgment is possible, an insured has a right to expect either independent representation or protection against loss of assets. The physician with $1 million in coverage with possible damages in excess of $1 million (such as a brain-injured baby case) has reason to worry. The insurance company may want to take the risk of a trial because its losses are capped at $1 million plus legal expenses.

The theoretical risk of verdicts in excess of policy should diminish as more states adopt periodic payments rules and caps on damages. However, historical data indicate that the bulk of claims dollars are paid for settlements and verdicts below the level of caps on damages. It is possible that insurers could agree to protect physicians against excess judgments without increasing their costs. This will become more probable as the lowest policy limits approach the caps on damages. If physicians cannot buy policies for less than $1 million coverage and the statutory cap is $1 million, then there cannot be an excess judgment.

The effect of protecting insureds against excess judgments is to remove the inherent conflict of interest between the insurer and its insureds. If this conflict were removed, the insurer could modify its contract of insurance to allow greater latitude for managing its litigation. This could be combined with a requirement that all litigation information be released to the insurer. Under these contractual provisions, the insurer would be free to present the best defense of the common assets, to the benefit of all insureds.

This rationalization of litigation would be especially important in cases involving multiple defendants. Under most policies, each defendant is entitled to an independent counsel. This can lead to an explosion of defense costs. More troubling, unlike single-defendant cases, a defendant in a multiple-party case can avoid liability by blaming another defendant, increasing the probability of an adverse settlement or judgment. It also pits one company's insureds against each other and against the company, with disastrous public relations consequences.

BEING AN EFFECTIVE INSURANCE BUYER

There are three critical considerations for buying malpractice insurance. First, policies must be evaluated on their potential long-term costs. It is foolish to change carriers because of a loss-leader rate that may evaporate at renewal time. Physicians must determine the company's timing for anticipated rate increases and their potential size. Second, policies that give the defendant undue influence on the conduct of the litigation will be more costly to all of the insureds. Physicians must realize that every dollar the company spends in the defense of individual claims comes out of their own pockets.

Third, and most important, when buying insurance physicians must determine the cost and terms of availability for the tail coverage. This involves the question of the company's financial stability; insurance is useless if the insurer is bankrupt. Although it is difficult to determine if the company is honest in its projections, it is useful to investigate the company's historic behavior and its behavior in other states. In the insurance business, once a scoundrel, always a scoundrel.

BIBLIOGRAPHY

Abraham KS: Medical liability reform. A conceptual framework. JAMA 1988 Jul 1; 260(1):68–72.
Brennan TA; Leape LL; Laird NM; et al.: Incidence of adverse events and negligence in hospitalized patients: Results of the Harvard Medical Practice Study I. N Engl J Med 1991; 324:370–76.
Fortess EE; Kapp MB: Medical uncertainty, diagnostic testing, and legal liability. Law Med Health Care 1985; 13:213–18.
GAO (I): *Medical Malpractice: A Framework for Action.* GAO/HRD-87-73. 1987.
GAO (II): *Medical Malpractice: Case Study on California.* GAO/HRD-87-21S-2. 1986.
GAO (III): *Medical Malpractice: Case Study on Florida.* GAO/HRD-87-21S-3. 1986.
GAO (IV): *Medical Malpractice: Case Study on New York.* GAO/HRD-87-21S-5. 1986.
GAO (V): *Medical Malpractice: Characteristics of Claims Closed in 1984.* GAO/HRD-87-55. 1987.
GAO (VI): *Medical Malpractice: Insurance Costs Increased But Varied Among Physicians and Hospitals.* GAO/HRD-86-112. 1986.
GAO (VII): *Medical Malpractice: Six State Case Studies Show Claims and Insurance Costs Still Rise Despite Reforms.* GAO/HRD-87-21. 1986.
Harrington S; Litan RE: Causes of the liability insurance crisis. Science 1988 Feb 12; 239(4841 Pt 1):737–41.
Harris JE: Defensive medicine: It costs, but does it work? JAMA 1987; 257:2801–2.
Huber P: Injury litigation and liability insurance dynamics. Science 1987 Oct 2; 238(4823):31–36.
Kapp MB: Defensive Medicine (letter). JAMA 1987; 258:1176.
Kapp MB: Solving the medical malpractice problem: Difficulties in defining what "works." Law Med Health Care 1989 Summer; 17(2):156–65.
Leape LL; Brennan TA; Laird NM; et al.: The nature of adverse events in hospitalized patients: Results of the Harvard Medical Practice Study II. N Engl J Med 1991; 324:377–84.
Localio AR; Lawthers AG; et al.: Relation between malpractice claims and adverse events due to negligence: Results of the Harvard Medical Practice Study III. N Engl J Med 1991; 325:245–51.

Medical Malpractice: Report of the Secretary's Commission on Medical Malpractice. DHEW publication (OS)73-88. 1973.

Miller AR; Moreland T; Donovan G; Richards EP: Birth Clustering. 1990 American Statistical Association Proceedings of the Social Statistics Section pp. 245–252.

Miller AR; Richards EP: Incident Reporting Times. American Statistical Society Proceedings of the Business and Economics Statistics Section pp. 327–339 (1989).

Mills DH, ed.: *California Medical Association and California Hospital Association Report on the Medical Insurance Feasibility Study.* 1977.

Patients, Doctors, and Lawyers: Medical Injury, Malpractice Litigation, and Patient Compensation in New York: The Report of the Harvard Medical Practice Study to the State of New York. 1990.

Pearse WH: Professional liability: Epidemiology and demography. Clin Obstet Gynecol 1988 Mar; 31(1):148–52.

Rostow VP; Osterweis M; Bulger RJ: Medical professional liability and the delivery of obstetrical care. N Engl J Med 1989 Oct 12; 321(15):1057–60.

Rushford G: Data bank has a deficit; Doctors who settle malpractice claims keep names out of monitoring system. Leg Times 1991 April; 22:1.

Sanazaro PJ; Mills DH: A critique of the use of generic screening in quality assessment. JAMA 1991; 265:1977–81.

Schwartz WB; Mendelson DN: The role of physician-owned insurance companies in the detection and deterrence of negligence. JAMA 1989 Sep 8; 262(10):1342–46.

Sloan FA; Mergenhagen PM; Burfield WB; Bovbjerg RR; Hassan M: Medical malpractice experience of physicians; Predictable or haphazard? JAMA 1989; 262:3291.

Schwartz WB; Mendelson DN: Physicians who have lost their malpractice insurance: Their demographic characteristics and the surplus-lines companies that insure them. JAMA 1989; 262:1335–41.

8

Management of Medical Information

| CRITICAL POINTS | • Medical records are critical to all medical-legal issues.
• The purpose of the medical record is to facilitate good medical care.
• More information does not always make for better records.
• Records must never be altered or fabricated.
• Physicians must not disclose a patient's medical information unless authorized by the patient or public health and safety laws. |
|---|---|

The starting point for all medical legal inquiries is the medical record. Many physicians have come to regard the medical record as a legal document, kept for reasons separate from patient care. Discussions about medical malpractice usually portray the good medical record as a totem to ward off litigation. Good medical practice is the only cure for malpractice litigation. Medical records are good only to the extent that they facilitate quality medical care.

MEDICAL RECORDS

Good Records

Ironically, the focus on the medical record as a legal document has reduced both its legal and its medical effectiveness. Medical personnel, constantly told that "the good medical record is the best defense," miss the point that the good medical record is valuable only to the extent that it documents the actual rendering of good medical care. A medical record can be legally disastrous if it demonstrates the incompetence of the underlying medical care. Poor documentation is actually an advantage to an incompetent defendant whose best defense is obfuscation. A poor record may prevent the medical care providers from establishing the good care they gave the patient, but a good record is not a substitute for good care.

The confusion between good medical records and good medical care has helped destroy the usefulness of medical records. Many records administrators believe that the more information in the record, the better the record is. Even if this excess information is accurate and well organized, it dilutes the medically

95

necessary information. Physicians and nurses will have difficulty finding medically necessary information in a timely manner. This leads to substandard medical care and potential medical malpractice litigation. Bigger medical records are not better medical records.

Medical Records in Litigation

The medical record is the basic legal document in medical malpractice litigation. A well-organized, well-written record is the best defense for the competent health care provider. A poorly-written, disorganized record is strong evidence of an incompetent health care provider. The poorly-kept record is not, in itself, proof of negligence on the part of the health care provider, but it is proof of substandard care.

Medical malpractice litigation is built around the medical record, which provides the only objective record of the patient's condition and the care provided. Records are particularly important for a physician's defense. It is the physician's responsibility to keep the medical record. The patient has injuries to show the court; the physician or other health care provider has only the medical records to prove that the injuries were not due to negligence. If the record is incomplete, illegible, or incompetently kept, this is the physician's failure. Although courts and juries usually give a physician the benefit of the doubt on ambiguous matters, this does not extend to ambiguities created by incompetent record keeping.

Medical Records as a Plaintiff's Weapon

When an injured patient seeks legal advice about filing a medical malpractice lawsuit, the attorney's first task is to review the medical records. The attorney is looking for specific acts of negligence and at the overall quality of the record. The strongest medical malpractice lawsuits are based on well-documented, specific acts of negligence. In most cases, however, the negligence is inferred from documented and undocumented events. If the patient's case depends at least partially on assuming that certain events were not recorded, the attorney must be able to cast doubt on the credibility of the record.

The least credible records are those that are internally inconsistent—for example, the physician's progress notes report that the patient was doing well and improving steadily, but the nurses' records indicate that the patient had developed a high fever and appeared to have a major infection. More commonly, the credibility of the records is attacked through demonstrating that it is incomplete. If it is clear that medically important information is missing from the record, then it is easier to convince a jury that the missing information supports the patient's claims.

Defensible Records

Viewing the medical record from outside, without reference to its role in medical care, leads to the *defensible record*, one that does not facilitate good care but does contain enough information to allow a plausible defense for the physician's actions. For example, recording a child's height and weight without plotting a growth chart would allow the defense that the physician was aware of the child's development. Plotting the information, however, might have caused the physician to investigate growth retardation and treat underlying medical problems. This would mitigate the child's injury and reduce the probability of litigation.

From the point of view of prevention, the best medical record is one that facilitates good care. If the patient's care is good, the probability of a successful medical malpractice lawsuit is low. If, in addition to facilitating good care, the record fully documents the patient's course and the care provided, then it is unlikely that a knowledgeable plaintiff's attorney will even proceed with a case. This appears to be happening with structured prenatal care records. These are printed medical records with check-offs for all routine prenatal care, combined with extensive patient education handouts. There have been many fewer than expected claims against physicians using these records. (See Chapter 27.) Given the financial and emotional cost of medical malpractice litigation, the best record is the one that convinces a plaintiff's attorney that it is not worth filing a lawsuit.

A HISTORICAL PERSPECTIVE

Medical record keeping evolved during the early part of the twentieth century, before there were health care delivery teams and free-floating hospital-based specialists. A physician took care of his own patients, and patients generally had only one physician. When a consultant was used, the consultant consulted; he did not take over the care of the patient.

Hospitals provided nursing, custodial, food, and hotel services. Nursing was low-technology patient care. Little laboratory work was performed, and the physician usually participated in this work himself. The nurses, often nuns, were available night and day. They knew the patient's condition and needs, and they talked to the physicians. Medical records served as documentation but were not a primary vehicle for communication between health care providers. Simple narrative reporting was used because there were few events to record and little need for retrieving information from the record.

Modern health care delivery has abandoned the one physician–one nurse model for the health care team. Many physicians care for a single patient; some of them are unknown to the patient and the primary physician. Nurses are employees with regular shifts and multiple responsibilities. The medical record is now the basic vehicle for communication among members of the health care team. Confusion arises because records are also kept to satisfy accreditation standards, legal requirements, accounting demands, and other nonpatient care purposes.

These nonpatient care demands have distracted providers from the three primary uses for a medical record: (1) providing rapid access to recent information (about the patient's condition, laboratory tests, and drugs, for example); (2) ensuring continuity of care as responsibility for patient care shifts between different providers; and (3) as an audit tool to gauge the quality of medical care. These primary uses for medical records must not be sacrificed to facilitate secondary goals such as medical malpractice defense and billing.

PHYSICIAN'S OFFICE RECORDS

Traditionally, physician's office records were for a single physician treating a group of long-term patients. The record served to remind the physician of the patient's medical history and to record the patient's treatment for billing purposes. With the advent of specialty and subspecialty care, private physicians began to see more limited-term patients, increasing the number of separate individuals in the physician's practice and reducing the number of times a physician sees a patient. Although physicians keep records in a manner that assumes that they know each patient personally, many of the patients are strangers to the physician. Add to this the enormous increase in available therapies, the high probability that the patient will be cared for by more than one physician, and the increase in multiple physician clinics, and the traditional physician office record is hopelessly out of date.

The Joint Commission on Accreditation of Healthcare Organizations (JCAHO) provides detailed requirements for the maintenance of medical records in the hospital, but there is no comparable set of standards for physicians' private office records. Consequently there is a tremendous variation in the quality of physicians' office records. As with hospital medical records, private office record-keeping styles evolved during a period that demanded less comprehensive record keeping than is necessary today. Physicians should use a standard medical record format such as the problem-oriented medical record for all their medical records. (See the section in the Bibliography on problem-oriented medical records for a detailed discussion of this record format.)

Basic Patient Information

The most important information is the basic patient data. The chart must contain enough information for a physician unfamiliar with the patient to provide appropriate care. This should include physiological information, therapeutic information, and any special patient characteristics such as allergies or handicaps. This information should be summarized on a cover sheet. There are several acceptable styles for providing this summary, but they share an emphasis on rapid identification of abnormal findings, the recording of problems that will require attention on future visits, and a way to ensure that the physician is notified if the patient misses a follow-up visit.

In clinics with several physicians, the demands on the medical record begin to resemble those of a hospital medical record. All of the physicians in the group must keep records in the same format, record enough information to allow any other physician in the group to treat the patient, and identify patient problems with great specificity to ensure continuity of care.

Multiphysician clinics create the opportunity for patient problems to be ignored through shared authority for patient care. As with hospital-based care, there must be one physician in charge of the patient's overall care, and the chart must identify this physician. The chart must also be returned to this physician for review whenever the patient is treated by another member of the clinic group. This review allows the primary physician to reconcile the care of the other providers. If there are problems, the patient can be contacted. If there are no problems, the reviewing physician can add whatever notes are necessary to ensure that the next physician to see that patient has the proper information.

Maintaining the Records

Chapter 3 discussed the hearsay rule and medical records as business records. As such, medical records are subject to the specific legal requirements for keeping records that may be used in court: (1) the record must be made in the regular course of the business; (2) the record must be kept by a person who has personal knowledge of the act, event, or condition being recorded; (3) the record must be made at or near the time that the recorded act, event, or condition occurred or reasonably soon thereafter; and (4) the record must be kept in a consistent manner, according to a set procedure.

Readability

An illegible medical record is doubly damaging to a physician: it obscures necessary information, and it makes the physician who wrote the entry look less than professional. A favorite strategy of plaintiffs' attorneys is to make enlargements of illegible medical records and use them to belittle the defendant physician in front of the jury. Despite the jokes about physicians' handwriting, juries are not tolerant of illegible records.

The best way to ensure that records are legible is to dictate them. This may be done on a pocket tape recorder while the physician is still with the patient or immediately after. In all cases, the dictation must be done before the physician sees another patient. If record keeping is delayed, it is inevitable that entries will be lost or distorted. The tape should be transcribed daily and the transcription entered into the chart. This entry may be made by affixing the actual typescript to the medical record. If a computer or memory typewriter is used for the transcription, then the entry, after proofing, may be printed on the chart page itself.

Handwritten notes should always be made in the chart in case the transcription is delayed or lost. The transcribed notes should not be pasted over the handwritten notes; both sets of notes are part of the legal record and must be preserved. If the chart entries are not dictated, all entries should be made in black ink—*never* in pencil. It is best if they are printed, but legible cursive handwriting is acceptable. The records should be spot-checked for legibility from time to time. Taking the time to write one legible sentence makes for a better record than a hastily scrawled page of illegible notes.

Altered Records

It is important to be consistent in the keeping of records. Attorneys and juries are suspicious of inconsistencies. If records are usually handwritten, a dictated note will be questioned. Conversely, a handwritten note in a series of dictated notes will be suspect. As discussed in the section on business records, the essence of a credible record is that it appears to have been maintained in the regular course of business. Anything that indicates special treatment for a record reduces its credibility.

Physicians should not alter their medical records under any circumstances. Hospitals guard medical records from alterations, but there is no such watchdog in a physician's office. Even an inconsequential alteration throws the validity of the entire record into question. Innocent mistakes, such as the loss of a few pages of a record, will be construed as an intentional cover-up. Under no circumstances should liquid correction fluid be applied to the record in order to correct an entry. If an entry must be changed, a single line should be drawn through the entry, taking particular care to make sure that the original entry is clearly legible.

The new entry should be written above or next to the old entry, with the date of the new entry and the initials of the person making the entry recorded. It is important that *the* entry include the reason for its inclusion—perhaps newly available laboratory information, addenda to explain a previous note, or just that it is a supplemental note. As long as it is clear that no deception is intended, physicians should not hesitate to supplement chart notes. A note supplemented two weeks after the original entry is more credible than attempts to supplement it on the witness stand five years later.

Protecting Records

Medical records are the basic tangible assets of a private practice. If these records are lost through fire or theft, the medical care of many patients may suffer. If a physician's office records were to be lost, it could be difficult to defend a claim brought by a patient who had been treated by the physician. As with any other business, the physician will also face potential financial ruin from the loss of customer lists and billing records. Unlike many other businesses, however, physicians rarely use specific techniques for protecting their business records.

Paper records should be stored in fire-resistant filing cabinets that are locked whenever the office is closed to provide some protection from fire and theft. Computer records should be copied (backed up) to removable media, either disks or tape, daily, with at least two sets of backup media. This practice ensures that one set will be preserved if a mistake is made in the backup process. These sets are alternated, with one being used on Monday, Wednesday, and Friday and the other on Tuesday, Thursday, and Saturday. It is better to have a set of backup media for each working day. Most businesses keep at least one set of backup media in a different building from the computer. A duplicated backup is made on this remote set at least once a week to prevent a complete loss of information if the building is destroyed.

If the physician's office is destroyed, the first step is to contact all of the physician's patients, for two reasons: to remind patients in need of continuing care that they must contact the new office for an appointment and to reassure patients that the physician will reopen the office and that they need not seek medical care elsewhere. Contacting the patients will be much easier if the physician maintains a patient list in a secure place away from the office in which the records are kept. This list should contain enough information to locate patients and, ideally, to reconstruct a skeleton of the patient's medical history. Keeping such a list is time-consuming, but it can be an effective marketing tool. A physician can use routine mailings to established patients to build loyalty. Mailings directed at patients with chronic conditions can be used to remind them to come in for follow-up care. This is good business and good medical management.

Retention of Records

There are few statutory requirements on how long a physician must retain private office records. From a risk management point of view, it is desirable for all records to be retained indefinitely in the physician's office. Unfortunately, this may be economically unfeasible and interfere with access to active records. All physicians' offices should have a formal records retention policy that balances convenient and economic storage with easy access to active records.

Records for any patient seen in the last two years must be considered active unless the patient has died. If the patient has not been seen for two years and does not have a continuing medical condition, the physician may consider putting the patient's records into less accessible storage while retaining the cover sheet of the chart in case the patient is seen again. The cover sheet will facilitate urgent care in either the office or the emergency room before the full record can be retrieved.

The physician must maintain a separate tracking system for all patients with implants of any kind. While this has always been done for heart valves and pacemakers, it is important for other implants that either need replacing or are subject to FDA recalls or reviews. This includes intrauterine devices and implantable contraceptives. The tracking system should identify each patient with an implant, the type of implant, the last patient visit, and any necessary review dates. For implantable contraceptives, for example, the patient should be seen each year and should be notified in the fourth year that the contraceptive effect is wearing off.

The physician should contact patients with chronic medical problems who have not been seen recently. If the patient is being treated by a new physician, that physician's name should be noted in the chart. If the patient cannot be found and is not in need of specific follow-up care, the physician should send a postcard to the patient's last known address. If the card is returned as undeliverable, it should be put in the chart to document that the physician tried to keep track of the patient. Once the patient has been accounted for, the chart may be moved to storage. If there are patients in need of follow-up care, they should be managed as discussed in Chapter 9.

From a strictly legal point of view, the statute of limitations for medical malpractice in the state where the physician practices is the absolute minimum period that records should be maintained. Depending on the local state laws, adults have from one to four years after the occurrence of an injury to file a claim for medical malpractice. For children, this period is usually extended until the patient reaches age 20 to 24.

The problem with the statute of limitation is that states tend to measure the period differently. The statute of limitations may begin to run: (1) on the date when the malpractice occurred, whether the patient knew about the malpractice or not; (2) on the date when the physician last treated the patient for the condition at issue; or (3) on the date the patient knew, or should have known, that he or she was a victim of malpractice. In states in which the running of the statute period of limitations starts from the discovery of the malpractice, it is conceivable that a malpractice suit could be filed 10, 15, 20, or more years after the patient was treated.

Statutory Requirements on Record Keeping

Federal and state laws govern the retention and release of medical records. Some Medicaid/Medicare records must be available for verification of charges for a five-year period. OSHA (Occupational Safety and Health Administration) regulations govern the retention and release of certain occupational health records. (See Chapter 31.) Any physicians involved in substance abuse treatment or occupational medicine should request more information about these laws from their attorneys. A federal law strictly regulates the release of medical information and the management of records for persons undergoing treatment for substance abuse. Any physician who treats patients for substance abuse should seek assistance in complying with these regulations from the participating governmental agency or a private attorney.

Destroying Records

Records may be destroyed only in limited circumstances. The clearest is when the patient dies. A reasonable period of time after the patient's death—perhaps the statute of limitations for medical malpractice in the state—the chart may be destroyed. It is always recommended that the family of a deceased patient be given a chance to request a copy of the chart before it is destroyed because it may provide invaluable medical information for other family members.

If a physician dies and his or her records are not transferred to another physician, these records may be destroyed a reasonable time after the physician's death. The executor of the physician's estate should attempt to contact all patients before destroying the records. All patients should be sent a certified letter at the time of the physician's death notifying them that the physician has died and that they may claim their medical records within a set time, say, three months. Once the time for claiming records has elapsed, the executor may begin to destroy the records of patients who have not been seen for several years. The records of current patients should be maintained for several years before being destroyed. If possible, these records should be transferred to a local physician or hospital.

Off-Chart Records

Poor organization, combined with illegible handwriting, leads many medical care providers to use temporary notes, such as index cards, to coordinate care. These notes are used as a source of immediate information. Entries in the official medical record may be written long after the care is delivered. Given the added dimension of hindsight, it is impossible to avoid slanting entries to reflect what should have happened, as opposed to what did happen. This is legally dangerous because it is difficult to maintain consistency in entries that are biased by hindsight. It is very damaging if a patient's attorney can discredit the record through internal inconsistencies and thereby raise questions about the good faith of the providers, as well as the quality of care.

Physicians in training and nurses maintain most extra-chart records. Residents often use 3- × 5-inch index cards with a brief history, the attending physician, recent test results, pending test results, and what needs to be done next. Residents keep their own cards, and these may be passed on at shift change or may serve as a memory jogger to fill in the new residents in charge, who transfer the information to their own set of cards.

Nursing personnel keep elaborate extra-chart bedside records. Individual nurses keep personal notes, and often the nursing service maintains a centralized extra-chart record-keeping system. These records exist outside both legal and administrative control. The records are kept in pencil, and old data are erased to make room for new data, ensuring that decisions are based on current information. This process of creating and erasing temporary records also carries over to the processing of physician orders, which are transcribed from the medical record into the extra-chart record. Once in the extra-chart system, it is easy to erase or mark out orders as they are performed.

From a patient care perspective, extra-chart records provide a way to coordinate patient care and provide ready access to laboratory test results. But these records are deficient in that they provide no historical information. Extra-chart records inevitably corrupt the accuracy of the chart itself because the extra-chart record becomes the record that is filled out first, with the chart becoming a secondary record, filled out when time allows. Secondary records often reflect what should have been done rather than what was done. This causes medical problems if the extra-chart system breaks down (someone loses the index cards, for example) and legal problems if the care is challenged in court.

Physicians should never use off-chart records. All patient information must originate in the chart and be transferred to notecards or other temporary records from the chart. If notes are made separate from the chart, these notes should be glued into the chart. They should not be copied over into the chart. Notepaper with strippable adhesive should never be used for keeping medical notes. If they are inadvertently used, they should be glued into the chart with a permanent adhesive.

Releasing Medical Records
Medical records are a peculiar type of business record. The physical record (paper, microfilm, or something else) belongs to the physician making the record or the employing clinic. The information belongs to the patient in the sense that the patient has a right to control the release of the information to self and others. Some states limit the patient's access to potentially damaging psychiatric information, but in general the patient has a right to the information in the medical record. The parent or legal guardian of minors and the guardian of an incompetent adult may exercise this right on behalf of the minor or ward.

The physician does not need the patient's permission to report communicable diseases, unusual outbreaks of illness, child abuse, violent injuries, or other legally reportable conditions. In most other situations, the physician should not release information from the patient's chart without the patient's written permission. At the first patient encounter, the physician should have the patient sign an authorization to release information as necessary for the patient's treatment. This includes release to consulting physicians, laboratories, and other health care providers.

The physician must always have the patient's permission to release information for nontherapeutic purposes—for example, collecting insurance, determining job fitness, documenting sick leave, and other situations in which the release of information is not related to the patient's medical treatment. The physician should ask the patient to sign a written authorization to release this nontherapeutic information. The written permission should be dated, state to whom the information is to be released, which information may be passed on to that party, and when the permission to obtain information expires.

With the growing concern over AIDS-related discrimination, some patients will not authorize the release of their medical information to third parties. If the patient refuses to release information to consultants or other necessary medical care providers, the physician may not be able to manage the patient's condition properly. (This is the same ethical dilemma as a patient who refuses necessary medical treatment.) The physician has no right to release the information without the patient's permission. Conversely, the patient may not coerce the physician into rendering improper care. The physician should inform the patient of the problem and document this in the chart. If the physician refuses to treat the patient on this basis, the patient must be informed of the medical rationale for this refusal.

A physician has a duty to ensure that information is released only to properly authorized individuals. Assume, for example, that a patient has signed an authorization to release information to an employer. The physician can legally release information to the employer, but he or she must ensure that the person requesting the information is the one authorized to have it. This might require that the information be sent to the personnel department rather than be given to a caller on the telephone.

If someone presents an authorization that the patient has signed, the physician should endeavor to determine if the release is valid. If the release is over a few months old or appears irregular, the physician should attempt to contact the patient before releasing the information. If the patient cannot be located, the physician should contact the person seeking the information and try to verify the authenticity of the release. If the physician is still suspicious, he or she should request the person seeking the information to have the patient contact the physician.

A physician has a right to charge a nominal fee for a copy of the patient's medical record. This fee should reflect the actual charge for copying the chart. If the patient is indigent, the physician should provide the chart at no cost. Under no circumstances should the physician attempt to hold the chart hostage for an unpaid medical fee or to prevent the patient from seeking care elsewhere. This is bad public relations and may cause the patient to sue to obtain the record.

Selling Medical Records

In most situations, the selling of a private medical practice is little more than selling patients' medical records. While there may be costs allocated to goodwill, this is meaningless when the practice is sold to a physician previously unknown to the selling practitioner. Any premium over the net present value of the furnishings, real estate, or lease represents a sale of medical records.

Interestingly, there have been few legal actions against physicians who sell medical records. In many states, it is illegal to transfer medical information for nontherapeutic purposes without the patient's explicit permission. In these states, the law would seem to require that each patient be contacted for permission to transfer the records. If the permission is denied, the selling physician will have to retain the records. If the patient cannot be located, then the record might be transferred under seal to the buying physician, to be opened only if the patient contacts the physician in the future.

It is expected that HIV/AIDS will precipitate a reexamination of the selling of medical records. This will be especially threatening in states that make violations of patient confidentiality a criminal act. Even in states that allow the transfer of medical records as part of the sale of a practice, this transfer is limited to another physician, not a lay practice broker.

HOSPITAL MEDICAL RECORDS

Each hospital has its own rules for maintaining medical records; most of these derive from the standards set by the JCAHO, which provide a detailed guide to keeping records. Relevant sections of the *Hospital Accreditation Manual* are reproduced in the chapter appendix because every physician who practices in an accredited hospital should be familiar with its requirements for medical records management. As plaintiffs' attorneys become more sophisticated, it is increasingly likely that physicians accused of poor record-keeping practices will be examined in court on these standards.

APPENDIX 8A: MEDICAL RECORD SERVICES

TEXT: MR.1 The hospital maintains medical records that are documented accurately and in a timely manner, are readily accessible, and permit prompt retrieval of information, including statistical data.

MR.1.1 An adequate medical record is maintained for each individual who is evaluated or treated as an inpatient, ambulatory care patient, or emergency patient.

MR.1.2 All significant clinical information pertaining to a patient is incorporated in the patient's medical record.

MR.1.3 The content of the medical record is sufficiently detailed and organized to enable

MR.1.3.1 the practitioner responsible for the patient to provide continuing care to the patient, determine later what the patient's condition was at a specific time, and review the diagnostic and therapeutic procedures performed and the patient's response to treatment;

MR.1.3.2 a consultant to render an opinion after an examination of the patient and a review of the medical record;

MR.1.3.3 another practitioner to assume the care of the patient at any time; and

MR.1.3.4 the retrieval of pertinent information required for utilization review and quality assessment and improvement activities.

MR.1.4 A system is established by the organization to routinely assemble all divergently located record components when a patient is admitted to the hospital or appears for a prescheduled ambulatory care appointment.

MR.2 The medical record contains sufficient information to identify the patient, support the diagnosis, justify the treatment, and document the course and results accurately.

MR.2.1 Although the format and forms in use in the medical record will vary, all medical records contain the following:

MR.2.1.1 identification data;

MR.2.1.2 the medical history of the patient;

MR.2.1.3 as appropriate to the age of the patient, a summary of the patient's psychosocial needs;

MR.2.1.4 reports of relevant physical examinations;

MR.2.1.5 diagnostic and therapeutic orders;

MR.2.1.6 evidence of appropriate informed consent;

MR.2.1.6.1 A policy on informed consent is developed by the medical staff and governing body and is consistent with any legal requirements.

MR.2.1.6.2 The medical record contains evidence of informed consent for procedures and treatments for which it is required by the policy on informed consent.

MR.2.1.7 clinical observations, including the results of therapy;

MR.2.1.8 reports of procedures, tests, and their results; and

MR.2.1.9 conclusions at termination of hospitalization or evaluation/treatment.

Source: Accreditation Manual for Hospitals (1992, pp. 49–54). Copyright © Joint Commission on Accreditation of Healthcare Organizations.

MR.2.2 Inpatient medical records also include at least the following:
  MR.2.2.1 the patient's name, address, date of birth, and next of kin;
  MR.2.2.2 the medical history of the patient including the following information:
    MR.2.2.2.1 the chief complaint;
    MR.2.2.2.2 details of the present illness, including, when appropriate, assessment of the patient's emotional, behavioral, and social status;
    MR.2.2.2.3 relevant past, social, and family histories appropriate to the age of the patient; and
    MR.2.2.2.4 an inventory by body systems;
  MR.2.2.3 in regard to services for children and adolescents,
    MR.2.2.3.1 an evaluation of the patient's developmental age;
    MR.2.2.3.2 consideration of educational needs and daily activities, as appropriate;
    MR.2.2.3.3 the parent's report or other documentation of the patient's immunization status; and
    MR.2.2.3.4 the family's and/or guardian's expectations for, and involvement in, the assessment, treatment, and continuous care of the patient;
  MR.2.2.4 the medical history, which is completed within the first 24 hours of admission to inpatient services;
  MR.2.2.5 the report of the physical examination;
    MR.2.2.5.1 The report reflects a comprehensive current physical assessment.
    MR.2.2.5.2 The physical assessment is completed within the first 24 hours of admission to inpatient services.
      MR.2.2.5.2.1 If a complete physical examination has been performed within 30 days prior to admission, such as in the office of a physician staff member or, when appropriate, the office of a qualified oral-maxillofacial surgeon staff member, . . . a durable, legible copy of this report may be used in the patient's hospital medical record, provided there have been no changes subsequent to the original examination or the changes have been recorded at the time of admission.
    MR.2.2.5.3 The recorded physical examination is authenticated by a physician or, when appropriate, by a qualified oral-maxillofacial surgeon member of the medical staff.
  MR.2.2.6 a statement of the conclusions or impressions drawn from the admission history and physical examination;
  MR.2.2.7 a statement of the course of action planned for the patient while in the hospital;
    MR.2.2.7.1 There is a periodic review of the planned course of action, as appropriate.
  MR.2.2.8 diagnostic and therapeutic orders;
    MR.2.2.8.1 Verbal orders of authorized individuals are accepted and transcribed by qualified personnel who are identified by title or category in the medical staff rules and regulations.
    MR.2.2.8.2 The medical staff defines any category of diagnostic or therapeutic verbal orders associated with any potential hazard to the patient.
      MR.2.2.8.2.1 Such orders are authenticated within 24 hours by the practitioner responsible for the patient.

MR.2.2.9 progress notes made by the medical staff and other authorized individuals;

MR.2.2.10 consultation reports;

MR.2.2.11 nursing notes and entries by nonphysicians that contain pertinent, meaningful observations and information;

MR.2.2.12 reports of procedures, tests, and their results;

> MR.2.2.12.1 All diagnostic and therapeutic procedures are recorded and authenticated in the medical record.
>
> MR.2.2.12.2 When there is a transcription and/or filing delay, a comprehensive operative progress note is entered in the medical record immediately after surgery to provide pertinent information for use by any individual who is required to attend to the patient.

MR.2.2.13 reports of pathology and clinical laboratory examinations, radiology and nuclear medicine examinations or treatment, anesthesia records, and any other diagnostic or therapeutic procedures; and

MR.2.2.14 conclusions at termination of hospitalization.

> MR.2.2.14.1 All relevant diagnoses established by the time of discharge, as well as all operative procedures performed, are recorded, using acceptable disease and operative terminology that includes topography and etiology, as appropriate.
>
> MR.2.2.14.2 The clinical resume concisely recapitulates the reason for hospitalization, the significant findings, the procedures performed and treatment rendered, the condition of the patient on discharge, and any specific instructions given to the patient and/or family, as pertinent.
>
>> MR.2.2.14.2.1 Consideration is given to instructions relating to physical activity, medication, diet, and follow-up care.
>
> MR.2.2.14.3 A final progress note may be substituted for the resume in the case of patients with problems of a minor nature who require less than a 48-hour period of hospitalization, and in the case of normal newborn infants and uncomplicated obstetric deliveries.
>
>> MR.2.2.14.3.1 The final progress note includes any instructions given to the patient and/or family.
>
> MR.2.2.14.4 When an autopsy is performed, provisional anatomic diagnoses are recorded in the medical record within three days, and the complete protocol is made part of the record within 60 days, unless exceptions for special studies are established by the medical staff.

MR.3 Medical records are confidential, secure, current, authenticated, legible, and complete.

MR.3.1 The hospital is responsible for safeguarding both the record and its informational content against loss, defacement, and tampering and from use by unauthorized individuals.

MR.3.2 Written consent of the patient or the patient's legally qualified representative is required for the release of medical information to persons not otherwise authorized to receive the information.

> MR.3.2.1 There is a written hospital and medical staff policy that medical records may be removed from the hospital's jurisdiction and safekeeping only in accordance with a court order, subpoena, or statute.

MR.3.3 When certain portions of the medical record are so confidential that extraordinary means are necessary to preserve their privacy, such as in the treatment of some psychiatric disorders, these portions may be stored separately, provided the complete record is readily available when required for current medical care or follow-up, review functions, or use in quality assessment and improvement activities.

MR.3.3.1 The medical record indicates that a portion has been filed elsewhere, in order to alert authorized reviewing personnel of its existence.

MR.3.4 The quality of the medical record depends in part on the timeliness, meaningfulness, authentication, and legibility of the informational content.

MR.3.4.1 Entries in medical records are made only by individuals given this right as specified in hospital and medical staff policies.

MR.3.4.2 All entries in the record are dated and authenticated, and a method is established to identify the authors of entries.

MR.3.4.2.1 Identification may include written signatures, initials, or computer key.

MR.3.4.2.2 When rubber-stamp signatures are authorized, the individual whose signature the stamp represents places in the administrative offices of the hospital a signed statement to the effect that he/she is the only one who has the stamp and is the only one who will use it.

MR.3.4.2.2.1 There is no delegation of the use of such a stamp to another individual.

MR.3.4.3 The parts of the medical record that are the responsibility of the medical practitioner are authenticated by the practitioner.

MR.3.4.4 When members of the house staff are involved in patient care, sufficient evidence is documented in the medical record to substantiate the active participation in, and supervision of, the patient's care by the attending physician responsible for the patient.

MR.3.4.5 Any entries in the medical record by house staff or nonphysicians that require countersigning by supervisory or attending medical staff members are defined in the medical staff rules and regulations.

MR.3.5 Each clinical event is documented as soon as possible after its occurrence.

MR.3.6 The records of discharged patients are completed within a period of time that in no event exceeds 30 days following discharge.

MR.3.6.1 The period of time is specified in the medical staff rules and regulations.

MR.3.6.2 A medical record is ordinarily considered complete when the required contents, including any required clinical resume or final progress note, are assembled and authenticated, and when all final diagnoses and any complications are recorded, without use of symbols or abbreviations.

MR.4 The medical record department is provided with adequate direction, staffing, and facilities to perform all required functions.

MR.4.1 Medical record services are directed by a qualified medical record administrator or technician who possesses the administrative skills necessary to provide effective leadership and management of medical record information systems.

MR.4.1.1 When employment of a registered or accredited individual is impossible, the hospital secures the consultative assistance of a qualified registered record administrator or accredited record technician.

MR.4.2 The length of time that medical records are to be retained is dependent on the need for their use in continuing patient care and for legal, research, or educational purposes and on law and regulation.

MR.4.3 Whatever filing and storage system is used, it provides for easy retrievability of records.
 MR.4.3.1 Retrievability of pertinent information is assured by the use of an acceptable coding system for disease and operation classifications, and by the use of an indexing system to facilitate the acquisition of medical statistical information.
 MR.4.3.2 Verification checks for accuracy, consistency, and uniformity of data recorded and coded for indexes, statistical record systems, and use in quality assessment and improvement activities are a regular part of the medical record abstracting process.
MR.5 The role of medical record personnel in the hospital's overall program for the assessment and improvement of quality and in committee functions is defined.

BIBLIOGRAPHY

Problem-Oriented Medical Records

Cross HD. *The Problem-Oriented System in Private Practice in a Small Town.* 1972.

Donnelly WJ: Righting the medical record—Transforming chronicle into story. JAMA 1988; 260:823–25.

Froom J: Conversion to problem-oriented records in an established practice. Ann Intern Med 1973; 78:254.

McDonald CJ; Hui SL; Smith DM; et al: Reminders to physicians from an introspective computer medical record: A two-year randomized trial. Ann Intern Med 1984; 100:130–38.

Maness F: Unsigned medical orders: A common problem magnified by automation. Nurs Adm Q 1986 Winter; 10(2):51–56.

National Center for Health Services Research: *Automation of the Problem-Oriented Medical Record.* DHEW publication (HRA 77-3177). 1977.

PROMIS III: *Adult Medical History Questionnaire for Problem Oriented Practices.* 1988.

Weed LL: *Medical Records, Medical Education, and Patient Care.* 1971.

General References

Berg RN: Disposition of a deceased physician's patient records. J Med Assoc Ga 1979 Jan; 68(1):56–57.

Blume SB: Changing the federal regulations on confidentiality of alcohol and drug abuse patient records: Views of clinical staff. J Stud Alcohol 1981 Mar; 42(3):344–49.

Bok S: The limits of confidentiality. Hastings Cent Rep 1983 Feb; 13(1):24–31

Brahams D: Duty to disclose medical records. Lancet 1989 Aug 19; 2(8660):460.

Coleman V: Why patients should keep their own records. J Med Ethics 1984 Mar; 10(1):27–28.

DeGeorge DB: A physician's anticipatory release of patient medical records to a professional liability insurer. Breach of confidentiality or justifiable release? J Leg Med (Chic) 1988 Mar; 9(1):123–59.

Gordis L; Gold E: Privacy, confidentiality, and the use of medical records in research. Science 1980 Jan 11; 207(4427):153–56.

Hiller MD: Computers, medical records, and the right to privacy. J Health Polit Policy Law 1981 Fall; 6(3):463–87.

Hirsh HL: Legal implications of patient records. South Med J 1979 Jun; 72(6):726–29, 733.

Hirsh HL: Medical records: Medicolegal balm or bomb? Med Law 1987; 6(6):525–35.

Hirsh HL; Rosenfeld J; Taffet GA; Passarelli T: Physician medical records: Why, whether, wherefore, how and their longevity. Med Law 1985; 4(2):141–54.

Jowers LV: It's your job: The contract to treat injuries includes an evidentiary responsibility. J Leg Med 1977 Apr; 5(4):8S–8V.

Kenny DJ: Confidentiality: The confusion continues. J Med Ethics 1982 Mar; 8(1):9–11.

Kinzie JD; Holmes JL; Arent J: Patients' release of medical records: Involuntary, uninformed consent? Hosp Community Psychiatry 1985 Aug; 36(8):843–47.

Miller RD: Confidentiality or communication in the treatment of the mentally ill. Bull Am Acad Psychiatry Law 1981; 9(1):54–59.

Miller RD; Morrow B; Kaye M; Maier GJ: Patient access to medical records in a forensic center: A controlled study. Hosp Community Psychiatry 1987 Oct: 38(10):1081–85.

Pfafflin F: Federal Supreme Court restricts psychiatric patients' right to inspect records. Med Law 1985; 4(4):389–91.

Poirier S; Brauner DJ: Ethics and the daily language of medical discourse. Hastings Cent Rep 1988 Aug–Sep; 18(4):5–9.

Showalter CR: Patient access to psychiatric records: A psychodynamic perspective. Med Law 1985; 4(4):351–60.

Stratton WT: May a physician release medical records upon receipt of a subpoena? Kans Med 1989 Apr; 90(4):94.

van Eys J: Confidentiality of medical records in pediatric cancer care: Myths, perceptions, and reality. Am J Pediatr Hematol Oncol 1984 Winter; 6(4):415–23.

Watson BL: Disclosure of computerized health care information: Provider privacy rights under supply side competition. Am J Law Med 1981 Fall; 7(3):265–300.

II Physicians and Patients

9

Physician-Patient Relationship

CRITICAL POINTS

- The physician's legal duty to the patient begins when the physician-patient relationship is formed.
- The physician-patient relationship can be formed through informal contacts, such as telephone calls.
- The physician's duty to the patient does not end until the physician-patient relationship is formally terminated.
- Contracts with third-party payers may reduce physicians' freedom to choose whom they will treat.

The basic legal relationship in medicine is between the physician and the patient. This book also discusses various other legal relationships—the physician-hospital relationship and partnerships, for example—but these are business relationships and are not very different from business relationships in other regulated businesses. The physician-patient relationship is different from these business relationships because it encompasses many nonfinancial considerations. This relationship has become legally problematic because the historic values that it embodies do not represent the realities of present-day medical care delivery. For example, the law anticipates that each patient's care is supervised by a single, identifiable physician. This reflects traditional medical practice, not the team care model used in many hospitals and clinics. When there is a conflict between legal standards and medical practice, the probability of medical malpractice litigation increases. Sometimes these conflicts result from outdated legal assumptions, but in others they result from the business side of medicine's improperly influencing the physician's duties to the patient.

ESTABLISHING THE RELATIONSHIP

Historically, the primary legal characteristic of the physician-patient relationship was that it was voluntary. The physician was free to choose which patients to treat. The patient, in theory, was free to choose a physician. This legal fiction of voluntariness has persisted, despite its inapplicability in situations ranging from racial discrimination to emergency treatment. With certain exceptions, the law still assumes that a physician must accept a patient voluntarily before the physician-patient relationship is legally binding. The exceptions involve physicians who have contractually agreed to treat certain classes of patients, such as those in maintenance organizations or emergency room groups. These exceptions have greatly reduced the latitude of most physicians to refuse to treat a given patient.

Explicitly Accepting the Patient

The clearest way to form a physician-patient relationship is for the physician to accept the patient explicitly. The physician and the patient may enter into a written contract, or the physician may just say that he or she accepts the patient. This explicit acceptance happens most frequently when the patient is seeking elective medical care that is not reimbursable by a third-party payer. Physicians delivering such care use written contracts to ensure that the patient will pay for the treatment. These explicit agreements are uncommon. Usually the physician's acceptance of the patient must be inferred from the physician's conduct.

A physician-patient relationship begins when a physician begins to evaluate the patient's medical condition—perhaps in an examining room, talking to him or her in an emergency room, or taking his or her pulse at an accident site. In general, the physician's right to refuse to accept the patient must be exercised before the physician evaluates the patient. If the physician evaluates the patient and determines that he or she is in need of immediate care, then the physician is responsible for ensuring that the necessary care is provided. If the patient is not in need of immediate care, the physician may terminate the relationship.

When a patient makes an appointment with a physician, the patient expects to be seen by the physician. This expectation does not create a problem if the physician sees every patient who makes an appointment. The patient's expectations become an issue when the physician evaluates the patient's insurance status after making an appointment. The physician may refuse to accept a patient for financial reasons, but this right is limited once a physician-patient relationship is initiated. Making an appointment may create a limited physician-patient relationship. The test would be the extent to which the patient will suffer because he or she has relied on the appointment. This requires balancing the severity of the patient's condition with the delay between making the appointment and seeing the physician.

If the patient must wait two months to see the physician and will have to wait two months to see another physician, a jury is likely to find that the patient should have been seen, irrespective of financial considerations. Conversely, if the patient has waited only a few hours and other care is readily available, the physician has greater freedom to refuse to see the patient. If the patient has an emergent condition, such as chest pain or a threatened miscarriage, the physician must attend to the patient irrespective of the availability of alternative care.

Exercising Independent Medical Judgment

Legally, a physician-patient relationship is formed when the physician exercises independent medical judgment on the patient's behalf. *Independent medical judgment* is a vague term that is defined by the facts of the given situation. It may involve making a diagnosis, recommending treatment, or implying that no treatment is necessary. As a legal concept, the key is reliance: Did the patient reasonably rely on the physician's judgment?

A physician may exercise independent medical judgment explicitly or implicitly. A physician who evaluates a patient and establishes a differential diagnosis recognizes that he or she has exercised independent medical judgment. Legal problems usually arise from the implicit exercise of medical judgment. If a physician is not aware of initiating a physician-patient relationship, he or she may injure the patient through inattention. The implicit exercise of medical judgment is best understood through a discussion of common practice situations in which medical judgment is at issue. Since telephone calls pose the most difficult problems in determining whether a physician-patient relationship has been formed, they serve as a useful model to discuss these issues.

Telephone Calls

Telephone calls are problematic because the caller and the physician often have different expectations. Some patients call physicians day or night about every minor medical question that comes to mind. Many patients call physicians after office hours only when they believe that they have a serious problem. From the physician's perspective, most calls involve minor problems. This creates a sense of complacency that may lead physicians to mishandle telephone calls by underestimating the severity of the patient's condition.

Physicians have an ethical duty to see that patients with emergent conditions get proper treatment. For persons who do not have a preexisting relationship with the physician, this duty can be fulfilled by sending the patient to a properly equipped emergency room. If the physician becomes more involved, such as by calling the ambulance, he or she must carry out these actions correctly—perhaps by calling the emergency room later and inquiring after the patient. A physician who listens to the patient's complaints assumes the duty to make a triage decision about the patient's condition: recommending treatment, no treatment, or that the patient see a physician in person.

From a medical perspective, new patients and new problems should not be evaluated over the telephone. If the patient has a medical complaint, the only question would be whether an ambulance should be sent to pick up the patient or whether the patient can find transportation to a medical care facility. Patient and physician resources make this an unreasonable ideal. In many situations patients must be evaluated without a hands-on examination. This should not blind physicians to the medical and legal hazards implicit in such indirect evaluations.

Prescribing medication is an exercise of independent medical judgment and creates a physician-patient relationship. It does not matter whether the physician recommends a prescription drug or an over-the-counter medication. Recommending aspirin is just as much as an exercise of judgment as prescribing digitalis. Telling the patient to "take two aspirin and call the office in the morning" assumes that the physician has ruled out the presence of any serious conditions that would require prompt attention.

Recommending treatment over the telephone is best reserved for patients with whom the physician already has a relationship. If the physician has not seen the patient before, he or she does not have the necessary context to judge the patient's condition. Is a headache due to a cold or out-of-control blood pressure? When dealing with existing patients, the physician must ensure that he or she has enough information to evaluate the patient's condition properly. If the physician has not seen the patient recently enough to remember him or her accurately and does not have the patient's chart available, the patient should be seen or referred to an emergency room.

A physician who listens to a patient's complaints and then recommends no treatment is implicitly telling the patient that he or she does not need immediate medical services. Usually the physician does intend for the patient to assume that he or she does not need further medical care. Occasionally, however, the physician does not want to treat the patient personally; he or she does not intend to imply that the patient does not need medical care. Once a physician has listened to the patient's complaints, he or she has assumed a limited duty to that patient. It is this limited duty that creates the inference that not prescribing treatment is the same as telling the patient that he or she does not need treatment. A physician who does not want to accept responsibility for the patient must pass the patient on to another physician. This must be done expeditiously to avoid responsibility for determining that the patient is not in need of immediate care.

All telephone conversations that involve medical decision making should be documented. If the call concerns an existing patient, the record of the call should be added to the patient's chart. If the call involves a person that the physician accepts as a new patient, a preliminary record should be opened for that patient. If the call involves a person whom the physician refers to another medical care provider, including an emergency room, a referral record should be created.

These records have two purposes. For existing patients, recording telephone calls is necessary to ensure that the patient's medical chart is complete. For persons who are not patients, the record of the call prevents later misunderstandings about what the physician told the patient. The record should contain the time and date of the call, the identity of the caller, how he or she came to call the physician (name out of the telephone book, for example), the nature of the complaint, exactly what the physician told the person, and where the patient was referred.

Private Office Walk-in Patients

The most basic consideration in patient screening in the office is whether the patient is calling for an appointment in the future or is standing in the office requesting care. There are many options for dealing with a patient on the telephone, but the patient in the office requires an immediate decision. The law does not impose a duty to treat every patient who walks into a private medical office; however, there are several exceptions that do recognize a duty to treat certain patients. More important, it would be ethically impermissible to turn away a patient for whom this would mean certain injury. The basic duty to a walk-in patient is to determine which patients to treat and which to refer. Few physicians understand their duty to provide immediate treatment to forestall further injury. In the private office, this duty is limited to situations in which a patient presents with a major problem such as a heart attack in progress or anaphylactic shock. The situation is most likely to occur if the physician's office is in an office complex with nonphysician tenants—a risk particularly for physicians in shopping center offices. This type of event is unusual, but it is potentially catastrophic and demands some type of screening for all walk-in patients.

In the limited context of an unknown walk-in patient in a private medical office, the first level of medical screening is to determine if the patient needs emergency treatment. For most patients, this simply requires asking the patients why they want to see the physician. Patients should not be relied upon for a definitive diagnosis, but they can recount the natural history of the complaint. If the symptoms were of sudden and recent onset or if the patient appears seriously ill, it is critical that a more complete medical examination be done at once.

If the patient is found to need urgent care, that care must be rendered to the extent that the practitioner is capable. The central problem for a physician facing a medical emergency outside his or her expertise is determining the extent of care that must be rendered before the patient can be transferred. For example, any physician should be able to manage anaphylactic shock; a dissecting aneurysm will require emergency transport to a fully equipped surgical center. The issue is the physician's general knowledge and the available facilities, not his or her self-selected specialty. A gynecologist and an allergist would have the same duty to treat a patient in anaphylactic shock, although the gynecologist would have no obligation to treat a routine allergy patient. If the patient can be managed without transport, the physician may determine later if he or she wants to continue the physician-patient relationship beyond the acute episode.

If the physician determines that the patient is not in need of urgent treatment, certain obligations remain. If the physician chooses to accept the person as a regular patient, these obligations will be discharged. If the physician chooses not to continue treating the patient, then he or she must ensure that the patient is told all the pertinent information about the condition, including the need for further treatment. If the condition is such as to require continuing treatment, the physician must be sure that the person understands the need for this treatment. The physician must be careful to distinguish between telling the patient that no treatment is required and telling this person to seek treatment elsewhere. The best course is to refer the person formally to the appropriate physician or hospital for treatment.

Invisible Patients

Radiologists, pathologists, and other strictly consultative specialists have the same medical and legal responsibilities as direct patient care physicians. Their role is to evaluate certain test results in the context of the patient's overall medical condition. When they exercise independent medical judgment, they enter into a physician-patient relationship with their invisible clientele. Because these specialists usually perform their work at the request of a primary treating physician, they often see their duty as flowing to the physician rather than to the patient—a concept that creates risks for the patient and both physicians.

Unlike nonphysician technical personnel, physicians always retain their independent duty to evaluate the patient's condition. This duty is most obvious in cases in which a consultant specialist is asked to perform an invasive test such as an intravenous pyelogram (IVP). In this case the radiologist has the duty to determine if the patient is in acceptable physical condition to undergo the test and whether the test is appropriate to the diagnostic question at issue. He or she also has a duty to interpret the results of the test properly.

Complying with these duties sometimes requires the consultant specialist to evaluate the patient's condition personally by reviewing the medical chart and examining the patient. The consultant physician usually relies on the ordering physician to provide this information. If the information provided is incorrect, the consultant specialist will be legally liable for any injuries the patient suffers as a result. If an IVP throws the patient into renal failure because the attending physician made a mistaken diagnosis, the radiologist would be liable because he or she did not rectify the mistake.

More problematically, nonpatient care specialists have the duty to ensure that patients are properly informed of the results of their evaluations and the need for any further care. Traditionally, this duty has been delegated to the ordering physician. The consultative specialist will send a report to the ordering physician or have this report entered into the patient's hospital chart. It is assumed that the ordering or treating physician then has the duty to ensure that the patient is properly informed and managed.

This assumption is not well grounded legally. Putting aside the independent professional duty implicit in the physician-patient relationship, these specialists bill patients directly for their services. When jurors are shown that a patient received substantial bills for professional services, they see this as the strongest evidence of a physician-patient relationship. And, they will assume that if the physician managed to get a bill to the patient, he or she could have gotten the test results and recommendations to the patient. Consultative specialists must ensure that systems failures do not injure the patients with whom they share a physician-patient relationship.

Informal Consultations

One of the banes of physicians is the curbside consult. These are best handled in the same way as a telephone call. A nonpatient who needs care should be referred in a manner appropriate to the urgency of the presenting condition. If the physician consults with a patient, appropriate records should be kept. The critical issue is that exercising independent medical judgment creates an ongoing responsibility to the patient.

With one caveat, informal consultations should be documented in the same manner as telephone calls. When a person telephones a physician, that person has demonstrated a much greater level of concern than someone who just makes conversation with a physician at a party. All telephone calls should be documented, but it is not necessary to record every social conversation that turns to a person's medical condition. The physician should record substantive discussions with existing patients in the patient's medical record and any consultations in which he or she recommended treatment or referred the patient for evaluation of an emergent condition.

Free-Standing Ambulatory Care Centers

Free-standing ambulatory care centers occupy a curious legal position. When a physician at one of these centers evaluates a patient, a physician-patient relationship is formed. In this sense, these centers are no different from a private medical office. The difficulty arises because these centers operate on the premise that the physician-patient relationship is terminated with the patient encounter. They do not accept the ongoing duty to care for the patient. There has been litigation on this point, but this limitation on future obligations may be hard to defend.

Refusing to Treat Patients

Physicians do not have unlimited discretion to refuse to accept a person as a new patient. Because much of medicine is involved with federal regulations, physicians cannot refuse to accept a person for ethnic, racial, or religious reasons. Nor can they discriminate based on the person's sex, unless the sex of the patient is relevant to the physician's specialty. Outside these protected areas, physicians have great latitude in refusing to accept persons as patients.

The most common reason for refusing to accept a patient is the patient's potential inability to pay for the necessary medical services. Patients should be given some indication of the financial requirements when they make an appointment for treatment to prevent them from delaying making other arrangements for care while waiting for an appointment at which they will receive no treatment. While it has not been clearly established that making an appointment creates a physician-patient relationship, it would be difficult to explain to a jury why someone in urgent need of care was turned away after having waited for an appointment. A defensible decision not to accept a patient for financial reasons can appear questionable in retrospect if the person was injured by the subsequent delay in receiving medical care.

Some physicians will not treat certain individuals or classes of patients. Perhaps the most common restriction is refusing to treat patients involved in accidents that will lead to litigation. Some physicians refuse to treat attorneys. Many obstetricians refuse to treat a pregnant woman who first seeks care after the sixth month of pregnancy. These decisions are shortsighted in a competitive market and ethically questionable in a market where they may make it difficult for the affected persons to obtain care; but they are not illegal.

Contractual and Statutory Duties to Treat

Hospitals with emergency facilities must provide treatment to all persons in need of lifesaving care, including delivering the baby of a woman in labor. Violating this duty can subject the hospital and the physician to a substantial fine and extensive civil liability. (See Chapter 32.) Most hospital bylaws require medical staff members to assist in the delivery of emergency care if needed or to participate in a specialty call system. This is a contractual agreement between the physician and the hospital. In return for staff privileges, the physician gives up the right to refuse to treat persons that the hospital requests him or her to treat. If a physician refuses to treat a patient when requested under this agreement, the hospital has the contractual right to cancel the physician's medical staff privileges. The patient who is refused treatment may sue the physician and the hospital if he or she is injured by the refusal.

With the recent growth of HMOs and similar other arrangements, many physicians have contracted with insurance carriers to treat any patient insured by that carrier. This obviates the physician's right to refuse to treat such insured patients. A person who is injured because a physician wrongfully refuses to accept him or her as a patient may sue the physician based on this contractual agreement with the insurance company. These contractual and statutory requirements can be understood as creating a physician-patient relationship with a class of persons rather than with an individual. When a member of this class requests treatment, the physician has the responsibility to treat that person as an accepted patient.

While patients traditionally had a free choice of physicians, it is becoming common for insurance companies to limit this choice in an attempt to control the cost of medical care. These limitations change the physician-patient relationship. From the patient's perspective, these limitations make the physician an "insurance company" physician, as opposed to the patient's physician. This difference in the perception of the physician's loyalties is most acute in health maintenance organizations (HMOs).

Closed-panel HMOs are the most restrictive type of health insurance scheme. The degree of restriction on the patient's choice of physicians varies among organizations, but in general, HMO patients have a physician assigned to care for them. The physicians have even less choice of which patients they may treat. In this situation, the traditional assumption of a freely determined physician-patient relationship is inapplicable.

In preferred provider organizations (PPOs) and other contractual arrangements in which the patients have a smaller co-payment if they are treated by certain physicians, the choice of physicians is limited, but unless the list is very short, the patients still perceive that they are choosing the physician. The physicians' position is more ambiguous. They may retain the right to refuse to treat patients of their choosing, but it is more usual that the PPO contract requires them to treat any PPO patient who presents in the office, subject to limitations of scheduling and specialty practice.

SPECIALTY CARE

Most physicians engage in a specialty practice, with almost all new licensees being specialists. Specialties range from narrow interests in an obscure disease to family practice. The more narrow the specialty is, the smaller is the potential patient population. If patients selected physicians at random, then narrow interest specialists would spend all their time turning away patients. The reality is that specialists with narrow interests traditionally depend upon referrals from other physicians rather than marketing their services to patients directly.

The most important limitation on a physician's willingness to accept a patient is that of a self-imposed specialty. Although there is nothing in the law to prevent a dermatologist from practicing general medicine, most dermatologists will decline to regulate a patient's diabetes. In the same sense, a family physician may be willing to treat acne and diabetes but unwilling to perform surgery. These limitations cause a problem only if they are not known to the patient when making an appointment. For example, a patient with severe hypertension makes an appointment with an internist. After taking the patient's medical history, the physician tells the patient that he limits his practice to gastroenterology. The patient would be justified in refusing to pay for the visit. More important, this unnecessary appointment may delay proper treatment for the patient's condition. In this situation, the physician should arrange for a referral and send the patient to an emergency room if he is concerned with the delay in seeing the second physician.

THE TREATING SPECIALIST

Treating specialists have limited their practice to a certain specialty area but treat patients independent of a primary care physician. This includes most of the nonhospital based specialties, such as endocrinology, gastroenterology, and gynecology. The duty to treat is more stringent for treating specialists because of the prescreening that their patients undergo. Unlike family practitioners, whose patients are mostly self-selected, specialists evaluate a patient before determining if they will accept the patient. Thus, the specialists have much more freedom to refuse to treat a patient, creating a greater duty to continue treating the patient once the patient has been accepted.

Within certain limitations, a specialist may examine and diagnose a patient without creating a physician-patient relationship. Assuming nonemergency care and no contractual obligations to the patient (such as PPO or HMO relationships), the specialist may determine if the patient falls into his or her chosen area of expertise. This opportunity to evaluate a patient before accepting him or her carries a corresponding duty to continue treating the patient. This duty is predicated upon the patient's greater reliance upon the specialist, as evidenced by the greater amount of time and money expended to be accepted for care by the specialist. This greater duty is tempered by the specialist's greater freedom to transfer the patient for complaints unrelated to the original disease that brought the patient under the specialist's care.

Referral is one of the most difficult judgments in specialty practice. Specialists have a duty to continue treating a patient until the person may be safely released from treatment or until a proper transfer of care may be arranged. The problem is the patient who develops conditions outside the specialist's area of expertise but for whom no substitute physician can be found. The choice is between treating a condition outside the specialist's chosen area or not treating the secondary problem. For example, assume that an obstetrician has a patient who is several months pregnant. This patient develops a serious sinus infection, but the obstetrician is unable to find a specialist willing to see the patient. In this situation, the obstetrician would be obligated to treat the infection, despite its being outside his or her chosen area of expertise.

The more difficult problem is the patient who develops a condition that the specialist cannot treat alone but the management of which is part of his or her specialty—for example, a gastroenterologist who finds that the patient has an acute appendicitis. The physician cannot perform the surgery, but it would be unacceptable to try to treat the patient without surgery. The gastroenterologist must be able to arrange proper surgical referrals as part of his or her duty to the patient. The patient is entitled to assume that the specialist is prepared to coordinate all of the personnel necessary to treat the patient's gastrointestinal problems. This expectation of comprehensive services will be discussed in the chapters that deal with specific specialties; it is a growing problem as traditional care patterns are fragmented.

EXPECTATION OF CONTINUED TREATMENT

There is a presumption that treating a patient creates an ongoing physician-patient relationship. This presumption derives from the traditional ongoing relationship between physicians and their patients. It is questionable how effectively it describes modern innovations such as ambulatory care centers in shopping malls and contract emergency room physicians. The extent of the physician's continuing responsibility to the patient is predicated on whether the patient has a reasonable expectation of continued treatment, the nature of the patient's illness, and whether the physician explicitly terminates the relationship.

There are four traditional models of physician practice: the family practice model, the treating specialist model, the consultant model, and the company doctor model. These traditional models have recently been joined by the ambulatory care center and the HMO models. Each of these models has a slightly different approach to the problem of the continuing duty to treat. This chapter will discuss the family practice model as the archetypical physician-patient relationship. The other models are discussed in other chapters.

The family doctor is the idealized physician-patient relationship beloved of nostalgia buffs and television script writers. In this romantic notion of medical practice, these physicians are intimately acquainted with all the details of their patients' lives, payment is never an issue, and the patients have unlimited resources to comply with the physician's recommended treatment. Life was never this way. The central problem for family physicians or general practitioners is to reach an accommodation between their style of practice and patients' expectations. This accommodation helps prevent legal misunderstandings, but its most important goal is preserving trust and mutual respect between physicians and their patients. How this accommodation is reached depends on the type of practice each physician is engaged in.

The law requires a family physician to provide treatment to a patient until that patient can be transferred to another physician safely or can be released from care. The physician is not required to provide that treatment personally, but responsibility for after-hours care and emergency care is always a vexing issue. This is easier to manage in urban settings because of the availability of alternative medical care. Urban physicians usually have arrangements with other physicians to share calls, reducing the burden of 24-hour responsibility for patient care. The availability of emergency room facilities can relieve the burden of after-hours care, although these facilities are more important for patients who may need more extensive care than is available in the office. The problem of urban practitioners is educating patients about the use of these alternative sources of care.

The main problem with small town practice is the lack of backup coverage, either through fellow practitioners or easily accessible emergency room facilities. Physicians in this situation will face the "super doc" dilemma: the "If I don't treat them, nobody will!" mind-set. While there is great ego gratification in being indispensable, this leads to burnout and the compromising of professional standards. Physicians must take personal time for relaxation and education and arrange for backup medical care for those times.

TERMINATING THE RELATIONSHIP

The initiation and termination of physician-patient relationships are legally risky events. At both times, it is critical that the physician and the patient have the same expectations and that the patient's health not be compromised by the physician's actions. Terminations are becoming increasingly risky because market pressures are making it more difficult for physicians to maintain long-term relationships with their patients.

Abandoning Patients

Abandonment is the legal term for terminating the physician-patient relationship in such a manner that the patient is denied necessary medical care. This should always be avoided. The legal liability becomes significant when the patient is injured by the failure to receive medical care. Abandonment can be intentional or inadvertent. *Intentional abandonment* is legally riskier because a jury may choose to award punitive damages as punishment for intentionally putting a patient's health at risk.

The most common reason for intentional abandonment of a patient is failure to pay the physician's fees, either by the patient or by the patient's insurance company. This is also legally the least justifiable. Juries have little sympathy for physicians who deny a patient necessary care because the patient is unable to pay the bill. Perhaps the worst case occurs when the physician denies the patient care because the patient's insurance company has refused to pay. If the insurance company has mistakenly denied coverage, the jury may take its anger out on the physician for allegedly conspiring with the insurance company to deny the patient medical care. A physician who is considering refusing to treat a patient for any reason, including failure to pay, should make sure that he or she can ensure that the patient will not be injured by this action.

Inadvertent abandonment usually occurs through misunderstandings about backup coverage when the physician is unavailable. While a jury will be much more sympathetic if the physician was unavailable because of a medical emergency, as opposed to a social event, the reason makes little difference to the patient in need of care. Many physicians would never go to a party without arranging to receive their calls or providing someone else to cover emergencies, but they frequently become involved in lengthy hospital procedures that render them unavailable without arranging any coverage.

Failure of the system for backup coverage can result in constructive abandonment. A physician who is part of a group that shares call on a set schedule can get in trouble if the person on call does not show up. The physician's duty is to his or her patient. If the patient is injured because of a problem with the call schedule, it is the patient's original physician, not the on-call physician, who is ultimately liable. It is important to verify call arrangements each time rather than relying on habit or custom.

Patients may be abandoned through failures in the scheduling system. The appointment clerk may functionally abandon a patient by refusing to let a patient talk to the medical personnel, by scheduling an appointment too far in the future, or by filing away the chart of a patient who failed to keep an important follow-up appointment. (This is discussed more fully in Chapter 15.)

Patient-Initiated Terminations

In the simplest scenario, the patient voluntarily terminates the physician-patient relationship and seeks care from another physician. Unfortunately, patients sometimes stop coming before they are fully recovered from the acute condition that brought them to the physician. When this happens, the physician must make some effort to determine whether the patient is knowingly forgoing further care, has found another physician, or is staying away out of ignorance or a misunderstanding of the physician's instructions. As discussed later under "documentation," the process of investigating the patient's disappearance also generates the necessary record that the physician has discharged the duty to the patient.

An adult patient has the right to refuse to follow the physician's advice. If this person understands the need for further treatment and the consequences of not having that treatment, the physician has no legal liability for the patient's subsequent course. (The physician's duty is different for a minor patient.) The problem arises in establishing what the patient was told. A jury will presume that a severely injured patient would not have refused to follow the physician's instructions if he or she had understood the consequences of the refusal. An example of this problem arose when a woman died of cervical cancer and her family sued the physician for failure to diagnose (*Truman v. Thomas,* 1980). The physician argued that she had refused a Pap smear, and this prevented him from making a proper diagnosis. The physician lost. The jury did not believe that he had properly informed her of the value of the test. His credibility was undermined because she had dutifully returned for gynecological checkups, including pelvic examinations. It was hard to believe that she would go to this much trouble and refuse a minor diagnostic test.

Problems also arise if the patient has misunderstood either the physician's directions as to the need for further care or the seriousness of forgoing further care. In this case the patient is not intentionally accepting the risk of injury. The physician may be liable if it can be established that the patient was not properly informed about the need for further treatment. There are steps the physician may take to ensure that the patient receives the proper information, but nothing can ensure that the patient understands this information. Since the goal of the physician is to prevent patient injuries whenever possible, he or she should make some effort to follow up with patients who do not return for needed visits.

Patients sometimes discharge their physicians explicitly. They may fire the physician over a disagreement or courteously inform the physician that they are seeking care elsewhere. In either case, the physician should endeavor to identify the subsequent treating physician and document the patient's decision to seek care elsewhere. If the patient has a new physician, the patient should be asked to write down the name of the new physician so that records may be forwarded. If the patient has not made arrangements for care, the physician should reiterate the need for care and offer to help the patient find a new physician. These efforts will help ensure that the patient receives proper care. If, despite the physician's efforts, the patient does not follow through in seeking proper care, there will be evidence that the original physician made a good-faith effort to help the patient.

Many medical insurance schemes use financial incentives to coerce patients into abandoning their usual physicians. The purpose is to shift patients to the care of physicians who have agreed contractually with the insurance company to accept reduced fees, modify their way of practice, or both. The effect is that the patient is forced to discontinue an established medical relationship and seek care from a new physician who is unfamiliar with the patient's condition. This poses a legal risk to physicians who subsequently treat these patients. Patients who are forced to abandon a long-standing relationship with a physician may be very demanding of a physician they see under duress. This increases the probability that misunderstandings and bad results will escalate to litigation. It also puts the physician at a technical disadvantage. He or she is expected to pick up the patient's care exactly where the previous physician left off, without the benefit of the previous physician's knowledge of the patient.

The physician who accepts a new patient who has sought care voluntarily is not expected to have all the knowledge of the patient's condition that the previous physician possessed. A physician who participates in a coercive effort to force patients to enter his or her practice cannot complain of being handicapped in any treatment of the patient by a lack of prior information. This is a natural consequence of the physician's actions, and he or she will be legally responsible if it causes the patient harm.

Physician-Initiated Termination of Care

When a physician-patient relationship must be terminated, the physician must carefully document the circumstances in the patient's medical record. This termination note should review the patient's previous medical treatment and the current state of the patient's health. If the termination will not affect the patient's health, this should be stated and explained. If the patient is in need of continuing care, the note must explain how the physician has ensured that the termination will not compromise the patient's health.

For patients in need of continuing care, there must be documentation of the arrangements made for the patient's subsequent care. If no arrangements have been made, there needs to be a detailed discussion of why the relationship is being terminated and why it was not possible to make follow-up arrangements.

There are several acceptable reasons for terminating the relationship with a patient who is still in need of medical care for an acute problem. One is that the patient has refused to follow the physician's advice to the extent that it becomes impossible to care for the patient in a professional manner. For example, a severely hypertensive patient may refuse to take medication. Assuming this refusal is not based on a reasonable concern with the side effects of the medicine, the physician is not bound to try to continue treating a patient who refuses what the physician believes to be essential therapy. The recent case of *Bouvia v. Superior Ct.* (1986), in which a person with cerebral palsy sought the legal right to force a hospital to starve her to death is an extreme example of this problem.

Changing circumstances in a physician's practice may make it difficult to care for a patient in a professional manner. The physician may be changing the nature of the practice (such as working part time), moving to a different geographic area, or joining a corporate practice that will make it difficult to continue treating former patients.

DOCUMENTING THE TERMINATION

When the relationship between a physician and patient is terminated, the exact circumstances of the termination must be documented. The patient's condition should be summarized in the same manner as a discharge note in a hospital record. For each ongoing medical problem that is identified, there should be evidence that the patient was notified of the problem and the need for further care. If the physician knows who the patient is transferring to, this should be recorded in the termination note.

A physician who terminates the physician-patient relationship must document that the patient was properly notified. The physician should write the termination note in the patient's chart, and the patient should be contacted and told of the physician's decision, its medical implications, and where to obtain further care, if needed. This should be put in a letter that repeats the information in the medical record.

If possible, the patient should sign a copy of this letter during a visit with the physician. The physician should give the patient the original letter, keeping the signed copy for files. If this is not possible, the letter should be sent by certified mail, with a return receipt requested. The certified mail number should be noted in the letter, and a copy of the letter and the return receipt should be put in the patient's medical record. If the letter is returned and efforts to find a correct address fail, the unopened letter in the patient's record will document that a diligent effort was made to contact the patient.

Patient-initiated terminations must be carefully documented. While the patient always has the right to terminate the physician-patient relationship, this is usually done not by confronting the physician but passively by not returning for care. It is the physician's responsibility to follow up on patients who disappear if they have conditions that require continuing medical care. (It is also good business to keep track of patients and their reasons for seeking care elsewhere.) These conditions may be acute, such as an orthopedic patient who does not return to have a cast removed, or chronic, such as a diabetic.

Following up on missing patients requires that medical records be kept in such a manner that the physician is aware that a patient has been lost to follow-up. Tickler files serve as reminders that a patient is due to return for care. These may be computerized, or simply noted as an extra entry on the office calendar. When a patient misses an appointment, the physician should call to find out what has happened to the patient. If the patient cannot be located, refuses to come back, or has found care elsewhere, the physician should document this information in the chart. The physician should send the patient a certified letter explaining why the patient should return or find alternate care.

BIBLIOGRAPHY

Patient Attitudes and Behaviors

Block MR; Coulehan JL: A taxonomy of difficult physician-patient interactions. Fam Med 1988 May–Jun; 20(3):221–23.

Boza RA; Milanes F; Slater V; Garrigo L; Rivera CE: Patient noncompliance and overcompliance: Behavior patterns underlying a patient's failure to "follow doctor's orders." Postgrad Med 1987 Mar; 81(4):163–70.

Connelly JE; Campbell C: Patients who refuse treatment in medical offices. Arch Intern Med 1987 Oct; 147(10):1829–33.

Conrad P: The noncompliant patient in search of autonomy. Hastings Cent Rep 1987 Aug–Sep; 17(4):15–17.

Hahn SR; Feiner JS; Bellin EH: The doctor-patient-family relationship: A compensatory alliance. Ann Intern Med 1988 Dec 1; 109(11):884–89.

Holloway RL; Matson CC; Zismer DK: Patient satisfaction and selected physician behaviors: Does the type of practice make a difference? J Am Board Fam Pract 1989 Apr–Jun; 2(2):87–92.

John C; Schwenk TL; Roi LD; Cohen M: Medical care and demographic characteristics of "difficult" patients. J Fam Pract 1987 Jun; 24(6):607–10.

Lazare A: Shame and humiliation in the medical encounter. Arch Intern Med 1987 Sep; 147(9):1653–58.

Like R; Zyzanski SJ: Patient requests in family practice: A focal point for clinical negotiations. Fam Pract 1986 Dec; 3(4):216–28.

Ling JC; Barefield P: Building bridges between doctors and patients. World Health Forum 1989; 10(1):28–29.

Merrill JM; Laux L; Thornby JI: Troublesome aspects of the patient-physician relationship: A study of human factors. South Med J 1987 Oct; 80(10):1211–15.

Moore C: Need for a patient advocate. JAMA 1989 Jul 14; 262(2):259–60.

Ouellette Kobasa SC: Patients' perception of their care. Cancer 1989 Jul 1; 64 (1 Suppl): 295–97; discussion 298–301.

Richards CG: The other end of the telephone. Arch Dis Child 1989 Jun; 64(6):886–88.

Root MJ: Communication barriers between older women and physicians. Public Health Rep 1987 Jul–Aug; Suppl:152–55.

Roter DL; Hall JA; Katz NR: Relations between physicians' behaviors and analogue patients' satisfaction, recall, and impressions. Med Care 1987 May; 25(5):437–51.

Schwenk TL; Marquez JT; Lefever RD; Cohen M: Physician and patient determinants of difficult physician-patient relationships. J Fam Pract 1989 Jan; 28(1):59–63.

Shreve EG; Harrigan JA; Kues JR; Kagas DK: Nonverbal expressions of anxiety in physician-patient interactions. Psychiatry 1988 Nov; 51(4):378–84.

Sinusas K: Patients' attitudes toward the closing of a medical practice. J Fam Pract 1989 May; 28(5):561–64.

Truman v. Thomas, 27 Cal 3d 285, 611 P2d 902, 165 Cal Rptr 308 (1980).
Weisman CS: Communication between women and their health care providers: Research findings and unanswered questions. Public Health Rep 1987 Jul–Aug; Suppl:147–51.
Weiss GL; Ramsey CA: Regular source of primary medical care and patient satisfaction. QRB 1989 Jun; 15(6):180–84.
Wilson J: Patients' wants versus patients' interests. J Med Ethics 1986 Sep; 12(3):127–32.

Physician Attitudes and Behaviors

Arnold RM; Martin SC; Parker RM: Taking care of patients—does it matter whether the physician is a woman? West J Med 1988 Dec; 149(6):729–33.
Bergman JJ; Eggertsen SC; Phillips WR; Cherkin DC; Schultz JK: How patients and physicians address each other in the office. J Fam Pract 1988 Oct; 27(4):399–402.
Branch WT: The language of patient care (editorial). J Gen Intern Med 1989 Jul–Aug; 4(4):359.
Campbell ML: The oath: An investigation of the injunction prohibiting physician-patient sexual relations. Perspect Biol Med 1989 Winter; 32(2):300–8.
Davidhizar RE; Wehlage DF: Telephone "emergencies": How to respond appropriately and effectively. Postgrad Med 1987 Feb 1; 81(2):61–68.
Diamond EL; Grauer K: The physician's reactions to patients with chronic pain. Am Fam Physician 1986 Sep; 34(3):117–22.
Gjerdingen DK; Simpson DE; Titus SL: Patients' and physicians' attitudes regarding the physician's professional appearance. Arch Intern Med 1987 Jul; 147(7):1209–12.
Jahnigen DW; Schrier RW: The doctor/patient relationship in geriatric care. Clin Geriatr Med 1986 Aug; 2(3):457–64.
Johnson CG; Levenkron JC; Suchman AL; Manchester R: Does physician uncertainty affect patient satisfaction? J Gen Intern Med 1988 Mar–Apr; 3(2):144–49.
Koenig HG; Bearon LB; Dayringer R: Physician perspectives on the role of religion in the physician–older patient relationship. J Fam Pract 1989 Apr; 28(4):441–48.
Lavin M: What doctors should call their patients. J Med Ethics 1988 Sep; 14(3):129–31.
Matthews E: Can paternalism be modernized? J Med Ethics 1986 Sep; 12(3):133–35.
Mishler EG; Clark JA; Ingelfinger J; Simon MP: The language of attentive patient care: A comparison of two medical interviews. J Gen Intern Med 1989 Jul–Aug; 4(4):325–35.
Novack DH; Detering BJ; Arnold R; Forrow L; Ladinsky M; Pezzullo JC: Physicians' attitudes toward using deception to resolve difficult ethical problems. JAMA 1989 May 26; 261(20):2980–85.
Parker LM: Doctor-patient communication and ethical issues (editorial). J Clin Oncol 1989 Sep; 7(9):1182–83.
Quill TE: Recognizing and adjusting to barriers in doctor-patient communication. Ann Intern Med 1989 Jul 1; 111(1):51–57.
Robins LS; Wolf FM: Confrontation and politeness strategies in physician-patient interactions. Soc Sci Med 1988; 27(3):217–21.
Roskin G; Marell SK: Differences in attitudes toward patients among medical specialties. Int J Psychiatry Med 1988; 18(3):223–33.
Roter DL; Hall JA: Physicians' interviewing styles and medical information obtained from patients. J Gen Intern Med 1987 Sep–Oct; 2(5):325–29.
Shore BE; Franks P: Physician satisfaction with patient encounters: Reliability and validity of an encounter-specific questionnaire. Med Care 1986 Jul; 24(7):580–89.
Stein HF: "Sick people" and "trolls": A contribution to the understanding of the dynamics of physician explanatory models. Cult Med Psychiatry 1986 Sep; 10(3):221–29.
Wilson-Barnett J: Limited autonomy and partnership: Professional relationships in health care. J Med Ethics 1989 Mar; 15(1):12–16.
Zinn WM: Doctors have feelings too. JAMA 1988 Jun 10; 259(22):3296–98.

10

Conflicts of Interest

CRITICAL POINTS
- Many medical business practices violate the Medicare fraud and abuse law.
- Financial incentives to change medical decision making can violate physicians' fiduciary duty to their patients.
- Physicians can be sued and criminally prosecuted for unknowingly violating statutory and common law duties to patients.
- Attorneys often fail to get physicians' full informed consent when setting up medical care business deals.

Medical practice is rife with conflicts of interest between physicians and patients. Some conflicts, such as sexual relations with patients, are ages old. Others, such as managed care incentive plans, are new manifestations of the competitive marketplace for medical care services. In the past, individual physicians were free to make their own accommodations to the conflicts of interest inherent in practice. There have always been physicians who are driven by money, but this was a personal choice. The vast majority of physicians put patients' interests first, even if it reduced the physician's income. Now these ethical choices are dictated by medical care business. Physicians are forced to put the third-party payer interests first or be driven out of practice. Managing these conflicts is critical to the survival of medicine as a profession (Bailey 1990).

This chapter reviews the physician-patient fiduciary relationship and the conflicts that it engenders. It is well established that patients can sue their physicians for breaching their fiduciary duties (Morreim 1989). Despite this right, few patients have sued their physicians over fiduciary issues. We believe that the paucity of litigation stems from the nearly insurmountable legal impediments to patient-initiated litigation for breaches of fiduciary duty. While these impediments may protect physicians from suit by patients, it is not patient-initiated litigation that physicians should fear (Hyman 1990).

A little-heeded corollary to medical care as a business is that medical businesses are subject to the same legal threats as other businesses. These include the antitrust laws (discussed in Chapter 18) and federal racketeering laws. Perhaps the greatest threat is the Medicare/Medicaid fraud and abuse law, as strengthened by the recent safe harbor regulations. Physicians often fail to study these laws, believing them to apply only to criminals. But many common medical business practices violate technical provisions of these laws. These violations can subject physicians to suit by other medical providers, third-party payers, and state and federal prosecutors.

THE FIDUCIARY RELATIONSHIP

The physician-patient relationship is a member of a special class of legal relationships called *fiduciary relationships*. Through the creation of fiduciary duties, the law recognizes that there are relationships in which the parties inherently have unequal power. In the words of one court:

> [T]he physician-patient relationship has: . . . its foundation on the theory that the former [physician] is learned, skilled and experienced in those subjects about which the latter [the patient] ordinarily knows little or nothing, but which are of the most vital importance and interest to him, since upon them may depend the health, or even life, of himself or family. [T]herefore, the patient must necessarily place great reliance, faith and confidence in the professional word, advice and acts of the physician. (*Witherell v. Weimer*, 1981)

The essence of the fiduciary relationship is that the patient's interests must be paramount. This is in contrast to the usual legal rule of caveat emptor ("let the buyer beware"). In most businesses, the law assumes that there is an arms'-length transaction: the buyer and the seller have, in theory, the same access to information and the same bargaining power. For example, a merchant in a retail store encourages customers to buy the items that have the greatest profitability for the store. The merchant may not lie about the goods but is allowed to puff: to volunteer only favorable information and to make reasonable overstatements of the products' virtues. In contrast, the physician is expected to recommend treatments based only on the patient's medical and psychological needs.

Physicians should be familiar with fiduciary duties from the literature on informed consent to medical treatment. The fiduciary duty extends to all aspects of the physician-patient relationship. Breaching the financial aspects of the fiduciary duty to a patient can subject the physician to liability under commercial laws. Understanding the factors that make the physician-patient relationship a fiduciary one will help physicians recognize potential violations.

Training and Licensure

The fundamental difference between physicians and patients is knowledge. The physician has power over the patient by virtue of greater knowledge gained through training and experience. The physician must complete many years of professional training before being allowed to practice medicine. This training is available to only a small number of individuals in the population, and it consumes many societal resources. This contributes to the societal policy that physicians should not take advantage of patients by virtue of their superior knowledge. Even more important to this policy is the limitation of the right to practice medicine to persons with this professional training.

The medical license carries with it five rights: the right to diagnose illness, the right to treat that illness by medical means, the right to prescribe drugs, the right to supervise nonphysicians in the provision of medical services, and the right to collect fees for medical services provided by oneself and others. Some of these rights are shared by other licensed health care practitioners (chiropractors may diagnose illness), but taken together they give the physician a unique monopoly position in health care delivery. In return for these rights, particularly the unique right to prescribe drugs, society expects physicians to exercise concern for the interests of patients. If licensing and knowledge were the only sources of power in the physician-patient relationship, there would be no need to extend this fiduciary duty to physicians in need of medical care. In fact, the duty owed to physicians in need of medical care is only slightly less than that owed to laypeople because the law recognizes other factors that affect the bargaining power of the patient.

Market Factors
Another limitation on a patient's choice of health care services is the limited availability of market information. Although the Federal Trade Commission (FTC) has eliminated many of the traditional bans on physician advertising, the highly personal nature of medical care makes it difficult to compare prices and services. It is also difficult to obtain a personalized bid for medical services. This lack of information increases the physician's duty to provide the comparative information to the patient that is necessary to make an informed choice of treatment. (This is discussed in detail in Chapter 11.)

Even patients with information about the market for medical services are often financially limited in their ability to choose a physician. These financial limitations stem from attempts by employers and their insurance companies to limit the cost of medical care. The two primary vehicles for reducing costs are health maintenance organizations (HMOs) and preferred provider organizations (PPOs). It is important to recognize that the more the patient's choice of physician is limited, the greater is that physician's duty to protect the patient's interests. If the plan is sufficiently restrictive (as is often true for specialty care in an HMO or PPO), this duty to guard the patient's interests may extend to the administrators of the plan and the employer that selects the plan.

Market models also assume that there is time to collect and evaluate market information, but many serious medical problems arise quickly and must be treated quickly, limiting the patient's choice of physicians to whomever is geographically available. Even in nonemergency cases, the discomfort and risk involved in shopping for physicians severely limit the patient's ability to choose a physician. An equally serious problem is financial limitations. The poor have always been limited in their choices of medical care providers—a limitation increasingly being felt by the middle class.

Finally, market models are based on the fungibility of goods: that ability to substitute one good for another. Patients do not like to treat physicians as fungible. One traditional definition of a profession was that it mattered who did the work, not just the price of the job. While the medical profession does not like to stress the differing abilities of its practitioners, physicians who seek medical care are usually particular about who renders that care. Since it is difficult for laypersons to evaluate professional services, patients usually reward physician fidelity with loyalty.

Physicians who behaved in a responsible manner could assume that the patient would continue to return for care. Acting in the patient's interest might cost the physician profits in the short term, but it led to a stable practice and long-term profitability. The changing nature of the medical care reimbursement system is forcing many patients to move from physician to physician. This destabilizes physician practices and increases the pressure to consider the short-term profitability of patient care alternatives, and it increases the physician's conflicts of interest.

TRADITIONALLY RECOGNIZED CONFLICTS

Informed Consent
When obtaining informed consent, the physician is expected to present an unbiased view of the proposed treatment, presenting the risks as well as the benefits. While this informed consent is important, the most important decision is which treatments to recommend. If the physician's impartiality in the selection of treatments is compromised, then providing the patient with information about the compromised choice is meaningless. This problem is most extreme in the managed care plans that request the physician not to inform the patient about alternative treatments or tests. This benefits the plan by preventing patient complaints about being denied alternative treatments. It completely defeats informed consent, however, and leaves the physician in an indefensible posture if the patient is injured.

Treating Family Members
This is probably the most commonly recognized conflict of interest. It has been traditional for physicians to treat their colleagues' families without charge to discourage physicians from treating their own families (Wasserman et al. 1989). This professional courtesy is a recognition that objective decision making is critical to medical care and that this objectivity is impossible for someone who is emotionally involved with the patient. Treating one's own family can lead to disharmony and guilt if the treatment is not successful. Although it is generally not illegal to treat a family member, many states limit the drugs that may be prescribed. Ideally, physicians and their family members will seek care from physicians who are not close friends or colleagues. This helps ensure objectivity and avoids the conflicts inherent in confiding personal information to colleagues or friends (Lane et al. 1990).

Hospitals
Physicians were traditionally prohibited from owning an interest in a hospital. (There was always an exception for small towns in which the physician might be the only person able to finance and oversee the hospital.) It was accepted by a consensus of the profession that it would be difficult for physicians to evaluate the need for hospital care objectively if they would financially benefit from putting the patient in the hospital.

The disappearance of this prohibition does not result from today's physicians' being more objective than their predecessors. It results from the increased profitability of hospital ownership, which may intensify the potential conflict of interest.

Laboratories
Just as ownership in a hospital potentially interferes with the physician's objectivity when evaluating the need for hospital care, ownership in a laboratory can encourage the ordering of unnecessary laboratory tests. Since there is no legal evidence that defensive medicine (the ordering of diagnostically unnecessary

tests) reduces the probability of a medical malpractice lawsuit, many critics of this practice attribute it to direct and indirect financial incentives to order tests. The extent to which test ordering is influenced by nonmedical considerations will become critical as shifts to prospective reimbursement systems reverse these incentives and begin to penalize physicians for ordering tests. There are risks associated with ordering unnecessary tests but much greater risks in failing to order a necessary test.

Sexual Relationships with Patients

The sexual exploitation of patients has been a high-visibility malpractice issue for psychiatrists. In psychiatry the conflict of interest is clear because the patient is definitionally at a psychological disadvantage. The conflict is also clear in any situation in which the sexual relations could be termed sexual assault. (See Chapter 6.) This includes any sexual relations in a medical care delivery setting with a patient who is not the medical care provider's spouse or significant other.

The more common problem is the physician who becomes romantically involved with a nonpsychiatric patient. It is important that the physician not continue providing major medical care for such a patient, and it is preferable that the patient be referred to another physician for all medical treatment.

TECHNICAL FRAUD: THE MEDICARE STATUTE

Physicians and institutions that deal with the Medicare and Medicaid (hereafter referred to jointly as Medicare) programs are subject to the Medicare fraud and abuse statute and regulations. The relevant provisions are short and simple:

> **42 USCA 1320a–7b(b) Illegal remunerations**
> (1) whoever knowingly and willfully solicits or receives any remuneration (including any kickback, bribe, or rebate) [defined broadly as anything of value] directly or indirectly, overtly or covertly, in cash or in kind—
> (A) in return for referring an individual to a person for the furnishing or arranging for the furnishing of any item or service for which payment may be made in whole or in part under subchapter XVIII of this chapter or a State health care program, or
> (B) in return for purchasing, leasing, ordering, or arranging for or recommending purchasing, leasing, or ordering any good, facility, service, or item for which payment may be made in whole or in part under subchapter XVIII of this chapter or a State health care program,
> shall be guilty of a felony and upon conviction thereof, shall be fined not more than $25,000 or imprisoned for not more than five years, or both.

This is a criminal law that subjects violators to fines and imprisonment. Since criminal prosecutions are not covered by malpractice or general indemnification insurance, physicians must pay attorneys' fees for contesting charges brought against them. These fees can easily exceed $100,000. Physicians convicted under the law can also lose their license to practice medicine.

Given the clarity of the law and the severity of the penalties, it would seem that physicians and their attorneys would be scrupulous in adhering to the requirements of the law. This is not the case:

> "I've talked about it with a lot of laboratory clients, and the reasoning almost always comes back, 'The competition is doing it, so we have to do it to stay in business.'"

The "it" in that observation by a Washington health care attorney refers to financial considerations built into business relationships between clinical labs and physician/hospital referral sources. (Column 1986)

To be more specific, the "it" is a renumeration prohibited under the Medicare fraud and abuse law. A substantial percentage of medical businesses engage in prohibited practices, and most of these prohibited practices occur in business arrangements structured and approved by lawyers. The interesting question is not that physicians might unknowingly violate the provisions of a given law but that their attorneys would counsel them to violate the law.

Constitutionality of the Fraud and Abuse Statute

Statutes are not the law when the courts find them unconstitutional or otherwise invalid. Currently there were three federal appeals court decisions involving criminal prosecutions under the fraud and abuse laws. The first dealt with a physician, Greber, who ran a laboratory service that provided Holter monitors (*United States v. Greber*, 1985). These monitors were ordered by cardiologists. Greber's business fitted them to the patient, collected the data, and prepared the data for reading by the ordering cardiologist. The ordering cardiologist was paid a consultant's fee for analyzing a patient's Holter monitor data. In the defendant's criminal prosecution for fraud, the government asserted that this fee was an illegal inducement to persuade physicians to use Greber's services.

Greber argued that these were not illegal inducements to refer patients but legitimate fees for evaluating the Holter monitor data. The court's record does not indicate that these consultants' fees were higher than the fee that would have been paid to a cardiologist who was retained to analyze the data but who had not ordered a Holter monitor. There was evidence, however, that some physicians received consulting fees when Greber had already evaluated the Holter monitor data. Perhaps most telling for the government's case was Greber's own testimony in a related civil case: "In that case, he had testified that '. . . if the doctor didn't get his consulting fee, he wouldn't be using our service. So the doctor got a consulting fee'" (*Greber*, p. 70).

The Court found that "if the payments were intended to induce the physician to use Cardio-Med's services, the statute was violated, even if the payments were also intended to compensate for professional services" (*Greber*, p. 72). This interpretation was upheld in a subsequent case in which the Court found that "the jury could convict unless it found the payment 'wholly and not incidentally attributable to the delivery of goods or services' (*United States v. Kats*, 1989). This ruling made it clear that the prohibited conduct was any payment that accompanied a referral, irrespective of whether the physician receiving the payment provided some goods or services in return.

A case involving payments allegedly intended to influence a decision to award an ambulance contract approved of the *Greber* decision and extended it to cover subsequent modifications that had been made in the law (*United States v. Bay State Ambulance and Hospital Rental Service*, 1991). This case directly considered the constitutionality of the Medicare fraud and abuse law: "Defendants next claim that, if we read the Medicare Fraud statute to criminalize, under certain circumstances, reasonable payment for services rendered, the statute becomes unconstitutionally vague" (*Bay State*, p. 33). The Court rejected this reasoning, finding that Congress's broad power to regulate commerce included the power to prohibit practices that might induce referrals, even if they had other, proper, motives (Holthaus 1989).

The Everyone-Does-It Defense
There have been few prosecutions under the fraud and abuse laws. As one attorney put it:

> Gaynor says the standard set in the *United States v. Greber* case is clear: If one purpose of payment is to induce future referrals, the Medicare statute has been violated. But, he adds, it is not followed absolutely. "You've got this case law that says everybody goes to jail and you know that can't be right." The question then becomes which of the transactions is more likely to stimulate the interest of a prosecutor, he says. (Hudson 1990)

For unstated reasons, the Justice Department has not enforced the fraud and abuse law in any meaningful way, leaving physicians and their attorneys in an ethical quandary. If physicians follow the law and the cases interpreting the law, they will be at a tremendous competitive disadvantage. Under the plain language of the law, its interpretation by the courts, and the administrative agency regulations, attorneys are compelled to recommend against many common medical care business practices. If attorneys do so, their clients will seek counsel who are more realistic.

The ethics are further complicated because some of the business practices that are outlawed are beneficial to patients and may even lower Medicare costs. This is not unusual; many business laws are imperfect. The legal test is not that the law be perfect in its application, only that it be rationally related to the ends sought to be achieved. Physicians and their attorneys are drawn into rationalizations that the law could not really mean what it says because that would outlaw many beneficial practices. While it may be ethically defensible to engage in civil disobedience to protest an unjust law, we do not believe that physicians are intentionally violating the law to protest its results.

Recently, there have been efforts to eliminate gross violations, such as any payments tied to referral volume, but these do not reach the structural problems in many deals (Hudson 1990). Physicians and their attorneys continue to believe that as long as they do not intend to commit fraud, their technical violations are acceptable. Even articles warning of the risk of deals such as joint ventures between hospitals often concentrate on the business risks and do not emphasize the potential for fraud and abuse prosecutions (Burke 1991).

Implications of the Safe Harbor Regulations
On July 29, 1991, the Office of the Inspector General of the Department of Health and Human Services (OIG) promulgated the final "safe harbor" regulations. When Congress amended the fraud and abuse law, it directed the OIG to develop guidelines to help physicians avoid unintentional violations of the law. The proposed regulation was published in January 1989, and the agency received extensive comments from physicians and other medical care businesses.

The final safe harbor regulation is much more restrictive than many physicians anticipated. Rather than expanding the range of allowable activities, the regulations stick close to the statutory language that prohibits all inducements to refer patients. This disturbed many, who expected the regulations to accept the legality of current business (the following comments and responses are taken from the safe harbor regulation):

> Comment: Numerous commenters expressed concern about the difficulty in revising a business arrangement that they entered into with a good-faith belief that the arrangement did not violate the statute, but which they now find does not qualify under one of the safe harbor provisions. They suggested that the OIG either "grandfather" these arrangements or provide a reasonable period of time before initiating enforcement action to enable health care providers to restructure their arrangements to meet the safe harbor provisions.
>
> Response: The failure of a particular business arrangement to comply with these provisions does not determine whether or not the arrangement violates the statute because, as we stated above, this regulation does not make conduct illegal. Any conduct that could be construed to be illegal after the promulgation of this rule would have been illegal at any time since the current law was enacted in 1977. Thus illegal arrangements entered into in the past were undertaken with a risk of prosecution. This regulation is intended to provide a formula for avoiding risk in the future.
>
> We also recognize, however, that many health care providers have structured their business arrangements based on the advice of an attorney and in good-faith believed that the arrangement was legal. In the event that they now find that the arrangement does not comply fully with a particular safe harbor provision and are working with diligence and good faith to restructure it so that it does comply, we will use our discretion to be fair to the parties to such arrangements.
>
> Nonetheless, we believe that it would be inappropriate for us to provide a blanket protection, even for a limited period of time, for all business arrangements that do not qualify for a safe harbor. As we stated above, certain business arrangements that do not qualify may warrant immediate enforcement action. (56 Federal Register 35952 1991)

The safe harbor regulations draw a bright line between many acceptable and unacceptable business practices. Some practices, such as the sale of an ongoing practice to a hospital, have been specifically disallowed. Others, such as businesses that do not meet the percentage ownership requirements for nonreferring investors, are in clear violation of at least some aspects of the law. The legal significance of the regulations is that they put physicians on notice that they are violating the law. This leaves physicians with the question of what to do next.

The Temptation of Business as Usual

The OIG rejected grandfathering in existing medical businesses. Its position is clear: physicians who show good faith by getting out of businesses that violate the law might not be prosecuted. This creates a conflict for attorneys advising physicians about health care deals. Following the OIG's regulations would force an attorney to advise clients to get out of prohibited deals—inconvenient and expensive for the affected physicians. The conflict arises if the attorney also structured or advised on the deals that now must be undone.

The safe harbor regulations make it clear that they do not prohibit any previously allowed behavior. Anything that is prohibited by the regulations has been illegal since 1977. Physicians who entered into these deals after a full disclosure of the potential legal risks and ambiguities inherent in them have no reason to criticize their counsel. Physicians who were not informed of the tenuous footing of the deals may rightfully question their initial legal advice. This may make some attorneys reticent to stress the importance of modifying these deals. Until the OIG starts prosecuting physicians at a higher rate, it is tempting to ignore the regulations. It may be that the OIG will never prosecute any significant number of physicians, effectively nullifying the law.

The Risks of Business as Usual

There is a significant question as to the ethics of continuing to participate in a prohibited activity. A low probability of being prosecuted is not an adequate excuse for breaking the law. While it may be ethically defensible to engage in civil disobedience to protest a law, this should be done with an acceptance of the consequences of the action. It also is hard to assert that actions taken in private, with substantial financial benefits, are civil disobedience rather than merely seeking to profit from illegal activities.

It is ethically defensible to continue a practice that is beneficial and not clearly prohibited by the law. The promulgation of the final safe harbor regulations limits the availability of this ambiguity defense. These regulations and the accompanying fraud alerts also limit the extent that a physician may rely on the advice of counsel as to the acceptability of a regulated activity. Reliance on the advice of counsel is not a defense to criminal activity. At best, it can be used to show that the defendant did not intentionally break the law. This does not excuse breaking the law, but it may persuade the judge to impose a reduced sentence. Ultimately each individual is responsible for knowing and obeying the law. Physicians cannot insulate themselves from liability by selecting counsel who will claim the practice is not prohibited.

Ethical questions aside, an analysis of the severity and probability of the risk of prosecution weighs against continuing to participate in prohibited activities. While in the past there have been few criminal prosecutions, physicians have gone to jail under this law. In other cases, physicians have avoided criminal prosecution by paying substantial fines to the OIG. In one settlement, the physician agreed to pay $875,000 (Burda 1991a). Fighting the claim can be devastating. A dentist who rejected the chance to settle a case for a small amount was assessed a penalty in excess of $18 million in the trial of the case (Burda 1991b).

Fraud and abuse settlements and court-imposed fines are not insurable; these must be paid out of the physician's own funds. Accused physicians also must pay for legal representation. This can be several thousand dollars for a simple negotiated settlement or tens of thousands of dollars to defend a criminal prosecution against a single physician. A criminal prosecution generates substantial adverse publicity and can take the physician away from practice for weeks during a trial.

The Politics of Prosecution

The decision to prosecute medical businesses under the fraud and abuse law has always been a political decision. The law has been clear since 1977; the only reason that it has been questioned is that it was not enforced. The delays and acrimony over the promulgation of the safe harbor regulations were because of the large number of noncomplying physicians and medical businesses, not because of the complexity of the regulations. The final regulations themselves are quite short and simple. While the OIG has been silent on its reluctance to recommend prosecution in the past, even this reluctance may have been understated.

The OIG has allowed many physicians and medical businesses to enter into settlements that are confidential and thus make it difficult for physicians and their attorneys to estimate the true risk of violating the laws and regulations. These settlements were agreed to before the final safe harbor regulations were promulgated. It is likely that most of the settlements were made for business practices approved by attorneys.

It is reasonable to assume that the OIG's strict interpretation of allowable practices, as reflected in the final safe harbor regulations, indicates a more aggressive posture toward prosecuting physicians and medical business. Other political signs point to increased prosecution. Congress and the administration have posed revised Medicare/Medicaid reimbursement guidelines that will reduce the overall payments to physicians. Increased fraud and abuse prosecutions are a convenient way to deflect criticism from medical groups seeking to ensure adequate reimbursement levels.

TECHNICAL FRAUD: RICO VIOLATIONS

The Medicare fraud and abuse law is not the only restriction on physician business practices. The greatest threat is that physicians will violate the federal Racketeering Influenced Corrupt Organizations Act (RICO). Losing defendants in a RICO action are subject to treble damages: the payment of the plaintiff's attorney's fees, confiscation of their assets, and incarceration. The implications of these potential damages are illustrated in the recent medical care RICO case that resulted in a judgment for $100 million (BNA 1989). As with the Medicare fraud and abuse provisions, physicians may commit RICO violations without engaging in what is traditionally thought of as illegal activities.

It is controversial to discuss routine medical practices as potential RICO violations. As with the fraud and abuse laws, there have been few RICO lawsuits or prosecutions against physicians. This lack of litigation, combined with a belief that RICO applies only to criminals, has led most lawyers to reject RICO as a problem for physicians and medical care businesses. Few physicians have been counseled about the risks of RICO yet, but many unknowingly engage in practices that could subject them to RICO liability. Understanding how this might happen requires an understanding of the RICO law.

Understanding RICO

RICO is a conspiracy law. Congress's intent in passing it is unclear. Many businesspersons assert that it was intended only to apply to gangsters, but one of the drafters of RICO counters that it was intended to be a sort of national deceptive business practices act. Irrespective of congressional intent, the U.S. Supreme Court has ruled that RICO is not restricted to organized crime enforcement. This is consistent with the plain language of RICO. It is also more reasonable to assume that a plaintiff would be inclined to sue a businessperson rather than a gangster.

A person violates RICO by engaging in a conspiracy—a joint effort with at least one or more individuals or organizations—to break any of a lengthy list of specific state and federal laws. Violating one of the listed laws is called a *predicate act*. Physicians are at risk because breaching their fiduciary duty to patients, or violating other technical laws such as the Medicare fraud and abuse provisions, can support fraud allegations that are predicate acts under RICO.

Mail and Wire Fraud

Most RICO cases are based on violations of the federal mail and wire fraud statutes. Any fraudulent conduct that directly or indirectly uses the mails or telephone is a violation of the federal mail and wire fraud laws. The courts use a spacious definition of fraud in mail and wire fraud cases:

> It is a reflection of moral uprightness, of fundamental honesty, fair play and right dealing in the general and business life of members of society. . . . As Judge Holmes so colorfully put it "[t]he law does not define fraud; it needs no definition; it is as old as falsehood and as versatile as human ingenuity." (*Gregory v. United States*, 1958)

The Supreme Court reiterated the expansive reach of mail and wire fraud in the 1987 case of *Carpenter v. United States*. It affirmed the mail fraud conviction of a *Wall Street Journal* reporter who used the paper's confidential information in an inside trading scheme. The reporter was held to have violated his fiduciary obligation to protect his employer's confidential information:

> We cannot accept petitioners' further argument that Winans' conduct in revealing pre-publication information was no more than a violation of workplace rules and did not amount to fraudulent activity that is proscribed by the mail fraud statute. [The statutes] . . . reach any scheme to deprive another of money or property by means of false or fraudulent pretenses, representations, or promises. . . . [T]he words "to defraud" in the mail fraud statute have the "common understanding" of "wronging one in his property rights by dishonest methods or schemes," and "usually signify the deprivation of something of value by trick, deceit, chicane or overreaching." (*Carpenter v. United States*, 1987)

The duty of fidelity between the employer and employee that was at issue in this case is precisely the same type of common law fiduciary duty as that between physician and patient. Providing incentives to physicians to change the medical care offered their patients is a breach of fiduciary duty. The nature of the motive behind such incentives is judged from the patient's perspective, not the persons offering the incentives. For example, it is common for managed care plans to give physicians an incentive to reduce specialty referrals in an effort to control medical care costs. While this might seen be a laudatory action on the part of the managed care plan, the individual patient denied a referral will probably see it as an improper interference with the physician-patient relationship. Irrespective of the payer's motive, these incentives are legally indistinguishable from giving bribes to employees to violate their duty to their employers.

Incentives and Commercial Bribery

In most states HMOs, PPOs, and other managed care plans do not directly employ and supervise physicians. The physicians are either employed by physician's associations that contract with the plan or independent practitioners who contract directly with the plan. These contracts contain provisions that are intended to encourage the physicians to change the medical care decisions that they would have made in the absence of the plan.

Some of these provisions, such as those governing the submission of bills and discount schedules for prompt payment, have no effect on medical care decision making. Others have profound effects on physician decision making. The most benign of these incentives are disallowing or heavily discounting procedures that the plan wants to discourage. This gives physicians the option to offer the care and absorb the reduced reimbursement. These become more troubling when they are coupled with provisions that prevent discounting care. This prevents physicians from providing the treatment at cost to help needy patients. The most ethically and legally problematic provisions are those that prohibit the physician from rendering the necessary care.

Some plans attempted to have physicians contractually agree not to provide routine ultrasound to pregnant women and not to inform the women that routine ultrasound was available. By preventing women from knowing about the procedure, the plans hoped to avoid complaints from women who wanted ultrasound.

Total capitation plans pose the greatest conflicts of interest. A total capitation scheme makes the physicians or clinic group the insurer of the patient by requiring that they provide all necessary patient care for a fixed payment. Services that the physician cannot perform personally must be bought out of this allocation. These plans shift the risk of insurance onto the physicians or clinic—a powerful disincentive for the physician to order tests or consult with outside specialists about the patient's care. These plans are dangerous for all but clinics large enough to employ all necessary specialists and with enough patient volume to average out the risks. Smaller entities face the risk that a run of seriously ill patients will deplete the clinic's assets, making it unable to buy the necessary care for the patients.

While these incentive plans are ubiquitous, their legal status is quite uncertain. (The Wall Street insider trading scandals and the prosecution of savings and loan executives illustrate that generally accepted business practices may nonetheless be illegal.) Perhaps the clearest threat to these arrangements are state commercial bribery statutes. These laws are based on the Model Penal Code, section 224.8: Commercial Bribery and Breach of Duty to Act Disinterestedly:

(1) A person commits a misdemeanor if he solicits, accepts or agrees to accept any benefit as consideration for knowingly violating or agreeing to violate a duty of fidelity to which he is subject as:
   ... (c) lawyer, physician, accountant, appraiser, or other professional adviser or informant; ...
(3) A person commits a misdemeanor if he confers, or offers or agrees to confer, any benefit the acceptance of which would be criminal under this Section.

The Model Penal Code broadly defines the "benefit or consideration" as "gain or advantage, or anything regarded by the beneficiary as gain or advantage."

It is clear that incentive plans affect physicians' clinical judgment; physicians make different therapeutic decisions under incentive systems (Hemenway et al. 1990). Under the technical provisions of most commercial bribery, this is illegal, irrespective of whether it harms the patient. If the incentive denies patients care that they would otherwise have received, it is illegal under all the state commercial bribery laws. The test is whether the fiduciary duty is breached when viewed from the patient's perspective, not the plan's.

Violating a state commercial bribery statute is a predicate act for RICO only if the statute provides for imprisonment for greater than one year. Several states specifically prohibit physician incentives under their commercial bribery laws and provide for imprisonment for more than a year. In these states, physician incentive plans are clearly predicate acts for RICO. Some states do not specifically mention physicians in their commercial bribery statutes but prohibit bribing physicians. These states have case law that defines a physician as fiduciary. Even in states that do not directly criminalize physician incentives under a commercial bribery statute, a plaintiff can argue that the model penal code prohibitions on bribing physicians are evidence that incentive plans violate the physician's common law fiduciary duty. These breaches of the physician's fiduciary duty can be the basis for mail and wire fraud, which are predicate acts for RICO.

The Pattern of Racketeering

Engaging in one predicate act, such as accepting a bribe, is not enough to trigger RICO. The defendant must engage in a pattern of racketeering. The risk of physicians' being charged with RICO violations was increased by the 1989 ruling in *H. J. Inc. v. Northwestern Bell Telephone Company*, in which the Supreme Court completed the expansion of RICO that began with the 1985 decision in *Sedima, S.P.R.L. v. Imrex Co.* In *Sedima*, the Court held that RICO defendants need not be convicted of the underlying predicate acts that were used to charge a pattern of racketeering. This ruling greatly simplified criminal prosecutions and private civil actions brought under RICO because the prosecutors or plaintiffs were no longer compelled to wait until the defendants were tried for the underlying predicate acts. The Sedima ruling left open the definition of a pattern of racketeering, allowing some courts to limit the application of RICO by defining a pattern of racketeering as sustained criminal activity involving many, even hundreds, of predicate acts.

The Supreme Court in *Northwestern Bell* held that the RICO pattern requirements were meant to have a broad reach. In particular, the Court stressed that RICO was meant to apply to situations "in which persons engaged in long-term criminal activity often operate wholly within legitimate enterprises." The Court also reiterated that a pattern might be as few as three predicate acts. This ruling makes clear that a legitimate business, such as a medical care enterprise, that commits three or more predicate acts can be charged with the requisite pattern of racketeering for a RICO action.

Prosecuting a RICO Claim

RICO is a criminal law prosecuted by the Justice Department. The Justice Department has sued physicians under RICO for submitting false insurance claims using the mails and telephone (*United States v. Bachynsky*, 1991). RICO also has a private attorney general provision; this allows individuals who have been harmed by the RICO violations to sue for treble damages and attorney's fees. Their damages are trebled to punish the defendant. As with the antitrust laws, RICO is intended to compensate only for economic injuries. RICO cannot be used in place of a medical malpractice lawsuit by an injured patient.

The most likely RICO plaintiffs will be other physicians or health care business (Hinsdale 1988). Plaintiffs do not need to be a direct target of the illegal activity to recover under RICO. They need only be injured through the pattern of racketeering. For example, assume that a managed care plan provides illegal incentives to participating physicians. Some physicians in the community are injured because they refuse to participate in a plan that requires them to compromise their medical care decision making. If this plan has enough market share, these physicians will lose business. If the insurance company insures a substantial percentage of the community, the nonparticipating physicians may be driven out of business. The nonparticipating physicians could sue the insurance company and the physicians who "stole" their patients by participating in the plan.

Peer review actions could be fertile ground for RICO litigation. Any physician participating in a peer review action who also receives illegal incentives is at risk for a RICO lawsuit. The plaintiff might be a physician who is being reviewed by a peer review committee for a PPO that provides incentives to encourage physicians to reduce hospitalization. Assume that the physician is being reviewed because she keeps patients in the hospital too long and orders too many tests. There is no evidence that she harms the patients, but she does cost the PPO a lot of money. If the peer review committee sanctions the physician, she could sue independent contractor physicians and the PPO for conspiring to sanction physicians who did not support the scheme to reduce hospitalizations.

The physician would argue that the peer review committee members were given financial incentives to put financial considerations above their fiduciary obligations to the patient. Since the federal law protecting peer review activities (see Chapter 19) does not protect actions taken in bad faith, this physician could get to the jury because the illegal incentive plan would be evidence of bad faith.

Failing medical business will also generate RICO claims as creditors and debtors look for solvent parties to share the costs. A hypothetical example might be Doctors' Hospital, which begins providing incentives to physicians to admit insured patients to its facility. These physicians begin to divert to Doctors' Hospital insured patients who otherwise would have been admitted to Holy Name Hospital. The patient mix at Holy Name Hospital shifts to medically indigent patients, and the hospital goes bankrupt. Holy Name Hospital was injured by the incentives provided by Doctors' Hospital. If Holy Name Hospital can establish that these incentives were predicate acts under the definition in RICO, it can sue Doctors' Hospital and the individual members of its medical staff under RICO. The damages in such a lawsuit could easily exceed $100 million. The individual physicians would share responsibility for paying the verdict.

PHYSICIANS AND FRAUD

We have been criticized for being unrealistic in our characterization of many medical business practices as criminal activities (Doherty 1989). This view confuses actions with actors. Under the plain reading of the statutes and cases, many common medical business practices, including the structural arrangements of some managed care plans, violate various laws. This does not mean that the physicians and others involved in these plans are calculated criminals. The laws discussed in these articles do not require an intent to be a criminal. Persons who violate the technical provisions of these laws are committing crimes, even if they do so unknowingly and with unimpeachable intent.

We also do not believe that every medical business practice that is technically illegal will or should be prosecuted. There are prohibited practices that benefit patients and lower the costs of medical care. We do believe that physicians have been much too ready to compromise their fiduciary duties. This is not solely the fault of physicians. When the issue is put directly to physicians, as it was in the Supreme Court case upholding restrictions on abortion counseling in Title X clinics, most physicians believe that they have a fiduciary duty to protect their patient's interests:

> Similarly entrenched in the common law and medical ethics are the responsibilities that flow from the trust on which the physician-patient relationship is based. "Because patients must be able to rely on their physicians to act in good faith and in their best interest," the common law treats the duties owed by doctors to patients as "fiduciary" in nature. Once having begun to serve a patient, a physician is ethically and legally obligated to speak honestly with that patient. In particular, physicians' "high ethical obligation to avoid coercion and manipulation of their patients" requires physicians to avoid "the withholding or distortion of information in order to affect the patient's beliefs and decisions." (Brief 1991)

The problem is not so much physician ignorance as a failure of informed consent in the physician-attorney relationship. Many questionable medical business practices are the consequence of joint ventures and other business arrangements that were structured by attorneys. Most of these business deals were not clearly illegal at the time they were established. They were, however, clearly questionable, and some have subsequently been declared illegal. Yet few physicians were apprised of the risks of these deals. They relied on their attorneys' expert judgment, just as patients must rely on their physicians' expert judgment when consenting to medical care.

CONCLUSIONS

Physicians must determine if any of their business practices breach their fiduciary duty to their patients or are otherwise legally improper:

1. All physicians must personally read the safe harbor regulations and the accompanying preface by the OIG.
2. They must determine their state's laws on physicians as fiduciaries. This includes commercial bribery laws and cases holding that the physician is a fiduciary.
3. If the attorney who drafted or reviewed their medical business arrangements did not provide full information about the potential risks of these arrangements, they must request this information.
4. If they did receive a disclosure of risks, they must ask their attorney if the safe harbor regulations have modified these risks.
5. If they are in a noncomplying deal, a written opinion on the specific problems and how they might be remedied is needed.
6. If they feel they were not properly advised of the risks when entering into the arrangement, they should consider getting a second opinion from an attorney who was not involved with the original attorney or the original deal.

Physicians must educate themselves about the problems of financial conflicts of interest with their patients. Conflicts should be avoided when possible and disclosed when they cannot be avoided. In some cases, such as the disclosure of the selection criteria for physician referral services, disclosure is legally required. In all cases, there is an ethical duty to disclose interests in medical care businesses and other potential conflicts of interest.

The nature of the fiduciary relationship is such that disclosure does not cure conflicts of interest. The physician-patient relationship is a fiduciary relationship precisely because patients must rely on their physician's integrity. Disclosing a conflict of interest does not help the patient avoid the effects of the conflict. Disclosure can show good faith but will not make an improper activity legally acceptable.

Managing conflicts of interest poses a profound ethical problem for physicians and for the rest of society. They underlie questions about appropriate termination of life support, access to care for indigents, and many other critical medical care problems. If physicians and their attorneys continue to ignore the significance of financial conflicts of interest, they should not be surprised by ever more draconian laws regulating medical business practices.

BIBLIOGRAPHY

Articles

Bailey BJ: Somehow we have to stop the train wreck; Part 1. Arch Otolaryngol Head Neck Surg 1990 June; 116:669–70.

Berenson RA: Capitation and conflict of interest. Health Aff (Millwood) 1986 Spring; 5(1):141–46.

BNA: Court approves settlement in physicians' suit against HMO. Sec Reg L Rep 1989 Feb 24; 21(8):313.

Burda D: AHM to pay $500,000 to settle dispute. Mod Healthcare 1991a Apr 8:32.

Burda D: Watchdog gets tough on Medicare fraud; Inspector general has strong-armed nearly $10 million in hospital settlements. Mod Healthcare 1991b Apr 8:32.

Burke M: Hospital-MD joint ventures move forward despite hurdles. Hospitals 1991; 65(9):22.

Column: Caution advised in relations with laboratory referral sources. Med Lab Observer 1986 Jul; 18:23.

Dalton R; Forman MA: Conflicts of interest associated with the psychiatric hospitalization of children. Am J Orthopsychiatry 1987 Jan; 57(1):12–14.

Doherty JF Jr: Doctors' bills can come under RICO's scope. Nat L J 1989 Sep 25:12.

Ellsbury KE: Can the family physician avoid conflict of interest in the gatekeeper role? An affirmative view. J Fam Pract 1989 Jun; 28(6):698–701.

Feinstein RJ: Physician payment plans and conflicts of interest. J Fla Med Assoc 1986 May; 73(5):387–89.

Hemenway D; Killen A; Cashman SB; Parks CL; Bicknell WJ: Physicians' responses to financial incentives. N Engl J Med. 1990; 322:1059–63.

Holthaus D: Courts broadly interpret antikickback laws. Hospitals 1989; 63(19):44.

Hudson T: Fraud and abuse rules: Enforcement questions persist. Hospitals 1990; 64(5):36.

Hyman DA: Conflicts of interest, continued (letter). JAMA 1990; 263:1199–1220.

Lane LW; Lane G; Schiedermayer DL; Spiro JH; Siegler M: Caring for medical students as patients. Arch Int Med 1990 Nov; 150(11):2249.

Lynn J: Conflicts of interest in medical decision-making. J Am Geriatr Soc 1988 Oct; 36(10):945–50.

McDowell TN Jr: Physician self referral arrangements: Legitimate business or unethical "entrepreneurialism." Am J Law Med 1989; 15(1):61–109.

Morreim EH: Conflicts of interest; Profits and problems in physician referrals. JAMA 1989; 262:390–94.

Relman AS: Dealing with conflicts of interest (editorial). N Engl J Med 1985 Sep 19; 313(12):749–51.

Schiedermayer DL: La Puma J; Miles SH: Ethics consultations masking economic dilemmas in patient care. Arch Intern Med 1989 Jun; 149(6):1303–5.

Schwartz H: Conflicts of interest in fee for service and in HMO's. N Engl J Med 1978 Nov 9; 299(19):1071–73.

Southgate MT: Conflict of interest and the peer review process (editorial). JAMA 1987 Sep 11; 258(10):1375.

Stephens GG: Can the family physician avoid conflict of interest in the gatekeeper role? An opposing view. J Fam Pract 1989 Jun; 28(6):701–4.

Wasserman RC; Hassuk BM; Young PC; Land ML: Health care of physicians' children. Pediatrics 1989; 83:319–22.

Cases

Brief of the American College of Obstetricians and Gynecologists, the American Academy of Family Physicians, the American Fertility Society, the American Medical Association, the American Medical Women's Association, Inc., as amici curiae in support of petitioners. *Rust v. Sullivan*, 111 SCt 1759 (1991).

Carpenter v. U.S., 484 US 19 (1987).
Gregory v. U.S., 253 F2d 104, 109 (5th Cir 1958).
H.J. Inc. v. Northwestern Bell Telephone Company et al., 492 US 229 (1989).
Hinsdale Women's Clinic, S.C. v. Women's Health Care of Hinsdale, 690 F Supp. 658 (NDIll, Jun 20, 1988).
Sedima, S.P.R.L. v. Imrex Co., 473 US479, (1985).
U.S. v. Bachynsky, 934 F2d 1349 (5th Cir 1991).
U.S. v. Bay State Ambulance and Hospital Rental Service, Inc., 874 F2d 20 (1st Cir), May 02, 1989).
U.S. v. Greber, 760 F2d 68 (3d Cir), Apr 30, 1985).
U.S. v. Kats, 871 F2d 105 (9th Cir), Apr 3, 1989).
Witherell v. Weimer, 421 NE2d 869 (1981).

11

Consent to Medical Treatment

CRITICAL POINTS
- Informed consent is a cornerstone of modern medical practice.
- Informed consent does not make the patient an equal partner in the therapeutic relationship.
- A proper informed consent must reflect the individual patient's special circumstances.
- Informed consent is a vehicle for fostering communication between physicians and patients.

The notion that patients have the right to know what is to be done to them and to have some voice in whether it is done has caused more confusion than any other medical legal doctrine. This chapter reviews the history of informed consent and discusses the different standards governing simple and informed consent. These standards reflect the conflict between legal ideals of medical care and its reality. Patient advocates and many physicians view informed consent as a way to empower patients, thereby making them equal partners in the therapeutic relationship.

This is a naive view of informed consent. As discussed in Chapter 10, informed consent does not affect the disparity in power and knowledge between physicians and patients. Informed consent is very important at the margin, when there are clear, simple-to-understand choices. It cannot protect patients from overreaching by physicians or from antiscientific delusions about medical treatments. Good science and proper standards for medical practice are more empowering than elaborate informed consent rituals. Informed consent is a laudable goal, but it is possible to comply with the legal standards for informed consent without effectively involving the patient in the decision-making process. When this happens, physicians lose the true value of informed consent: reducing conflicts with patients through dissipating unreasonable expectations.

DEFINING CONSENT

In 1914 in *Schoendorff v. Society of New York Hospital,* Justice Cardozo wrote the classic judicial statement of a person's right to consent to medical care:

> Every human being of adult years and sound mind has a right to determine what shall be done with his own body; and a surgeon who performs an operation without his patient's consent commits an assault for which he is liable in damages. This is true except in cases of emergency, where the patient is unconscious and where it is necessary to operate before consent can be obtained.

Historically, consent meant no more than getting the patient's permission before commencing treatment. This permission required only that the patient be told what would be done, not the risks or alternatives to treatment.

Medical care, especially surgical care, is the most intrusive private action that may be done to a free person. Society may imprison or execute, but one private citizen may not cut or medicate another without permission from the intended patient and a license from society. A person's right to consent to medical treatment has always been an important part of medical care. It was not a topic of general interest until the war crimes trials at Nuremberg shocked the world medical community with revelations about the experiments carried out by physicians in the death camps. Blurring the line between experimentation and torture, these experiments moved the discussion of consent to medical care from the philosophical to the practical.

As a pure legal issue, forcing treatment on an unwilling person is no different from attacking that person with a knife. The legal term for touching a person without permission is *battery*. Battery is a criminal offense, and it can also be the basis of a civil lawsuit. The key element of battery is that the touching be unauthorized, not that it be intended to harm the person. Battery requires a complete failure of consent. In medical care situations, the patient has usually implicitly authorized some treatment by voluntarily seeking medical care. This implied consent would prevent a claim of battery in most medical care situations.

Battery is a legal threat only when the patient is either technically incompetent to consent to care or when the patient has refused care. As discussed later, a patient who refuses care may not be treated without the authorization of a court. Yet even when a patient has refused care, the physician is unlikely to be charged with a crime if the treatment was meant to be beneficial. This is not an endorsement for acting against a patient's will. It is a recognition that the criminal law is reticent to punish physicians unless it is clear that they intended to cause harm.

EXCEPTIONS TO THE REQUIREMENT OF CONSENT

There are two well-recognized exceptions to the need for informed consent to medical treatment. The more common is a medical emergency, in which an unconscious or delirious patient cannot consent. The second is rare and involves certain court-ordered treatments or treatments and tests mandated by law. There is also a pseudo-exception: the therapeutic exception, which ostensibly allows the physician to withhold information from a patient if that information would psychologically harm the patient and thus imperil the patient's physical health.

The Emergency Exception
The emergency exception to the need for informed consent (or any consent) is based on the premise that a reasonable person would not want to be denied necessary medical care because he or she happened to be too incapacitated to consent to the treatment.

The legal strictures on the emergency exception are very limiting: the patient must be incompetent to consent and in need of treatment to save his or her life or to prevent permanent disability. This often involves children, who may be medically able to consent to treatment but are legally unable to consent because of their age. An example is the problem of the 14 year old who has broken an arm and is brought to the hospital by a neighbor. Neither the child nor the neighbor is legally able to consent to treatment. The physician may rely on the emergency exception to consent if immediate care is necessary to preserve the use of the child's arm.

The case law on the definition of an emergency is restrictive because the only cases that are brought to court involve bizarre facts, such as children being brought in for elective surgery without, or against, their parent's consent. If parents were suing a physician because he or she relieved their child's suffering, the issue would quickly shift from the physician's liability for malpractice to the parents' liability for child abuse and neglect. In general, it is better for the physician to be explaining to a jury why he or she helped someone rather than stand by and watch the child lose life or limb.

A rare abuse of the emergency exception involves patients who have refused to consent to specific medical care. The refusal may be based on religious beliefs, such as refusing blood transfusions, or on a personal decision, such as refusing intensive care. If the physician disagrees with such a decision, the time to fight the decision is when it is made. There is no legal justification for waiting until the patient is unconscious or for physically or chemically restraining a patient and then rendering care against the patient's consent. This would not constitute an emergency exception to the need for consent. On the contrary, it would constitute battery.

The major abuse of the emergency exception to the need for consent is its use as a justification for treating chronically ill patients who are incompetent to consent to medical care. The emergency exception is just that—an exception limited to emergencies. These may be in the emergency room, or they may involve patients in the hospital who have an unexpected event such as a cardiac arrest. The emergency exception does not apply to an incompetent patient in need of routine care. Chronically incompetent patients should have a legal guardian.

Legally Mandated Treatment

A court with proper jurisdiction may appoint a guardian to consent for a patient, or a court may issue an order for treatment under the authority of the public health laws. (See Chapter 20.) Medical treatment mandated under the public health laws poses a peculiar informed consent problem. The patient cannot refuse the treatment but is probably entitled to be informed about the nature of the treatment. This anomalous situation arises because a legal action for failure of informed consent requires the patient to prove that he or she would have refused the treatment if he or she had been properly informed. Since refusal is not an option, the legal action would fail. Conversely, it is repugnant to our sense of freedom to force treatment on a person without at least explaining what is being done and why.

The Therapeutic Exception

The therapeutic exception to the need for informed consent arises from a now-discredited view that information about risks of treatment or the existence of diseases such as cancer should be withheld from patients to foster the proper mental attitude for recovery. Most of the court opinions and legal articles dealing with informed consent take care to acknowledge that there may be circumstances when it is in the patient's best interest not to be informed of the risks of the proposed treatment. Although the courts constantly reaffirm the existence of the therapeutic exception, they uniformly reject it as a defense in specific cases.

The public debate that surrounded the question of telling patients about their cancer has made the courts wary about establishing standards that would deny patients information. But the courts have not explicitly overruled the cases that discuss the therapeutic exception; they have just refused to find that a therapeutic exception existed in the cases that have been before them. They have stated that the alleged harm cannot be the refusal of the treatment.

The courts are particularly loath to accept the therapeutic exception in cases in which the physician withheld information to encourage the patient to undergo treatment. In cases involving mental patients, courts have refused to accept the withholding of information about risks based on concerns that the patients would otherwise refuse the necessary treatments. In a case involving a patient under psychiatric care, the court held that it was improper not to tell the patient about the risk of tardive dyskinesia. The defendant physician argued that had the patient been told of the risk, he would have refused the treatment. The court rejected this argument, finding that the policy behind informed consent was precisely to allow patients to choose to refuse treatment. If the physician believes that a patient must be deceived into necessary therapy, the proper course is to obtain a guardianship.

Implicit in the narrowing of the basis for the therapeutic exception is the belief that if a patient is sufficiently psychologically fragile as to be harmed by the consent process, then perhaps that patient is not competent to consent to care. If a physician really believes that it would do significant harm to a patient to tell that person the risks of a proposed treatment, then it would be appropriate to consider petitioning the court to determine if that patient should have a guardian appointed to make medical decisions.

INFORMED CONSENT

The acceptance of informed consent to medical treatment as a routine part of medical practice is less than 20 years old. While the cult of currency hastens the diffusion of scientific knowledge in medical teaching, social and philosophical information diffuses much more slowly. Random gossip spreads more quickly through the health care system than does accurate information. It is this misinformation that has shaped most physicians' perceptions of informed consent, causing much consternation in the process. Despite many physicians' belief that informed consent is a creature of legal fiat, it is the natural societal response to the demystification of medicine. As medicine has moved from the shaman's tent into the research laboratory, it has adopted the cloak of logical decision making. A natural response is the assumption by the lay public that, given enough information, they may rationally make their own medical decisions.

Technology-Oriented Medicine
The post-Nuremberg period coincides with the growth of technology-based medicine. While the Nuremberg Doctrine provided the moral force for transforming

consent to medical treatment, the growth of technology determined the direction of this transformation. The interval between the advent of scientific medicine in the late 1890s and the rise of technological medicine in the 1950s was a period with relatively few effective treatments. The patient's choices were usually limited to one treatment or no treatment at all. Perhaps most important, few conditions had been medicalized. Symptomatic disease, rather than laboratory values, drove patients to seek treatment.

In this context, patients expected physicians to make all necessary medical decisions. This was an extension of the traditional paternalistic physician-patient relationship. It was also a reasonable response. The decision on treatment was based mostly on technical medical considerations. Without the luxury of several effective treatments, the paternalistic model of medical decision making did not deprive patients of meaningful autonomy.

The Demise of Paternalism

Traditional medical paternalism was based on the importance of faith in the absence of effective treatments. Physicians occupied a quasi-religious role, providing solace rather than salvation. With the rise of more invasive medical procedures, more finely tuned but highly toxic drugs, and more diseases defined by a medical finding rather than by a patient's symptoms, the underpinnings of this paternalistic role deteriorated. Choosing treatments is no longer the simple exercise of diagnosing the patient's condition and having that diagnosis determine therapy. A diagnosis now triggers a universe of possible actions. The selection of a treatment from this universe becomes a value judgment based on the relative risks and benefits of the various actions. The risks to be considered include patient-specific psychological and social risks.

Physicians may be expert in determining the medical risks of a treatment, but it is only the patient who can determine the relative acceptability of these risks. For example, some patients will risk substantial disability on a chance of a complete cure of chronic pain. For others, chronic but bearable pain is preferable to the chance of disability secondary to treatment. This weighing of risks is idiosyncratic to the patient's individual risk-taking behavior and cannot be predicted by a physician.

Following the paternalistic model, physicians assumed the task of making these risk-benefit decisions for the patients. Problems arose as patients began to question the consequences of these decisions. Once patients realized that there might be more than one way to treat their conditions, they began to question the physician's authority to make unilateral treatment decisions.

Changing Values

Patients expressed their dissatisfaction with paternalism through lawsuits. In a small number of cases in the 1970s, physicians were sued for obtaining consent without informing patients of the risks of the proposed treatments. In almost every one of these cases, the failure to consult with the patient properly was only one facet of substandard care. A few courts held that a patient was entitled to be informed of the risks of treatment as part of the consent process. These opinions were seized upon by legal scholars, who then fashioned the theory of informed consent to medical care.

As more courts began to recognize a patient's legal right to be informed about the risks of treatment, this was transformed into an individual liberties issue.

Physicians who did not inform patients adequately have been accused of oppressing their patients. This legal view of informed consent as a liberty issue created a bitter dispute over the role of the physician. Physicians felt that their integrity was being challenged over their good-faith attempts to shield patients from unpleasant medical information. The courts, despite much language about the special relationship between physicians and patients, have inexorably moved to the position that physicians who assume the right to make decisions for their patients also assume the consequences of those decisions.

Legal Standards for Informed Consent
The core of the controversy over informed consent is the choice of a standard by which informed consent is judged. Physicians argue, correctly, that they have always talked to patients about proposed treatments. It is not talking to patients that they object to; it is the court's intrusion into what is said. Many states have sought to minimize this intrusion by adopting disclosure standards based on physician expectations: the community standard. Other states have adopted standards based on patient expectations: the reasonable-person standard.

Both the community standard and the reasonable-person standard are used for judging the information to be given to passive patients, who do not ask questions. If the patient does ask questions, the physician must answer these questions truthfully. More important, the answers must be sufficiently complete to convey the requested information accurately. The physician cannot hide behind the patient's inability to phrase a technical question properly. Under either standard, a patient who asks to be told all the risks of a procedure is entitled to more information than a patient who sits mutely. Failure to disclose a risk in reply to a direct question may constitute fraud, even if the appropriate standard for judging informed consent would not require that the risk be disclosed.

The Community Standard
The community standard is the older standard and reflects the traditional deference of the law toward physicians. It is based on what physicians as a group do in a given circumstance. The community standard requires that the patient be told what other physicians in the same community would tell a patient in the same or similar circumstances. "Community" refers both to the geographic community and to the specialty (intellectual community) of the physician.

The community standard usually requires that the patient be told little about the risks of the treatment or possible alternatives. In the extreme case, the community standard can shelter, telling the patient nothing other than the name of the proposed treatment and a brief description of it. In this extreme situation, physicians choose not to inform patients about the risks of the treatment.

The community standard has the most extreme results in very limited subspecialty areas of practice. In these areas, the number of practitioners is small, and there are only a few training centers. This results in an intellectually homogeneous group of physicians who tend to approach patient care in a similar manner. It is common for subspecialty practitioners to become true believers in the efficacy of a given treatment and to promote that treatment to patients. In this situation, the community standard will be to offer the patient only enough information to convince him or her to have the treatment. Risks will be ignored because the physicians have convinced themselves that it would be unreasonable to refuse the treatment.

Another area in which the community standard becomes a problem occurs when a small group of a larger specialty adopts a therapy that is rejected by the majority of the specialty. Since informing their patients of the majority view would make it impossible to perform the procedure, the minority-view physicians must ignore the controversy. For example, there has been a great controversy in ophthalmology over performing radial keratotomies. A small group of ophthalmologists began performing this procedure on large numbers of patients without traditional controlled studies on the benefits and long-term risks of the procedure (Freifeld 1985). A disclosure based on the views of the majority of the profession would have required that the patient be told that this was an unproved, experimental treatment that carried potentially severe long-term risks. Few patients would consent to an essentially cosmetic procedure if given this information. As a result, the majority view was discounted, and patients were told little about the uncertainty concerning the existing and future risks of the treatment. When a national study panel disputed this practice and called for proper studies of the procedure, the advocates of radial keratotomies sued the members of the study panel for antitrust violations (Norman 1985). The court found these allegations groundless and ruled for the study panel members (*Schachar v. Society of New York Hospital* 1989).

The Uncertainty of the Community Standard
From a physician's perspective, the community standard provides little guidance in deciding what to tell patients. Physicians do not routinely discuss what they tell patients; medical journals do not publish articles on the proper disclosure for specific treatments; professional societies do not promulgate standards for disclosure because they fear antitrust litigation by physicians who are offering unorthodox treatments. A physician who wants to comply with the community standard has a difficult task in establishing what disclosure the standard would mandate for a given treatment.

This uncertainty arises because the community standard is not rooted in medical practice. It is a legal rule that determines how a jury is to decide if a specific patient was given enough information. The community standard is a defensive standard. The jury is not allowed to judge the physician's disclosure on a commonsense basis. The patient must find a physician to testify that certain disclosures should have been made. It is usually possible to find a physician to testify that whatever complication the patient suffered is part of the community standard for disclosure. This leaves a physician who has not disclosed the risk, based on a good-faith belief that the disclosure was not required, without an objective standard to argue to the jury.

Reasonable-Person Standard
The courts and legislatures of several states have abandoned the community standard in favor of the more patient-oriented reasonable-person standard. The reasonable-person standard requires that a patient be told all of the material risks that would influence a reasonable person in determining whether to consent to the treatment. While hardly less ambiguous than the community standard, the reasonable-person standard has the advantage of encouraging physicians to discuss the proposed treatment with the patient more fully.

This new standard is not accepted by all states, but it is spreading. As courts in community standard states grapple with the perceived abuses of corporate medical practice, it is expected that they will move to the reasonable-person standard. Even in states that retain the community standard, a plaintiff's expert will present a hybrid standard to the jury based on the increased information given patients in states that have adopted the reasonable-person standard. Since the standards for specialty practice are national, physicians in reasonable-person jurisdictions will set the minimum disclosure, which will then have to be followed in the community standard states. By this incremental increasing of the standards for disclosure, the reasonable-person standard will become the de facto national standard.

When a standard is based on reasonableness, it means that jurors are allowed to use their common sense to determine what should have been done. In an informed consent case, the jurors decide what they would have wanted to be told about the proposed treatment. This weights the standard toward disclosure, since each juror is more likely to add to the list of necessary information than to argue that another's concerns are unreasonable. The reasonable-person standard does not always work to the patient's benefit. If the patient's personal demands for information seem unreasonable, the jurors may reject the claim even if the disputed information is usually given to patients.

Alternative Treatments
The reasonable-person standard both increases the amount of information that the patient must be given and changes the substance of that information. The community standard is concerned with the old question of treatment versus no treatment. The reasonable-person standard is concerned with the modern problem of choosing among alternative treatments. To make an informed choice, the patient must be told about the risks and benefits of all the acceptable treatments. This becomes a sensitive issue because specialty practice lines are often based on a particular approach to treatment. Surgeons do not like to discuss the medical management of patients, and family practitioners are reticent to recommend highly technical procedures for conditions that may be managed more conservatively.

The disclosure of alternative treatments is crucial when the physician is being pressured by a third-party payer to steer the patient to less expensive treatments. The patient must be informed of alternative treatments and their relative benefits. If the physician believes that an alternative treatment is preferable to the treatment that the third-party payer is advocating, the patient must be told of this conflict. The physician must never imply that a financially motivated treatment decision is medically preferable. Financial considerations must be explicitly discussed, or the physician commits a fraud on the physician-patient relationship.

Perhaps the most significant difference between the community standard and the reasonable-person standard is the presentation of the physician's personal recommendations. The community standard rests on the inherent coercion of forcing the patient to choose between treatment and no treatment: between continued care by the physician and loss of care. The reasonable-person standard, with its emphasis on alternatives, allows the patient to reject a given treatment without rejecting the physician. This change in emphasis reflects the reality of contemporary medical practice. In a competitive marketplace, physicians need patients as much as patients need physicians. This recognition of mutual dependence is beneficial unless it results in physicians' advocating trendy treatments to gain a marketing edge.

Statutory Disclosure Standards

Certain states and the federal government mandate specific disclosures in certain situations. (For an example of a federal requirement, see Chapter 25.) Texas is a good example because it has the most detailed requirements. The Texas Medical Disclosure Panel, a statutory body consisting of physicians and lawyers, promulgates lists of procedures and the risks that a patient must be told about each procedure. In some cases, the panel mandates more disclosure than was usual in the community, and in others it has lowered the level of disclosure.

This law was passed to reduce the threat of informed consent litigation. It is difficult to determine if it has been effective because there was very little informed consent litigation in Texas before the law was passed. What it has done is make it very easy to sue physicians who do not comply with the statutory requirements. It has also reduced the effectiveness of informed consent as a risk management tool. Rather than using the consent process to ensure that the patient understands what is to be done, physicians simply have patients sign the promulgated forms.

The best risk management advice for physicians in states with statutory disclosure standards is to tell the patient everything a reasonable person would want to know and then be sure that the patient signs the appropriate statutory consent forms. Physicians should ask their attorney if their state has any statutory disclosure requirements. If so, these should always be complied with. They are not, however, a substitute for obtaining a full informed consent.

Fraud

Fraud arises when a physician intentionally misleads a patient about the risks and benefits of a treatment. It becomes a serious legal (and criminal) issue when a patient is induced to accept substandard care by forgoing beneficial treatment or submitting to an unorthodox treatment. Concerns about fraud often arise when a physician begins to specialize in an unorthodox treatment. The most common examples are weight loss clinics that employ unusual and unapproved regimens, such as giving patients human chorionic gonadotrophin injections or pesticide pills. A patient who can establish fraud may be entitled to punitive damages. Fraudulent dealings may also subject the physician to criminal prosecution and the loss of his or her license. One physician who was involved with a fraudulent weight loss clinic was successfully prosecuted under the federal racketeering laws (*U.S. v. Bachynsky* 1991).

The Commonsense Approach

The doctrine of informed consent is a special case of the broader notion of assumption of risk. Whenever a person knowingly engages in a risky activity, that person consents to the risks of the activity. For this consent to be effective (1) the person must know the risks that are being assumed; (2) he or she must assume these risks voluntarily; and (3) it must not be against public policy to assume the risks. When a person makes a formal agreement (usually written) to accept the risks of an activity, that agreement is called a *waiver*. A properly executed informed consent is a waiver of the risks of medical treatment. To be effective, a waiver of the risks of medical treatment must meet the same three criteria as other waivers. Informed consent serves an additional, perhaps more important, purpose. In the process of discussing the risks, benefits, and potential alternatives to a given treatment, the physician and the patient have an opportunity to ensure that there are no misunderstandings about the patient's complaint and the proposed treatment.

Knowable Risks

People can assume only risks that they know about. For most commonplace activities, such as driving a car, the risks are well known and are implicitly assumed by engaging in the activity. It is possible to assume implicitly the risks of medical care. For example, a physician undergoing general anesthesia would be assumed to know that general anesthesia carries a risk of anoxic brain damage. He or she would implicitly assume this risk without the need for an explicit informed consent.

Most patients do not have the background medical knowledge implicitly to assume specific risks of treatment. Prior to the advent of informed consent, the patient was assumed to know that medical treatment was risky. Since the person had sought treatment knowing that it was risky, he or she was assumed to have accepted that the risk of treatment was less than the risk of the medical condition. The law was not concerned with the particular form that a risk might take. Under the doctrine of informed consent, this implicit assumption of risk no longer applies to medical care.

Advances in medical technology have caused a proliferation of choices in medical therapy. Patients are no longer limited to the choice between treatment or no treatment. This undermines the theory that the patient has accepted that the undifferentiated risks of medical therapy outweigh the risks of the condition. With many possible therapies for a given condition, the courts have rejected this implicit assumption of risk. A patient must now be told of the risks that he or she is assuming. The more particularized the information is about the potential adverse consequences of a treatment, the more effective is the assumption of risk.

Unknowable Risks

Medicine is not a perfect science. All medical care is associated with unknown, and perhaps unknowable, risks. The physician must tell the patient of the known risks of treatment, but this is not a guarantee that other problems cannot occur. Patients may assume these unknown risks if three conditions are met:

1. The risk is unknown (or of such a low probability that it is not known to be causally related to the procedure).
2. The patient is informed that the disclosed risks are not the only possible risks.
3. The medical rationale for the treatment is sound.

Condition 3 means that a patient cannot assume the risks of a negligently recommended treatment, an important issue with marginal treatments and vanity surgery. A patient who suffers a complication from an improper treatment may always sue the physician who recommended the treatment. A detailed consent form, listing all the risks of a treatment, is no protection if the treatment is unnecessary. If a patient can prove that a treatment was unnecessary or contraindicated, then the consent to risks of the treatment becomes ineffective.

Voluntariness

Consent to medical care can be truly voluntary only when it is reasonable to reject the care. Certain religious groups aside, a patient cannot be said to assume the risks of lifesaving care voluntarily. The law recognizes this in its requirement that a patient convince the jury that he or she would have forgone the treatment had the risk in question been made clear. The more clearly necessary a treatment is, the less meaningful is the idea of informed consent. Yet even in life-threatening situations, voluntariness can be an issue if there is more than one appropriate treatment. The patient might not reasonably reject all treatment but may justifiably argue that he or she might have chosen a different treatment.

Voluntariness becomes a legal issue if the physician coerces the patient into accepting a treatment for which there are acceptable alternatives. This coercion may be explicit—telling the patient that he or she will die without the proposed treatment at once—or implicit—ignoring the discussion of alternatives or financial intimidation. Physicians who cooperate with third-party payers to limit patients' treatment options undermine the voluntariness of patient consent. They should not be surprised if a court determines that this renders the patient's informed consent invalid.

Public Policy

A patient may assume only risks that arise from appropriate care. For example, any operation done under general anesthesia carries a small risk of anoxic brain damage. Assume that a patient consents to general anesthesia, including acknowledging the risk of brain damage. The anesthesiologist then negligently overdoses the patient with an anesthetic agent, fails to monitor the patient, and discovers the mistake only after the patient is brain injured. The patient's informed consent to the risks of anesthesia would not prevent the patient from suing for the negligent administration of anesthesia.

The law does not allow a patient to assume the risks of negligent medical care because of the involuntary nature of medical care. A person providing a necessary service has a duty to provide that service in a proper manner. This policy is intended to preserve the quality of necessary services. Conversely, it does not apply to services that the consumer may freely reject. For example, in most states, a skydiving service can successfully require that a customer waive the right to sue for all risks, including those from negligent acts of the service. This is accepted because skydiving is a purely voluntary activity.

Medically Unnecessary Procedures

The most difficult informed consent problems are those that arise from competently performed but medically unnecessary procedures. The extreme cases are those that involve vanity procedures, such as facelifts, liposuction, and breast enhancements. These procedures pose an informed consent dilemma. As medically unnecessary procedures, they may be rejected in the same way that skydiving may be rejected. From this perspective, a physician should be allowed to require a patient to assume all the risks of a vanity procedure, including the risks of negligent treatment.

A more moralistic perspective is that it is improper for physicians to use their skills and position of respect to perform purely commercial treatments. This attitude would view the vanity surgery patient as a victim who should not bear the risks of the physician's greed. This would lead to the rejection of assumption of risk for all risks, leaving vanity surgeons as guarantors of a good result.

Jurors tend toward the moralistic view. While they are constrained to accept a proper informed consent, they are very suspicious of the motives of vanity surgeons. If the consent has any ambiguities or if there is evidence of overreaching (such as aggressive advertising that implies that the risks are minimal and the benefits fantastic), then they tend to rule against the physician.

The Medical Value of Informed Consent

The informed consent document, carefully filed in the patient's medical records, has only legal value. It is the process of obtaining the informed consent that is medically valuable. Obtaining an informed consent should be seen as a quality control review of the patient's care. A proper informed consent must deal with the key elements in medical decision making: the patient's physical condition, the patient's subjective complaints and expectations, and the appropriateness of a proposed treatment.

Few patients are sophisticated health care consumers. They lack technical knowledge about medicine, and it is difficult for them to be objective about their health. Despite a physician's best efforts, questioning about medical history sometimes leads to an incorrect assessment of the patient's condition. This may arise because the patient misstates the severity of the condition, either denying or overstating its seriousness, or because the physician unconsciously directs the patient's answers toward the medical conditions that the physician is most interested in. Irrespective of how these misunderstandings arise, they dangerously distort the factual basis for medical decision making.

A careful discussion of the risks of the proposed treatment may cause the patient to reconsider the actual severity of his or her problem. The physician must be open to indications that the patient is growing uncomfortable about undergoing the proposed treatment. Synergistic misunderstandings can arise when the physician overestimates the severity of the patient's problem and recommends a major intervention. The patient then believes that the problem must be serious because the physician has recommended such a major treatment. Unless the physician carefully questions the patient after the treatment has been proposed but before it is carried out, the patient's belief that he or she must be sick because the physician wants to treat him or her as sick will not surface until the patient is injured.

The Patient's Expectations

Unreasonable expectations are at the heart of most medical malpractice lawsuits. It is important not to overstate the benefits of a proposed treatment, most critical if the treatment is for a minor condition or if there are effective alternative treatments. It is simple enough for a physician to avoid overstating the benefits of a treatment in talking with the patient. It is much more difficult to combat the unreasonable expectations that patients get from the constant news about medical breakthroughs. With patients treated to the spectacle of routine heart transplants and perfect test-tube babies on the evening news, it becomes very difficult to explain that heart disease is a chronic illness without a quick fix and that a certain percentage of all babies have some type of birth defect.

A physician must assume that every patient has an unreasonable expectation of the benefits of medical treatment. Whether these unreasonable expectations arise from overly optimistic news reports or medical advertising, they must be rooted out and dispelled. The physician must specifically ask the patient what the patient expects the treatment to do and believes the risks to be. This will allow the physician to deal explicitly with the patient's misinformation rather than blindly giving the patient more facts to confuse. In a variant of Gresham's law, it is clear that good information does not drive out bad information; it increases a patient's misperceptions. Patient misperceptions should be documented and a notation made about the correct information given.

Even when the physician and the patient agree on the severity of the complaint and the risks of the treatment, they will not necessarily make the same decision about undergoing the treatment. Physicians and patients have different risk-taking behavior, and patients differ in their risk-taking behaviors. Some are gamblers, and some keep their money under the mattress.

One patient will present with chronic pain and be satisfied to find out that it is only a bone spur, having assumed it must be cancer. Another patient with the same problem will want the physician to try to correct the spur surgically, despite the risks of anesthesia and potential disability. Patients who do not like to take risks are poor candidates for treatment if their untreated prognosis is good and the available treatments are risky. Patients who are aggressive risk takers may want "kill-or-cure" treatments, but they may also be more aggressive about suing when the treatments fail.

The patient's occupation and avocation can strongly affect his or her tolerance of certain risks. People who engage in activities that involve fine motor skills are susceptible to subtle injuries that might not be noticed by other patients. A routine arterial blood gas sample drawn from the radial artery could diminish the coordination of an accomplished violinist. The same injury in an attorney whose hobby was gardening would go unnoticed. Accommodating treatment to the patient's life-style should be part of medical decision making but is sometimes overlooked. Moreover, for esoteric skills, the patient who is an expert in the skill will be a better judge of its demands than the physician who may never have encountered the problem before. In this situation, the patient may teach the physician, if the physician is careful to listen to the patient.

DOCUMENTING CONSENT

There are two goals to achieve when documenting informed consent. The more important is using the process of documentation to ensure that the physician and the patient have the same understanding of the care being rendered—its risks, benefits, and alternatives. The secondary goal is to document this understanding in such a way that a third person, such as a juror, can determine both what the patient was told and whether the patient had some reasonable understanding of the implications of what was told.

Most of the literature on informed consent focuses on the consent form. While it is true that an undocumented consent is legally difficult to defend, informed consent is more than just getting a form signed. A proper informed consent starts with a discussion between the treating physician and the patient. In this discussion, the physician discusses the risks of proposed treatment and its alternatives. Most important, these risks and alternatives must be discussed in the context of the patient's prognosis. For example, the same risks of general anesthesia have profoundly different implications for a patient having a tooth pulled compared to a patient with an ectopic pregnancy. The consent form serves to document the discussion between the physician and the patient. It cannot substitute for it.

The Form of the Documentation
There is no single best way to document informed consent. In some situations, such as an immunization clinic, having the patient sign a preprinted consent form is optimal. In other situations, such as elective experimental treatment, a videotape of the physician's talking to the patient may be desirable. The form of documentation must fit the circumstances of the actual transaction between the physician and the patient. The most important consideration is that the documentation reflect the physician's conversation with the patient. "The patient was given the appropriate information and consented to the treatment" is too brief and vague. Long preprinted forms tend to be so broad that it is not possible to establish that they describe the actual conversation with a specific patient.

Blanket Consent Forms
The worst solution to documenting informed consent is the form that blankets all possibilities. The typical blanket form recites that the physician and his or her designees may do what they think is necessary. These forms usually contain language about how the physician has discussed the treatment with the patient and that the patient has had an opportunity to ask questions. Such a form may protect the physician from accusations of battery. As the sole records of consent, these forms are worthless.

Treatment-Specific Consent Forms
These prepared forms act as an information sheet for the proposed treatment. They can be very useful as a patient education tool but must be part of a detailed conversation with the patient. If the form alone is used, the consent may be effective, but the risk management benefit of informed consent will be lost because the physician will not learn about the patient's special concerns.

Patient-Specific Consent Forms
These are the ideal consent forms. They contain information on the patient's condition, the proposed treatments and alternatives, and any special considerations. It is an administrative nightmare to collect this information and type up a form for each patient. The best solution is to write (legibly) a detailed note in the patient's medical record as the actual conversation takes place. The patient should be given the note to read and should sign it as part of the medical record. This makes a legally robust document and impresses the patient with the individualization of his or her care.

Non-English Speakers
It is possible to develop foreign language consent forms, but medical terms are often idiosyncratic to regional dialects. For example, there are many patient education materials available in Spanish. These materials may be in textbook Spanish, perfectly intelligible to nonnative Spanish speakers who learned Spanish in school. They may be in the dialect of the translator. They may be hybrid documents in a pan-American patois. Whatever the case, they may be unintelligible to Spanish speakers who did not learn formal Spanish.

The major problem with dialects is not just that parts of a translated form will not be intelligible to the patient. The same idiomatic medical terms may be used in different dialects but with different meanings. Sometimes this is just embarrassing. Usually it results in the patient's believing that he or she understands the form, which he or she does in the context of the dialect, but misunderstanding what is about to be done. This problem is similar to the functional illiterate who recognizes some words but cannot make out the subtle meaning of the document.

The best solution for non-English speakers who may not read standard-school Spanish or another well-defined national languange is to have someone who is medically knowledgeable explain the treatment to the patient in his or her own dialect, with the physician present to answer questions. Ideally the physician should be able to understand enough of the patient's language to know if the translation is appropriate. Real informed consent is very difficult if the patient and the physician have no common language.

Illiterate Patients

The ritual of the patient's reading and signing a form or chart note is meaningless if the patient is illiterate. Studies in the United States have found a substantial fraction of the population to be functionally illiterate—unable to read well enough to carry out day-to-day tasks. When the material that must be read is relatively technical in nature, such as a description of the risks and benefits of medical treatment, the number of persons capable of understanding the material drops substantially.

The first problem is determining if the patient is literate. This is not always easy, for there are some intelligent, successful people who have developed elaborate strategies to conceal their illiteracy. Moreover, many people in the United States are literate and well educated in a language other than English, so for them an English-language form is useless. While this is obvious to the physician obtaining the consent, it seldom stops administrative personnel from having the patient sign the routine consent form. This undermines the documentation of the oral consent by calling into question the integrity of the process.

This problem requires a translator familiar with the patient's dialect and with the medical terms. The translator should be identified in the medical record. If possible, the translator's address and background should be on file with the hospital or physician. The translator may also serve as the witness if no one else fluent in the patient's language is available. The translator should be cautioned not to speak for the patient but to indicate if the patient's answer is inappropriate. The translator should write a brief note in the chart as to the patient's understanding and linguistic abilities.

Documenting the Oral Consent

The best form of documentation is a recording, either audio or video. These are cheap and easy to make but difficult to store. Medical records departments are equipped to store flat, relatively indestructible materials; lumpy items get lost or destroyed. This will change as medical images start being stored electromagnetically, but for the near future, the storage problems for recordings are a major impediment to their use. For this reason, recordings should be used only when the medical procedure or the patient pose particular problems. Unusual treatments include heart or liver transplants, experimental heroic measures such as artificial hearts, or refusal of lifesaving treatment by salvageable young people. Problem patients include minors undergoing nontherapeutic procedures (such as kidney donors), involuntary patients such as prisoners, patients with transient mental disabilities, and others for whom their state of mind at the time may become a significant issue.

When the person is illiterate but speaks and understands English, consent is usually documented with a witness. Ideally, this should be an impartial witness. The problem with an impartial witness is finding one. A family member may remember only what the patient remembers, while a nurse will be seen as an interested party. Clergy, a volunteer from a service agency, or another person not clearly identified with either the physician or the patient is the best choice. The witness must be present at the discussion with the patient and must make some independent record of his or her observations. This independent record may be simply initialing sections of the consent form or a note that certifies that the patient was asked a given question and made the appropriate reply.

BIBLIOGRAPHY

Baker LA: "I think I do": Another perspective on consent and the law. Law Med Health Care 1988 Fall–Winter; 16(3–4):256–60.

Baker MT; Taub HA: Readability of informed consent forms for research in a Veterans Administration medical center. JAMA 1983 Nov 18; 250(19):2646–48.

Baum M: Do we need informed consent? Lancet 1986 Oct 18; 2(8512):911–12.

Boisaubin EV; Dresser R: Informed consent in emergency care: Illusion and reform. Ann Emerg Med 1987 Jan; 16 (1):62–67.

Borak J; Veilleux S: Informed consent in emergency settings. Ann Emerg Med 1984 Sep; 13 (9 Pt 1):731–35.

Brenner LH; Gerken EA: Informed consent: Myths and risk management alternatives. QRB 1986 Dec; 12(12):420–25.

Capron AM: Uniform Law Commissioners' Model Health-Care Consent Act. Considerations against adoption. J Leg Med (Chic) 1983 Dec; 4(4):513–24.

Curran WJ: Law-medicine notes: Informed consent in malpractice cases: A turn toward reality. N Engl J Med 1986 Feb 13; 314(7):429–31.

Deutsch E: The right not to be treated or to refuse treatment. Med Law 1989; 7(5): 433–38.

Douglas S; Larson E: There's more to informed consent than information. Focus Crit Care 1986 Apr; 13(2):43–47.

Engelhardt HT Jr: Information and authenticity: Rethinking free and informed consent (editorial). J Gen Intern Med 1988 Jan–Feb; 3(1):91–93.

Freifeld K: Myopic haste? (100,000 plus have had new eye surgery). Forbes 1985 May 6; 95(2):135.

Gutheil TG; Bursztajn H; Brodsky A: Malpractice prevention through the sharing of uncertainty. Informed consent and the therapeutic alliance. N Engl J Med 1984 Jul 5; 311(1):49–51.

Helfand M: Understanding how physicians think: Medical decision making and informed consent. Pharos 1983 Fall; 46(4):31–36.

Kapp MB: Enforcing patient preferences: Linking payment for medical care to informed consent. JAMA 1989 Apr 7; 261(13):1935–38.

Kapp MB: Informed consent for federal clinicians. Milit Med 1989 May; 154(5):238–42.

Kee F: Risk management, public policy and informed consent: A case study. Public Health 1989 Jul; 103(4):281–87.

Lasagna L: The professional-patient dialogue. Hastings Cent Rep 1983 Aug; 13 (4):9–11.

Levine RJ: Medical ethics and personal doctors: Conflicts between what we teach and what we want. Am J Law Med 1987; 13(2–3):351–64.

Lidz CW; Meisel A; Munetz M: Chronic disease: The sick role and informed consent. Cult Med Psychiatry 1985 Sep; 9 (3):241–55.

Lidz CW; Meisel A; Osterweis M; Holden JL; Marx JH; Munetz MR: Barriers to informed consent. Ann Intern Med 1983 Oct; 99(4):539–43.

Mazur DJ: Informed consent: Court viewpoints and medical decision making. Med Decis Making 1986 Oct–Dec; 6(4):224–30.

Mazur DJ: Why the goals of informed consent are not realized: Treatise on informed consent for the primary care physician. J Gen Intern Med 1988 Jul–Aug; 3(4):370–80.

Minogue BP; Taraszewski R; Elias S; Annas GJ: The whole truth and nothing but the truth? Hastings Cent Rep 1988 Oct–Nov; 18(5):34–36.

Norman C: Clinical trial stirs legal battles: Legal disputes in Atlanta and Chicago over surgery for myopia raise issue of how controversial surgical techniques should be assessed. Science 1985; 1316(3):227.

Rosenberg JE; Towers B: The practice of empathy as a prerequisite for informed consent. Theor Med 1986 Jun; 7(2):181–94.

Schachar v. American Academy of Ophthalmology, Inc., 870 F2d 397 (7th Cir 1989).

Schoendorff v. Society of New York Hospital, 105 NE 92, 93 (1914).

Taub HA; Baker MT; Kline GE; Sturr JF: Comprehension of informed consent information by young-old through old-old volunteers. Exp Aging Res 1987 Winter; 13(4):173–78.

U.S. v. Bachynsky, 934 F2d 1349 (5th Cir 1991).

Wallace LM: Informed consent to elective surgery: The "therapeutic" value? Soc Sci Med 1986; 22(1):29–33.

Zerubavel E: The bureaucratization of responsibility: The case of informed consent. Bull Am Acad Psychiatry Law 1980; 8(2):161–67.

12

Special Consent

CRITICAL POINTS
- Patients may use a power of attorney to designate a surrogate to consent to their medical care.
- Surrogates and guardians must be provided all the information that the patient would have been given.
- Minors' medical records should specify who may consent to their care.
- In many situations, children may be treated without parental consent.

This chapter discusses power of attorney to consent to routine medical care, guardianships, and consent to medical care for minors. The special problems of terminating and refusing life support and the issues raised by involuntary surrogate decision making are discussed in Chapter 13. Obtaining and documenting consent are inseparable activities. This is especially true when the consent is obtained from someone other than the patient. For substituted or proxy consent to be effective, the physician must know the extent of the authority of the proxy to act on behalf of the patient and the circumstances when the proxy may not act.

PROXY CONSENT

Proxy consent is the process by which people with the legal right to consent to medical treatment for themselves or for a minor or a ward delegate that right to another person. There are three fundamental constraints on this delegation:

1. The person making the delegation must have the right to consent.
2. The person must be legally and medically competent to delegate the right to consent.
3. The right to consent must be delegated to a legally and medically competent adult.

There are two types of proxy consent for adults. The first, the power of attorney to consent to medical care, is usually used by patients who want medical care but are concerned about who will consent if they are rendered temporarily incompetent by the medical care. A power of attorney to consent to medical care delegates the right to consent to a specific person. The second type is the living will. These are discussed in Chapter 13.

Power of Attorney to Consent to Medical Care

The basic vehicle for an adult to delegate his or her right to consent to medical care is the power of attorney to consent to medical care. In the simplest case, the person delegates all medical decision making power to another competent adult, for a fixed period of time or an indefinite period. A competent patient may always revoke a power of attorney to consent to medical care.

Few states have laws forbidding the use of a power of attorney to delegate the right to consent to medical care. Conversely, many states do not specifically outline what a power of attorney may be used for. While the U.S. Supreme Court has not ruled that the right to delegate medical decision making is protected by the Constitution, it has endorsed the use of powers of attorney to consent to medical care. (See Chapter 13.) In the absence of a specific state law or state court decision forbidding the use of a power of attorney to delegate the right to consent to medical care, this is a valid method of proxy consent for adults.

The person making the delegation must be legally and medically competent at the time the power of attorney is signed. These documents are usually notarized, but the notarization has little legal significance. The notary public may testify as to the person's appearance to a layperson, but this is not persuasive if the patient's competency is at issue. If the person delegating the power to consent to medical care has a condition that might affect his or her competency, a physician, preferably not the patient's usual attending physician, should evaluate the patient and swear to the patient's competence. This should be incorporated into the power of attorney to forestall attacks on its validity.

The person to whom the right to consent has been delegated must be medically and legally competent to exercise this right. If he or she is not competent, the patient must be informed and asked to appoint a new person to consent to care. If both the patient and the person to whom the right to consent has been delegated are incompetent, then a court order must be sought to determine who is legally able to consent to the patient's care. Being medically incompetent refers to mental function, not medical training. The person designated to make decisions for the patient should not be a physician or a nurse involved in the care.

Conflicts of Interest

The person to whom the power to consent will be delegated should not have any conflicts of interest—emotional, financial, or professional—with the patient. The most obvious conflict is between the physician and the patient. While the physicians caring for the patient certainly have the patient's best interests in mind, they cannot both propose treatments and consent to them. Physicians and other health care providers should not allow themselves to be given the right to consent to care by a patient for whom they may have to provide treatment. This does not prevent physicians' acting for friends or relatives when their role is to act as the patient's advocate.

There are two types of conflict of interest between family members: conflicts related to loss of objectivity about the medical problems of a loved one and conflicts related to interests in the property or authority of the relative. For example, assume that a woman authorizes her husband to consent to her medical care during a severe illness. When significant treatment decisions must be made, the husband will find it difficult to put aside his concern for his wife and make objective decisions. He may feel guilty that she is ill and he is not. He may feel that he has contributed to her illness. He may even resent her illness and seek to punish her for being ill. The result is irrational decision making. The husband may blindly accept the proposed treatments or, less frequently, unreasonably refuse to consent to necessary treatments.

This issue should be discussed with patients who seek to execute a power of attorney to consent to medical care. It is important that patients realize the heavy burden that accompanies the right to consent to medical care for a loved one. They should consider whether they have a close friend or more distant relative who would be better able to make objective decisions and weather the pressures associated with the decisions.

Financial conflicts of interest also are inherent in family relationships. Returning to the example of the husband who has power of attorney to consent to his wife's care, if their resources are limited or the proposed treatment is very expensive, the husband will have to choose between paying for his wife's care or the needs of other members of the family. A third party can make more reasoned decisions about allocating resources and is less likely to consent to questionable treatments that the couple cannot afford.

Limitations

A power of attorney to consent to medical care may be limited in whatever way the person delegating the right wishes, consistent with public policy. Put simply, a person may not use a power of attorney to force treatment decisions that would otherwise be improper. For example, the person with a power of attorney may not authorize active euthanasia or force the physician to provide care that the physician would not otherwise provide.

If the person delegating the authority to consent is suffering from a terminal illness, it is usual to state that the power of attorney to consent to medical care is to remain in effect until revoked. It is also usual for spouses to execute prospective powers of attorney that are of indefinite duration, called *durable powers of attorney*. A durable power of attorney remains in force if the patient becomes legally incompetent. In some states, a power of attorney expires when the patient is declared legally incompetent. In all states, the court may supersede a power of attorney by appointing a guardian for the person. The courts are interested in perpetuating the person's wishes and will usually honor a guardian who is proposed in the power of attorney. For the power of attorney to be durable, it must recite that the patient wants the power of attorney to remain effective if he or she becomes incompetent. If the person is concerned only with temporary incapacity secondary to medical treatment, the power of attorney to consent to medical care should have an expiration date.

A power of attorney to consent to medical treatment may be unlimited, or it may authorize only certain medical decisions. It is even possible to execute more than one power of attorney to consent to medical treatment, as long as each document is limited and does not conflict with the others. This might happen when the person executes a general power of attorney to consent to routine medical care and a specific power of attorney to refuse or terminate life support.

In some situations, it is difficult to determine what authority the patient intended to delegate. The patient may have delegated the right to consent to more than one person. The power of attorney may be inconsistent, delegating the right to consent to only part of the necessary care or delegating the authority to consent to improper care. A physician confronted with an ambiguous delegation of the authority to consent to treatment or with improper delegations should ask a court for clarification.

GUARDIANSHIPS

All states provide legal mechanisms to manage the affairs of persons who have become incompetent through illness or injury. While the names of these proceedings vary, they have the common goal of determining whether the person is competent and appointing a surrogate if he or she is not. This surrogate is usually called the *guardian*, and the person who has been declared incompetent is usually called the *ward*. The guardian has a fiduciary duty to look out for the patient's best interests and may be required to have court approval for decisions that have a potential adverse impact on the ward.

The guardian becomes the legal alter ego of the ward. When a court appoints a guardian for an individual, the physician must then obtain all consent to medical care from the guardian. The guardian must be given the same information that the patient would have been given. The guardian is also under a duty to ask questions and determine if the treatment is in the patient's best interests. The physician is no longer obliged to obtain consent from the patient. If the patient is conscious, the physician does have a duty to explain what will be done and to preserve the patient's dignity as much as possible.

Establishing the Authority of a Guardian

The most critical element in surrogate consent is establishing the legal standing of the surrogate. Physicians are frequently confronted with friends or relatives of an incompetent patient who claim to be the patient's guardian. It is imperative that these persons be asked to provide a copy of the legal order that establishes their status as guardian. A copy of this order should be made a part of the patient's chart and should be referred to in every consent form.

In most cases, guardianship proceedings are uncontested. The proceedings are instituted by a family member, social worker, health care provider, or other concerned person for the protection of the incompetent person. The incompetent's friends and relatives, if any, may testify that the appointment of the guardian is in the patient's best interests. In uncontested guardianships, consent for medical care should be documented in the same way as a consent from a competent patient. The same type of chart note and consent form should be used, with the additional language about the consent being obtained from the guardian.

Some guardianships are contested. The most common contest involves the appointment of a guardian to consent to medical care for a child whose parents do not want the child treated. The duty to inform the guardian is the same in these cases, but the necessary documentation is more extensive. In addition to incorporating the guardianship papers in the patient's medical record, an attorney should review these papers to ensure that they are in order. This review is to determine if there are any limitations on the guardian's authority. Since these cases usually involve hospitalization, the physician should also discuss the guardianship with the hospital's attorney.

Once a guardian has been appointed for a given purpose, the court does not second-guess the guardian's decisions. It does attempt to ensure that the guardian is acting properly, and persons may ask the court to remove the guardian if they believe that he or she is acting improperly. If a physician is treating a patient who has a guardian, the physician does not need to ask the court to approve each of the guardian's decisions. The physician should be prepared to explain how he or she and the guardian arrived at those decisions. The detail necessary for this explanation depends on whether anyone is contesting the guardianship.

Emergency Guardianships

In two situations it is necessary to obtain an emergency guardianship: (1) when a parent refuses to authorize necessary care for a minor child and (2) when an adult refuses care in a situation in which the health care provider believes the refusal should not be honored. In both situations, the care at issue must be necessary to save life or limb or to prevent serious permanent injury. If the care is for a minor condition or has little hope of benefiting the patient, the patient's or parent's wishes should be heeded while applying for a guardianship on a nonemergency basis.

In an emergency guardianship, the judge appoints a temporary guardian for the patient. The appointment may be made over the telephone if the hospital has previously arranged a protocol with the appropriate judges. This protocol must address the care that is needed, the consequences of delaying the care while a hearing is scheduled, and an explanation of why the patient or parent will not consent to the care. Ideally, the patient will be examined by an independent physician who can certify that the care is needed to preserve the patient's life or limb. The judge will often speak to the parents or the patient, if possible.

If the judge determines that an emergency guardianship is warranted, a temporary guardian will be appointed. The judge will usually limit the scope of the guardian's authority to consenting to care that is needed to prevent permanent harm or death. This guardian may be a hospital administrator, but it is preferable to appoint a person who is independent of the hospital and health care providers. The temporary guardian serves until the court can have a hearing with all the concerned parties. The hearing will be held as soon as the parties can be notified and a courtroom scheduled, sometimes within 24 hours.

Minors

When a parent refuses necessary medical care for a child, it is usually for religious reasons. Parents may refuse all care or just specific treatments, such as blood transfusions. They may belong to an organized religious group such as the Christian Scientists or have personal beliefs that may be shared with only a few other people. The strength and importance of their religious beliefs can sometimes be determined by how the child was brought to the health care provider. If the parents brought the child to the physician or emergency room, they should be assumed to want help. However, if the child is brought in by neighbors or the police, the physician should expect no cooperation from the parents.

The child should be evaluated at once to determine if immediate care is needed. If it is, a judge should be contacted to arrange a temporary guardianship. The child welfare department should also be notified because denying a child necessary medical care is neglect in most states. Since many states allow children who are abused or neglected to be treated with parental consent, the child welfare agency may be able to authorize treatment for the child without a court order. Although the court may decide to accede to the parents' religious beliefs, the physician's duty is to advocate for the child until the court rules that the child need not be treated.

Adults

An adult who refuses emergency medical care poses a difficult problem. Society does not give parents the right to kill a child through neglect, but it does allow an adult to commit suicide by refusing life-saving medical care. The only conditions are that the adult must demonstrate that he or she is mentally sound and that the care is being refused for a proper reason, such as a religious objection to care or the presence of a terminal illness. (See Chapter 13.) These two conditions often merge. If the court finds the reason for refusing care frivolous, this will be taken as evidence of an unsound mind.

As with a child, the patient should be evaluated to determine the needed care and the consequences of not providing that care. A judge should be contacted at once. If the patient remains conscious, the grounds for the refusal of care should be explored and carefully documented. A full medical status examination should be documented in the chart. A psychiatric consult can document the patient's fitness to make reasoned decisions. The attending physician should prepare a care plan that attempts to intrude as little as possible on the patient's beliefs, while still preventing permanent harm. Such a specific, limited-care plan will encourage the judge to allow the patient to be treated until the case can be reviewed in a formal hearing.

The Interim until the Judge Rules

Even an emergency guardianship takes time. The purpose of an emergency guardianship would be defeated if the patient were to die or be permanently injured before the guardianship could be obtained. This would be especially tragic for a child, because the courts almost always appoint a guardian to consent to necessary care for children. If the child will suffer by a delay in care, then the child should be treated while the guardianship is being arranged. This is a technical violation of the parents' right to consent to the child's medical care, but it is unlikely that a jury would punish a physician for trying to help the child. Conversely, if the child is allowed to die or become permanently injured, the physician's behavior will be hard to explain to a jury.

Competent adults who refuse care because of religious beliefs pose a more difficult problem. If the physician chooses to treat the patient without consent, the treatment should not be limited in any way that will reduce its effectiveness. Legally, the most damaging outcome is ultimately to save the patient but only after he or she is permanently disabled.

CONSENT FOR MINORS

Until the late 1800s, parents had almost unlimited power over their children. Physical abuse of children was tolerated, and neglect, even to the point of death, was common. Children were treated as the property of the father. This presumption of complete power over the child was challenged under the laws designed to prevent cruelty to animals. Specific child protective laws followed, and now all states attempt to protect children from abuse and neglect. These laws, combined with public health laws and the U.S. Supreme Court decisions on reproductive rights, have greatly limited parental rights to deny children needed medical care.

In general, persons under 18 years old do not have the right to consent to their own medical care. Unless the parents' legal rights have been terminated, the parents of a minor have the sole authority to consent to medical care for the minor. In most states, if the parents are married to each other, they have an equal right to consent to medical care for the children of that marriage. If the parents are divorced or were never married, the parent with legal custody of the child may have the sole right to consent to care for the child. This does not give the physician the legal right to force care on a mature minor, nor may the physician render medically questionable care, such as a sterilization, at the parents' request.

Proxy Consent for Minors
Since there is no legal right to provide nonemergency care without parental consent, the child is usually denied care if the parent is not available. A typical case involves a child who is injured while visiting with friends in another community. Less commonly recognized is the problem of children who are visiting with a noncustodial parent in a state that does not give that parent the right to consent to medical care for the children.

Parents or guardians may delegate the right to consent to medical care for a child to another competent adult. Physicians should encourage patients to identify persons who may consent to their child's care if they are not available. As with all other delegations of authority to consent to medical care, these persons must be competent adults. If the child's medical record contains an authorization for proxy consent, the physician will be able to treat the child even if a parent is not available. Most parents have signed a proxy consent form for school or summer camp. Few parents think about signing a proxy consent when the child visits with an out-of-town relative.

The basic form for proxy consent for a child identifies the child, the person delegating the right to consent, the legal relationship of the person to the child, the care for which the delegation is made, and the duration of the delegation. It is also important to include specific medical information if the child has special medical needs. The extent to which the right to consent is delegated should depend upon the expected delay in notifying the person with the legal right to consent. The form to allow the teacher at a day school to take a child to the emergency room would be much more limited than the form for a teenager going on a six-week wilderness trip in Alaska.

Special Circumstances
When a child's parents are divorced or legally separated, the physician can no longer assume that both parents have the right to consent to care for the child. The right to consent depends on the state law and the court's orders in the specific case. The parent with legal custody usually has the authority to consent to care for the child; however, the physician seldom knows which parent has legal custody. This is especially problematic in states that allow joint custody.

The child's legal status should be recorded in the medical record. The physician should tell the parents of minor patients to notify him or her of divorces and marriages, as well as address changes. If the physician knows that a couple is separating, he or she should ask who has the right to consent to the child's care. In states that do not allow the noncustodial parent to consent to care, the physician should discuss proxy consent with the custodial parent. A physician should not deny a child needed medical care because of uncertainty about the child's legal status. Conversely, the physician should not knowingly continue to treat a child with a questionable status without attempting to determine who has the legal right to consent to the care.

Many states give certain adult relatives of a child the right to consent to medical care for the child. The parents should be encouraged to use a proxy consent form to clarify their wishes and to broaden the emergency care authority granted in state statutes.

If the child stays or travels with friends and neighbors, the parent or guardian should execute a proxy consent allowing these persons to consent to care for the child. If the parents are not comfortable with giving this proxy, they should reconsider whether they should leave the child with this person.

The extent of proxy consent for institutions depends on the proximity and availability of the parents and the medical resources of the school. If the institution has a physician available or if the parent will not be readily available, the proxy consent should be more encompassing. The maximum delegation involves institutions that stand in loco parentis ("in the place of the parent"). These institutions should ask the parent to delegate full rights to consent to the institution. The neighborhood public school needs little right to consent to care for a child. The boarding school that caters to diplomats' families needs full rights to consent.

Guardians

Many children are not in the custody of either biological parent. They may be in foster care, under the care of a relative, with a potential adoptive parent, or in other situations in which their caregiver is not a biological parent. If the child has a legally appointed guardian, the guardian must consent to the child's care in the same fashion as for an adult ward.

In some of these cases, no one has asked the court to appoint a guardian for the child. These children are in legal limbo; no one may consent to their care, but it is unthinkable to deny them necessary care because of their legal status. A child in need of immediate care should be treated as necessary while the hospital seeks to have the caregiver appointed as temporary guardian for the child. If the child is in need of simple elective care, that care should be postponed until a guardian is appointed. The physician should always notify child protective services when a child needs a legal guardian.

Conflict between Parents

Children can be pawns in marital battles. This becomes an issue in medical care if the child is being abused or if the parents disagree on medical treatment for a child. As discussed in Chapter 20, suspected child abuse must always be reported to child protective services. If the disagreement over medical care threatens to escalate into neglect or physical harm, this must also be reported to child protective services.

The most difficult cases are those involving disputes over elective care. Legally, consent from one parent is sufficient. When the child is too young to have an independent opinion, the physician may choose to treat the child based on the consent of one parent. If the physician has been refused consent by one parent, it is less clear that the physician may then seek consent from the other parent. Children who are mature enough to have an independent opinion should also be consulted. If the child and one parent agree on a medically reasonable course, the physician should follow that course. Conversely, since physicians should not force unwanted care on a mature minor in general, they should be especially reticent to do so if a parent agrees with the minor.

Conflicts between Parents and Children
The parents of a 17 year old may legally retain the right to determine the minor's medical care; however, the courts have been reluctant to allow parents to deny mature minors elective care. While a physician should find out the legal requirements in his state, in general physicians may provide birth control information and counseling, treatment for substance abuse, and treatment for communicable diseases to mature minors. In some states, minors may be entitled to consent to such care without their parents' being informed.

The more difficult cases involve attempts by parents to force care on mature minors. The most common scenario involves involuntary psychiatric care for an allegedly drug-abusing or crazy teenager. There is sometimes a fine line between self-destructive behavior and normal adolescent rebellion. Physicians have an ethical obligation not to allow psychiatric care to be used to manipulate or punish a recalcitrant child. Legally, the child could sue for malpractice the physician who recommends unnecessary psychiatric care.

Documentation
Documenting consent to medical care for minors is a special case of the general problem of documenting proxy consent: the person who may consent to the care is not the person receiving the care. The physician must first document the relationship between the person giving consent and the patient and then document the risks and alternative treatments that the consenting person was informed of. If the patient is a mature minor, the physician should also discuss the treatment with the minor and document this discussion.

If there are disputes between the parents about the treatment or about who has the authority to consent, these disputes should be documented. It is important to document the rationale for deciding to accept the consent for treatment. The medical necessity of the treatment should be stressed. All contacts with child protective services should be documented. If the child is hospitalized, this information should be copied into the hospital medical record. Physicians who render necessary care to children are seldom sued for failure of consent. Proper documentation is important to reduce the chance that the physician will be sued as an ancillary party in child custody battles.

Statutory Right to Treat Minors
All states have laws that allow children to be treated without the parents' or guardian's consent in certain circumstances. These laws are designed to protect either the child or the public health of the community.

All states allow persons in need of emergency care to be treated without consent; nevertheless, many hospitals and physicians have been reticent to treat children without parental consent. To encourage the prompt treatment of sick and injured children, many states have passed laws that allow certain relatives of a child to consent to emergency medical care when the parents are unavailable. Since consent to treatment is not required in true emergencies, the primary purpose of these laws is to assuage physicians' fears of litigation.

Most states allow a physician to treat a child who is suspected of being the victim of abuse or neglect, without the consent of the parents. These laws also require that the physician notify the proper authorities so that the case may be investigated and the child protected if necessary.

Most states allow a child to be treated for communicable and venereal diseases without parental permission. This treatment benefits the child and also helps prevent the spread of disease in the community. This exception to the need for parental consent is usually limited to diseases that are reportable under the state's communicable and venereal disease reporting laws. These diseases must be reported and the child welfare agency notified in certain cases where the disease (such as venereal disease in a young child) raises the suspicion of abuse.

Many states allow minors to seek treatment for alcohol and drug abuse without parental permission. These laws may or may not require child welfare agencies to be notified. Because of the prolonged nature of these treatments and the possibility of hospitalization, it is usually impossible to carry out the treatment without involving the parents. (Very few hospitals accept a minor without parental permission and a guarantee of payment.) These laws are most valuable when dealing with runaways and abandoned minors.

Pregnancy and childbirth pose the most legally difficult conflicts between the rights of parents and those of their children. State laws differ greatly and are frequently modified by U.S. Supreme Court decisions. The courts are attempting to balance the rights of the minor to determine her own medical care, the rights of a parent to control the medical care that a child receives, and the rights of the fetus. In general, the laws allow and encourage pregnant minors to seek prenatal care. There is also a more limited right to birth control information and devices. The most limited right is abortion, which is discussed in Chapter 25.

Emancipated Minors

Most states have a legal proceeding that allows a person under the age of majority to petition the court for full rights as an adult. This grant of adult rights is based on the maturity of the minor and the minor's need for adult status. This need is based on the minor's living alone or other factors that make it inappropriate for the minor's parents to retain control over the minor. Marriage usually qualifies the minor to consent to medical care, as does service in the armed forces.

BIBLIOGRAPHY

Minors

Abel GG; Becker JV; Cunningham-Rathner J: Complications, consent, and cognitions in sex between children and adults. Int J Law Psychiatry 1984; 7(1):89–103.

Chabon RS: The physician and parental consent. J Leg Med 1977 Jun; 5(6):33–37.

Dickey SB: Informed consent and health decisions of adolescents—why the dilemma? Pa Nurse 1983 Oct; 38(10):4, 11.

Engum ES: Expanding the minor's right to consent to non-emergency health care. A psycho-legal rationale. J Leg Med (Chic) 1982 Dec; 3(4):557–615.

Erickson S; Hopkins MA: Gray areas: Informed consent in pediatric and comatose adult patients. Heart Lung 1987 May; 16(3):323–25.

Holder AR: Disclosure and consent problems in pediatrics. Law Med Health Care 1988 Fall–Winter; 16(3-4):219–28.

Klein A: Physical restraint, informed consent and the child patient. ASDC J Dent Child 1988 Mar–Apr; 55(2):121–22.

Kourany RF; Hill RY; Hollender MH: The age of sexual consent. Bull Am Acad Psychiatry Law 1986; 14(2):171–76.

Lesko LM; Dermatis H; Penman D; Holland JC: Patients', parents', and oncologists' perceptions of informed consent for bone marrow transplantation. Med Pediatr Oncol 1989; 17(3):181–87.

Nilson DR; Steinfels MO: Parental consent and a teenage sex survey. Hastings Cent Rep 1977 Jun; 7(3):13–15.

Perr IN: Confidentiality and consent in psychiatric treatment of minors. J Leg Med 1976 Jun; 4(6):9–13.

Restaino JM Jr: Informed consent: Should it be extended to 12-year-olds? A surgeon's view. Med Law 1987; 6(2):91–98.

Silva MC: Assessing competency for informed consent with mentally retarded minors. Pediatr Nurs 1984 Jul–Aug; 10(4):261–65, 306.

Walker CL: Informed consent with children. J Assoc Pediatr Oncol Nurses 1988; 5(1–2):38–40.

Mentally Incompetent Patients

Beck JC; Staffin RD: Patients' competency to give informed consent to medication. Hosp Community Psychiatry 1986 Apr; 37(4):400–2.

Drane JF: Competency to give an informed consent. A model for making clinical assessments. JAMA 1984 Aug 17; 252(7):925–27.

Dyer AR; Bloch S: Informed consent and the psychiatric patient. J Med Ethics 1987 Mar; 13(1):12–16.

Hes JP; Hecht P; Levy A: Some psychological and legal considerations in the determination of incompetence in the elderly. Med Law 1988; 7(2):151–59.

Hipshman L: Defining a clinically useful model for assessing competence to consent to treatment. Bull Am Acad Psychiatry Law 1987; 15(3):235–45.

Irwin M; Lovitz A; Marder SR; Mintz J; Winslade WJ; Van Putten T; Mills MJ: Psychotic patients' understanding of informed consent. Am J Psychiatry 1985 Nov; 142(11): 1351–54.

Kemna DJ: Current status of institutionalized mental health patients' right to refuse psychotropic drugs. J Leg Med (Chic) 1985 Mar; 6(1):107–38.

Mann L; Whall A: Informed consent and the deinstitutionalized patient. J Psychosoc Nurs Ment Health Serv 1984 Jan; 22(1):22–27.

Munetz MR; Lidz CW; Meisel A: Informed consent and incompetent medical patients. J Fam Pract 1985 Mar; 20(3):273–79.

Ratzan RM: Informed consent from the mentally incompetent elderly. Postgrad Med 1986 Oct; 80(5):81–88.

Sadoff RL: Competence and informed consent. New Dir Ment Health Serv 1985 Mar; 25:25–34.

Schwartz HI; Blank K: Shifting competency during hospitalization: A model for informed consent decisions. Hosp Community Psychiatry 1986 Dec; 37(12):1256–60.

Tancredi L: Competency for informed consent: Conceptual limits of empirical data. Int J Law Psychiatry 1982; 5(1):51–63.

Power of Attorney

Bernstein BE: Legal needs of the ill: The social worker's role on an interdisciplinary team. Health Soc Work 1980 Aug; 5(3):68–72.

Doudera AE: Developing issues in medical decision making: The durable power of attorney and institutional ethics committees. Prim Care 1986 Jun; 13(2):315–26.

Gillon R: Living wills, powers of attorney and medical practice (editorial). J Med Ethics 1988 Jun; 14(2):59–60.

Hoffman DE: Planning for medical decision making: Living wills and durable powers of attorney. Md Med J 1989 Feb; 38(2):154–58.

Kapp MB: Advance health care planning: Taking a "medical future." South Med J 1988 Feb; 81(2):221–24.

Peters DA: Advance medical directives: The case for the durable power of attorney for health care. J Leg Med (Chic) 1987 Sep; 8(3):437–64.

Solnick PB: Proxy consent for incompetent non-terminally ill adult patients. J Leg Med (Chic) 1985 Mar; 6(1):1–49.

Warren JW; Sobal J; Tenney JH; Hoopes JM; Damron D; Levenson S; DeForge BR; Muncie HL Jr: Informed consent by proxy: An issue in research with elderly patients. N Engl J Med 1986 Oct 30; 315(18):1124–28.

Wencel S: Wisconsin's durable power of attorney. Wis Med J 1989 Mar; 88 (3):25–26, 28.

13

Substituted Consent and Terminal Illness

CRITICAL POINTS
- Patients have a right to refuse emergency medical care and to request that life-supporting care be stopped.
- Physicians may follow appropriate refusals of care without seeking a court order.
- Physicians have an ethical duty to seek judicial intervention when patients unreasonably refuse care for themselves or their children.
- Substituted consent will undermine the physician-patient relationship if accepted as a general legal principle.

This chapter discusses the problem of substituted consent and decisions to terminate life support. (*Substituted consent* is defined as consent by a person who is neither a guardian appointed by the court nor a surrogate appointed by the patient.) Patients' right to die preoccupies bioethicists. We believe this is a misplaced concern; with the exception of a small number of well-publicized cases such as that of Nancy Cruzan, current reimbursement policies shift the concern from right to die to right to live. The greatest threat is the conflict between substituted consent for incompetent, terminally ill patients and substituted consent for competent patients seeking controversial care, such as abortion and reproductive medicine. Our analysis of recent U.S. Supreme Court decisions leads to the conclusion that if the Court is persuaded to accept substituted consent for terminally ill patients, it also will allow substituted consent in other contexts, such as giving husbands a right to be consulted about their wives' reproductive care.

FRAMING THE ETHICAL DEBATE

The ethical questions arising out of termination of life support for incompetent adults may be categorized by the interests of the various stakeholders: patients, physicians, hospitals, families, and society. These stakeholders have both conflicting and complementary interests. The shifting of these interests through time has shaped the history of thinking about termination of life-support decisions.

Parts of this chapter originally appeared in *Journal of Intensive Care Medicine*.

Balancing these interests requires finding an ethical course of action within the constraints imposed by the legal system (Carton 1990).

Patients' Interests

The interests of patients have changed dramatically through time. In the medieval period, the church proscribed medical treatment by Christians. Religious orders were involved with caring for the sick, but this was palliative care intended only to smooth the transition into heaven. Life was seen as a veil of tears to be passed through, not an end in itself. Modern notions of prolonging life would have been considered blasphemous. (As is usually the case, these prohibitions fell mostly on the poor. Wealthy individuals and the nobility often had Jewish or Muslim court physicians.)

During the period between the development of modern medicine and the advent of life support technologies, patients' interests shifted to curative, rather than merely palliative, care. After World War II, the U.S. government began to subsidize and otherwise encourage the construction of hospitals and the training of physicians. Technology became more important in medical practice, and private medical insurance companies proliferated as employers saw medical insurance as an attractive and inexpensive employee benefit. This trend continued through the 1950s, with technology-based medicine becoming the norm in the 1960s.

Two events in the 1960s had direct bearing on the problem of artificial prolongation of life. The first was the maturation of technology and its integration into routine practice. Ventilators, cardiac monitors, and other life-support devices were improved and became widely available. Physicians became comfortable with these devices and learned how to optimize their effectiveness through better infection control and nursing practices.

The second event was the introduction of Medicare and Medicaid. Medicare was particularly important because it removed many of the cost constraints on the care of elderly patients, the class of patient most likely to need life support. This ushered in the era of patient demands for all possible medical technology.

The growth of technological medicine was accompanied by a developing concern for patient autonomy. The strongest force shaping demands for autonomy was the Nuremberg trials of the Nazi war criminals, which documented the medical experiments performed by physicians. Although directed at medical experimentation, the resulting Nuremberg Doctrine set out the rights of patients to determine freely the course of their medical care. Patients' concerns with the right to choose their own care began to include a concern for the right to refuse care as the risk of being reduced to a persistent vegetative state became better publicized (Cranford 1988; Brody 1988; Wikler 1988).

Physicians' Interests

From early Greece, physicians have been committed to curative treatment whenever possible. Physicians have always used whatever technology was available, sometimes without regard to its effects on patients. The Hippocratic Oath's proscription of cutting for stone was based on the operation's uniform failure rate, not an aversion to technology. Physicians embraced life-support technologies as they became available. While originally intended to support metabolism while the patient recovered from a specific pathology, patient demands and insurance incentives soon made life support an end as well as a means.

While physicians have financial interests in life-support decisions, they are not as great as those of hospitals. The physicians' stakes are much more emotional than financial. Physicians are torn between the urge to help specific identified patients avoid unnecessary suffering and a traditional reluctance to talk to patients about death and dying. Irrespective of their personal feelings, they are under pressure from hospitals, managed care providers, and the federal government to save money by denying and terminating life support. This pressure is directed at all patients, not just those who are clearly terminally ill.

Hospitals

The growth of intensive care medicine has paralleled the increase in hospital autonomy. Hospitals have evolved from "physicians' workshops" to independent agents in health care delivery. It is hospitals, rather than physicians, that bear the financial impact of termination of life-support decisions. Most legal challenges to termination of life-support decisions have been brought by hospitals rather than physicians.

The most controversial issue in critical care medicine is the extent to which financial concerns have driven hospital attitudes on termination of life-support decisions. Until the prospective payment system was put in place, termination of life support also meant the termination of a substantial income stream from the patient's insurer. While it would be unfair to see reimbursement considerations as controlling, it is clear that they have had an impact on ethical decision making. It is likely that the technological imperative was greatly strengthened by its profitability (Powerly 1989). The troubling question now is the extent to which prospective payment systems lead to the denial of necessary medical care (Dougherty 1989).

Families

Families often have deeply ambiguous feelings about termination of life support. In general, families want their loved ones given all the benefits of medical technology, including advanced life support. The family's interests become compelling when a patient with dependent children refuses life-saving treatment. At the same time, families are the main witnesses to the suffering and degradation that accompany the long-term life support of an incompetent patient. This creates a humanitarian urge to terminate life support, which is often complicated by unresolved feelings of guilt over family issues unrelated to life support. For example, a family may want to use every possible avenue to prolong the grandmother's life because they feel guilty for putting her in a nursing home.

In the worst cases, family interests are shaped by potential inheritances. Since many wills contain clauses that shift the distribution of the estate depending on the time of death, there can be substantial financial interests in either artificially prolonging or shortening life. A major function of probate courts is to resolve family members' conflicts over estates. It would be unrealistic to assume that these conflicts had no influence on family decisions on termination of life support.

Society's Interests

Until recently, American society was uncritically committed to prolonging the life of all citizens. Insurance payments influenced physicians through direct financial incentives and through the indirect incentive of societal approbation. Insurance companies, as powerful representatives of society, clearly approved of the prolongation of life with advanced life-support technologies. This ratified the life-at-any-cost mentality that physicians were adopting in the 1960s and 1970s.

In conflict with this interest is the problem of resource allocation. Resources expended on supporting the life of a patient are not available for other objectives, such as education or preventive medical care (Murphy and Matchar 1990). The enactment of the Medicare prospective payment system is one manifestation of this concern. Implicit in the prospective payment system is a repudiation of the life-at-all-cost signal sent by the previous cost-based reimbursement system (Veatch 1988).

Societal interests have become more complicated as antiabortion forces have sought legislation that demands that the state favor life under all circumstances. While intended to limit abortions, such statutory presumptions can also be read as limiting termination of life-support decisions. This is at issue in the *Cruzan* decision by the Missouri Supreme Court. The court held that its refusal of an order to terminate life support for an incompetent person was mandated by a prolife statutory provision in the state's antiabortion law.

THE CRUZAN CASE

On June 15, 1990, the U.S. Supreme Court rendered its long-awaited decision in the Cruzan "right-to-die" case. The actual law established by this case is very narrow and is only tangentially related to the termination of life support. This decision has discomfited many physicians because it does not establish an easy-to-administer, national standard for the termination of life support. *Cruzan* is an important decision because it clarifies several issues surrounding the termination of care for incompetent patients. While it does not resolve the dilemmas posed by incompetent patients who have not properly formalized their wishes concerning continued care, *Cruzan* may prove to be a wise compromise for a difficult problem.

The specific facts of the *Cruzan* case are compelling: a young woman, brain injured in an automobile accident, was trapped in a persistent vegetative state for years. Brain atrophy made recovery or rehabilitation hopeless, and her family requested that her life support be terminated, but the state refused.

Cruzan is a hard case, and hard cases make bad law because they tempt judges and juries to help the injured party rather than follow the law. Physicians are not strangers to hard cases. Every birth injury case tempts juries to help the baby by disregarding the legal standard for proof of malpractice. The facts in *Cruzan* call out to the court to ignore the traditional rule of patient autonomy and allow the family to terminate a patient's life support. This would be a good result in *Cruzan*, but would it best serve the needs of future patients and their health care providers?

The Missouri Supreme Court Ruling

The *Cruzan* case began in a Missouri public hospital. Nancy Cruzan was in a persistent vegetative state secondary to anoxia suffered during an automobile accident in 1983. She maintained sufficient brain function to breathe on her own and to respond to painful stimuli. She was fed through a gastrostomy tube but was not otherwise medicated or instrumented. Her parents, who had been appointed her legal guardians, sought to have her nutrition and hydration terminated. The state hospital opposed this request. A case was initiated in state trial court, and a guardian ad litem was appointed to protect the patient's interests.

The trial court sought to determine Nancy Cruzan's wishes. Since she had neither executed a living will nor used a durable power of attorney to appoint a surrogate to make decisions in her stead, there was no formal record of her intent. The trial court did find that she had once discussed termination of life support with a roommate, indicating in a general way that she did not want to live in a vegetative state. The trial court accepted this conversation as sufficient evidence of Nancy Cruzan's wish not to be maintained in a persistent vegetative state and authorized the termination of her feedings.

The Missouri Supreme Court accepted the guardian ad litem's appeal of the trial court's decision. The Missouri Supreme Court reversed the trial court's authorization to terminate Nancy Cruzan's nutrition and hydration. This opinion addressed two central points: were Nancy Cruzan's wishes knowable, and, if not, did her parents have the authority to terminate her life support as an independent decision?

The court found that Missouri law did not give Nancy Cruzan's parents, as guardians, the right to authorize the termination of her nutrition and hydration. The court did not find that such authority would be constitutionally impermissible, only that it was not explicitly provided in the state's guardianship statute. Having determined that Cruzan's parents did not have the authority to discontinue her life support, the Missouri Supreme Court sought to determine whether Nancy's own wishes were knowable.

The Missouri Supreme Court started with the premise that the traditional concept of informed consent applied to decisions to refuse care, as well as decisions to accept care. Under this standard, there would have to be evidence that Nancy Cruzan did not want to be maintained in a vegetative state and appreciated the significance of terminating her nutrition and hydration. The court also required that the patient's intentions be proved by "clear and convincing evidence." This is a standard that is stricter than the preponderance-of-the-evidence rule (51 percent) used in most civil cases but less strict than the beyond-a-reasonable-doubt rule required to prove guilt in criminal cases.

The clear-and-convincing-evidence standard is used in civil cases when an individual's liberty, rather than just money, is at issue. These situations include involuntary commitment for mental illness, deportation hearings, and proceedings to terminate parental rights (*Addington v. Texas*, 1979). Courts choose the clear-and-convincing-evidence rather the preponderance-of-the-evidence standard as "a societal judgment about how the risk of error should be distributed between the litigants" (*Santosky v. Kramer*, 1982). The *Cruzan* court chose this standard because of the gravity of a decision to terminate life support.

Using this heightened standard of proof, the court then reviewed the evidence presented to the trial court. The court did not find that the testimony in the trial court's record provided clear and convincing proof of Nancy Cruzan's intentions. In particular, the court found that the reported conversations were only general reactions to other persons' medical care and not an informed statement of her intention to refuse life support if she were in a persistent vegetative state.

The disqualification of Nancy Cruzan's parents and the rejection of the evidence of her own desires forced the court to look for other sources of direction for determining whether it should authorize the termination of life support. The court's decision to reverse the trial court's order to terminate Nancy Cruzan's life support was compelled by a Missouri statute passed as part of the state's anti-abortion laws: "At the beginning of life, Missouri adopts a strong predisposition in favor of preserving life. Section 188.010, RSMo 1986, announces the 'intention of the General Assembly of Missouri to grant the right to life to all humans, born and unborn. . . . ' " (*Cruzan v. Harmon*, 1988 p. 419). While the legislators who passed this law had intended it to apply to abortions only, the court was compelled by its plain language to apply it to all human beings, including Nancy Cruzan. This decision was appealed to the U.S. Supreme Court.

The U.S. Supreme Court's Ruling

Chief Justice William Rehnquist wrote the majority opinion that establishes the legal rule of the *Cruzan* case. Four additional justices joined in this opinion, and four justices dissented. With the exception of Justice Antonin Scalia, all of the justices were willing to agree, for the purpose of this case, that a competent person has a right to refuse life-saving medical treatment. (When judges assume something for the purpose of a case, it means that what they are assuming is not critical to their decision and may be reevaluated in other cases.) Justice Scalia refused to accept this assumption because he believed that this would undermine the state's authority to forbid suicide.

Both the majority and dissenting opinions accepted that the patient's intentions should be controlling if they are known. The majority found it proper for Missouri to require these intentions to be proved in a clear and convincing manner, preferably through a living will or durable power of attorney. The dissent found the requirement of such formality to be unconstitutionally burdensome, arguing that the court hearing a termination of life-support case should be bound by the testimony of the patient's family and friends. While accepting such informal evidence would seem to ease the resolution of these cases, it rejects the general rule disallowing oral testimony entirely:

> It is also worth noting that most, if not all, States simply forbid oral testimony entirely in determining the wishes of parties in transactions which, while important, simply do not have the consequences that a decision to terminate a person's life does. At common law and by statute in most States, the parole evidence rule prevents the variations of the terms of a written contract by oral testimony. The statute of frauds makes unenforceable oral contracts to leave property by will, and statutes regulating the making of wills universally require that those instruments be in writing. (*Cruzan v. Director, Missouri Dept. of Health*, 1990 p. 2854)

The states prohibit oral testimony about wills because the person whose intentions are being sought is dead and thus unavailable to contest the testimony. This rule evolved as the courts found determining the wishes of dead people to be an invitation to fraud and family conflict. Given that a patient in a persistent vegetative state, is, for the purpose of contesting testimony, equivalent to a dead person, the majority did not find it unconstitutionally burdensome to require these same protections for termination of life-support decisions.

There is a contentious debate between the majority and dissenting opinions over the use of the clear-and-convincing standard for proving a patient's wishes. This debate is less important for its own merits than as a surrogate for the fundamental disagreement between the majority and dissenting opinions in *Cruzan*: Is Nancy Cruzan really dead? Justice Rehnquist's majority opinion and, more strongly, Justice Scalia's concurring opinion treat Nancy Cruzan as a living person with liberty interests that are entitled to constitutional protection. The dissenting justices, led by now-retired Justice Brennan, treat Nancy Cruzan as a dead person who has slipped through the cracks in the usual medical tests for death.

The majority opinion specifically rejected a constitutional right of family members to terminate care for patients whose wishes are not known. This ruling is consistent with the Court's previous cases protecting competent patients from requirements that husbands have a voice in determining their wives' medical care. The Court ruled that people of the states, through their legislative processes, are empowered to establish guidelines for medical decision making for incompetent patients who have not otherwise properly documented their wishes. (The effect of this ruling is to leave all existing state laws in place; *Cruzan* does not require any changes in established procedures to terminate life support.)

The Persistent Vegetative State
The dissenting justices would give families a constitutional right to substitute their decisions for those of incompetent patients who had not made their treatment preferences known. The dissent rejected a state right to require that patients formalize their intentions in living wills or durable powers of attorney as too burdensome. In contrast to the majority, the dissenting judges would exclude the state from participation in termination of treatment decisions, finding families better judges of the patient's best interests. Ironically, in a case decided the same day as *Cruzan*, these same dissenting justices decried even notifying the family of a minor seeking an abortion (*Ohio v. Akron*, 1990).

The apparent inconsistency of relying solely on the family for termination of life support but rejecting even limited family involvement in other medical decision making is resolved by a close reading of Justice Brennan's discussion of balancing the risks and benefits of medical treatment: "For many, the thought of an ignoble end, steeped in decay, is abhorrent. A quiet, proud death, bodily integrity intact, is a matter of extreme consequence.... A long, drawn-out death can have a debilitating effect on family members" (*Cruzan*, p. 2868). It is clear that Justice Brennan regards these patients as dying, or already dead, in the same way that brain-dead patients are legally dead although still physiologically functioning.

This assumption that Nancy Cruzan and other patients in her condition are effectively dead is a useful starting point for reconceptualizing the debate on substituted consent. It is the rare patient who survives in a persistent vegetative state while manifesting significant brain atrophy. Such patients should be dealt with by a modified definition of death. The courts and legislatures have been more willing to accept changing definitions of death than they have been to reduce the autonomy and protections of patients still considered alive (AMA(1) 1990). A definition of death that includes Nancy Cruzan is more practical and ethically defensible than a definition of life that abets the denial of care to potentially salvageable patients.

LIVING WITH CRUZAN

The *Cruzan* ruling is intrinsically limited because it is only permissive. It upholds Missouri's law that prohibits guardians from authorizing the termination of life support for their wards but does not prevent other states from allowing guardians such authority. It upholds Missouri's right to require a patient's intentions to be proved by clear and convincing evidence but does not prevent states from using less rigorous criteria to determine a patient's wishes. *Cruzan* does not change the law of any state; it merely allows the states latitude to change their own laws.

Justice Rehnquist, in a rare example of preventive law advice from the bench, stressed the importance of using living wills and durable powers of attorney. Since these were not at issue in the case, this advice is not law, but it is a useful prediction of the court's future direction.

Medical care providers in states such as Missouri should note that the majority opinion, and Justice Sandra Day O'Connor's concurring opinion, imply that the state may be bound to follow the requests of a patient-appointed surrogate. This would give a surrogate appointed by a patient's durable power of attorney more authority than a guardian appointed under restrictive state guardianship laws (Mishkin 1990).

It is critical to appreciate that the public debate over termination of life support is driven in part by a desire not to waste medical care on patients who will not benefit from it. The problem is determining just who these patients are. Nancy Cruzan clearly does not benefit (in the sense of improved prognosis) from her medical care. Yet there are thousands of close calls for everyone in a similar condition. Given the enormous pressure by medical insurers and the federal government on physicians' and patients' families to terminate medical care, relaxed rules for substituted consent may not be the best solution to the problems of those in the Cruzan's condition.

Formalizing the Patient's Wishes

Every person, and especially every patient, should consider some formal provision for decision making should he or she become incompetent. The implication of the *Cruzan* decision is that a durable power of attorney may be the strongest legal provision. There are other benefits to using a durable power of attorney rather than a living will (Orentlicher 1990). Physicians do not like to discuss living wills with patients because it makes the patient face the issue of death. Living wills are also troublesome because they must anticipate future circumstances. Conversely, a durable power of attorney may be discussed in terms of the patient's potential temporary incompetence during treatment. Durable powers of attorney are also flexible because they substitute a fully empowered decision maker who can carry out the patient's intentions in the face of changing circumstances.

The Duty to Counsel

The Patient Self-Determination Act of 1990 requires health care providers to counsel patients about the use of living wills, advance directives, and powers of attorney to consent to medical care (Cotton 1991). Each patient must be provided written information concerning:

(i) an individual's rights under State law (whether statutory or as recognized by the courts of the State) to make decisions concerning such medical care, including the right to accept or refuse medical or surgical treatment and the right to formulate advance directives (as defined in paragraph (3)), and

(ii) the written policies of the provider or organization respecting the implementation of such rights;

(B) to document in the individual's medical record whether or not the individual has executed an advance directive;
(C) not to condition the provision of care or otherwise discriminate against an individual based on whether or not the individual has executed an advance directive;
(D) to ensure compliance with requirements of State law (whether statutory or as recognized by the courts of the State) respecting advance directives at facilities of the provider or organization; and
(E) to provide (individually or with others) for education for staff and the community on issues concerning advance directives.
Subparagraph (C) shall not be construed as requiring the provision of care which conflicts with an advance directive.

The following information must be provided:

(A) in the case of a hospital, at the time of the individual's admission as an inpatient,
(B) in the case of a skilled nursing facility, at the time of the individual's admission as a resident,
(C) in the case of a home health agency, in advance of the individual coming under the care of the agency,
(D) in the case of a hospice program, at the time of initial receipt of hospice care by the individual from the program, and
(E) in the case of an eligible organization . . . [HMOs and certain other managed care providers] at the time of enrollment of the individual with the organization.
(3) In this subsection, the term "advance directive" means a written instruction, such as a living will or durable power of attorney for health care, recognized under State law (whether statutory or as recognized by the courts of the State) and relating to the provision of such care when the individual is incapacitated. (1395cc(f))

COMPLYING WITH A PATIENT'S REFUSAL OF CARE

The American legal system is based on achieving politically acceptable rules within the limits posed by the Constitution. The courts are loath to interfere in the medical care decisions of competent adults, a product of the high value placed on patient autonomy. It also reflects judicial economy. Unlike attorneys, judges prefer to minimize the number and types of disputes that must be judicially resolved. The courts will upset the decision of a competent patient only when other stakeholders present a compelling argument for overriding the patient's interests.

Once patients have indicated their desires in a living will or by a surrogate decision maker appointed by a power of attorney, physicians should heed these instructions. Unnecessarily delaying the termination of life support, or forcing unwanted life support while contesting the patient's decisions in court is legally risky. On its face, this assertion seems too simplistic. It appears to ignore the raging debate among ethicists over the proper role of physicians in termination of life-support decisions. On closer analysis, however, it is clear that following the patient's wishes is both ethically correct and legally safe.

The Role of Courts
Until recently, decisions about the withdrawal or withholding of death-delaying treatment were debated by ethicists and civil libertarians but were not a fundamental problem for practicing physicians. Decisions were made, the courts were seldom involved, and there were few malpractice lawsuits or criminal prosecutions. While it is tempting to assume that this benign neglect of the law can continue without risk, it is a badly premised assumption. The historical societal premise in critical care medicine was that health care providers would do everything possible for the patient.

With the advent of diagnosis-related groups (DRGs) and other forms of prospective payment, the general public is beginning to be concerned that health care providers are doing less for patients for whom it is financially rewarding to do less. This erosion of public confidence, combined with the real pressure on physicians to do less for DRG patients, makes it imperative that decisions that will lead to premature death be carried out in a legally impeccable manner. Ultimately, adhering to legal principle is the best defense against administrative pressures to compromise patient care for the sake of optimal reimbursement.

Following the Patient's Wishes
If a competent patient refuses care, either directly or through a living will or surrogate, the physician is bound to respect those wishes. This does not apply to euthanasia or living wills that violate state law. Until recently, however, physicians have been able to treat critical care patients against their will because the courts were reluctant to punish a physician for delaying a patient's death. As the courts become more sophisticated about these cases, they are less willing to tolerate these intrusions on patient autonomy. One court has already assessed damages against a hospital that refused to terminate life support for a patient who was brain dead (*McVey v. Englewood Hospital Association,* 1987). Courts are also likely to assess attorney's fees and damages against physicians who ignore clearly effective living wills in order to avoid terminating life support.

Physicians should expect to see patients who reject living wills and demand life support. Patients do not have the right to unnecessary medical care, including intensive care unit care that cannot affect the outcome of their condition. If the patient demands all available care, the physician must be careful to document the therapeutic rationale behind decisions to deny or terminate life support for these patients. In all cases, it is easier not to start a therapy than to terminate it. This is a very slippery slope, however, as hospitals and third-party payers increase the pressure on physicians and families to refuse or terminate life support.

At least one hospital openly challenged the right of patients and their families to demand the application and continuation of life support. This hospital sought a court order to terminate life support for a patient whose clearly expressed wishes, and those of her husband, were to continue the life support. The court refused the order, finding no compelling reason to overrule the patient's decision. Most hospitals apply less open but nonetheless real pressure on families and physicians. Physicians should be careful that it is medical considerations and not financial pressures that underlie the decision to refuse life support to patients. Many physicians correctly worry about the denial of resources to other patients with a better prognosis. This does not make physicians who are determining the care for individual patients the proper agents to refuse care to benefit society. While managed care plans stress cost-effective care, this is under the constraint that the patient must receive the same quality care. Only the government can change the legal standard and allow classes of patients to be denied care to benefit society as a whole.

Judicial Intervention

There are two important caveats to nonjudicially supervised termination of life-support decisions. The first, and more critical, is that the patient must be a competent adult at the time the decision is made. The second is that the patient must clearly state his or her intentions, and these must be properly documented. Unless required by state law, this documentation need not be a witnessed living will. It can be a properly recorded conversation with the physician or the written request by a patient-appointed surrogate. The termination of life-support for minors, long-term medically incompetent patients, and patients who have not made their wishes known while competent are more complex and generally require the intervention of a judicially appointed guardian.

The most compelling cases for judicial intervention are those in which a patient who refuses curative therapy has dependent family members. These are almost exclusively persons with religious objections to some or all medical care. This may be because refusing curative treatment without a religious rationale results in the patient's being treated as an incompetent. While courts have ordered treatment in some cases, the most recent case law, in the decision of *Fosmire v. Nicoleau* (1990), affirmed the right of a pregnant woman to refuse blood transfusions despite the risk to her fetus:

> In sum, the patient as a competent adult, had a right to determine the course of her own treatment, which included the right to decline blood transfusions, and there is no showing that the State had a superior interest, in preventing her from exercising that right under the circumstances of this case. (*Fosmire*, 1990 p. 84)

Cases such as *Fosmire* are ethically the most difficult to resolve. The case is brought on behalf of family members, usually minor children, who depend on the patient. If the necessary treatment is forced on the patient, the patient will recover and the issue will be resolved. The appellate judges in *Fosmire* had the luxury of upholding the patient's autonomy without having blood on their own hands: the trial court's order to give blood had been carried out immediately. The appeal sought only to second-guess its validity.

Physicians in a case like *Fosmire* would properly question whether it would be ethical, although legal, to stand by and not seek a court order to force treatment. Societal interest in the well-being of the dependents would also favor intervention. The trial court's ordering of the treatment might offend some people, but it would not shock the conscience of members of the general public. It is cases such as this that fuel ethical debates, yet these cases have little to do with termination of life-support issues.

Termination of life-support cases, in general, do not involve the refusal of curative therapy. If a competent adult refuses curative life support for religious reasons, these cases should be treated separately from the termination of noncurative life support. It is legally permissible to comply with such requests without legal process. It is ethically questionable, however, to accept a refusal of curative therapy without using judicial process at least to verify the sincerity of the request. In extreme situations, the patient's request is tantamount to a request for assistance in committing suicide (Kane 1985).

The Simple Cases

Few termination of life-support cases present irreconcilable ethical problems (Weir 1990). Most of the patients involved are going to die relatively quickly, irrespective of treatment. All but a few of the rest will be condemned to a persistent vegetative state, which they have previously rejected as unacceptable. Family members may have personal psychological reasons to resist the termination of life support. These are not compelling, however, because of the patient's inability to contribute either personally or financially to family life. Unlike refusal of curative therapy, there is no compelling ethical basis for a physician or hospital to resist the termination of essentially futile treatment. Once treatment becomes both ineffective and unacceptable to the patient, society's interest is to preserve its resources for other patients (Callahan 1990).

This leaves a residuum of hard cases, cases such as that of Hector Rodas. Rodas suffered an accidental brain injury that left him mentally competent but otherwise totally dependent on life-support technology. He could neither speak nor swallow. He could respond to yes or no questions by nodding his head, which allowed him to spell out messages with the help of a therapist pointing to letters on a board. By this means, Rodas requested that he no longer be fed or hydrated. The hospital required Rodas, through his lawyer, to seek a court order discontinuing life support. The court ultimately ruled that Rodas could refuse nutrition and hydration while remaining in the hospital (Miller 1988).

The physicians and the hospital in this case were reluctant to terminate treatment without a court order, but it is difficult to imagine a court refusing Rodas's request to be allowed to die. According to Mishkin (1990), allowing Rodas to die without a court order is certainly legally proper. Considering the prolongation of Rodas's suffering caused by the court action and his extremely limited prognosis, it may be more than merely legal. In cases such as this one, where none of the stakeholders other than the patient has a compelling interest, the delays and suffering inherent in judicial process make such a course of action ethically questionable.

THE IMPACT OF CRUZAN

The *Cruzan* decision disappointed those who had hoped that the Supreme Court would find that families have a constitutional right to terminate a patient's life support (AMA(2) 1990). The American Medical Association has supported substituted decision making for termination of life support, both because of concern with family suffering and because it is convenient for the physicians (AMA 1989). The dissent in *Cruzan* implied that without substituted decision making, physicians would be forced to keep most patient in critical care alive forever.

Would that we were so effective at keeping patients alive as the dissent in *Cruzan* implies. The dissent in *Cruzan* profoundly misinterprets the nature of most termination of life-support decisions. Cases like Nancy Cruzan's are rare rather than typical of termination of life-support situations. Most termination of life-support decisions for incompetent patients are questions of a few hours or days of extra care, not years or decades. While not diminishing the familial suffering that can be caused by unnecessary delays of even a few days in terminating life support, this is not a problem that rises to constitutional significance. Current trends in health care finance have already begun to make controversies over a patient's right to die an anachronism.

In the 1970s and early 1980s, the confluence of effective new technologies and reimbursement schemes that encouraged doing everything for that patient created the popular illusion of critical care physicians as technovampires who would never let patients die. Those days are gone. Third-party payers pressure physicians to admit fewer patients to intensive care units and discharge admitted patients sooner. Increased copayments and medical insurance policies with high stop-loss provisions put most families of critically or terminally ill patients in an intense financial conflict of interest. In this environment, the risks of substituted consent far outweigh its administrative convenience.

The right-to-die debate blinds the public to the real crisis in intensive care: ensuring that every person who might benefit from medical care receives that care. Peter Medawar put it best:

> The tenacity of our hold on life and the sheer strength of our preference for being alive whenever it is an option is far better evidence of a life instinct than any element of human behavioral repertoire is evidence of a death instinct. It is odd, then that nothing in modern medicine has aroused more criticism and resentment than the lengths to which the medical profession will go to prolong the life of patients who need not die if any artifice can keep them going.... Charity, common sense, and humanity unite to describe intensive care as a method of preserving life and not, as its critics have declared, of prolonging death. (Medawar 1990)

The Drawbacks of Substituted Consent

The Judicial Council of the American Medical Association has endorsed the concept of allowing spouses and relatives to consent to the care of incompetent patients. Several state legislatures have considered or passed laws that empower physicians to seek informal consent from the relatives of incompetent patients. Physicians have supported these efforts because they make the physician's life simpler by limiting the need for guardianship proceedings. Unfortunately, these efforts may have profound and unintended consequences for the physician-patient relationship.

Substituted consent is a devil's bargain. First, the assumption that family members always have their relatives' best interests at heart is contradicted by the bulk of family law cases and many of the cases involving wills. Even a loving family is no insurance against conflicts:

> Close family members may have a strong feeling—a feeling not at all ignoble or unworthy, but not entirely disinterested, either—that they do not wish to witness the continuation of the life of a loved one which they regard as hopeless, meaningless, and even degrading. But there is no automatic assurance that the view of close family members will necessarily be the same as the patient's would have been had she been confronted with the prospect of her situation while competent. (*Cruzan*, p. 2855)

There is a particular irony in *Cruzan*. Justice Brennan's dissent in the case asserted that the family had a constitutional right to substitute its wishes for the unknown desires of the patient. This dissent was prefaced with a glowing description of the concern that all families feel for their loved ones and how it was cruel for the majority to imply that the family might not have the patient's best interests at heart. In a case decided the same day, Justice Brennan joined in a dissent portraying the families of girls seeking abortions as uncaring monsters who had no right to be informed or participate in the decision to have an abortion. Most bioethicists see a critical distinction between substituting consent for terminally ill incompetents and other patients. Unless this is based on the hidden belief that these incompetents are actually dead, it is legally unsupportable. Our belief is that the Supreme Court will not treat substituted consent for medical incompetents as a special case, separate from that of legal incompetents, including minors.

While preserving patient autonomy is inconvenient for terminally ill incompetent patients, once autonomy is lost, the consent process will be a battleground for control of the physician-patient relationship. The legal basis of this relationship is the same personal autonomy that this substituted consent denies. If the Supreme Court creates a constitutional right for families to substitute their decisions for patients, this right will not be limited to termination of life-support cases. For example, such a constitutional right would be a sufficient precedent for laws requiring husbands to be consulted about their wives' access to contraception or wives to be consulted about their husbands' cardiac surgery. It would be especially troubling for minors because minors are incompetents according to the law. The convenience of simplifying a limited number of termination of life-support decisions could be rapidly overshadowed by unprecedented intrusions into the physician-patient relationship.

The Problem of Relatives

If it is accepted that family members and spouses have a right to substitute their decisions for a patient, then physicians will find themselves talking to relatives in other situations, such as abortion counseling. Protecting patient autonomy has a great benefit to physicians: the physician always knows who has the right to consent to medical care. While physicians dislike being involved in guardianship proceedings, the alternative is uncertainty in obtaining consent. Relatives frequently disagree over the care a patient should receive. The physician must choose the relatives with whom to consult. This raises questions such as whether two children trump one spouse. Does any relative with an attorney trump the rest of the family?

If the physician chooses whom to consult for consent, he or she will also be legally liable if the choice is incorrect. If no family member has a right to consent, then no family member has the right to sue for failing to be consulted about the patient's care. Conversely, if family members may be consulted, then they have a right to sue if they are unhappy with the physician's decisions.

BIBLIOGRAPHY

Addington v. Texas. 441 US 418 (1979).
AMA(1); Council on Scientific Affairs and Council on Ethical and Judicial Affairs: Persistent vegetative state and the decision to withdraw or withhold life support. JAMA 1990; 263:426–30.
AMA(2); Office of the General Counsel, Orentlicher D: The right to die after Cruzan. JAMA 1990; 264:2444–46.

AMA, Council on Ethical and Judicial Affairs, American Medical Association: AMA ethical opinion 2.20: Withholding or withdrawing life-prolonging medical treatment. Curr Opin 1989; 13.

Brody BA: Ethical questions raised by the persistent vegetative atate patient. Hast Cent Rep 1988; 18(1):330.

Callahan D: Setting limits: Ethics and resource allocation. In Lumb PD; Shoemaker WC: *Critical Care: State of the Art.* 1990.

Carton R: The road to euthanasia. JAMA 1990; 263:2221.

Cotton P: Providers to advise of "medical Miranda." JAMA 1991; 265:306.

Cranford RE: The persistent vegetative state: The medical reality (getting the facts straight). Hast Cent Rep 1988; 18(1):27.

Cruzan by Cruzan v. Director, Missouri Dept. of Health. 497 US 261, 110 S Ct 2841 (1990).

Cruzan v. Harmon, 760 SW2d 408 (Mo, 1988)

Dougherty CJ: Ethical perspectives on cost containment. Hast Cent Rep 1989; 19(1):5.

Fosmire v. Nicoleau. 551 NE2d 77 (NY 1990).

Kane EI: Keeping Elizabeth Bouvia alive for the public good. Hast Cent Rep 1985; 15(6):5.

McVey v. Englewood Hospital Association. 216 NJ Super 502, 524 A2d 450 (1987).

Medawar PB: The threat and the glory: Reflections on science and scientists. Quoted in Perutz MF: High on science, NY Rev Books, 1990 Aug 16; 37(13):12.

Miller DH: Right to die damage actions. Denver L Rev 1988; 65:184.

Mishkin DB: You don't need a judge to terminate treatment. J Intensive Care Med 1990; 5(5):5201–4.

Murphy DJ; Matchar DB: Life-sustaining therapy: A model for appropriate use. JAMA 1990; 264:2103–8.

Ohio v. Akron Center for Reproductive Health. 110 S Ct 2972 (1990).

Orentlicher D: Advance medical directives. JAMA 1990; 263:2365.

Powerly KE; Smith E: The impact of DRGs on health care workers and their clients. Hast Cent Rep 1989; 19(1):16.

Richards EP: Ethical considerations in non-judicial termination of life-support decisions. J Intensive Care Med 1990; 5(5):193–96.

Richards EP: Making sense of Cruzan: Implications of the Supreme Court's right to die decision. J Intensive Care Med 1990; 5(6):241–45.

Santosky v. Kramer. 455 US 745, 755 (1982).

Veatch RM: Justice and the economics of terminal illness. Hast Cent Rep 1988; 18(4):34.

Weir RF; Gostin L: Decisions to abate life-sustaining treatment for Nonautonomous patients: Ethical standards and legal liability for physicians after Cruzan. JAMA 1990; 264:1846–153.

Wikler D: Not dead, not dying? Ethical categories and persistent vegetative state. Hast Cent Rep 1988; 18(1):41.

14

Medical Research

CRITICAL POINTS
- Medical research is strictly regulated by international codes and federal laws.
- Physicians who violate federal research regulations can lose their grants and be prosecuted under the criminal laws.
- Federal research regulations apply to financial conflicts of interest, as well as patient safety issues.
- Federal insider trading laws apply to physicians involved in research joint ventures or consulting agreements.

There has been more medical legal scholarship on the conduct of medical research involving human subjects than any other topic—in interesting contrast to the nearly complete lack of litigation alleging injuries from improperly conducted research. Medical research is controversial because of the abuses that occurred in the not-too-distant past, rather than a current litigation threat. Ranging from the medical experiments conducted by the Nazis to the Tuskegee syphilis experiment (Jones 1981) conducted by the U.S. Public Health Service, these abuses resulted in the promulgation of two major international codes and extensive congressional regulation (Katz 1972). Any patient injured by an experiment that violates these codes or regulations can sue the physician for medical malpractice. More commonly, however, investigators or their institutions are sanctioned by the Department of Health and Human Services or the U.S. Public Health Service for not complying with governmental regulations.

In one area, litigation (and criminal investigation) is probable. The growth of joint research agreements between universities and medical businesses, combined with the involvement of medical scientists in for-profit ventures, has put many scientists in violation of laws dealing with conflicts of interest and stock fraud. The Public Health Service has also promulgated rules governing misconduct in science, which could be the basis for fraud-related litigation. Lawsuits asserting financial fraud are not covered by medical malpractice insurance and are especially dangerous to physicians. The physician-scientist must pay the defense costs for such actions and any fines or damages if the defense is unsuccessful.

INTERNATIONAL CODES

Two primary international codes govern the conduct of medical research involving human subjects. The Declaration of Helsinki is a document promulgated by the World Medical Association "as a guide to each doctor in clinical research." The Nuremberg Code arose from the Nuremberg trials of Nazi war criminals accused of conducting medical experiments on prisoners that caused great suffering and many deaths. The code sets forth principles designed to protect human subjects from abuses related to medical research. The code's statement of the ethical framework for medical research is considered to be the policy behind federal and state regulation of human-subject-based research.

Neither of these codes has the force of law, but they set the moral tone for all medical research, including research unregulated by state or federal law. These codes are admissible in court as evidence of the proper standard of care for medical experimentation. Every physician who is involved in medical research should read and be familiar with these codes.

The Nuremberg Code

The Nuremberg Code arose as part of the trial of the *United States v. Karl Brandt*. Karl Brandt and others were tried at Nuremburg for crimes against humanity committed in their roles as the Nazi high command. The code has ten requirements:

1. The voluntary consent of the human subject is absolutely essential. This means that the person involved should have legal capacity to give consent: should be so situated as to be able to exercise free power of choice without the intervention of any element of force, fraud, deceit, duress, overreaching, or other ulterior form of constraint or coercion and should have sufficient knowledge and comprehension of the elements of the subject matter involved as to enable him to make an understanding and enlightened decision. This latter element requires that before the acceptance of an affirmative decision by the experimental subject there should be made known to him the nature, duration, and purpose of the experiment; the method and means by which it is to be conducted; all inconveniences and hazards reasonably to be expected; and their effects upon his health or person which may possibly come from his participation in the experiment.

   The duty and responsibility for ascertaining the quality of the consent rests upon each individual who initiates, directs, or engages in the experiment. It is a personal duty and responsibility which may not be delegated to another with impunity.
2. The experiment should be such as to yield fruitful results for the good of society, unprocurable by other methods or means of study, and not random and unnecessary in nature.
3. The experiment should be so designed and based on the results of animal experimentation and a knowledge of the natural history of the disease or other problem under study that the anticipated results will justify the performance of the experiment.
4. The experiment should be so conducted as to avoid all unnecessary physical and mental suffering and injury.
5. No experiment should be conducted where there is a prior reason to believe that death or disabling injury will occur, except perhaps, in those experiments where the experimental physicians also serve as subject.

6. The degree of risk to be taken should never exceed that determined by the humanitarian importance of the problem to be solved by the experiment.
7. Proper preparations should be made and adequate facilities provided to protect the experimental subject against even remote possibilities of injury, disability or death.
8. The experiment should be conducted only by scientifically qualified persons. The highest degree of skill and care should be required through all stages of the experiment of those who conduct or engage in the experiment.
9. During the course of the experiment the human subject should be at liberty to bring the experiment to an end if he has reached the physical or mental state where continuation of the experiment seems to him to be impossible.
10. During the course of the experiment the scientist in charge must be prepared to terminate the experiment at any stage, if he has probable cause to believe, in the exercise of the good faith, superior skill, and careful judgment required of him, that a continuation of the experiment is likely to result in injury, disability, or death to the experimental subject. (The Nuremberg Code)

World Medical Association

It is the mission of the doctor to safeguard the health of the people. His knowledge and conscience are dedicated to the fulfillment of this mission.

The Declaration of Geneva of the World Medical Association binds the doctor with the words: "The health of my patient will be my first consideration"; and the International Code of Medical Ethics which declares that "Any act of advice which could weaken physical or mental resistance of a human being may be used only in his interest."

Because it is essential that the results of laboratory experiments be applied to human beings to further scientific knowledge and to help suffering humanity, the World Medical Association has prepared the following recommendations as a guide to each doctor in clinical research. It must be stressed that the standards as drafted are only a guide to physicians all over the world. Doctors are not relieved from criminal, civil and ethical responsibilities under the laws of their own countries.

In the field of clinical research a fundamental distinction must be recognized between clinical research in which the aim is essentially therapeutic for a patient, and clinical research the essential object of which is purely scientific without therapeutic value to the person subjected to the research.

I. Basic Principles

1. Clinical research must conform to the moral and scientific principles that justify medical research, and should be based on laboratory and animal experiments or other scientifically established facts.
2. Clinical research should be conducted only by scientifically qualified persons and under the supervision of a qualified medical man.
3. Clinical research cannot legitimately be carried out unless the importance of the objective is in proportion to the inherent risk to the subject.
4. Every clinical research project should be preceded by careful assessment of inherent risks in comparison to foreseeable benefits to the subject or to others.
5. Special caution should be exercised by the doctor in performing clinical research in which the personality of the subject is liable to be altered by drugs or experimental procedure.

II. Clinical Research Combined with Professional Care

1. In the treatment of the sick person the doctor must be free to use a new therapeutic measure if in his judgment it offers hope of saving life, re-establishing health, or alleviating suffering.

If at all possible, consistent with patient psychology, the doctor should obtain the patient's freely given consent after the patient has been given a full explanation. In case of legal incapacity consent should also be procured from the legal guardian; in case of physical incapacity the permission of the legal guardian replaces that of the patient.

2. The doctor can combine clinical research with professional care, the objective being the acquisition of new medical knowledge, only to the extent that clinical research is justified by its therapeutic value for the patient.

III. Non-therapeutic Clinical Research

1. In the purely scientific application of clinical research carried out on a human being it is the duty of the doctor to remain the protector of the life and health of that person on whom clinical research is being carried out.
2. The nature, the purpose, and the risk of clinical research must be explained to the subject by the doctor.
3a. Clinical research on a human being cannot be undertaken without his free consent, after he has been fully informed; if he is legally incompetent the consent of the legal guardian should be procured.
3b. The subject of clinical research should be in such a mental, physical, and legal state as to be able to exercise fully his power of choice.
3c. Consent should as a rule be obtained in writing. However, the responsibility for clinical research always remains with the research worker; it never falls on the subject, even after consent is obtained.
4a. The investigator must respect the right of each individual to safeguard his personal integrity, especially if the subject is in a dependent relationship to the investigator.
4b. At any time during the course of clinical research the subject or his guardian should be free to withdraw permission for research to be continued. The investigator of the investigating team should discontinue the research if in his or their judgment it may, if continued, be harmful to the individual.

Consent Under the International Codes

The core value of both international codes is that medical research cannot be performed without the freely given (uncoerced) consent of the potential subjects. In a refinement of the Nuremberg Code, the Declaration of Helsinki distinguishes between therapeutic and nontherapeutic research, requiring the physician to exercise special care in performing research that cannot personally benefit the patient. Legally, informed consent shifts the risk of nonnegligent injury to the patient in therapeutic research. In nontherapeutic research, however, it is arguable that the physician-experimenter is strictly liable (regardless of negligence) for injuries to the patient. This distinction is reflected in the federal regulations with the requirement that the risk of the experiment be compared to both the benefits to the patient and to society.

Private Research

These international codes have been superseded by U.S. Department of Health and Human Services (HHS) regulations for most traditional institution-based research. They are still important for private research that is not done under HHS auspices. For example, pharmaceutical firms have always engaged in and contracted for private research. These firms have been criticized for testing drugs in Third World countries to avoid legal liability. In general, however, this research has been well designed and controlled to ensure that the resulting data will be acceptable to the U.S. Food and Drug Administration (FDA).

More problematic are independently run trials that implicitly promise therapeutic benefit from experimental drugs. Some of these trials are run on a money-making basis, allowing wealthy patients to buy access to experimental drugs. Others, such as certain clinics treating AIDS patients, are humanitarian efforts to increase access to experimental drugs. Both efforts have serious methodological flaws because they are dependent on self-selected populations with a high probability of manipulating their care outside the research protocol. This sample selection and compliance problem undermines the potential value of the research. At some point, the potential societal benefit of the research is so small that it is no longer ethical to conduct the research.

HHS REGULATIONS ON PROTECTING HUMAN SUBJECTS

The Department of Health and Human Services has promulgated regulations for the protection of human research subjects, enforced through the creation of institutional review boards (IRBs) at each participating institution. They apply to all research done by covered institutions or individuals, including research done outside the United States. The regulations stipulate the composition and duties of an IRB, establish standards for informed consent, provide for sanctions against institutions and individuals who violate the regulations, and require more intensive scrutiny of research involving fetuses, in vitro fertilization, pregnant women, prisoners, and children. These regulations do not supersede other state and federal laws; they create additional duties for persons involved in research involving human subjects.

Researchers who run afoul of these regulations can lose their current research funding, can become ineligible for future funding, and can be forced to repay funds improperly expended. In practical terms, a researcher who is disciplined under the regulations will be at a disadvantage for future funds from HHS and other government agencies. Researchers in competitive areas may find it impossible to continue their careers as principal investigators. For this reason, it is imperative that every person contemplating research involving human subjects have a basic understanding of the HHS regulations.

In this chapter, the regulations have been edited and paraphrased for easier reading. This abridged presentation is intended to help researchers understand when they must submit their research design to an IRB and the general constraints of the IRB process. The general provisions of these regulations probably will be constant; nevertheless, their details are subject to change. Any physician engaged in covered research should consult with the appropriate IRB for current regulations.

Scope of the Regulations

With certain delineated exceptions, the HHS regulations apply to all research conducted with HHS funds, both inside and outside the United States. All institutions receiving HHS funding in any area must have an ethical policy governing all human research conducted at that institution, regardless of the source of funding. Many institutions have also assured HHS that all research in the institution, irrespective of HHS funding, will be reviewed and conducted pursuant to the HHS regulations. These regulations require investigators supervising cooperative research projects to ensure that all other participants abide by the HHS regulations:

Cooperative research projects are those projects, normally supported through grants, contracts, or similar arrangements, which involve institutions in addition to the grantee or prime contractor (such as a contractor with the grantee, or a subcontractor with the prime contractor). In such instances, the grantee or prime contractor remains responsible to the Department for safeguarding the rights and welfare of human subjects. Also, when cooperating institutions conduct some or all of the research involving some or all of these subjects, each cooperating institution shall comply with these regulations as though it received funds for its participation in the project directly from the Department, except that in complying with these regulations institutions may use joint review, reliance upon the review of another qualified IRB, or similar arrangements aimed at avoidance of duplication of effort. (sec. 46.114)

Research Involving Human Subjects

"Research" means a systematic investigation designed to develop or contribute to generalizable knowledge. Activities which meet this definition constitute "research" for purposes of these regulations, whether or not they are supported or funded under a program considered research for other purposes. For example, some "demonstration" and "service" programs may include "research activities."

"Human subject" means a living individual about whom an investigator (whether professional or student) conducting research obtains (1) data through intervention or interaction with the individual, or (2) identifiable private information. "Intervention" includes both physical procedures by which data are gathered (for example, venipuncture) and manipulations of the subject or the subject's environment that are performed for research purposes. "Interaction" includes communication or interpersonal contact between investigator and subject. "Private information" includes information about behavior that occurs in a context in which an individual can reasonably expect that no observation or recording is taking place, and information that has been provided for specific purposes by an individual and which the individual can reasonably expect will not be made public (for example, a medical record). Private information must be individually identifiable (for example, the identity of the subject is or may readily be ascertained by the investigator or associated with the information) in order for obtaining the information to constitute research involving human subjects.

"Minimal risk" means that the risks of harm anticipated in the proposed research are not greater, considering probability and magnitude, than those ordinarily encountered in daily life or during the performance of routine physical or psychological examinations or tests. (sec. 46.102)

General Exceptions

(b) Unless otherwise required by department or agency heads, research activities in which the only involvement of human subjects will be in one or more of the following categories are exempt from this policy:

(1) Research conducted in established or commonly accepted educational settings, involving normal educational practices, such as (i) research on regular and special education instructional strategies, or (ii) research on the effectiveness of or the comparison among instructional techniques, curricula, or classroom management methods.

(2) Research involving the use of educational tests (cognitive, diagnostic, aptitude, achievement), survey procedures, interview procedures or observation of public behavior, unless:

(i) Information obtained is recorded in such a manner that human subjects can be identified, directly or through identifiers linked to the subjects; and (ii) any disclosure of the human subjects' responses outside the research could reasonably place the subjects at risk of criminal or civil liability or be damaging to the subjects' financial standing, employability, or reputation.

(3) Research involving the use of educational tests (cognitive, diagnostic, aptitude, achievement), survey procedures, interview procedures, or observation of public behavior that is not exempt under paragraph (b) (2) of this section, if:

(i) The human subjects are elected or appointed public officials or candidates for public office; or (ii) federal stature(s) require(s) without exception that the confidentiality of the personally identifiable information will be maintained throughout the research and thereafter.

(4) Research, involving the collection or study of existing data, documents, records, pathological specimens, or diagnostic specimens, if these sources are publicly available or if the information is recorded by the investigator in such a manner that subjects cannot be identified, directly or through identifiers linked to the subjects.

(5) Research and demonstration projects which are conducted by or subject to the approval of department or agency heads, and which are designed to study, evaluate, or otherwise examine:

(i) Public benefit or service programs; (ii) procedures for obtaining benefits or services under those programs; (iii) possible changes in or alternatives to those programs or procedures; or (iv) possible changes in methods or levels of payment for benefits or services under those programs. (sec. 45 CFR 46.101)

Provisions for Children

The general exceptions to the necessity of IRB review apply to children with two exceptions. The exemption for research involving the observation of public behavior applies only when the investigator does not participate in the activities being observed, and the exemption for research involving survey or interview procedures, does not apply to research involving children.

Research That Will Involve Human Subjects in the Future

Certain types of applications for grants, cooperative agreements, or contracts are submitted to HHS departments or agencies with the knowledge that subjects may be involved within the period of funding, but definite plans would not normally be set forth in the application or proposal. These include activities such as institutional type grants when selection of specific projects is the institution's responsibility; research training grants in which the activities involving subjects remain to be selected; and projects in which human subjects' involvement will depend upon completion of instruments, prior animal studies, or purification of compounds. These applications need not be reviewed by an IRB before an award may be made. However, except for research described in § 46.101(b) or (i), no human subjects may be involved in any project supported by these awards until the project has been reviewed and approved by the IRB, as provided in this policy, and certification submitted by the institution, to the department or agency. (sec. 46.118)

Institutional Review Boards

Every institution receiving HHS funds for research involving human subjects must set up an IRB. The IRB must review all research that is subject to HHS regulation. In most institutions the IRB will conduct a preliminary review of all research involving human subjects, exempting projects that are not subject to

HHS regulation from a full review as mandated by the statute. The institution must provide the staff, meeting space, and supplies necessary for the IRB to conduct its reviews and properly document its findings.

IRB Membership

(a) Each IRB shall have at least five members, with varying backgrounds to promote complete and adequate review of research activities commonly conducted by the institution. The IRB shall be sufficiently qualified through the experience and expertise of its members, and the diversity of the members, including consideration of race, gender, and cultural backgrounds and sensitivity to such issues as community attitudes, to promote respect for its advice and counsel in safeguarding the rights and welfare of human subjects. In addition to possessing the professional competence necessary to review specific research activities, the IRB shall be able to ascertain the acceptability of proposed research in terms of institutional commitments and regulations, applicable law, and standards of professional conduct and practice. The IRB shall therefore include persons knowledgeable in these areas. If an IRB regularly reviews research that involves a vulnerable category of subjects, such as children, prisoners, pregnant women, or handicapped or mentally disabled persons, consideration shall be given to the inclusion of one or more individuals who are knowledgeable about and experienced in working with these subjects.

(b) Every nondiscriminatory effort will be made to ensure that no IRB consists entirely of men or entirely of women, including the institution's consideration of qualified persons of both sexes, so long as no selection is made to the IRB on the basis of gender. No IRB may consist entirely of members of one profession.

(c) Each IRB shall include at least one member whose primary concerns are in scientific areas and at least one member whose primary concerns are in nonscientific areas.

(d) Each IRB shall include at least one member who is not otherwise affiliated with the institution and who is not part of the immediate family of a person who is affiliated with the institution.

(e) No IRB may have a member participate in the IRB's initial or continuing review of any project in which the member has a conflicting interest, except to provide information requested by the IRB.

(f) An IRB may, in its discretion, invite individuals with competence in special areas to assist in the review of issues which require expertise beyond or in addition to that available on the IRB. These individuals may not vote with the IRB. (sec. 45 CFR 46.107)

Composition of IRBs Where Prisoners Are Involved

When prisoners are involved as human subjects, the IRB must meet additional requirements:

> A majority of the Board (exclusive of prisoner members) shall have no association with the prison(s) involved, apart from their membership on the Board.
>
> At least one member of the Board shall be a prisoner, or a prisoner representative with appropriate background and experience to serve in that capacity, except that where a particular research project is reviewed by more than one Board only one Board need satisfy this requirement. (sec. 46.304)

Criteria for IRB Approval of Research

(a) In order to approve research covered by these regulations the IRB shall determine that all of the following requirements are satisfied:

(1) Risks to subjects are minimized: (i) By using procedures which are consistent with sound research design and which do not unnecessarily expose subjects to risk, and (ii) whenever appropriate, by using procedures already being performed on the subjects for diagnostic or treatment purposes.
(2) Risks to subjects are reasonable in relation to anticipated benefits, if any, to subjects, and the importance of the knowledge that may reasonably be expected to result. In evaluating risks and benefits, the IRB should consider only those risks and benefits that may result from the research (as distinguished from risks and benefits of therapies subjects would receive even if not participating in the research). The IRB should not consider possible long-range effects of applying knowledge gained in the research (for example, the possible effects of the research on public policy) as among those research risks that fall within the purview of its responsibility.
(3) Selection of subjects is equitable. In making this assessment the IRB should take into account the purposes of the research and the setting in which the research will be conducted and should be particularly cognizant of the special problems of research involving vulnerable populations. . . .
(4) Informed consent will be sought from each prospective subject or the subject's legally authorized representative, in accordance with, and to the extent required by . . . [these regulations].
(5) Informed consent will be appropriately documented, in accordance with, and to the extent required by . . . [these regulations].
(6) Where appropriate, the research plan makes adequate provision for monitoring the data collected to insure the safety of subjects.
(7) Where appropriate, there are adequate provisions to protect the privacy of subjects and to maintain the confidentiality of data.
(8) Where some or all of the subjects are likely to be vulnerable to coercion or undue influence, such as children, prisoners, pregnant women, mentally disabled persons or economically or educationally disadvantaged persons, appropriate additional safeguards have been included in the study to protect the rights and welfare of these subjects. (sec. 46.111)

General Requirements for Informed Consent

Except as provided elsewhere in this policy, no investigator may involve a human being as a subject in research covered by these regulations unless the investigator has obtained the legally effective informed consent of the subject or the subject's legally authorized representative. An investigator shall seek such consent only under circumstances that provide the prospective subject or the representative sufficient opportunity to consider whether or not to participate and that minimize the possibility of coercion or undue influence. The information that is given to the subject or the representative shall be in language understandable to the subject or the representative. No informed consent, whether oral or written, may include any exculpatory language through which the subject or the representative is made to waive or appear to waive any of the subject's legal rights, or releases or appears to release the investigator, the sponsor, the institution or its agents from liability for negligence. (sec. 45 CFR 46.116)

Except as . . . [modified by the IRB], in seeking informed consent the following information shall be provided to each subject:

(1) A statement that the study involves research, an explanation of the purposes of the research and the expected duration of the subject's participation, a description of the procedures to be followed, and identification of any procedures which are experimental;

(2) A description of any reasonably foreseeable risks or discomforts to the subject;
(3) A description of any benefits to the subject or to others which may reasonably be expected from the research;
(4) A disclosure of appropriate alternative procedures or courses of treatment, if any, that might be advantageous to the subject;
(5) A statement describing the extent, if any, to which confidentiality of records identifying the subject will be maintained;
(6) For research involving more than minimal risk, an explanation as to whether any compensation and an explanation as to whether any medical treatments are available if injury occurs and, if so, what they consist of, or where further information may be obtained;
(7) An explanation of whom to contact for answers to pertinent questions about the research and research subjects' rights, and whom to contact in the event of a research-related injury to the subject; and
(8) A statement that participation is voluntary, refusal to participate will involve no penalty or loss of benefits to which the subject is otherwise entitled, and the subject may discontinue participation at any time without penalty or loss of benefits to which the subject is otherwise entitled.

Additional Elements of Informed Consent

(b) When appropriate, one or more of the following elements of information shall also be provided to each subject:

(1) A statement that the particular treatment or procedure may involve risks to the subject (or to the embryo or fetus, if the subject is or may become pregnant) which are currently unforeseeable;
(2) Anticipated circumstances under which the subject's participation may be terminated by the investigator without regard to the subject's consent;
(3) Any additional costs to the subject that may result from participation in the research;
(4) The consequences of a subject's decision to withdraw from the research and procedures for orderly termination of participation by the subject;
(5) A statement that significant new findings developed during the course of the research which may relate to the subject's willingness to continue participation will be provided to the subject; and
(6) The approximate number of subjects involved in the study.

Research

Expedited review procedures for certain kinds of research involving no more than minimal risk, and for minor changes in approved research.

(a) The Secretary, HHS, has established, and published as a Notice in the Federal Register, a list of categories of research that may be reviewed by the IRB through an expedited review procedure. The list will be amended, as appropriate after consultation with other departments and agencies, through periodic republication by the Secretary, HHS, in the Federal Register. A copy of the list is available from the Office for Protection from Research Risks, National Institutes of Health, HHS, Bethesda, Maryland 20892.
(b) An IRB may use the expedited review procedure to review either or both of the following:

(1) Some or all of the research appearing on the list and found by the reviewer(s) to involve no more than minimal risk,
(2) Minor changes in previously approved research during the period (of one year or less) for which approval is authorized.

Under an expedited review procedure, the review may be carried out by the IRB chairperson or by one or more experienced reviewers designated by the chairperson from among members of the IRB. In reviewing the research, the reviewers may exercise all of the authorities of the IRB except that the reviewers may not disapprove the research. A research activity may be disapproved only after review in accordance with the non-expedited procedure set forth in § 46.108(b).

(c) Each IRB which uses an expedited review procedure shall adopt a method for keeping all members advised of research proposals which have been approved under the procedure.

(d) The department or agency head may restrict, suspend, terminate, or choose not to authorize an institution's or IRB's use of the expedited review procedure. (sec. 45 CFR 46.110)

Documentation of Informed Consent

(a) Except as . . . [exempted by the IRB], informed consent shall be documented by the use of a written consent form approved by the IRB and signed by the subject or the subject's legally authorized representative. A copy shall be given to the person signing the form. . . .

(b) [T]he consent form may be either of the following:

(1) A written consent document that embodies the elements of informed consent required by . . . [the regulations]. This form may be read to the subject or the subject's legally authorized representative, but in any event, the investigator shall give either the subject or the representative adequate opportunity to read it before it is signed; or

(2) A "short form" written consent document stating that the elements of informed consent required by . . . [the regulations has] been presented orally to the subject or the subject's legally authorized representative. When this method is used, there shall be a witness to the oral presentation. Also, the IRB shall approve a written summary of what is to be said to the subject or the representative. Only the short form itself is to be signed by the subject or the representative. However, the witness shall sign both the short form and a copy of the summary, and the person actually obtaining consent shall sign a copy of the summary. A copy of the summary shall be given to the subject or the representative, in addition to a copy of the "short form."

(c) The IRB may waive the requirement for the investigator to obtain a signed consent form for some or all subjects if it finds either:

(1) That the only record linking the subject and the research would be the consent document and the principal risk would be potential harm resulting from a breach of confidentiality. Each subject will be asked whether the subject wants documentation linking the subject with the research, and the subject's wishes will govern; or

(2) That the research presents no more than minimal risk of harm to subjects and involves no procedures for which written consent is normally required outside of the research context.

In cases where the documentation requirement is waived, the IRB may require the investigator to provide subjects with a written statement regarding the research. (sec. 45 CFR 46.117)

Preemption of Other Laws Governing Informed Consent
The informed consent requirements in these regulations are not intended to preempt any applicable federal, state, or local laws which require additional information to be disclosed in order for informed consent to be legally effective. (sec. 45 CFR 46.116 [e])

Exemption for Emergency Care
Nothing in these regulations is intended to limit the authority of a physician to provide emergency medical care, to the extent the physician is permitted to do so under applicable federal, state, or local law. (sec. 45 CFR 46.116 [f])

Pregnant Women, Fetus, In Vitro Fertilization
The[se] regulations ... are applicable to all Department of Health and Human Services grants and contracts supporting research, development, and related activities involving: (1) The fetus, (2) pregnant women, and (3) human in vitro fertilization. (sec. 45 CFR 46.201)

Definitions

(b) "Pregnancy" encompasses the period of time from confirmation of implantation (through any of the presumptive signs of pregnancy, such as missed menses, or by a medically acceptable pregnancy test), until expulsion or extraction of the fetus.

(c) "Fetus" means the product of conception from the time of implantation (as evidenced by any of the presumptive signs of pregnancy, such as missed menses, or a medically acceptable pregnancy test), until a determination is made, following expulsion or extraction of the fetus, that it is viable.

(d) "Viable" as it pertains to the fetus means being able, after either spontaneous or induced delivery, to survive (given the benefit of available medical therapy) to the point of independently maintaining heart beat and respiration. The Secretary may from time to time, taking into account medical advances, publish in the Federal Register guidelines to assist in determining whether a fetus is viable for purposes of this subpart. If a fetus is viable after delivery, it is a premature infant.

(e) "Nonviable fetus" means a fetus ex utero which, although living, is not viable.

(f) "Dead fetus" means a fetus ex utero which exhibits neither heartbeat, spontaneous respiratory activity, spontaneous movement of voluntary muscles, nor pulsation of the umbilical cord (if still attached).

(g) "In vitro fertilization" means any fertilization of human ova which occurs outside the body of a female, either through admixture of donor human sperm and ova or by any other means. (sec. 45 CFR 46.203)

Ethical Advisory Boards
In addition to the review by the institution's own IRB, any research governed by this section must also be reviewed by a national ethical advisory board:

(a) One or more Ethical Advisory Boards shall be established by the Secretary. Members of these board(s) shall be so selected that the board(s) will be competent to deal with medical, legal, social, ethical, and related issues and may include, for example, research scientists, physicians, psychologists, sociologists, educators, lawyers, and ethicists, as well as representatives of the general public. No board member may be a regular, full-time employee of the Department of Health and Human Services.

(b) At the request of the Secretary, the Ethical Advisory Board shall render advice consistent with the policies and requirements of this Part as to ethical issues,

involving activities covered by this subpart, raised by individual applications or proposals. In addition, upon request by the Secretary, the Board shall render advice as to classes of applications or proposals and general policies, guidelines, and procedures.
(c) A Board may establish, with the approval of the Secretary, classes of applications or proposals which: (1) Must be submitted to the Board, or (2) need not be submitted to the Board. Where the Board so establishes a class of applications or proposals which must be submitted, no application or proposal within the class may be funded by the Department or any component thereof until the application or proposal has been reviewed by the Board and the Board has rendered advice as to its acceptability from an ethical standpoint.
(d) No application or proposal involving human in vitro fertilization may be funded by the Department or any component thereof until the application or proposal has been reviewed by the Ethical Advisory Board and the Board has rendered advice as to its acceptability from an ethical standpoint. (sec. 45 CFR 46.204) [At the time of this writing, none of the ethical advisory boards had been properly constituted; thus no research had yet been approved under this section.]

General Limitations

(a) No activity to which this subpart is applicable may be undertaken unless:

(1) Appropriate studies on animals and nonpregnant individuals have been completed;
(2) Except where the purpose of the activity is to meet the health needs of the mother or the particular fetus, the risk to the fetus is minimal and, in all cases, is the least possible risk for achieving the objectives of the activity.
(3) Individuals engaged in the activity will have no part in: (i) Any decisions as to the timing, method, and procedures used to terminate the pregnancy, and (ii) determining the viability of the fetus at the termination of the pregnancy; and
No procedural changes which may cause greater than minimal risk to the fetus or the pregnant woman will be introduced into the procedure for terminating the pregnancy solely in the interest of the activity.

No inducements, monetary or otherwise, may be offered to terminate pregnancy for purposes of the activity. (sec. 45 CFR 46.206)

Pregnant Women as Subjects

(a) No pregnant woman may be involved as a subject in an activity covered by this subpart unless: (1) The purpose of the activity is to meet the health needs of the mother and the fetus will be placed at risk only to the minimum extent necessary to meet such needs, or (2) the risk to the fetus is minimal.
(b) An activity permitted under ... this section may be conducted only if the mother and father are legally competent and have given their informed consent after having been fully informed regarding possible impact on the fetus, except that the father's informed consent need not be secured if: (1) The purpose of the activity is to meet the health needs of the mother; (2) his identity or whereabouts cannot reasonably be ascertained; (3) he is not reasonably available; or (4) the pregnancy resulted from rape. (sec. 45 CFR 46.207)

Activities Directed toward Fetuses In Utero as Subjects

(a) No fetus in utero may be involved as a subject in any activity covered by this subpart unless: (1) The purpose of the activity is to meet the health needs of the particular fetus and the fetus will be placed at risk only to the minimum extent necessary to meet such needs, or (2) the risk to the fetus imposed by the research is minimal and the purpose of the activity is the development of important biomedical knowledge which cannot be obtained by other means.

(b) An activity permitted under paragraph (a) of this section may be conducted only if the mother and father are legally competent and have given their informed consent, except that the father's consent need not be secured if: (1) His identity or whereabouts cannot reasonably be ascertained, (2) he is not reasonably available, or (3) the pregnancy resulted from rape. (sec. 45 CFR 46.208)

Fetuses Ex Utero, including Nonviable Fetuses

(a) Until it has been ascertained whether or not a fetus ex utero is viable, a fetus ex utero may not be involved as a subject in an activity covered by this subpart unless:

(1) There will be no added risk to the fetus resulting from the activity, and the purpose of the activity is the development of important biomedical knowledge which cannot be obtained by other means, or

(2) The purpose of the activity is to enhance the possibility of survival of the particular fetus to the point of viability.

(b) No nonviable fetus may be involved as a subject in an activity covered by this subpart unless:

(1) Vital functions of the fetus will not be artificially maintained,
(2) Experimental activities which of themselves would terminate the heartbeat or respiration of the fetus will not be employed, and
(3) The purpose of the activity is the development of important biomedical knowledge which cannot be obtained by other means.

(c) In the event the fetus ex utero is found to be viable, it may be included as a subject in the activity only to the extent permitted by and in accordance with the requirements of other subparts of this part.

(d) An activity permitted under ... this section may be conducted only if the mother and father are legally competent and have given their informed consent, except that the father's informed consent need not be secured if: (1) his identity or whereabouts cannot reasonably be ascertained, (2) he is not reasonably available, or (3) the pregnancy resulted from rape. (sec. 45 CFR 46.209)

Dead Fetuses, Fetal Material, or the Placentas

Activities involving the dead fetus, macerated fetal material, or cells, tissue, or organs excised from a dead fetus shall be conducted only in accordance with any applicable State or local laws regarding such activities. (sec. 45 CFR 46.210)

Prisoners

Inasmuch as prisoners may be under constraints because of their incarceration which could affect their ability to make a truly voluntary and uncoerced decision whether or not to participate as subjects in research, it is the purpose of this subpart to provide additional safeguards for the protection of prisoners involved in activities to which this subpart is applicable. (sec. 45 CFR 46.302)

Definitions

(c) "Prisoner" means any individual involuntarily confined or detained in a penal institution. The term is intended to encompass individuals sentenced to such an institution under a criminal or civil statute, individuals detained in other facil-

ities by virtue of statutes or commitment procedures which provide alternatives to criminal prosecution or incarceration in a penal institution, and individuals detained pending arraignment, trial, or sentencing.
(d) "Minimal risk" is the probability and magnitude of physical or psychological harm that is normally encountered in the daily lives, or in the routine medical, dental, or psychological examination of healthy persons. (sec. 45 CFR 46.303)

Restrictions on Prisoner Participation

Research on prisoners may be approved only if the IRB finds that

(2) any possible advantages accruing to the prisoner through his or her participation in the research, when compared to the general living conditions, medical care, quality of food, amenities and opportunity for earnings in the prison, are not of such a magnitude that his or her ability to weigh the risks of the research against the value of such advantages in the limited choice environment of the prison is impaired;
(3) The risks involved in the research are commensurate with risks that would be accepted by nonprisoner volunteers;
(4) Procedures for the selection of subjects within the prison are fair to all prisoners and immune from arbitrary intervention by prison authorities or prisoners. Unless the principal investigator provides to the Board justification in writing for following some other procedures, control subjects must be selected randomly from the group of available prisoners who meet the characteristics needed for that particular research project;
(5) The information is presented in language which is understandable to the subject population;
(6) Adequate assurance exists that parole boards will not take into account a prisoner's participation in the research in making decisions regarding parole, and each prisoner is clearly informed in advance that participation in the research will have no effect on his or her parole; and
(7) Where the Board finds there may be a need for follow-up examination or care of participants after the end of their participation, adequate provision has been made for such examination or care, taking into account the varying lengths of individual prisoners' sentences, and for informing participants of this fact. (sec. 45 CFR 46.305)

Permitted Research involving Prisoners

(a) Biomedical or behavioral research conducted or supported by DHHS may involve prisoners as subjects only if: (1) The institution responsible for the conduct of the research has certified to the Secretary that the Institutional Review Board has approved the research . . . ; and (2) In the judgment of the Secretary the proposed research involves solely the following:

(i) Study of the possible causes, effects, and processes of incarceration, and of criminal behavior, provided that the study presents no more than minimal risk and no more than inconvenience to the subjects;
(ii) Study of prisons as institutional structures or of prisoners as incarcerated persons, provided that the study presents no more than minimal risk and no more than inconvenience to the subjects;
(iii) Research on conditions particularly affecting prisoners as a class (for example, vaccine trials and other research on hepatitis which is much more prevalent in prisons than elsewhere; and research on social and psychological problems such as alcoholism, drug addiction and sexual assaults) provided that the study may

proceed only after the Secretary has consulted with appropriate experts including experts in penology medicine and ethics, and published notice, in the Federal Register, of his intent to approve such research; or

(iv) Research on practices, both innovative and accepted, which have the intent and reasonable probability of improving the health or well-being of the subject. In cases in which those studies require the assignment of prisoners in a manner consistent with protocols approved by the IRB to control groups which may not benefit from the research, the study may proceed only after the Secretary has consulted with appropriate experts, including experts in penology medicine and ethics, and published notice, in the Federal Register, of his intent to approve such research. (sec. 45 CFR 46.306)

Children

HHS has recently promulgated specific regulations for research involving children. These are in addition to the general IRB regulations.

(a) "Children" are persons who have not attained the legal age for consent to treatments or procedures involved in the research, under the applicable law of the jurisdiction in which the research will be conducted.
(b) "Assent" means a child's affirmative agreement to participate in research. Mere failure to object should not, absent affirmative agreement, be construed as assent.
(c) "Permission" means the agreement of parent(s) or guardian to the participation of their child or ward in research.
(d) "Parent" means a child's biological or adoptive parent.
(e) "Guardian" means an individual who is authorized under applicable State or local law to consent on behalf of a child to general medical care. (sec. 45 CFR 46.402)

Research Not Involving Greater Than Minimal Risk

HHS will conduct or fund research in which the IRB finds that no greater than minimal risk to children is presented, only if the IRB finds that adequate provisions are made for soliciting the assent of the children and the permission of their parents or guardians, as set forth in § 46.408. (sec. 45 CFR 46.404)

Therapeutic Research

HHS will conduct or fund research in which the IRB finds that more than minimal risk to children is presented by an intervention or procedure that holds out the prospect of direct benefit for the individual subject, or by a monitoring procedure that is likely to contribute to the subject's well-being only if the IRB finds that:
(a) The risk is justified by the anticipated benefit to the subjects;
(b) The relation of the anticipated benefit to the risk is at least as favorable to the subjects as that presented by available alternative approaches; and
(c) Adequate provisions are made for soliciting the assent of the children and permission of their parents or guardians, as set forth in § 46.408. (sec. 45 CFR 46.405)

Nontherapeutic Research

HHS will conduct or fund research in which the IRB finds that more than minimal risk to children is presented by an intervention or procedure that does not hold out the prospect of direct benefit for the individual subject, or by a monitoring procedure which is not likely to contribute to the well-being of the subject, only if the IRB finds that:
(a) The risk represents a minor increase over minimal risk;

(b) The intervention or procedure presents experiences to subjects that are reasonably commensurate with those inherent in their actual or expected medical, dental, psychological, social, or educational situations;
(c) The intervention or procedure is likely to yield generalizable knowledge about the subjects' disorder or condition which is of vital importance for the understanding or amelioration of the subjects' disorder or condition; and
(d) Adequate provisions are made for soliciting assent of the children and permission of their parents or guardians, as set forth in . . . [these regulations]. (sec. 45 CFR 46.406)

Research Not Otherwise Approvable

HHS will conduct or fund research that the IRB does not believe meets the requirements of . . . [these regulations] only if:
(a) The IRB finds that the research presents a reasonable opportunity to further the understanding, prevention, or alleviation of a serious problem affecting the health or welfare of children; and
(b) The Secretary, after consultation with a panel of experts in pertinent disciplines (for example: science, medicine, education, ethics, law) and following opportunity for public review and comment, has determined either: (1) That the research in fact satisfies the conditions of . . . [these regulations] as applicable, or (2) the following: (i) The research presents a reasonable opportunity to further the understanding, prevention, or alleviation of a serious problem affecting the health or welfare of children; (ii) The research will be conducted in accordance with sound ethical principles; and (iii) Adequate provisions are made for soliciting the assent of children and the permission of their parents or guardians, as set forth in [these regulations]. (sec. 45 CFR 46.407)

Consent

(a) In addition to the determinations required under other applicable sections of this subpart, the IRB shall determine that adequate provisions are made for soliciting the assent of the children, when in the judgment of the IRB the children are capable of providing assent. In determining whether children are capable of assenting, the IRB shall take into account the ages, maturity, and psychological state of the children involved. This judgment may be made for all children to be involved in research under a particular protocol, or for each child, as the IRB deems appropriate. If the IRB determines that the capability of some or all of the children is so limited that they cannot reasonably be consulted or that the intervention or procedure involved in the research holds out a prospect of direct benefit that is important to the health or well-being of the children and is available only in the context of the research, the assent of the children is not a necessary condition for proceeding with the research. Even where the IRB determines that the subjects are capable of assenting, the IRB may still waive the assent requirement under circumstances. . . .
(b) In addition to the determinations required under other applicable sections of this subpart, the IRB shall determine . . . that adequate provisions are made for soliciting the permission of each child's parents or guardian. Where parental permission is to be obtained, the IRB may find that the permission of one parent is sufficient for research to be conducted. . . . Where research . . . permission is to be obtained from parents, both parents must give their permission unless one parent is deceased, unknown, incompetent, or not reasonably available, or when only one parent has legal responsibility for the care and custody of the child.
(c) In addition to the provisions for waiver contained in . . . [these regulations] if the IRB determines that a research protocol is designed for conditions or for a

subject population for which parental or guardian permission is not a reasonable requirement to protect the subjects (for example, neglected or abused children), it may waive the consent requirements... provided an appropriate mechanism for protecting the children who will participate as subjects in the research is substituted, and provided further that the waiver is not inconsistent with Federal, state or local law. The choice of an appropriate mechanism would depend upon the nature and purpose of the activities described in the protocol, the risk and anticipated benefit to the research subjects, and their age, maturity, status, and condition. (sec. 45 CFR 46.408)

Wards

(a) Children who are wards of the state or any other agency, institution, or entity can be included in research approved under . . . [these regulations] only if such research is:

(1) Related to their status as wards; or
(2) Conducted in schools, camps, hospitals, institutions, or similar settings in which the majority of children involved as subjects are not wards.

(b) If the research is approved... the IRB shall require appointment of an advocate for each child who is a ward, in addition to any other individual acting on behalf of the child as guardian or in loco parentis. One individual may serve as advocate for more than one child. The advocate shall be an individual who has the background and experience to act in, and agrees to act in, the best interests of the child for the duration of the child's participation in the research and who is not associated in any way (except in the role as advocate or member of the IRB) with the research, the investigator(s), or the guardian organization. (sec. 45 CFR 46.409)

Penalties for Noncompliance

(a) The department or agency head may require that department or agency support for any project be terminated or suspended in the manner prescribed in applicable program requirements, when the department or agency head finds an institution has materially failed to comply with the terms of this policy.
(b) In making decisions about supporting or approving applications or proposals covered by this policy the department or agency head may take into account, in addition to all other eligibility requirements and program criteria, factors such as whether the applicant has been subject to a termination or suspension under paragraph (a) of this section and whether the applicant or the person or persons who would direct or has/have directed the scientific and technical aspects of an activity has/have, in the judgment of the department or agency head, materially failed to discharge responsibility for the protection of the rights and welfare of human subjects (whether or not the research was subject to federal regulation). (sec. 45 CFR 46.123)

FRAUD AND MISCONDUCT

Two federal laws speak to the subject of fraud and misconduct in research: an HHS regulation that requires institutions to develop policies governing misconduct and a National Science Foundation rule governing science and engineering research. This is a fledgling area of regulation, so it is difficult to predict how strong these laws will be in practice. Investigators must be aware that these regulations exist and ask their IRB for their university's policy governing compliance with them.

PHS/HHS Fraud and Misconduct

This ... [regulation] applies to each entity which applies for a research, research-training, or research-related grant or cooperative agreement under the Public Health Service (PHS) Act. It requires each such entity to establish uniform policies and procedures for investigating and reporting instances of alleged or apparent misconduct involving research or research training, applications for support of research or research training, or related research activities that are supported with funds made available under the PHS Act. This subpart does not supersede and is not intended to set up an alternative to established procedures for resolving fiscal improprieties, issues concerning the ethical treatment of human or animal subjects, or criminal matters. (sec. 50.101)

Misconduct

"Misconduct" or "Misconduct in Science" means fabrication, falsification, plagiarism, or other practices that seriously deviate from those that are commonly accepted within the scientific community for proposing, conducting, or reporting research. It does not include honest error or honest differences in interpretations or judgments of data. (sec. 50.102.)

Institutional Compliance

Institutions shall foster a research environment that discourages misconduct in all research and that deals forthrightly with possible misconduct associated with research for which PHS funds have been provided or requested. An institution's failure to comply with its assurance and the requirements of this subpart may result in enforcement action against the institution, including loss of funding, and may lead to the OSI's conducting its own investigation. (sec. 50.105)

National Science Foundation Regulations

(a) "Misconduct" means (1) fabrication, falsification, plagiarism, or other serious deviation from accepted practices in proposing, carrying out, or reporting results from activities funded by NSF; or (2) retaliation of any kind against a person who reported or provided information about suspected or alleged misconduct and who has not acted in bad faith.

(b) The NSF will take appropriate action against individuals or institutions upon a determination that misconduct has occurred in proposing, carrying out, or reporting results from activities funded by NSF. It may also take interim action during an investigation. (sec. 689.1)

Final Actions

(a) Possible final actions listed below for guidance range from minimal restrictions (Group I) to the most severe and restrictive (Group III). They are not exhaustive and do not include possible criminal sanctions.

(1) Group I Actions.
  (i) Send a letter of reprimand to the individual or institution.
  (ii) Require as a condition of an award that for a specified period an individual, department, or institution obtain special prior approval of particular activities from NSF.

(iii) Require for a specified period that an institutional official other than those guilty of misconduct certify the accuracy of reports generated under an award or provide assurance of compliance with particular policies, regulations, guidelines, or special terms and conditions.
(2) Group II Actions.
  (i) Restrict for a specified period designated activities or expenditures under an active award.
  (ii) Require for a specified period special reviews of all requests for funding from an affected individual, department, or institution to ensure that steps have been taken to prevent repetition of the misconduct.
(3) Group III Actions.
  (i) Immediately suspend or terminate an active award.
  (ii) Debar or suspend an individual, department, or institution from participation in NSF programs for a specified period after further proceedings under applicable regulations.
  (iii) Prohibit participation of an individual as an NSF reviewer, advisor, or consultant for a specified period. (sec. 689.2)

COMMERCIAL AND SECURITY LAW VIOLATIONS

There has been an explosive growth of joint ventures between medical schools and private businesses since the early 1980s, ranging from multimillion-dollar contracts and department-wide cooperative research agreements to informal, short-term contracts with individual researchers. To the extent that these agreements support research with commercial value, they subject the researchers to scrutiny under both the securities laws and the other laws that govern the control of proprietary information—for example, insider trading, a crime that cheats the shareholders of a company of potential profits.

Material Nonpublic Information

The laws governing insider trading are based on the idea of *material nonpublic information:* any information that would influence an investor's decision to buy or sell securities. The most common example is information that would influence the price of stock in a publicly traded corporation, say, information that a drug company has developed a promising treatment for AIDS. This is material because of the tremendous potential profits to be made from an effective AIDS treatment. If an international drug firm develops a slightly improved wart remover, this would probably not be material information because it would add little to the company's profits. This information about the same wart remover, however, might be material information to a small drug manufacturer with only a few products.

Nonpublic information is information that is not available to members of the general investing public. It is illegal for company insiders with access to this material nonpublic information to use it to profit from the stock market. This insider trading encompasses directly profiting from stock trades, indirectly profiting through the trades of family, friends, or business associates, and intentionally giving the information to other persons, who then profit from the information.

For example, assume that a small, publicly traded biotech research company discovers a method that may lead to an AIDS vaccine. This is material information; it will affect the price of the company's stock when it becomes public. The company insiders cannot trade in the stock until the shareholders are made aware of the new material information. If the information is presented at a small scientific meeting, it would be in the public domain, but it would not be reasonably available to shareholders until it was reported in a widely circulated publication such as the *Wall Street Journal*. If the company is small and the information is less newsworthy than an AIDS treatment, the information may never be published nationally. The company may have to send a letter to all shareholders to ensure that they are aware of the material information.

Determining Who Is an Insider

Trading on material nonpublic information is illegal only if the trader is an insider or obtained the information from an insider who has breached a duty of confidentiality to the company. For example, assume that a general practitioner who has no involvement with any research, owns no stock, and is not a party to any drug company consulting agreements is seated next to the executives of a drug company in a crowded restaurant. The executives are loudly celebrating a new discovery, and the physician cannot help overhearing that at a press conference the next morning they will be announcing the discovery of a new antiulcer drug. The physician has no relationship with the company; he may legally trade on the information, calling a broker and purchasing the stock before the press conference.

Most physician-researchers realize that insider trading is illegal; they do not realize when they may become an insider for security law purposes, however. This is simple for employees; all employees are insiders concerning their employer's information. More problematic is the status of independent contract physicians who have a relationship with the company. The closer this tie is to the company, the greater is the probability that the physician is an insider. Clearly any physician party to a formal research agreement with a company is an insider for any information that would be material to the company. The more difficult question is how far this relationship extends: Does it include every physician in a medical school department that signed the agreement? Every physician in the medical school? Every physician in the university? The answers to these questions depend on the nature of the research agreement. If the agreement is limited to part of the time of one physician, it may not make other members of the department insiders. If is signed by the university and involves many physicians and several departments, it probably makes everyone at the university an insider.

Misappropriation of Information

The securities laws are limited in scope. There are more general commercial laws that prohibit the misappropriation of confidential information. These laws apply to employee physicians and others who have a relationship with the company. Physicians have the same duty to protect the company's information that they have to protect a patient's confidences. Improperly disclosing confidential information or using it for personal benefit is illegal, regardless of whether it violates the securities laws against the insider trading of stock. For example, a physician who has access to a proprietary cell culture formula through a confidential research agreement may not use that formula for research that does not benefit the company. A person who breaches the duty of confidentiality to a company can be sued by the company and prosecuted criminally for theft.

Avoiding Commercial Law Problems

All cooperative research agreements and contracts for specific research should discuss specifically the ownership of the research data and who controls the dissemination of the data. The university and the individual researchers should have the agreements independently reviewed by their own attorneys. Physicians who are involved with companies through contract research or other relationships must disclose these to their university. The university should notify all persons who may be insiders due to these agreements of potential limitations on their use of material nonpublic information.

More generally, physician-researchers should avoid owning or trading in the stock of companies for which they do research to obviate questions of insider trading. Any researcher who has a financial interest in the outcome of a research project risks being attacked for bias and misconduct. An honest mistake in the collection or interpretation of data can take on sinister overtones when the researcher owns stock in the affected company. Universities with substantial cooperative research agreements also should not hold stock in the companies sponsoring the research.

BIBLIOGRAPHY

Appelbaum PS; Roth LH; Lidz CW; Benson P; Winslade W: False hopes and best data: Consent to research and the therapeutic misconception. Hastings Cent Rep 1987 Apr; 17(2):20–24.

Baum M: The ethics of clinical trials and informed consent. Experientia Suppl 1982; 41:300–8.

Brahams D: Randomised trials and informed consent. Lancet 1988 Oct 29; 2(8618):1033–34.

Breuer A: Can a healthy subject volunteer to be injured in research? Hastings Cent Rep 1986 Aug; 16(4):31–33.

Eighteenth World Medical Assembly, Declaration of Helsinki: Recommendations Guiding Medical Doctors in Biomedical Research Involving Human Subjects, 271 N Engl. J Med (1964):473.

Fletcher JC; Ryan KJ: Federal regulations for fetal research: A case for reform. Law Med Health Care 1987 Fall; 15(3):126–38.

Furlow TG: Consent for minors to participate in nontherapeutic research. Leg Med 1980;261–73.

Gillon R: Medical treatment, medical research and informed consent. J Med Ethics 1989 Mar; 15(1):3–5, 11.

Helmchen H: Problems of informed consent for clinical trials in psychiatry. Controlled Clin Trials 1981 May; 1 (4):435–40.

Hillebrecht JM: Regulating the clinical uses of fetal tissue. A proposal for legislation. J Leg Med 1989 Jun; 10(2):269–322.

Jones J: *Bad Blood.* 1981.

Katz J: *Experimentation With Human Beings.* 1972.

Kolata GB: The death of a research subject. Hastings Cent Rep 1980 Aug; 10(4):5–6.

Leenen HJ: The legal status of the embryo in vivo and in vitro: Research on and the medical treatment of embryos. Law Med Health Care 1986 Sep; 14 (3–4):129–32.

McKinlay JB: From "promising report" to "standard procedure": Seven stages in the career of a medical innovation. Milbank Mem Fund Q Health Soc 1981 Summer; 59(3):374–411.

Murray JC; Pagon RA: Informed consent for research publication of patient-related data. Clin Res 1984 Oct; 32(4):404–8.

Nuremberg Code, Trials of War Criminals before the Nuremberg Tribunals under Control Council Law No. 10. Reprinted in Levine R: *Ethics and Regulation of Clinical Research.* 1981.

Parker PM: Recognizing property interests in bodily tissues. A need for legislative guidance. J Leg Med 1989 Jun; 10(2):357–75.

Richards EP: Insider trading in research agreements, preventive law approach is required. Prev L Rptr 1990; (1):28.

Richards EP; Walter CW: Scientific misconduct: Part 2—What are your constitutional rights? IEEE Engin Med Biol 1992; 11(1):73–74.

Richards EP; Walter CW: Scientific misconduct: Part 1—The federal rules. IEEE Eng Med Biol 1991; 10(4):69–71.

Rothman DJ: Were Tuskegee and Willowbrook "studies in nature"? Hastings Cent Rep 1982 Apr; 12(2):5–7.

Taylor KM; Shapiro M; Soskolne CL; Margolese RG: Physician response to informed consent regulations for randomized clinical trials. Cancer 1987 Sep 15; 60(6):1415–22.

Walter CW; Richards EP: Employment obligations part I: Duties of an employee to his employer. IEEE Eng Med Biol 1990; 9(2):72–73.

Walter CW; Richards EP: Employment obligations part II: Duties of an ex-employee. IEEE Eng Med Biol 1990; 9(3):72–73.

Walter CW; Richards EP: Employment obligations part IV: University facultes and expert consultants. IEEE Eng Med Biol 1991; 10(1):95–97.

Walter CW; Richards EP: Employment obligations part III: Who is an independent contractor? IEEE Eng Med Biol 1990; 9(4):48–50.

World Medical Association: Declaration of Geneva: World Med Assn Bull 1949 Jul 3; 1:109.

III Physicians and Other Medical Personnel

15

Delegation of Authority

CRITICAL POINTS
- State and federal laws govern the delegation of authority to nonphysicians.
- Improper delegation of authority can result in civil and criminal liability.
- Proper protocols are critical to effective quality assurance.
- Protocols can reduce the overall paperwork burden in routine office practice.

This chapter examines the relationship between physicians and nonphysician health care providers. Whether in solo practice in a small town or as a member of a large multispecialty health care delivery team, all physicians delegate certain professional duties to physician extenders (PEs). (This term is used to denote physician's assistants, nurse-practitioners, child health associates, public health nurses, and other personnel when they are engaged in medical practice under the authority of a physician.) Physicians must recognize when they have implicitly delegated duties for which they retain legal responsibility. When PEs injure patients because they have been delegated tasks beyond their abilities, the rules of vicarious liability attribute their negligence to the supervising physician.

LEGAL AND ETHICAL ISSUES

State and federal laws governing the delegation of authority to nonphysician personnel are much more restrictive than medical practice would indicate. These laws include medical practice acts, state and federal controlled substances laws, administrative rules governing protocol-oriented quality assurance activities, and laws and regulations limiting physician reimbursement for work performed by nonphysician personnel. Physician extenders resist these rules because their training creates the expectation that they will be able to operate as autonomous professionals. Physicians tend to overdelegate authority because it allows them to have more patients go through offices. However, this natural reaction to the pressure to deliver cost-effective medical care can compromise the quality of medical care if the PEs are not carefully managed through direct supervision and formal protocols.

The most probable consequence of improperly delegating authority to nonphysician personnel is a medical malpractice lawsuit. The general legal rule is that a physician may delegate authority but not responsibility to nonphysician personnel. Physicians always remain legally liable for the actions of personnel under their control. (See the section on employment in Chapter 6.) This keeps the insurance rates for nonphysician personnel artificially low, masking the real risks of improper delegation.

Improper delegation of authority is grounds for limiting or terminating a physician's license, although very few boards of medical examiners enforce the rules against improper delegation of authority or unauthorized practice of medicine by nonphysician personnel. This is expected to change as the federal government pressures the states to improve the regulation of medical practice. The most likely enforcement action will come from the state board of pharmacy, the federal Drug Enforcement Administration, or the Health Care Financing Administration. These agencies can recommend that action be taken against the physician's license, but they are more likely to bring a civil or criminal prosecution against the physician.

Aggressive delegation of authority is a symptom of deeper philosophical problems in medical care delivery. Some groups oppose physician-dominated medical care in favor of quasi-scientific schools of natural healing. Some PEs strive for greater autonomy, reflecting expectations garnered in training programs. Employers and others seeking to lower the cost of medical care assume that using PEs more will be cheaper than relying on physicians. Most sympathetically, advocates of reducing restrictions on delegation of authority point to the potential benefit to rural communities.

There is little evidence that the extensive use of autonomous PEs (as opposed to supervised PEs working off proper protocols) reduces the cost or increases the availability of medical care. In most practices, PEs are used to allow physicians to spend more time on costly procedures and less on routine, inexpensive patient evaluation. The systems that have the most difficulty in supervising PEs are those that use several PEs to each physician in one office. These are nearly always urban or suburban practices. Rural practices cannot generate the patient flow to support practices with several PEs per physician.

MEDICAL JUDGMENT

The right to exercise independent medical judgment separates physicians from nonphysician personnel. This is a statutory distinction; the right to practice medicine is defined and granted by the state government. That is, the state may restrict acts of medical practice to physicians, allow them to be performed by other medical personnel, or forbid anyone to perform certain of them. States follow a common path and define medical practice functionally. Physicians are defined according to what they are given the exclusive right to do—for example, performing a procedure, writing a prescription, or making a diagnosis. A functional definition, however, does not define the practice of medicine sufficiently clearly to establish which acts can be delegated and which cannot.

In medicine, independently observable phenomena are called signs, as distinguished from symptoms, which are reported by the patient. Much of medicine is practiced on the assumption that these objective phenomena can be categorized and measured as accurately by nonphysician personnel as by physicians. This is certainly true of phenomena such as blood pressure and temperature, which can be measured and recorded unambiguously by nonphysician, or even lay, personnel. But if the phenomena being observed are not easily quantified, the training and biases of the observer begin to affect the consistency of the observations. Medicine contributes further to this ambiguity by using terms of diagnosis interchangeably with terms of description. For example, hypertension is both a disease process and the state of having a higher than normal blood pressure.

Making observations often involves the exercise of medical judgment. When a medical care provider examines a patient's throat, the provider must decide whether the throat displays objective signs of illness. This is simple in extreme cases of raging tonsillitis, but in more ambiguous cases, the provider must exercise judgment to decide whether the patient's throat should be recorded as normal or diseased. These expert observations blur the distinction between objective information and medical decision making. Physicians may delegate the task of making expert observations to nonphysician personnel, but the delegating physician retains responsibility for the accuracy of the observations. Physicians should not delegate diagnostic or therapeutic decisions that require analysis beyond the application of the rules in a strict protocol.

LIMITATIONS ON DELEGATION OF AUTHORITY

A physician's right to delegate authority is governed by both statutory and contractual limitations. Failure to comply with these limitations can subject the physician to civil liability and, for drug law violations, loss of licensure and criminal prosecution. Physicians must be personally familiar with the terms of these statutes; they cannot rely on nursing personnel or clinic administrators to ensure that their practice complies with the law.

Every state has a medical practice act and a board of medical examiners. These set the requirements for obtaining a license to practice medicine in the state, oversee the processes of licensure, and provide for the revocation of licenses or for disciplinary action against those who are accused of violating the terms of licensure. All physicians should read the medical practice act for the states in which they hold licenses. Those who supervise PEs should read the specific provisions of the medical practice act that govern such supervision.

Copies of a state's medical practice act can be obtained from the state's board of medical examiners. Physicians should ask for all applicable administrative regulations as well. These regulations are enacted by the board rather than the state legislature but nevertheless have the force of law. Physicians should make sure that the law and regulations are still in force as written. Changes in the law or regulations can take months or years to appear in the written materials provided by the regulatory agency.

Most medical practice acts are understandable to physicians who read them carefully. They do not need to consult a lawyer on the intent of the regulations. Moreover, most attorneys, including those who practice health care corporate law or medical malpractice defense, are unfamiliar with the laws and regulations that govern medical practice in private physicians' offices. If sections of the law are unclear or seem contrary to common practice, an official of the medical board or an attorney who is knowledgeable in medical practice regulations can be consulted.

Nursing Practice

Nursing is a licensed profession with the same types of laws, licenses, and regulations as the medical profession. Physicians who supervise nurses directly or who authorize nurse practice should be familiar with the state's nursing practice act and its attendant regulations. Beyond the personal risks of improperly delegating authority to nurses, a physician who does not comply with the state's nursing laws will endanger the licenses of the nursing staff. Unlike boards of medical examiners, boards of nursing examiners have enforced rules against the unauthorized practice of medicine.

All nurses providing medical care must do so on either the independent authority of a nursing license or on the delegated authority of a properly licensed physician. All parties to the care—the nurse, the patient, and the physician—must understand and agree on who is responsible for what. If a physician writes an order for, say, 250 mg of amoxicillin by mouth three times a day, the nurse administers the medicine on the authority of the physician. The nurse has an independent responsibility to ensure that the drug, the dose, and the schedule for administration are consistent with established nursing practice.

When nurses are working from standing orders or protocols, their authority is derived from the physician's authority, but the lines of responsibility are less obvious. Intensive care nurses may be authorized to look at a cardiac monitor and to give a bolus of lidocaine when the monitor shows premature ventricular contractions. The nurses may not realize that they are not doing this on their own judgment or responsibility. The protocols are authorized by the physician in charge of the intensive care unit. If no physician has authorized the protocols, the nurse is practicing medicine without a license.

Nursing training recognizes many different specialties and practice styles. Some states recognize these additional certifications beyond the basic registered nurse license, but many do not. Nurses and physicians should know the laws of their state concerning specialty nursing. A nurse midwife or a board-certified nurse-practitioner may be able to get a license that permits a more advanced level of care than is permitted for a simple registered nurse. It is important to know, however, that the board of nursing examiners may recognize nurse specialists without the state law's granting them any extraordinary privileges over other registered nurses. A nurse-practitioner may simply be recognized as one of a class of nurses who are skilled at working independently under protocol. Physicians cannot assume that specially certified nurses may be delegated more responsibility than other registered nurses.

Nurse-practitioners may have unrealistic expectations, fostered by their academic training programs, about independent practice. They may have been taught to diagnose many common ailments without realizing that making these diagnoses is likely to be outside the scope of practice allowed to nurses. The shelves of the medical bookstores are filled with books of nurse-practitioner protocols with differential diagnoses. These are teaching protocols, however; they are not suitable for delegation of authority for medical practice from a physician to a nurse.

Contractual Limitations

Medical care providers such as hospitals and managed care plans may never authorize the delegation of more authority than is permitted by state law, but they may impose limitations on the delegation of authority that are more restrictive than the state laws. These limitations are generally covered in the employee policies and procedures and the medical staff rules. Typically nurses and technicians may accept orders only from physician members of the medical staff. Those in the employ of a physician may work in the hospital only after an independent review of credentials and with a specific scope of practice. The penalty for violating these policies is loss of the job for those who are hospital employees or loss of staff privileges for the physicians. These policies also may be admissible in a medical malpractice lawsuit as evidence of the proper standard of care.

Drug Laws
Drug law violations account for most instances in which physicians lose their medical licenses or go to jail. Drug law enforcement against physicians is often done by the same agents who pursue drug dealers. These agents do not show the same deference to physicians as do boards of medical examiners' investigators.

Drugs are a particularly touchy area for nonphysician practice. The states vary widely in the laws governing prescribing and dispensing drugs; some allow limited prescribing by nurse-practitioners or physician's assistants, but most do not. Some laws are inconsistent, perhaps allowing prescribing or dispensing by individuals who are prohibited from this by the medical or nursing practice act. As a rule, a physician should not allow a PE to write prescriptions and should not allow dispensing except under strict protocol.

Office dispensing has been casual in the past, but heightened awareness of the role of prescription drugs in drug addiction is causing states and the federal government to tighten drug laws and their enforcement. For example, the federal regulations on distributing drug samples are much more restrictive than in the past. A physician's signature and Drug Enforcement Administration (DEA) number are required before the drug company representative may leave samples of prescription drugs. These samples must be kept secure and dispensed in the same manner as other prescription drugs. Some states require samples to be dispensed personally by physicians.

Physicians should contact their state board of pharmacy and local office of the DEA to obtain a copy of the restrictions on prescribing drugs. If a clinic or physician group plans to buy drugs in bulk and package them for dispensing, it should inquire about a pharmacy or dispensing license and a federal repackaging permit. Most states allow physicians to dispense drugs if they bottle and label the pills personally and give them to the patient directly, but the states are increasing the physician's record-keeping requirements.

Faith Healers
Some states specifically exempt faith healers from the legal restrictions on medical practice. All states must recognize the right of a consenting adult to follow personal religious beliefs in making choices about health care. This does not mean that a physician must participate in medically questionable care. It is unwise for physicians to work with faith healers in the care of a patient in the way that they would work with a nurse or a psychologist. The fundamental theories of treatment are not compatible. Legally physicians are held to the general standards of care for allopathic or osteopathic medicine, not to the standards of the religion.

This does not mean that physicians may not tailor medical care to meet the needs of patients with specific religious beliefs. Concerned physicians have become specialists in providing surgical care for Jehovah's Witnesses and family planning for Roman Catholic couples. Many hospitals have chaplaincy programs that minister to the spiritual needs of patients during the stressful times of birth, illness, and death. The physician must avoid becoming the religious adviser rather than the medical care provider. A Roman Catholic physician who is asked about the advisability of oral contraceptives should discuss the medical risks and benefits, not the religious implications. A physician who is asked to participate in a prayer session for faith healing should decline.

DELEGATION OF AUTHORITY

There are three issues to consider when delegating authority: (1) the legality of the delegation, (2) the proper method of delegation, and (3) the physician's oversight responsibilities for the delegated duties. These issues must be considered within the context of the three classes of medical tasks.

The first class is tasks that are freely assignable; they are not unique to medical care delivery and do not require the exercise of professional judgment. They include billing and patient accounts, maintaining simple medical equipment, and other nonpatient care activities that accompany the practice of medicine. The supervising physician must ensure that the activities meet the necessary legal standards for protecting patient confidentiality and any other statutory requirements.

The tasks in the second class are those that may be assigned to a limited class of persons. These tasks such as nursing activities and laboratory analyses, require professional skills and judgment. They also may include activities that require physician supervision, such as taking clinical information from patients.

Activities in the third class of medical tasks are reserved solely to physicians; delegation may violate criminal laws against aiding in the unauthorized practice of medicine. These activities include performing surgery, directly supervising nonphysician personnel in physician-only activities, and writing prescriptions for controlled substances. State law and tradition determine which specific activities cannot be delegated, but generally nonassignable tasks involve the exercise of independent medical judgment.

Explicit Delegation of Authority

Explicit delegation of medical authority occurs when a physician uses protocols to authorize nonphysician personnel to render medical care directly to patients. The physician is allowing the PE to practice medicine by following written protocols that allow the extender to determine the physician's judgment in the specific limited situation. This works well if both physicians and extenders understand that all medical judgments must be made by physicians. Under the law in most states, PEs may not substitute their personal judgment in any decision that requires medical judgment. Even if a state allows PEs to practice independently, any physician nominally directing their actions will be legally liable for their malpractice if it involves an error in medical judgment.

Implicit Delegation of Authority

Implicit delegation of authority occurs when the physician allows nonphysician personnel to act on their own initiative, by carrying out medical tasks without strict protocols. This is not a problem if these personnel are under the direct supervision of the physician, as a nonphysician surgical assistant is. Physicians are legally responsible for the actions of these personnel, but they also can recognize and correct any improper actions.

Problems arise in two situations: when nonphysician personnel initiate care outside the physician's direct supervision and when the physician allows these personnel to perform tasks that the physician is not competent to perform. The physician remains legally responsible but can no longer prevent improper actions. The classic example of this type of implicit delegation of authority was the medical equipment sales representative showing the surgeon how to place a hip prosthesis. The salesman scrubbed and participated in the operation, to the point of placing the prosthesis. There was much consternation about a sales-representative in the operating room, but this was no more legally significant than the use of a nonlicensed surgical assistant. The physician could not supervise the sales representative's actions because the physician did not know how to do the procedure. Despite the proximity of the physician, knowledgeable supervision was impossible.

Triage by the front desk clerk is a common and legally dangerous form of implied delegation of authority, particularly in large group practices and clinics. In this situation, the physician implicitly authorizes the appointments clerk to determine whether a patient needs follow-up care. Certainly this is not the physician's intent, but it happens when the office manager or clerk is permitted to deny appointments to patients who are behind in paying their bills or when there are no provisions for evaluating patients who may need to be seen more quickly than the physician's appointment calendar allows.

If the front office tells patients that they will not be seen until they pay their bills, this is implicitly determining that the patient does not need the return appointment. If, as frequently happens, the patient does not return for care, the physician will be liable for any consequences that flow from the denial of care. This is also the case when the patient is made to wait more than the medically acceptable time for a follow-up appointment. If the obstetrician tells a patient to come back in three days for a preoperative visit because it is time to put a stitch in her incompetent cervix, the appointment clerk must not schedule her for an appointment in three weeks. The obstetrician would be liable if the patient lost the baby during this delay. Physicians must ensure that a patient's medical condition is considered when appointments are being scheduled. They should always be consulted before a patient is denied a timely appointment.

Physicians sometimes implicitly delegate the evaluation of medical test results to their filing clerk. This happens when the office charting system is not set up to ensure that every test result is reported to the physician. From both a legal and a medical standpoint, a test should not have been ordered if the results do not warrant evaluation. Deciding that a report is normal for a patient is a medical judgment. A physician may reasonably delegate many of these evaluations to laboratory or nursing staff—the gynecologist does not need to see every normal Pap smear report that comes back—but there should be a formal system for checking in the reports, and it should be explicit about what can be filed and what must be evaluated by the physician. If a laboratory report did not come back at all, it needs to be located or the test repeated.

Physicians do not need to review every piece of paper that comes to the office. Consequently the nonphysician personnel must have specific written orders or protocols for handling reports and for finding lost reports. The receptionist must have a tracking system that identifies and locates patients who miss appointments or fail to make return appointments the physician has recommended. For example, if a report comes back with a notation that the patient has trichomonas, some action should be taken. Nurses in the office might have a protocol that allows them to arrange treatment and a follow-up visit, or the secretary might have instructions to pull the chart and leave it with the report on the physician's desk.

Physicians sometimes delegate authority by allowing others to practice medicine at times when it is inconvenient for them to attend to the patient. A common complaint of nurse-anesthetists is that they are competent only at night: they are allowed to do cases at 3:00 A.M. that are beyond their expertise at 10:00 A.M. This is legally and medically indefensible. The determination of whether a task may be done by a nonphysician cannot depend on when the task must be performed. If the time of day matters at all, it mitigates against delegation of authority at night when physician backup is not readily available.

PHYSICIAN'S ORDERS

The most common way of delegating authority is to write an order in a hospital chart or otherwise formally record orders for PEs. The physician may write the order in person, or a nurse may enter it in the chart at the physician's direction. Formal orders are valuable for clarifying the delegation of authority in that setting though they are less commonly used in private offices.

Standing orders, which include protocols, are a special case of written physician's orders. A *standing order* is an order conditioned upon the occurrence of certain clinical events. The important characteristic of a standing order is that all the patients who meet the criteria for the order receive the same treatment. A common use of standing orders is in public health clinics that treat specific diseases. A venereal disease control program will use the Centers for Disease Control (CDC) protocols for antibiotic dosages. Once the specific venereal disease is identified, the nurse administers the antibiotics as specified by the CDC protocol and authorized by the physician directing the clinic. In this situation, the CDC protocol is a standing order from the medical director, and the conditional event is the diagnosis of a specific venereal disease.

It is important to differentiate standing orders from *preprinted orders:* orders that the physician uses repeatedly and has photocopied to save the trouble and potential errors of rewriting each time they are used. Although the orders are the same for all patients, they are not standing orders because they are not conditional. The physician, not the nurse, determines whether the printed orders will be used in a given case. Unlike a standing order, until the physician incorporates the printed order into the chart, the nurse cannot initiate treatment. Preprinted orders are a useful tool, but they can lead to problems if a patient requires a variation in the usual printed order. These variations must be carefully marked on the orders and the nursing staff notified.

Direct orders are voice orders that are given directly to nonphysician personnel. Sometimes these orders are documented in the medical records, but usually they are carried out at once and not recorded. For example, when a surgeon directs the operating room nurse assisting in a procedure, some of the surgeon's orders will be documented, but most will not. Documenting the individual orders is not a problem in this situation because the physician is directly supervising the nurse's work. The satisfactory completion of the nurse's work will be documented as part of the operative report.

In office practice, neither the voice orders nor their satisfactory completion will necessarily be documented in the patient's chart. This makes it difficult to determine whether the physician has given a direct order, or the nonphysician personnel are acting out of routine. Unless these routine actions are carried out according to a strict protocol, the physician will not be able to ensure that the proper nursing functions have been carried out. If the physician is sued over a question about the nurse's actions, there will be no record to establish what was done to the patient.

PROTOCOLS

The term *protocol* is widely used in health care to refer to a variety of documents. We use protocol to refer to written guidelines directing the practice of nurses and other PEs. These protocols are not intended to be clinical algorithms; unlike clinical algorithms, which are intended to assist medical decision making, protocols are intended to circumscribe clinical decision making (Hadorn DC, McCormick K, and Diokno A 1992).

Few medical offices use the detailed, deterministic protocols described in this chapter. Such protocols require substantial effort to compile and tailor to the needs of an individual physician's office. In the long term, however, they become time-effective by rationalizing quality assurance efforts and the analysis of work flow in the office. More important, systematically using structured protocols reduces the burden of routine documentation of patient encounters. If an office relies on standard protocols to determine the diagnosis and treatment of common conditions, these protocols become generic documentation for those conditions. As long as the physician can convince a court that the protocols are enforced, the protocol becomes evidence of a pattern of behavior. In this case, the burden of proof is shifted to the plaintiff, who seeks to dispute that the protocol was not followed. If the office does not rigorously enforce the use of protocols, each patient encounter must be fully documented. In effect, the core of what would be the protocol must be written as a chart entry every time the condition is treated. Failing in this repetitive documentation shifts the burden of proving what care was rendered to the physician.

Physician Protocols

Many group practice organizations use physician protocols to standardize medical practice within the group. The goal may be to improve consistency of care when a patient is likely to be seen by different doctors, to limit the number of drugs in the formulary, or to ensure that the physicians are following recognized standards, such as CDC protocols, in their practices. Physician protocols do not place legal limitations on the physicians; they are characterized by their allowance for independent medical judgment. They are a voluntary agreement by the physicians to follow certain patterns when practicing within the group.

A common example is a protocol for treating an HMO patient for essential hypertension. Typically this protocol would not include a definition of essential hypertension; every treating physician would be expected to be able to make the diagnosis. The protocol would contain a list of the diagnostic procedures to be done on a new patient. These might be arrived at by consensus after an analysis of the costs and benefits of each test. Every patient might have a blood count but only those over age 40 years would have an electrocardiogram. The protocol would then list the drugs to be prescribed for certain types of patients. A beta-blocker might be first choice, with an alpha-blocker substituted if the patient does not respond well or is over 60 years old. The drugs on the list also would be in the formulary.

The physician protocol guides rather than dictates patient care. If a physician wants to use a different drug from the established standard, the reasons for deviation should be documented, but the physician is legally free to make the change. In contrast, a PE would not be allowed to use such a protocol becasue it leaves the diagnosis open and allows choice in the use of medicines, both of which require exercising medical judgment.

Teaching Protocols

Teaching protocols also called teaching algorithms, fall somewhere between strict protocols and physician protocols; they guide students through the exercise of professional judgment. Teaching protocols thus fill the dual purpose of providing consistency of care and allowing students to learn how to make good judgments.

The hallmark of a teaching protocol is a differential diagnosis list, which is generally unnecessary in a physician protocol and not proper in a protocol intended for PEs. The classic example of a group of teaching protocols is the *Washington Manual of Medical Therapeutics,* often called the "intern's brain." The entries in this manual include a general definition of the condition and a list of other possible causes of the patient's problems. It then explains how to treat the patient, with reasons for some of the recommendations. Medical students use this source to learn about basic treatments. Residents use it as a treatment guide and for help in solving unfamiliar problems. Established physicians consult it when caring for patients with a problem they have not treated recently or for which treatment standards have changed. Each would learn from the protocols and use them according to their level of training and licensure.

PE Protocols: Strict Protocols

Protocols that are used to allow nonphysicians to do tasks that are generally reserved for licensed physicians must be much more rigid and specific than physician protocols or teaching protocols. No judgment or discretion is allowed to the PE; the judgment remains with the physician who authorized the protocols. The extender must follow the protocol to the letter, without deviation or the exercise of independent judgment. If state law allows PEs to practice medicine without supervision, strict protocols are not necessary, but even in such a state, strict protocols are desirable for risk management, quality assurance, and compliance with federal laws.

Sample Protocol

This section works through a sample protocol for strep throat to aid readers in understanding how to produce and use legal strict protocols for PEs. In some states it may not be necessary for extenders to act under strict protocol. Nevertheless, in any jurisdiction, physicians should use caution in authorizing practice by nonphysicians without strict protocols.

Diagnostic Criteria
This section defines the condition that triggers the use of the particular protocol. There may be more than one set of criteria that trigger the same protocol. The criteria will be very specific. A differential diagnosis has no place in a strict protocol.

Diagnostic Criteria for Strep Throat

1. Positive strep culture or rapid strep test on pharyngeal swab.
2. Sore throat or cervical adenopathy in a household or day care contact to a laboratory-confirmed case of strep throat.
3. Asymptomatic member of a household with two or more laboratory-confirmed cases of strep throat.
4. Established patient with two or more laboratory-confirmed episodes of strep throat who now has symptoms that are typical for strep in this patient.
5. Any sore throat in a patient with a history of rheumatic fever.

This list gives five circumstances that trigger the protocol and allow the PE to treat the patient for strep throat. The criteria take into account medical history, physical examination, patient complaints, laboratory tests, and living situation. The PE may do the entire history, examination, and laboratory tests but is not called upon to judge what constitutes the need for treatment of strep throat. This diagnostic judgment is made by the physician in authorizing the protocol. A nurse who treated a patient for strep throat because he or she thought the throat was so red that it could not be anything else would be acting outside the protocol.

Examination/Laboratory
This section of the protocol specifies the extent of the examination and testing to be done to stay within the scope of the protocol. This should include everything necessary to establish that diagnostic criteria have been met and everything that might require consultation or referral.

Examination/Laboratory

1. Examine throat, ears, neck, and chest in all patients.
2. Obtain a pharyngeal swab for strep testing on one family member at a time until two family members have positive tests.

The extent of examination required does not have to be this specific. The physician and the PE may have decided on the type of examination that is appropriate in a particular type of case. Nevertheless, the PE must take a history and do a physical examination extensive enough to gather the information required to meet the diagnostic criteria or the criteria for referral. In our example, the history must include household and day care information, and the physical must include examination of the throat and cervical lymph nodes and listening for a heart murmur.

Treatment
It is critical for legal protection and for quality of patient care that this section of the protocol be clear and specific. There may not be a selection of therapies. It

should be clear from the specifics of the particular patient what course of therapy should be followed.

Treatment
1. Rest, humidity, acetaminophen for fever and body aches.
2. Antibiotics
    a. penicillin V potassium 250 mg q.i.d. in adults, 30 mg/kg per day in 4 divided doses for children
    b. If the patient has red TMs or pustular tonsils, give amoxicillin 250 mg t.i.d. in adults and children over 45 lb, 125 mg t.i.d. in children over 15 lb.
    c. If the patient is allergic to penicillin, give erythromycin estolate 250 mg q.i.d. for adults, 30 mg/kg per day in 4 divided doses for children.
    d. If the patient is intolerant of both penicillin and erythromycin, consult the physician.

Following this treatment protocol requires reasonable skill by the PE in determining the correct medicine and calculating doses. It does not, however, allow any exercise of judgment as to which drug to use. That is defined by the characteristics of the patient.

Follow-up
When PEs are working from protocols, it is particularly important that patients be given specific instructions about when to be rechecked. There is too much delegated medical judgment involved to assume that the patient has received all the necessary and appropriate care.

Follow-up
1. Return to the clinic if not improved in three days or if fever continues this long.
2. Return to the clinic in two weeks for recheck.
3. Return to the clinic immediately or go to the emergency room if you develop respiratory distress, rash, or fever greater than 102°F.

Referral
Inherent in the practice of protocol medicine is the need for physician backup when the problem falls outside the scope of the protocol or the particular practice. A family physician may make a practice of referring all patients with cardiac arrhythmias to a cardiologist. This is not a legal requirement; it is just good sense. A nurse-practitioner who is working off protocols must refer patients who have problems beyond the scope of the protocols or the practice. The inclusion in the protocol of specific reasons for referring allows the physician to highlight conditions that are of particular concern. The protocol also may branch to other protocols if indicated.

Refer
1. Refer to the physician all patients with a rash, a heart murmur, or who appear toxic.
2. Consult the physician on all patients who cannot take penicillin or erythromycin.
3. Consult the physician on all patients under 6 months of age.

4. Refer to the emergency room by EMS all patients with respiratory distress or stridor. DO NOT EXAMINE.
5. Refer to the "Otitis Media" protocol all cases that involve concurrent ear infection.

Epidemiology

Any disease that is reportable or that involves the treatment of exposed individuals should have these requirements included in the protocol. This is as much a part of the treatment as doing laboratory tests or dispensing medicine.

Epidemiology
1. Strep infections are reportable weekly, by numerical totals only, to the health department at 555-1234.
2. Household members should be screened for all patients with more than one strep throat in two months.

Notes

This is the part of the strict protocol that should be used for all the educational information. It might include a differential diagnosis of the condition or the reasons for some of the choices made in establishing the protocol. This section also might contain prescribing information for the convenience of the physician. It should be clear to all parties involved that this section does not authorize any actions by the PE.

Notes
1. There are no clinical signs or symptoms that differentiate strep throat from viral pharyngitis.
2. Sensitivities are not necessary since community-acquired strep is uniformly sensitive to all the penicillins.
3. Strep is not generally susceptible to sulfas.
4. The rapid strep now used by our lab is 85 percent sensitive.

SUPERVISING PEs

Physicians who employ PEs should be very careful in their supervision. A physician should never accept responsibility for a PE without having the authority to supervise or decline to practice with the person. The physician is liable for negligent medical care rendered by PEs. The physician is also liable for nonmedical actions by the extender, such as sexual assault, if the physician is negligent in screening or supervising the extender.

The first step in selecting or accepting supervision of a PE is to check the person's credentials personally and carefully. The extender's license status must be checked in every applicable state, not just the state where he or she will work. The physician should find out the specifics of the PE's training and previous experience to gauge skill levels. Finally, the physician should talk to other physicians who have worked with this extender, asking specifically about the extender's willingness to accept physician authority, clinical skills, and readiness to ask for consultation from the physician. A PE who worked well with a physician who checks every patient and chart entry may not be compatible with a physician who prefers to delegate by written protocols.

The physician should observe a newly hired PE in providing patient care and repeating the physical assessment. It is not possible to know if the extender recognizes a bulging eardrum until the physician has reevaluated both negative and positive findings by the extender. This also gives the extender the opportunity to learn the physician's preferences and practice habits.

Scope of Practice

Every PE should have a written scope of practice that specifically states what the extender may do on his or her own initiative, what requires protocol authorization, and what must be referred to the physician. It should include specific instructions for handling emergencies and urgent situations when the physician is unavailable. It should specify types of patients that the extender should or should not accept for care. If the extender is a licensed nurse, the scope of practice should delineate which activities are nursing and which are delegated medical care. Like protocols, this scope of practice should be agreed upon and signed by both the physician and the extender. The scope of practice should explicitly deal with both nursing diagnoses and what constitutes unauthorized practice of medicine.

Unreasonable Expectations

If a nurse wants to provide primary health care under the strict supervision of a physician without making independent judgments, becoming a nurse-practitioner is a good career. If the nurse wants to provide primary health care without having to follow every physician instruction to the letter, the appropriate course is to go to medical school. Nurses who are unwilling to accept restrictions on their practice prerogatives can compromise patient care and create substantial legal liability for themselves and physicians.

Nursing Diagnosis

Nursing diagnosis is a term that has come into use in recent years through nursing education. It has physicians confused and some health care attorneys concerned. For the most part, making a diagnosis is an act of medical judgment that may be done only by a licensed physician. From the risk management standpoint, it may be wise not to use the term. There are some types of diagnosis that a nurse may do independently—for example, wound care. A nurse does not need the authorization of a physician to diagnose a superficial abrasion of the knee. The nurse is doing the same thing a physician would be doing, and it is not necessary to qualify the term as a nursing diagnosis.

The term and the concept of nursing diagnosis have no place in an outpatient medical record. Typically, chart entries are made by physicians and nurses in the same set of progress notes. Any use of the term *diagnosis* will be perceived as a true diagnosis in the medical sense. A nurse making a diagnosis must be working under strict protocol or direct supervision of a physician. Any other diagnosis made by a nurse constitutes the unauthorized practice of medicine.

The term *nursing diagnosis* is often used as the title of a nursing care plan. This is confusing but legally acceptable if the nurse is not making a diagnosis or ordering care. Problems arise when the nurse fails to understand the difference and writes a medical diagnosis on a patient. As an example, a patient admitted to a hospital with a physician's diagnosis of congestive heart failure might have a nursing diagnosis of "complete bed rest for congestive heart failure." This compliments the physician's diagnosis and order for bed rest and does not lead to confusion.

If the physician has admitted the patient with a diagnosis of "rule out congestive heart failure, rule out renal failure," and the nursing diagnosis is "complete bed rest for congestive heart failure," then the nursing diagnosis can be revised in response to the change in the medical diagnosis. If, however, the nursing diagnosis is recorded as "congestive heart failure," the nursing notes and the physician's problem sheet are in conflict, and the patient's care may suffer. Other physicians and nurses caring for the patient will be treating the patient for the wrong problem if they rely on the nursing diagnosis.

Documentation

Careful documentation is particularly important when PEs are practicing medicine under supervision, but it is not necessary or desirable to document every positive and negative physical finding. Such charts will be hard to read and are unlikely to be reviewed completely by the supervising physician. The important items to document are the subjective and objective findings that support the diagnosis under the protocol, the decision-specific assessment, and the treatment and instructions authorized under the protocol. Using the example of strep throat, an adequate visit entry might read as follows:

S: sore throat × 3 days
O: TMs clear, chest clear, throat red, no adenopathy
rapid strep +
A: strep pharyngitis
P: Penicillin V K 250 mg q.i.d. × 10—dispensed
Tylenol, rest, liquids
RTC 2 weeks for recheck, sooner if problems

This chart entry, made in a timely fashion and legibly, provides all the necessary documentation for this encounter. It documents the trigger for the protocol and that the protocol was followed in testing, treatment, and follow-up. The protocol itself will provide the additional information to flesh out the chart note.

Quality Assurance

Quality assurance is as important in the private office as in large health care institutions. In hospitals or HMOs, there are many people who may observe the medical practitioner. In small offices, if the physician is not checking on the people he or she supervises, dangerous deficiencies may go unnoticed. The simplest form of quality assurance for PEs is to have the physician read and sign every chart. This will allow correction of errors and ongoing education of the nurse or physician's assistant.

There also should be a formal quality assurance program, usually a chart audit. Sample charts should be reviewed for every provider and for a range of patient problems. Each case should be evaluated to see if the protocols were followed and if the care was documented properly. General considerations, such as whether the entries were made at the time the care was rendered and whether they can be read by the other providers, should be included in the audit. At intervals, the actual care rendered should be checked. The chart entry may be perfect yet bear no relationship to the patient's actual condition.

Every quality assurance program should have a system for correcting all identified deficiencies. It must have provisions for changing questionable practices and for immediately suspending anyone who may be dangerous to patients for any reason.

BIBLIOGRAPHY

Avery JK: Vicarious liability and the physician's assistant. J Tenn Med Assoc 1985 Jan; 78(1):31–32.
Bailey E: Legal notes: Vicarious liability. Nurs Focus 1980 Sep; 2(1):21–22.
Berg RN: Physician liability under the "borrowed servant" rule. J Med Assoc Ga 1989 May; 78(5):291–92.
Chaney EA: Personal and vicarious liability. J Pediatr Nurs 1987 Apr; 2(2):132–34.
Creighton H: Failure to adequately supervise PAs. Nurs Manage 1982 Dec; 13(12):44–45.
Finch J: Law: Vicarious liability. Nurs Mirror 1983 Dec 7; 157(23):42.
Firman GJ: Ostensible agency: Another malpractice hazard. Am J Psychiatry 1988 Apr; 145(4):510–52.
Gabel W: Vicarious liability. J Am Optom Assoc 1987 Jul; 58(7):599–601.
Hadorn DC; McCormick K; Diokno A: An annotated algorithm approach to clinical guideline development. JAMA 1992 Jun 24; 267:3311–3314.
Hickman JR: The physician's liability for the acts of others—changing concepts of "the captain of the ship" and respondeat superior doctrines. Med Leg Bull 1969 Apr; 18(4):1–6.
Hosoda Y: Gerry James: The captain of the ship. Sarcoidosis 1987 Sep; 4 Suppl 1:20–24.
Istre GR; Gustafson TL; Baron RC; Martin DL; Orlowski JP: A mysterious cluster of deaths and cardiopulmonary arrests in a pediatric intensive care unit. N Engl J Med 1985 Jul 25; 313(4):205–11.
James AE Jr; Garrett WJ; Bundy A; Fleischer AC; Vallentine JR: The commonality and contrasts of agency law and relationships in sonography. Australas Radiol 1986 Nov; 30(4):298–301.
Kapp MB: Supervising professional trainees: Legal implications for mental health institutions and practitioners. Hosp Community Psychiatry 1984 Feb; 35(2):143–47.
Kucera WR: Imputed negligence: The captain of the ship is sinking. AANA J 1980 Apr; 48(2):162–64.
Price SH: The sinking of the "captain of the ship." Reexamining the vicarious liability of an operating surgeon for the negligence of assisting hospital personnel. J Leg Med 1989 Jun; 10(2):323–56.
Reiss J: Captain of the ship doctrine. Am J Proctol 1966 Aug; 17(4):310–32.
Rozovsky LE; Rozovsky FA: Is the O.R. supervisor the captain of the ship? Can Oper Room Nurs J 1985 May–Jun; 3(3):28, 30.
Tamelleo AD: Legal case briefs for nurses. AL.: Wrong anesthetic: Vicarious liability. N.C.: Incorrect needle count: Complications. Regan Rep Nurs Law 1989 Jun; 30(1):3.
Tammelleo AD: Agency nurses and vicarious liability. Case in point: *Joyce v. National Medical Registry, Inc.* (524 N.E. 2d 243—IL (1988). Regan Rep Nurs Law 1988 Aug; 29(3):4.
Tammelleo AD: Borrowed servant doctrine: Anesthesia death. Case in point: *Fortson v. McNamara* (508 So. 2d 35—FL). Regan Rep Nurs Law 1987 Aug; 28(3):2.
Tammelleo AD: Captain of ship doctrine: Vicarious liability. Case in point: *Krane v. Saint Anthony Hosp. Systems* (738 P. 2d 75—CO). Regan Rep Nurs Law 1987 Aug; 28(3):4.
Tammelleo AD: Legal case briefs for nurses. NE.: Sexual assault: Respondeat Superior issue; N.Y.: Physician's failure to communicate: Orders. Regan Rep Nurs Law 1989 Feb; 29(9):3.

Thrasher JE; McNicholas AJ III: Borrowed servant doctrine. J Fla Med Assoc 1980 Jun; 67(6):556.
Trandel-Korenchuk D; Trandel-Korenchuk K: Borrowed servant and captain-of-the ship doctrines. Nurse Pract 1982 Feb; 7(2):33–34.
Walzer RS: Legal aspects of employing "counselors" in a clinical practice. Conn Med 1989 Mar; 53(3):147–51.

16

Referral and Consultation

CRITICAL POINTS
- The law expects that patients will have a single physician responsible for coordinating their care.
- Consultants can be liable if the attending physician fails to report their recommendations to the patient.
- Consultations and referrals require the patient's consent.
- Consultations and referrals with midwives pose special problems.

The legal rules governing referral and consultation evolved in earlier times when patients tended to have long-term relationships with individual physicians. With the advent of team care and the corporatization of medical practice, sorting out the individual responsibilities for a patient's care has become a difficult problem, complicated by the economics of current medical practice. Referrals are sometimes a battleground in the fight to retain well-insured patients while minimizing responsibility for uncompensated care. These financial issues complicate malpractice litigation arising from referral-related injuries.

The distinction between a consultation and a referral has become blurred. Nevertheless, it is legally important because it determines whether the responsibility for the patient's care shifts from one physician to another or whether it simply encompasses more physicians. In a *consultation*, the original physician retains the duty to oversee the patient's care. Consultants have an independent duty to the patient, but this does not supplant the duty of the attending physician. In a *referral*, the responsibility for the patient's care shifts from the original physician to the recipient of the referral, who then becomes the attending physician. The consultant relationship is problematic because consultants such as pathologists and radiologists mistakenly assume that they work for the attending physician rather than the patient. Sending a report to the attending physician does not satisfy their independent duty to the patient if the attending fails to inform the patient of the problem.

OBTAINING A CONSULTATION

Virtually every physician sometimes must rely on specialty consultants because of the nature of modern medical practice. No physician can be all things to all patients. Consultations can offer patients the comfort and continuity of receiving care from a single physician, while benefiting from the expertise of specialists. The attending physician benefits from the help and advice of other physicians but retains the primary relationship with the patient.

Consultations have two functions. More commonly, they allow physicians to manage problems that require additional expertise but are within the physician's general area of skill. They are also useful in helping physicians determine if a patient's problem is beyond their skills or available facilities, thus necessitating a referral. The consultation itself does not transfer the responsibility for the patient's care, but the consultant does assume certain duties to the patient. Since the primary physician retains the responsibility for the patient's care, it is this physician, not the consultant, who makes the final treatment decisions. Responsibility becomes an issue only when the consultant and the attending physician disagree about the proper course of action.

The attending physician's better knowledge of the patient and the history of the condition may lead him or her to decide against the recommendations of a consultant, or the attending physician may find that the consultant is not as knowledgeable or skilled as was thought at the time the consultation was requested. When the attending physician disagrees with the consultant, both parties should discuss the disagreement with the patient and their reasons for recommending differing courses of action. It is best for the attending physician and the consultant to talk with the patient at the same time. In discussing the differing recommendations, it is important to differentiate between facts such as laboratory tests and opinions such as interpretation of a panel of tests. This avoids misunderstandings and can sometimes result in a negotiated care plan that meets the needs of all parties. The attending physician should consider a second consultation, but this should not be seen as a poll of the best two out of three. No matter how many consultations are obtained, the medical responsibility remains with the attending physician. It is critical to obtain the patient's informed consent when choosing to ignore the recommendations of a consultant. If the patient decides to follow the advice of the consultant rather than that of the attending physician, the latter should discuss whether the patient needs a different attending physician.

Requesting a Consultation

In most cases the decision to ask for a consultation is a medical judgment. A physician who believes that the patient's care would benefit from another opinion should ask for a consultation. Sometimes hospital or insurance company rules require a consultation before certain therapy begins. For instance, if a patient may not be admitted to the coronary care unit without a cardiology consultation, the general internist has a duty to obtain the consultation to provide the patient with the needed care.

Often a physician must consult another physician to obtain a certain test for a patient. The attending physician may believe that a specific cardiologist is skilled at doing stress tests and cardiac catheterizations but is too quick to recommend bypass surgery. In this case, the attending physician should let the patient know in advance why his or her recommendations may differ from those of the consultant. The attending physician should ensure that the cardiologist understands that this is a consultation, not a referral. Conversely, the cardiologist may believe that the attending physician is endangering the patient by downplaying the seriousness of the condition. The cardiologist has a duty to inform the patient of this opinion, but it is better if this is done in cooperation with the attending physician.

Physicians often obtain informal consultations from colleagues without appreciating the legal significance of this process. Informal consultations are valuable and should be used, but they have limitations. First is the patient's right to privacy and to choose physicians. An informal consultation should be anonymous. Any information that would disclose the identity of the patient should be withheld. In small communities, the physician should ask the patient to consent to an informal consultation. The physician should ensure that informal consultations do not violate any state or federal laws, as might be the case for substance abuse patients.

Patient Choice

Most practitioners are aware of the patient's right to choose a physician for consultation. In the outpatient setting, the patient is unlikely to go to another physician if he or she does not want the consultation. A hospital patient has this same right to choose whether another physician will be consulted. When a consultation is considered, the patient should be informed and given the opportunity to refuse the consultation or the consultant proposed.

When a patient refuses a necessary consultation, the physician should first determine whether the refusal is based on financial concerns. If the patient's insurer will not pay for consultation, the physician has a duty to try to persuade the insurer that the care is necessary. If this fails, the physician should try to persuade the consultant to waive or reduce the fee. If the patient's refusal is not based on financial concerns, the physician should carefully explain (and document) the necessity of the consultation. The problem then becomes the general problem of a patient who refuses necessary care. While the physician should try to continue treating the patient, this may be impossible; the physician may be forced to terminate the physician-patient relationship. (See Chapter 9.)

Using Consultants Properly

An attending physician has the legal responsibility to obtain consultations when necessary for the patient's well-being. Physicians must choose consultants carefully, both as to specialty and personal competence. The attending physician must then oversee the actions of the consultant while continuing to provide the patient's general care. When orders are written or accepted by the attending physician, he or she has implicitly ratified the correctness of those orders. It is not a defense to say that the order was written at the suggestion of a consultant.

Physicians may be held liable for substandard care if they fail to obtain a consultation in a case that falls outside their areas of expertise or in a case in which only a consultant can provide necessary tests or procedures. If an internist who cannot do endoscopy is caring for a patient with occult intestinal bleeding, the internist has a duty to consult an endoscopist to obtain the procedure for the patient. The attending physician cannot force a patient to undergo the procedure but must ensure that the test and the consultation are available. If the attending physician leaves the arrangement of the consultation to the patient, the patient may later contend that he or she had no real opportunity for this care.

A physician has a duty to choose consultants wisely. The physician should know the consultant's qualifications and be assured of the person's competence before asking for a consultation. Usually the attending physician can rely on the process of admission to hospital staff as adequate verification of another physician's qualifications. This reliance assumes that the attending physician has no reason to suspect the consultant. If a consultant does not appear to have appropriate skills or is impaired, the attending physician has a duty to investigate before consulting that particular physician. For example, a surgeon typically may accept as an anesthesiologist any member of the anesthesia group that serves the hospital; the qualifications of the individual anesthesiologists have been checked by the hospital staff committee and the anesthesia group. If, however, the surgeon smells liquor on the anesthesiologist and notices impaired coordination, the surgeon has a duty to protect the patient by refusing the anesthesiologist's services.

An attending physician is liable for negligent care that a patient receives from a consultant because the attending physician retains responsibility for the patient's care. An attending physician should never simply turn over the care of the patient to a consultant. The attending should be informed of all actions taken by the consultant and should order all tests, medications, and other changes in the patient's care. If the attending physician does not wish to accept responsibility for the patient's care, the patient should be referred to the consultant or another physician.

Documenting a Consultation
The entire process of consultation should be documented in the patient's chart: the request for consultation or, in the hospital, an order for the consultation; all physical findings and test results; a clear evaluation and recommendation; the attending physician's evaluation of the consultation and his or her own recommendations; and any differences of opinion between the physicians and the basis for the difference. The last should be done clearly and factually, without subjective comments. The chart should reflect that the attending physician appreciated and differed with the consultant's findings. Neither party should denigrate or belittle the other's analysis. Offhand remarks can take on unintended significance when presented in a legal proceeding.

REFERRAL

A referral is the correct choice for a physician when a patient's condition requires care that the attending physician cannot provide—perhaps because of a lack of proper facilities, because it is an area in which the physician lacks sufficient training, or because the physician does not choose to practice medicine in that area. By a proper referral, the original physician may shift the responsibility for the patient's general care or refer the patient only for specialty treatment. In either case, the physician who accepts the referral accepts responsibility for care of the patient.

A physician may refer a patient for specialty care without transferring all responsibility for care. For example, a pediatrician may refer a patient to an otorhinolaryngologist for evaluation and insertion of tympanotomy tubes. This referral is necessary if the pediatrician lacks the training and surgical privileges necessary to provide the needed service. The referring pediatrician could remain the primary physician for the child's preventive care and for other acute problems.

After the surgery and necessary postoperative care, the otorhinolaryngologist sends the child back to the referring pediatrician. However the responsibility for the patient's future care is allocated, it is critical that the physicians involved understand their continuing areas of responsibility. The pediatrician should not assume that the otorhinolaryngologist will provide general medical care to the child; the otorhinolarygologist should not assume that the pediatrician can manage postoperative complications. Both physicians must take responsibility for the care of the whole patient, with each concentrating on his or her appropriate area of expertise.

The referring physician has a limited duty to ensure the competence of the receiving physician. This is primarily a duty to determine if the physician provides the type of care the patient requires. If the referring physician has reason to believe that the receiving physician is incompetent, there may be liability for an improper referral. If there are questions about the appropriateness of the referral, the referring physician should follow the patient's progress until he or she is confident that the patient is receiving appropriate care.

Duty to Refer

A physician may have the personal skills necessary to provide certain types of specialty care but lack the necessary resources. For example, an internist may be trained in cardiology but be practicing in a hospital that does not have an intensive care unit, or a patient may have a rare disease that can be treated by experimental drugs but the drugs are licensed only to research centers. In such cases, the patients should be referred to a physician and medical center that have the necessary resources. Physicians must resist institutional pressures not to transfer insured patients if the original institution cannot provide appropriate facilities.

Providing very specialized care may require transferring the patient to a specialty hospital or regional center where none of the staff is known to the referring physician. In this case, the referring physician may have difficulty ensuring the quality of care that the patient will receive. To a large extent, the referring physician may have to rely on the reputation of the center; nevertheless, it is always a good idea to keep in touch with the patient and to request reports from the caregivers to ensure that the referral was appropriate and that the patient is receiving appropriate care.

Duty to Refer to a Nonphysician

In many situations a physician has a duty to refer a patient to a nonphysician for special care. In some cases, such as patients with psychological problems, there may be physicians who could provide the care, but better or more cost-effective service may be available from a psychologist or professional counselor. Many problems are treated only by nonphysicians. A pediatrician who detects a speech defect in a school-aged child has a duty to see that the child is evaluated and treated by a qualified speech therapist, although the speech therapy itself is beyond the realm of pediatric practice. As with other referrals, a referral to a nonphysician should be discussed with the patient.

A physician has the same duties to ensure quality care for patients with referrals to nonphysicians as when referring to another physician. The attending physician must know that the party accepting the referral is qualified to provide the needed care and willing to accept the care of this patient. The physician does not have an ongoing responsibility to monitor the care provided by the nonphysician but should intervene if there are problems with the care rendered.

Referring to Institutions
Physicians often refer patients to institutions rather than to other physicians, a situation that can pose some difficult problems for both patient and the physician. Most major specialty institutions have specific eligibility criteria and various funding requirements. A children's hospital may not accept patients who are more than 18 years old but make exceptions for patients who have had surgical repairs of congenital defects in that hospital. A cancer center may not accept patients who do not have private health insurance unless the patient is willing to participate in a research protocol that has outside funding. A physician who wishes to refer a patient to such an institution must make sure that the patient is eligible for care and that the institution is willing to accept him or her. The best way to do this is to call someone in charge of admissions at the institution and follow up the conversation with a letter. If the patient is not eligible for that institution, care can be sought elsewhere quickly and without the inconvenience of being turned away.

Eligibility may be based on the patient's financial status or residence. Public charity hospitals normally serve residents of a specific area who have incomes below a certain level. These hospitals do not provide free care to everyone. A patient who has no medical insurance may be considered indigent by a private hospital but not be eligible for services at the county hospital. Before referring a patient to a charity hospital, the physician should check to make sure that the patient will be accepted, as he or she would with any other institutional referral. The referring physician also must be aware of federal antidumping regulations that carry a fine of up to $50,000 against the physician personally for improper transfers to charity hospitals. The fine is beyond any malpractice claim that might be paid by insurance. (See Chapter 32.)

The Duty to Find Care
The regionalization of care poses problems for even the best-insured patients. A regional facility, with its complement of subspecialist practitioners, has a substantial stake in keeping specialty beds full. This situation can lead to overinclusive policies on the necessity for specialty care. Neonatologists in some centers, for example, establish standards of care that require pediatricians to refer as many babies as possible to the neonatologists for care. A failure to make these referrals could be malpractice by a pediatrician. The pediatrician, however, does not have the power to force acceptance of a particular patient. If the regional care system is full, the problem of finding a place for a severely premature baby falls to the pediatrician because there is no duty for the neonatologists to transfer less ill infants to make room for more ill patients.

A physician with a patient who needs special care must pursue all options until a place is found for that patient. In some celebrated cases involving indigent, premature babies, this has required searching in several states and calling on the military for emergency transport. The physician's best allies in such situations are a newspaper reporter and a public interest attorney. The threat of adverse publicity and litigation can work wonders in finding care for an individual patient.

If rejections happen too frequently, community physicians should work with the regional centers to correct the problem. Specific guidelines should be established that specify which patients have priority for the space available and which patients will be moved or discharged first when a higher-priority patient comes in. It is hard to defend keeping a terminal cancer patient in the only intensive care bed available if it means that a patient with a heart attack may die for lack of care. Physicians who practice in communities that do not provide adequate indigent or specialty medical care services must warn their patients that they may be denied necessary care. Physicians in these areas also should assist patients in using the federal and state laws to gain access to medical care.

Continuing Care

Before referring a patient to a specialty institution, the physician and the patient should decide to what extent the physician will provide continuing care to that patient. Even physicians who no longer provide care after the referral should follow up to make sure that the referral was received and that the patient is being cared for. If the original physician will continue to provide some care for the patient or take the patient back after the special care, he or she should keep abreast of the patient's care at the referral center. Too often, the patient is the only source of information the community physician has. Checking with the patient or family during the course of treatment helps maintain a good relationship and may allow the physician to intervene if necessary.

The referring physician should make sure that complete records on what was done at the referral center accompany the returning patient. The referring physician should insist on receiving copies of any operative reports, significant test results, and discharge summaries. If it is difficult to get such information from the referral center, the physician should consider getting a release from the patient and requesting a copy of the entire chart. The medical records administrator of a large hospital is likely to be prompter and more thorough in honoring such requests than a resident who has moved to another service.

Liability for Improperly Managed Referrals

Referring a patient to another physician generally relieves the original physician of responsibility for the patient's care and reduces his or her liability. However, if the referral is not made correctly, the liability of the referring physician may increase. The referral must be acceptable to all three parties involved: the referring physician, the receiving physician, and the patient. (If the patient requires emergency care or is in labor, the referring physician must comply with the federal laws discussed in Chapter 32.)

Patients have the right to refuse referral without relieving their attending physicians of responsibility. To refer patients against their wishes and then withdraw from the patient's care constitutes abandonment. Historically, abandonment did not result in substantial tort losses because patients could usually find substitute care. This is no longer true in many parts of the United States. Abandoned patients, particularly pregnant women, may not be able to find care until they can qualify for emergency care under the federal laws. Referrals must be made so that the patient is assured of the availability of ongoing care.

When a patient refuses to be referred to another physician, the attending physician should find out why and attempt to correct any problem. If the patient is opposed to the specific physician recommended, another physician should be sought. If the patient's insurance will not pay for the care, the attending physician should help the patient deal with the insurance carrier. If the patient does not want to change physicians, the attending physician should carefully explain to the patient why this is impossible. (Perhaps the physician does not have the skills or resources needed to continue the case.) The patient should understand that after making appropriate care available, the attending physician will withdraw from the case.

A physician may refuse a referral for a variety of reasons but not if he or she has a preexisting duty to care for the patient. (See Chapter 9.) The neurosurgeon whose hospital staff privileges are dependent on his accepting referrals from the emergency room, for example, has a duty to treat an accident victim referred from the emergency room. In practice, this duty does not help the emergency room physician or the patient if the neurosurgeon refuses to come in. The emergency room physician must care for the patient until appropriate specialty care becomes available.

The attending physician should ensure that the receiving physician will accept the patient before making the referral. This may be on a patient-by-patient basis or through an ongoing agreement. If the receiving physician refuses to accept the patient, the referring physician must make other arrangements. If the physician refusing the referral has an obligation to accept the referral and still refuses, the referring physician should report the refusal to the proper agency: a hospital medical staff committee, a contractual provider of medical services such as an HMO, or the state board of medical examiners. Physicians should keep in mind that they may become liable for the lack of adequate staff coverage or the misbehavior of other physicians if they acquiesce in the misbehavior.

BEING A CONSULTANT

As attorneys become more sophisticated about team medical care delivery, plaintiffs are increasingly suing consultants. Hospital and laboratory-based consultants commonly assume that they work for the physician who orders the tests. Legally, this is not so: physician consultants who do individual patient evaluations for the welfare of the patient enter a physician-patient relationship, with all its attendant duties. If a consultant relies on the treating physician to communicate with the patient, the consultant is liable if the patient does not receive the necessary information. The consultant must balance the conflicting roles of adviser to both patient and treating physician. This can lead to some difficult decisions for the consultant when an attending physician does not follow recommendations. Consequently, a consultant must be as careful in choosing which physicians to consult for as an attending physician must be in choosing consultants.

The Consultant-Patient Relationship

Traditionally, the consultant relationship is seen as a physician-to-physician relationship, a view that derives from the business side of consultant practice. Until the recent growth in managed care plans, consultants were dependent on the goodwill of attending physicians for referrals. Specialists who took patients from primary care physicians by turning consultations into referrals saw their consultations dry up, as did those who questioned the probity of the attending physician's care of the patient. The law, however, insists that the consultant's primary duty is to the patient, not the treating physician.

A physician who is requested to consult on a particular case must first establish a physician-patient relationship with the patient—usually accomplished by an introduction to the patient and an explanation of the consultation requested. A consultant should never assume that the patient has consented to the consultation simply because the attending physician has requested it. Consultants should not rely on blanket consents such as those that authorize treatment from "Dr. Smith and other physicians he or she may designate." Although these are adequate for radiology and pathology consultations and others that do not require direct patient contact, they should be avoided by other consultants. Observing the courtesy of consultation is important. Treating the patient rudely increases the probability of a lawsuit if anything goes wrong and will encourage the patient to refuse to pay for the consultant's services if they are not fully covered by insurance.

The consultant should discuss with the patient what has been said about the consultation and any tests or procedures that will be done. It is wise to make sure that the expectations of the patient and the attending physician are not too high. The consultant should give the patient any additional information that may be needed but dissuade the patient from the idea that specialists can work miracles. A patient who has a close and long-standing relationship with his or her attending physician is likely to blame the impersonal consultant for problems that arise. This is sometimes implicitly encouraged by attending physicians, who may raise patient expectations unreasonably.

Consultants should do a complete evaluation of the case as soon as the patient accepts the consultation: reviewing the patient's chart, examining the patient fully, and talking with both the patient and the attending physician. Relying on information gathered second hand is dangerous. The assumption in bringing a consultant into a case is that the attending physician is not as skilled or as knowledgeable about the problem as the consultant. This makes it unacceptable to rely entirely on the history and physical in the chart. Items critical to the specialty consultation should be verified by the consultant.

Tests and Procedures

Consultants who conduct tests or procedures on a patient must first obtain proper informed consent. They must inform the patient of any risks involved and any available alternatives. In the case of diagnostic tests, the patient should be told about the reliability of a test and whether it will make any difference in the choice of therapy. A patient is likely to be angry if he or she is injured by a test that is of diagnostic interest to the physician but has no bearing on how the patient will be treated. Informed consent to dangerous tests is sometimes complicated by the unwillingness of the attending physician to acknowledge the risks of the procedure, thus undermining the consent obtained by the consultant.

Consultants should always determine for themselves if any contraindications exist to a particular procedure or therapy. For example, it is not a defense to say that the chart did not record that a patient was allergic to iodine. The radiologist is responsible for taking an adequate history to determine that it is safe to do an iodine dye study. And the nephrologist who orders an intravenous pyelogram (IVP) should personally ascertain that the patient is not dehydrated, is not pregnant, and is not allergic to the dye. The legal expectation is that all the physicians involved in the procedure will exercise caution to prevent avoidable injuries to the patient.

The results of tests and the recommendations of the consultant must be transmitted to the attending physician in a manner consistent with the urgency of the patient's condition. For example, a cardiologist who reads all electrocardiograms in a hospital may have the reading posted on the chart by the next morning. If a routine ECG turns out to have a life-threatening arrhythmia on it, the cardiologist must ensure that the patient is treated immediately. This duty is not discharged by noting the arrhythmia on the report and sending the report to the patient's chart, to be seen many hours later.

Informing the Patient

Consultants have a duty to make sure that a patient is informed about the results of the consultation. Since a consultation is intended to assist the attending physician in making medical decisions, it may seem that informing the attending should be sufficient. It is not. The consultant has established a physician-patient relationship with the patient, a relationship that continues until the consultant is released from the case. Discussing findings with the patient gives the consultant the opportunity to ensure that his or her recommendations and findings are known and understood by the patient. It also gives the consultant the opportunity to withdraw from the case and relinquish responsibility to the attending physician. This gives the patient and the nursing staff a clear understanding of who is in charge of care of the patient.

Sometimes a consultant has a duty to intervene in a patient's care. In the case of the cardiologist who discovers a life-threatening arrhythmia, it is unlikely that the patient or the attending physician will object to emergency orders if the attending is not available. When the attending and consulting physicians do not agree, the consultant usually should not countermand the orders of the attending physician. It is best to discuss the problem with the attending physician before talking to the patient. The attending physician may be able to provide additional information or insight that will obviate the disagreement. If the consultant and the attending still disagree, the consultant must fully inform the patient, or the person legally authorized to consent to the patient's medical care, about the disagreement and the options for care.

Patients retain the right to choose their physicians and their care. In some cases, the patient will choose to follow the advice of the attending physician. If so, the consultant should document any disagreements and the patient's choice and then formally withdraw from the case if the disagreements are important enough to warrant this decision. With a hospitalized patient, the consultant should file an incident report if he or she believes the patient is at risk. If the patient chooses to follow the advice of the consultant, the consultant should be prepared to act as attending physician for the patient. If the consultant cannot act as attending physician, both physicians should be ready to assist the patient in finding another physician who meets the patient's needs. Neither physician should abandon the patient.

Record Keeping

Consultants are held to the same standards for record keeping as attending physicians. All pertinent information—history, physical findings, consent, test results, and contacts with the patient—should be reflected in the chart. In addition, the consultant should provide a written consultation report to the attending physician. The consultant's report should be complete and understandable and avoid the use of abbreviations and specialty jargon. A PPD, for example, is an intradermal test for tuberculosis infection to an infectious disease physician but postpartum depression to a psychiatrist. Distinguishing the two is very important in a postpartum patient suffering from fatigue. A consultant creates unnecessary legal liability if the recommendations are not clear and understandable.

Public Duties

The practice of medicine encompasses specific duties to the public and society. These duties apply to all physicians, attending and consulting.

Every jurisdiction in the United States requires the reporting of certain infectious diseases and certain types of injury that may result from a criminal act. (See Chapter 20.) A radiologist who sees suspicious injuries on a child's X ray has the duty to report these findings to the child protection agency. The consultant's duty to report is independent of previous reports by the attending physician. The consultant should not be a party to any agreements by the attending physician not to comply with the reporting laws.

INSTITUTIONAL CONSULTANTS

Physicians whose specialty requires a hospital-based practice are often practicing as consultants without realizing it. The contracts under which they practice in the hospital make them formal consultants for most of the patients admitted. The consultations are done as a matter of routine, often without the patient and physician ever seeing one another. Nevertheless, the consultations and the accompanying charges for service establish a physician-patient relationship, with all its attendant duties.

Radiology

The usual system for providing radiology services in a hospital is a contract between the hospital and an individual physician or a practice group. The group agrees to supervise technical personnel and to read and interpret all tests. The hospital gives the group an exclusive contract to provide these services and requires that all tests done in the hospital be done through the group. Patients eventually receive a bill from the radiology group.

One source of liability for radiologists is improper supervision of nonphysician technical personnel and equipment. Physicians are responsible for ensuring that the personnel are adequately trained and doing their jobs properly. Patients must be protected from falls and other simple injuries. The radiologists must ensure that all equipment is functioning, that the tests are technically adequate, and that patients are not exposed to excessive doses of radiation.

Radiologists must carry out special tests and procedures safely and accurately. Whenever there are special procedures, the radiologist should review the patient's history, do a physical examination as necessary to verify critical information, and obtain informed consent for the procedure. For example, if the attending physician has ordered an IVP and the patient is dehydrated, the radiologist has a duty to cancel or postpone the test until the patient is able to tolerate it. If the IVP was done by a technician without the radiologist's evaluating the patient, the radiologist is responsible, not the attending physician. The attending physician could argue that determining the patient's fitness for the test at the scheduled time is the radiologist's responsibility.

Radiologists should interpret tests as completely as possible. There is an unfortunate tendency to equivocate on reports as a way of avoiding responsibility. Giving a report of "possible pneumonitis" instead of "right lower lobe infiltrates consistent with bacterial pneumonia" does not provide the attending physician with the benefit of the expert opinion that a radiologist is expected to provide. Vague readings increase the consultant's liability when they mask serious conditions or substitute for an in-depth review of the film.

Radiologists have a duty to make sure attending physicians are informed quickly of any serious or life-threatening conditions found on a test. Technicians should routinely inform their supervising radiologists about any serious results or results that are strange or unusual. Radiologists also must ensure that the patient is informed of test results and their significance. Usually this is done by alerting the attending physician, who in turn informs the patient and recommends any necessary care. This discharges the radiologist's duty to inform the patient personally.

Problems arise when the attending physician does not inform the patient of the test results. In this case, the radiologist's duty is not discharged, and the patient will have a cause of action against the radiologist for delayed or missed diagnosis. In almost all cases, this failure to inform the patient is due to a failure in the reporting system; the radiology report does not reach the physician's office, or it is filed without being seen by the attending physician. Radiologists must have a system for following up serious findings to ensure that they have been received by the attending physician and transmitted to the patient. Radiologists and other physicians who provide information to attending physicians rather than patients may contract for indemnification if the attending fails to transmit the test results and recommendations to the patient. This does not affect the patient's right to sue the radiologist but will shift the burden of paying the award to the attending physician. More important, it clarifies the duty of the attending to pass on the information to the patient.

Pathologists

Pathologists' liability stems primarily from quality control and communication problems. Pathologists depend on the attending physician for the collection of samples to be analyzed. When mistakes in labeling result in a patient with a benign condition being subjected to a mutilating surgical procedure, lawsuits are inevitable. Pathologists should ensure that samples are unambiguously labeled upon receipt, when it may still be possible to correct mistakes. If there is any question about the origin of a sample, the attending physician must be notified at once.

Pathologists should follow the same procedures as radiologists to determine that significant laboratory findings are received and appreciated by the attending physician. This is particularly important for rapidly evolving conditions or life-threatening conditions. This type of information should be handled differently from information that is not time critical. Pathologists who practice alone in small laboratories should see to it that the laboratory has formal mechanisms for communicating time-critical information. If the communication of these results depends on ad hoc calls to the attending physician by the pathologist, there is a high probability that the system will break down if a substitute pathologist fills in during a vacation or illness.

Cardiology
Many hospitals have instituted quality assurance systems that require that all EKGs be read by a hospital cardiologist, just as X rays are read by a hospital radiologist. Cardiologists who review routine EKGs must realize that this creates a duty to ensure that the results of the reading are acted on properly. These duties may be more extensive than the duties of a pathologist or a radiologist because cardiologists also act as treating consultants. A cardiologist is expected to know whether the drugs the patient is taking are appropriate to someone with particular EKG findings and to intervene if they are not. A dangerous finding on an EKG may create a duty for the cardiologist to do a full evaluation and consultation in order to ensure that the patient is being cared for properly.

Intensive Care
There is much confusion about who is in charge of a patient in an intensive care unit. (The responsibilities and problems of intensive care medicine are covered more fully in Chapter 33.) The most important concept in caring for a patient in an intensive care setting is that there must be one physician who is fully responsible for the care that the patient receives or does not receive. The patient, the patient's family, and all physicians and nurses involved in the care must know who the responsible physician is.

WORKING WITH MIDWIVES
One of the most difficult areas in referral and consultation is the relationship between obstetricians and midwives in states that allow the independent practice of midwifery. Some states allow midwives to practice only under a physician's supervision. In these states, the relationship between physicians and midwives is governed by the principles discussed in Chapter 15. Midwives pose unique problems because of the view that pregnancy is a natural function that does not require sophisticated medical attendance.

The level of maternal and fetal morbidity and mortality is unacceptable for any woman accustomed to modern medicine. An effective midwifery system depends on the patients of independently practicing midwives' being assured of access to necessary medical and surgical care. European midwifery practice is often touted as a model of such a system, but the model is not directly applicable to the United States because of profound differences in the underlying health care systems.

Except for women having contractions, there is no guaranteed access to medical care for pregnant women in the United States. (See Chapter 32.) In many states, there is little regulation of the training and competence of lay midwives. The underlying morbidity and mortality of the population generally, and pregnant women in specific, is higher than in Europe, and it is dramatically higher in many low-income areas. These factors increase the percentage of women who will need physician-directed care during pregnancy or delivery. Most problematically, women who choose midwives because they believe that the perfect baby results from a natural pregnancy will be especially intolerant of pregnancy-related morbidity or neonatal mortality. The anger, and litigation, will be directed at the obstetrician because the midwife will usually transfer the patient before the disaster.

These factors contribute to, and reflect, the lack of a rational system for midwifery practice in the United States. This makes it legally risky for obstetricians to work with independently practicing midwives. Midwives also pose ethical problems for the physicians who are called on to treat their patients. It is not unusual for lay midwives in states with weak regulations to avoid physician referrals until there is a crisis, and then to refer the patient to the emergency room. Many obstetricians want to help the patients of such midwives but do not want to be seen as endorsing their practices.

Financial issues complicate the relationship between obstetricians and midwives. Some obstetricians oppose midwife practice as unwanted competition, while others employ midwives to increase their patient base. In smaller communities that can support only one or two obstetricians, extensive midwifery practice drains off the routine deliveries that are the financial base for obstetric practice. This increases the pressure on the obstetricians to shift to gynecology-only practices or to leave the community, compromising the availability of surgical deliveries and other medical interventions for all pregnant women in the community.

Classes of Midwives

Referral and consultation practices vary with the class of midwife. Nurse-midwives are registered nurses with specialty training in midwifery. All laws governing nursing licensure and practice apply to nurse-midwives. As a consequence, nurse-midwife practice is usually well regulated and reliable even in states that do not otherwise regulate midwives. Although there are special considerations in working with independently practicing nurses, referral and consultation with nurse-midwives does not pose the ethical and legal problems of working with lay midwives.

The training of lay midwives varies enormously. Some have been through extensive training and apprenticeship programs; some may be physicians or nurses who are not licensed in the United States; others are self-taught from books or experience; and some have virtually no training or skills. A state may license and regulate lay midwives as extensively as nurses or physicians, but few do. There are contradictory reasons for allowing lay midwifery. Some groups argue for lay midwives because of their opposition to the medicalization of pregnancy. Others believe that lay midwifery compromises the health and safety of pregnant women. They point to the lack of lay cardiologists and urologists as evidence that lay practice on women is tolerated only because of the low status of women in the legal system.

Physicians must be wary about practicing with lay midwives. If they are inadequately trained, they are much more likely to delay physician referrals until the patient is in grave danger. The most dangerous situation is lay midwives who practice under the umbrella of an antimedical religious group. Religious healers may be specifically exempted from state laws forbidding the practice of medicine without a license. Even states that forbid or regulate independent midwifery may allow religious practitioners to practice without supervision.

States that regulate the practice of midwifery are often lax in enforcing these regulations. A physician who knows that an individual is practicing midwifery in violation of the law must report such practice to the proper authorities—the board of medical examiners, the board of nursing examiners, or the police—and not practice with such an individual under any circumstances. However, the physician should assist a patient who is in danger, even if that means taking over the patient from the illegal midwife. Reporting the illegal practice establishes that the physician was not condoning or participating in the practice.

Referrals and Consultations

Consulting and referrals with midwives are complicated because the tort law generally assumes that physicians are in charge whenever they work with nonphysician personnel in medical settings. A physician who consults on a case for a midwife is in a very different legal position than if the consultation were for another physician. If the consulting physician determines that physician procedures or prescription medications are necessary, carrying out these recommendations is the responsibility of the attending physician. With no attending physician, the responsibility remains with the consultant because the midwife cannot deliver the necessary care. The physician must ensure that the patient appreciates the limitations of the midwife's authority and understands the necessity for the recommended care and that it can be delivered only by a physician. Since a consultation, even for limited tasks such as ordering screening blood tests, creates a physician-patient relationship, the physician may have a duty to render the needed treatment if requested by the patient.

Referrals from midwives are less problematic than consultations because the physician will assume responsibility for the patient's ongoing care. There must be a good working relationship that ensures that referrals are made before the patient's medical condition deteriorates. In the ideal medical arrangement, the midwife and the physician discuss each new patient to evaluate future medical needs. The midwife then confers with the physician whenever something unusual develops in the patient's condition. Legally, such close cooperation would result in the physician's being found liable for the patient's medical care. If the physician is confident of the midwife's skills and judgment, assuming liability for the care is preferable to not being involved in the prereferral care.

BIBLIOGRAPHY

General

Ballard WP; Gold JP; Charlson ME: Compliance with the recommendations of medical consultants. J Gen Intern Med 1986 Jul–Aug; 1(4):220–24.

Byrd JC; Moskowitz MA: Outpatient consultation: Interaction between the general internist and the specialist. J Gen Intern Med 1987 Mar–Apr; 2(2):93–98.

Detsky AS: Problems in consultation medicine: Why they occur and what can be done about them. J Gen Intern Med 1988 Nov–Dec; 3(6):596–601.

Dinubile MJ; Rudd P: Subspecialty consultations in internal medicine: Uses, misuses, and abuses. J Gen Intern Med 1988 Nov–Dec; 3(6):589–95.

Goldman L; Lee T; Rudd P: Ten commandments for effective consultations. Arch Intern Med 1983 Sep; 143(9):1753–55.

Hampton JR: The GP and the specialist. Cardiology. Br Med J (Clin Res) 1982 June 19; 284(6332):1841–42.

Hansen JP; Brown SE; Sullivan RJ Jr; Muhlbaier LH: Factors related to an effective referral and consultation process. J Fam Pract 1982 Oct; 15(4):651–56.

Horwitz RI; Henes CG; Horwitz SM: Developing strategies for improving the diagnostic and management efficacy of medical consultations. J Chronic Dis 1983; 36(2):213–18.

Lee T; Pappius EM; Goldman L: Impact of inter-physician communication on the effectiveness of medical consultations. Am J Med 1983 Jan; 74(1):106–12.

McPhee SJ; Lo B; Saika GY; Meltzer R: How good is communication between primary care physicians and subspecialty consultants? Arch Intern Med 1984 Jun; 144(6):1265–68.

Marshall JB: How to make consultations work. Postgrad Med 1988 Aug; 84(2):253–54, 256–57.

Pupa LE Jr; Coventry JA; Hanley JF; Carpenter JL: Factors affecting compliance for general medicine consultations to non-internists. Am J Med 1986 Sep; 81(3):508–14.

Sears CL; Charlson ME: The effectiveness of a consultation. Compliance with initial recommendations. Am J Med 1983 May; 74(5):870–76.

Strohmeyer RW Jr; Shula RJ: Physician's liability for failure to consult with and/or refer a patient to a specialist. Indiana Med 1988 Jan; 81(1):45–47.

Wark PM: Malpractice liability of referring and consulting physicians. J S C Med Assoc 1981 Nov; 77(11):563–66.

Wilson MA: Improvement in referral practices elicited by a redesigned request format. Radiology 1983 Mar; 146(3):677–79.

Institutional Consultants

Baker SR; Stein HD: Radiologic consultation: Its application to an acute care surgical ward. AJR 1986 Sep; 147(3):637–40.

Baker SR: The operation of a radiology consultation service in an acute care hospital. JAMA 1982 Nov 5; 248(17):2152–54.

Besterman EM: Changes in cardiological practice over the past eighteen years. Practitioner 1982 Mar; 226(1365):487–88, 490, 493.

Clinger NJ; Hunter TB; Hillman BJ: Radiology reporting: Attitudes of referring physicians. Radiology 1988 Dec; 169(3):825–26.

Golden WE; Lavender RC: Preoperative cardiac consultations in a teaching hospital. South Med J 1989 Mar; 82(3):292–95.

Halvorsen JG; Kunian A: Radiology in family practice: Experience in community practice. Fam Med 1988 Mar–Apr; 20(2):112–17.

Kleiman MB: The infectious disease consultant and the telephone consultation. Pediatr Infect Dis 1986 Jan–Feb; 5(1):51–53.

Kolner EH: Ten ways to get more out of your radiologist. Wis Med J 1983 Apr; 82(4):8–10.

Lafortune M; Breton G; Baudouin JL: The radiological report: What is useful for the referring physician? J Can Assoc Radiol 1988 Jun; 39(2):140–43.

Levin HS: Operating room consultation by the pathologist. Urol Clin North Am 1985 Aug; 12(3):549–56.

Mackenzie TB; Popkin MK; Callies AL; Jorgensen CR; Cohn JN: The effectiveness of cardiology consultation. Concordance with diagnostic and drug recommendations. Chest 1981 Jan; 79(1):16–22.

Malkasian GD Jr: Cytopathological interpretation and medical consultation. JAMA 1989 Aug 18; 262(7):942.

Meaney TF: The decline of diagnostic radiology: Call to action. 1989 Dotter lecture. Radiology 1989 Sep; 172(3 Pt 2):889–92.

Monsees B; Destouet JM; Evens RG: The self-referred mammography patient: A new responsibility for radiologists. Radiology 1988 Jan; 166(1 Pt 1):69–70.

Morris KJ; Tarico VS; Smith WL; Altmaier EM; Franken EA Jr: Critical analysis of radiologist-patient interaction. Radiology 1987 May; 163(2):565–67.

Myers JP: Curbside consultation in infectious diseases: A prospective study. J Infect Dis 1984 Dec; 150(6):797–802.

Oneson RH; Minke JA; Silverberg SG: Intraoperative pathologic consultation. An audit of 1,000 recent consecutive cases. Am J Surg Pathol 1989 Mar; 13(3):237–43.

Schreiber MH; Winslade WJ: Rights, roles, and relationships in radiology. Radiology 1987 Apr; 163(1):269–70.

Seltzer SE; Beard JO; Adams DF: Radiologist as consultant: Direct contact between referring clinician and radiologist before CT examination. AJR 1985 Apr; 144(4):661–64.

Shuman WP; Heilman RS; Larson EB: DRGs and the radiologist as a consultant (editorial). AJR 1984 Jul; 143(1):193–94.

Sickles EA: Mammography screening and the self-referred woman (editorial). Radiology 1988 Jan; 166(1 Pt 1):271–73.

Stempsey WE: The virtuous pathologist: An ethical basis for laboratory medicine. Am J Clin Pathol 1989 Jun; 91(6):730–38.

17

Teaching

CRITICAL POINTS
- Patients have the right to refuse to participate in teaching programs.
- Students must not impersonate physicians.
- Most patients are willing to participate in teaching if they are treated honestly.
- Many training programs do not comply with legal standards for supervising their students.

While only a few physicians are full-time members of medical school faculties, most physicians have to deal with students and residents, at least occasionally, when they hospitalize or refer a patient. It is important for physicians to understand the extent to which they may rely on students and residents to care for patients. Improper delegation of authority to students and residents can subject attending physicians to medical malpractice liability, license review, and criminal investigation. The case of Libby Zion is a rare but poignant reminder of the risks of improper supervision in a medical teaching situation (Colford 1989).

Libby Zion, a young woman in generally good health, was admitted to a New York hospital for an acute illness. She died several hours later, after questionable care from residents who had been on duty for an extended period. A grand jury investigation found no criminal conduct but recommended shorter hours and more supervision for residents (Asch and Parker 1988).

Most private physicians do not appreciate the risks of working with an improperly supervised teaching program. There are few large malpractice verdicts against teaching programs. There are, however, many cases in which a teaching program, protected by governmental immunity, is dropped from the case for a token settlement, leaving the private physician to fight the case alone. Improperly billing for work done by students or residents may subject the physician to civil and criminal prosecution for Medicare/Medicaid fraud.

PATIENTS' RIGHTS

Physicians who work with teaching services should be careful to protect their patients' autonomy. Patients are entitled to control who is entrusted with their medical care and their medical information. Ethically, a patient's method of payment, or the absence of payment, does not affect the right to receive care from a licensed physician. This is also the legal rule unless modified by state law. While a state might pass a law conditioning the provision of charity care on the acceptance of care by students and residents, this might pose equal protection problems under the Constitution. If a patient is brought into a county charity hospital that uses students and interns extensively in first-line care and demands a "real doctor," the hospital must produce a licensed physician to provide care. It is not acceptable to tell the patient that no physician is available.

Patients also are entitled to know, when they first seek care from a physician, whether they will be asked to participate in a teaching program. Private physicians who make teaching a part of their practice should inform their patients at the first patient visit that they are entering a teaching practice but that they have the right to refuse to be cared for by students and residents or by a given resident or student.

Patients should not be introduced to a student and then asked if they are willing to participate as teaching material. Most patients are willing to participate in teaching, but the physician must be prepared to honor the request of patients who do not want to participate. Ethically, the patient's decision to accept or refuse to participate in a teaching program should have no bearing on whether the physician will treat the patient. Linking the participation in the teaching program to access to medical care creates an improper coercive atmosphere. Legally, the physician must honor the patient's refusal but may refer the patient to another physician if the referral would otherwise be acceptable.

The physician should document the patient's wishes as to participating in teaching. Once general permission is obtained, simple consent is required before a specific medical student or resident may participate in a patient's care. This is obtained by introducing the student to the patient and asking the patient if the student may participate in the care. If the patient has concerns about privacy, the students and residents should be instructed to respect the patient's wishes. Some teaching programs generally ignore concerns with privacy of medical information, but they are not excluded from either the state or federal laws that govern access to medical information.

Faculty Physicians

Physicians who are medical school faculty without private practices must balance the realities of their practices against patients' right to choose who delivers their medical care. This dilemma is exacerbated when the teaching program has assumed the obligation to care for classes of patients other than those who voluntarily choose to be treated at a teaching facility: emergency patients, indigent patients (when the teaching program has charge of an indigent care program), and patients with a contractual right to be treated, such as members of a managed care plan for which the medical school has contracted to provide care. Persons in these classes retain their right to refuse the care of students and residents.

Faculty physicians should obtain their patients' permission to be included in the teaching program in the same way that a private physician would. Except in emergencies when consent is not required, this permission should be obtained before the patient is seen by students or residents. In teaching programs with insufficient attending staff supervision that rely on students or residents for primary patient contact, the first person to see the patient should obtain the patient's consent. To lessen the implicit coercion in such a situation, the patients should be told that they have a right to refuse care from a resident or a medical student. Most patients consent to be treated by students and residents; the teaching program and the nursing personnel must respect the wishes of patients who refuse this care. The patient's right of privacy should not be violated for the convenience of the teaching staff.

Fraud

Medical students and residents who misrepresent themselves as fully licensed physicians or as specialists in some area of medicine defraud the patient and increase the probability of a malpractice lawsuit if the patient is injured or just angered by the care. It also may constitute Medicare/Medicaid fraud if the patient is billed for the student's or resident's services. All patients should be made aware of the status of all the people involved in their care and the identity of their attending physician. If a patient signs a consent for a procedure, it should clearly state who will be doing the procedure. (See Chapter 34.) Patients may choose to receive care from someone other than the attending physician, but they should never be misled.

If the patient understands that the person providing care is in training and if the trainee is properly supervised by a licensed physician, the patient may consent to care from a student or resident. The patient may not, however, waive the laws governing independent medical practice, and the providers may not subvert the patient's right to consent.

MEDICAL STUDENTS, RESIDENTS, AND FELLOWS

Academic medical centers are characterized by the variety of their graduate and postgraduate students. This can lead to confusion about who may do what to patients and who may supervise whom. In the extreme case, nonmedical personnel, such as graduate students in the basic sciences, may be confused with physician fellows and given clinical responsibilities. More generally, teaching programs are often lax in their supervision of unlicensed physicians and medical students, giving them authority beyond their legal scope of practice (Gleicher 1991). This creates medical malpractice liability for the attending physician when a patient is injured through the improper actions of a student or resident. Treatment by an unauthorized person can support a lawsuit for battery. Moreover, juries are unsympathetic to physicians who shirk the duty to care for patients personally.

Residents and Fellows

Legally, the most important question about residents and fellows is whether they are licensed to practice in the state where they are training. A resident who does not have either a personal license or an institutional license has no legal right to exercise independent medical judgment. This is often the case for first-year residents in states that require one year of postgraduate training for licensure. Since these residents are part of a properly supervised training program, there are seldom legal questions about their status.

The legal status of residents and fellows becomes an issue when an academic appointment is used to shelter the practice of an improperly trained or unlicensible individual: foreign medical graduates with questionable credentials, physicians with substance abuse problems, or physicians who have been disciplined by the board of medical examiners in another state. Juries and boards of medical examiners take a jaundiced view of subterfuges that allow unqualified physicians to practice on unsuspecting patients. Such personnel are not proper candidates for standard training programs. They should be accommodated in programs that explicitly recognize their disabilities and provide close supervision.

A physician receiving postgraduate training may be practicing under an institutional license, either formal or informal. Most states allow or tolerate limited medical practice by residents and fellows within a formal teaching system and under supervision. The terms of this institutional licensure are very limiting. The practice must be under genuine supervision and be limited to the institution. Institutional licensees frequently get into trouble by writing prescriptions for outpatients. While state law may allow the physician to write medication orders on inpatients, this privilege seldom extends to outpatients. When such physicians work in a clinic, their prescription must be signed by a fully licensed physician with appropriate state and federal drug licenses.

Physicians and organizations outside the teaching institution should be careful to confirm that residents are practicing within the law before accepting them into a practice. If there is any question about the scope of the institutional licensure, practitioners should allow only independently licensed residents in their private practices and then only to the extent approved by their malpractice insurance carrier.

Besides externships, many residents accept short locum tenens, weekend call, or emergency room coverage to make extra money. Candidates for such jobs should be treated like any other physician seeking work. They must have an independent license to practice medicine and privileges that are extensive enough to cover foreseeable circumstances at any hospital at which they practice. The employing physician should ensure that they have adequate malpractice insurance coverage for the job. If a physician or hospital routinely uses moonlighting residents to provide emergency coverage, it is also a good idea to limit the amount of time the resident works in the combined programs. If the residents look upon the moonlighting as a paid rest, they are not going to be able to provide proper emergency coverage. Eventually, an overtired resident will face a major emergency with unfortunate results.

Medical Students

Medical students are often enthusiastic about new clinical opportunities, and it is tempting to let them try their hand at patient care, particularly if the problem seems simple. This situation can jeopardize a student's future. A medical student who is accused of practicing medicine without a license, even if it is at the instigation of a supervising physician, may not be allowed to complete his or her degree. Even if the school awards the student a degree, it may be difficult or impossible for the student to get a license, residency training, or malpractice insurance. Supervising physicians must protect themselves and their students from the temptation to delegate too much authority.

The practice of introducing a medical student to patients as "doctor," "young doctor," or a "student doctor" is fraud. A reasonable person introduced to a doctor in a medical setting assumes that this term denotes a licensed physician with a doctoral degree in medicine. Even holders of other doctoral degrees should not be introduced to patients as a doctor. A medical student who has a Ph.D. should not use the title in a medical setting in situations when it can lead to confusion. If a person with a Ph.D. is working in a medical setting, the difference should be explained to every patient. An example of a proper introduction might be introducing a clinical pharmacologist to a patient by saying: "This is Doctor Jones. Dr. Jones is a doctor of pharmacology who is trying to help us work out the problem with your medications." This tells the patient that Doctor Jones is not a medical doctor and why a pharmacologist is involved in the patient's care.

No matter how capable the student or how close to finishing training, medical students do not have the legal authority to practice medicine. Everything that a student does must be reviewed and checked by a licensed physician. The student should not be allowed even as much independence as a nurse or a paraprofessional. It may be permissible for a physician to delegate certain tasks to a nurse under protocol that should not be delegated to a medical student. The legal assumption is that the student is there to be taught. If the student knew the tasks well enough to be allowed to do them unsupervised, then he or she would not need to be doing them.

Under no circumstances should the student be used as a substitute for the physician in completing routine physician tasks. It is tempting to use medical students to do admission histories and physicals or to evaluate a patient, but it is very dangerous legally. If anything untoward happens to the patient, the physician will be responsible and will be in the position of having injured a patient by not fulfilling his or her medical duties. The attending physician must personally review the history and physical, not just cosign the work of a nonphysician.

The writing of orders and prescriptions is limited to physicians and other health care professionals who are properly licensed in the state. This may never be done by a medical student. A student may act as a transcriber of orders if it is the licensed physician who signs or approves them. Hospital and office staff should never act on an order from a medical student until it has been cosigned or otherwise endorsed by the attending physician. Even in an emergency, a nurse should follow established protocols and the orders of an appropriate physician, not the advice of a medical student.

It is particularly important to follow the laws of medical practice when prescribing or ordering drugs. Most boards of medical examiners tend to be lenient toward physicians and medical students in the division of work. State and federal drug enforcement agencies are much less understanding. The rule is simple: only licensed persons may prescribe or dispense drugs. Those who violate this rule may be subjected to criminal prosecution and the punishments prescribed by law. The fact that the unlicensed prescriber is a student will only make prosecution politically easier.

Nursing and Other Students

The rules that apply to medical students apply to other types of students: their work must be supervised, and they may not do anything that requires licensure or certification.

As a practical matter, much of what other students do does not require licensure or is already supervised by a physician. For instance, an unlicensed individual may be authorized to draw blood or administer medication. A medical student or a nursing student also may be authorized to draw blood or give medicines. Caution must be used to make sure that these students are following specific orders and not using their own judgment. If there is an order from a physician saying that a blood glucose should be drawn at 8 A.M., a student may do the task. If the blood is being drawn under a protocol for registered nurses that says that the test should be done when the patient shows signs of hyperglycemia, a nurse's professional judgment is required; no student should assume responsibility for doing or not doing the test.

THE REALITY OF TEACHING PROGRAMS

The conflict between legal norms and medical practice is great in teaching programs. The improper supervision and delegation of work is a perennial problem in medical care delivery, and it is most troublesome in teaching programs. The medical-ethics and medical-legal literature contain elaborate theories of patient autonomy and student supervision that represent the expectations of the law. They bear little resemblance to medical training, however. The usual practice in teaching hospitals and medical schools has been to use medical students and residents for patient care with little or no attention to their legal status. Patients are implicitly (and sometimes explicitly) deceived about who is a licensed physician and about their right to refuse to participate in teaching programs (Asch and Parker 1988).

This conflict between legal expectations and medical practice has persisted for two reasons: (1) it is convenient for the physicians participating in the teaching programs, and (2) boards of medical examiners have had little interest in enforcing the provisions of the law that relate to patient autonomy and physician-endorsed unauthorized practice of medicine. Malpractice lawsuits become an issue only when a patient is severely injured. Even then, many programs are sheltered under various forms of governmental immunity, pushing the onus for paying the resulting claims onto any private physicians involved in the care of the injured patient.

Importance of the Law

Three themes in contemporary medical practice bode ill for physicians who continue to participate in illegally managed teaching programs. The first is the growing reluctance of medical malpractice insurers to continue to insure physicians who have preventable claims against them. If a physician's insurer pays off on a case involving an improperly supervised student, the physician may have difficulty in renewing the policy or in obtaining coverage from another insurer.

Second, with the demise of charitable immunity and the growth of formal risk management and quality assurance programs, hospitals are demanding that physicians supervise the care of their patients personally. Third, outside pressures are increasing the enforcement of the laws governing the supervision of nonphysician personnel. The driving force behind this enforcement has been the Medicare/Medicaid programs. Physicians who bill for work performed by students and residents violate the federal law against fraud and abuse. Private insurance companies are increasing their supervision of billing practices associated with teaching programs. The growing concern among politicians about the illicit use of drugs will result in more vigorous enforcement of the rules on who may write prescriptions and dispense drugs.

It is not necessary to deceive patients to persuade them to participate in teaching programs. Many patients enjoy having students involved in their care. The students generally have much more time to spend with an individual patient than do either the residents or the attending physician. As medical schools have been forced to rigid policies of disclosure to patients, the students have not been driven from the hospitals.

In the past, properly supervising medical students and residents was more expensive than not supervising them. This is changing, however, as the federal government and third-party payers become more reluctant to pay for student work. An institution that is subject to an enforcement action for fraud can see its revenue stream from the federal government frozen for months or years. The physicians who are personally accused of fraud must expend tens of thousands of dollars of their own funds on defense lawyers because these actions are not covered under medical malpractice insurance companies. If the defense is not successful, the physician is subject to large fines, loss of licensure, and imprisonment.

Working with a Teaching Program

The critical legal issue in working with a teaching program is ensuring that the patient's care is always supervised by a properly trained and licensed physician. No matter how many residents, fellows, or medical students are participating in the care of a patient, it is the staff physician who is responsible. All the rules that apply to working with a consultant apply to this staff physician. If the patient is not referred to the teaching service for all care, then the original physician should be careful to supervise the patient's care personally.

When private physicians refer patients to a teaching hospital, they should make sure that the referral is to a fully licensed physician, not to a resident or a medical student. It may be a student who takes the telephone call, but the referral is to that student's supervising physician. If the referring physician is not certain who is taking the referral, then this should be determined or the patient should be referred elsewhere. If a physician refers a patient to a student or a resident and the supervising physician does not accept the patient, the referring physician has abandoned the patient and is liable for any problems that arise.

If a physician requests a consultation from a teaching service, both the physician and the patient should know who on the service will be primarily responsible for the work and who is the supervising staff physician. If problems arise during the consultation, these should be worked out between the attending physician and the supervising staff physician.

Maintaining Supervision

A staff physician should never turn over care of the patients on the service to an unsupervised resident. If the staff physician is unavailable to supervise the service, another equally qualified physician must assume this responsibility. Although residents and fellows may have independent licenses to practice medicine, they are viewed as students and therefore not appropriate substitutes for their teachers.

A physician who undertakes the education of students, whether in private practice or in the school, has a fundamental duty to supervise their activities. The most important part of this supervision is making sure that the student does not harm the patients or interfere with the physician-patient relationship. As a recent study illustrates, this is complicated by the tendency of residents to hide their mistakes from their attending physicians, as well as their patients (Wu et al. 1991). This deception can have profound risk management consequences (Persson 1991). The students must understand the importance of reporting all problems to the attending physician. It must be clear that it is expected that students make mistakes (Bosk 1979). It is covering up a mistake that is unacceptable. The physician also must ensure that the student does not violate the law or go beyond the allowable scope of practice.

Preventing harm to the patients requires close supervision of everything the student does to or for a patient. It is acceptable to have a student write orders if the nursing staff knows that the orders are only advisory and cannot be acted upon until reviewed and approved by the attending physician. If it is not possible to ensure that student orders will not be acted on, as is the case in most private hospitals, students should not write orders in the patient's chart. If a student is going to do a procedure on a patient, the attending physician should personally assist the student to prevent wrong actions or take over the procedure if the student has difficulty.

Maintaining the integrity of the physician-patient relationship is important to successful teaching within a private practice. Patients may choose whether they wish to participate in the teaching program. The student should understand that he or she must be as unobtrusive as possible. If the patient is uncomfortable with the situation, then compliance is likely to suffer and the quality of care will deteriorate. The attending physician's first duty is always to the patient.

The Physician-Student Relationship
The duty to teach students is sometimes contractual but usually only an ethical obligation. Faculty members who receive a salary for teaching must educate the students under their supervision. Physicians who accept staff privileges at a teaching hospital also may have a contractual duty to teach. If teaching is a requirement for staff membership, accepting the staff privileges means accepting the teaching responsibility. For most physicians, there is no formal contract that requires teaching, but there is an ethical duty to improve the practice of medicine and to educate new physicians. If the physician derives any benefit from the presence of students, this ethical duty becomes very strong.

In theory, a student should not be allowed to do anything to a patient that the supervising physician cannot legally authorize a layperson to do. The physician should verify everything the student does. For instance, if a medical student does a history and physical examination and dictates the findings, the physician must repeat the history and physical to determine their accuracy before signing the dictation. Otherwise, the physician would be illegally delegating the practice of medicine to the student.

If the person doing the history and physical is a resident in a teaching hospital, it may not be necessary for the attending physician to repeat all the work. The resident may have a limited license to practice medicine through his or her training institution. It is important to know the legal status of the student or resident. A student doing an intern-like rotation is still a student and may not do any medical practice. A resident who has no independent license is restricted to practicing within the limitations of whatever institutional license he or she may have. Even an independently licensed resident physician may be limited in the scope of practice by the residency policies. These may not carry the force of law, but they may affect malpractice insurance coverage.

Whether a physician has the right to refuse to treat a patient who will not participate in a teaching program depends on the circumstances of the physician's practice and the laws in that jurisdiction. A private practicing physician who chooses to act as a preceptor has the right to turn away patients who object to this, if the proper steps are taken to provide the patient with alternative care.

Otherwise this might constitute abandonment. If the patient is entitled to care from the physician because of contractual arrangements, such as an HMO or because of emergency care laws, the physician does not have the right to force the patient to accept care from a student.

Payment for Services

Federal programs and most state and private third-party payers will not pay for any service performed by a student or a physician in a training program. Payment can be expected if a student or resident performs the activity under the direct supervision of a licensed physician. If a medical student dictates a history and physical on a patient who is being admitted to the hospital and the attending physician cosigns this dictation after doing a history and physical, the physician may bill for the service. A physician who cosigns the dictation without doing the work is not entitled to payment for a service he or she did not perform. The physician also may violate the terms of his or her hospital privileges or the laws on delegation of medical authority.

It is particularly important that consent and billing for surgical procedures be done appropriately. If a resident is going to be performing a surgical procedure, the patient must be aware of this and the attending surgeon must be scrubbed into the surgery and directly supervise the entire procedure. It is not good enough to be available if needed. In the first case, the attending surgeon is arguably doing the surgery through the resident. In the second case, he or she is simply trying to collect a fee for services not rendered. If the patient has signed a consent for the attending surgeon to do the surgery, the absent surgeon is also perpetrating a fraud.

BIBLIOGRAPHY

Asch DM, Parker RM: The Libby Zion case: One step forward or two steps backward? N Engl J Med 1988; 318:771–775.

Bosk C: *Forgive and Remember: Managing Medical Failure.* 1979.

Calhoun JG; Woolliscroft JO; Hockman EM; Wolf FM; Davis WK: Evaluating medical student clinical skill performance: Relationships among self, peer, and expert ratings. Proc Annu Conf Res Med Educ 1984; 23:205–10.

Carney SL; Mitchell KR: Satisfaction of patients with medical students' clinical skills. J Med Educ 1986 May; 61(5):374–79.

Colford JM Jr; McPhee SJ: The ravelled sleeve of care: Managing the stresses of residency training. JAMA 1989; 261:889–893.

Dworkin G: The "student doctor" and a wary patient. Commentary. Hastings Cent Rep 1982 Feb; 12(1):27–28.

Farber NJ; Weiner JL; Boyer EG; Robinson EJ: Residents' decisions to breach confidentiality. J Gen Intern Med 1989 Jan–Feb; 4(1):31–33.

Freedman ML: Medical education in geriatrics: Ethical and social concerns. Bull N Y Acad Med 1985 Jul–Aug; 61(6):501–5.

Gartrell N; Herman J; Olarte S; Localio R; Feldstein M: Psychiatric residents' sexual contact with educators and patients: Results of a national survey. Am J Psychiatry 1988 Jun; 145(6):690–94.

Gleicher N: Expansion of health care to the uninsured and underinsured has to be cost-neutral. JAMA 1991; 265:2388–90.

Gorovitz S: Preparing for the perils of practice. Hastings Cent Rep 1984 Dec; 14(6):38–41.

Hoffman LM: Housestaff activism: The emergence of patient-care demands. J Health Polit Policy Law 1982 Summer; 7(2):421–39.

Holmes DB; Mann KV; Hennen BK: Defining fitness and aptitude to practice medicine. Proc Annu Conf Res Med Educ 1988; 27:32–37.

Irby DM: Peer review of teaching in medicine. J Med Educ 1983 Jun; 58(6):457–61.

Kaplan JM: Medical students as child abusers. Bull Am Acad Psychiatry Law 1986; 14(1):31–36.

Kapp MB: Rights training for providers: Education as advocacy. Law Med Health Care 1982 Dec; 10(6):270–72.

Morgan D: Liability for medical education. J Leg Med (Chic) 1987 Jun; 8(2):305–38.

Persson A: Letter concerning: Do house officers learn from their mistakes? JAMA 1991; 266:512–13.

Puckett AC Jr; Graham DG; Pounds LA; Nash FT: The Duke University program for integrating ethics and human values into medical education. Acad Med 1989 May; 64(5):231–35.

Richardson PH; Curzen P; Fonagy P: Patients' attitudes to student doctors. Med Educ 1986 Jul; 20(4):314–17.

Robinson J: Are we teaching students that patients don't matter? J Med Ethics 1985 Mar; 11(1):19–21, 26.

Rush JP; Chambers LW; Keddy W: A study to identify who is the responsible physician for each patient in a teaching hospital. QRB 1986 Dec; 12(12):426–30.

Stillman PL; Swanson DB: Ensuring the clinical competence of medical school graduates through standardized patients. Arch Intern Med 1987 Jun; 147(6):1049–52.

Strauss A: "Shpos." South Med J 1983 Aug; 76(8):981–84.

Thomas R; Nieman LZ; Holbert D: The medical record and the medical interview: An evaluation of student case histories. Fam Med 1987 Nov–Dec; 19(6):449–52.

Vogel LL: University teaching hospital liability. Med Law 1985; 4(2):177–87.

Wu AW; Folkman S; McPhee SJ; Lo B: Do house officers learn from their mistakes? JAMA 1991; 265:2089–94.

18

Peer Review

CRITICAL POINTS
- The law allows the medical profession to self-police through peer review.
- Peer review activities can violate the federal antitrust laws.
- Improperly conducted peer review can subject the reviewing physician to substantial liability that may not be covered by malpractice insurance.
- Physicians must understand how peer review law has been changed by the Health Care Quality Improvement Act of 1986.

Peer review is the review of a physician's professional competence by another physician or group of physicians. In most circumstances, this review is done privately rather than under the authority of state or federal law. Peer review is a contentious process. It cannot be both effective and collegial because the stakes in medical practice are too high: an adverse peer review decision can destroy a practice, but overly solicitous peer review can endanger patients' lives. While physicians resist the substitution of state regulation for private peer review, the conflicts of interest inherent in private peer review make it legally risky. This chapter reviews the basic legal constraints on peer review and how these are modified by federal law. Chapter 19 discusses how to conduct legally defensible peer review.

CONTEMPORARY PEER REVIEW

The most common arena for peer review is the hospital medical staff committee. Until recently, this was also the arena that had the most direct effect on a physician's practice. Now, peer review efforts by third-party payers, such as professional review organizations (PROs), PPOs, HMOs, and even traditional health insurers, are gaining in importance. These reviews share many characteristics of hospital privileges reviews. The hospital medical staff model for peer review is a good starting point for all types of peer review, but it should be modified for the special circumstances of other peer review environments.

The law grants the professions remarkable latitude in disciplining their own, a practice rooted in a historical context that is very different from current practice.

Historically, the professions were seen as a calling, not a business. It was acceptable to discriminate against practitioners for racial, cultural, ethnic, gender, and anticompetitive reasons. The essence of peer review was to ensure that professionals were both technically qualified and socially acceptable. Since these were qualities that the professions were uniquely suited to judge, the law allowed them to be self-governing. In medicine, medical professional societies were granted the authority to determine where and whether a physician could practice. Hospital medical staffs were given the authority to grant or deny the privilege to practice in a given hospital. This delegation of authority has survived, but it is now an anachronism.

The reality of contemporary peer review is frequently in conflict with the medical profession's history. Conflict arises because the trappings of peer review remain, but much of the authority has been eroded.

This erosion of authority began with the civil rights laws. In most parts of the United States, medical practice was completely segregated, and this segregation was enforced through the medical societies. With the enforcement of the civil rights laws, the stranglehold of local medical societies on medical practice was broken. Rulings that hospital privileges could not be predicated on medical society membership quickly followed. (This principle is still flouted in practice by requirements that a physician be eligible for membership in the local medical society.)

The Federal Trade Commission

The next assault on the self-regulation of the professions came in the 1970s from the concern of the courts and the Federal Trade Commission about anticompetitive practices. This was not the first-time the FTC had entered medical society politics. As early as the 1930s, it had brought legal action against certain medical societies for blacklisting physicians who participated in prepaid medical plans. These antitrust efforts died out during World War II and were not resumed in earnest until the 1970s.

The case that finally reached the Supreme Court involved attempts by a bar association to fix fees. In *Goldfarb v. Virginia State Bar* (1975), the U.S. Supreme Court held that the delegation of authority to professional societies to conduct peer review did not encompass a grant of authority to engage in price fixing. This decision was followed by a ruling against an engineering society that held that attempts to manipulate technical standards to benefit one competitor over another, hidden in the guise of standards to protect the public, would not be allowed (*American Society of Mechanical Engineers v. Hydrolevel* 1982). The result of these rulings has been an effort by the FTC and private litigants to force professional societies to refrain from anticompetitive actions.

The effect of FTC enforcement actions and private litigation has been perverse. Exemplary attempts to establish objective standards for medical practice (such as the Academy of Pediatrics's "Blue Book") have been thwarted because of the fear of litigation. Simultaneously, some practitioners have used threats of antitrust litigation to suppress criticism of questionable procedures or marketing practices. A cynical observer might say that the FTC has removed curbs on unprofessional practices, which has increased the cost of medical care by increasing the marketing of dubious procedures. Except for the certification activities of the large professional societies, the control of medical staff privileges has passed from local medical societies to hospital and other corporate committees.

Medical Staff Committees

Hospital medical staff committees, especially those involved in staff credentialing decisions, exist in a legal limbo. With the exception of some hospitals in small communities that are short of physicians, the members of a hospital's medical staff are competitors. Thus, medical staff committees are groups of independent small businesspersons making decisions that affect the ability of other small businesspersons to compete with them. This is facilitated by a larger business, the hospital, that controls essential facilities, delegating critical management decisions to this group of independent contractors.

Hospital administration based on decision making by independent committees of physicians can be traced to the Joint Commission on the Accreditation of Healthcare Organizations (JCAHO). The JCAHO was originally a joint endeavor by the American Hospital Association (AHA) and the American College of Surgeons (ACS). The AHA wanted to professionalize the management of hospitals but needed the support of the physicians. The ACS could see the benefit in the professionalism of hospital management but did not want to concede to physicians the power to control the medical staff appointments process. Out of these needs and aspirations the JCAHO was born. The surgeons agreed to support efforts to reform hospital management as long as the hospital administrators agreed not to interfere with the prerogatives of the medical staff. The result was an uneasy truce between administrators and physicians on the medical staff.

Because of its basic nature as a group of competitors conspiring to set the terms of the competition, the authority of a medical staff committee is legally suspect. We concede that this view is the inverse of the prevailing opinion that medical staff committees are legally favored, except when they make biased decisions. It is important to understand the basis for turning this view on its head. If medical staff committees are legally favored unless they make biased decisions, then it should be relatively easy to establish criteria for making decisions that will avoid the biases that concern the courts. If, on the other hand, medical staff committees are inherently suspect, attempts to make their decisions legally supportable will result in ever more complicated rules and procedures, and these rules and procedures will be constantly under attack with the development of new legal theories. This has been the case, prompting the Congress to pass a law attempting to preempt legal attacks on peer review actions. (See Chapter 19.)

The Legal Status of Medical Staff Committees

A hospital medical staff is an unusual entity. It serves the interests of the hospital but is not part of the hospital corporation. Since most states prohibit physicians from working for hospitals directly, the hospital does not employ or control the actions of the members of the committee. A medical staff committee may be a part of the hospital if it is staffed by physicians who are employees of the hospital. The medical staff is legally separate from the constituent physicians' practices. They may engage in joint decision making for the hospital, but they are not a joint venture. It is important to note that the courts have found that the members of a hospital medical staff are, by definition, a conspiracy.

This view was articulated in *Weiss v. York Hospital* (1984), an antitrust case. The plaintiff in *Weiss* had sued some of the individual physicians on the medical staff, but he had also sued the medical staff itself as an independent entity. The court found that the medical staff had no independent legal existence but accepted the plaintiff's allegation that the individual physicians were engaged in a conspiracy as defined in section 1 of the Sherman Antitrust Act:

> We agree with the Plaintiffs that, as a matter of law, the medical staff is a combination of individual doctors and therefore that any action taken by the medical staff satisfies the "contract, combination, or conspiracy" requirement of section 1. (*Weiss,* p. 815)

The key to this case is the distinction between the medical staff as an entity unto itself and the individual physicians who make up the medical staff. Although the trial court instructed the jury that the medical staff was an "unincorporated division" of the hospital and thus the two were a "single entity," incapable of conspiring, it was careful to distinguish the actions of the individual members of the medical staff:

> The Court also instructed the jury, however, that if they found that some or all of the individual Defendants took action against the Plaintiffs "in whole or in part in their individual capacities and motivated in whole or in part by independent personal economic interests, then such individual-named Defendants are, under the law, independent economic entities . . . legally capable of conspiring with York Hospital or its Medical and Dental Staff." (*Weiss,* p. 813)

In the case of *Quinn v. Kent General Hospital* (1985), the court expanded on this distinction between the medical staff and the individual physicians:

> It is certainly true that, regardless of their specialty, the members of the Hospital's active medical staff have a financial interest in limiting the number of physicians admitted to active staff privileges at the Hospital, for all admitting staff members compete with each other. . . . The active staff cannot be regarded as a single economic unit, but must be viewed as a collection of independent economic actors who are capable of combining or conspiring with each other for purposes of the Sherman Act."(*Quinn,* p. 1242)

The holdings of the *Weiss* and *Quinn* courts represent the view that medical staff committees satisfy the legal definition of a *conspiracy:* an informal relationship between independent parties to carry out joint action. Conspiracy is generally used as a pejorative term, but here it is presumed that the conspiracy is for good, not evil. Nonetheless, it means that medical staff committees that act improperly are subject to the same federal laws that govern traditional illegal conspiracies.

LEGAL CLIMATE FOR PEER REVIEW

While the law grants professionals substantial latitude in self-governance, under some circumstances their decisions are reviewable in court. If peer review decisions are based on fair criteria, fairly applied, they will be legally defensible. Legally defensible is not enough, however, because the cost of defending a peer review decision can be overwhelming for a small hospital or individual committee member. It is critical that peer review actions incorporate preventive law strategies to prevent lawsuits or reduce the cost of defending those that are brought.

Adverse peer review decisions damage and destroy careers. The termination of medical staff privileges can deprive a physician of the ability to continue to practice in his or her chosen community. More seriously, it can hamper his or her ability to obtain privileges at other hospitals. If professionals undertake private peer review activities (as opposed to state governmental activities), they should not be surprised when they are sued. There is a substantial penalty for being your brother's keeper.

The corporatization of medicine makes defensible peer review problematic. There is increasing pressure to expand peer review to include cost control matters. Hospitals and managed care plans want to eliminate physicians who do not comply with managed care guidelines, a controversial legal issue because the legal authority to do peer review does not obviate the laws governing anticompetitive conduct. Traditionally, allegedly anticompetitive actions have been attacked as violations of the antitrust laws. Increasingly, however, they are being seen as potential violations of business fraud laws such as the Racketeering Influenced Corrupt Organizations Act (RICO). A peer review action that violates RICO will subject the medical staff committee members to individual liability for treble damages, attorney's fees, and potential jail time. It is not a crime to deny physicians medical staff privileges wrongfully, but it may be a crime if it is done as part of a conspiracy to eliminate competition or to compromise the rights of patients.

While it is understandable that an aggrieved physician would sue after an adverse peer review decision, many physicians are baffled by the ready acceptance of these lawsuits by the courts and the public. This is easily explained. Average citizens (jurors) do not believe that there should be special legal provisions for professionals. They do not understand why a drunk physician who endangers the lives of patients is judged by colleagues rather than by the criminal justice system, as a drunk truck driver would be. Peer review is obviously biased in favor of the medical establishment. It is only to be expected that established practitioners will use it against physicians they do not like or who pose a competitive threat.

Litigation arising out of peer review decisions is so dangerous because the potential damages are large. A physician wrongly deprived of his or her livelihood can sue for the cash value of that livelihood. Even if only his or her reputation is injured, the traditional rules for libel and slander place a high value on the reputation of a professional. High damages attract attorneys. (See Chapter 4.) If the physician has been in practice for a substantial period, he or she is usually willing and able to pay to defend that practice. If the physician is young, with good prospects, an attorney may be willing to take the case on a contingent basis. If either the conspiracy or the antitrust laws have been violated, the plaintiff may recover treble damages and attorney's fees. It is these multiplied damages that drive attorneys to sue for antitrust violations.

State Law Violations

Many lawsuits contesting peer review decisions include state law claims, but these are usually secondary to federal actions. Most states have made it difficult for aggrieved physicians to contest peer review decisions under state law, due, in part, to state statutes immunizing peer review activities. In larger part, it is due to state discovery rules that block access to hospital records related to peer review. Plaintiffs cannot present their cases in court if they are denied access to the records that document their claims.

Defamation is harming a person's reputation through lies. Defamation may be slander—speaking the lies—or libel—writing them down. In neither case must the statements be true. If the story is horrible but true, spreading it may invade the person's privacy, but it is not libel or slander. A physician may maintain that the fact that his or her medical staff privileges were terminated constitutes slander. More commonly, slander claims are based on specific comments about the physician. For example, if the chairperson of the peer review committee characterizes a surgeon as a butcher, this is likely to result in a slander claim.

Most state laws prevent a physician from suing a member of a peer review committee for libel or slander for actions arising out of the peer review process. Unfortunately, many physicians forget that this protection does not extend beyond the formal peer review proceedings. Calling a colleague a ham-handed idiot may be protected in a peer review committee meeting; repeating the remark on the golf course is not protected. Physicians must restrict critical remarks to formal peer review proceedings.

A second state law action is *tortious interference* with the physician's business relationships. This is a special type of anticompetitive action but one that arises under the common law rather than the antitrust laws. The basis of this action is that legitimate competition is encouraged, but it is wrong to destroy a competitor's business with lies or improper interference. For example, assume that there are two surgeons on the medical staff of a hospital. Assume further that this is a small town with only one hospital. If surgeon Y starts a rumor that surgeon X is a drunk and is dangerous to his patients, this is slander. If surgeon Y starts this rumor to improve his or her practice by destroying surgeon X's practice, this is also tortious interference with surgeon X's business relationships.

Another form of tortious interference is to entice business associates not to honor their contractual obligations. For example, a physician group that tries to persuade a hospital to break its exclusive contract with a radiology group would be liable for tortious interference with a contractual relationship. In many states, tortious interference resembles invasion of privacy more than it does defamation. The truth of the accusation used to inflame the physician's business associates is not a defense. Even if the physician does cheat patients, it is improper to use this information to persuade the physician's business associates to change their allegiance. The proper course is to initiate appropriate disciplinary proceedings.

Federal Law Violations

Peer review actions are most commonly contested in federal court under federal laws. This allows the aggrieved physician to escape state law protections for peer review actions. More important, the federal courts do not recognize state laws that protect peer review committee minutes and related records from discovery. Some federal laws also provide for treble damages and attorney's fees if the plaintiff prevails. Without the possibility of this increased recovery, it would not make economic sense to contest most improper peer review actions. Laws that pay a bonus to a successful plaintiff are called *private attorney general laws*. These provisions are intended to encourage private enforcement of the law through civil litigation, saving the government the cost of prosecuting violators in the criminal justice system. Both the antitrust laws and RICO contain these private attorney general provisions.

Due Process Violations

Due process is legal shorthand for a set of notions regarding fairness. Daniel Webster defined this phrase to mean a law that "hears before it condemns, which proceeds on inquiry, and renders judgment only after trial" (*Trustees of Dartmouth College v. Woodward*, p. 518). Courts divide their inquiry into the fairness of the law (substantive due process) and the fairness of the application of the law (procedural due process). Due process is a consideration in peer review in two situations: when the hospital or other entity carrying out the review is a governmental entity and if the review is governed by specific state or federal laws.

In governmental entities, such as a city or county hospital, the actions of the peer review committee are imputed to the state. Since the Constitution requires the states to deal fairly with citizens, these entities are required to provide some level of due process. The more severe is the deprivation that might result from the state action, the more elaborate is the required procedure. In the medical context, the criminal prosecution of a physician for violating the controlled substances act would require the most elaborate protection of the physician's rights. If a due process hierarchy were established, it would be: (1) criminal law prosecutions, (2) state or federal civil law prosecutions, (3) private civil law actions, (4) actions involving the physician's license, (5) peer review actions at governmental entities, (6) private peer review regulated by state or federal law, (7) private peer review of independent contractors, and (8) private peer review of employee physicians.

With two exceptions, the due process requirements for peer review in private institutions are limited to the contractual provisions of the medical staff bylaws. This is sometimes extended by state law provision, but the major exception is the federal Health Care Quality Improvement Act of 1986. As discussed in Chapter 19, this law does not set due process requirements. It encourages private institutions to provide due process protections by giving them conditional immunity from state and federal lawsuits over peer review activities.

Substantive due process is an old legal notion that more nearly approximates a lay idea of fairness. Courts use a substantive due process standard to invalidate rules or laws with which they disagree. A peer review example would be a medical staff rule banning osteopaths from the staff. A court might find that this rule, however fairly and uniformly applied, violates substantive due process. This would be an expression of the court's belief that the exclusion of osteopaths would not serve to enhance the quality of the medical care in the hospital. The court would be ruling on the substance of the rule rather than its fair application.

Substantive due process is a consideration in peer review only if the review criteria exclude classes of practitioners without evidence that this exclusion is reasonably related to the quality of medical care. An example of a current controversy is the blanket exclusion of podiatrists from medical staffs. Podiatry is not a recognized medical specialty, but its practitioners are licensed by the state to provide medical care. These state licensing laws also establish the scope of a professional's practice. In some states, hospital care is within the allowable practice of a podiatrist. In these states, a podiatrist could argue that a governmental hospital that excluded all podiatrists was violating their right to substantive due process. Whether the courts would agree is another question.

Procedural due process refers to the procedure used to conduct the peer review. The procedure must be fair. Accused physicians must be allowed to present their case to an impartial decision maker. This may include examining the evidence, presenting and questioning witnesses, and appealing the decision to a neutral reviewer. It is not necessary to conduct the proceedings as if they are part of a court proceeding. The process may be informal, as long as it is consistent and the physicians subject to review know the rules.

Antitrust Laws
The federal antitrust laws, embodied in the Sherman and Clayton acts, are intended to protect competition that affects interstate commerce. These laws apply to all medical practice activities because of the court's broad definition of interstate commerce. Antitrust laws have three attractions to physicians attacking peer review proceedings. As federal laws, they obviate state law peer review protections. In other business contexts, they are used to attack exclusionary agreements that have a surface resemblance to medical staff contracts. Finally, prevailing plaintiffs can recover three times the proved damages plus their attorney's fees.

The antitrust laws do not condemn bigness in itself, but they prevent a business from using its size or control of the market (monopoly power) against its competitors. The antitrust laws also prevent competitors from reaching agreements to divide markets (horizontal restraints) or otherwise reduce competition. The policy of the antitrust laws is to protect competition, not competitors. There are certain actions, such as price fixing, that are illegal without reference to their effect on the market. These are called *per se violations;* they are illegal irrespective of the market power of the offenders. For all other violations, the plaintiff must prove that the business, or businesses, involved in the alleged violation have a dominant market position.

Market Share
The effect of the market share requirement is that unless the hospital is the major provider in a small community or is possessed of a unique community resource (say, the only federally funded level 3 nursery in the community), then the court will reject antitrust claims against it. Even if a hospital has sufficient market share, the court is concerned with the impact of the practices on the consumer, not on the competitors. The court will not be concerned if the hospital uses its market power in a way that injures an individual physician, as long as it does not injure consumers. This was the heart of the *Jefferson Parish Hospital District No. 2 v. Hyde* case (1984), which is taken as sanctioning exclusive contracts with medical staff members.

In this case the plaintiff was an anesthesiologist. He applied for medical staff privileges at Jefferson Parrish Hospital and was rejected because the hospital had an exclusive contract with a group of anesthesiologists. Hyde sued, alleging that this exclusive contract was a violation of the antitrust laws in that it interfered with his right to practice in the hospital.

While there were several other issues in the case, the heart of the U.S. Supreme Court's ruling was that Hyde only wanted to join the conspiracy. He did not claim that he would compete with the existing group and thus benefit the public through lower prices or better service. He just complained that he was denied the opportunity to profit from the price fixing and work allocation aspects of the exclusive contract granted to the existing anesthesia group. Finding that this would be of no benefit to the community, the Court rejected Hyde's claim. Rather than an endorsement of exclusive contracts as a way to allocate medical staff privileges, this case should be seen as the Court's lack of sympathy for would-be conspirators who are left out. The Court did not rule on the fate of exclusive contracts in the face of an attack by a physician who offered a competitive alternative in the delivery of services.

State Action Immunity
There is an exemption to the federal antitrust laws for actions taken by states. This is called the *Parker v. Brown* immunity, after a famous 1943 case upholding the right of California to enforce agreements to protect raisin growers. The agreements at issue in the "raisin case" allocated market share to the various growers. This guaranteed a profit to the growers in the scheme, artificially raised the prices for raisins, and excluded new growers. While it would have been illegal for the growers themselves to have entered into these agreements, the Court found that a state may proscribe competition among its own citizens. Several courts tried to use this principle to block peer review lawsuits in states where the board of medical examiners had some role in reviewing peer review decisions.

This state action immunity was at issue in the much publicized case of *Patrick v. Burget* (1988), which involved the sole hospital in a small community. Because of geographic isolation, this hospital had monopoly power in the local market. As a result of a business disagreement, the other members of the medical staff conspired to terminate Dr. Patrick's staff privileges. This was a blatant conspiracy that included even attempts to manipulate the state board of medical examiners. Dr. Patrick won a multimillion dollar verdict at trial, and the case was appealed to the federal circuit court. Several medical groups filed briefs urging the court to overturn the verdict while acknowledging that the review itself was grossly unfair. The appeals court found that the termination of Dr. Patrick's staff privileges did violate the antitrust laws. The court also found that the peer review process in Oregon was not an independent activity conducted by private individuals but an extension of state power and thus subject to active supervision by the state. Based on this regulation by the state, which, on paper at least, is quite detailed, the court found that the defendant's conduct was immune from legal challenge.

Dr. Patrick appealed the circuit court's decision to the U.S. Supreme Court, with his request for review supported by the FTC. The FTC argued that there was insufficient state involvement to justify state action immunity. The Supreme Court found:

> Because we conclude that no state actor in Oregon actively supervises hospital peer-review decisions, we hold that the state action doctrine does not protect the peer-review activities challenged in this case from application of the federal antitrust laws. In so holding, we are not unmindful of the policy argument that respondents and their Amici have advanced for reaching the opposite conclusion. They contend that effective peer review is essential to the provision of quality medical care and that any threat of antitrust liability will prevent physicians from participating openly and actively in peer-review proceedings. This argument, however, essentially challenges the wisdom of applying the antitrust laws to the sphere of medical care, and as such is properly directed to the legislative branch. (*Patrick*, p. 105)

The *Patrick* case may be a classic example of the cliché that hard cases make bad law. The egregious facts in the case made it unlikely that the Supreme Court would find that Oregon supervised the review of Dr. Patrick's competence. To have accepted that the *Patrick* case was a valid exercise of state oversight would have only shifted the issue to a due process claim based on improper state action. While many physicians are concerned that the *Patrick* holding will cripple peer review, the Health Care Quality Improvement Act immunizes properly conducted peer review irrespective of state action.

RICO

We believe that RICO will supplant antitrust laws as a basis for challenging improper medical business practices, including peer review proceedings. (See Chapter 10 for a discussion of RICO.) As with the antitrust laws, RICO provides for treble damages plus attorney's fees. RICO actions are potentially much more threatening than antitrust actions because RICO does not require either market share or monopoly power. Physicians who engage in fraudulent peer review activities may be sued irrespective of the health care business's share of the relevant market. While RICO has been little used in medical law, its explosive growth in other areas makes it probable that it will soon reach medical businesses.

The predicate acts for a RICO action contesting a peer review decision could be commercial bribery, mail, and wire fraud. Commercial bribery laws prohibit using financial incentives to influence the decisions of physicians and other fiduciaries. Since these laws prohibit hospitals and third-party payers from providing financial incentives to influence physicians' decisions about their patients, physicians who receive these incentives are technically receiving bribes. If these incentives are involved in an improper peer review action, the injured physicians may claim under the RICO laws. An example would be a medical staff under a total capitation agreement that removed a physician for medically justified but financially troublesome admissions.

The mail and wire fraud statutes merely require plaintiffs to prove that the defendants used the mail or telephone ancillary to their fraudulent activities. The plaintiff does not need to prove that the use of the mail or wire was an essential element of the fraud. A peer review committee meeting that was scheduled by telephone or with a letter would satisfy the requirement for mail or wire fraud if the committee performed a fraudulent review.

RICO is not intended to provide a remedy for anticompetitive actions covered under the antitrust laws. It does apply if other fraudulent activities are involved with the antitrust violations. A medical staff committee that uses sham quality-of-care issues to deprive competitors of their medical staff privileges would be engaged in fraud beyond the anticompetitive activities. If these fraudulent activities involve the use of the mails or the telephone, they violate the federal mail or wire fraud statutes. Although it has not been specifically litigated, a hospital medical staff may satisfy the RICO definition of an enterprise. Combining this enterprise with a pattern of mail and wire fraud violations will subject all members of the medical staff committee and the hospital itself to liability for RICO violations.

CONCLUSIONS

Peer review is critical to maintaining quality medical care, but it is a suspect activity when carried on by the competitors of the physician being reviewed. As a commonsense matter, jurors may assume that an action by a group of physicians against one of their competitors was done for anticompetitive reasons.

Physicians must not be overcautious when conducting peer review. If the hospital allows an incompetent physician to continue practicing, persons injured by the physician may sue the hospital for negligent peer review. The members of the medical staff also will have a duty to protect their patients from incompetent physicians (no more referrals or consultations). In many states, they also have a duty to notify the state board of medical examiners.

BIBLIOGRAPHY

Cases
American Society of Mechanical Engineers v. Hydrolevel. 456 US 556 (1982).
Goldfarb v. Virginia State Bar. 421 US 733 (1975).
Jefferson Parish Hospital District No. 2 v. Hyde. 466 US 2 (1984).
Parker v. Brown. 317 US 341 (1943).
Patrick v. Burget. 486 US 94 (1988).
Quinn v. Kent General Hospital. 716 F Supp 1226 (1985).
Trustees of Dartmouth College v. Woodward. 17 US 518 (1819).
Weiss v. York Hospital. 745 F2d 786 (Cir 3 1984).

Articles
American Medical Association: *Collective Negotiation and Antitrust.* 1991.
Bell J: Does peer review work? JAMA 1988 Dec 2; 260(21):3213.
Borenstein DB: Standards of proof for ethics committees of professional organizations. Hosp Community Psychiatry 1987 Jul; 38(7):711–12, 717.
Burda D: Public gains access to peer review data. Hospitals 1987 Jan 20; 61(2):57.
Caplan RA; Posner K; Ward RJ; Cheney FW: Peer reviewer agreement for major anesthetic mishaps. QRB 1988 Dec; 14(12):363–68.
Chambers LW; Sibley JC; Spitzer WO; Tugwell P: Quality of care assessment: How to set up and use an indicator condition. Clin Invest Med 1981; 4(1):41–50.
Colin N: Clinical trial stirs legal battles: Legal disputes in Atlanta and Chicago over surgery for myopia raise issue of how controversial surgical techniques should be assessed. Science 1985 Mar 15; 227:1316.
Curran WJ: Medical peer review of physician competence and performance: Legal immunity and the antitrust laws. N Engl J Med 1987 Mar 5; 316(10):597–98.
Dolin LC: Antitrust law versus peer review. N Engl J Med 1985 Oct 31; 313(18):1156–57.
Freidheim JE: Doing something about "bad doctors." IMJ 1986 May; 169(5):257.
Gibbs CE; Cheetham PS: Voluntary review of obstetric and gynecologic services. QRB 1988 Sep; 14(9):290–93.
Grol R; van Eijk J; Mesker P; Schellevis F: Audit: A project on peer review in general practice. Fam Pract 1985 Dec; 2(4):219–24.
Hastings DA: Legal issues raised by private review activities of medical peer-review organizations. J Health Polit Policy Law 1983 Summer; 8(2):293–313.
Koska MT: ACOG program eases peer review conflicts. Hospitals 1988 Apr 20; 62(8):58.
Koska MT: Proper procedures are key to peer review legality experts say. Hospitals 1988 Jun 20; 62(12)65.
LaCombe MA: Peer review (Part 1). Am J Med 1987 Aug; 83(2):336–37.
Logan WS: The evaluation of the impaired physician. New Dir Ment Health Serv 1989 Spring; 41:33–53.
Merry MD: A physician's perspective on proper design of quality assessment criteria. QRB 1982 Oct; 8(10):3–4.
Newald J: Watchful eyes to follow physicians through '87. Hospitals 1987 Jan 5; 61(1):49.

Pattee JJ: Utilization review committee as a peer review mechanism. J Am Geriatr Soc 1980 Apr; 28(4):190–91.

Prout DM: Checks and balances in peer review: Advice from the Patrick case (editorial). Ann Intern Med 1988 Nov 1; 109(9):689–90.

Relman AS; Angell M: How good is peer review? (editorial; comment). N Engl J Med 1989 Sep 21; 321(12):827–29.

Rennie D; Knoll E: Investigating peer review (editorial). Ann Intern Med 1988 Aug 1; 109(3):181.

Riffer J: Antitrust law and peer review remain at odds. Hospitals 1986 Feb 5; 60(3):58.

Riffer J: Peer review gets a big legal push. Hospitals 1986 Nov 20; 60(22):78.

Todd JS: Physicians looking at themselves (editorial). JAMA 1989 Sep 8; 262(10):1376–77.

Winickoff RN; Coltin KL; Morgan MM; Buxbaum RC; Barnett GO: Improving physician performance through peer comparison feedback. Med Care 1984 Jun; 22(6):527–34.

19

The Federal Peer Review Law

CRITICAL POINTS
- The Health Care Quality Improvement Act provides vital protections for peer review activities.
- Peer review activities must follow the specific requirement of the the federal law to qualify for federal protection.
- The conditions for protected peer review will make it more difficult to control some medically dangerous practices.
- The key to protected peer review is a well-developed and well-documented record of the proceedings.

This chapter focuses on *42 USCA s 11101, et seq.*, the codification of the Health Care Quality Improvement Act of 1986, which provides immunity for physicians who conduct good-faith peer review. It also creates a national database on physician peer review matters. If peer review activities comply with the act, physicians and others conducting these reviews cannot be sued under state or federal civil laws, including the antitrust and RICO statutes. This protection may be more illusionary than real, however. The courts have never allowed aggrieved physicians to recover for good-faith peer review activities—only for those that violated a law. Such violations, by definition, are not good faith.

The more important provision of the act may be the National Practitioner Data Bank. This is meant to be a clearinghouse for information on peer review actions, payments in medical malpractice cases, and other information bearing on the competence of physicians. The intent of the data bank is to facilitate peer review and to prevent physicians from escaping disciplinary actions by moving to a different state. This information is available to malpractice plaintiffs in only very limited circumstances.

REQUIREMENTS OF THE ACT

The act's intent is clear from its subtitle: "Encouraging Good Faith Professional Review Activities." The act establishes the basic constraints on peer review. While its immunity and attorney's fees provisions will discourage some lawsuits, its limitations on reviewing improper delegation of authority will generate others. The creation of nationally available physician dossiers will improve the quality and reduce the cost of peer review. But it will generate additional litigation because it will destroy the practices of physicians who are stigmatized by an improper peer review action.

So far, the act has been subject to very little court review and no major appellate decisions. Physician and hospital objections to the procedures for maintaining the data bank delayed its initiation until September 1990. Since there are no provisions for retrospective reporting, it will be several years before the data bank is fully operational.

This review of the act is based on the statutory language, with annotations to improve the clarity. The act is divided into the following sections: Protection from Liability, Adequate Notice and Hearing, Reporting Malpractice Payments, Duty of Hospitals to Obtain Information, Definitions and Reports, and Attorney's Fees.

The need for this law was based on the following congressional findings:

(1) The increasing occurrence of medical malpractice and the need to improve the quality of medical care have become nationwide problems that warrant greater efforts than those that can be undertaken by any individual State.
(2) There is a national need to restrict the ability of incompetent physicians to move from State to State without disclosure or discovery of the physician's previous damaging or incompetent performance.
(3) This nationwide problem can be remedied through effective professional peer review.
(4) The threat of private money damage liability under Federal laws, including treble damage liability under Federal antitrust law, unreasonably discourages physicians from participating in effective professional peer review.
(5) There is an overriding national need to provide incentive and protection for physicians engaging in effective professional peer review. (sec. 11101)

Protection from Liability

If a professional review action (as defined in the Act) of a professional review body meets all the standards specified in the Act, then the professional review body, any person acting as a member or staff to the body, any person under a contract or other formal agreement with the body, and any person who participates with or assists the body with respect to the action, shall not be liable in damages under any law of the United States or of any State (or political subdivision thereof) with respect to the action.

This immunity does not extend to civil rights violations, nor does it apply to civil or criminal actions brought by the United States or any Attorney General of a State. There is no immunity for the peer review activities of an institution that does not comply with the reporting requirements of the Act. These protections apply to peer review actions taken on or after October 14, 1989, unless a state chooses, by legislation, to exempt itself from the protections of the Act. (sec. 11111)

Standards for Professional Review Actions
To qualify for immunity, a professional review action must be taken:

(1) in the reasonable belief that the action was in the furtherance of quality health care,
(2) after a reasonable effort to obtain the facts of the matter,

(3) after adequate notice and hearing procedures are afforded to the physician involved or after such other procedures as are fair to the physician under the circumstances, and
(4) in the reasonable belief that the action was warranted by the facts known after such reasonable effort to obtain facts and after required notice and hearing

A professional review action shall be presumed to have met the preceding standards unless this presumption is rebutted by a preponderance of the evidence. (sec. 11112)

Definition of Acceptable "Professional Review Action"

The term "professional review action" means an action or recommendation of a professional review body which is taken or made in the conduct of professional review activity, which is based on the competence or professional conduct of an individual physician (which conduct affects or could affect adversely the health or welfare of a patient or patients), and which affects (or may affect) adversely the clinical privileges, or membership in a professional society, of the physician. Such term includes a formal decision of a professional review body not to take an action or make a recommendation described in the previous sentence and also includes professional review activities relating to a professional review action. . . . [A]n action is not considered to be based on the competence or professional conduct of (a) a physician if the action is primarily based on—the physician's association, or lack of association, with a professional society or association; (b) the physician's fees or the physician's advertising or engaging in other competitive acts intended to solicit or retain business; (c) the physician's participation in prepaid group health plans, salaried employment, or any other manner of delivering health services whether on a fee-for-service or other basis; (d) a physician's association with, supervision of, delegation of authority to, support for, training of, or participation in a private group practice with, a member or members of a particular class of health care practitioner or professional; (e) or any other matter that does not relate to the competence or professional conduct of a physician. (sec. 11151[9])

Limitations of the Act

Nothing in the Act shall be construed as requiring health care entities to provide clinical privileges to any or all classes or types of physicians or other licensed health care practitioners.

This Act only applies to physicians. It does not affect the activities of professional review bodies regarding nurses, other licensed health care practitioners, or other health professionals who are not physicians.

Nothing in this Act shall be construed as affecting in any manner the rights and remedies afforded patients under any provision of Federal or State law to seek redress for any harm or injury suffered as a result of negligent treatment or care by any physician, health care practitioner, or health care entity, or as limiting any defenses or immunities available to any physician, health care practitioner, or health care entity. (sec. 11115)

Adequate Notice and Hearing

A health care entity is deemed to have met the adequate notice and hearing requirement of the Act with respect to a physician if the following conditions are met or are waived voluntarily by the physician. . . . A professional review body's failure to meet the conditions for notice and hearing described in the Act shall not, in itself, constitute failure to meet the standards of the Act. (sec. 11112)

Notice of a Right to a Hearing

The physician has been given notice stating—that a professional review action has been proposed to be taken against the physician, the reasons for the proposed action, that the physician has the right to request a hearing on the proposed action, any time limit (of not less than 30 days) within which to request such a hearing, and a summary of the rights in the hearing. (sec. 11112)

Notice of the Nature of the Hearing

If a hearing is requested on a timely basis the physician involved must be given notice stating—the place, time, and date, of the hearing, which date shall not be less than 30 days after the date of the notice, and a list of the witnesses (if any) expected to testify at the hearing on behalf of the professional review body. The right to the hearing may be forfeited if the physician fails, without good cause, to appear. (sec. 11112)

Economic Competition

If a hearing is requested on a timely basis—the hearing shall be held (as determined by the health care entity) before an arbitrator mutually acceptable to the physician and the health care entity, before a hearing officer who is appointed by the entity and who is not in direct economic competition with the physician involved, or before a panel of individuals who are appointed by the entity and are not in direct economic competition with the physician involved. (sec. 11112)

Rights in the Hearing

In the hearing the physician involved has the right—to representation by an attorney or other person of the physician's choice, to have a record made of the proceedings, copies of which may be obtained by the physician upon payment of any reasonable charges associated with the preparation thereof, to call, examine, and cross-examine witnesses, to present evidence determined to be relevant by the hearing officer, regardless of its admissibility in a court of law, and to submit a written statement at the close of the hearing. (sec. 11112)

Rights at the Completion of the Hearing

Upon completion of the hearing, the physician involved has the right—to receive the written recommendation of the arbitrator, officer, or panel, including a statement of the basis for the recommendations, and to receive a written decision of the health care entity, including a statement of the basis for the decision. (sec. 11112)

Emergency Procedures

Nothing in the Act shall be construed as—requiring the notice and a hearing where there is no adverse professional review action taken; or in the case of a suspension or restriction of clinical privileges, for a period of not longer than 14 days, during which an investigation is being conducted to determine the need for a professional review action; or precluding an immediate suspension or restriction of clinical privileges, subject to subsequent notice and hearing or other adequate procedures, where the failure to take such an action may result in an imminent danger to the health of any individual. (sec. 11112)

Reporting Malpractice Payments

Each entity (including an insurance company) which makes payment under a policy of insurance, self-insurance, or otherwise in settlement (or partial settlement) of, or in satisfaction of a judgment in, a medical malpractice action or claim shall report, in accordance with this Act [discussed below], information respecting the payment and circumstances thereof. (In interpreting information reported under this subchapter [of the act], a payment in settlement of a medical malpractice action or claim shall not be construed as creating a presumption that medical malpractice has occurred. (sec. 11137)

The information to be reported under includes—the name of any physician or licensed health care practitioner for whose benefit the payment is made, the amount of the payment, the name (if known) of any hospital with which the physician or practitioner is affiliated or associated, a description of the acts or omissions and injuries or illnesses upon which the action or claim was based, and such other information as the Secretary determines is required for appropriate interpretation of information reported under this section.

Any entity that fails to report information on a payment required to be reported under this section shall be subject to a civil money penalty of not more than $10,000 for each such payment involved. (sec. 11131)

Reporting by Boards of Medical Examiners

Each Board of Medical Examiners which revokes or suspends (or otherwise restricts) a physician's license or censures, reprimands, or places on probation a physician, for reasons relating to the physician's professional competence or professional conduct, or to which a physician's license is surrendered, shall report, the name of the physician involved, a description of the acts or omissions or other reasons (if known) for the revocation, suspension, or surrender of license, and such other information respecting the circumstances of the action or surrender as the Secretary deems appropriate.

If, after notice of noncompliance and providing opportunity to correct noncompliance, the Secretary determines that a Board of Medical Examiners has failed to report information in accordance with the Act, the Secretary shall designate another qualified entity for the reporting of the required information. (sec. 11132)

Reporting by Health Care Entities

Each health care entity which takes a professional review action that adversely affects the clinical privileges of a physician for a period longer than 30 days shall report to the Board of Medical Examiners. This duty also applies when the health care entity accepts the surrender of clinical privileges of a physician while the physician is under an investigation by the entity relating to possible incompetence or improper professional conduct, or in return for not conducting such an investigation or proceeding; or in the case of such an entity which is a professional society, takes a professional review action which adversely affects the membership of a physician in the society.

The information to be reported is—the name of the physician or practitioner involved, a description of the acts or omissions or other reasons for the action or, if known, for the surrender, and such other information respecting the circumstances of the action or surrender as the Secretary deems appropriate.

A health care entity that fails substantially to meet the reporting requirements of this Act shall lose the protections of section otherwise provided by the Act. This suspension of immunity does not become effective until the Secretary publishes the name of the entity as provided in the Act. (sec. 11133)

Form of Reporting

The information required to be reported under the Act shall be reported regularly (but not less often than monthly) and in such form and manner as the Secretary prescribes. Such information shall first be required to be reported on a date (not later than one year after November 14, 1986) specified by the Secretary. The information required to be reported under the Act shall be reported to the Secretary, or, in the Secretary's discretion, to an appropriate private or public agency which has made suitable arrangements with the Secretary with respect to receipt, storage, protection of confidentiality, and dissemination of the information under this subchapter.

Information about malpractice lawsuit settlement payments or adverse verdicts shall also be reported to the appropriate State licensing board (or boards) in the State in which the medical malpractice claim arose. (sec. 11134)

Protection for Persons Providing Information

Notwithstanding any other provision of law, no person (whether as a witness or otherwise) providing information to a professional review body regarding the competence or professional conduct of a physician shall be held, by reason of having provided such information, to be liable in damages under any law of the United States or of any State (or political subdivision thereof) unless such information is false and the person providing it knew that such information was false. (sec. 11111)

Duty of Hospitals to Obtain Information

It is the duty of each hospital to request from the Secretary (or the agency designated by the Secretary), at the time a physician or licensed health care practitioner applies to be on the medical staff (courtesy or otherwise) of, or for clinical privileges at, the hospital, information reported under this Act concerning the physician or practitioner. Every two years the hospital shall request updated information concerning any physician or such practitioner who is on the medical staff (courtesy or otherwise) of, or has been granted clinical privileges at, the hospital. A hospital may request information at other times.

With respect to a medical malpractice action, a hospital which does not request information respecting a physician or practitioner as required by this Act is presumed to have knowledge of any information reported under this subchapter to the Secretary with respect to the physician or practitioner. Each hospital may rely upon information provided to the hospital under this Act and shall not be held liable for such reliance in the absence of the hospital's knowledge that the information provided was false. (sec. 11135)

Access to Information

The Secretary or the agency designated under the Act shall, upon request, provide information reported under the Act with respect to a physician or other licensed health care practitioner to State licensing boards, to hospitals, and to other health care entities (including health maintenance organizations) that have entered (or may be entering) into an employment or affiliation relationship with the physician or practitioner or to which the physician or practitioner has applied for clinical privileges or appointment to the medical staff. (sec. 11137)

Disclosure and Correction of Information

With respect to the information reported to the Secretary (or the agency designated under the Act) respecting a physician or other licensed health care practitioner, the Secretary shall, by regulation, provide for—disclosure of the information, upon request, to the physician or practitioner, and procedures in the case of disputed accuracy of the information. (sec. 11136)

Confidentiality of Information

Information reported pursuant to the Act is considered confidential and shall not be disclosed (other than to the physician or practitioner involved) except with respect to professional review activity, as necessary to carry out the provisions of the Act or in accordance with regulations of the Secretary promulgated pursuant to the Act. Nothing in this subsection shall prevent the disclosure of such information by a party which is otherwise authorized, under applicable State law, to make such disclosure. Information that is in a form that does not permit the identification of any particular health care entity, physician, other health care practitioner, or patient shall not be considered confidential.

Any person who improperly discloses this information shall be subject to a civil money penalty of not more than $10,000 for each such violation involved. Information provided under the Act is intended to be used solely with respect to activities in the furtherance of the quality of health care. (sec. 11137)

Definitions and Reports (Sec. 11151)

1. *"adversely affecting"*
   The term "adversely affecting" includes reducing, restricting, suspending, revoking, denying, or failing to renew clinical privileges or membership in a health care entity.
2. *"Board of Medical Examiners"*
   The term "Board of Medical Examiners" includes a body comparable to such a Board (as determined by the State) with responsibility for the licensing of physicians and also includes a subdivision of such a Board or body.
3. *"clinical privileges"*
   The term "clinical privileges" includes privileges, membership on the medical staff, and the other circumstances pertaining to the furnishing of medical care under which a physician or other licensed health care practitioner is permitted to furnish such care by a health care entity.
4. *"health care entity"*
   The term "health care entity" means—a hospital that is licensed to provide health care services by the State in which it is located, an entity (including a health maintenance organization or group medical practice) that provides health care services and that follows a formal peer review process for the purpose of furthering quality health care, a professional society (or committee thereof) of physicians or other licensed health care practitioners that follows a formal peer review process for the purpose of furthering quality health care.

   The term "health care entity" does not include a professional society (or committee thereof) if, within the previous 5 years, the society has been found by the Federal Trade Commission or any court to have engaged in any anticompetitive practice which had the effect of restricting the practice of licensed health care practitioners.
5. *"hospital"*
   The term "hospital" means an institution which—is primarily engaged in providing, by or under the supervision of physicians, to inpatients (A) diagnostic services and therapeutic services for medical diagnosis, treatment, and care of injured, disabled, or sick persons, or (B) rehabilitation services for the rehabilitation of injured, disabled, or sick persons. In the case of an institution in any State in which State or applicable local law provides for the licensing of hospitals, (A) is licensed pursuant to such law or (B) is approved, by the agency of such State or locality responsible for licensing hospitals, as meeting the standards established for such licensing. (42 USCA sec. 1395x(e)(1)&(7))
6. *"licensed health care practitioner"*
   The terms "licensed health care practitioner" and "practitioner" mean, with respect to a State, an individual (other than a physician) who is licensed or otherwise authorized by the State to provide health care services.
7. *"medical malpractice actions or claim"*
   The term "medical malpractice action or claim" means a written claim or demand for payment based on a health care provider's furnishing (or failure to furnish) health care services, and includes the filing of a cause of action, based

on the law of tort, brought in any court of any State or the United States seeking monetary damages.

8. *"physician"*
The term "physician" means a doctor of medicine or osteopathy or a doctor of dental surgery or medical dentistry legally authorized to practice medicine and surgery or dentistry by a State (or any individual who, without authority holds himself or herself out to be so authorized).

9. *"professional review activity"*
The term "professional review activity" means an activity of a health care entity with respect to an individual physician—to determine whether the physician may have clinical privileges with respect to, or membership in, the entity, to determine the scope or conditions of such privileges or membership, or to change or modify such privileges or membership.

10. *"professional review body"*
The term "professional review body" means a health care entity and the governing body or any committee of a health care entity which conducts professional review activity, and includes any committee of the medical staff of such an entity when assisting the governing body in a professional review activity.

11. *"Secretary"*
The term "Secretary" means the Secretary of Health and Human Services.

12. *"State"*
The term "State" means the 50 States, the District of Columbia, Puerto Rico, the Virgin Islands, Guam, American Samoa, and the Northern Mariana Islands.

13. *"State Licensing Board"*
The term "State licensing board" means, with respect to a physician or health care provider in a State, the agency of the State which is primarily responsible for the licensing of the physician or provider to furnish health care services.

Attorney's Fees

In any suit brought against a defendant, if the court finds that the defendant has met the standards set forth in the Act, and the defendant substantially prevails, the court shall, at the conclusion of the action, award to the defendant the cost of the suit attributable to such claim, including a reasonable attorney's fee, if the claim, or the claimant's conduct during the litigation of the claim, was frivolous, unreasonable, without foundation, or in bad faith. A defendant shall not be considered to have substantially prevailed when the plaintiff obtains an award for damages or permanent injunctive or declaratory relief. (sec. 11113)

THE PROBLEM OF GOOD FAITH

The crux of the immunity provisions of the act is the determination of whether a peer review action is made in "the reasonable belief that the action was in the furtherance of quality health care" and does not violate the list of forbidden criteria for peer review. This will rule out immunity for cases such as *Patrick v. Burget* in which the plaintiff's case was based on the allegation that the peer review action was based on anticompetitive rather than quality-of-care grounds. (See Chaapter 18.) More generally, good-faith quality-of-care decisions have always been a defense to actions contesting peer review. If the defendants can establish that the action was intended to protect patients, they will win the case. Moreover, since the determination of reasonableness is a jury matter, the act will not allow the judge to dismiss the plaintiff's complaint before trial if there is a factual question about the reasonableness of the committee's actions. The most meaningful effect of the immunity provisions may be the allowance of attorney's fees in frivolous cases. This should be a useful deterrent to cases that are filed merely to delay proceedings or to intimidate the members of the peer review committee.

The act's immunity is important if the jury finds that the peer review action was taken in the reasonable belief that it would further the quality of medical care but nonetheless violated a federal law. This might help when physicians on the peer review committee violate other laws but conduct the peer review properly. For example, assume that the physicians on the committee were engaged in anticompetitive activities that do not concern the practice of the physician they are reviewing. If they conduct a proper peer review activity, the act might prevent an aggrieved physician from alleging that the peer review action was tainted by the racketeering activities.

A more interesting question is whether the act would allow peer review activities designed to improve medical care by reducing competition. For example, specialty surgeons must get several cases of each unusual condition to keep their skills keen. If competition between two surgeons denies both the necessary level of cases to maintain their skills, this will adversely affect the quality of medical care in the community. It might be appropriate for a peer review committee to consider the adequacy of the patient base when granting or renewing a specialist's hospital privileges. The act, however, defines these considerations as per se improper:

> Action is not considered to be based on the competence or professional conduct of a physician if the action is primarily based on— . . . [any] matter that does not relate to the competence or professional conduct of a physician.

Thus, if the specialty surgeons were still competent (before competition reduced their skills), the act seems to forbid peer review actions necessary to maintain that competence. Once the competition had reduced the surgeons' competence, the committee might be able to act to reduce competition. At this point, however, it might be impossible to justify penalizing one surgeon to the benefit of the other. This also may affect the general issue of the hospital's using medical staff privilege decisions to shape the package of services it offers.

POTENTIAL ADVERSE IMPACTS

While physicians see the act as protecting them from lawsuits by the disgruntled victims of peer review, this may not be the act's major effect. The act evidences the disparate agendas of its drafters. The central intent of Congress was to mandate a national clearinghouse for peer review actions and medical malpractice payments. This was the quid pro quo for granting the physicians' request that they get immunity for engaging in peer review. Unfortunately, many nonphysician groups, including nonscientific providers such as chiropractors, were successful in excluding from immunity the review of physicians who improperly delegate authority to nonphysician providers.

The act will make it more difficult to curb the inappropriate delegation of authority to nonphysician personnel as managed care plans and hospitals attempt to use nonprofessional staff to care for patients (Adelman 1991). This is an understandable though not necessarily a correct response to cost containment. This will be harder to attack because the act defines as improper any peer review activities based on "a physician's association with, supervision of, delegation of authority to . . . a member or members of a particular class of health care practitioner or professional." This provision will make it more difficult to discipline physicians who allow nurses, physician extenders, or others to practice medicine on their licenses. This practice can have a devastating effect on the quality of patient care, yet the act seems to preclude it as a ground for peer review. This is aggravated in states that have uncritically incorporated the federal provisions into their own peer review laws.

THE PROBLEM OF BIAS

Until recently, the definition of a peer-for-peer review purpose was based on the historical notion of a peer. A "jury of one's peers" once meant a jury composed of persons who personally knew both the defendant and the community. These peers were assumed to be better able to determine the truth of the case than persons who did not know the participants and their history. The legal system gradually rejected the use of knowledgeable peers because of the problem of bias. The courts shifted their concern with the jurors' knowing the facts of the case to a concern that the jurors would let their prejudices for or against the defendant affect their ruling. Contemporary court rules allow the exclusion of jurors who know the parties or any facts of the case. Concern for bias is forcing peer review committees to make the same move to the unknowledgeable peer.

Bias has always been an issue in peer review. Until the Congress passed the Civil Rights and the Equal Employment Opportunity acts, women and blacks were routinely excluded from medical staffs. It would be naive to assume that such forbidden criteria have been eliminated from all peer review decisions. Physicians with unconventional practice styles or uncollegial personalities pose a difficult problem of balance. While it is unreasonable to expect every physician to behave in the same way, unconventional practice styles or personality problems may be evidence of substance abuse or psychological impairment. Peer review activities should not be conducted by physicians with outspoken biases against either the individual being reviewed or the aspects of the individual's practice that are being reviewed.

Peer review has always had an economic component. Hospital medical staffs tried to balance the needs of the community with the economic interests of the existing staff. Sometimes this meant preventing new physicians from starting practice in the community, but as often it resulted in efforts to encourage physicians in needed specialties to set up practice in the community. As physicians and hospitals have been forced into competition, economic biases have become a major confounding factor in peer review activities.

In most communities, physicians practicing the same specialty are either in business together or are competitors. Even in large cities, physicians and hospitals compete with their geographic neighbors. This competition is exacerbated by the blurring of specialty lines. As the number of physicians in a community increases, subspecialists often practice general medicine to supplement their incomes. General medicine physicians and others cross specialty lines to offer lucrative procedures such as liposuction. The act's requirement that hearing officers and panels must not be in "direct economic competition with the physician involved" seems to preclude traditional peer review committees composed of physicians in the same specialty or practice area who practice in the same community as the physician under review.

CONDUCTING THE REVIEW

The act states that its notice and hearing requirements are not the only way to provide adequate due process for peer review. The courts, however, will tend to regard these statutory requirements as minimums. These requirements were developed in court cases against governmental health care institutions. The effect of the act is to require private institutions seeking immunity to comply with the same due process requirements as public institutions. Since most private hospitals already meet this standard, this should not require substantial changes in hospital procedures. It will require other health care entities, such as private clinics, to use formal, hospital-style proceedings rather than the informal procedures that are the norm in these environments.

The act only covers peer review activities carried out in a reasonable belief that they will improve the quality of medical care. The best evidence of a good-faith peer review decision is a written set of standards that explain what is expected of a physician practicing in the entity. These should be detailed and straightforward. They must be intelligible to jurors and physicians, as well as to attorneys. For hospitals, most of the relevant standards are already in force as part of the JCAHO requirements. The problem is that few physicians are familiar with these requirements. These standards must be made available to members, and prospective members, of the medical staff. Adherence to these standards must be an explicit condition of medical staff privileges.

It is critical that the health care entity enforce all standards uniformly. There cannot be a double standard based on economic performance or personality. If, for example, delinquent chart completion is used as a ground for the termination of staff privileges, then the hospital must ensure that other members of the medical staff complete their charts on time. Disparate enforcement of standards is less defensible than having no standards.

The only way to provide even-handed enforcement of standards is to shift from exception-oriented review to review based on statistical and population analysis. In some areas such as completion of medical records, the hospital keeps data on every physician. The data can be compiled into profiles to establish the norm and standard deviations for chart completion. Physicians exceeding a set deviation would be flagged and counseled. If their performance did not improve, they would be terminated. In other areas, such as surgical complications, indirect measures are much less effective. These require that a random sample of charts from every physician be reviewed for problems.

DOCUMENTING THE PEER REVIEW PROCESS

The key to preventing litigation over peer review proceedings is careful documentation of a well-organized, exemplary process. It is not enough for an individual member to act properly. Every member of the committee must be above reproach because it is the committee that acts and will be sued. The hospital bylaws should require each committee member to disclose all personal and business dealings with members of the medical staff who might come before the committee. This information can be protected from general disclosure, but it should be available to the other committee members. The committee members should demand that the hospital or other institution indemnify them against any losses related to the peer review activities.

Defensible peer review depends on creating a clear record of the alleged deviations from standard practice. The record also should demonstrate that none of the reviewers was an economic competitor of the physician being reviewed. If it is impossible to assemble a review panel without financial conflicts, the committee should employ an outside reviewer or consulting service. Given the reality of medical business practices, it would seem necessary to use outside reviewers in all but the largest hospitals. Even in these facilities, subspecialty care will require outside review.

This record must be specific as to the facts of each incident, how these facts deviate from accepted practice, and the actual or potential harm resulting from this deviation from accepted standards. If there is no demonstrable harm or potential harm from the deviation, the deviation does not affect patient care and is not a proper basis for an adverse peer review action. The record should be objective and should be free of personal attacks on the physician in question. Copies of patient records should be attached and annotated as necessary to establish the validity of the facts in question. All complaints by patients and other health care providers should be investigated and incorporated into the record.

The record should demonstrate that the physician was warned about the deviations from standard practice and was given an opportunity to correct these deviations. These warnings should be communicated in writing, with the physician asked to respond in writing. If the nature of the deviation was such as to necessitate immediate suspension of medical staff privileges, this should be documented. The arrangements to care for the suspended physician's patients should be discussed, as should patients' reaction to their physician's suspension. Emergency suspensions are merited only when there has been little delay between the institution's learning of the problem and its taking action against the physician. It is impossible to defend an emergency action taken after months of discussion.

BIBLIOGRAPHY

Federal Laws

42 CFR Part 1003: Civil Money Penalties for Failure to Report Medical Malpractice Payments and for Breaching the Confidentiality of Information—Final Regulations, Friday, June 21, 1991.

45 CFR Part 60: National Practitioner Data Bank for Adverse Information on Physicians and Other Health Care Practitioners—Final Regulations, Monday, April 1, 1991.

45 CFR Part 60: National Practitioner Data Bank for Adverse Information on Physicians and Other Health Care Practitioners: Confirmation of Effective Date and Technical Amendments, Tuesday, December 4, 1990.

45 CFR Part 60: National Practitioner Data Bank for Adverse Information on Physicians and Other Health Care Practitioners—Final Rules, Tuesday, October 17, 1989.

Articles

Adelman SH: Ways that hospitals control their physicians. Am Med News 1991 June 10; 34(22):26.

Gelber BR: The Health Care Quality Improvement Act of 1986 (editorial). Nebr Med J 1988 Aug; 73(8):261.

George JE; Rouse AR: The Health Care Quality Improvement Act of 1986. N J Med 1987 Jun; 84(6):401–3.

Holthaus D: Federal law offers protection for peer review. Hospitals 1988 Jul 5; 62(13): 46, 48.

How the National Practitioner Data Bank can affect you. JAMA 1991 May 1; 265:2239.

Hudson T; Koska MT: The data bank: Final regulations. Hospitals 1989 Dec 5; 63(23):33–36.

Iglehart JK: Congress moves to bolster peer review: The Health Care Quality Improvement Act of 1986. N Engl J Med 1987 Apr 9; 316(15):960–64.

Johnson ID: Reports to the National Practitioner Data Bank (from the office of the general counsel). JAMA 1991 Jan 16; 265:407–8, 410–11.

Koska MT: HCQIA (Health Care Quality Improvement Act): CA doctors decide to opt out. Hospitals 1988 Jul 5; 62(13):56.

Myers SA; Gleicher N: A successful program to reduce cesarean section rates: Friendly persuasion. QRB 1991 May 17:162–66.

Pearson JH: Health Care Quality Improvement Act of 1986: A personal opinion. Hawaii Med J 1987 Aug; 46(8):310–11.

Ronai SE; Meng ME: Civil liability of peer review participants: *Patrick v. Burget* and the Health Care Quality Improvement Act of 1986. Conn Med 1988 Sep; 52(9):537–40.

Scholten MG: Reflections on the Health Care Quality Improvement Act (editorial). WV Med J 1988 May; 84(5):193–94.

Trostorff DL: Medical staff privileging: How to avoid pitfalls in the administrative process. QRB 1987 Jun; 13(6):198–204.

Wright RF: State level expert review committees—Are they protected? Public Health Rep 1990 Jan–Feb; 105:13–23.

IV Physicians and Public Health

20

General Public Health

CRITICAL POINTS
- All physicians have duties under the public health laws.
- The power to protect the public health is fundamental to a nation.
- The validity of all health measures depends on accurate birth and death records.
- Failing to report child abuse or violent injuries can subject a physician to criminal prosecution.

Most medical specialties are defined by organ systems or treatment modalities; public health is defined by the legal authority to protect the health and safety of the community. Public health authority is usually vested in a local health officer. The health officer's authority extends to physicians' health services practices when they encounter conditions that threaten the public health. The internist who diagnoses salmonellosis in a patient, the emergency room physician who suspects that a child may have been abused, and the family practitioner who signs a death certificate wear the cloak of public health in these endeavors. Many physicians are unaware of these public health responsibilities. This chapter discusses the authority for public health practice and the nondisease control obligations of physicians. (Some of this material is adapted from Richards 1989.)

THE HISTORY OF PUBLIC HEALTH AUTHORITY

Sanitary laws were the first public health measures. An early record of these laws is in Leviticus 11–16. The Romans developed the discipline of sanitary engineering—building water works and sewers. The next advance in public health was the quarantine of disease-carrying ships and their passengers, instituted in response to the diseases brought back by the Crusaders. The word *quarantine* derives from *quadraginta*, meaning "forty." It was first used between 1377 and 1403 when Venice and the other chief maritime cities of the Mediterranean adopted and enforced a forty-day detention for all vessels entering their ports (Bolduan and Bolduan 1941).

The English statutory and common law recognized the right of the state to quarantine and limit the movement of plague carriers. Blackstone observed that disobeying quarantine orders merited severe punishments, including death. The American colonies adopted the English laws on the control of diseases. When the Constitution was written, public health power was left to the states, because it was considered fundamental to the state's police power:

> It is a well-recognized principle that it is one of the first duties of a state to take all necessary steps for the promotion and protection of the health and comfort of its inhabitants. The preservation of the public health is universally conceded to be one of the duties devolving upon the state as a sovereignty, and whatever reasonably tends to preserve the public health is a subject upon which the legislature, within its police power, may take action. (*In re Halko*, 1966)

Soon after the Constitution was ratified, the states were forced to exercise their police power to combat an epidemic of yellow fever that raged in New York and Philadelphia. The flavor of that period was later captured in an argument before the Supreme Court:

> For ten years prior, the yellow-fever had raged almost annually in the city, and annual laws were passed to resist it. The wit of man was exhausted, but in vain. Never did the pestilence rage more violently than in the summer of 1798. The State was in despair. The rising hopes of the metropolis began to fade. The opinion was gaining ground, that the cause of this annual disease was indigenous, and that all precautions against its importation were useless. But the leading spirits of that day were unwilling to give up the city without a final desperate effort. The havoc in the summer of 1798 is represented as terrific. The whole country was roused. A cordon sanitaire was thrown around the city. Governor Mifflin of Pennsylvania proclaimed a non-intercourse between New York and Philadelphia. (*Smith v. Turner*, 1849)

The extreme nature of the actions, including isolating the federal government (sitting in Philadelphia at the time), was considered an appropriate response to the threat of yellow fever. The terrifying nature of these early epidemics predisposed the courts to grant public health authorities a free hand in their attempts to prevent the spread of disease:

> Every state has acknowledged power to pass, and enforce quarantine, health, and inspection laws, to prevent the introduction of disease, pestilence, or unwholesome provisions; such laws interfere with no powers of Congress or treaty stipulations; they relate to internal police, and are subjects of domestic regulation within each state, over which no authority can be exercised by any power under the Constitution, save by requiring the consent of Congress to the imposition of duties on exports and imports, and their payment into the treasury of the United States. (*Holmes v. Jennison*, 1840)

Few cases have challenged the constitutionality of state actions taken to protect citizens from a communicable disease. The only successful attacks on such exercises of state police power have been based on federal preemption of state laws that restricted interstate commerce. Yet even interference with interstate commerce is not always fatal to health regulations. If a state regulation is substantially related to health and safety, the Supreme Court will uphold it. This is true even if the regulation interferes with interstate commerce, such as would result from a cordon sanitaria in which all travel is forbidden. From vaccinations to quarantines, laws enacted to protect society have been upheld even when they force individuals to sacrifice liberty and privacy.

LEGAL STANDARDS FOR PUBLIC HEALTH AUTHORITY

As courts have reviewed the constitutionality of laws that ostensibly protect the public health and safety, they have developed consistent standards for defining an acceptable exercise of public health authority. The courts have allowed substantial restrictions on individual liberty pursuant to public health laws that seek to prevent future harm rather than to punish past actions. If a court finds that a law is directed at prevention rather than punishment, it will allow the state to:

1. Rely on expert decision makers.
2. Provide for judicial review through habeas corpus proceedings rather than through prerestriction hearings.
3. Use a scientific, rather than a criminal law, standard of proof.

Although a state's power to protect the public health is broad, it is restricted to preventing future harm. The state may not punish a person under its public health police powers. Administrative deprivations of liberty are tolerated only if their purpose is not punitive. The distinction between allowable restrictions and forbidden punishment is sometimes finely drawn. For example, being put in the community pesthouse was seldom a pleasant prospect, and with the closing of pesthouses, public health restrictions have frequently been carried out in prisons and jails. In one such case, the court rejected the petitioner's claim that he was being punished without due process, concluding, "While it is true that physical facilities constituting part of the penitentiary equipment are utilized, interned persons are in no sense confined in the penitentiary, and are not subject to the peculiar obloquy which attends such confinement" (*Ex parte McGee,* 1919).

Expert Decision Makers

Public health jurisprudence is based on a deference to scientific decision making. This deference may be expressed by incorporating scientific standards into legislation or by delegating the right to make public health decisions to boards of health or individual health officers who are skilled in the science of public health. This deference is illustrated in the best known of the traditional public health cases, *Jacobson v. Massachusetts* (1905), in which the scientific basis of a Massachusetts law requiring vaccination for smallpox was challenged.

Mr. Jacobson believed that the scientific basis for vaccination was unsound and that he would suffer if he was vaccinated. The Massachusetts Supreme Court found the statute consistent with the Massachusetts state constitution, and Jacobson appealed to the U.S. Supreme Court. The Court first ruled that being subject to vaccination was the price for living in society. (See Chapter 28.) The Court then considered Jacobson's right to contest the scientific basis of the Massachusetts vaccination requirement. Accepting that some reasonable people still questioned the efficacy of vaccination, the Court nonetheless found that it was within the legislature's prerogative to adopt one from many conflicting views on a scientific issue:

> It is no part of the function of a court or a jury to determine which of two modes was likely to be most effective for the protection of the public against disease. That

was for the legislative department to determine in the light of all the information it had or could obtain.

In a recent case upholding the closing of a bathhouse as a disease control measure, the court showed the same deference to discretionary orders by public health officers:

It is not for the courts to determine which scientific view is correct in ruling upon whether the police power has been properly exercised. The judicial function is exhausted with the discovery that the relation between means and ends is not wholly vain and fanciful, an illusory pretense. (*City of New York v. New Saint Mark's Baths*, 1986)

Reviewing Public Health Orders

Traditional public health laws do not require the health officer to obtain a court order before acting. Instead, the propriety of public health restrictions is determined by postrestriction habeas corpus proceedings brought on behalf of the restricted individual. Although courts have recognized that public health measures may involve grave intrusion into an individual's expectation of liberty, the control of communicable diseases and unsanitary conditions has been found to outweigh the individual privacy interest. Perhaps the clearest difference between public health detentions and criminal arrests is that public health detentions are not bailable:

To grant release on bail to persons isolated and detained on a quarantine order because they have a contagious disease which makes them dangerous to others, or to the public in general, would render quarantine laws and regulations nugatory and of no avail. (*Varholy v. Sweat*, 1943)

The court's deference to public health authority finds further expression in rulings on the appropriate standard of proof for restricting an individual's liberty. When persons detained under the public health authority petition for habeas corpus relief, the courts use a *reasonable-belief* standard for determining the validity of the detention or testing orders. Reasonable belief may be based on individual specific information, such as a diagnosis of tuberculosis, which may be obtained through voluntary testing of individuals at risk. In modern public health practice, statutorily required disease reports usually provide the basis for the reasonable belief that an individual is infected and should be restricted to protect the public health:

No patient can expect that if his malady is found to be of a dangerously contagious nature he can still require it to be kept secret from those to whom, if there was no disclosure, such disease would be transmitted. The information given to a physician by his patient, though confidential, must, it seems to us, be given and received subject to the qualification that if the patient's disease is found to be of a dangerous and so highly contagious or infectious a nature that it will necessarily be transmitted to others unless the danger of contagion is disclosed to them, then the physician should, in that event, if no other means of protection is possible, be privileged to make so much of a disclosure to such persons as is necessary to prevent the spread of the disease. (*Simonsen v. Swenson*, 1920)

Due Process and Privacy

It has become fashionable to criticize public health laws as antiquated and thus unconstitutional. The argument is that traditional public health laws do not provide the privacy or due process protections required under modern constitutional law. It is true that standards for protecting privacy and for criminal due process protections were strengthened under the Earl Warren Court. None of these decisions, however, changed the traditional standards for public health practice. Rather than extend the protections of the Warren Court to public health matters, more recent Supreme Court cases clearly favor the state's right to control dangerous individuals.

The more dangerous flaw in the argument that public health laws should provide extensive procedural protections is that it ignores the costs of those protections. Court proceedings take time and money. No health departments have sufficient legal staffs to have a court hearing before every enforcement action. This has been specifically recognized in several U.S. Supreme Court decisions (*Camara v. Municipal Court of City and County of San Francisco*, 1967). The administrative costs of elaborate due process requirements prevent the enforcement of public health laws.

Some states have rewritten their communicable disease laws to provide more than the protections mandated by the Constitution. These protections interfere with local health authorities' ability to deal with diseases such as drug-resistant tuberculosis. In many jurisdictions, health offices must bring their enforcement actions through the district attorney's office. These offices are so buried under crimes such as murder that it is impossible to get timely assistance with public health orders.

VITAL STATISTICS

The keeping of good vital statistics is important to a society for several reasons. Infant mortality is generally considered the best indicator of the health of a population. Accurate records allow for allocation of health care funds to areas of greatest need. These records are of great historical value as well. On the individual level, the documentation of a birth certificate establishes the individual's legal existence and basic legal relationships like citizenship and parentage.

Vital statistics records are not uniform among the states. The forms, the information required, and the keeper of the records differ. Usually a county office houses these records. The records may be open to public view, access may be limited, or the records may be confidential. These records are always available to the person on whom they are kept or to a court. These records also fall under the full faith and credit clause of the Constitution. A state must honor the birth and death records of another state.

Historically, vital statistics records were kept in the locality where the event occurred rather than the place of current residence or a unified state office. A person born in Boston who moved to Los Angeles as an infant and lived there until he was killed in a Chicago plane crash would have a Massachusetts birth certificate and an Illinois death certificate. There would be no record of this person in the California vital statistics records. Another problem is that parents may not remember accurately where and when their children were born, making it impossible for these offspring to obtain their birth certificates. It also makes it difficult to match birth and death certificates to determine if a person has taken a false identity. It is anticipated that vital statistics records will become a more useful resource as states centralize their records and begin to correlate them with other states and the federal social security records.

Birth Certificates

Normally the law requires that the person who attended the birth or delivered the baby must file a birth certificate within a specified time of a few days. Although the physician is responsible for the accuracy of the medical information and the timely filing, most states allow the certificate to be completed and certified by someone other than the attending physician. In most hospitals, someone from the medical records department obtains the necessary information from family members and prepares the certificate. This medical information is useful for public health. The attending physician should ensure that it is completed fully and accurately.

Birth certificates also contain social information, such as the name of the baby's father. This should be completed accurately if the information is known, but the physician is allowed to rely on the family for the necessary information. There may be doubts about the accuracy of information such as parentage or citizenship, but this is not the physician's concern; there is no duty to investigate social information. On many certificates the source of this information is listed, and this person may be asked to sign the certificate.

It is important that the birth attendant file the birth certificate promptly. The certificate must be filed before a certified copy can be issued. The child cannot get a social security number without the certified copy of the birth certificate. If the family receives any type of public assistance, federally funded assistance programs limit the amount of time that a child may be carried on the program without a social security number and case file.

Naming the Child

State laws on choosing children's surnames vary substantially. Some states allow the mother to choose any surname; others allow any surname except that of a putative but unacknowledged father; some require that the child be given the surname of a legal recognized relative. The highest federal court to consider this issue found that the parents' privacy interest did not supersede the state's interest in having children named for a legal parent. This case arose in Nebraska, which requires that a child be named for a legal relative. Two mothers challenged the law. One wanted to give her baby the surname of its father, which was different from her husband. The other mother just liked the name *McKenzie* and wanted to use it for her child's surname (*Henne v. Wright*, 1990).

Lower courts in two states had found a constitutional right to give children any desired name. This decision was based on the parents' right of privacy. The appeals court considering the Nebraska case agreed that the parents had a privacy right in naming their children, but it found that the state's right to orderly record-keeping procedures and certainty of parentage outweighed the parent's privacy interest. Since the U.S. Supreme Court refused to review this case, it can be assumed that the state may restrict the allowable names for a child.

The name on the birth certificate does not establish the child's paternity. It may be evidence of paternity if the named father agreed to the use of his name, but it does not affect the state's legal procedures for establishing paternity. (See Chapter 24.) State restrictions on choosing names on a child's birth certificate do not prevent the parents or the child from petitioning the court for a name change after the birth certificate proceeding.

Stillbirths

Some states use a separate form for filing a report of stillbirth. Other states require the birth attendant to file both a birth certificate and a death certificate.

The gestational age that constitutes a stillbirth differs from state to state but is usually around 20 weeks. In some cases, an induced abortion may require registration.

The stillbirth certificate may be the appropriate form even if the child is born alive. Separate birth and death certificates are required usually only if the child is potentially viable and lives for some period. If a fetus of any gestational age shows signs of life such as heartbeat or respiratory effort, it is best to file the appropriate certificates.

A reasonable attempt to determine the cause of death should be made for stillborn infants. Prematurity is usually a result of some underlying medical condition, not the cause itself. Prematurity is obviously not the cause of intrauterine death. Since some causes of stillbirth, such as infection or uterine abnormality, are treatable, the physician who does not establish the cause of a stillbirth may be liable for similar problems in a subsequent pregnancy.

Death Certificates

The quality of death records in the United States is generally poor because physicians are not well trained in filing these reports. Death certificates are problematic for several reasons: unexpected deaths frequently occur outside the hospital; the cause of death may not be immediately obvious; there may be no one to provide information on the identity of the person who died; occasionally there may be a question of criminal activity having been involved in the death.

The cause of death is the most important information on a death certificate and is generally the most inadequate. Preferably the causes of death listed would be codable from the International Classification of Disease. But for many certificates, the actual cause of the death is not clear, let alone codable. "Cardiac arrest" is a result of death, not a cause. A death certificate that lists cardiac arrest as the cause of death and respiratory arrest following shock as the contributing causes may be for a patient who died of a gunshot wound or a terminal cancer patient or a patient with underlying heart disease. The cause of death should tell a reader what killed the patient—not what the terminal events were.

It is important that the death certificate contain the information that a death was caused or contributed to by infectious disease, cancer, toxic exposure, violent injury, or congenital defect. These causes may be reportable to the health department, child welfare, the police, or a state disease registry. An unusual number of deaths from a specific cause may lead to investigation of the problem and preventive measures.

An inaccurate death certificate may make it difficult for the survivors to collect benefits and insurance. If the death certificate lists septic shock and cardiac arrest as the cause of death in a patient who was involved in a motor vehicle accident, the widow may have difficulty collecting on an insurance policy that pays only upon accidental death. Normally a certified copy of the death certificate must accompany every claim for death benefits.

Declaration of Death

Generally a physician must make the determination that a person is dead. The physician then makes a formal declaration of the death and a record of the time of death. In a hospital setting, the physician who declares the death may not be the one who signs the death certificate. A resident or the physician covering the emergency room may be asked to pronounce the death of a patient who was under another doctor's care. The attending physician would be expected to determine the cause of death and file the death certificate. The physician who pronounces the death must simply determine that the patient is dead.

If the determination of death is difficult, a physician should consult with others and know the legal definition of death in the state. A patient may be legally dead because of lack of brain function but still have a heartbeat when on a mechanical ventilator. There is no point in ventilating a dead patient, but stopping the ventilator before the legal criteria for death have been met may involve the physician in both civil and criminal proceedings.

The legal time of death may be a long time after the death actually occurred. Many accident victims are obviously dead at the scene of the accident but are pronounced dead officially on arrival at a hospital because no physician was at the scene. When homicide is suspected or in large cities where the police handle large numbers of accidental deaths, a medical examiner may be on call to pronounce death at the scene and to determine the cause of death.

The time of death may be important because of survivorship clauses in wills. For example, a man may leave all his property to his wife unless she does not survive him by at least 30 days, in which case the property goes to a hospital fund. The wife might have a will that leaves everything to her son. If they are in a common disaster that kills him outright but leaves her comatose for 30 days, the determination of the time of brain death may well decide whether the hospital or the son receives the property. In such a case, a physician who had an interest in the hospital might be considered to have a conflict of interest in determining death.

Coroner Cases and Autopsies

A death is a coroner's case if it is unexpected or if there is any possibility that a law has been broken. Not every death that occurs outside a hospital is a coroner's case. If the deceased had a physician who is reasonably certain of the cause of death and is willing to sign a death certificate, further medical examination may not be required.

The coroner system in the United States is in difficulty. Only the largest cities have forensic pathologists to act as coroner and do the medical examinations. In small, rural counties, the coroner may be a physician who has no forensic training, or it may be the sheriff or the mortician. A physician who is asked to act as county coroner should try to learn something about forensic medicine and should be quick to ask for assistance from experts when it is needed. The time of death or the angle of gunfire may determine whether the person committed suicide or was murdered.

The percentage of deaths that are autopsied has been falling for many years. Autopsies benefit society by providing information about hidden pathologies and about the accuracy of medical diagnoses. But they do not benefit the patient, and they are sometimes opposed by physicians who do not want the accuracy of their diagnoses challenged. Because of these factors, there is little money available to pay for autopsies. Even when it is feasible to do an autopsy, many physicians do not know how to obtain consent. Physicians should be familiar with the state law in their jurisdictions governing the persons who may consent to an autopsy. If there is any question of criminal activity, the autopsy may be ordered by a court.

Disease Registries

Disease registries are a special class of reporting laws. Since the objective is not to control a communicable disease, there is often no penalty for failing to report to a disease registry. Most disease registries are statewide and involve either cancer or occupational illness; some, such as the Centers for Disease Control (CDC) registry of cases of toxic shock syndrome, are national. Reporting cases to the registry may be mandatory or voluntary, but it is always desirable to have a complete registry. These registries are used to determine the extent of certain problems in the community and to try to determine causes. If they are inaccurate, they may give false correlations and become useless for research and prevention.

Consider a cancer registry that contains only half the cases of a particular kind of cancer. If a local industry tries to determine whether its workers are exposed to something that causes the cancer, it will look at the rate among its exposed workers and the rate in the general population. If the company finds all the cases among its workers but the cancer registry has only half the cases in the general population, then an exposure that does not cause the cancer will look like it does by a factor of two. An epidemiologist may know that this is wrong, but the reporter from the local paper may not.

LAW ENFORCEMENT REPORTING

Every jurisdiction requires physicians to report certain types of injuries to law enforcement officials or protection agencies. Generally these laws require reporting of assaults, family violence, and criminal activity. Physicians should avoid the tendency to investigate the crime before reporting it. Particularly in cases of family violence, the victim may have a plausible explanation of the injury and be anxious to avoid reporting. The injured person may fear reprisals or may be under investigation already. Proper reports should be made despite the victim's wishes. It will be up to the law enforcement agency to determine what use will be made of the report.

Child Abuse

Whenever a physician or other care provider suspects that a child has been abused or neglected, that suspicion should be reported to the child protective agency immediately. Child abuse is not a diagnosis; it is a legal finding. Medical personnel who try to investigate this crime may confuse the evidence to the point that the law enforcement agency cannot protect the child. Physicians should defer to experts in child abuse and neglect rather than attempt to make an independent determination of abuse. These experts will act as consultants to the courts and protective services.

As with other reporting laws, neither the patient nor the parents nor the physician have the right to stop the reporting or to withhold information from the law enforcement agency. A parent may refuse to answer an investigator's questions under the Fifth Amendment protections against self-incrimination. This part of the process should not involve the physician. The physician should provide all the known information in as objective a manner as possible.

Health care providers should be very careful about vouching for the character of parents. It is not possible to know that parents are not abusive based on their behavior during office visits. Particularly with sexual abuse cases, the physician who has trouble dealing with the reality of child abuse may suffer from denial when dealing with an individual case. Keep in mind that the child is the patient and all the duties of the physician are to the patient, not the parents.

Violent Injuries

Generally physicians have a responsibility to report violent or suspicious injuries—all gunshot wounds, knifings, poisonings, serious motor vehicle injuries, and any other wounds that seem suspicious—to the local law enforcement agency. The legal assumption is that anyone who has knowledge that a crime may have been committed has a duty to report the possible crime to the police. If the patient is brought to the hospital in the custody of the police or from the scene of a police investigation, the physician may safely assume that the police have been notified. In all other cases, the physician should call the police and make the report.

Such injuries should be reported despite the wishes of the patient. The patient who has been shot escaping from the scene of a crime will be more interested in the wound's not being reported than the patient who is embarrassed about mishandling a gun while cleaning it. Some states have made domestic violence a reportable offense. In states where such reporting is not required, the physician should determine if battered spouses or partners may be reported under general violent injury laws. This is very important because of the high probability that the victim will be severely injured or killed eventually. In some cases, the couple will have made up by the time the stitches are in and the X rays are read. This should not stop the physician from reporting. In others, the victim will be too terrified to complain. If the woman who came in saying her husband cut her now claims she injured herself cooking, the injury must be reported nevertheless. Domestic violence is one of the most dangerous areas of police work, and the rate of repeat violence is very high. Health care providers should not try to handle these cases privately in emergency rooms.

Intoxications

Unlike child abuse or gunshot wounds, most jurisdictions do not have a law requiring physicians to report intoxications to police authorities. Without reporting laws that override the patient's rights of privacy, physicians should remember that they may not volunteer information about a patient without the patient's permission. As with other forms of medical care, physicians may not do testing without the patient's consent. Physicians have the right and the duty to assert their patient's right of confidentiality when questioned by police officers about the patient's medical condition. If the physician's testimony is legally required, the court can order the physician to testify; the investigating officer cannot.

Although the consent of the patient is required for any type of medical care, physicians usually do not think about obtaining consent for routine laboratory procedures such as blood chemistry or urinalysis. It is assumed that the patient and the physician take the general consent to care to include these. In addition, the patient may refuse to allow the drawing of the blood or to provide the urine for testing. This type of nonspecific consent should not be used when testing for intoxicants. The legal problems that may arise from positive tests make it necessary for the physician to obtain a valid, specific informed consent from the patient before doing the test.

If this testing is being done for medical reasons the rules of consent are like those for any other medical procedure. If a patient is brought into the emergency room unconscious, the emergency exception to consent will apply. This does not allow the substituting of consent from a third party, such as a spouse or a police officer. It simply relieves the physician of the necessity of obtaining consent for emergency care. If the normal medical evaluation of an unconscious patient includes a drug screen or a blood alcohol level, these tests should be done and recorded in the patient's medical records, just like a blood glucose or a skull X ray. They are part of the emergency medical care of the patient. Testing that is not necessary for the care of the patient may not be done under the emergency exception. If the physician does not normally do a blood alcohol level to evaluate an unconscious patient, then he or she should not include it at the request of a police officer.

If the patient is conscious and able to consent to medical care, then no matter how serious the medical condition may be, normal consent is necessary. A physician who wishes to do any testing for intoxicants must obtain the explicit consent of the patient. If the patient refuses to consent to such testing, the physician must respect the refusal even if it makes the care of the patient more difficult. If the patient is intoxicated with an illegal drug, the legal risks of testing may be much greater than the risks of less informed medical care. A physician should never take a blood sample for a glucose level and do drug testing on the remainder. If the physician believes that the refusal to test threatens the patient's life, a court order may be sought for testing.

Physicians may order testing for intoxicants for purely legal purposes but should be cautious about doing so. Unlike having communicable diseases, substance abuse is both a public health threat and a criminal act. A physician has a duty to protect the patient's confidences in criminal matters. The physician must comply with state laws on testing and reporting drug abuse but should fully inform the patient before the specimen is taken. The patient should be aware that there is no medical indication for the test and that the physician cannot know what the results will be. If the patient has the right to refuse the test, the consent should be in writing, signed and witnessed, and it should contain the name and identifying information on the officer requesting the testing as well as the patient. If the physician has reason to think that the consent is being coerced from the patient, then he or she should not accept the consent or do the testing.

Dealing with Peace Officers

There are two important questions that a physician should ask in dealing with a police officer in a medical care setting: Is the patient in custody? Is there a court order involving medical care? If the patient is not in custody, the police officer is a third party, with no right to information about the patient or the medical care. Medical information may become available to the officer later through a court action for the medical records, but that does not allow the officer to question the physician without the express permission of the patient. If the patient is unable or unwilling to give permission, the officer should be politely but firmly shown the door.

If the patient is in custody, the officer still has no right to consent to or know about the patient's medical care beyond the specific requirements of the state's laws. Being under arrest increases the importance of the patient's right of privacy. The physician must be careful not to interfere with the officer's duties, just as the physician should not allow the officer to interfere with the patient's medical care. If privacy is required for the medical examination, the patient's dignity should be protected as much as possible consistent with preventing the patient's escape. The physician should not interfere with actions that are necessary to maintain custody of a conscious and potentially dangerous prisoner.

Court-ordered medical care is different from care requested by a peace officer. A police officer does not have the right to overrule a patient's decisions on medical consent; a court does. A physician who is presented with a valid court order to do something to or for a patient may either honor the order or get a lawyer to fight the order. Physicians who are routinely involved with court-ordered care should be well versed in the procedures. The emergency physician in the county hospital may be routinely ordered to do drug testing on specific prisoners. This physician or the nurses who work there regularly may know the forms and the judges' names and have no problem with honoring the order. The physician in a private hospital who is presented with an order should contact the hospital attorney or someone in the court system for a clarification of the order.

Some medical records are protected even from court orders, but these are usually in the custody of agencies that know the extent of their authority to withhold records. Venereal disease control programs frequently receive subpoenas for medical records that are protected from subpoena by state law. The judge in a divorce proceeding may not know about the law protecting these records or may have authorized that subpoena as one in a large group. The public health program will routinely request that the subpoena be quashed. A physician in public health or drug rehabilitation who deals regularly with protected records must view the possibility of spending some time in jail on a contempt citation as an occupational hazard. The physician who does not deal with these matters frequently should consult an attorney when presented with a court order.

BIBLIOGRAPHY

Police Power

Bolduan C; Bolduan N: *Public Health and Hygiene.* 1941.
Camara v. Municipal Court of City and County of San Francisco. 387 US 523 (1967).
City of New York v. New Saint Mark's Baths. 497 NYS2d 979, 983 (1986).
Ex parte McGee. 105 Kan 574, 581, 185 P 14, 16 (1919).
Holmes v. Jennison. 39 US (14 Pet) 540, 616 (1840).
In re Halko. 246 Cal 2d 553, 556, 54 Cal Rptr 661, 663 (1966).
Jacobson v. Massachusetts. 197 US 11 (1905).
Richards EP: The jurisprudence of prevention: Society's right of self-defense against dangerous individuals. Hast Const L Q 1989:16; 329.
Simonsen v. Swenson. 104 Neb 224, 228, 177 NW 831, 832 (1920).
Smith v. Turner. 48 US (7 How) 283, 340–41 (1849).
Varholy v. Sweat. 153 Fla 571, 575, 15 So 2d 267, 270 (1943).

Vital Statistics

Cole SK: Accuracy of death certificates in neonatal deaths. Community Med 1989 Feb; 11(1):1–8.

Davis BR; Curb JD; Tung B; Hawkins CM; Ehrman S; Farmer J; Martin M: Standardized physician preparation of death certificates. Controlled Clin Trials 1987 Jun; 8(2): 110–20.

Duley LM: A validation of underlying cause of death, as recorded by clinicians on stillbirth and neonatal death certificates. Br J Obstet Gynaecol 1986 Dec; 93(12):1233–35.

Haines JL; Conneally PM: Causes of death in Huntington disease as reported on death certificates. Genet Epidemiol 1986; 3(6):417–23.

Hanzlick R: Death certificates, natural death, and alcohol: The problem of underreporting. Am J Forensic Med Pathol 1988 Jun; 9(2):149–50.

Hardy AM; Starcher ET II; Morgan WM; Druker J; Kristal A; Day JM; Kelly C; Ewing E; Curran JW: Review of death certificates to assess completeness of AIDS case reporting. Public Health Rep 1987 Jul–Aug; 102(4):386–91.

Harter L; Starzyk P; Frost F: A comparative study of hospital fetal death records and Washington State fetal death certificates. Am J Public Health 1986 Nov; 76(11): 1333–34.

Henne v. Wright. 904 F 2d 1208 (CTA 8 1990).

Kelson MC; Farebrother M: The effect of inaccuracies in death certification and coding practices in the European Economic Community (EEC) on international cancer mortality statistics. Int J Epidemiol 1987 Sep; 16(3):411–14.

Kelson MC; Heller RF: The effect of death certification and coding practices on observed differences in respiratory disease mortality in 8 E.E.C. countries. Rev Epidemiol Sante Publique 1983; 31(4): 423–32.

Kircher T; Anderson RE: Cause of death. Proper completion of the death certificate. JAMA 1987 Jul 17; 258(3):349–52.

Mackeprang M; Hay S; Lunde AS: Completeness and accuracy of reporting of malformations on birth certificates. HSMHA Health Rep 1972 Jan; 87(1):43–49.

Williams RL; Chen PM: Controlling the rise in cesarean section rates by the dissemination of information from vital records. Am J Public Health 1983 Aug; 73(8):863–67.

Zumwalt RE; Ritter MR: Incorrect death certification. An invitation to obfuscation. Postgrad Med 1987 Jun; 81(8):245–47, 250, 253–54.

Reporting

Brahams D: Standard of proof in evidence of child abuse. Lancet 1988 Feb 6; 1(8580): 311–12.

Gaus SM: Reporting child abuse. "Whistle blower protection" and physician responsibility. Mich Med 1988 Apr; 87(4):191–93.

George JE; Quattrone MS: Reporting child abuse: Duties and dangers. JEN 1988 Jan–Feb; 14(1):34–35.

Hollander N: Homicides of abused children prematurely returned home. Forensic Sci Int 1986 Feb–Mar; 30(2–3):85–91.

Johnson CF; Showers J: Injury variables in child abuse. Child Abuse Negl 1985; 9(2):207–15.

McGrath P; Cappelli M; Wiseman D; Khalil N; Allan B: Teacher awareness program on child abuse: A randomized controlled trial. Child Abuse Negl 1987; 11(1):125–32.

Morris JL; Johnson CF; Clasen M: To report or not to report. Physicians' attitudes toward discipline and child abuse. Am J Dis Child 1985 Feb; 139(2):194–97.

Rhodes AM: The nurse's legal obligations for reporting child abuse. MCN 1987 Sep–Oct; 12(5):313.

Rosenthal JA: Patterns of reported child abuse and neglect. Child Abuse Negl 1988; 12(2):263–71.

Saulsbury FT; Campbell RE: Evaluation of child abuse reporting by physicians. Am J Dis Child 1985 Apr; 139(4):393–95.

Schetky DH; Haller LH: Parental kidnapping. J Am Acad Child Psychiatry 1983 May; 22(3):279–85.

Schoeman F; Reamer FG: Should child abuse always be reported? Hastings Cent Rep 1983 Aug; 13(4):19–20.

Smith SR; Meyer RG: Child abuse reporting laws and psychotherapy: A time for reconsideration. Int J Law Psychiatry 1984; 7(3–4):351–66.

Watson H; Levine M: Psychotherapy and mandated reporting of child abuse. Am J Orthopsychiatry 1989 Apr; 59(2):246–56.

Weinstock R; Weinstock D: Child abuse reporting trends: An unprecedented threat to confidentiality. J Forensic Sci 1988 Mar; 33(2):418–31.

21

Disease Control

CRITICAL POINTS
- Traditional communicable diseases are increasing because of homelessness, inadequate childhood immunizations, and HIV-induced immunosuppression.
- Physician-initiated disease reports are essential to controlling communicable diseases.
- Failing to comply with reporting laws can be the basis for malpractice litigation and license revocation.
- Isolation and quarantine are still appropriate to protect the community from communicable diseases such as drug-resistant tuberculosis.

The control of communicable disease, the essence of traditional public health, is not the same as the internal medicine subspecialty of infectious disease treatment. This subspecialty is concerned with the treatment of individual patients infected with viral and bacterial organisms, and the training is oriented to individual patients, not the community. In contrast, disease control is concerned with the prevention of the spread of diseases in the community rather than the treatment of individual patients.

Disease control was the core of public health until the last polio epidemics in the 1950s and the recognition of the communicability of AIDS in the early 1980s. With the development of antibiotics and effective immunizations, the public lost its fear of communicable diseases, undermining public support for disease control in the general populace and in schools of public health. Since the 1960s, public health has become a broad umbrella, encompassing every cause from nuclear war to controlling cholesterol levels. This loss of focus has weakened the disease control programs in all health departments. The diminished support for disease control is exacerbated by the burden of indigent health care. While indigent health care is a critical community service, it is so expensive and demanding that it saps the resources of the much smaller preventive programs.

Since the 1980s, there has been a resurgence of communicable disease in the United States. The most visible disease has been HIV infection, but tuberculosis and other traditional scourges are returning with the increasing population of persons who are most susceptible to communicable diseases: the homeless, immigrants exposed to communicable diseases in their homelands and refugee camps, and persons without access to preventive medical care, especially immunizations (Carrell and Zoler 1990). The increase in this population, combined with the weakening of health department disease control programs, makes disease control an important concern.

DISEASE CONTROL

Disease control is the one area of medicine in which treatment of the patient is not paramount. Certainly patients are treated, but the benefits to them are ancillary to preventing the spread of their disease. It is good that the penicillin shots that make syphilis patients noninfectious also cure them. Erythromycin therapy makes a pertussis patient noninfectious without altering the course of the disease. Whatever risks this may pose to the patient are justified by the need to protect others. Neither patient will be given the choice of refusing therapy and remaining in the community.

Disease Control and the Individual

The price of disease prevention in the group may be injury to an occasional individual. The fact that polio vaccine prevents thousands of cases of paralytic polio is little comfort to the rare individual who gets polio from the vaccine. Most mandatory immunization laws contain exceptions for individuals who have a high probability of being injured by an immunization. Many of these laws also exempt persons who have religious objections to immunization. The U.S. Constitution allows mandatory immunization of religious objectors, but most states do not take advantage of this power.

The effectiveness of the immunization laws depends on compliance by physicians and parents. If physicians give medical exemptions to a large percentage of their patients, the level of immunity in their school system might drop low enough to support a disease epidemic. The physician might be liable for the results of the disease in any child he or she exempted improperly. The physician also might be liable for injuries to children who are not the physician's patients who would not have been exposed to the disease but for the physician's improper behavior.

Herd immunity is important because an infectious disease epidemic must have a large group of susceptible people to continue its spread, just as a fire must have fuel. (See Chapter 28.) If enough people are immune to the disease, the epidemic will die out. Although some people remain susceptible, they are diluted sufficiently that the probability of an infected person's contacting a susceptible person is low. If the disease has a short period of infectivity, the infected persons will become noninfectious before they have a chance to spread the disease.

Compulsory immunization laws take advantage of herd immunity to control or eliminate certain diseases from the community. Most of these laws are directed at children because school entry is the only opportunity to ensure immunization status for patients without regular medical care. School children are the best vectors or the major reservoir of disease for many diseases. Many communicable diseases are less serious in school-age children. Rubella is benign in the children who carry it but can be devastating to a fetus. Immunizing children against rubella prevents the exposure of women in their childbearing years and thereby prevents congenital rubella. Mumps, too, is much more serious in adults than in children.

Immunization programs have suffered from fears of legal liability and increased vaccine costs. (See Chapter 28.) Immunization levels for many diseases are at lower levels than they were in 1978. In 1978 the CDC set the goal of eliminating measles by October 1982. In 1990, there were more than 20,000 cases, more than at any other time in the previous 20 years because of falling immunization levels and the problem of infections in children who are too young to be reached by school-entry-driven programs. Most children, even indigent children, will see a physician during the first few years of life, but many of those physicians do not see to it that the child is properly immunized. The physician may send the child to the health department for immunizations, but parents may never follow up to take the child to be immunized.

Epidemics and Plagues

The technical meaning of the word *epidemic* is an "excess of cases of a disease over the number expected in a given population." This is an important concept for a physician who may be required to report any unusual disease or group expression of disease to the health department. Influenza normally infects large numbers of people every winter. A few cases of influenza may herald the beginning of the season, but they are expected. Public health reports on the epidemic may even use the term "excess deaths." Only when a substantial number of people are ill and medical resources are strained does it become an epidemic. In contrast, one or two cases of a rare disease may constitute an epidemic. The occurrence of a case of diphtheria anywhere in the United States is an epidemic because we do not expect any cases of this disease.

To most people, the word *plague* brings to mind images of the decimation of Europe by the black death in the Middle Ages. *Plague* is not a technical term like *epidemic*. It is generally used to describe epidemic disease that is perceived as a disaster for a community or a specific group. A plague of locusts may be a disaster, but it is not an epidemic. The potential for disease epidemics that qualify as plagues is ever present. Many of these diseases appear and disappear without warning or in cycles that are poorly understood. The sudden appearance of HIV infection is not unusual for a plague. Bubonic plague goes through cycles that last about 400 years; on this cycle, we are due for another worldwide epidemic of bubonic plague. The population of rodents and fleas that is necessary to fuel such an epidemic is present, and the disease is endemic in most of the western United States. The question is not what would start such an epidemic but why it has not already started.

Public health procedures backed by strong laws are necessary to combat plagues. If disease control measures are postponed while policy is debated, the disease may spread so widely that no measure can contain it. We believe that more vigorous public health efforts, such as closing gay bathhouses as soon as it became obvious how AIDS was spread, might have reduced the extent of the epidemic. Had the bathhouses been closed in the late 1970s when it became obvious that they were the vector for the spread of hepatitis b (HBV), HIV might have emerged slowly enough that gay men could have learned of its existence before infection became so widespread.

Carrier State

Typhoid Mary has become a general term for a person spreading a communicable disease. Typhoid Mary was an actual person, and typhoid carriers are not unusual. Most big cities have typhoid carriers who are registered with the health department, and they are living and working in the community. Because the carrier state cannot be cured with antibiotic treatment, the carriers must live with certain restrictions: they may not work as food handlers or as child care attendants. They can safely work in such establishments at other jobs—for example, as a restaurant accountant. This is an example of the restrictions on personal freedom that a health officer has the legal authority to impose on an individual as a disease control measure.

If a carrier is under orders to restrict activities and does not comply with the orders, the health officer may take stronger actions, including quarantine or incarceration. Typhoid Mary was a threat because she worked as a cook and refused to stop this work. Every time the health department located her, usually through a new outbreak of typhoid, she would move and change her name but not her occupation. She was finally placed under house arrest to keep her from cooking and infecting others. Typhoid Mary infected more than a hundred people, killing several of them, before the more restrictive measures were imposed.

A 1941 case involving a typhoid carrier is a good example of the court's view of the appropriateness of disease control measures. The case concerned whether the identity of typhoid carriers could be disclosed when necessary to prevent their handling food and thus exposing others to their disease:

> The Sanitary Code which has the force of law . . . requires local health officers to keep the State Department of Health informed of the names, ages and addresses of known or suspected typhoid carriers, to furnish to the State Health Department necessary specimens for laboratory examination in such cases, to inform the carrier and members of his household of the situation and to exercise certain controls over the activities of the carriers, including a prohibition against any handling by the carrier of food which is to be consumed by persons other than members of his own household. . . . Why should the record of compliance by the County Health Officer with these salutary requirements be kept confidential? Hidden in the files of the health offices, it serves no public purpose except a bare statistical one. Made available to those with a legitimate ground for inquiry, it is effective to check the spread of the dread disease. It would be worse than useless to keep secret an order by a public officer that a certain typhoid carrier must not handle foods which are to be served to the public. (*Thomas v. Morris*, 1941)

Disease Control and the Physician-Patient Relationship

Basic to all public health is the reporting of communicable diseases and hazardous conditions to the public health officer. This information is used for tracking the course of epidemics and for intervening to protect the public health.

Reporting duties transcend the patient's right of privacy and the physician's obligation to protect the patient's confidential information. For some diseases, physicians are required to report only the number of cases they see. Other diseases and conditions require physicians to provide identifying information, such as name, address, occupation, or birth date of the patient, as well as information on the disease. For many diseases, the health department will contact the affected person and obtain information about additional persons who may have been exposed to the disease.

CDC in Atlanta, Georgia, is the federal agency responsible for accepting disease reports and participating in national and international disease control efforts. It is the U.S. agency that participates in the World Health Organization and the Pan American Health Organization. CDC maintains many disease-specific programs, such as venereal disease control and tuberculosis control. It also stocks and distributes specialty drugs and biologicals either because these are not approved for distribution in the United States or because the need is limited. CDC maintains the Epidemic Investigation Service, which may be called in by a local health authority to assist with a difficult disease problem. Except for a few specific programs, the CDC does not accept disease reports directly. The programs work through state and territorial health departments.

All jurisdictions in the United States have laws that require the reporting of certain diseases to a local or state health officer (Chorba and Berkelman, 1989). The laws differ on which diseases are reportable, who must report, how the reports are made, and who accepts the reports, but the substance of the law changes little. Reportable conditions are infectious diseases or toxic exposures that endanger the community. All states require that physicians report these diseases and conditions, and many extend this requirement to include nurses, dentists, veterinarians, laboratories, school officials, administrators of institutions, and police officials. Failure to report a reportable disease may constitute a criminal offense, and it creates civil liability if someone is hurt by it. Required reporting is exempt from confidentiality limitations and physician-patient privilege. The patient's right of privacy gives way to the societal need to prevent the spread of disease. Physicians must not abuse this privilege and unnecessarily divulge a patient's medical information. (See Chapter 8.)

Reportable Diseases

Table 21-1 lists diseases that are commonly reportable. Most of these are reportable in all jurisdictions; the remainder are of public health interest irrespective of their reportability in a given jurisdiction. They are divided into categories according to the mode of spread or the programs used to control them. This list is not comprehensive. State-specific information on what to report and to whom can be obtained from the state health department. Generally if a disease is affecting an unusually large number of people or if it is a disease that may become epidemic, it should be reported. Except for HIV, most health departments accept reports for diseases that are not on the state list of reportable diseases. The health department may choose not to act on the reports, but physicians have no legal liability for making a report that is not required.

Complying with Reporting Duties

Irrespective of personal beliefs, physicians must comply with reporting laws. A physician should never withhold information or give false information to protect a patient's privacy. Although violators are seldom prosecuted, interfering with a public health investigation is a crime in most states. There is a much greater chance that a failure to comply with a reporting duty will result in a medical malpractice lawsuit. Failure to report an infectious person or a dangerous condition can make the physician liable for any harm to the patient or anyone else that compliance with the reporting duty would have protected.

Legally required disease control reporting is not subject to informed consent; the patient has no right to veto the reporting. The reportability of a disease should not be part of the informed consent for laboratory tests. Information about the reportability of a disease might deter some patients from consenting to testing. While this might protect the patient's autonomy, it can threaten the

Table 21-1. Commonly Reportable Diseases

Disease categories	Specific diseases
animal bites	AIDS
any group expression of diseases	amebiasis
cancer	animal bites
congenital anomalies	anthrax
foodborne diseases	ascariasis
infestations	aspergillosis
occupational illness and injury	blastomycosis
sexually transmitted diseases	botulism (adult and infant)
toxic exposures	brucellosis
vector-borne diseases	Campylobacter infection
zoonoses	chancroid
	chicken pox
	chlamydia trachomatis infection
	cholera
	coccidioidomycosis
	Colorado tick fever
	congenital infections (all types)
	dengue fever
	diphtheria
	encephalitis (all types)
	pertussis syndrome (including parapertussis)
	food poisoning
	giardiasis
	gonorrhea
	granuloma inguinale
	Haemophilus influenzae infections
	Hansen's disease (leprosy)
	hepatitis (all types)
	histoplasmosis
	HIV infection
	HIV-related illness
	influenza and flulike illness
	Kawasaki syndrome
	Lassa fever
	legionellosis
	leishmaniasis
	leprosy
	leptospirosis
	listeriosis
	Lyme disease
	lymphogranuloma venereum
	malaria
	measles (rubeola)
	meningitis—bacterial (all types)
	meningococcal infections
	mumps
	paratyphoid
	pelvic inflammatory disease

Table 21-1. (Continued)

Disease categories	Specific diseases
	pinta
	plague
	pneumonia
	poliomyelitis
	psittacosis
	Q fever
	rabies
	rat bite fever
	relapsing fever
	respiratory fungal infections
	Reye's syndrome
	rheumatic fever
	Rocky Mountain spotted fever
	rubella
	rubella, congenital
	salmonellosis
	scabies
	schistosomiasis
	shigellosis
	smallpox
	streptococcal disease
	syphilis
	teniasis (tape worm)
	tetanus
	toxic shock syndrome
	toxoplasmosis
	trachoma
	trichinosis
	tuberculosis
	tularemia
	typhoid
	typhus fever (epidemic, murine, and scrub)
	vibrio infections
	viral hemorrhagic fevers
	visceral larva migrans
	yaws
	yellow fever

public's health. The physician does not need a medical records release for disease reporting because neither the physician nor the patient has the right to refuse the release of information.

Physicians must never knowingly report false information to public health authorities. The physician is liable for any injuries occasioned by the false report. This does not mean that the physician must personally investigate the information that patients provide. It does mean that the physician must truthfully report what is known to him or her. The reality is that very few physicians do not know their patients' correct names and addresses. It is the rare patient who pays cash for medical care and never requires a prescription or other order that requires correct identity.

A physician who provides information in good faith is not liable if the information is incorrect. Conversely, a physician who intentionally provides false information may be liable for negligence per se. This means that the reporting statute establishes the proper standard of care and the physician is liable as a matter of law. (See Chapter 6.) Depending on the nature of the state's reporting laws, a physician's malpractice insurance may not cover damages due to knowingly breaking the law. Most states also allow the board of medical examiners to restrict or revoke a physician's license for failing to comply with reporting laws.

Most state laws also require laboratories to report communicable diseases. The physician reports the clinical diagnosis, and the laboratory reports the results of tests that indicate the presence of a reportable disease. When the laboratory reports a disease, this does not obviate the physician's duty to report. Physicians who run laboratories in their offices may have to file duplicate reports if they perform the laboratory tests that establish the diagnosis.

Warning Third Parties

Any physician who diagnoses a contagious disease has a duty to counsel the patient about the communicability of the disease and to ensure that any other persons at risk are warned. This duty has been clear and explicit in the laws of this country since the nineteenth century. This duty can be discharged directly, by warning the exposed individuals, or indirectly, by reporting the disease to public health officials or by counseling the patient to warn persons at risk. The proper method of discharging this duty to warn is shaped by the applicable reporting and privacy laws. The patient's privacy is best protected by indirect warnings through the health department. This route may be ineffective, however, in jurisdictions where the health department declines to warn persons who are exposed to communicable diseases such as HIV. For example, a physician who treated a married man with syphilis would have to report the disease to the local health department, which would contact the man's wife. They would interview her to determine if there were other contacts who might require treatment. The physician would have discharged his or her duty to warn the wife and to report disease. The health department also protects the patient's confidence. A disease investigator does not tell a contact to a communicable disease carrier who the carrier is—simply that there has been a contact.

In this case, if the wife has not had sexual relations with anyone except her husband, she will know who her contact was. It is important to keep in mind that the resulting family problems are not the fault of the reporting physician if the health department does the warning. Conversely, if a physician attempts to warn a person at risk and does so negligently, the physician may be liable for the ensuing marital disharmony.

In the classic case, the physician diagnosed syphilis in a married woman. The physician then told the woman to tell her husband that he might be infected and to come in for testing. The consequences of this negligent diagnosis and counseling were suspicion, disharmony, and divorce. The court found that the physician was responsible for this result and had to pay damages to the husband for negligent infliction of mental distress (*Molien v. Kaiser Foundation Hospitals*, 1980). Had the physician reported the disease to the health department and relied on it to warn the husband, the potential liability for marital distress would have been reduced or eliminated.

This case is especially interesting because the strategy of counseling patients to warn their own contacts is often recommended for HIV-infected persons. Under this court's analysis, instructing an infected plaintiff to warn others and ask them to come in for testing can leave the physician liable for any negligently inflicted mental distress suffered by the patient's contacts.

Such potential liability, coupled with the greater expertise of the health department disease investigators, means that physicians should rely on the health department to warn persons at risk. Most health departments, however, refuse to trace and warn the contacts of HIV carriers. In such states, physicians are in a difficult bind: they have a duty to warn but may be liable for consequences of negligent warnings, delivered by either the patient or the physician. If they warn without the patient's consent, they also may be liable for violating the patient's privacy. If the state law permits the physician to warn third persons without the patient's permission, the physician must be careful not to disclose the disease carrier's identity, even if the contact clearly knows the identity and asks the physician to confirm it. Laws allowing the physician to warn still leave the physician liable for the consequences of a negligent warning.

The problem of warning third parties is exacerbated if a contact is a patient of the physician, commonly the case for family physicians. Physicians who treat families can obviate the confidentiality problem by asking patients to authorize sharing necessary medical information with other family members. This should be done on the first patient visit to prevent the violation of state laws requiring the physician to protect each individual patient's confidential information. If the patient refuses, the physician must be careful not to violate his or her confidences. Even if the patient agrees, which she did in the *Molien* case, this is no protection against negligently inflicted harm.

Coercive Measures

State and federal public health laws provide the authority to restrict the liberty of individuals to protect the public health and safety. This includes the power to isolate individuals (quarantine), to force individuals to be immunized or treated, and to restrict the activities in which the individual may engage. Forced quarantine has fallen into disuse since antibiotics, and the use of specific behavioral restrictions has made it possible to allow infected individuals more personal freedom without endangering others. However, quarantine is still used on some patients, such as typhoid carriers who take jobs as food handlers or tuberculosis carriers whose disease is resistant to all the antituberculosis drugs available. Mandatory immunization or incarceration for treatment is still used by public health officials.

Involuntary Testing

The least intrusive coercive public health measure is the involuntary testing of populations at risk for communicable disease. The most common example is testing for tuberculosis in high-risk populations. Involuntary testing has three benefits. First, it allows public health officials to learn the prevalence of a disease in the community. This is difficult to accomplish with voluntary testing because of the statistical problems associated with self-selected data sets. Second, it identifies infected individuals who may benefit from treatment. Third, it identifies individuals who may need to be restricted to protect the public health.

Involuntary testing for communicable diseases is legally different from testing for personal behavior such as drug use or the propensity to steal from an employer. The presence or absence of a communicable disease may be objectively determined, and the risk it poses is easily quantified. There are no criminal law consequences to the diagnosis of a communicable disease, so there is no need for protection against self-incrimination in disease screening. In many cases, treatment will eradicate the condition. Even when treatment is impossible, only rare circumstances demand more than minimal workplace restrictions to prevent the spread of the disease. When these restrictions are required, they are solely to protect others, not to punish the affected individual.

Contact Tracing
This is the method that has been used in the control of endemic contagious disease for decades (Hethcote and Yorke 1984). A disease investigation begins when an individual is identified as having a communicable disease. An investigator interviews the patient, family members, physicians, nurses, and anyone else who may have knowledge of the primary patient's contacts, anyone who might have been exposed, and anyone who might have been the source of the disease. Then the contacts are screened to see if they have or have ever had the disease. The type of contact screened depends on the nature of the disease. A sexually transmitted disease will require interviewing only infected patients and screening only their sex partners. A disease that is spread by respiratory contact, such as tuberculosis, may require screening tens to hundreds of persons, such as other inmates in a prison.

Many persons object to contact tracing as an invasion of privacy. Since contact tracing is constitutionally permissible, these objections are often disguised as criticisms of the cost of contact tracing. Contact tracing is an expensive process but one that is cost-effective because it is highly efficient in finding infected persons (Potterat et al. 1989). This was best demonstrated in the campaign to eradicate smallpox.

Contrary to popular belief, smallpox was not controlled by immunizing every person on earth. It was controlled by extensive contact tracing to find infected individuals. Smallpox could be controlled only because the sores and scars prevented infected persons from escaping detection (Carrell and Zoler 1990). Fellow villagers and tribesmen were encouraged in various ways to identify infected persons. When a person with smallpox was identified, he or she was quarantined, and all the persons in the surrounding community or village were vaccinated. In this way smallpox was eventually reduced to isolated outbreaks and then eradicated.

While many health departments have resisted contact tracing for HIV infection, the resurgence of infectious tuberculosis secondary to HIV-induced immunosuppression is forcing them to reexamine this policy (CDC 1991). Recent outbreaks of drug-resistant tuberculosis have intensified the concern with contact tracing. Drug-resistant tuberculosis poses great public health problems because of its often fatal course and the inability to render the carriers noninfectious (CDC 1990).

Mandated Treatment
Implicit in the power to protect the public health is the power to treat disease carriers against their objections. Since treatment is a less restrictive alternative to

quarantine or isolation, it is favored as a disease control measure. A patient who refuses to accept treatment for a contagious disease may be ordered to accept the treatment by a health officer or, depending on the jurisdiction, a court. A common practice is to incarcerate a recalcitrant patient until the patient consents to the treatment. This coerced consent is not obtained as a sham on an informed consent but to obviate the need for physically subduing the patient. It also gives the patient an opportunity to contest the treatment through a habeas corpus proceeding.

Although coerced treatment for a communicable disease violates a person's autonomy, it is permissible under the U.S. Constitution. The alternative is to allow the infected person to threaten the health and life of others. With tuberculosis, failure to force a contagious homeless person to accept treatment may result in the infection of other persons with whom the person comes into contact in shelters. Since many of these contacts, especially the children, are poorly nourished or chronically ill, they will be susceptible to fast-spreading infection that is difficult to treat. This problem is already evident in the high rates of tuberculosis spread in homeless shelters.

Quarantine and Isolation

As a public health measure, quarantine has come to mean the restriction of disease carriers to an environment where their contact with outsiders is limited. Quarantine was widely used until the 1950s. For self-limited diseases such as measles, the infected person was required to stay home and not have visitors. For diseases such as infectious tuberculosis before antitubercular agents were available, the quarantine might be at a sanitarium with other tuberculosis patients.

Isolation, a special case of quarantine, is almost always used in an institutional setting. It may be reverse isolation, to protect the person being isolated. The most famous reverse isolation case was the "bubble baby," the child who was raised in an isolation chamber because he did not have a functioning immune system. The medical and psychological sequellae of indefinite length long-term protective isolation were sufficiently daunting to discourage its further use. Nevertheless, it is used routinely for short, controlled periods for patients undergoing certain types of chemotheraphy and organ transplantation.

Isolation is used for diseases that are transmitted through casual contact or respiratory transmission. Strict isolation is used for highly infectious agents that may travel long distances through the air or be caught from cutaneous contact with sores or secretions. Strict isolation requires restriction to a private room with controlled air flow. Persons entering the room must wear gowns, gloves, and respirators capable of filtering out micron-level particles. Surgical masks give no protection for respiratory isolation, which is used for diseases such as tuberculosis that are spread through the inspiration of infected particles but have only limited spread through contact with wounds or secretions. Respiratory isolation requires the same precautions as strict isolation but without the extensive gowning and gloving. Contact isolation is for diseases that spread by direct contact and limited droplet spread. It requires personal protective measures but not a controlled air supply (Coleman 1987).

Strict and respiratory isolation must be meticulously maintained to be effective. Patients may not leave the room without supervision to ensure that they do not remove their respirators. Staff must never break isolation, and visitors must be carefully monitored. The patient rooms must be at negative pressure to doors and hallways. The room air must be exhausted outside, preferably through high-efficiency air particulate air filters. Ultraviolet lights may also be used to reduce the spread of infectious particles. All treatment rooms must meet these isolation standards, including the control of personnel entering and leaving the room (Drug-resistant TB outbreak, 1991).

Using Isolation and Quarantine
When it became clear that AIDS was a communicable disease, there was discussion of quarantining persons with AIDS to prevent the spread of disease. Although this was never seriously considered, the resulting outcry made public health authorities reluctant to use or discuss quarantine and isolation in any circumstances. Some states even rewrote their disease control laws to make it difficult to restrict disease carriers. The repercussions of these policies are evident in the growing number of reports of the spread of tuberculosis and other diseases from known carriers to health care providers and members of the general community. These cases might have been prevented with the effective use of isolation (CDC 1990).

The transmittal of drug-resistant tuberculosis to health care workers is increasing (TB not limited, 1991). About 10 percent of otherwise healthy people who are infected develop acute disease, which is often impossible to cure and difficult to render noninfectious. A person with infectious tuberculosis must be put in respiratory isolation. This isolation lasts a short time for drug-sensitive tuberculosis, but it may last until the end of the patient's life for drug-resistant tuberculosis.

The biggest problem with quarantine and isolation is not the patient's civil rights but the logistics. Few city or county governments want to pay for feeding, housing, and caring for patients placed under isolation. The public health nurse may not consider doing grocery shopping and laundry for a quarantined patient as a proper part of nursing duties. Hospitals do not like to take in infectious patients who require extensive isolation precautions. The cost of these precautions is seldom reimbursed fully, and the patient cannot be discharged until noninfectious. Controlling the spread of disease is particularly difficult in jails. This reticence to bear the responsibility of quarantine and isolation is often concealed behind a facade of concern for the individual's civil rights. The result in some jurisdictions is that people, including health care providers, continue to be exposed to carriers of easily communicated, deadly diseases such as pan-drug-resistant tuberculosis.

FOOD SANITATION

Community hygiene is an important part of public health that most physicians know little about, yet most physicians will have a case of food poisoning themselves at some time in their lives, besides treating cases in their patients. These cases usually involve food handled improperly in the home, such as tuna salad that was saved a little longer than it should have been. Generally the physician need only make the report of a case of food poisoning to the local health department and remind the patient, "When in doubt throw it out."

Most community outbreaks of food poisoning arise from the same sources as individual cases. Potluck dinners and socials at churches and schools give more people food poisoning than any other source in the United States. The local health department usually has jurisdiction to deal with such outbreaks through local ordinances supported by state law. It is important that such outbreaks be reported to the health department because locating the problem and educating the leaders of the organization may avert future outbreaks.

Local health departments usually have jurisdiction over the preparation or sale of food in the community, although their control over schools and public institutions may be limited. Federal laws govern such matters as the handling of food in interstate commerce, the licensing of drugs, and special hazards such as seafood and meat processing. Physicians should try to cooperate with health authorities to protect the food supply. Recognizing and reporting cases of food poisoning is the first step. Powerful institutional providers may bring great pressure to bear on health officials and physicians to overlook deficiencies. A college physician may be encouraged to substitute a diagnosis of gastroenteritis for one of food poisoning if the presumed source of the problem is the college food service. This would violate professional ethics, reporting laws, and the physician's duty to patients. A better response is for the physician to work with public health authorities to correct the problems that are causing the food poisoning. A physician who did not make proper diagnoses and reports might be held liable for illness in subsequent patrons of the establishment.

There also will be times when food poisoning will result from food that is damaged before it reaches the retail level. Most people are familiar with the recall of canned food that appears to have been contaminated during manufacture. This is usually discovered by an attentive private physician who recognizes botulism or other unusual diseases. Food may also become unfit for consumption because of improper handling. If a carload of fish has lost refrigeration and spoiled, it may cause a local disease outbreak of considerable magnitude. A physician who recognizes and reports an early case may save many people from illness. The health department would have the opportunity to locate the problem and supervise the destruction of the contaminated food.

ENVIRONMENTAL HEALTH

Local health departments have a general responsibility for protecting the community from environmental hazards. These duties range from stray animal control to coordinating the cleanup of a toxic waste dump. Community physicians should cooperate with the health officials and report problem cases. This will help the public health physicians to draw on the many resources available through the public health system and national organizations such as chemical manufacturers.

A private physician should be cautious about making pronouncements on environmental hazards to patients or the news media. An association between exposure and disease may seem obvious to a physician who has seen only a couple of cases yet be incorrect. A physician who publicly accuses a business of wrongdoing may be open to suit for damages to the business. Public health officials are protected from such suits when they are acting as officers of the state. Their job is made more difficult by the publicity that often arises when individual physicians seek to publicize public health risks. It is better to discuss the problem with the health department personnel before attempting to publicize a risk that may not be significant. If, however, the health department is unresponsive, the physician might want to contact a state or national environmental protection group.

BIBLIOGRAPHY

Anderson RM; May RM: Vaccination and herd immunity to infectious diseases. Nature 1985 Nov 28–Dec 4; 318(6044): 323–29.

Bouvier B; Octavio J: A model system for reporting communicable diseases to local health agencies. Am J Infect Control 1988 Apr; 16(2):35A–36A.

Bradley BL; Kerr KM; Leitch AG; Lamb D: Notification of tuberculosis: Can the pathologist help? Br Med J (Clin Res) 1988 Sep 3; 297(6648):595.

Carrell S; Zoler ML: Defiant diseases: Hard-won gains erode. Med World News 1990 31 12(7):20.

Carroll P; Maher VF: Legal aspects of contagious infectious disease. Adv Clin Care 1989 Jul–Aug; 4(4):6.

Cates W Jr: Priorities for sexually transmitted diseases in the late 1980s and beyond. Sex Transm Dis 1986 Apr–Jun; 13(2):114–17.

CDC: Outbreak of multidrug-resistant tuberculosis—Texas, California, and Pennsylvania. MMWR 1990 39 (22):369.

CDC: Transmission of multidrug-resistant tuberculosis from an HIV-positive client in a residential substance-abuse treatment facility—Michigan. MMWR 1991; 40(8):129.

Chorba TL; Berkelman RL; Safford SK; Gibbs NP; Hull HF: Mandatory reporting of infectious diseases by clinicians. JAMA 1989; 262:3018–26.

Coleman D: The when and how of isolation. RN 1987 Oct; 34:50.

Davis RM; Markowitz LE; Preblud SR; Orenstein WA; Hinman AR: A cost-effectiveness analysis of measles outbreak control strategies. Am J Epidemiol 1987 Sep; 126(3):450–59.

Davis RM; Whitman ED; Orenstein WA; Preblud SR; Markowitz LE; Hinman AR: A persistent outbreak of measles despite appropriate prevention and control measures. Am J Epidemiol 1987 Sep; 126(3):438–49.

Drug-resistant TB outbreak highlights need for screening. AIDS Alert 1991 May; 6(5):96.

Etkind P; Wilson ME; Gallagher K; Cournoyer J: Bluefish-associated scombroid poisoning. An example of the expanding spectrum of food poisoning from seafood. JAMA 1987 Dec 18; 258(23):3409–10.

Francis H: Understanding medical officers of health. Public Health 1988 Nov; 102(6):545–53.

Grist NR; Reid D; Young AB: Herd immunity to infections. Health Bull (Edinb) 1981 Jul; 39(4):211–17.

Gross TP; Rosenberg ML: Shelters for battered women and their children: An underrecognized source of communicable disease transmission. Am J Public Health 1987 Sep; 77(9):1198–1201.

Henderson DA: Principles and lessons from the smallpox eradication programme. Bull WHO 1987; 65(4):535–46.

Hethcote HW; Yorke JA: *Gonorrhea Transmission Dynamics and Control*. 1984.

Kane MA; Alter MJ; Hadler SC; Margolis HS: Hepatitis B infection in the United States. Recent trends and future strategies for control. Am J Med 1989 Sep 4; 87(3A):11S–13S.

Miller CH: Tracing the routes of disease transmission. RDH 1989 Mar; 9(3):48, 64.

Molien v. Kaiser Foundation Hospitals. 616 P2d 813 (1980).

Potterat JJ; Spencer NE; Woodhouse DE; Muth JB: Partner notification in the control of human immunodeficiency virus infection. Am J Public Health 1989 Jul; 79(7):874.

Silber P; Alexander WJ; Harden JW Jr; Housch JG; Cutter GR; Maetz HM: A study of the cost of tuberculosis contact investigation related to non-tuberculous mycobacterial isolation in Jefferson County, Alabama. Public Health 1987 Jul; 101(4):297–304.

Steele JH: The zoonoses. Int J Zoonoses 1985 Jun; 12(2):87–97.

Stevenson CS; Sterne GS; Stephens KO: Liability for infectious diseases in day care: Legal and practical considerations. Rev Infect Dis 1986 Jul–Aug; 8(4):644–47.

TB not limited to AIDS patients, can affect workers. AIDS Alert 1991 Jan; 6(1):9.

Thomas v. Morris. 286 NY 266, 269, 36 NE2d 141, 142 (1941).

22
AIDS

CRITICAL POINTS
- The HIV epidemic is exacerbating problems in the medical care delivery system.
- Public health authorities have been constrained in their response to the HIV epidemic.
- The legal problems posed by HIV are not unique but only mirror problems seen in other communicable diseases.
- HIV dementia and secondary infections pose real risks in the workplace.

Acquired immunodeficiency syndrome (AIDS) is the most legally troubling problem facing the health care system in the United States. The epidemic has frightened the public, highlighted the flaws in our public health system, and exacerbated the inequities in the health insurance and indigent care systems. Many authors have stressed the special problems of AIDS and why traditional medical and public health practices are inappropriate for AIDS and HIV infection. In our view, AIDS poses no new and unique medical problems. It is unique only when the history of communicable disease control in this century is ignored.

This is not intended to diminish the significance of AIDS or, more properly, HIV infection. Careful study of epidemiologic models without the distortions induced by politicization of HIV leads us to conclude that HIV will reach a higher equilibrium prevalence than is predicted by current models (Brookmeyer 1991). We also believe that dementia and communicable secondary infections such as tuberculosis will make the management of HIV infection much more complex than is anticipated. The efforts to quell fears of the casual spread of HIV have made it controversial to discuss any risks posed by HIV-infected persons. This denies the reality of the disease and risks a backlash that will further stigmatize HIV-infected persons.

HIV infection is a difficult subject for a chapter in a book because our knowledge changes so rapidly. This chapter reviews the political and medical history of HIV as necessary to provide a context for the discussion of the legal problems posed by the disease. This is not a survey of applicable state laws or a comprehensive discussion of HIV-related illness. Physicians must ascertain the current laws concerning HIV and AIDS reporting, counseling, and warning in their states. The objective of this chapter is to help physicians understand the legal issues posed by HIV infection within the larger context of public health law and practice.

HISTORY

Antibodies to HIV were found in blood and tissue samples as early as 1969. Retrospectively, it is believed that there may have been sporadic cases of the disease in the United States since 1965. The clinical syndrome of AIDS was first recognized among gay men in San Francisco and New York in 1981. The isolated cases of Kaposi's sarcoma and uncontrollable infections with normally nonpathogenic organisms were quickly recognized to be part of single pathologic process. This identification was possible because the syndrome occurred in a subpopulation that was easily recognizable and well known to venereologists and infectious disease experts. Had an equally small number of cases been diluted in the general population, it might have taken several more years to recognize that AIDS was an epidemic infectious disease.

Hepatitis B in the Bathhouses

The emergence of a new disease, particularly if it affects a particular group, always suggests an infectious agent or a toxin of some type. In AIDS, the disease appeared in a subpopulation that was known to have significant risk for venereal infection and for illicit drug use: the small population of gays whose life-style included high-frequency, anonymous sex in bathhouses, frequently accompanied by the use of amphetamines and amyl nitrate.

The high-frequency, anonymous sex in the bathhouses made them ideal places to spread infections of all types. In addition to gonorrhea and syphilis, hepatitis B was spread widely through homosexual bathhouses. The epidemiology of this disease was studied intensively as part of the effort to develop a hepatitis B vaccine. It was evident that hepatitis B was spread by both sexual activity and by sharing needles when using intravenous drugs. By 1980 a high percentage of those who frequented bathhouses regularly were infected with hepatitis B.

The most interesting aspect of this hepatitis B epidemic was that few people in public health tried to stop it. Hepatitis B is a debilitating, sometimes fatal disease and the leading cause of cancer worldwide. Although only a small percentage of infected persons die of acute fulminate hepatitis, a substantial number of infected persons become chronic carriers, who may continue to spread the disease for years. These chronically infected persons develop liver cancer or cirrhosis at a much higher rate than the general population.

Despite the personal and public health costs of the disease, public health officials did not want to jeopardize their relationship with the gay community by closing the bathhouses, and they argued that this would compromise other disease control efforts. More fundamentally, it would have been political suicide. In New York City, San Francisco, Los Angeles, and Houston, gay men were a well-organized, powerful political lobby. Mayors did not want to risk offending them by supporting the control of a communicable disease with which their own community was not concerned. Thus, the rights of gay men were protected by denying them public health protections. This was the precedent for nonintervention that characterized the first several years of the AIDS epidemic.

The History of AIDS and ARC

The terms *AIDS* (acquired immunodeficiency syndrome) and *ARC* (AIDS-related complex) are historical artifacts, dating from the period between the recognition of an immunosuppression syndrome in gay men and the identification of HIV. In 1981 physicians in San Francisco and New York City began to see a pattern of unusual infections and cancers in young and otherwise healthy homosexual men. The first report in *Morbidity and Mortality Weekly Report* (MMWR) focused on the men's infection with an atypical pneumonia and a cancer that had been previously seen only in elderly men of Mediterranean descent (Karposi's sarcoma and pneumocytis pneumonia among homosexual men, 1981).

Early research quickly pointed to common trends among cases, but these were obscured by many extraneous factors. The most suggestive of these was the use of drugs, such as inhalant stimulants, by some of the affected men. As these leads were being pursued, more cases of the syndrome were diagnosed. While epidemiologically inconsistent with the toxin hypothesis, they had the same distribution as hepatitis B. Many victims were positive for hepatitis B acquired in the bathhouses. The most crucial evidence for an infectious agent was the appearance of the disease in persons who had no visible link with the bathhouses.

While a toxic agent might have caused the disease among homosexuals and intravenous drug users, it did not explain the development of the disease among recipients of blood and blood products. Initially a mystery, these cases were soon traced back to the blood donors: homosexual men dead or dying of AIDS. The traditional test for an infectious agent was satisfied, and the parallel to hepatitis B was complete. When the antibody test for HIV became available, it was found in frozen blood samples that had been saved during the study of hepatitis B in the late 1970s.

There was some controversy over what to call this syndrome. Terms such as *GRID* (gay-related immunodeficiency disease) were considered but rejected in favor of the more neutral *AIDS* (Shilts 1987). The CDC promulgated a broad surveillance definition of what it called acquired immunodeficiency syndrome to facilitate the reporting and investigation of this new syndrome:

> For the limited purposes of epidemiologic surveillance, CDC defines a case of AIDS as a reliable diagnosed disease that is at least moderately indicative of an underlying cellular immunodeficiency in a person who has had no known cause of underlying cellular immunodeficiency or any other underlying reduced resistance reported to be associated with that disease. (Leads from MMWR, 1983)

As cases were reported and analyzed under the broad CDC definition, common patterns emerged. It was found that various combinations of unusual infections, indirect measures of immune system function, and a rare cancer, Kaposi's sarcoma, characterized most of the reported cases. This lead the CDC to revise its definition of AIDS to reflect the most common manifestations presented by the reported cases (CDC 1985). The revised criteria took the form of a list of the unusual infections and cancers, abnormal immune system tests, and other diagnostic findings that were significantly correlated with symptomatic HIV infection.

These revised criteria were sufficiently restrictive to create a class of persons who were infected with HIV and had symptomatic disease but did not meet the

CDC criteria for AIDS. These persons were identified as having ARC. Persons with ARC were not reportable, and their numbers did not count toward the CDC's running total of AIDS cases. Persons with ARC also had difficulty in qualifying for categorical programs funded for treating AIDS patients. Moreover, persons who were positive for the then newly discovered HIV but had no symptomatic disease were not reported and followed to track the epidemiology of the disease.

In 1987 the CDC definition of AIDS was broadened to include neurological symptoms, wasting syndrome, and more common infections such as tuberculosis (CDC 1987). This redefined many persons with ARC as persons with AIDS. In our view, once it was possible to test for the presence of HIV and it was proved that persons with AIDS or ARC were infected with HIV, then the presence of HIV or its antibodies should have become the reportable condition. Most states, however, persist in requiring AIDS cases to be reported but do not require the reporting of HIV-infected persons. This masks the epidemiology of the disease in women who do not fit the male-oriented standards for HIV (Chu, Buehler, and Berkelman 1990). Given that the latency of AIDS may exceed ten years, counting AIDS cases rather than HIV infection makes it difficult to predict accurately the movement of the disease into new population groups. If the CDC again revises the definition of AIDS to include low T4-cell counts, it is estimated the number of persons with AIDS will double.

Origin of Infectious Disease

AIDS is not the first disease that just appeared as if from nowhere. The classic example is syphilis. We often hear of the syphilization of Europe being attributed to Columbus's sailors bringing the disease back from the New World. However, since the disease was a major problem in the armies of both France and Naples in a war that broke out four months after the return of the explorer's ships to Spain, it is unlikely that a handful of sailors can be responsible. A spirochetal disease similar to yaws had been well known in northern Africa for centuries. It is probable that syphilis was a mutation of this disease. For the first 40 years that the disease existed, it was much more severe than syphilis is today. Secondary syphilis had a mortality rate of 20 to 40 percent during this early time. The virulence of the disease then decreased to the level we know today.

Changing virulence is a common phenomenon in infectious diseases. The great plagues of the Middle Ages came and went in waves that had little to do with medical care, hygiene, or immunity in the general population. Today plague is endemic in Asia and the western United States. We have the necessary insect vectors, the animal reservoir of infection, and the potential human exposure yet only sporadic cases instead of epidemics. At the beginning of this century, streptococcal disease was dreaded. Even well-nourished and well-cared-for children died of strep throat and rheumatic fever. The severity of this disease has decreased so much that many states have removed it from the list of reportable diseases. Although it has been attributed to penicillin, the change occurred before the era of antibiotics and extends to children who have not received treatment. The cycle now is reversing as the severity of strep and the incidence of rheumatic fever increase (Carrell 1990).

Initial Concentration in the Gay Community

Three factors were responsible for the original concentration of AIDS in the male homosexual population in the United States. First, it appears that AIDS originated in Africa as a mutation of an endemic virus and was carried from there to Haiti. Haiti was a popular vacation spot for homosexuals, and male prostitution was widespread among the impoverished Haitians. Irrespective of how the initial introduction of the disease occurred, the second factor was the existence of the bathhouses. These provided large numbers of sexual contacts and a high incidence of other sexually transmitted diseases. It is likely that genital lesions secondary to these other venereal diseases made the spread of HIV easier.

Most important, the rate of spread of diseases is proportional to the frequency of contact with potentially infected individuals and the effectiveness of those contacts in spreading the disease. This becomes critical for diseases such as HIV with a low probability of transmission in a given sexual encounter. Some bathhouse patrons had more than 1000 sexual contacts a year. A very sexually active heterosexual man might have 100 contacts a year. Although HIV was probably introduced into the heterosexual population simultaneously as in the homosexual population, the spread would be less than one-tenth as fast. (While female prostitutes do have large numbers of sexual contracts, women are less effective at infecting their sexual contacts than are men.)

It is important to note that AIDS in Africa is primarily a disease of heterosexuals. It may be spread by nonsexual rituals and the reuse of needles in medical practice. The number of people infected, evidence about modes of transmission, and other vital information have been hard to obtain on these populations. It is clear, however, that the spread follows traditional prostitution patterns. There is also evidence that HIV is primarily transmitted heterosexually in Central and South America.

Currently the percentage of AIDS cases attributable to heterosexual spread is much lower than the number of cases secondary to homosexual contact or drug abuse. The rate of increase of heterosexual cases parallels the rate among homosexual men early in the epidemic. Given that an AIDS case diagnosed in 1990 may represent an infection acquired in 1983 and given the lower rate of spread among heterosexuals, the number of heterosexual cases should continue to increase for many years.

PARALLELS WITH OTHER DISEASES

Although HIV is a new disease organism, the problems it poses are common to several other diseases that have been dealt with by the public health system in the United States. The devastating sequelae of HIV infection make controlling the spread of the disease so important. Unlike an easily communicated disease such as measles, individuals can protect themselves from HIV. But because it is a sexually transmitted disease, it is certain to be a serious threat until a cheap, highly effective vaccine is developed. Even easily treated venereal diseases such as syphilis and gonorrhea are increasing rather than moving toward extinction.

When the AIDS syndrome was first described, it represented the end stage of the disease. AIDS was 100 percent fatal, with a short mean lifetime between diagnosis and death. As the syndrome became better defined, it was diagnosed earlier, and the mean survival time increased. With the ability to diagnose asymptomatic HIV infection came the realization that some persons infected with HIV could live ten or more years. It is expected that current drug therapies for HIV infection will again increase the survival of HIV-infected persons.

Nevertheless, it is assumed that HIV infection is still 100 percent fatal, with a mean survival time exceeding ten years.

It is unusual for a communicable disease to have a 100 percent mortality. Rabies is 100 percent fatal, and the disease usually progresses rapidly in humans. Several cancers are 100 percent fatal. In addition, there are many infectious diseases that have a very high mortality rate even with adequate therapy. Although such diseases are difficult for many health care providers to deal with, we do manage to care for the patients adequately.

HIV is not unique as an infectious agent. More than 60 infectious diseases are reportable in various states and are a common part of public health practice. HIV is less difficult to work with and control than many other diseases because it is less easily spread. Diseases that may be spread through respiratory casual contact, for example, can be much more difficult to prevent and control. Tuberculosis was controlled before it was treatable. Other diseases with carrier states must be managed without definitive therapy. Standard public health such as public education, screening, and contact tracing also are effective in the control of HIV.

Fear of Disease

Fear is both a problem and an opportunity in disease control. Public hysteria can make rational disease control measures impossible. Yet without some level of fear, it is impossible to keep the public and their elected representatives interested in disease control. During the polio epidemics of the 1930s and 1940s, people cancelled group meetings of all kinds, threw away food because a fly had lighted on it, and defied school attendance laws. The advent of Salk's vaccine brought the polio epidemics and the associated hysteria to an end. Less than 30 years later, it is difficult to maintain proper levels of immunization against measles because parents believe the disease is eradicated and do not have their children immunized.

The double-edged nature of fear has stymied effective HIV control stratagems. The efforts to downplay the risk of HIV to heterosexuals slowed the flow of research dollars at the beginning of the epidemic. The general community's lack of fear of HIV allowed the bathhouses to remain open despite clear evidence of their role in the spread of HIV. Irrational fears that HIV may be spread through casual contact have resulted in discrimination against HIV carriers, but efforts to control these fears have encouraged employers and others to ignore the real problems of HIV-induced dementia and secondary infections.

Risks Posed by HIV Infection

HIV is spread through consensual behavior. Accidental transinsular is a risk only in medical care settings or other situations were there can be contact with blood or bodily fluids. Infected patients pose a risk to their medical care providers. There is a much greater risk of death from workplace-acquired hepatitis B than from workplace-acquired HIV. The risk of transmission of HIV from health care providers to patients is just being explored. There is a risk of transmission during invasive procedures that must be considered. (See Chapter 23.) Except in certain medical care situations, it is HIV dementia and secondary infections, not HIV transmission, that endanger others.

HIV directly affects the central nervous system (CNS). This is independent of infections of the CNS that are secondary to immune system failure (Wilkie et al.

1990). While originally thought to be a late sequella of AIDS, HIV CNS signs may be the first manifestation of the disease (Stern et al. 1991). Central nervous system HIV infection may manifest as an acute encephalopathy within a few weeks of infection, or it may have a gradual course. It may affect all CNS functions, both motor and cognitive. Its symptoms include short-term memory loss, impaired motor function, and emotional disturbances (Lunn et al 1991). This has profound implications for professionals such as physicians and pilots, and others, such as truck drivers, in whom mental impairment case endanger themselves and others (Fulghum 1990). (See Chapter 23.)

Secondary infections with conventional pathogens pose the only risk to the casual contacts of HIV carriers. Some cities have seen a substantial increase in new cases of tuberculosis because of a high prevalence of HIV infection. An HIV carrier infected with an easily communicated secondary infection poses the same risk to co-workers as any other person with the same communicable disease. There has already been documented spread of tuberculosis to health care workers in a clinic administering pentamidine to HIV-infected persons (CDC 1988). The potential spread of secondary infections by HIV carriers may be increased by the difficulty of controlling infections in immunosuppressed persons.

DISEASE CONTROL FOR HIV

The failure to institute traditional disease control measures for HIV infection indicates the disorganization of the American public health system. Even public health professionals became caught up in the rhetoric that since HIV is untreatable, there is no justification for using proved disease control techniques to control its spread. The rationale was that since carriers could not be cured and their contacts could not be immunized, there was no reason to report infected persons and to trace the contacts of these persons. This rationale ignores the success in controlling tuberculosis before it was treatable and the current efforts to control incurable viral illnesses.

Control of HIV has been unique in providing a common political ground for radical homosexual activists and the religious right. Homosexual activists fought efforts to control the spread of HIV because they did not want restrictions on their sexuality. The religious right fought disease control efforts because they saw AIDS as an expression of God's wrath about homosexual practices. The result was to paralyze the public health establishment for the critical first years of the epidemic. The same paralysis now extends to the conflict between draconian laws against illicit drug use and public health measures to limit the spread of bloodborne pathogens among intravenous drug users.

Patient Education

The surgeon general's report on AIDS in 1986 emphasized the need for public education to control the spread of HIV infection in the United States. The full report, in a readable pamphlet form, is available from the CDC and many state and local health departments. One of the most controversial aspects of this report was the recommendation that frank sex education be provided to children who are not yet sexually active.

Patient education is an obvious adjunct to public education. Physicians who care for adolescent children must be knowledgeable about the risk of HIV and the safer sex practices that can limit its spread. Those who care for patients who are sexually active or are exposed to blood or tissue products must include information about the spread and prevention of HIV infection in routine patient counseling.

The duty to warn third parties is discussed in Chapter 21. There is also a duty to counsel the patient as to the prevention of harm to others. This duty has allowed persons injured by a patient whose driving was impaired by medication to sue the prescribing physician. If these third parties are able to prove that the physician did not warn the patient of the dangers of driving while on the medication, they may recover from the physician. It is clear that persons subsequently infected by an HIV carrier can recover if the treating physician did not properly instruct the patient in how to prevent the spread of the disease. There has been at least one large settlement by a physician who did not counsel a woman exposed to HIV by a blood transfusion to practice safer sex with her husband.

Physicians have a special responsibility to counsel women who seek medical advice on contraception. When physicians prescribe contraceptives, they imply that the prescribed contraceptive is safe to use. They may be held liable if the woman is injured by an undisclosed risk of the contraceptive. Thus, a woman who is prescribed oral contraceptives is given detailed information about the risks of smoking and vascular problems. The same woman should be warned about the risk of contracting HIV if she relies on oral contraceptives rather than condoms for contraception. As HIV spreads to the heterosexual population, forms of contraception that do not involve barriers and spermicides are increasingly inappropriate for women who are not in long-term, monogamous relationships. (See Chapter 25.)

Traditional Disease Control
There has been little support for using traditional disease control measures for HIV infection. (See Chapter 21.) States that use these measures find Congress limiting their actions through refusal to fund disease control commensurate with treatment and research and shifting funds away from states with lower numbers of HIV cases, which might have a better ability to control the future spread of the disease. There are three main arguments against disease control measures.

The first is the apocalyptic view: so many people are infected that nothing will help. While the current estimate of 1 million infected persons is probably low, even doubling the estimate would still be only 1 infected person in 125. This seems to leave considerable room for the prevention of future spread.

The Peak Argument
The second argument is that the epidemic is already under control. This is based on the declining rate of reports of new AIDS cases.

Models that predict that the transmission of HIV has peaked are premised on the assumption that AIDS cases are an effective index of HIV transmission. (They also assume that most AIDS cases are reported, which is not supported by death certificate studies.) The long latency of infection and the dramatically different dynamics of spread in most heterosexual groups lead to an underestimate of the latency of spread into the general community. Models based on back calculation of infection rates from AIDS case reports are sensitive to the rate of spread in the community being modeled and the latency of the disease. If the latency is longer than the model assumes, the model underestimates the infection rate—and the lower infection rate lowers the predicted equilibrium rate of infection, the point at which new cases equal deaths or cures. If the disease spreads fast enough and kills quick enough, it can go to extinction: it consumes the susceptible population.

Overestimating the rate of transmission also lowers the predicted equilibrium rate of infection. This happens because the time to reach equilibrium is dependent on the size of the population modeled, the percentage of infected persons at the point when the prediction is made, and the rate of transmission. Other things held constant, the faster the rate of infection is, the faster the system reaches equilibrium. Thus, at a given time after the introduction of the disease into the community, the faster the rate of transmission is, the closer the disease is to equilibrium. This is mathematically the same problem as chemical reactions: the faster the reaction is, the sooner the reaction is at equilibrium.

The high rate of sexual activity among gay men frequenting bathhouses resulted in a high rate of transmission, and the disease rapidly reached equilibrium in the community. Conversely, the slower rate of transmission of HIV in the heterosexual community means that current levels of AIDS cases are further from the equilibrium levels. If the models of heterosexual transmission overestimate the rate of transmission, they will underestimate the time to reach equilibrium. This leads to the conclusion that current levels of infection are closer to equilibrium levels than would be the case if a lower transmission rate was used.

The confounding factor in heterosexual transmission is that the heterosexual population is multimodal: there are several subgroups of heterosexuals with substantially different transmission rates, with approximately 10 percent of persons having a much higher rate of transmission than the remaining population. This has been well established in models of other sexually transmitted diseases (Hethcote and Yorke 1984). It is reasonable to assume that current AIDS cases in heterosexuals disproportionately represent transmission in the 10 percent with high rates of sexual activity. If this is the case, the rate for the remaining 90 percent of the heterosexual community is much lower than has been assumed in the models of HIV transmission.

This lower rate of transmission of HIV in heterosexuals means that the predicted equilibrium rates will be much higher and will take much longer to achieve. If this analysis is correct, the rate of new AIDS cases in heterosexuals should slowly increase until at least the year 2000. Ultimately, however, this low rate of transmission will limit the equilibrium level in heterosexuals because of the low infectivity of HIV. Outside the highly sexually active subgroup, the average number of lifetime contacts with an infected person will be low enough to limit the transmission of HIV among heterosexuals to much lower levels than the 50 percent or greater that were seen in highly sexual active gay men.

The Community Education Argument

The third argument against intrusive disease control measures is that they are unneeded because community education programs can control spread of HIV infection. This is supported by reference to the reduced number of new AIDS cases in the San Francisco gay community. This low rate of new AIDS cases, however, represents saturation. Saturation occurs with HIV when the probability of a sexual contact between an infected and an uninfected person drops below the probability of transmitting the disease through a given contact. Most of the highly sexually active individuals were infected in the late 1970s and very early 1980s. This accounted for perhaps 50 percent of the gay men in San Francisco.

Saturation in this subgroup does not mean that the disease is under control. Sexual contact networks are relatively stable, with relatively little intermixing of the various social subgroups. If the subgroup contains few or no HIV-infected persons, there will be slow or no transmission of HIV in the group. The great majority of the most sexually active gay men have already died of the disease. While most of the remainder have reduced their unsafe sexual activity, many were never highly promiscuous.

The gay man with 1000 sexual contacts a year is an unfortunate stereotype that does not, and never did, describe most gay men. Sexual activity in the gay community has a multimodal that parallels the heterosexual community. This has the same implications for gay men as it does for the heterosexual community: the high rate of HIV transmission and the rapid saturation of the the most sexually active subgroup mask the lower but inexorable rise of HIV infection in the much less sexually active majority of gay men.

A greater threat to controlling the transmission of HIV is the influx of young gay men into San Francisco who are engaging in high-risk sexual activity at much higher rates than the existing community. It appears that it is not community education that reduces the incidence of unsafe sexual activity but the personal experience of witnessing the sickness and death of one's friends. While this personal experience may profoundly affect the behavior of older gay men in urban centers, it is largely irrelevant to younger gay men, intravenous drug users, and women.

Perhaps the most important factor that limits the usefulness of the experience of older, urban gay men is the special demographics of that community—a relatively affluent, well-educated group without dependent children. They bear little resemblance to the poor, minority, young, and increasingly female populations accounting for many new cases of HIV infection. These women are less able to protect themselves by safer sexual practices because these depend on the cooperation of their male partners. They are at the mercy of their partners both to take precautions and to inform them of their HIV status. These women can benefit from disease reporting and contact tracing to warn them when they and their children are at risk of HIV infection.

Testing

The first effective test for HIV infection was the ELISA test that was developed to test blood in blood banks. This test has been widely used to test high-risk individuals for infection. At the time the test was first marketed, it was thought that alternative test sites were needed to keep people from using blood banks as a way to find out if they were infected. These alternative sites were to be for people who wanted to find out their antibody status easily and confidentially. The only way they were expected to affect the control of the epidemic was to keep high-risk people out of the blood banks. These test sites quickly came to be viewed as an alternative to the traditional disease control program of testing, reporting, and contact tracing. This deprived patients of the safeguards found in properly run public health programs. One the most prevalent problems was the improper use of the ELISA test.

Following up on a positive ELISA is an important problem, both medically and legally. Patients who are incorrectly identified as HIV positive based on an unconfirmed ELISA are needlessly subjected to extreme anxiety. The ELISA is a screening test, not a diagnostic test. It is very sensitive but not very specific. The

ELISA, as with all other screening tests, is designed to have very few false-negative results, at the cost of many false-positive results. Every positive ELISA test should be followed by a more specific test, such as the Western blot. The problem has been that the Western blot is expensive and takes more time than the ELISA. In testing programs with limited resources, there has been a tendency to rely on the ELISA test alone if the individual being tested is at high risk. This should never be done. Many factors can cause false-positive ELISA tests. Positive ELISA results should not be reported until they have been confirmed by Western blot or other highly specific tests, such as the pneumocystis carinii pneumonia reaction.

Reporting
The greatest failing in the management of the HIV epidemic has been limiting case reporting to CDC-defined cases of AIDS. When a test for HIV infection became available, the CDC should have demanded that local and state public health departments require the fully identified reporting of every HIV carrier. Irrespective of whether this information was used for contact tracing or other disease control interventions, it is fundamental to any epidemiologic investigation of the epidemic. While a few jurisdictions required the reporting of HIV infection shortly after the ELISA and Western blot tests became available, only recently has reporting become the norm. Unfortunately, even states that require reporting have been forced to provide for anonymous testing. California and New York, the states with the largest number of HIV carriers, continue to refuse to require or accept reports of HIV infection.

Gay advocates and civil libertarians opposed the reporting of HIV because of their fear that the lists of infected persons would be used for intimidation and harassment. This was an especially strong fear in jurisdictions where homosexual sexual practices were illegal. The irony is that lists of gay men already existed in health departments nationwide in the reports of infection with early syphilis or hepatitis B, both reported by name, means of infection, and potential contacts. The most prominent of these diseases was syphilis. Infectious syphilis was predominantly a homosexual disease during the 1970s and the early 1980s. Most of the first victims of AIDS were already on health departments' lists of persons infected with syphilis. When the lists of persons who had been infected with syphilis were combined with the lists of persons who had been infected with hepatitis B, the result was a fairly complete roster of gay men who engaged in high-risk sexual behavior. Had law enforcement personnel wanted to use health department information to persecute homosexuals, they would not have needed HIV lists to identify their targets.

Because of the failure to require the reporting of HIV carriers, it is impossible to know how many persons are already infected with HIV or to evaluate the dynamics of spread into new risk groups. The emphasis on reporting AIDS cases ensures that all the information about the spread of HIV is out of date by the average delay between initial infection and diagnosis of AIDS. By the time the first AIDS cases appear in a new risk group, many individuals at risk in the group will already be infected with HIV. This was the situation with homosexual men, then IV drug users, and now inner-city adolescents. This lack of current information also masks the transformation of HIV into a heterosexual venereal disease.

Contact Tracing

Contact tracing has not been widely used in the control of the HIV epidemic. Many public health professionals believe that a disease that has no treatment cannot be controlled by contact tracing. Civil libertarians and gay rights advocates fought reporting and contact tracing out of fear of social and economic reprisals against members of their groups. Diseases such as whooping cough and typhoid are controlled through contact tracing and patient counseling because they have no curative treatment. Concerns about discrimination should be addressed through antidiscrimination legislation, not through changes in disease control programs. Several states have used reporting and contact tracing since 1985, with good results and none of the problems that were predicted (Potterat et al. 1989).

Contact tracing for HIV has three objectives. The first is to explore the epidemiology of the disease. The statistics used in epidemiology may be a mathematical problem, but all analysis must begin with "shoe leather" epidemiology to collect data. Because the states with the majority of HIV carriers have not conducted contact tracing, HIV epidemiology is based on the theoretical projections drawn from nonrandom subpopulations rather than actual case counts.

The second objective of contact tracing is highly personalized education. As with other forms of public health education, general exhortations have little effect on individual behavior. Individuals become motivated to change their behavior when the threat becomes personalized. When contacts of an HIV carrier are notified that they have been exposed to the virus, they can no longer indulge in the self-denial that HIV is not their problem. Because the risk of HIV to heterosexuals has been downplayed, contact tracing often alerts unsuspecting persons to their exposure to HIV. This warning is valuable for HIV control because HIV is difficult to transmit. Many persons at risk will be warned before they have been infected.

The third objective is the converse of warning the unknowing contact: detecting irresponsible individuals who continue to engage in high-risk behavior. Public health officials have the authority under the U.S. Constitution to restrict the liberty of persons who pose a threat to the public health. This power has been used only sparingly for HIV control. As the epidemic spreads, however, there will be situations when it is necessary to restrict certain persons, such as prostitutes, who are repeatedly identified as contacts.

There has been a concerted effort to replace the term *contact tracing* with the more positive term *partner notification*. Partner notification is appropriate terminology for stable relationships. It does not fit so well when applied to a brief, anonymous encounter with a prostitute or to the denizens of a crack house. *Partner notification* and *contact tracing* are used interchangeably in HIV control.

The failure to require the reporting of HIV and conduct contact tracing saddles physicians with the burden of deciding whether to warn third parties whom their patients put at risk. This duty to warn is usually transferred to the health department when the physician reports a communicable disease. If the health department finds that third parties are at risk, health department personnel warn them. Physicians in states that accept and investigate reports of HIV infection discharge their duty to warn when they report the case to the health department.

Physicians in states that do not accept and investigate reports for HIV must either violate their patients' confidence or violate their duty to the public at large. The worst situation may be states that allow physicians to warn third parties but do not provide expert assistance. The physician may be sued for failing to warn, for warning the wrong person, or for defamation if the patient is not infected with HIV. (See Chapter 21.) In contrast, a properly written reporting statute can have the state assume the physician's duty to warn when the patient is reported to the health department and provide immunity from failure to warn lawsuits if the physician reports the case (Richards 1989).

Screening versus Anonymous Testing
Screening high-risk groups is a useful tool in disease control if it is combined with treatment and contact tracing. Such screening will help identify truly high-risk groups and provide information about the patterns of spread of the disease. Anonymous testing of volunteers does not accomplish these goals; it does not give prevalence or incidence data because there is no way to know the numerator or the denominator. If there are 100 tests done and 10 are positive, one does not know if 100 people were tested and 10 of them were positive or if 10 people were tested 10 times and only 1 of them was positive.

Calculating the costs of screening for HIV infection must include the value of information about the spread of a new disease. With an established disease such as syphilis, which is at equilibrium in the population, the probability of finding the disease in a given population is known. This allows a meaningful calculation of the cost-benefit ratio for case finding. The prevalence of HIV is unknown in almost all populations. While the cost of finding a case in a given population may be high, this may be offset by the value of knowing the prevalence in that population.

The problem of the delay between initial infection and the presence of detectable antibodies has been greatly overstated. The development of antibodies appears to be an exponential process. Most persons develop detectable antibodies within six months, but a small number will go for years without testing positive on antibody-based tests (Imagawa et al. 1989). This is termed the *window period*. Screening a given population will not ensure that all HIV carriers are detected, but it will detect much in excess of 90 percent of carriers. Shifting to direct tests for viral components such as the polymerase chain reaction will allow detection within a short period of infection (Eisenstein 1990). This will narrow the window period to the point where screening will identify over 99 percent of infected persons (Daar et al. 1991).

Restrictions and Quarantine
Quarantine is not usually appropriate for the control of HIV because HIV cannot be contracted through casual contact. Counseling the HIV-infected patient and anyone who may have had sexual or blood contact with the patient is more effective and less restrictive than quarantine. Specific restrictive measures are the accepted alternative to general quarantine. It is more difficult to defend partial restrictions than quarantine, however. In a common example, the health department may order an HIV-infected prostitute to stay off the street. This will not prevent her from working; it will reduce her contacts and encourage her to find other work. Such a limited restriction will be attacked in court as unreasonable because it does not eliminate all risk. Since it is not perfect, it is not worth inconveniencing the prostitute. The same court might be more willing to allow the quarantine, but few health departments have the resources to quarantine.

The issue of quarantine is complicated by cross-over with the criminal justice system. Prostitution and IV drug abuse are illegal in every state, and homosexual sexual activity is illegal in about 50 percent of the states. Many others criminalize reckless endangering of another person, the usual criminal charge for exposing a person to a communicable disease. There is increasing pressure to prosecute HIV carriers who endanger others. Many cases of HIV carriers who continue to engage in reckless behavior involve persons with some degree of HIV dementia. Given the poor medical conditions in most jails and prisons, it may be more humane to encourage civil commitment under the public health laws than to introduce these persons into the criminal justice system.

MEDICAL DUTIES

The medical duties to an HIV-infected patient are the same as to any other patient infected with a communicable disease. Physicians treating HIV-infected persons also have a duty to the community to cooperate in efforts to prevent the spread of the disease. When a physician enters a physician-patient relationship, he or she accepts the responsibility to care for that patient until the relationship is appropriately terminated. (See Chapter 9.) The physician's wishes or convenience are not a justification for abandoning a patient, and his or her fear of contagion is not an excuse for abandonment. HIV-infected persons are entitled to the same notice and continued care as any other patient.

The more difficult question is whether HIV-infected persons are entitled to special protections not available to other patients. Should it be unethical to refuse to treat a person with AIDS, yet acceptable to refuse to treat patients with other diseases? Should it be considered unethical for a family practitioner to refuse to treat insulin-dependent diabetics because it is too complicated? Physicians are discouraged from requiring patients to be tested for HIV, yet it is just as diagnostically important as a Pap smear or fasting blood sugar. Most incongruous, in our opinion, is that it is considered more ethical to worry about being paid than about being infected with a communicable disease. While access to care for HIV-infected persons is a real problem, it pales when compared to the problem of access to care for the poor. Often it becomes the same problem: the various medical associations that have deemed it unethical to refuse to treat HIV-infected persons limit this prohibition to HIV-infected persons who can pay for their care.

Legal Discrimination

Preventing discrimination has shaped the medical and public health response to AIDS and HIV. This task is complicated by the double nature of the discrimination. While many AIDS patients were discriminated against because of their disease, most of the discrimination against homosexuals was because of a traditional condemnation of homosexuality rather than a new-found fear of AIDS. This discrimination against homosexuals is deplorable, but it is legal, except in certain jurisdictions that have enacted specific legislation prohibiting discrimination based on gender preference. As Chief Justice Warren Burger wrote in a case upholding the authority of Georgia to outlaw homosexual sodomy:

> Decisions of individuals relating to homosexual conduct have been subject to state intervention throughout the history of Western Civilization. Condemnation of those practices is firmly rooted in Judeo-Christian moral and ethical standards. . . .

The common law of England, including its prohibition of sodomy, became the received law of Georgia and the other Colonies. In 1816 the Georgia Legislature passed the statute at issue here, and that statute has been continuously in force in one form or another since that time. To hold that the act of homosexual sodomy is somehow protected as a fundamental right would be to cast aside millennia of moral teaching. This is essentially not a question of personal "preferences" but rather of the legislative authority of the State. I find nothing in the Constitution depriving a State of the power to enact the statute challenged here. (*Bowers v. Hardwick, 1986*).

Because the Supreme Court found it legal to discriminate against homosexuals, gay rights advocates were left with a dilemma: they did not want to advocate going back into the closet, but a positive HIV test might also be seen as a positive test for homosexuality. For many, the way out of the dilemma was to attribute all discrimination to fear of HIV and discount the traditional bias against homosexuals. This led to the belief that the only way to prevent discrimination was to keep HIV infection hidden from employers and others. The campaign to hide HIV resulted in political pressure to make it difficult for physicians to test for HIV and to prevent physicians from disclosing a patient's HIV status.

This campaign was premised on the assumption that physicians, and especially public health departments, were derelict in their duty to protect patient records. In 1987 the Association of State and Territorial Health Officers convened a panel to report on the problem of confidentiality of medical records of HIV status. This panel polled health departments, civil rights commissions, and homosexual advocacy groups around the United States in an attempt to document as many incidents of discrimination secondary to breaches of confidentiality as possible. Few incidents could actually be documented. Of these, most were due to breaches of confidentiality by private physicians. There were no instances of breaches of confidentiality by health departments. Most commonly, the patient divulged the information to friends or coworkers (ASTHO 1988).

Another rationale for concealing a patient's HIV status was that insurance companies would not insure an HIV-infected person. Insurance companies treat HIV carriers just as they do other persons with a chronic, expensive medical condition. Certainly it is poor public policy to exclude sick people from insurance, but there is no justification for creating special rules to protect HIV carriers while ignoring persons with asthma, multiple sclerosis, and the myriad of other conditions that render a person uninsurable. This attempt to get special consideration for insurance was couched in terms of confidentiality. The physician would protect the patient's confidence by not testing the patient for HIV and by not entering information about HIV status in the patient's medical records. The result would be to deny insurers information that they could use to evaluate the risk of insuring the patient.

Consent to HIV Testing

There is no medical risk to HIV testing. The law of informed consent deals with informing patients of the medical risks of medical tests and treatments. (See Chapter 11.) There is no legal duty to inform a patient of the political risk of a medical test or procedure. Despite this clear legal precedent, physicians and hospitals have been convinced that consent for HIV testing requires a recitation of political risks, such as job and housing discrimination. Unfortunately, during the recitation of political risks, the medical risks of not being tested are usually overlooked.

Many consent forms for HIV testing do not discuss the medical benefits of diagnosing HIV early in the course of the disease. Even before it was recognized that certain drugs can slow the progress of the disease, it was useful to know that the patient's immune system was potentially depressed. Infections can be managed more aggressively, and the patient can be counseled to avoid certain immunizations and sources of dangerous infections. If patients are given a consent form that does not recite the medical benefits of testing, they may make an uninformed refusal of care. If such a patient is then injured by refusal to be tested, he or she may sue for failure of informed consent in the same way that a patient who refused a Pap smear may sue if she was not properly informed of the risks of cervical cancer. The detailed consent form listing political risks but not medical risks will be the patient's best evidence of the failure of informed consent.

The controversy over HIV testing has obscured the physician's basic duty to provide proper medical care for patients. Early diagnosis of HIV infection benefits the patient's medical care and improves society's knowledge of the spread of the disease. A patient who refuses an HIV test is no different from a patient with chest pain who refuses an EKG or one with potential diabetic neuropathy who refuses a blood sugar test. Most patients consent to testing if properly informed of the medical benefits; the patients who refuse create a legal problem for physicians. A physician's ethical duty to treat a patient does not include the duty to practice substandard medicine at the patient's request. The physician must carefully document the patient's refusal of testing and establish that the patient was fully informed of the medical indications for the test. If the physician believes that the patient's HIV status is necessary medical information, the physician may ethically demand that the patient either agree to the test or find another physician. (See Chapter 9.)

BIBLIOGRAPHY

ASTHO (Association of State and Territorial Health Officers' report); *Guide to Public Heath Practice: Principles to Protect HIV-Related Confidentiality and Prevent Discrimination.* 1988.

Bowers v. Hardwick. 478 US 186 (1986).

Brookmeyer R: Reconstruction and future trends of the AIDS epidemic in the United States. Science 1991; 235:37–42.

Carrell S; Zoler ML: Defiant diseases: Hard-won gains erode. Med World News 1990; 31(12):20.

CDC: Mycobacterium tuberculosis transmission in a health clinic—Florida 1988. MMWR 1989; 38:256–58, 263–64.

CDC: Revision of the case definition of acquired immunodeficiency syndrome for national reporting—United States. MMWR 1985; 34:373–75.

CDC: Revision of the CDC surveillance case definition for acquired immunodeficiency syndrome. MMWR 1987; 36(suppl 1S).

Chu SY; Buehler JW; Berkelman RL: Impact of the human immunodeficiency virus epidemic on mortality in women of reproductive age, United States. JAMA 1990; 264: 225–29.

Colgate SA; Stanley EA; Hyman JM; Layne SP; Qualls C: Risk behavior-based model of the cubic growth of acquired immunodeficiency syndrome in the United States. Proc Natl Acad Sci USA 1989 Jun; 86(12):4793–97.

Curran JW; Jaffe HW; Hardy AM; Morgan WM; Selik RM; Dondero TJ: Epidemiology of HIV infection and AIDS in the United States. Science 1988 Feb 5; 239(4840):610–16.

Daar ES; Moudgil T; Meyer RD; Ho DD: Transient high levels of viremia in patients with primary human immunodeficiency virus type 1 infection. N Engl J Med 1991; 324(14):961.

Des Jarlais DC; Friedman SR; Stoneburner RL: HIV infection and intravenous drug use: Critical issues in transmission dynamics, infection outcomes, and prevention. Rev Infect Dis 1988 Jan–Feb; 10(1):151–58.

Eisenstein BI: The polymerase chain reaction: A new method of using molecular genetics for medical diagnosis. N Engl J Med 1990; 322(3):178.

Fox DM: AIDS and the American health polity: The history and prospects of a crisis of authority. Milbank Q 1986; 64 Suppl 1:7–33.

Fulghum JS: Letter. JAMA 1990; 264:3147–48.

Guidelines for prevention of transmission of human immunodeficiency virus and hepatitis B virus to health-care and public-safety workers. MMWR 1989 Jun 23; 38 Suppl 6:1–37.

Hethcote HW; Yorke JA: *Gonorrhea Transmission Dynamics and Control.* 1984.

Horwath E; Kramer M; Cournos F; Empfield M; Gewirtz G: Clinical presentations of AIDS and HIV infection in state psychiatric facilities. Hosp Comm Psychiatry 1989 May; 40(5):502–6.

Imagawa DT et al.: Human immunodeficiency virus type 1 infection in homosexual men who remain seronegative for prolonged periods. N Engl J Med 1989; 320(22):1458.

Janssen RS; Cornblath DR; Epstein LG; McArthur J; Price RW: Human immunodeficiency virus (HIV) infection and the nervous system: Report from the American Academy of Neurology AIDS Task Force. Neurology 1989 Jan; 39(1):119–22.

Kaposi's sarcoma and Pneumocystis pneumonia among homosexual men—New York City and California. MMWR 1981 Jul 3; 30(25):305–8.

Kelen GD; DiGiovanna T; Bisson L; Kalainov D; Sivertson KT; Quinn TC: Human immunodeficiency virus infection in emergency department patients. Epidemiology, clinical presentations, and risk to health care workers: The Johns Hopkins experience. JAMA 1989 Jul 28; 262(4):516–22.

Kuller LH: A policy to control the spread of HIV infection. Yale J Biol Med 1988 May–Jun; 61 (3):269–76.

Leads from MMWR, current trends; update: acquired immunodeficiency syndrome (AIDS)—United States. JAMA 1983; 250:1016.

Lunn S; Skydsbjerg M; Schulsinger H; Parnas J; Pedersen C; Mathiesen L: A preliminary report on the neuropsychologic sequelae of human immunodeficiency virus. Arch Gen Psychiatry 1991; 48:139–42.

Maki DG: AIDS: Serologic testing for the human immunodeficiency virus—to screen or not to screen. Infect Control Hosp Epidemiol 1989 Jun; 10(6):243–47.

Potterat JJ; Spencer NE; Woodhouse DE; Muth JB: Partner notification in the control of human immunodeficiency virus infection. Am J Public Health 1989; 79(7):874.

Richards EP: Colorado public health laws: A rational approach to AIDS. Dev U L R 1989; 65:127.

Shilts R: *And the Band Played On.* 1987.

Stern Y et al.: Multidisciplinary baseline assessment of homosexual men with and without human immunodeficiency virus infection; III. Neurologic and neuropsychological findings. Arch Gen Psychiatry 1991; 48:131–38.

Wilkie FL; Eisdorfer C; Morgan R; Loewenstein DA; Jose Szapocznik J: Cognition in early human immunodeficiency virus infection. Arch Neurol 1990; 47:433–40.

23

Communicable Diseases in the Workplace

CRITICAL POINTS
- Communicable diseases are an increasing problem in the workplace.
- Employers are legally liable for workers and others infected in the workplace.
- Chronic diseases carriers are protected by the Americans with Disabilities Act.
- Immunosuppressed workers pose special problems, with no simple legal solutions.

AIDS is changing public perceptions about communicable diseases. Although AIDS is not communicable in most workplaces, it is alerting lawyers to the compensability of workplace-acquired infections. Concern with discrimination against the disabled and HIV-infected persons led Congress to pass the Americans with Disabilities Act (ADA) in 1990. As discussed in Chapter 30, the ADA reduces employers' right to ask about a potential employee's health. It also limits the right of employers to refuse to hire persons who are at increased risk of injury in the workplace or who may pose a risk to others.

These limitations come as the courts and legislatures are expanding employers' duty to protect workers and the public. With diseases such as tuberculosis on the rise, employers need comprehensive plans to manage communicable diseases in the workplace. With the ADA's stress on the individual evaluation of employees, physicians must play the central role in these communicable disease plans. This requires assessing the risk posed by individual infected employees and developing legally sound protocols for balancing the risk of contagion against the employee's right to continued employment. The ADA and its administrative regulations provide little guidance because they are silent on all communicable diseases except for those that are foodborne. This chapter presents a general approach to communicable diseases in the workplace. Medical care workplaces have been treated as a special case of the general communicable disease plan.

THE INCREASE OF COMMUNICABLE DISEASES IN THE WORKPLACE

The morbidity and mortality from communicable diseases is increasing in the United States. While much of this is secondary to the HIV epidemic, traditional threats such as tuberculosis and measles are also increasing. HIV also has overshadowed new epidemic diseases, such as Lyme disease. Paradoxically, the legal risks of communicable diseases are increasing because the diseases themselves are still relatively rare. If an epidemic afflicts most of the population, it is difficult to link an individual case to a workplace exposure. However, if outbreaks of the disease are infrequent, it will be obvious when an employee's exposure occurred at work.

Immunizations and Antibiotic Misuse

The root cause of the increase of immunizable diseases in the United States is public compliancy. After one or more generations of a successful immunization program, the targeted disease becomes rare and no longer frightening. Once the public is no longer concerned about a disease, the financial and political support for disease control measures such as mass immunizations disappears. This creates cohorts of susceptible adults who were neither immunized nor exposed as children, a dangerous situation for employers because many childhood diseases are much more serious in adults. For example, before mumps immunizations, epidemics of mumps would pass through a community regularly, and most of the susceptible population would become immune through having the disease. Complications in these susceptible children were rare, and most children had the disease before reaching puberty. Now, through vaccine failure, lack of exposure to disease or vaccine, and waning immunity, workplace epidemics of mumps can occur. These adult epidemics are dangerous because adults are prone to severe sequelae, with attendant high workers' compensation costs.

Controlling communicable diseases is complicated by the rise of drug resistance secondary to the misuse of antibiotics. Overprescription by physicians, sharing prescriptions by patients, the use of massive amounts of antibiotics in animal husbandry, and the absence of international controls on antibiotics leads to the evolution of antibiotic-resistant strains of common diseases. Tuberculosis is the best example of the problem. There are only a few effective antitubercular drugs. These are all prescription drugs in the United States, but some are available in over-the-counter cough syrup in Mexico. The tuberculosis bacillus is hard to kill and prone to develop drug resistance. The repeated exposure of tuberculosis carriers to ineffective doses of antitubercular drugs dramatically increases the incidence of drug-resistant tuberculosis.

Immunosuppression

The wide use of immunosuppressive drugs and HIV infection has resulted in a large number of workers with suppressed immune systems who are more susceptible to infectious diseases in the workplace. They also may spread diseases such as tuberculosis to others. (See Chapter 21.) Until recently, significant immunosuppression was not a workplace issue because it occurred only secondary to severe illness. Because otherwise healthy immunosuppressed workers are a new phenomenon in the workplace, their legal status is not well defined.

Immunosuppressed individuals are disabled under the federal law and are entitled to work if they meet the other requirements of the law. If a secondary infection such as active tuberculosis threatens other workers or third parties, the infected person may be removed from the workplace. The difficult question is whether immunosuppressed persons may be denied employment to protect them from workplace-acquired infections. It is argued that the worker has the right to accept the risk of infection. Worker's compensation laws, however, do not allow the worker to accept the financial risk of workplace injury. The employer must pay for the costs of treatment or disability if the immunosuppressed worker becomes infected in the workplace, irrespective of the employee's assumption of the risk of infection.

THE LEGAL RISKS OF COMMUNICABLE DISEASES

Communicable diseases in the workplace pose three classes of risk: (1) worker's compensation liability, (2) third-party liability, and (3) productivity losses. All three are potentially very expensive yet have been accorded scant attention from employers or employees. The HIV epidemic has sensitized employees and employers to the problems of workplace-acquired infections. As declining health insurance coverage forces more persons to seek compensation through the courts for illness, worker's compensation claims for workplace-acquired infections will increase.

Worker's compensation laws are not limited to accidents or occupational illnesses; they cover all illnesses and injuries acquired in the workplace, including communicable diseases and intentional injuries such as rape in the workplace. The employee is entitled the cost of medical care, disability, and lost time for work. In return, the law prevents the employee from suing the employer for the more extensive damages available in tort litigation. This exemption is important because some usually mild diseases can cause serious injuries in adults. Mumps can cause sterility, measles sometimes kills, chicken pox can cause brain injury, and tuberculosis can require long-term treatment. Drug-resistant tuberculosis, on the increase in the United States, cannot be effectively treated; it requires prolonged hospitalization and eventually kills many of its victims.

Earlier in this century, it was common for employees to claim compensation for communicable diseases such as typhoid caught from the company water supply. As the public awareness of communicable diseases diminished, claims for workplace-acquired infections decreased. Even health care workers, who have a high rate of morbidity from workplace infections, have tended to rely on group health coverage for workplace-acquired infections rather than worker's compensation. Progressive reductions in group health coverage and reduced job security are causing workers to seek worker's compensation for illnesses that in the past would not have resulted in compensation claims. This will require physicians to be more sensitive to the epidemiology of workplace-acquired infections.

Third-Party Liability

Employers are liable to nonemployees, called third parties, who are injured by negligent employees. These third parties can sue the employer for all the damages allowed in tort litigation. While the worker's compensation costs of a communicable disease cannot be ignored, they pale before the costs of third-party liability. Hiring a truck driver with severe heart disease or an alcoholic physician would be negligent, making the company liable to anyone the employee injured. Allowing an employee with infectious tuberculosis to work in a day care center or a demented HIV carrier to be an airplane pilot also would be negligent.

The most likely third-party victims of workplace-acquired infections are the family members or the unborn children of the worker. When a worker infects a family member with a workplace-acquired infection, the family member may sue the employer. The most serious risks to third parties are those to unborn children. A pregnant worker cannot be excluded from the workplace to protect her fetus. (See Chapter 30.) Under current law, if that fetus is injured by a workplace exposure, perhaps to rubella, the employer could be liable for the resulting injuries.

The risk of third-party infections is greatest for foodborne illnesses and highly contagious diseases such as measles that are spread by contact or respiratory transmission. Less infectious respiratory illnesses such as tuberculosis require close or prolonged contact with the infected person. These pose the greatest threat in service industries such as day care centers, where there is close contact between the employees and the customers. Bloodborne illnesses such as hepatitis B virus (HBV) and HIV pose a threat to customers only when there is a chance of exposure to contaminated blood. This is usually thought to be limited to medical care but can happen in any activity where a customer's skin is pierced. Tattooing, for example, has been implicated in HBV transmission and could transmit HIV.

Immunosuppressed family members or other third parties pose difficult legal problems. There is no simple legal rule for determining when a company should be liable for a workplace-related infection to an immunosuppressed worker or third party. Traditional tort law holds that negligent persons take their plaintiffs as they find them: if an employer negligently allows a chicken pox–infected employee to stay in the workplace, the employer would be liable if an immunosuppressed customer contracts chicken pox encephalitis from the employee. Conversely, the doctrine of foreseeability acts as a brake on unlimited liability: if a customer catches a cold from an employee, and then falls off a cliff while sneezing, the employer would not be liable for the fall. It will be difficult to reconcile jurors' tendency to hold employers liable for injuries to third parties with the ADA's strict limitations on the employer's right to exclude infected workers from the workplace.

Productivity

A workplace epidemic can bring the operations of the business to a halt. If the mail clerk comes to work with the flu and gives it to every secretary, three days later most of the secretarial force may call in sick. If the doughnut vendor gives everyone hepatitis A, the onset of the disease will not be simultaneous, but the disease will last long enough that at some point many workers will be absent. In years past, it was common to close the elementary school for an epidemic of a childhood disease. High-technology service industries that are dependent on skilled personnel are particularly vulnerable: "Between August 18 and December 25, 1987, 116 employees at the three futures exchanges in Chicago developed clinically diagnosed mumps. Three cases subsequently occurred in household contacts of affected exchange employees. Twenty-one persons developed complications; nine were hospitalized" (Mumps in the workplace, 1988). The direct medical costs were over $56,000, with the total work loss probably in excess of 700 days. The potential tort liability was significant: the mumps virus induced premature labor in a pregnant employee. Fortunately, the labor was arrested, preventing a premature birth with the attendant liability for possible brain injury to the infant. The report of this epidemic does not discuss whether any of the infected men were rendered sterile. This corporate epidemic was costly and completely preventable. Yet like most other employers, the futures exchange did not recognize communicable diseases as a workplace issue.

COMMUNICABLE DISEASES AS A HANDICAP OR DISABILITY

The ADA incorporates and expands existing protections provided in section 504 of the Rehabilitation Act. In cases decided under this predecessor act, the U.S. Supreme Court held that a person with a communicable disease (tuberculosis) was handicapped under the definitions of the law (*School Board of Nassua County v. Arline*, 1987). This case involved a school teacher with a history of recurrent activation of her tuberculosis who was fired after becoming sputum positive. While acknowledging that Arline was covered under the provisions of the act, the Court was left with the question of whether she was otherwise qualified to be a school teacher: (See Chapter 30.)

> The remaining question is whether Arline is otherwise qualified for the job of elementary school teacher. To answer this question in most cases, the District Court will need to conduct an individualized inquiry and make appropriate findings of fact. Such an inquiry is essential if § 504 is to achieve its goal of protecting handicapped individuals from deprivations based on prejudice, stereotypes, or unfounded fear, while giving appropriate weight to such legitimate concerns of grantees as avoiding exposing others to significant health and safety risks. The basic factors to be considered in conducting this inquiry are well established. In the context of the employment of a person handicapped with a contagious disease, we agree with amicus American Medical Association that this inquiry should include:
> "[findings of] facts, based on reasonable medical judgments given the state of medical knowledge, about (a) the nature of the risk (how the disease is transmitted), (b) the duration of the risk (how long is the carrier infectious), (c) the severity of the risk (what is the potential harm to third parties) and (d) the probabilities the disease will be transmitted and will cause varying degrees of harm."
> In making these findings, courts normally should defer to the reasonable medical judgments of public health officials. The next step in the "otherwise-qualified" inquiry is for the court to evaluate, in light of these medical findings, whether the employer could reasonably accommodate the employee under the established standards for that inquiry. (pp. 1130–31)

The Supreme Court did not decide if Arline was otherwise qualified. The case was remanded to allow the trial court to obtain evidence on whether, after appropriate accommodations, Arline posed a threat of infection to the students. The evidence presented to the trial court established that Arline's tuberculosis was under control to the satisfaction of the public health authorities. Since she did not pose a threat of infection, she was reinstated and given back pay.

ADDITIONAL REQUIREMENTS OF THE ADA

The ADA and its administrative regulations (29 CFR 1630, July 16, 1991) introduced the concepts of direct threat and significant risk of substantial harm. These narrow the traditional right of an employer to exclude workers who might be injured or injure others. The following regulations must be combined with the requirements of *Arline* to determine the proper balance between employee rights and the duty to protect the employee and the public:

> Direct Threat means a significant risk of substantial harm to the health or safety of the individual or others that cannot be eliminated or reduced by reasonable accommodation. The determination that an individual poses a "direct threat" shall be

based on an individualized assessment of the individual's present ability to safely perform the essential functions of the job. This assessment shall be based on a reasonable medical judgment that relies on the most current medical knowledge and/or on the best available objective evidence. In determining whether an individual would pose a direct threat, the factors to be considered include:

(1) The duration of the risk;
(2) The nature and severity of the potential harm;
(3) The likelihood that the potential harm will occur; and
(4) The imminence of the potential harm.

Determining whether an individual poses a significant risk of substantial harm to others must be made on a case by case basis. The employer should identify the specific risk posed by the individual. For individuals with mental or emotional disabilities, the employer must identify the specific behavior on the part of the individual that would pose the direct threat. For individuals with physical disabilities, the employer must identify the aspect of the disability that would pose the direct threat. The employer should then consider the four factors listed in part 1630:

(1) The duration of the risk;
(2) The nature and severity of the potential harm;
(3) The likelihood that the potential harm will occur; and
(4) The imminence of the potential harm.

Such consideration must rely on objective, factual evidence—not on subjective perceptions, irrational fears, patronizing attitudes, or stereotypes—about the nature or effect of a particular disability, or of disability generally. Relevant evidence may include input from the individual with a disability, the experience of the individual with a disability in previous similar positions, and opinions of medical doctors, rehabilitation counselors, or physical therapists who have expertise in the disability involved and/or direct knowledge of the individual with the disability.

An employer is also permitted to require that an individual not pose a direct threat of harm to his or her own safety or health. If performing the particular functions of a job would result in a high probability of substantial harm to the individual, the employer could reject or discharge the individual unless a reasonable accommodation that would not cause an undue hardship would avert the harm. . . .

The assessment that there exists a high probability of substantial harm to the individual, like the assessment that there exists a high probability of substantial harm to others, must be strictly based on valid medical analyses and/or on other objective evidence. This determination must be based on individualized factual data, using the factors discussed above, rather than on stereotypic or patronizing assumptions and must consider potential reasonable accommodations. Generalized fears about risks from the employment environment, such as exacerbation of the disability caused by stress, cannot be used by an employer to disqualify an individual with a disability.

THE ELEMENTS OF A COMMUNICABLE DISEASE POLICY

Paradoxically, the more the law stresses individual evaluation, the more the employer must rely on carefully drafted written policies. Individualized evaluation makes it easier for the employee to contest the employer's standards. While the employer may ultimately prevail in court, careful adherence to written guidelines can discourage attorneys from difficult-to-win lawsuits. If this policy is to be credible, it must be developed before the business is embroiled in controversy over potentially discriminatory actions against disease carriers.

Following is a framework for a disease control plan based on the analysis suggested in the Supreme Court decision in *Arline*. A completed disease control plan must detail the actual circumstances of the company and diseases that pose a risk in that environment. The medical information should be based on CDC recommendations and the American Public Health Association publication, *Communicable Diseases in Man*. The workplace-specific parts of the plan are more difficult because there are few good models for disease control plans. Although large companies have a corporate policy on AIDS, these plans are usually equal employment guidelines with no reference to other diseases.

Nature of the Risk

Nature of the risk is the Supreme Court's term for the method of spreading the disease. Airborne transmission poses the greatest risk and sexual transmission the smallest risk in the workplace. When analyzing communicability, the most important question is whether the mode of transmission for the disease in question occurs in the workplace. Airborne transmission occurs in all situations, while sexual transmission is usually not a workplace risk. Foodborne illnesses are a problem for food handlers in the employee cafeteria but do not pose a threat to assembly line or sales personnel.

Methods of Transmission

Airborne
These are diseases that may be spread through the air from the infected person to a healthy person. This may be direct spread, as when a disease carrier coughs near another person, or indirect spread, when the disease organisms spread through the air ducts in a building. Indirect spread can infect workers several floors away from the disease carrier.

Fomites
A fomite is an inanimate object that is contaminated with disease-causing microorganisms. Fomites may be too small to see, or they may be large objects such as contaminated clothing or safety equipment. Although not as dangerous as airborne transmission, fomite transmission, including fetal-oral transmission, can be a problem in child care and nursing situations.

Foodborne
Foodborne illnesses are a risk only if the disease carrier prepares or serves the food. Typhoid is the classic foodborne illness. Casual contact with a typhoid carrier will not spread the disease. Typhoid is spread when the carrier prepares food on which the typhoid organisms can grow. The typhoid carrier infects the food, which infects the person who eats it. The proposed administrative regulations for the ADA define what the CDC considers illnesses that are commonly foodborne: hepatitis A virus, Norwalk and Norwalk-like viruses, *Salmonella typhi*, *Shigella* species, *Staphylococcus aureus*, and *Streptococcus pyogenes*. The CDC has also identified a group of diseases that can be but are not commonly foodborne: *Campylobacter jejuni*, *Entamoeba histolytica*, enterohemorrhagic *Escherichia coli*, enterotoxigenic *Escherichia coli*, *Giardia lamblia*, nontyphoidal *Salmonella*, rotavirus, *Vibrio cholerae 01*, and *Yersinia enterocolitica*.

These proposed rules will prove troubling if they are not modified. The first problem is that the list will make it difficult to exclude a person with an unusual disease that is not on the list. A greater problem is that the rules imply that foodborne illness can be prevented by enforcing hand washing and the wearing of clean gloves or by excluding persons when they have diarrheal diseases. It is true that meticulous attention to hand washing and sanitation can reduce or eliminate the risk of transmission of foodborne illnesses. It also is impossible to ensure that such high levels of sanitation are observed. Even studies of physicians, who are much more sensitive to the need for hand washing than most food handlers, demonstrate frequent lapses in hand washing, with the resultant transmission of disease. Infected food handlers can promise to wear gloves and wash their hands, thus rendering themselves otherwise qualified to work with food. The employer will not be able to exclude the infected employee until it is proved that the employee has failed to abide by the agreement to wash properly. If the breach is discovered through the infection of a customer, the employer will be liable for not preventing the spread of the disease.

Insect Vectors
Many diseases are spread by insects. These are generally not a problem for office workers but can be a significant risk to persons working with animals, raw animal products, or in the outdoors. Insect-borne diseases that may be workplace problems include rocky mountain spotted fever, Lyme disease, and sleeping sickness.

Sexually Transmitted Diseases
Outside of a few brothels in Nevada, sexually transmitted diseases are not usually thought of as workplace hazards. They may, however, create a risk in health care or laboratory settings where personnel can come in direct contact with infected specimens or body fluids. It should be noted, however, that there may be liability if an employer is on notice of sexual relations between employees and customers and does not prevent them. This can be a problem in sex-oriented businesses or resorts where personnel may supplement their income through prostitution.

Bloodborne
Few diseases are strictly bloodborne. Most, like hepatitis B and HIV, are also transmitted through intimate contact. Bloodborne diseases are a risk only in workplaces where workers can come into contact with blood or other bodily fluids—most common in medical care delivery and laboratory work. It is also a consideration for employees who provide first aid to other employees or customers. Employers should be careful of hidden blood exposures. Ear piercing in a department store can effectively spread HBV between customers if the instruments are reused without sterilization.

Direct Contact
Some diseases and parasites are spread by direct contact between individuals or their personal items such as clothing. These include scabies, lice, and ringworm. These can be a substantial problem where employees share living quarters or coat closets. Other than inconvenience, however, infestations seldom pose any serious health risk.

Duration of the Risk
Duration of the risk is the Court's term for the period the carrier remains infectious. This period may be self-limited for diseases such as measles, limited by antibiotic treatment for diseases such as drug-sensitive tuberculosis, or unlimited, such as for HIV and the carrier states of typhoid and HBV. Employees remain disabled under the law after the disease is no longer infectious because the law also includes persons who are perceived to be disabled.

Severity
The Court was rightly concerned with the severity of the disease. This would be judged as a function of the morbidity of the disease, the duration of the disease, and whether the disease has permanent sequelae. It is important to note when the characteristics of the organism and the patient can increase the severity of the disease. Diseases such as influenza are mildly incapacitating in healthy workers but could be dangerous to the residents of a nursing home. The legal significance of a conversion to a positive tuberculosis skin test is uncertain. Active tuberculosis requires a long period of treatment and monitoring; there are potentially serious complications to the treatment and some persons do not respond to treatment.

While HIV is very serious for all infected persons, the complications of many communicable diseases are equally serious in a smaller percentage of cases. A small percentage of HBV-infected persons develop fulminant liver failure and die. A larger number become chronic carriers. These carriers have a high probability of developing liver cancer and may be limited in certain workplace activities such as performing invasive medical procedures. Childhood diseases can have devastating effects on adults.

Probability of Transmission and Complications
This is the final element in the Court's analysis, although it is more a synthesis of the first three elements. The probability of transmission depends on the mode of transmission and the infectivity of the diseases. This is sometimes called *contact effectiveness*. The higher the contact effectiveness is, the higher is the probability that a person coming into proper contact with a disease carrier will contract the disease. For example, HIV is a disease with a low contact effectiveness; a sexual encounter has a less than 10 percent chance of spreading the disease. There is no possibility of spreading HIV by casual contact such as coughing. Conversely, measles is a disease with a high contact effectiveness. A single exposure to a coughing person infected with measles usually results in infection among susceptible persons.

If the usual mode of transmission does not occur in the workplace, then there is a very low probability of transmission. This is the usual case for sexually transmitted diseases that are not otherwise bloodborne. If the mode of transmission occurs in the workplace but the contact efficiency is very low, there is also a low probability of transmission. This would be the case for a disease such as leprosy that is spread by physical contact but the contact efficiency is so low that it poses a risk only to intimate family members. Conversely, active tuberculosis, an airborne disease with a medium contact efficiency, poses a threat to anyone with whom the infected person has frequent contact.

The Court did not specifically address the problem of persons with special susceptibility to communicable diseases—primarily immunosuppressed persons and pregnant women. The court has ruled that fertile women as a class cannot be excluded from workplaces where there is exposure to teratogens. (See Chapter 30.) It is likely that current law prevents pregnant women from being excluded from workplaces where there is only a possibility of infection with a disease that adversely affects the fetus. If there is a high probability of exposure, as on a hospital service caring for persons infected with the disease, the court might allow some restrictions on pregnant workers. The limited set of infections that pose a risk to the fetus and the fixed length of pregnancy would make pregnancy-related restrictions unusual outside certain medical care workplaces.

Federal and State Requirements

The communicable disease plan should identify all applicable federal and state disease control laws and administrative regulations. These may include statutory reporting duties that apply to the company physician or laboratory, sanitation rules that govern the company cafeteria, or Occupational Health and Safety Administration (OSHA) regulations. OSHA has already issued compliance directives for bloodborne illnesses and will issue a final regulation with detailed specifications on the management of bloodborne infections in the workplace. Any relevant CDC recommendations should be incorporated in the plan, as should standard-setting documents from private professional groups and accrediting agencies.

Identifying Employees at Risk or Who Pose Risks

Employees who are inadequately immunized against diseases such as measles and mumps are susceptible to the workplace spread of these diseases. Medical care workers who are not properly immunized may become infected and spread these diseases to patients. Medical care workers who are not immunized against hepatitis B may contract the disease in the workplace. Farm workers may acquire tetanus if they have not been immunized within the past ten years. Animal control workers should be immunized against rabies. Employers should know the immunization status of all employees and ensure that all employees are adequately immunized. OSHA requires that HBV vaccine be provided free of charge to employees at risk of infection. While other immunizations may not be covered by OSHA requirements, the employer should provide them at no cost. The employer may require employees to be immunized as a condition of employment.

Screening for contagious disease may be done on the employees, clients, or both. Screening has a bad reputation among health care professionals because many of the old screening programs included diseases that were not spread in the workplace. The health card system for food handlers is a good example. Until recently, most states and cities required that restaurant workers get a health card, obtained after tests for syphilis and tuberculosis. The tuberculosis test was a holdover from earlier times when it posed a general workplace risk; syphilis, however, has never been associated with food handling.

In contrast, requiring an annual test for tuberculosis on medical care and social services personnel does protect clients and the employee from the risks of tuberculosis. This is critical for all persons who work closely with HIV-infected persons. A worker who smokes and has hay fever may have a highly contagious cough for months before realizing that it is due to tuberculosis. If an employee is found who has infectious tuberculosis or another communicable disease, the health department should be contacted at once. The health department, in cooperation with the corporate medical department if one is available, will screen co-workers as necessary to prevent further spread at the worksite. This screening is mandatory, and the employer should ensure that the health department's recommendations are fully implemented.

The Special Problems of Immunosuppression

Immunosuppressed workers pose a double-edged problem: they are more susceptible to workplace-acquired infections, and they may harbor infectious diseases such as tuberculosis that pose a threat to other workers. The conventional legal wisdom is that immunosuppressed workers did not need special protections in the workplace. This is predicated on *Pneumocystis carinii* pneumonia as the model secondary infection. *Pneumocystis carinii* is a ubiquitous organism that is acquired from the environment rather than personal spread. The person's risk of infection is not increased by being at work. More important, there is no way to prove that the organism was acquired at a workplace, so it is impossible for an infected person to claim for either worker's compensation or third-party tort damages.

The problems arise when the immunosuppressed person is infected with an agent that is traceable to the workplace. This could be a common communicable disease such as chicken pox, which injures the person because of the immunosuppression, or an unusual infection that is acquired because of the immunosuppression. Most employees are in workplaces that do not pose an increased risk of infection. The ADA prevents immunosuppressed workers from being excluded from such workplaces because of their general increased risk of infection. The employer must protect such employees from known risks posed by fellow employees or customers, but this protection must interfere as little as possible with the employee's opportunities in the company.

This might entail being removed from the workplace to avoid a customer with a known infectious disease. In general, the employer's duty will be to identify other employees with communicable diseases. If these employees pose a threat to other workers, they must be removed from the workplace while they are infectious. If these employees pose a threat only to the immunosuppressed employee, the infected employee may be moved away from the immunosuppressed employee during the infectious period. (Short-term illnesses and injuries are not covered by the ADA.)

Many workplaces pose an increased risk of infection: hospitals, medical offices, day care centers, and other workplaces that render personal services to populations that regularly include customers with communicable diseases. The Supreme Court's test from *Arline* was intended for judging the risk that an infected employee poses to others. If the court uses the same analysis to judge the risk to immunosuppressed persons, the employer must demonstrate substantial risk of harm before the employee can be excluded from the workplace. An infectious disease service in a large hospital might properly refuse to hire an immunosuppressed nurse or ward clerk. A plastic surgeon whose practice is limited to elective cosmetic surgery would not be able to refuse to hire an immunosuppressed person.

As the spread of tuberculosis secondary to HIV-induced immunosuppression demonstrates, immunosuppressed persons can bring communicable diseases into the workplace. This is a significant problem for workplaces such as day care centers or hospitals whose customers are at special risk of infection. Such persons should have special counseling about the risks of secondary infections and undergo periodic screening for tuberculosis and other diseases that are demonstrated to pose special problems. This is controversial, however, because it requires screening for HIV-infected employees.

BALANCING THE RISKS OF HIV IN THE WORKPLACE

HIV poses real risks in the workplace. It is difficult to determine their magnitude because HIV is a new disease. In 25 years we will have a good idea how to balance the risks of HIV in the workplace. The difficult problem is deciding who should bear the risk of loss during this interval. In analogous situations, state and federal laws allow the employer to manage the risks posed by impaired workers. An employer is not compelled to hire a person with a bad back for manual labor; this protects the worker from injury and the employer from loss. Employers are under enormous pressure to protect the public by screening employees for drug use. Yet it matters little to the injured third party whether the worker was impaired by drugs or disease.

Ungrounded Fears and Real Risks

In the early stages of the AIDS epidemic, there was a tremendous fear of being exposed to AIDS patients and HIV carriers. With education, this fear is diminishing, but it is still present in many workplaces, and it must be considered when managing HIV carriers in the workplace. Any effective program for managing HIV in the workplace must include a general education program on the methods of transmission of HIV. Fellow employees must be taught that there is no risk of contracting HIV in the usual course of work. Employers must be taught that there is no risk of their customers' becoming infected with HIV by an employee. Conversely, employers and physicians must recognize the real risks of HIV in the workplace.

Many physicians speak of their patients' right to privacy as though it transcends society's right to protect itself from the consequences of disease and impairment. This attitude threats the ability of employers to achieve a proper balance between individual rights and workplace safety.

Employers must not be cowed by threats from plaintiffs' attorneys. Plaintiffs' attorneys were first excited about antidiscrimination litigation. This interest is already shifting to concern for persons injured by HIV carriers. But plaintiffs' attorneys follow the dollars: a family injured by a demented truck driver makes a much more financially attractive client than does the truck driver who wants to protest his exclusion from the workplace.

Many persons infected with HIV suffer substantial mental impairment before they manifest signs of physical illness. Persons with dementia suffer cognitive, motor, and behavioral disabilities. "Early symptoms ... include difficulty with concentration and performance of complex sequential mental activities.... Difficulty in reading or carrying out more demanding mental efforts at work..." (Price 1988). These mental impairments are persistent and may appear soon after infection with HIV. Some persons progress to complete mental deterioration and death without developing any other symptoms of AIDS. Once dementia is grossly apparent, the person must be removed from any workplace activity where mental acuity is necessary: operating machinery, making complex decisions, and other activities that pose a risk of injury to the worker or others. In general, dementia disqualifies an employee from performing any activity in which being drunk or under the influence of other drugs would be a disqualification.

Employee Screening for HIV

The most politically sensitive issue arising from HIV in the workplace is the appropriateness of screening employees for HIV. Employers clearly have the legal authority and duty to screen for medical conditions that potentially endanger the employee, fellow workers, or the public. Employees are routinely screened for medical conditions that pose a potential workplace hazard. The CDC is now recommending that HIV-infected medical care providers refrain from performing invasive procedures. Some commentators believe this restriction should be voluntary, but such a position is legally unsupportable. No medical care institution with oversite authority for health care providers can afford not to require that they be screened for HIV. Such a failure will put the institution at substantial risk of punitive damages if a patient is infected.

Unless the preliminary estimates of the risk of transmission from medical care workers to patients are grossly understated, this concern with the transmission in the medical care workplace is misplaced. The greatest risks of HIV in all workplaces are the dementia and the secondary infections. One federal court has already upheld the legality of HIV screening based on the risk of transmission during invasive medical procedures (*Lecklet v. Board of Commissioners of Hosp. Dist. No. 1* 1990). While this was decided under section 504 of the Rehabilitation Act, it is expected that the screening of medical care workers will be allowed under the ADA. Outside medical care workplaces, screening for HIV is appropriate only if it is based on the risks of dementia or secondary infections and does not violate state law against HIV testing. Physicians advising employers must carefully monitor the literature on dementia and secondary infections. If these risks continue to increase, then employers will have a duty to screen for HIV and to develop proper accommodations for HIV-infected workers.

Reasonable Accommodation for HIV

Reasonable accommodations for HIV might include periodic mental and communicable disease evaluations. The potential of dementia might disqualify employees from driving a truck, but it would not affect their ability to load the truck. The difference is that the employer can monitor the loading of the truck and correct problems without risk to others. Close monitoring of employees' performance and neurological status is an appropriate accommodation for HIV-infected employees. This may not be possible for employees engaged in activities that are so hazardous that sudden impairment would subject others to substantial harm.

The most problematic cases are HIV-infected persons who are knowledge workers in health and safety occupations—air traffic controllers, physicians, and others who must exercise critical judgment. If such a person is identified as an HIV carrier, the employer must monitor him or her closely to detect any diminution of mental capacity. For a physician, this may require practicing with a preceptor who will perform frequent chart reviews and supervision of procedures. Once there is any evidence of mental impairment, the physician may be allowed to continue practice only under the direct supervision of another qualified physician. For difficult-to-supervise jobs such as air traffic controllers, the first evidence of mental impairment would disqualify the individual from continued employment.

BIBLIOGRAPHY
Non–Health Care Workers
Barnham M; Kerby J: Skin sepsis in meat handlers: Observations on the causes of injury with special reference to bone. J Hyg (Lond) 1981 Dec; 87(3):465–76.
Human cutaneous anthrax—North Carolina, 1987. MMWR 1988 Jul 8; 37(26):413–14.
Kaufmann AF; Fox MD; Boyce JM; Anderson DC; Potter ME; Martone WJ; Patton CM: Airborne spread of brucellosis. Ann NY Acad Sci 1980; 353:105–14.
Lutsky II; Baum GL; Teichtahl H; Mazar A; Aizer F; Bar-Sela S: Respiratory disease in animal house workers. Eur J Respir Dis 1986 Jul; 69(1):29–35.
Messner RL; Smith MN: Infection prevention and control in the workplace. AAOHN J 1986 Mar; 34(3):109.
Multistate outbreak of sporotrichosis in seedling handlers, 1988. MMWR 1988 Oct 28; 37(42):652–53.
Mumps in the workplace—Chicago. MMWR 1988 Sep 9; 37(35):533–38.
Oltmann M: Infectious disease protection of non–health care workers. AAOHN J 1988 May; 36(5):228–30.
Outbreak of occupational hepatitis—Connecticut. MMWR 1987 Feb 27; 36(7):101–2.
Polakoff PL: When disease strikes, victims' job may give clue to cause of illness. Occup Health Saf 1988 Jul; 57(7):33.
Price R; Sidtis JJ; Rosenblum M: The AIDS dementia complex: Some current questions. Ann Neurol 1988; 23(suppl):S27–S33.
Q fever among slaughterhouse workers—California. MMWR 1986 Apr 11; 35(14): 223–26.
Rubella outbreak among office workers—New York City. MMWR 1983 Jul 15; 32(27): 349–52.
Rubella outbreak among office workers—New York City. MMWR 1985 Jul 26; 34(29): 455–59.
Skinhoj P; Hollinger FB; Hovind-Hougen K; Lous P: Infectious liver diseases in three groups of Copenhagen workers: Correlation of hepatitis A infection to sewage exposure. Arch Environ Health 1981 May–Jun; 36(3):139–43.
Sporotrichosis among hay-mulching workers—Oklahoma, New Mexico. MMWR 1984 Dec 7; 33(48):682–83.

Health Care Workers
Buesching WJ; Neff JC; Sharma HM: Infectious hazards in the clinical laboratory: A program to protect laboratory personnel. Clin Lab Med 1989 Jun; 9(2):351–61.
Dworsky ME; Welch K; Cassady G; Stagno S: Occupational risk for primary cytomegalovirus infection among pediatric health-care workers. N Engl J Med 1983 Oct 20; 309(16):950–53.
Favero MS: Preventing transmission of hepatitis B infection in health care facilities. Am J Infect Control 1989 Jun; 17(3):168–71.
Guidotti TL: Occupational health for hospital workers. Am Fam Physician 1987 Feb; 35(2):137–42.
Gundlach DC: Protecting health care workers from the occupational risk of disease. QRB 1988 May; 14(5):144–46.
Hartstein AI; Quan MA; Williams ML; Osterud HT; Foster LR: Rubella screening and immunization of health care personnel: Critical appraisal of a voluntary program. Am J Infect Control 1983 Feb; 11(1):1–9.

Lecklet v. Board of Comm'rs of Hosp. Dist. No. 1. 941 F2d 1495 (1990).

Mycobacterium tuberculosis transmission in a health clinic—Florida, 1988. MMWR 1989 Apr 21; 38(15) 256–58, 263–64.

Patterson WB; Craven DE; Schwartz DA; Nardell EA; Kasmer J; Noble J: Occupational hazards to hospital personnel. Ann Intern Med 1985 May; 102(5):658–80.

Sandler BH; Harwood SE; Thurber CH; Infante PF: Development of the Occupational Safety and Health Administration's proposed standard to protect workers from contracting bloodborne diseases in the workplace. J Public Health Dent 1989 Spring; 49(2): 87–89.

School Board of Nassua County v. Arline. 107 S Ct 1123 (1987).

Suspected nosocomial influenza cases in an intensive care unit. MMWR 1988 Jan 15; 37(1):3–4, 9.

Thomas MC; Giedinghagen DH; Hoff GL: An outbreak of scabies among employees in a hospital-associated commercial laundry. Infect Control 1987 Oct; 8(10):427–29.

Update: Acquired immunodeficiency syndrome and human immunodeficiency virus infection among health-care workers. MMWR 1988 Apr 22; 37(15):229–34, 239.

Valenti WM: Infection control and the pregnant health care worker. Am J Infect Control 1986 Feb; 14(1):20–27.

Williamson KM; Selleck CS; Turner JG; Brown KC; Newman KD; Sirles AT: Occupational health hazards for nurses: Infection. Image J Nurs Sch 1988 Spring; 20(1):48–53.

V Physicians and the Family

24

Legal Aspects of Parental Rights

> **CRITICAL POINTS**
> - Husbands have a right to participate in a woman's decision to conceive a child.
> - Physicians must protect the interests of their pregnant patients.
> - Violating adoption laws can subject physicians to criminal prosecution.
> - Surrogate parenting cannot be used as a subterfuge for baby selling.

Medical technologies that disassociate sexual intercourse from reproduction plunge physicians into the age-old maelstrom surrounding legitimacy, fidelity, and heritage. Except for introducing ambiguity into maternity as well as paternity, medical technology has transformed old problems more than it has created new ones. The transformation has been to substitute medical technology for sexual intercourse. The medicalization of reproduction allows the participants to escape from the religious and social opprobrium that defined acceptable reproductive choices. This disassociation from traditional religious values and legal rules poses grave ethical and legal questions about the use of certain reproductive technologies. The problems of adoption are better understood, but they have also been complicated by reproductive technologies that confuse the problem of determining whose parental rights control the adoption. This chapter presents a basic legal framework for analyzing the issues arising from reproductive technologies. Chapter 26 discusses the medical and ethical issues of surrogacy arrangements.

These issues are addressed within the traditional context of adoption and parental rights determinations. This leads to a conservative approach based on the stricter state laws in each area. While this provides a more generally applicable legal and ethical approach to reproductive technologies, physicians in less restrictive states may choose to be more aggressive in their use of these technologies, consistent with appropriate legal and ethical guidelines. Since legitimacy determinations and adoption laws differ dramatically from state to state, it is important for physicians to ensure that they comply with applicable state laws. Procedures that are legal and acceptable in one state may subject the physician to criminal prosecution and imprisonment in a different state.

LEGAL ASPECTS OF PARENTAL RIGHTS

In most areas of medical practice, adult patients are entitled to make their own medical decisions. The state may limit these decisions, and the patient must make the decisions in consultation with a physician, but other private persons have no right to interfere with the patient's decisions. In reproductive medicine, however, a woman's partner has the right to veto her medical decisions that would lead to the conception of a child. Once the child is born, the legal parents have responsibility for the child's care and well-being. The legal parents, however, are not always the biological parents. Some of the most bitter ethical and legal disputes in reproductive medicine center on the determination of legal parentage and the subsequent right to custody of the child.

New reproductive technologies exacerbate the problem of determining parental rights rather than creating unique new problems. Although relatively few physicians are involved in providing high-technology reproductive services, most physicians who deal with families face the traditional problems raised by parental rights determinations. These include investigations of child abuse, examination of children and parents to determine medical and psychological fitness before termination of parental rights or adoption proceedings, and questions about the privacy of adoption records. Additionally, physicians are faced with questionable private placement adoptions and attempts to use reproductive technologies to avoid state restrictions on adoptions. These creative alternatives to state-regulated adoptions have been driven by the declining pool of infants available for adoption. If physicians involved with such practices violate the state laws governing adoption proceedings, they may be prosecuted for baby selling and be subject to discipline by the board of medical examiners and to adverse publicity:

> Petitioner, a physician licensed to practice in New York, is an obstetrician/gynecologist with a subspecialty in infertility. In May 1988, petitioner was arrested and charged with the unclassified misdemeanor of unlawfully placing a child for adoption in violation of Social Services Law § 374(2) and § 389. Petitioner pleaded guilty to the charge admitting that he had, in June 1986, arranged for the placement of a baby boy, now known as Travis Smigiel, for adoption by Joel Steinberg and Hedda Nussbaum without complying with the appropriate provisions of the Social Services Law.
>
> The mother of the baby boy, Nicole Smigiel, was an unwed teenager whose mother became suspicious of the pregnancy only a few days prior to the infant's birth.... Petitioner was contacted and he agreed to deliver the child and to cooperate with the adoption plans in secrecy. He insisted that the child be placed with Steinberg, his attorney and business associate. Petitioner had been treating Steinberg and Nussbaum for infertility for some time.... Petitioner did not seek or receive a fee for delivering or placing the boy and this was the only time he had ever participated in arrangements for an adoption. Petitioner told Smigiel that Steinberg and Nussbaum were a "wonderful couple" and the baby would be well taken care of. Petitioner learned otherwise when Steinberg was arrested and ultimately convicted of manslaughter in connection with the death of Steinberg's other illegally adopted child, Lisa....
>
> In connection with the criminal charge against petitioner, Criminal Court of the City of New York sentenced petitioner, an individual with no criminal history, to three years of probation, 100 hours of community service and a $1,000 fine. In its decision, the court noted that, although many physicians in New York were unfamiliar with Social Services Law § 374(2) and § 389 and may have unwittingly vi-

olated these provisions, "ignorance of the law is no excuse". Based on this criminal conviction, the Office of Professional Medical Conduct initiated a disciplinary proceeding against petitioner charging him with professional misconduct for having been convicted of an act constituting a crime. . . . The report by the Regents Review Committee . . . recommended . . . that petitioner's license to practice medicine be suspended for three years, with the last 30 months of said suspension to be stayed at which time petitioner would be placed on probation for 30 months. (*Sarosi v. Sobol*, 1990)

The Board of Regents (the medical licensing board in New York State) went beyond the committee's recommendation. Taking "a more serious view of petitioner's misconduct," it revoked the physician's license to practice medicine. The physician appealed this sanction, and the court found that the revocation was unnecessarily harsh, given the criminal sentence and adverse publicity that the physician had already endured. The court reiterated, however, that the defendant's good intentions and lack of knowledge of the technical requirements of the law were no defense to the charges. They served only to mitigate the physician's punishment.

Parental Rights
A legally recognized parent has the right to make decisions on a child's behalf and the responsibility to provide financial and emotional support for the child. Under the law in most jurisdictions, a child may have two parents (one father and one mother), one parent, or no parents. The identity of these parents can be determined by birth, marriage, or legitimation or paternity proceedings or through adoption. Since the rights and responsibilities attendant on parenthood are so encompassing, the law places certain restrictions on the rights of a woman to conceive a child without the permission of the man who will assume the legal duties of father to the child. The clearest restrictions are the requirements in artificial insemination statutes that a married woman have her husband's permission to be inseminated. Potential fathers have also asked courts to block the implantation of previously frozen embryos, although the absence of statutory guidance makes these cases more ambiguous. Outside of this right to veto certain reproductive procedures that will lead to the bearing of a child, fathers have no legal right to control the mother's medical care. Nor do they have the right to prevent or force a woman to have an abortion or to require that she use contraception. (See Chapter 25.)

It is important for a physician treating a child to know if the child has a legal father and whether the father has full parental rights. The rights of a legal father (not a merely biologic father) start at the child's birth and are coextensive with the mother's rights. This means that from the birth of the child on, a father and a mother have the same rights to determine the medical care their child will receive, where the child will live, and all the other decisions that parents normally make for their children. If the mother and father do not agree, it is the business of the family courts to decide who will care for the child.

The Presumption of Legitimacy
The law has always been concerned with paternity. Paternity was critical to the succession of monarchs and the inheritance of property. Paternity was a moral issue because of the church's insistence on fidelity in marriage and celibacy

outside marriage. Infidelity could mean disgrace for a man and death for a woman. The moral taint was so strong that law punished the child as well as the mother:

> All the disabilities of bastardy are of feudal origin. With us it is of Saxon origin. The term bastard being derived from a Saxon word, importing a bad, or base, original. The disabilities of bastardy are the same under the civil as under the common law, and in all ages and nations. He has no ancestor; no name; can inherit to nobody, and nobody to him; can have no collaterals nor other relatives except those descended from him. He can have no surname, until gained by reputation. (*Stevesons's Heirs v. Sullivant*, 1820)

The stigma of bastardy lasted a lifetime and could blight the lives of the next generation, as witnessed by the heraldic bend (or bar) sinister on the family crest, designating bastardy. In addition to inheritance, a bastard was denied entrance into several callings and certain civil rights. These harsh laws persisted until relatively recent times in England and the United States. The stigma of bastardy was such that the common law developed legal presumptions in favor of legitimacy.

> The presumption of legitimacy was a fundamental principle of the common law. Traditionally, that presumption could be rebutted only by proof that a husband was incapable of procreation or had had no access to his wife during the relevant period. As explained by Blackstone, nonaccess could only be proved "if the husband be out of the kingdom of England (or, as the law somewhat loosely phrases it, extra quatuor maria [beyond the four seas]) for above nine months...." And, under the common law both in England and here, "neither husband nor wife [could] be a witness to prove access or nonaccess." The primary policy rationale underlying the common law's severe restrictions on rebuttal of the presumption appears to have been an aversion to declaring children illegitimate, thereby depriving them of rights of inheritance and succession, and likely making them wards of the state. A secondary policy concern was the interest in promoting the "peace and tranquillity of States and families," a goal that is obviously impaired by facilitating suits against husband and wife asserting that their children are illegitimate. Even though, as bastardy laws became less harsh, "[j]udges in both [England and the United States] gradually widened the acceptable range of evidence that could be offered by spouses, and placed restraints on the 'four seas rule' . . . [,] the law retained a strong bias against ruling the children of married women illegitimate." (*Michael H. and Victoria D., Appellants v. Gerald D.*, 1989)

The *Michael H.* case is a good, if unusual, example of this legal rule. Carole and Gerald were married. During this marriage, Carole had an adulterous affair with Michael. Sometime after this affair, the child Victoria was born. During a brief separation from her husband, Carole and Michael had blood tests performed to determine Victoria's paternity. The tests established, according to the evidence presented to the court, a 98 percent probability that Michael was Victoria's father. After a period of living with Michael and treating Victoria as Michael's daughter, Carole reconciled with Gerald. Michael, as probable biologic father of Victoria, sought visitation rights with Victoria.

The California law, which was more than a century old, held that "the issue of a wife cohabiting with her husband, who is not impotent or sterile, is conclusively presumed to be a child of the marriage." Subsequent revisions allowed this presumption to be "rebutted by blood tests, but only if a motion for such tests is made, within two years from the date of the child's birth, either by the husband or, if the natural father has filed an affidavit acknowledging paternity, by the wife."

Gerald had always acknowledged Victoria as his daughter. Carole, having reconciled with Gerald, also refused to request the court to examine Victoria's paternity. Michael, as the probable biologic father, argued that this law denied him a constitutional right to establish a parental relationship with his daughter. The U.S. Supreme Court upheld the California law as a valid exercise of the state's right to protect the family relationship. The Court made it clear that biologic parenthood did not supersede legal parenthood as defined by a state statute reflecting the common law tradition.

Biological Fathers and Legitimation
All states have legal procedures for establishing the paternity of children born out of wedlock, or when the husband is found to not be the child's father, pursuant to state law:

> The Commonwealth has an interest in its infant citizens having two parents to provide and care for them. There is a legitimate interest in not furnishing financial assistance for children who have a father capable of support. The Commonwealth is concerned in having a father responsible for a child born out of wedlock. This not only tends to reduce the welfare burden by keeping minor children, who have a financially able parent, off the rolls, but it also provides an identifiable father from whom potential recovery may be had of welfare payments which are paid to support the child born out of wedlock. (*Rivera v. Minnich*, 1986)

If the mother is not married at the time of a child's birth, a father wishing to establish legal paternity must legally acknowledge the child as his own. In some states, this may be as simple as filing a form with the birth certificate. In other states, it may require a full court proceeding similar to an adoption. If the mother agrees that he is the father, a man seeking to acknowledge the child as his own usually does not have to prove that he is the biologic father to be declared the legal father of the child. If more than one man seeks to acknowledge the child or if the mother refuses to recognize the man as the father of the child, the courts in most states may order blood tests to determine paternity.

States also provide for the testing of potential fathers who do not voluntarily acknowledge their children. These lawsuits may be brought by the mother or by the state on behalf of the child. It is common for the state to require an unmarried woman seeking public assistance to identify the father (if known) of her children. While a state is free to establish a stricter standard of proof, the U.S. Supreme Court has found that it is constitutional to establish paternity with a preponderance of the evidence standard. By allowing this less strict standard of proof than the standard required for termination of parental rights, the courts recognize the strong societal interest in the legitimation of children. Once the court rules that a man is the legal father of the child, the man has the same rights and duties regarding the child as would the husband of the mother.

Termination of Parental Rights
Parental rights are not inalienable. Courts may terminate a parent's rights regarding a child if it is determined that the parent is unfit. In limited circumstances, a person may voluntarily relinquish his or her parental rights. The

standards for proving a case for terminating a parent's right are stricter than the standard for establishing those rights. While a court may determine paternity based on a preponderance of the evidence, the state must prove a parent's unfitness by clear and convincing evidence because of the importance attached to a person's right to be a parent. Unfitness is also narrowly defined as a physical or psychological threat to the child. This is in contrast to the "best interests of the child" standard used to decide which parent gets custody of the child in a divorce. It is not enough for the state to show that the child would be better off if a parent's rights were terminated. The state must show some fault on the part of the parent.

Since a parent's duty to support a child ends with a termination of that parent's rights, the states generally allow parents to waive their parental rights voluntarily only when they are putting a child up for adoption. Parents may waive their parental rights implicitly by abandoning the child. This is most commonly done by the fathers of illegitimate children, but it is increasingly common among mothers with AIDS or who are addicted to drugs. The state must still bring a formal termination proceeding, but it has a lower burden of proof than in a termination based on unfitness.

> When an unwed father demonstrates a full commitment to the responsibilities of parenthood by "com[ing] forward to participate in the rearing of his child," his interest in personal contact with his child acquires substantial protection under the due process clause. At that point it may be said that he "act[s] as a father toward his children." But the mere existence of a biological link does not merit equivalent constitutional protection. The actions of judges neither create nor sever genetic bonds. "[T]he importance of the familial relationship, to the individuals involved and to the society, stems from the emotional attachments that derive from the intimacy of daily association, and from the role it plays in 'promot[ing] a way of life' through the instruction of children as well as from the fact of blood relationship." (*Lehr v. Robertson*, 1982)

The implications of this holding extend beyond the termination of the rights of an absent father. By emphasizing the importance of the familial rather than the genetic relationship, the court also provides a hint about how it might analyze a contest between a birth mother and an embryo donor. A bias in favor of the birth mother would be consistent with the Supreme Court's determination later in this case that the law at issue did not violate the equal protection clause. The father argued that the law gave the mother's rights more protection than it did those of a putative father. The Court found that the statute protected all parents with a real, custodial relationship with the child. The mother's interests were protected because she gave birth to the child and took care of her after birth, not because she was the biological mother.

When a court grants a divorce, it also determines who gets custody of the children. States differ in the extent of the parental rights remaining to the noncustodial parent. This can pose problems when getting consent for the child's medical care. Even states that generally allow the noncustodial parent to consent to medical care for the child allow the court to deny the noncustodial parent the right to make decisions for the child.

Physicians should find out the applicable rules for their state. If the state does not allow the noncustodial parent to consent to or direct the child's medical care, the physician should ask custodial parents their wishes. If the custodial parent wants the noncustodial parent to be able to obtain medical care for the child and there is no court order to the contrary, the custodial parent should sign a delegation of authority to consent to the child's medical care. (See Chapter 11.) In all states, the physician should ask the custodial parent if there are any court-ordered limitations on the rights of the noncustodial parent. If a pregnant woman is divorced during the course of the pregnancy, the courts will sometimes make a determination of paternity as well as custody of the child. A physician should handle this the same way as any other child of divorce.

Adoption

Adoptions are proceedings that vest parental rights in a person who is not the child's legal parent. Adoption involves the termination of the legal parent's parental rights and the determination that the potential adoptive parents are fit. All conflicting parental rights must be terminated before an adoption is final. If a parent marries a person who is not the child's legal parent, this stepparent cannot exercise full parental rights unless he or she formally adopts the child. Such an adoption will require the rights of the previous parent, if known and still living, to be terminated. If a married couple, neither of them parents of the child, or a single adult seeks to adopt a child, the rights of both of the child's existing parents must be terminated. Parents may voluntarily relinquish their parental rights in an adoption proceeding, but most states protect the parent (usually the mother) from precipitous decisions concerning termination of parental rights. These protections may include a ban on agreements signed before the baby is born and a waiting period after birth during which the parent may revoke the decision to give up parental rights.

In most states it is illegal to pay parents to induce them to terminate their parental rights. It would be legal to give the mother almost anything as long as she did not give up her baby. It is only when she gives up the baby that coercion becomes an issue. It is acceptable to pay for the mother's medical expenses and support during the pregnancy, but this cannot be conditioned on a waiver of parental rights. Although the courts realize that this payment is an incentive, they treat it as a gift. Payments made after the birth of the baby are suspect because they have no relationship to providing for the mother's and baby's welfare during the pregnancy. Payments to husbands are impossible to characterize as anything other than bribes to terminate their parental relationship. While it is acceptable for physicians to receive their routine fees from an agency or prospective parent, any payment in excess of the fees charged in other situations could subject the physician to prosecution for receiving money in connection with an adoption.

In addition to bans on paying parents, the courts are sensitive to efforts to coerce parents into relinquishing their parental rights. This concern with coercion, combined with the fiduciary nature of the physician-patient relationship, makes it improper for physicians to participate in obtaining a waiver of parental rights from their patients. The physician's legal and ethical duty is to protect the patient's best interests, consistent with public health and safety. If the physician has doubts about the mother's fitness to care for the baby, they should be reported to the child welfare department. Such beliefs are not an excuse for helping the patient by participating in obtaining her waiver of parental rights so the baby can find a good home. Improper participation by physicians is grounds for setting aside the termination of parental rights. This imperils whatever good a physician seeks to do by expediting the child's placement in an adoptive home.

Matchmaking

In most states, the adoption laws provide that potential adoptive parents must be screened to determine if they will be fit parents. Unlike parental rights, which arise in the common law's overriding concern with the preservation of families, adoption has no common law heritage to give rise to special protections for the rights of potential adoptive parents. The states are free to establish strict criteria for evaluating prospective parents. While these criteria must not violate constitutional protections or federal law, persons may be denied the right to adopt for reasons that would not support terminating their parental rights were they already legal parents. This process has been criticized for giving babies to the highest-income couple whose religion and politics agree with those of the baby's case worker.

As the physician in the *Sarosi* case discovered, physicians should not second-guess this procedure by trying to set up matches between prospective parents and pregnant women. Physicians have neither the resources nor the authority to investigate prospective parents properly. No physician wants to face the nightmare of finding that the couple he or she recommended became child killers. It is to be expected, however, that some couples will seek private placement because they would be found unsuitable in a parental fitness evaluation. As with the physician's participation in obtaining a patient's waiver of parental rights, such matchmaking raises ethical questions about the coercion implicit in the physician-patient relationship. A patient may feel coerced into complying with the physician's recommendation on placement. As in the *Sarosi* case, this matchmaking can violate state adoption laws.

Physicians should be cautious about participating in adoptions that are arranged outside the state welfare system or recognized nonprofit agencies. Termination of parental rights and adoption are also implicated in fertility procedures that involve the transfer of a baby from the birth mother or her husband to the family contracting for her services. If the parents are profiting from the adoption, if the attorneys or physicians are being paid excessive fees, or if there is a broker, the transaction will violate the baby-selling laws in some states. In states that do not allow private nonagency placements, any involvement with private parties who are seeking to arrange or facilitate adoptions can be illegal. The physician should be especially cautious about participating in adoptions that cross state lines. If the transaction is illegal in either state, there can be prosecutions for kidnapping when the baby is moved across the state line. Physicians who assist private placements should always retain their own attorney to advise them on the legality of each transaction.

Evaluating Potential Adoptive Children

The publicity about crack babies and babies infected with HIV has made potential adoptive parents very concerned with the health of the baby in question. Less well publicized is the high level of tuberculosis in adoptive children from Third World countries.

Physicians examining babies for adoption are subject to malpractice lawsuits if they fail to diagnose conditions, within the standard of care for pediatrics, that would be grounds for not adopting the baby. In some states, physicians may be sued for fraud if they withhold information about the baby that would influence the adoption decision. Since such information may involve the mother's behavior, the physician must have a written authorization from the mother or a court order before transmitting such information to the adoption agency or prospective parents. There may be a conflict with the physician-patient relationship for family practitioners and others who are treating both the mother and the baby. Evaluating the infant for adoption may put the physician in conflict with the mother if the physician's determination is at odds with the mother's wishes.

In addressing the specific problem of HIV testing for children to be placed in foster care or adoptive homes, the American Academy of Pediatric's Task Force on Pediatric AIDS found:

> In response to the legitimate need for pre-placement HIV testing of the infant or child in areas of high prevalence of HIV infection in childbearing women, procedures should be established by foster care and adoption agencies in collaboration with health care facilities, to accomplish the following.
>
> 1. Develop the expertise to provide prospective foster care or adoptive families with comprehensive and up-to-date information regarding all aspects of pediatric HIV infection.
> 2. Establish a process that would accomplish, with the appropriate consent of the infant's legal guardian, the pre-placement HIV testing of infants or children, initiated either: (a) at the request of the prospective adopting or foster care parents through the physician who is responsible for that child's care, or (b) through the request of the infant's physician in response to his or her judgment that the mother is at high risk for HIV infection and that the infant's health supervision and/or placement may be affected by knowing the infant's antibody status.
> 3. Provide comprehensive and up-to-date interpretation of the meaning of test results, taking into account the age and health status of the child and the reliability of the test.
> 4. Establish a record-keeping system to contain information regarding the child's test results with access to such information strictly limited to those who need to know, but specifically including the informed adoptive or foster care family and the physician responsible for the infant's medical care.
> 5. Establish a procedure whereby all infants who have positive results on HIV antibody tests are retested on a regular basis to distinguish between passively transmitted antibody and true HIV infection in the infant. (Plotkin et al. 1989)

Access to Adoption-Related Records

One of the lingering controversies surrounding adoption is whether the process should be confidential. Irrespective of the physician's personal beliefs on the matter, the state law must be followed. A physician should not disclose information in violation of confidentiality provisions, but neither should persons be denied information that they are entitled to under state law. This question often arises when adopted children approach the physician who attended their delivery and request a copy of their birth record. (Most states leave the physician's and/or the hospital's name on the adoptee's birth certificate.) Unless the state has a specific provision in its access to medical records law, adult adoptees are entitled to read or copy any medical records that contain information about their birth or pediatric care.

As with all other medical records, the physician is advised not to alter or mutilate the records to disguise the birth mother's name. If the physician is concerned about the child's access to the records, the state agency regulating adoptions should be contacted for advice. It may be able to provide medical information to the child without violating anyone's privacy. Most states also have a registry system whereby former parents can express their wish to contact or provide medical information to the children they relinquished for adoption. If the parent has notified the state of such a wish, the registry can direct the child to the parent without violating the laws governing adoption. A physician treating a person who has given up a child for adoption should inform the patient of any information about genetic diseases or other conditions (such as DES exposure, birth injuries, and congenital infections) that might be necessary medical information for the child.

LEGAL DECISIONS INVOLVING SURROGATE PARENTHOOD

Most of the legal disputes involving reproductive technologies have centered on the disputes over traditional parental rights to the resulting child or fertilized ova. Some cases, usually denominated as baby selling, are criminal prosecutions for failing to comply with the applicable adoptions laws. The most highly publicized cases have been custody disputes such as the *Baby M* case in New Jersey and the *Davis* divorce case in Tennessee. The *Davis* case, while involving more sophisticated technology, had a simpler legal solution. The only technology involved in the *Baby M* case was artificial insemination, but it had a much more complex legal result. In a thoughtful and articulate opinion, the New Jersey court discussed the legal problems posed by so-called surrogacy agreements and, implicitly, the general policy considerations in heterogeneous parentage situations. The following discussion includes quotation from the legal opinions themselves to convey the attitude of the courts as well as the legal rules in the cases. The holdings of these cases are limited to their respective states, but the attitude of the courts are representative of courts in other jurisdictions.

Davis v. Davis (1990)—The Tennessee Appeals Court Decision

In this divorce action, the sole issue on appeal is essentially who is entitled to control seven of Mary Sue's ova fertilized by Junior's sperm through the in vitro fertilization process. The fertilized ova are cryopreserved at the Fertility Center of East Tennessee in Knoxville.

The trial judge awarded "custody" of the fertilized ova to Mary Sue and directed that she "be permitted the opportunity to bring these children to term through implantation."

At the outset, it should be emphasized no pregnancy is involved. Both Mary Sue and Junior are now married to other spouses; moreover, neither wants a child with the other as parent.

There are significant scientific distinctions between fertilized ova that have not been implanted and an embryo in the mother's womb. The fertilized ova at issue are between 4 and 8 cells. Genetically each cell is identical. Approximately three days after fertilization the cells begin to differentiate into an outer layer that will become the placenta and an inner layer that will become the embryo. This "blastocyst" can adhere to the uterine wall, the hallmark of pregnancy. Once adherence occurs, the inner embryonic layer reorganizes to form a rudimentary "axis" along which major organs and structures of the body will be differentiated. It is important to remember when these ova were fertilized through mechanical manipulation, their development was limited to the 8 cell stage. At this juncture there is no development of the nervous system, the circulatory system, or the pulmonary system and it is thus possible for embryonic development to be indefinitely arrested at this stage by cryopreservation or "freezing".

Treating infertility by in vitro fertilization results in a low success rate. As one writer has observed:

> In IVF programs the embryo will be transferred to a uterus when it reaches the four-, six-, or eight-cell stage, some forty-eight to seventy-two hours after conception. It is also at this stage that the embryo would be cryopreserved for later use. . . . In vitro culture until the blastocyst stage may be possible, but beyond that it has not occurred. Finally, only one in ten pre-embryos at this stage goes on to initiate a successful pregnancy.

Moreover, cryopreservation poses risks to the fertilized ova, which have only a 70 per cent rate of viability after having been frozen.

The parties, after concluding a normal pregnancy was unlikely, jointly decided to attempt to have a child by in vitro fertilization and, after several attempts, nine of Mary Sue's ova were successfully fertilized in December of 1988. For the first time, their doctors advised that freezing was an option and would enable them to avoid all but the implantation phase of in vitro fertilization if later attempts were undertaken. The couple agreed to attempt implantation of two of the fertilized ova and to preserve the others. There was no discussion between them or their doctors about the consequences of preservation should the Davises divorce while the fertilized ova were stored. Mary Sue testified she had no idea that a divorce might be imminent and she would not have undergone the in vitro fertilization procedure had she contemplated divorce. Junior testified he believed the marriage was foundering but believed that having a child would improve the marriage and did not anticipate a divorce at the time of the in vitro fertilization procedure.

Davis v. Davis (1992)—The Tennessee Supreme Court Decision

Resolving disputes over conflicting interests of constitutional import is a task familiar to the courts. One way of resolving these disputes is to consider the positions of the parties, the significance of their interests, and the relative burdens that will be imposed by differing resolutions. In this case, the issue centers on the two aspects of procreational autonomy—the right to procreate and the right to avoid procreation. We start by considering the burdens imposed on the parties by solutions that would have the effect of disallowing the exercise of individual procreational autonomy with respect to these particular preembryos.

Beginning with the burden imposed on Junior Davis, we note that the consequences are obvious. Any disposition which results in the gestation of the preembryos would impose unwanted parenthood on him, with all of its possible financial and psychological consequences. The impact that this unwanted parenthood would have on Junior Davis can only be understood by considering his particular circumstances, as revealed in the record.

Junior Davis testified that he was the fifth youngest of six children. When he was five years old, his parents divorced, his mother had a nervous break-down, and he and three of his brothers went to live at a home for boys run by the Lutheran Church. Another brother was taken in by an aunt, and his sister stayed with their mother. From that day forward, he had monthly visits with his mother but saw his father only three more times before he died in 1976. Junior Davis testified that, as a boy, he had severe problems caused by separation from his parents. He said that it was especially hard to leave his mother after each monthly visit. He clearly feels that he has suffered because of his lack of opportunity to establish a relationship with his parents and particularly because of the absence of his father.

In light of his boyhood experiences, Junior Davis is vehemently opposed to fathering a child that would not live with both parents. Regardless of whether he or

Mary Sue had custody, he feels that the child's bond with the non-custodial parent would not be satisfactory. He testified very clearly that his concern was for the psychological obstacles a child in such a situation would face, as well as the burdens it would impose on him. Likewise, he is opposed to donation because the recipient couple might divorce, leaving the child (which he definitely would consider his own) in a single-parent setting.

Balanced against Junior Davis's interest in avoiding parenthood is Mary Sue Davis's interest in donating the preembryos to another couple for implantation. Refusal to permit donation of the preembryos would impose on her the burden of knowing that the lengthy IVF procedures she underwent were futile, and that the preembryos to which she contributed genetic material would never become children. While this is not an insubstantial emotional burden, we can only conclude that Mary Sue Davis's interest in donation is not as significant as the interest Junior Davis has in avoiding parenthood. If she were allowed to donate these preembryos, he would face a lifetime of either wondering about his parental status or knowing about his parental status but having no control over it. He testified quite clearly that if these preembryos were brought to term he would fight for custody of his child or children. Donation, if a child came of it, would rob him twice—his procreational autonomy would be defeated and his relationship with his offspring would be prohibited.

The case would be closer if Mary Sue Davis were seeking to use the preembryos herself, but only if she could not achieve parenthood by any other reasonable means. We recognize the trauma that Mary Sue has already experienced and the additional discomfort to which she would be subjected if she opts to attempt IVF again. Still, she would have a reasonable opportunity, through IVF, to try once again to achieve parenthood in all its aspects—genetic, gestational, bearing, and rearing.

Further, we note that if Mary Sue Davis were unable to undergo another round of IVF, or opted not to try, she could still achieve the child-rearing aspects of parenthood through adoption. The fact that she and Junior Davis pursued adoption indicates that, at least at one time, she was willing to forego genetic parenthood and would have been satisfied by the child-rearing aspects of parenthood alone.

Conclusion

In summary, we hold that disputes involving the disposition of preembryos produced by in vitro fertilization should be resolved, first, by looking to the preferences of the progenitors. If their wishes cannot be ascertained, or if there is dispute, then their prior agreement concerning disposition should be carried out. If no prior agreement exists, then the relative interests of the parties in using or not using the preembryos must be weighed. Ordinarily, the party wishing to avoid procreation should prevail, assuming that the other party has a reasonable possibility of achieving parenthood by means other than use of the preembryos in question. If no other reasonable alternatives exist, then the argument in favor of using the preembryos to achieve pregnancy should be considered. However, if the party seeking control of the preembryos intends merely to donate them to another couple, the objecting party obviously has the greater interest and should prevail.

But the rule does not contemplate the creation of an automatic veto, and in affirming the judgment of the Court of Appeals, we would not wish to be interpreted as so holding.

For the reasons set out above, the judgment of the Court of Appeals is affirmed, in the appellee's favor. This ruling means that the Knoxville Fertility Clinic is free to follow its normal procedure in dealing with unused preembryos, as long as that procedure is not in conflict with this opinion.

In the Matter of Baby M

In this matter the Court is asked to determine the validity of a contract that purports to provide a new way of bringing children into a family. For a fee of $10,000, a woman agrees to be artificially inseminated with the semen of another woman's husband; she is to conceive a child, carry it to term, and after its birth surrender it to the natural father and his wife. The intent of the contract is that the child's natural mother will thereafter be forever separated from her child. The wife is to adopt the child, and she and the natural father are to be regarded as its parents for all purposes. The contract providing for this is called a "surrogacy contract," the natural mother inappropriately called the "surrogate" mother.

In February 1985, William Stern and Mary Beth Whitehead entered into a surrogacy contract. It recited that Stern's wife, Elizabeth, was infertile, that they wanted a child, and that Mrs. Whitehead was willing to provide that child as the mother with Mr. Stern as the father.

The contract provided that through artificial insemination using Mr. Stern's sperm, Mrs. Whitehead would become pregnant, carry the child to term, bear it, deliver it to the Sterns, and thereafter do whatever was necessary to terminate her maternal rights so that Mrs. Stern could thereafter adopt the child. Mrs. Whitehead's husband, Richard, was also a party to the contract; Mrs. Stern was not. Mr. Whitehead promised to do all acts necessary to rebut the presumption of paternity under the Parentage Act. Although Mrs. Stern was not a party to the surrogacy agreement, the contract gave her sole custody of the child in the event of Mr. Stern's death. Mrs. Stern's status as a nonparty to the surrogate parenting agreement presumably was to avoid the application of the baby-selling statute to this arrangement.

Mr. Stern, on his part, agreed to attempt the artificial insemination and to pay Mrs. Whitehead $10,000 after the child's birth, on its delivery to him. In a separate contract, Mr. Stern agreed to pay $7,500 to the Infertility Center of New York ("ICNY"). The Center's advertising campaigns solicit surrogate mothers and encourage infertile couples to consider surrogacy. ICNY arranged for the surrogacy contract by bringing the parties together, explaining the process to them, furnishing the contractual form, and providing legal counsel.

Invalidity and Unenforceability of Surrogacy Contract

We have concluded that this surrogacy contract is invalid. Our conclusion has two bases: direct conflict with existing statutes and conflict with the public policies of this State, as expressed in its statutory and decisional law.

One of the surrogacy contract's basic purposes, to achieve the adoption of a child through private placement, though permitted in New Jersey "is very much disfavored." Its use of money for this purpose—and we have no doubt whatsoever that the money is being paid to obtain an adoption and not, as the Sterns argue, for the personal services of Mary Beth Whitehead—is illegal and perhaps criminal. In addition to the inducement of money, there is the coercion of contract: the natural mother's irrevocable agreement, prior to birth, even prior to conception, to surrender the child to the adoptive couple. Such an agreement is totally unenforceable in private placement adoption. Even where the adoption is through an approved agency, the formal agreement to surrender occurs only after birth, and then, by regulation, only after the birth mother has been offered counseling. Integral to these invalid provisions of the surrogacy contract is the related agreement, equally invalid, on the part of the natural mother to cooperate with, and not to contest, proceedings to terminate her parental rights, as well as her contractual concession, in aid of the adoption, that the child's best interests would be served by awarding custody to the natural father and his wife—all of this before she has even conceived, and, in some cases, before she has the slightest idea of what the natural father and adoptive mother are like.

The foregoing provisions not only directly conflict with New Jersey statutes, but also offend long-established State policies. These critical terms, which are at the heart of the contract, are invalid and unenforceable; the conclusion therefore follows, without more, that the entire contract is unenforceable.

A. Conflict with Statutory Provisions

The surrogacy contract conflicts with: (1) laws prohibiting the use of money in connection with adoptions; (2) laws requiring proof of parental unfitness or abandonment before termination of parental rights is ordered or an adoption is granted; and (3) laws that make surrender of custody and consent to adoption revocable in private placement adoptions.

(1) Our law prohibits paying or accepting money in connection with any placement of a child for adoption. Violation is a high misdemeanor. Excepted are fees of an approved agency (which must be a non-profit entity), and certain expenses in connection with childbirth.

Considerable care was taken in this case to structure the surrogacy arrangement so as not to violate this prohibition. The arrangement was structured as follows: the adopting parent, Mrs. Stern, was not a party to the surrogacy contract; the money paid to Mrs. Whitehead was stated to be for her services—not for the adoption; the sole purpose of the contract was stated as being that "of giving a child to William Stern, its natural and biological father"; the money was purported to be "compensation for services and expenses and in no way . . . a fee for termination of parental rights or a payment in exchange for consent to surrender a child for adoption"; the fee to the Infertility Center ($7,500) was stated to be for legal representation, advice, administrative work, and other "services." Nevertheless, it seems clear that the money was paid and accepted in connection with an adoption.

Mr. Stern knew he was paying for the adoption of a child; Mrs. Whitehead knew she was accepting money so that a child might be adopted; the Infertility Center knew that it was being paid for assisting in the adoption of a child. The actions of all three worked to frustrate the goals of the statute. It strains credulity to claim that these arrangements, touted by those in the surrogacy business as an attractive alternative to the usual route leading to an adoption, really amount to something other than a private placement adoption for money.

The evils inherent in baby-bartering are loathsome for a myriad of reasons. The child is sold without regard for whether the purchasers will be suitable parents. The natural mother does not receive the benefit of counseling and guidance to assist her in making a decision that may affect her for a lifetime. In fact, the monetary incentive to sell her child may, depending on her financial circumstances, make her decision less voluntary. Furthermore, the adoptive parents may not be fully informed of the natural parents' medical history.

The negative consequences of baby-buying are potentially present in the surrogacy context, especially the potential for placing and adopting a child without regard to the interest of the child or the natural mother.

(2) The termination of Mrs. Whitehead's parental rights, called for by the surrogacy contract and actually ordered by the court, fails to comply with the stringent requirements of New Jersey law. Our law, recognizing the finality of any termination of parental rights, provides for such termination only where there has been a voluntary surrender of a child to an approved agency or to the Division of Youth and Family Services ("DYFS"), accompanied by a formal document acknowledging termination of parental rights, or where there has been a showing of parental abandonment or unfitness.

Such an action, whether or not in conjunction with a pending adoption, may proceed on proof of written surrender, "forsaken parental obligation," or other specific grounds such as death or insanity. Where the parent has not executed a formal consent, termination requires a showing of "forsaken parental obligation," i.e., "willful and continuous neglect or failure to perform the natural and regular obligations of care and support of a child."

In this case a termination of parental rights was obtained not by proving the statutory prerequisites but by claiming the benefit of contractual provisions. From all that has been stated above, it is clear that a contractual agreement to abandon one's parental rights, or not to contest a termination action, will not be enforced in our courts. The Legislature would not have so carefully, so consistently, and so substantially restricted termination of parental rights if it had intended to allow termination to be achieved by one short sentence in a contract.

These strict prerequisites to irrevocability constitute a recognition of the most serious consequences that flow from such consents: termination of parental rights, the permanent separation of parent from child, and the ultimate adoption of the child.

The provision in the surrogacy contract, agreed to before conception, requiring the natural mother to surrender custody of the child without any right of revocation is one more indication of the essential nature of this transaction: the creation of a contractual system of termination and adoption designed to circumvent our statutes.

B. Public Policy Considerations

The contract's basic premise, that the natural parents can decide in advance of birth which one is to have custody of the child, bears no relationship to the settled law that the child's best interests shall determine custody.

The surrogacy contract guarantees permanent separation of the child from one of its natural parents. Our policy, however, has long been that to the extent possible, children should remain with and be brought up by both of their natural parents. The impact of failure to follow that policy is nowhere better shown than in the results of this surrogacy contract. A child, instead of starting off its life with as much peace and security as possible, finds itself immediately in a tug-of-war between contending mother and father. And the impact on the natural parents, Mr. Stern and Mrs. Whitehead, is severe and dramatic.

The depth of their conflict about Baby M, about custody, visitation, about the goodness or badness of each of them, comes through in their telephone conversations, in which each tried to persuade the other to give up the child. The potential adverse consequences of surrogacy are poignantly captured here—Mrs. Whitehead threatening to kill herself and the baby, Mr. Stern begging her not to, each blaming the other. The dashed hopes of the Sterns, the agony of Mrs. Whitehead, their suffering, their hatred—all were caused by the unraveling of this arrangement.

The surrogacy contract violates the policy of this State that the rights of natural parents are equal concerning their child, the father's right no greater than the mother's. The whole purpose and effect of the surrogacy contract was to give the father the exclusive right to the child by destroying the rights of the mother.

Here there is no counseling, independent or otherwise, of the natural mother, no evaluation, no warning. Under the contract, the natural mother is irrevocably committed before she knows the strength of her bond with her child. She never makes a totally voluntary, informed decision, for quite clearly any decision prior to the baby's birth is, in the most important sense, uninformed, and any decision after that, compelled by a pre-existing contractual commitment, the threat of a lawsuit, and the inducement of a $10,000 payment, is less than totally voluntary. Her interests are of little concern to those who controlled this transaction.

Worst of all, however, is the contract's total disregard of the best interests of the child. There is not the slightest suggestion that any inquiry will be made at any time to determine the fitness of the Sterns as custodial parents, of Mrs. Stern as an adoptive parent, their superiority to Mrs. Whitehead, or the effect on the child of not living with her natural mother. This is the sale of a child, or, at the very least, the sale of a mother's right to her child, the only mitigating factor being that one of the purchasers is the father. Almost every evil that prompted the prohibition on the payment of money in connection with adoptions exists here.

The differences between an adoption and a surrogacy contract should be noted, since it is asserted that the use of money in connection with surrogacy does not pose the risks found where money buys an adoption.

First, and perhaps most important, all parties concede that it is unlikely that surrogacy will survive without money. Despite the alleged selfless motivation of surrogate mothers, if there is no payment, there will be no surrogates, or very few. That conclusion contrasts with adoption; for obvious reasons, there remains a steady supply, albeit insufficient, despite the prohibitions against payment. The adoption itself, relieving the natural mother of the financial burden of supporting an infant, is in some sense the equivalent of payment.

Second, the use of money in adoptions does not produce the problem—conception occurs, and usually the birth itself, before illicit funds are offered. With surrogacy, the "problem," if one views it as such, consisting of the purchase of a woman's procreative capacity, at the risk of her life, is caused by and originates with the offer of money.

Third, with the law prohibiting the use of money in connection with adoptions, the built-in financial pressure of the unwanted pregnancy and the consequent support obligation do not lead the mother to the highest paying, ill-suited, adoptive parents. She is just as well-off surrendering the child to an approved agency. In surrogacy, the highest bidders will presumably become the adoptive parents regardless of suitability, so long as payment of money is permitted.

Fourth, the mother's consent to surrender her child in adoptions is revocable, even after surrender of the child, unless it be to an approved agency, where by regulation there are protections against an ill-advised surrender. In surrogacy, consent occurs so early that no amount of advice would satisfy the potential mother's need, yet the consent is irrevocable.

In the scheme contemplated by the surrogacy contract in this case, a middle man, propelled by profit, promotes the sale. Whatever idealism may have motivated any of the participants, the profit motive predominates, permeates, and ultimately governs the transaction. The demand for children is great and the supply small. The availability of contraception, abortion, and the greater willingness of single mothers to bring up their children has led to a shortage of babies offered for adoption.

The point is made that Mrs. Whitehead agreed to the surrogacy arrangement, supposedly fully understanding the consequences. Putting aside the issue of how compelling her need for money may have been, and how significant her understanding of the consequences, we suggest that her consent is irrelevant.

There are, in a civilized society, some things that money cannot buy. In America, we decided long ago that merely because conduct purchased by money was "voluntary" did not mean that it was good or beyond regulation and prohibition.

The long-term effects of surrogacy contracts are not known, but feared—the impact on the child who learns her life was bought, that she is the offspring of someone who gave birth to her only to obtain money; the impact on the natural mother as the full weight of her isolation is felt along with the full reality of the sale of her body and her child; the impact on the natural father and adoptive mother once they realize the consequences of their conduct. Literature in related areas suggests these are substantial considerations, although, given the newness of surrogacy, there is little information.

The surrogacy contract is based on principles that are directly contrary to the objectives of our laws. It guarantees the separation of a child from its mother; it looks to adoption regardless of suitability; it totally ignores the child; it takes the child from the mother regardless of her wishes and her maternal fitness; and it does all of this, it accomplishes all of its goals, through the use of money.

A sperm donor simply cannot be equated with a surrogate mother. The State has more than a sufficient basis to distinguish the two situations—even if the only difference is between the time it takes to provide sperm for artificial insemination and the time invested in a nine-month pregnancy—so as to justify automatically divesting the sperm donor of his parental rights without automatically divesting a surrogate mother.

This case affords some insight into a new reproductive arrangement: the artificial insemination of a surrogate mother. The unfortunate events that have unfolded illustrate that its unregulated use can bring suffering to all involved. Potential victims include the surrogate mother and her family, the natural father and his wife, and most importantly, the child. Although surrogacy has apparently provided positive results for some infertile couples, it can also, as this case demonstrates, cause suffering to participants, here essentially innocent and well-intended.

BIBLIOGRAPHY

Cases

Baby M, In the Matter of Baby M, 109 N.J. 396, 537 A.2d 1227 (1988).
Davis v. Davis. (Tenn. C. App. 1990) WL 130807. 1990.
Davis v. Davis. (Tenn. S. Ct. 1992) Tenn. LEXIS 400. 1992.
Lehr v. Robertson. 463 U.S. 248 (1982).
Michael H. and Victoria D., Appellants v. Gerald D. 491 U.S. 110 (1989).
Rivera v. Minnich. 506 A2d 879 (1986).
Sarosi v. Sobol. 155 A2d 125 (1990).
Stevensons's Heirs v. Sullivant. 18 U.S. 207 (1820).

Surrogacy

Annas GJ: Baby M: Babies (and justice) for sale. Hastings Cent Rep 1987 Jun; 17(3):13–15.
Annas GJ: Death without dignity for commercial surrogacy: The case of Baby M. Hastings Cent Rep 1988 Apr–May; 18(2):21–24.
Annas GJ: Fairy tales surrogate mothers tell. Law Med Health Care 1988 Spring–Summer; 16(1–2):27–33.
Annas GJ: Surrogate embryo transfer: The perils of patenting. Hastings Cent Rep 1984 Jun; 14(3):25–26.
Bezanson RP: Solomon would weep: A comment on In the Matter of Baby M and the limits of judicial authority. Law Med Health Care 1988 Spring–Summer; 16(1–2):126–30.
Brody EB: Reproduction without sex—but with the doctor. Law Med Health Care 1987 Fall; 15(3):152–55.
Cahill LS: The ethics of surrogate motherhood: Biology, freedom, and moral obligation. Law Med Health Care 1988 Spring–Summer; 16(1–2):65–71.
Chalmers DR: No primrose path. Surrogacy and the role of the criminal law. Med Law 1989; 7(6):595–606.
Charo RA: Legislative approaches to surrogate motherhood. Law Med Health Care 1988 Spring–Summer; 16(1–2):96–112.
Gersz SR: The contract in surrogate motherhood: A review of the issues. Law Med Health Care 1984 Jun; 12(3):107–14.
Hirsh HL: Surrogate motherhood: The legal climate for the physician. Med Law 1986; 5(2):151–67.

Holder AR: Surrogate motherhood and the best interests of children. Law Med Health Care 1988 Spring–Summer; 16(1–2):51–56.

Holder AR: Surrogate motherhood: Babies for fun and profit. Law Med Health Care 1984 Jun; 12(3):115–17.

Krimmel HT: The case against surrogate parenting. Hastings Cent Rep 1983 Oct; 13(5):35–39.

Lupton ML: The right to be born: Surrogacy and the legal control of human fertility. Med Law 1989; 7(5):483–503.

Macklin R: Is there anything wrong with surrogate motherhood? An ethical analysis. Law Med Health Care 1988 Spring–Summer; 16(1–2):57–64.

Perry C: Surrogate contracts. Contractual and constitutional conundrums in the Baby "M" case. J Leg Med (Chic) 1988 Mar; 9(1):105–22.

Rothenberg KH: Baby M, the surrogacy contract, and the health care professional: Unanswered questions. Law Med Health Care 1988 Spring–Summer; 16(1–2):113–20.

Smith GP II: The case of Baby M: Love's labor lost. Law Med Health Care 1988 Spring–Summer; 16(1–2):121–25.

Steinbock B: Surrogate motherhood as prenatal adoption. Law Med Health Care 1988 Spring–Summer; 16(1–2):44–50.

Taub N: Surrogacy: A preferred treatment for infertility? Law Med Health Care 1988 Spring–Summer; 16(1–2):89–95.

Adoption

Andersen RS: Why adoptees search: Motives and more. Child Welfare 1988 Jan–Feb; 67(1):15–19.

Brodzinsky DM; Singer LM; Braff AM: Children's understanding of adoption. Child Dev 1984 Jun; 55(3):869–78.

Curtis PA: The dialectics of open versus closed adoption of infants. Child Welfare 1986 Sep–Oct; 65(5):437–45.

Demick J; Wapner S: Open and closed adoption: A developmental conceptualization. Fam Process 1988 Jun; 27(2):229–49.

Deykin EY; Patti P; Ryan J: Fathers of adopted children: A study of the impact of child surrender on birthfathers. Am J Orthopsychiatry 1988 Apr; 58(2):240–48.

Freedman B; Taylor PJ; Wonnacott T; Brown S: Non-medical selection criteria for artificial insemination and adoption. Clin Reprod Fertil 1987 Feb–Apr; 5(1–2):55–66.

Friede A; Harris JR; Kobayashi JM; Shaw FE Jr; Shoemaker-Nawas PC; Kane MA: Transmission of hepatitis B virus from adopted Asian children to their American families. Am J Public Health 1988 Jan; 78(1):26–29.

Garfinkel FL; Goldsmith LS: Child welfare agencies: Possible bases of liability for placement of children with AIDS in adoptive or foster homes. J Leg Med 1989 Mar; 10(1):143–54.

Goldsmith MF: Forgotten (almost) but not gone, tuberculosis suddenly looms large on domestic scene. JAMA 1990; 264:165.

Gradstein BD; Gradstein M; Glass RH: Private adoption. Fertil Steril 1982 Apr; 37(4):548–51.

Hostetter MK; Iverson S; Dole K; Johnson D: Unsuspected infectious diseases and other medical diagnoses in the evaluation of internationally adopted children. Pediatrics 1989 Apr; 83(4):559–64.

Jenista JA; Chapman D: Medical problems of foreign-born adopted children. Am J Dis Child 1987 Mar; 141(3):298–302.

Kaunitz AM; Grimes DA; Kaunitz KK: A physician's guide to adoption. JAMA 1987 Dec 25; 258(24):3537–41.

Lange WR; Warnock-Eckhart E: Selected infectious disease risks in international adoptees. Pediatr Infect Dis J 1987 May; 6(5):447–50.

Lee RE; Hull RK: Legal, casework, and ethical issues in "risk adoption." Child Welfare 1983 Sep–Oct; 62(5):450–54.

Melina CM; Melina L: The physician's responsibility in adoption, Part II: Caring for the adoptive family. J Am Board Fam Pract 1988 Apr–Jun; 1(2):101–5.

Melina CM; Melina L: The family physician and adoption. Am Fam Physician 1985 Feb; 31(2):109–18.

Melina CM; Melina L: The physician's responsibility in adoption, Part I: Caring for the birthmother. J Am Board Fam Pract 1988 Jan–Mar; 1(1):50–54.

25

Contraception, Sterilization, and Abortion

CRITICAL POINTS
- Physicians must not let their personal beliefs about abortion deny their patients necessary medical information.
- The risk of HIV infection must be considered when recommending nonbarrier contraceptives.
- Minor and mentally impaired patients must not be sterilized without a court order.
- Physicians must protect their patients' rights while complying with state and federal laws on abortion and sterilization.

Decision making involving contraception, sterilization, and abortion has been the key nexus between medical practice and the law. The modern notions of patient autonomy and privacy arose from U.S. Supreme Court decisions on access to contraceptives and abortion. Most precedent-setting litigation on the physician-patient relationship has arisen in the context of contraception first, and then abortion, because these are areas with no general political consensus on the proper reach of the law. Even the *Cruzan* right-to-die decision (see Chapter 13) was based on a law passed as part of an antiabortion legislative package. In several states, a majority of the population believes that abortion should be illegal in all but the most extreme cases. In many states, a majority of the population believes that a minor should not be allowed to have an abortion without notifying her parents. While access to contraception has not been as emotionally charged an issue as abortion, a substantial percentage of the population would limit a minor's access to contraceptives unless she had parental permission.

Abortion promises to remain controversial. The U.S. Supreme Court is allowing the states more latitude to regulate abortions. This is resulting in the passage of very restrictive antiabortion laws in some states at the same time that others are considering allowing the use of new abortifacients such as RU-486.

While there has not been a corresponding turmoil in the laws governing access to contraceptives, products liability litigation has limited the availability of some contraceptive options. More fundamentally, HIV infection is changing the assumptions on which traditional contraception counseling is based. For some populations, the risk of HIV infections is sufficiently high as to make the use of nonbarrier contraceptives questionable at best. This will add to the already substantial risk of medical malpractice litigation surrounding contraception and sterilization. Properly managing the legal risks and ethical dilemmas of reproductive medicine requires physicians to understand the legal and emotional issues that this care engenders.

ETHICAL DILEMMAS IN REPRODUCTIVE CARE

Few other areas of medicine are as fraught with ethical and legal hazards as is reproductive care. Some physicians see abortion and contraception as sins; some find it immoral that women who are not able to support their existing children are not prevented from having more children; most consider it unethical to deny women medical control over their own bodies. Charting a legally and ethically defensible path through this minefield is difficult. The fundamental principle that must underlie all medical care is that of honesty:

> The principle of autonomy requires that a patient be given complete and truthful information about her medical condition and any proposed treatment. Only with such information is she able to exercise her right to make choices about health care. If complete information is not available, existing uncertainty should be shared with the patient. It is inappropriate for a physician to assume that he or she is better able to assess what the patient would want to know than is the patient herself. In general, a patient benefits from a full understanding of her medical condition, its prognosis, and the treatment available. The perception that a physician has concealed the truth or has engaged in deception will weaken the patient trust and undermine the physician-patient relationship. Thus the norm of honesty can be based on the principle of beneficence as well as on the principle of autonomy. (ACOG 136)

Honest and ethical reproductive care should ensure (1) that patients are given full information about any restrictions on reproductive care provided by the physician; (2) that physicians counsel patients about alternative care even if they do not provide the care; (3) that physicians are not bound to provide elective care that is abhorrent to their religious beliefs; (4) that physicians balance the medical necessity of sexual history taking with the patient's concern for privacy; and (5) that physicians do not compromise a patient's health by refusing to provide needed care in an emergency, even if the physician could refuse to provide the same services on an elective basis.

Balancing the Physician's and the Patient's Rights

The tension between a physician's right to refuse to participate in certain types of medical care and a patient's right to receive care begins in medical school and residency training. The constitutional right to exercise one's religion freely has always been limited by the state's right to pass laws that apply equally to all citizens. (This was most recently reaffirmed in the decision by the U.S. Supreme Court that a state could prohibit members of the Native American church from using peyote.) While the state has the right to specify the required training and knowledge of persons it licenses to practice medicine, this is usually left to the discretion of accreditation agencies for medical training programs. These agencies determine the extent to which a medical student or resident may avoid certain procedures and still be allowed to be certified.

Medical training programs must meet the requirements of their accrediting organizations if their students and residents are to be eligible for licensing or advanced certification after completing their training. The federal courts have recently upheld the right of the Accreditation Council for Graduate Medical Education (ACGME) to require residents in an ACGME-accredited program to receive training in abortion, sterilization, and contraception. The case in question arose when the ACGME rescinded the accreditation of a residency based in a Catholic hospital. Many Catholic hospitals prohibit residents from performing these procedures in the hospital itself. This program was unusual in forbidding the residents to perform the procedures in other hospitals, thus ensuring that the residents did not learn techniques for abortion and sterilization or have training to provide information on contraception. The court found that the training requirement was not religiously motivated. Since the requirement did not advocate a religious doctrine and was nondiscrimatorily applied, it did not violate the First Amendment protections on free exercise of religion (*St. Agnes Hospital v. Riddick*, 1990).

Once they are in independent practice, physicians must make any self-imposed limitations on the care they offer clear to their patients as early in the encounter as feasible. Ideally, patients will be asked what care they are seeking when making their initial appointment. If the patient is seeking care that the physician is unwilling to provide, the patient can be directed elsewhere at once. Under no circumstances should physicians withhold their beliefs in an attempt to persuade the patient to change her mind. Implicitly or explicitly holding out the availability of services that are not in fact available is deception.

Putting the patient on notice of the physician's refusal to provide certain types of care does not obviate the physician's duty to inform the patient when this care is appropriate. For example, if the physician discovers that the patient has a medical condition that would make pregnancy difficult, the physician must counsel the patient on the availability of contraception and sterilization. The requirement that a physician refer a patient to an alternative source of care is the same whether the physician is unable to provide the care or the physician has personal objections to the care. A physician may not abandon a patient on religious grounds. The physician-patient relationship carries with it a duty to continue care until an alternative is provided.

Contractual Limitations on Refusing to Provide Care

Most physicians today have signed contracts obligating themselves to care for various patients who are insured with the contracting third-party payer. It is unusual for these contracts to exempt the physician from providing care that is morally abhorrent him or her. Without such a specific exemption, it is arguable that the physician is contractually obligated to provide all medically acceptable care that the patient requests.

Physicians who work in emergency rooms or in locum tenans situations are also subject to a contractual obligation to provide all care that is not specifically exempted from the contract. Even if the physician has a contract that allows certain care to be avoided, a patient seeking care at the emergency room has the expectation that any appropriate care will be available. If there is a threat of immediate danger to the patient or there has been no provision for an alternative source of care for patients in an ambulatory care practice, the physician will have to provide the necessary care without regard for his or her personal beliefs. Even religious hospitals are constrained in the care that they can deny to emergency patients if the denial of care would result in preventable injury. A patient who presented in shock from an incomplete abortion should have an immediate uterine evacuation. It is an unacceptable standard of care to wait to see if the fetal heart had ceased to beat.

Consent for Reproductive Care

A mentally competent adult woman has the sole authority to consent to her medical care in all but very limited circumstances. A woman's husband has the right to veto care that will result in the conception of a child without his explicit or implied consent. This is limited to vetoing artificial insemination or embryo transplants. A husband has no veto or right to be be informed of his wife's decisions on contraception, sterilization, or abortion. The state may also determine what care can be obtained or refused under its power to protect either the public health and safety or the best interests of an individual. Unless the state or federal government has passed a law governing consent or access to the care in question, the decision rests with the woman and her physician.

Physicians should encourage women to discuss reproductive choices with their husbands or significant others, but it is improper to require the husband's consent. No court has allowed a husband to recover from a physician on the theory that the husband had a right to be consulted about his wife's medical care. Physicians who obtain a husband's consent rather than the wife's (unless the husband is the legal guardian or has been delegated the right to consent in a durable power of attorney) can be liable for battery to the wife. A more subtle risk arises when the husband and wife are estranged or legally separated. In these cases, the wife's expectation of privacy is great, and a physician who consults her husband without her permission can be sued for breaching the confidential relationship. This becomes a serious medical risk if necessary care is denied or delayed because of a husband's wishes or because of a delay in finding the husband.

Physicians should be very careful about interfering in marital relationships and about giving out patient information to spouses. If a patient does not want a spouse or family member to be informed about medical care, this wish must be honored. In one case, a woman who did not want more children was taking oral contraceptives without her husband's knowledge. When the husband asked the family doctor why the couple had not conceived, the doctor told the husband about the pills. The husband went home and severely beat his wife. In this case, the physician could be held liable for the beating because it was a foreseeable consequence of the physician's improper disclosure of private medical information.

TAKING A SEXUAL HISTORY

All reproductive care begins with a sexual history. Traditionally physicians avoided discussing sexual practices with their patients, due partly to mutual embarrassment and, more recently, a fear of seeming judgmental. This reticence has contributed to the epidemic spread of sexually transmitted diseases, including HIV. It has also encouraged the perpetuation of the stereotyping of patients, especially women, by the physician's assumptions about their sexual behavior. Sexually active females were denied information because it was assumed they knew everything; those who were not were assumed not to need the information. Patients were sometimes injured by physicians who missed diagnosing sexually transmitted diseases because they assumed the patient was not sexually active.

Physicians can ignore patient sexuality no longer. They must ask patients about high-risk behavior and counsel them in the risks of such behavior:

> Counseling and testing are recommended in any medical setting in which women at risk are encountered, including private practices and clinics offering services for gynecologic and prenatal care, family planning, and diagnosis and treatment of sexually transmitted diseases. Voluntary and confidential HIV antibody testing, with appropriate counseling and consent, should be offered to all women and encouraged for those who are at risk for acquiring the disease.
>
> - The risk factors for acquiring HIV infection apply to a woman or to her sexual partner and include the following:
>   - Illicit drug abuse (especially intravenous drug use)
>   - Current or previous multiple sexual partners or prostitution
>   - Transfusion of blood or blood products before adequate screening began in the United States (between 1978–1985)
>   - Bisexual activity
>   - Origin in countries where the incidence of HIV is high
>   - Symptoms of HIV-related illnesses
>   - History of or current sexually transmitted diseases
>
> In addition, testing is recommended in the presence of tuberculosis or any illness for which a positive test result might affect the recommended diagnostic evaluation, treatment, or follow up. (ACOG 169)

This sexual history must be documented as carefully as any other part of the medical history. The physician should ask every patient the same basic questions. Even if a woman is self-identified as homosexual, she should be counseled to ensure that she understands the options for contraception and reproductive health. These matters may not be of immediate concern to her, yet many male and female homosexuals do enter into heterosexual relationships to conceive children or as a variant on their usual sexual activity. It is also important to ask self-identifed heterosexuals about homosexual activity. This is especially important for prisoners who may engage in homosexual activities in prison but self-identify as heterosexuals and have only heterosexual relationships outside prison.

The physician's duty to ask about a patient's sexual activity must be balanced against the patient's right of privacy. If a patient denies sexual activity and there is no objective evidence to the contrary, the physician should treat this information like any other patient-reported information. As with other changeable behavior, however, the physician has a duty to reexplore the area on future visits. Given the general unreliability of self-reported information about behavior that the patient may wish to conceal, the physician should continue to consider pregnancy and venereal diseases when indicated by the patient's objective medical condition. This is especially important if the physician is considering prescribing a drug that is a known teratogen.

CONTRACEPTION

The contraceptive options for women in the United States have been unnecessarily limited by inappropriate litigation and pseudoscientific fear mongering by groups that believe contraception should be risk free. The benefit-to-risk ratio for oral contraceptives is among the highest for any other pharmaceutical (ACOG 106). Even IUDs, which pose substantially greater risks than oral contraceptives, pose very low absolute risks (ACOG 104).

Contraception is medical therapy that is usually prescribed for healthy persons. As with childhood immunizations, the general populace have forgotten the risks of the alternative—be it unwanted pregnancy or pertussis. The very success of the drugs has contributed to the expectation that they should be risk free—not merely extremely safe.

The choice of a contraceptive is determined by physiological, behavioral, and psychological factors. Given that most women are physiologically able to tolerate oral contraceptives, IUDs, and barrier forms of contraception, behavioral and psychological factors have been most important. Until recently, these tended toward oral contraceptives. Women outside long-term relationships usually preferred the privacy and flexibility of IUDs or oral contraceptives. Because of the real and perceived risks of IUDs, the majority of these women choose oral contraceptives.

The standard of care for informed consent for oral contraceptives is set by contraceptive manufacturers, public health officials, and federal and state law. The standard for informed consent for IUDs is set by standard consent forms supplied by the IUD manufacturers.

The physician should inform a patient of risks and alternatives whether the contraceptives being used are prescription, over-the-counter, or so-called natural methods. It is important to consider the patient's life-style and health behavior in tailoring informed consent to the patient. A patient who smokes is a poor candidate for birth control pills. However, if the patient has religious objections to abortion and intrauterine devices because she believes they are abortive, then pills may be the only acceptable alternative. The physician should explain the risks carefully and encourage the patient to stop smoking as an alternative method of reducing the risks.

Balancing the Risk of Pregnancy

Except for the growing threat of HIV infection, the risks posed by pregnancy are the most important consideration in choosing a method of contraception. For the patient with a disease condition that makes pregnancy dangerous, effectiveness may be the most important consideration. The patient with heart disease should realize that a barrier method that is only 70 percent effective is probably not adequate to her needs. For the patient who could not accept induced abortion in any form, the safety of the fetus in the event of conception may be paramount. It would be unwise to insert an IUD in a patient who would not allow its removal if she became pregnant with the device in place. The physician might be liable for an injury to the patient even if she refused to follow his advice when the pregnancy occurred.

Legally Mandated Warnings for Oral Contraceptives

Oral contraceptives are unusual in that Congress mandates that each patient receive a package insert with the pills to supplement the information provided by physicians when obtaining informed consent to the use of these pills. Physicians cannot rely on the patient's reading this package insert. Effective informed consent requires that the patient receive the information—not merely that the information be available. Since the patient will not receive the package insert until after the decision to take the pills has occurred, it is arguable that even a patient who has read the insert has already committed to the treatment.

Congress established a warning requirement for these pills because it believed that "the safe and effective use of oral contraceptive drug products requires that patients be fully informed of the benefits and the risks involved in their use." While this law is aimed at persons dispensing and manufacturing oral contraceptives, it provides a useful benchmark for physicians counseling patients. The federal law requires patients to be given the following information with a prescription for oral contraceptives:

> The name of the drug.
> A summary including a statement concerning the effectiveness of oral contraceptives in preventing pregnancy, the contraindications to the drug's use, and a statement of the risks and benefits associated with the drug's use.
> A statement comparing the effectiveness of oral contraceptives to other methods of contraception.
> A boxed warning concerning the increased risks associated with cigarette smoking and oral contraceptive use.
> A discussion of the contraindications to use, including information that the patient should provide to the prescriber before taking the drug.
> A statement of medical conditions that are not contraindications to use but deserve special consideration in connection with oral contraceptive use and about which the patient should inform the prescriber.
> A warning regarding the most serious side effects of oral contraceptives.
> A statement of other serious adverse reactions and potential safety hazards that may result from the use of oral contraceptives.
> A statement concerning common but less serious side effects which may help the patient evaluate the benefits and risks from the use of oral contraceptives.
> Information on precautions the patients should observe while taking oral contraceptives, including the following:
> A statement of risks to the mother and unborn child from the use of oral contraceptives before or during early pregnancy;
> A statement concerning excretion of the drug in human milk and associated risks to the nursing infant;
> A statement about laboratory tests that may be affected by oral contraceptives; and
> A statement that identifies activities and drugs, foods, or other substances the patient should avoid because of their interactions with oral contraceptives.
> Information about how to take oral contraceptives properly, including information about what to do if the patient forgets to take the product, information about becoming pregnant after discontinuing use of the drug, a statement that the drug product has been prescribed for the use of the patient and should not be used for other conditions or given to others, and a statement that the patient's pharmacist or practitioner has a more technical leaflet about the drug product that the patient may ask to review.
> A statement of the possible benefits associated with oral contraceptive use. (21 CFR, sec. 310.501)

Physicians should obtain the mandated package insert for each oral contraceptive that they prescribe and discuss the relevant insert with the patient as part of the informed consent for taking oral contraceptives. This is best done with a detailed consent form that follows the package insert for the oral contraceptives being prescribed. The physician should give the patient a copy of the insert irrespective of where she will obtain the pills. If the physician also gives the patient a starter pack or otherwise dispenses oral contraceptives, the law requires that the patient be given a package insert with the pills: "Each dispenser of an oral contraceptive drug product shall provide a patient package insert to each patient (or to an agent of the patient) to whom the product is dispensed, except that the dispenser may provide the insert to the parent or legal guardian of a legally incompetent patient (or to the agent of either)."

IUDs

The adverse litigation climate created by the Dalkon shield threatened to drive all IUDs off the market in the United States. While IUDs are widely used worldwide, in the United States they are generally reserved for women for whom oral contraceptives are physiologically or behaviorally contraindicated. Once the IUD is placed and risk of uterine perforation is passed, the risks of the IUD are related to venereal diseases and other pelvic infections. IUDs are a poor choice of contraceptive for patients who do not have a long-term mutually monogamous relationship. There are several forms of epidemic venereal disease that can render a woman sterile or damage a fetus that are made worse by the presence of an IUD and may be prevented by the use of barriers or spermicides. Since a history of high-risk sexual activity or venereal disease is the best indicator of future risk, a complete sexual history is a necessary starting point for the decision whether to prescribe an IUD.

IUDs are not 100 percent effective. Generally they fail through expulsion from the uterus, but sometimes they are retained during the pregnancy. If they are removed during a pregnancy, there is a potential that the fetus will be miscarried. If they are left in place, they substantially increase the chance of serious infection during the term of the pregnancy. These risks must be explained before insertion. Unlike oral contraceptives or barrier contraceptives, IUDs provide no protection against ectopic pregnancy. This becomes a particular concern if the women is in a high-risk group for ectopic pregnancies.

IUDs should be inspected at one month postinsertion and annually thereafter until replacement (ACOG 104). Since the progesterone-impregnated IUDs must be replaced yearly, they will necessitate two patient encounters each year. At the first sign of infection, the patient must return for prompt treatment and potential removal of the IUD. These considerations make an IUD unsuitable for patients who are unlikely to return for periodic medical care.

As with other high-maintenance implantables, physicians have a duty to keep track of patients with IUDs. The patient should be given written information about the importance of follow-up care and the symptoms that should prompt an immediate call to the physician. The physician should contact the patient for the one-month postinsertion visit and for the yearly checkup or replacement visit. If the patient cannot be contacted, the physician should send a certified letter to the patient's last known address and document that it was either received or returned.

Implantable Contraceptives

The FDA has recently approved levonorgestrel implants (Norplant, Wyeth-Ayerst Laboratories, Philadelphia, Pennsylvania) as a long-term, reversible contraceptive system (Nightingale 1991). According to the manufacturer's promotional information, the product is highly effective with few side effects. Initially it is contraindicated in most physiologic conditions that are contraindications for oral contraceptives. It must be implanted by a physician or nurse who has received special training by the manufacturer.

The product comes with a detailed consent form that should be adequate for most situations. Since this is a new product without an established history of use in the United States, we advise physicians to be scrupulous about using a detailed consent form with this product. In addition, physicians should use the same tracking system for patients with implantable contraceptives as for patients with IUDs. These patients should be seen at least once a year for evaluation of potential side effects and must be seen at the end of five years to remove or replace the implants. While implantable contraceptives do not facilitate pelvic infections as do IUDs, they do nothing to prevent the spread of sexually transmitted diseases (STDs), including HIV. Physicians should be careful to counter the idea that using an implantable contraceptive means not having to think about contraception for five years.

Natural Family Planning

The rhythm method has been expanded to include several methods of determining the time of ovulation. While most physicians do not recognize rhythm as a medical matter, it is a form of contraception their patients may use or ask about. There are risks to this method, and these risks should be explained to patients.

The most obvious risk is pregnancy. This is an effective method if used properly in selected patients, but it requires training and good record keeping. In addition, the woman must consider the social problems of abstinence. One study of the effectiveness of rhythm was discontinued after several study subjects were beaten by their husbands for refusing intercourse. Another risk is the use of rhythm as an adjunct to barrier methods by a patient who is not trained. Many couples will not use barriers if the woman is menstruating in the mistaken belief that conception is not possible. This last risk should be discussed with patients who choose to use barrier contraceptives because it may increase the incidence of pregnancy.

HIV Infection and AIDS

HIV is already one of the most common venereal diseases. Its low infectivity has slowed its spread, but as an incurable disease with a long asymptomatic latency, its predicted equilibrium level is very high. There is nothing unique about the problems posed by HIV as an STD. The widespread reliance on oral contraceptives and IUDs has contributed to the very high levels of other STDs such as gonorrhea and chlamydia. It is the catastrophic consequences of HIV, rather than its epidemiology, that commands our attention.

As HIV infection spreads in the United States, oral contraceptives, IUDs, and other nonbarrier contraceptives are no longer acceptable choices as the sole form of birth control for women outside long-term monogamous relationships. While the known failure rates of condoms as birth control devices makes it dishonest to speak of "safer sex," it is clear that condoms, combined with certain spermicides, appear to provide substantial protection against infection with HIV. It has already become a standard of care to counsel about the risk of HIV infection whenever contraception is discussed with a patient:

Historically, birth control and sexually transmitted disease control were closely linked. Abstinence and condoms were birth control options that also prevented the spread of sexually transmitted diseases. A changing attitude toward sex and improved contraceptive technology, however, has effectively severed the tie between birth control and control of sexually transmitted diseases. Users of intrauterine devices, birth control pills, and sterilization, though effectively protected from pregnancy, are still at risk of sexually transmitted diseases. AIDS has signaled the need to reintegrate these aspects of gynecologic care. When contraception is discussed, women should be informed about HIV transmission and how to lower the risk of sexual transmission. (ACOG 169)

Every patient must be counseled about the risks of HIV infection. Patients in long-term, monogamous relationships should be given the surgeon general's AIDS information pamphlet and be informed that the disease is spreading in the population. These persons are not at risk if their relationship is monogamous, but studies repeatedly demonstrate that a significant percentage of apparently long-term, monogamous relationships are neither. Sexually active patients who have multiple partners over a period of years or those whose partners are not exclusive are at increasing risk of contracting HIV. These patients must be counseled that methods of birth control other than condoms subject them to a substantial risk of HIV infection. The patient may choose to accept this risk, but the physician must be able to prove that the risk was assumed knowingly. The physician must carefully document that the patient was counseled about the risk of HIV infection, that HIV infection leads to AIDS in both mother and child, and that HIV is increasingly a problem for heterosexuals.

An ethical question posed by HIV and contraceptive choice is the extent to which patient choice is swayed by physician recommendations. Many patients rely on their physician to let them know what is medically dangerous. If the physician tells them to give up bacon and eggs forever because their cholesterol is elevated but the same physician continues to renew their oral contraceptive prescriptions, the implicit message is that HIV is less of a threat than a greasy breakfast. This does not mean that physicians should refuse to prescribe oral contraceptives for woman who are not in long-term monogamous relationships. It does mean that the physician must take care that warnings about HIV are not lost in the general noise of good health tips and recommendations that are given each patient. Patients who engage in high-risk sexual activity must be helped to understand the seriousness of the threat of HIV infection. This information should be reiterated whenever contraception is discussed or a prescription for oral contraceptives is refilled.

Minors' Access to Contraception
Minors are constrained in their ability to consent to medical care. Ideally the minor and his or her parent will agree on the need for contraception, and the parent will authorize the medical care. However, many parents do not want their sons and daughters to use contraceptives because they believe that this availability will encourage sexual activity. Minors may purchase nonprescription contraceptives in all states, and many states explicitly allow mature minors to consent to prescription contraceptives. Physicians also may counsel minors about contraception without parental consent.

Some states do not explicitly allow minors to consent to prescription contraceptives, but no state prohibits minors from receiving prescription contraceptives. The federal family planning legislation (Title X) encourages medical care providers to make contraceptives available to minors. While this legislation has a provision requiring the parents of minor patients to be notified after the minors receive care, the enforcement of this provision has been enjoined by the courts. Ethically, physicians have a duty to respect the privacy of minors. Legally, however, many states allow physicians to breach the physician-patient relationship and notify parents of medical care rendered to their minor children. Currently, no state requires parents to be notified when a minor is prescribed contraception. In general, physicians should respect a minor's privacy, but there are situations when it is advisable to involve her parents—for example, ancillary conditions, such as suicidal tendencies, that are detected as part of the medical encounter. The mere fact of sexual activity does not justify breaching the minor's confidence although it may be grounds for suspecting abuse or neglect if the minor is younger than 14.

Medical Issues in Contraception for Minors

Contraceptives should be prescribed only if medically indicated and desired by the minor (ACOG 145). Most physicians worry about the risks of giving minors prescription contraceptives without parental consent. Parental pressure to force contraceptives on an unwilling minor is a more subtle problem. A minor who is forced to use contraceptives by a parent or guardian cannot be said to have voluntarily assumed the risks. If this minor were to suffer a stroke or other serious side effect, the physician could be sued for failure of consent. The physician should talk to the minor alone and attempt to determine if she truly wants the contraceptive. If the minor is reluctant, the physician should refuse to prescribe a contraceptive for her.

Adolescents are at special risk for STDs:

> Adolescent contraceptive practices affect the risk of infections. Many adolescents never use a method or rely solely on the oral contraceptive. Whether or not oral contraceptives increase susceptibility to certain infections, they clearly reduce the impetus to use a barrier method or to involve males in prevention. Adolescents who decide or can be persuaded to use barrier methods seldom use them consistently and often use them incorrectly. IUD are rarely advised for adolescents and should never be considered for those at high risk for infection or for poor compliance with close follow-up. (Brookman 1990)

Physicians prescribing contraceptives should provide the minor with all the information that is usually provided to adult patients. If the contraceptives are prescribed without parental permission, then it is advised that additional information be considered and recorded in the medical record:

1. Inquiry should always be made as to the feasibility of parental consent.
2. A full case history, including preexisting sexual activity, should be obtained and maintained, and it should demonstrate that the physician has considered the "total situation" of the patient.
3. A record should be kept of the "emergency" need and a judgment by the physician that pregnancy would constitute a serious health hazard, one more serious than the possible disadvantages of the prescription.

4. The minor should be clearly aware of the problems presented and the nature and consequences of the procedures suggested, including very specific discussions of the side effects of contraceptive pills if those are to be prescribed. She should be required to sign a consent form so stating.
5. Where follow-up care is indicated, it should be insisted on. (Holder 1985)

To this list and the consent form should be added a discussion of the risks of STD infection, with particular reference to HIV.

STERILIZATION

Legally a physician is held to the same standards of informed consent for procedures affecting reproductive capacity as for any other type of procedure. Realistically a physician should be particularly careful that the patient understands the procedure and its risks and limitations. It is also important to make sure that any patient undergoing treatment that will cause sterility or reproductive problems knows and understands this fact. A woman may freely consent to a hysterectomy for fibroid tumors without understanding that this will make her unable to bear a child. The level of knowledge of reproductive physiology in the general public is not high. The physician who performs the hysterectomy may incur considerable liability for rendering this woman sterile without her informed consent.

Informed consent for sterilization requires the disclosure of the risks and failures of the procedure involved and appropriate alternatives. A physician should be very careful not to overestimate the effectiveness of a particular procedure and not to oversell the patient. Most malpractice litigation arising from sterilizations concerns the reversibility of the procedure. Traditionally, patients sued physicians when the procedure spontaneously reversed, resulting in an unwanted pregnancy. These complaints are now joined by lawsuits alleging that the physician indicated that the sterilization could be reversed, but the reversal has been unsuccessful. Both of these claims arising from reversibility can be prevented by obtaining proper consent for the sterilization.

Every patient undergoing a sterilization procedure should understand that the procedure could fail and allow conception. The patient should be told that such failures may occur immediately or years in the future. The physician must ensure that the woman is not already pregnant when the sterilization is performed (ACOG 113). The couple deciding on a procedure should also understand that it is possible to check the success of the procedure in a man but not in a woman. This may alter their decision on which procedure to choose. It is unwise to assume that any patient is in fact sterile. If there is any question of conception after a sterilization, the patient should be evaluated thoroughly. A physician who tells a vasectomy patient that he must be sterile may precipitate a messy divorce and paternity actions as well as a lawsuit for malpractice.

Patients must understand the permanency of surgical sterilization. No one should undergo a sterilization procedure with the idea that it can be easily reversed with a change of mind. A patient may keep that idea whatever the physician may say, but the physician should not encourage the patient to think of sterilization as reversible. The physician who does surgical repairs of sterilizations should make sure that the patient who is being sterilized does not assume that this physician has some special ability to do temporary sterilizations.

Determining Which Partner to Sterilize
Informed consent to a sterilization should include information on the alternatives, among them the sterilization of the other partner. Many couples are not aware that tubal ligation on a woman is major surgery requiring general anesthesia, while vasectomy on a man is minor surgery that can be done under local anesthesia. A gynecologist should offer the alternative to a woman before doing a tubal ligation. Gynecologists who do not do vasectomies should refer the couple to a physician who can provide the service they desire. The limits of a particular physician are no excuse for limiting a patient's choices.

The Childless Patient
The childless patient who requests sterilization leads to a quandary for most physicians because some of these patients may later wish they had not been sterilized. In most cases, physicians have the right to refuse to perform the surgery. But too often the only reason for the refusal is the physician's imposing his own social values on the patient. Similarly, physicians may be too quick to agree to sterilize a patient if the patient has a number of children. The patient who wants a vasectomy because his marriage is in trouble and he does not trust his wife to take prescribed oral contraceptives may regret the decision just as much in his next marriage as the bachelor who thought he would not want children.

A teaching obstetrician-gynecologist developed a system for sterilization procedures that is a useful model of how to provide these services. The patients had a full range of services available and the opportunity to make informed decisions. This physician first arranged to provide vasectomies through other members of his physician group so that he could offer couples the choice of who would be sterilized without having to refer to an outside physician. Second, he made it a policy that all patients who requested sterilization give him a written explanation of why they wanted to be sterilized. This allowed him to be sure that the patient had considered the procedure carefully.

The single man in his early twenties who wrote on the note pad, "My father has Huntington's chorea," was scheduled for surgery immediately. But the single man who simply stated that he did not like children was also scheduled. The important point was that the patient was able to state reasons for making the decision. The reasons did not affect whether the patient would be operated on unless they were medically unsound. If a patient had unfounded fears of genetic disease, these could be discussed so the patient could reevaluate the decision in the light of accurate information. Many patients decided against sterilization when they were required to consider the decision carefully.

Sterilizing Minors and Incompetents
The sterilization of legal and mental incompetents is a legally risky endeavor because of a strong societal policy against forcing or coercing individuals to be sterilized. If a physician or other person uses the threat of withdrawal of federally funded services to coerce a person into agreeing to be sterilized, he or she commits a federal crime and is subject to imprisonment. The problem is that the courts tend to assume that coercion is involved whenever a minor or incompetent is sterilized. When a sterilization is otherwise medically and ethically indicated (ACOG C.O. 63), the physician should seek a court order approving the procedure. Under no circumstances should a minor be sterilized without the approval of the appropriate court in the state where the procedure is to take place.

Federal Law Requirements

Congress has passed specific, detailed laws governing consent to sterilizations performed under federal programs. With one exception, these laws are also a useful guide to the information that must be provided to all patients considering a sterilization procedure. The exception is that the federal law requires a 30-day waiting period between signing the consent to sterilization and the actual procedure. There is a waiver provision in cases of emergency abdominal surgery and premature delivery (as long as the form was signed more than 30 days before the estimated date of delivery), but these waivers require at least a 72-hour delay.

The waiting period and other federally mandated requirements must be followed by all physicians who deliver services in "programs or projects for health services which are supported in whole or in part by Federal financial assistance, whether by grant or contract, administered by the Public Health Service." These physicians must use the statutorily approved consent form and patient information brochures mandated in the federal law. These materials are available from the U.S. Public Health Service. Following is the summary of the information that must be provided and the structure of the consent form:

Informed Consent

Informed consent does not exist unless a consent form is completed voluntarily and in accordance with all the requirements of this [law].

A person who obtains informed consent for a sterilization procedure must offer to answer any questions the individual to be sterilized may have concerning the procedure, provide a copy of the consent form, and provide orally all of the following information or advice to the individual who is to be sterilized:

> Advice that the individual is free to withhold or withdraw consent to the procedure any time before the sterilization without affecting his or her right to future care or treatment and without loss or withdrawal of any federally funded program benefits to which the individual might be otherwise entitled;
> A description of available alternative methods of family planning and birth control;
> Advice that the sterilization procedure is considered to be irreversible;
> A thorough explanation of the specific sterilization procedure to be performed;
> A full description of the discomforts and risks that may accompany or follow the performing of the procedure, including an explanation of the type and possible effects of any anesthetic to be used;
> A full description of the benefits or advantages that may be expected as a result of the sterilization; and
> Advice that the sterilization will not be performed for at least 30 days except under the circumstances specified in § 50.203(d) of this subpart.

An interpreter must be provided to assist the individual to be sterilized if he or she does not understand the language used on the consent form or the language used by the person obtaining the consent.

Suitable arrangements must be made to insure that the information specified in paragraph (a) of this section is effectively communicated to any individual to be sterilized who is blind, deaf or otherwise handicapped.

A witness chosen by the individual to be sterilized may be present when consent is obtained.

Informed consent may not be obtained while the individual to be sterilized is:

In labor or childbirth;
Seeking to obtain or obtaining an abortion; or
Under the influence of alcohol or other substances that affect the individual's state of awareness.

Any requirement of State and local law for obtaining consent, except one of spousal consent, must be followed. (42 CFR sec. 50.204)

Required Consent Form

The consent form appended to this subpart or another consent form approved by the Secretary must be used.

Required Signatures

The consent form must be signed and dated by:

The individual to be sterilized; and
The interpreter, if one is provided; and
The person who obtains the consent; and
The physician who will perform the sterilization procedure.

Required Certifications

The person obtaining the consent must certify by signing the consent form that:

Before the individual to be sterilized signed the consent form, he or she advised the individual to be sterilized that no Federal benefits may be withdrawn because of the decision not to be sterilized,
He or she explained orally the requirements for informed consent as set forth on the consent form, and
To the best of his or her knowledge and belief, the individual to be sterilized appeared mentally competent and knowingly and voluntarily consented to be sterilized.

The physician performing the sterilization must certify by signing the consent form, that:

Shortly before the performance of the sterilization, he or she advised the individual to be sterilized that no Federal benefits may be withdrawn because of the decision not to be sterilized,
He or she explained orally the requirements for informed consent as set forth on the consent form, and
To the best of his or her knowledge and belief, the individual to be sterilized appeared mentally competent and knowingly and voluntarily consented to be sterilized.

Except in the case of premature delivery or emergency abdominal surgery, the physician must further certify that at least 30 days have passed between the date of the individual's signature on the consent form and the date upon which the sterilization was performed.

If premature delivery occurs or emergency abdominal surgery is required within the 30-day period, the physician must certify that the sterilization was performed less than 30 days but not less than 72 hours after the date of the individual's signature on the consent form because of premature delivery or emergency abdominal surgery, as applicable. In the case of premature delivery, the physician must also state the expected date of delivery. In the case of emergency abdominal surgery, the physician must describe the emergency.

If an interpreter is provided, the interpreter must certify that he or she translated the information and advice presented orally, read the consent form and explained its contents and to the best of the interpreter's knowledge and belief, the individual to be sterilized understood what the interpreter told him or her. (42 CFR sec. 50.205)

ABORTION

Abortion is the most contentious issue in contemporary medical practice. It divides physician from patient and physician from physician; it submerges deep ethical problems such as the destruction of physicians duty of fidelity to their patients; and, perhaps most troubling, leads physicians to support legal positions that are destructive of the privacy of the physician-patient relationship.

Abortion also poses medical malpractice risks because the courts do not give physicians a right to veto a woman's decision to have an abortion. Even when the courts limit a woman's access to an abortion, they still leave the decision to the woman. This becomes a malpractice issue when a fetus potentially suffers from a genetic disease or congenital anomaly. If a woman is denied information about the availability of prenatal testing and abortion, the physician may be held liable for the costs of caring for the damaged infant.

The Politics of Abortion

The U.S. Supreme Court has never ruled that abortion is legal or, conversely, that it is illegal. Abortion itself is not a constitutional issue. The Supreme Court decisions that have shaped access to abortion have been based on the legal theory of privacy. The Court has been concerned with the extent to which legislatures may regulate the physician-patient relationship, not with abortion as a right independent of the physician-patient relationship. Legally, it matters little that the cases that are prosecuted concern abortion rather than orthopedic surgery. Politically, there is no strong lobby group pushing legislatures to regulate or deregulate access to orthopedic surgery. Concerned citizens do not seek injunctions to prevent strangers from having an arthroplasty.

Over the past several thousand years, the legality of abortion has changed with cultural norms. The antiabortion laws that were found to violate a woman's privacy unconstitutionally in *Roe v. Wade* were passed in the nineteenth century to protect women from the medical hazards of unsterile abortions. Abortion was legal when the Constitution was adopted but had been illegal in earlier periods. It is meaningless to argue that there is a historical justification for either banning abortion or making it universally available. Medieval societies banned abortion, but they also banned medical treatment in general. Societies that allowed abortion were frequently oppressive to women in other fundamental ways. Whatever legal course society chooses for abortion must be rooted in contemporary needs and values.

The Problem of Privacy

The recognition of personal privacy, as distinguished from privacy in one's possessions, is a relatively new legal concept. It is also a limited right. In the 1988 case of *Bowers v. Hardwick*, the U.S. Supreme Court refused to extend the right of privacy to include homosexual activity between consenting adults. The Court reiterated that privacy considerations cannot be used to shelter socially unacceptable behavior such as drug use, possession of prohibited munitions, dangerous behavior, and behavior that offends deeply held societal norms. With this language, the Court shifted the balance between individual rights and societal stability toward community values.

In the 1989 *Webster v. Reproductive Health Services* decision, the Court broadened the authority of states to regulate the availability of abortions. The Court found that there was no overriding privacy right that supersedes the states' traditional right to regulate medical practice to protect the public health and safety. While this decision was heralded by antiabortion physicians, it should give all medical practitioners pause. The extent to which the state may regulate the availability and performance of abortions is precisely the extent to which the state may regulate all other aspects of medical care delivery. A state that may condition practice in state facilities, or with state funds, on the banning of abortions could use these same powers to determine which patients physicians may treat and what treatments will be allowed. The same authority that allows states to ban the routine treatment of addicts with controlled substances would allow the state to ban facelifts or any other medical treatment.

Protecting Personal Beliefs

The states and the federal government have passed laws that allow medical care professionals, with some exceptions, to refuse to participate in abortions. These laws are strictly the result of political compromises, not constitutional rights. While most medical care providers who oppose abortion do so on religious grounds, this does not trigger the First Amendment's protection of the free exercise of religion. A law that regulated abortion or any other medical treatment on religious grounds would constitute an illegal establishment of religion.

These laws are limited in two respects. First, they apply to actions, not to patient counseling. A physician cannot appeal to a conscience law to defend a medical malpractice lawsuit based on failure to counsel a patient about the medical indications for abortion. Second, they have limited applicability in emergency situations. If a woman presents to the emergency room in extremis because of an incomplete abortion, the emergency room physician cannot hide behind a conscience law and allow the woman to die. Fortunately, almost all medical care providers treat saving a mother's life as of a higher ethical urgency than their personal religious beliefs.

Limiting Governmental Support

The most perverse aspect of abortion law in the United States is that it affects only poor women. The Supreme Court has ruled that it is not discriminatory for a governmental agency to refuse to pay for medical care that is otherwise available in the medical marketplace. Most states and the federal government will not allow the use of governmental funds to pay for abortions or abortion referral services. The restrictions on the federal Title X family planning grants are typical:

> Because Title X funds are intended only for family planning, once a client served by a Title X project is diagnosed as pregnant, she must be referred for appropriate prenatal and/or social services by furnishing a list of available providers that promote the welfare of mother and unborn child. . . . A Title X project may not use prenatal,

social service or emergency medical or other referrals as an indirect means of encouraging or promoting abortion as a method of family planning, such as by weighing the list of referrals in favor of health care providers which perform abortions, by including on the list of referral providers health care providers whose principal business is the provision of abortions, by excluding available providers who do not provide abortions, or by "steering" clients to providers who offer abortion as a method of family planning. (42 CFR sec. 59.8)

These restrictions were recently upheld by the U.S. Supreme Court, which found that the regulations did not interfere with physicians' right of free speech. Referring to its previous decisions upholding the right of the government not to fund abortions, the Court reiterated the rule that refusing to fund the exercise of a right is not the same as prohibiting that right. As with other voluntary employment situations, the Court found that the employer has the right to restrict the workplace activities:

> The same principles apply to petitioners' claim that the regulations abridge the free speech rights of the grantee's staff. Individuals who are voluntarily employed for a Title X project must perform their duties in accordance with the regulation's restrictions on abortion counseling and referral. The employees remain free, however, to pursue abortion related activities when they are not acting under the auspices of the Title X project. The regulations, which govern solely the scope of the Title X project's activities, do not in any way restrict the activities of those persons acting as private individuals. The employees' freedom of expression is limited during the time that they actually work for the project; but this limitation is a consequence of their decision to accept employment in a project, the scope of which is permissibly restricted by the funding authority. (*Rust v. Sullivan*, 1991)

The Implications of Title X Restrictions

The Court found that the regulations were limited to a prohibition on abortion as a means of birth control. It specifically found that the personnel in Title X–funded facilities were free to discuss abortion and refer patients when the abortion was medically necessary:

> On their face, the regulations cannot be read, as petitioners contend, to bar abortion referral or counseling where a woman's life is placed in imminent peril by her pregnancy, since it does not seem that such counseling could be considered a "method of family planning" under § 1008, and since provisions of the regulations themselves contemplate that a Title X project could engage in otherwise prohibited abortion-related activities in such circumstances. (*Rust v. Sullivan*, 1991)

The Court was careful to distinguish Title X regulations from a more general prohibition on abortion counseling:

> Nor is the doctor-patient relationship established by the Title X program sufficiently all-encompassing so as to justify an expectation on the part of the patient of comprehensive medical advice. The program does not provide postconception medical care, and therefore a doctor's silence with regard to abortion cannot reasonably be thought to mislead a client into thinking that the doctor does not consider abortion an appropriate option for her. The doctor is always free to make clear that advice regarding abortion is simply beyond the scope of the program.

Assuming that these restrictions are not modified by Congress, clinics providing Title X services should track this language to explain the limitations on their services. Every woman should be told specifically that abortions cannot be discussed as a birth control option and that she will have to seek that information elsewhere. While the clinic personnel cannot refer women to abortion counselors, they can make sure the women know that the Title X clinic is not a full-service facility and that advice should be sought elsewhere. Information about abortion counseling can be provided outside the clinic as long as it is not provided by clinic personnel. If the clinic is in a multipurpose building, a separate office with separate funding could be setup next to the family planning clinic to provide abortion counseling.

Consent to Abortion
In 1992 the Supreme Court affirmed that a woman of adult years and sound mind has the same exclusive right to consent to an abortion as to any other medical care (*Planned Parenthood v. Casey* 1992). Putative fathers and husbands have no right to be informed or consulted about the woman's decision to have an abortion. The rights of minors are more limited. Although the U.S. Supreme Court has not allowed states to prevent minors from having abortions, states can require minors who do not have parental consent for an abortion to seek consent from a court and to demonstrate that the abortion is in their best interest. At least one state (Utah) has passed a law forbidding most abortions for both minors and adult women. While this law is still under judicial review, it is to be expected that the Supreme Court will allow further restrictions in the availability of abortions. Physicians should keep informed on the current laws in their state of practice.

Physicians should counsel their patients about the emotional consequences of an abortion and their need for social support. If the patient can discuss the matter with friends or family, that is preferable to keeping the decision to herself. But physicians should never abuse their position of trust by coercing a patient into revealing confidential information or reversing her own decision. Physicians who are personally unprepared to counsel their patients about abortion should refer them to another physician or a counselor trained in reproductive matters.

Informing the Patient
As with contraception, physicians who do not perform abortions must fully inform all obstetrics patients of this restriction at the first patient visit, with this information documented in the patient chart. If a physician suspects that a pregnant patient may have a medical reason for terminating the pregnancy or may be carrying a defective fetus, the physician has a duty to inform the patient of the problem and the options available to her. If the patient decides to have an abortion, the physician is not obliged to perform the abortion but has a duty to refer the woman to a physician who will.

The information given to the patient should be complete and reasonably objective. A physician should never withhold information or downplay the seriousness of a problem in an attempt to guide a patient's decision. The essence of informed consent is that the patient has all the information necessary to make the decisions. A failure to inform the patient properly can create liability for the torts of wrongful life and wrongful birth.

Adoption Alternatives

A patient faced with a problem pregnancy may seek advice from her physician. If there is no medical reason for terminating the pregnancy, adoption should be discussed as an alternative to abortion. A physician should refer a patient to an approved adoption agency if the patient wants to place the child for adoption. The physician should be careful to avoid any conflict of interest in making this referral (see Chapter 24). No matter who pays the bills or arranges the care, the physician's duties are to the patient, not the agency or adoptive parents.

Time Constraints

The Supreme Court decision that upheld a woman's right of privacy in deciding on abortion limited this right to the period when the fetus is not viable. As a purely medical matter, the safety and ease of induced abortion decrease as the pregnancy progresses. This puts a time restraint on the provision of abortion services. A patient must be provided necessary information and care in a time frame that maintains her options and safety.

When physicians first see patients in the second trimester, they must make special efforts to get test results or referral appointments quickly. The physician who knows that time is short should personally ensure that the patient has access to timely care. A physician whose delay prevents the patient from aborting a damaged baby can be liable for the consequences.

The Changing Nature of Abortion

While abortion is still a surgical procedure in the United States, this will rapidly change as RU 486 and second-generation progesterone inhibitors become available. These drugs make it possible to perform 95 percent of first-trimester abortions as outpatient procedures. This is disturbing to antiabortion activists because it does away with easily targeted abortion clinics. As states begin to restrict the availability of legal abortions, the demand for RU 486 will become enormous. Since RU 486 also has value in the treatment of disorders such as progesterone-dependent cancer, it is anticipated that it will be licensed for cancer chemotherapy but not abortions. This will allow physicians to use it as an abortifacient because the use of prescription drugs is not limited to FDA-approved uses. (If drugs could be used only for FDA-approved uses, there would be very few drugs available for pregnant women.)

If the FDA refuses to license RU 486, it may become available on the black market either from supplies diverted from European clinics, or illegally manufactured in the United States. Given that an illegal abortion can cost several hundred dollars, the profit margin on a dose of RU 486 and a prostaglandin would be much higher than on cocaine. Restrictive abortion laws probably will add RU 486 and its analogues to the profitable inventory of the illicit drug industry. This will pose a dilemma for physicians who will be asked by patients to obtain RU 486 or supervise the administration of patient-acquired RU 486. While physicians should not deal with illegally obtained drugs, ethical demands to help a patient otherwise unable to obtain an abortion will be strong.

BIBLIOGRAPHY

Contraception
ACOG: Technical Bulletin 136, *Ethical Decision-Making in Obstetrics and Gynecology.* (Nov 1989).

ACOG: Technical Bulletin 169, *Human Immune Deficiency Virus Infections.* (June 1992).
ACOG: Technical Bulletin 104, *The IUD.* (May 1987).
ACOG: Technical Bulletin 106, *Oral Contraception.* (July 1987).
ACOG: Technical Bulletin 145, *The Adolescent Obstetric-Gyncologic Patient.* (Sept 1990).
ACOG: Technical Bulletin 113, *Sterilization.* (Feb 1988).
Beck JG; Davies DK: Teen contraception: A review of perspectives on compliance. Arch Sex Behav 1987 Aug; 16(4):337–68.
Brookman RR: Adolescent sexual behavior. In Holmes KK et al.: *Sexually Transmitted Diseases.* 1990.
Chamberlain A; Rauh J; Passer A; McGrath M; Burket R: Issues in fertility control for mentally retarded female adolescents: I. Sexual activity, sexual abuse, and contraception. Pediatrics 1984 Apr; 73(4):445–50.
Chng CL: The male role in contraception: Implications for health education. J Sch Health 1983 Mar; 53(3):197–201.
DuRant RH; Sanders JM Jr; Jay S; Levinson R: Analysis of contraceptive behavior of sexually active female adolescents in the United States. J Pediatr 1988 Nov; 113(5):930–36.
Forrest JD; Fordyce RR: U.S. women's contraceptive attitudes and practice: How have they changed in the 1980s? Fam Plann Perspect 1988 May–Jun; 20(3):112–18.
Goldscheider C; Mosher WD: Religious affiliation and contraceptive usage: Changing American patterns, 1955–82. Stud Fam Plann 1988 Jan–Feb; 19(1):48–57.
Goldstuck ND; Hammar E; Butchart A: Use and misuse of oral contraceptives by adolescents attending a free-standing clinic. Adv Contracept 1987 Dec; 3(4):335–39.
Hein K; Coupey SM; Cohen MI: Special considerations in pregnancy prevention for the mentally subnormal adolescent female. J Adolesc Health Care 1980 Sep; 1(1):46–49.
Holder AR: *Legal Issues in Pediatrics and Adolescent Medicine,* 2d ed. 1985.
Isaacs SL; Holt R: Drug regulation, product liability, and the contraceptive crunch. Choices are dwindling. J Leg Med (Chic) 1987 Dec; 8(4):533–53.
Jones EF; Beniger JR; Westoff CF: Pill and IUD discontinuation in the United States, 1970–1975: The influence of the media. Fam Plann Perspect 1980 Nov–Dec; 12(6):293–300.
Kulig JW: Adolescent contraception: Nonhormonal methods. Pediatr Clin North Am 1989 Jun; 36(3):717–30.
Lovett J; Wald MS: Physician attitudes toward confidential care for adolescents. J Pediatr 1985 Mar; 106(3):517–21.
Nightingale SL: From the Food and Drug Administration. JAMA 1991; 265:847.
Notelovitz M: The use of oral contraceptives past the age of 35: Bridging the gap. Int J Fertil 1988; 33 Suppl:13–20.
Orr MT: Private physicians and the provision of contraceptives to adolescents. Fam Plann Perspect 1984 Mar–Apr; 16(2):83–86.
Rust v. Sullivan. 111 S. Ct. 1759 (1991).
Tanfer K; Horn MC: Contraceptive use, pregnancy and fertility patterns among single American women in their 20s. Fam Plann Perspect 1985 Jan–Feb; 17(1):10–19.
Tanfer K; Rosenbaum E: Contraceptive perceptions and method choice among young single women in the United States. Stud Fam Plann 1986 Nov–Dec; 17 (6 Pt 1):269–77.

Sterilization

ACOG: Committee Opinion 63, *Sterilization of Women Who are Mentally Handicapped.* (Sept 1988).
Annas GJ: Sterilization of the mentally retarded: A decision for the courts. Hastings Cent Rep 1981 Aug; 11(4):18–19.
Dickens BM: Retardation and sterilization. Int J Law Psychiatry 1982; 5(3–4):295–318.
Lachance D: In re Grady: The mentally retarded individual's right to choose sterilization. Am J Law Med 1981 Winter; 6(4):559–90.
Rousso A: Sterilization of the mentally retarded. Med Law 1984; 3(4):353–62.

Shain RN; Miller WB; Holden AE: Factors associated with married women's selection of tubal sterilization and vasectomy. Fertil Steril 1985 Feb; 43(2):234–44.

Sobel RJ; Gert B: Definitive birth control and the physician—ethical issues. Isr J Med Sci 1986 Nov; 22(11):841–46.

Soskin RM: Sterilization of the mentally retarded. The rules change but the results remain the same. Med Law 1983; 2(3):267–76.

West NJ: Parens patriae: Judicial authority to order the sterilization of mental incompetents. J Leg Med (Chic) 1981 Dec; 2(4):523–42.

Abortion

Agnes Hospital v. Riddick. 748 F. Supp. 319 (1990).

Annas GJ: The impact of medical technology on the pregnant woman's right to privacy. Am J Law Med 1987; 13(2–3):213–32.

Annas GJ: Webster and the politics of abortion. Hastings Cent Rep 1989 Mar–Apr; 19(2):36–38.

Bowers v. Hardwick. 478 U.S. 186 (1986).

Cahill LS: "Abortion pill" RU 486: Ethics, rhetoric, and social practice. Hastings Cent Rep 1987 Oct–Nov; 17(5):5–8.

Callahan D: How technology is reframing the abortion debate. Hastings Cent Rep 1986 Feb; 16(1):33–42.

Henshaw SK; Silverman J: The characteristics and prior contraceptive use of U.S. abortion patients. Fam Plann Perspect 1988 Jul–Aug; 20(4):158–68.

Mahowald M; Abernethy V: When a mentally ill woman refuses abortion (editorial). Hastings Cent Rep 1985 Apr; 15(2):22–23.

Milby TH: The new biology and the question of personhood: Implications for abortion. Am J Law Med 1983 Spring; 9(1):31–41.

Planned Parenthood v. Casey. 60 U.S.L.W. 4795 (1992).

Schedler G: Women's reproductive rights. Is there a conflict with a child's right to be born free from defects? J Leg Med (Chic) 1986 Sep; 7(3):357–84.

Shore BD: Marital secrets. The emerging issue of abortion spousal notification laws. J Leg Med (Chic) 1982 Sep; 3(3):461–82.

Webster v. Reproductive Health Services. 492 U.S. 490 (1989).

Westfall D: Beyond abortion: The potential reach of a human life amendment. Am J Law Med 1982 Summer; 8(2):97–135.

26

Genetic Counseling and Fertility Treatment

CRITICAL POINTS

- Failing to counsel a patient about genetic diseases can result in substantial legal liability.
- Physicians must not let their personal views about abortion influence their counseling about genetic diseases.
- Physicians must follow state laws on regulated procedures such as artificial insemination and surrogate parenting.
- Physicians must never compromise their duty to the birth mother.

The topics of genetic counseling and the treatment of infertility are related in several ways. First, both arise from a patient's desire to have a child. Second, infertility treatments ranging from artificial insemination (AI) to in vitro fertilization and embryo transplantation are increasingly seen as alternatives for couples who are at high risk for genetic disease. Third, improper genetic counseling and negligent fertility treatment share the common risk of the birth of an injured child.

Perhaps most important, genetic counseling and fertility treatment medicalize one of the central mysteries of life. Whether it is the traditional bans on AI as adultery or fears that in vitro fertilization will result in the discarding of embryos, this area of medical practice is complicated by cultural and religious taboos. The goal of this chapter is to present the issues that every physician providing family medical care or obstetric services should consider in routine practice. Specialists in fertility practice and physicians who are involved in any way with surrogacy transactions should seek personal legal counsel on these matters.

PREVENTING BIRTH-RELATED TORTS

When a baby is born with a severe genetic disease or intrauterine injury, the parents often blame themselves for the injury. If there is any indication that the physician might have been at fault, this guilt can rapidly turn to anger and a lawsuit. These lawsuits often can be particularly acrimonious because the parents may be driven by an emotional need to shift the guilt as much as by the potential monetary recovery.

There are two potential injured parties when a defective child is born: the parents or guardian and the child. The parents' lawsuit, termed a *wrongful birth action*, will claim for the extra cost of the medical and other services required to treat their child's condition. The traditional component of this claim is for these expenses during the child's minority, or the child's lifetime, if the child will be permanently incompetent. (See Chapter 4.) The more controversial claim is for the mental anguish for having to observe the child's suffering and for the disruption in family life. The courts are suspicious of such claims, recognizing that even injured children provide an emotional benefit to most parents.

The value of the parents' claim for mental anguish will be based on the court's perception of the set-off of having the child. This set-off is greatest in the failure-of-sterilization cases. Assuming that there was no medical injury to the mother or the baby, the courts have generally found that the benefit of a healthy baby exceeds the detriment of having an unwanted child. Conversely, parents are most likely to recover when the child is badly damaged; an extreme case would be the birth, through the failure of genetic counseling, of a child with Tay-Sachs disease.

The courts have been much more hostile to lawsuits brought by injured children. If the child states a specific damage claim for an expense necessitated by the injury that is not covered by the parents' claim, then some courts will allow for this expense to be recovered. These claims are seen as related to the cases in which the child is affirmatively injured, such as the Rh sensitization cases. (See Chapter 27.) The controversy arises over what are termed *wrongful life claims*. A wrongful life claim asserts that the child would have been better off not having been born. The set-off and public policy issues are very strongly against recovery on such claims:

> Ultimately, the infant's complaint is that he would be better off not to have been born. Man, who knows nothing of death or nothingness, cannot possibly know whether that is so. We must remember that the choice is not between being born with health or being born without it; it is not claimed that the defendants failed to do something to prevent or reduce the ravages of rubella. Rather the choice is between a worldly existence and none at all.... To recognize a right not to be born is to enter an area in which no one could find his way. (*Gleitman v. Cosgrove*, 1967)

Preconception Versus Postconception Remedies

Abortion creates a critical ethical and legal distinction between pre- and postconception care. Abortion is ethically abhorrent to a substantial minority of persons in the United States. (Some antiabortion groups also oppose the use of contraception, but contraception has become so widely accepted that its use generates no moral outrage comparable to abortion.) Even persons who support a woman's right to choose to terminate an unwanted pregnancy are not necessarily proabortion but see it as a necessary evil. As a matter of public policy and individual patient welfare, it is preferable that reproductive decisions be made before conception.

In a failure of preconception counseling, the parents must prove that had they been properly informed of the risk of having an injured child, they would have chosen not to conceive the child. In contrast, when the information is sought after conception, the parents must convince the jury that they would have aborted the baby had they known of the risk. Juries are clearly more sympathetic to decisions not to conceive than to decisions to abort. As a result, they are willing to believe that a couple would choose not to conceive based on the risk of minor conditions such as congenital deafness. Conversely, it is be much more difficult to convince a jury that the same condition, discovered postconception, would justify an abortion.

Patients' Views about Abortion

A patient's personal beliefs about abortion change the risk-benefit determinations for genetic counseling and, to a lesser extent, for fertility treatment. Physicians must not assume, however, that a patient who is opposed to abortion in the abstract will not consider abortion if she is personally faced with a high probability of giving birth to a child with a severe defect. All women, even those who are opposed to abortion, should be offered all appropriate testing and counseling. This does not mean that a physician should advocate abortion. Ideally, a patient should receive the necessary information about genetic diseases and the risks of fertility treatment without reference to either her or her physician's views about abortion. The woman's personal views about abortion should shape the risks that she is willing to assume of conceiving a child with a genetic disease, the prenatal testing to which she will consent, and under which circumstances, if any, she will terminate a pregnancy.

Physicians who do not perform abortions because of personal ethical beliefs should ensure that their beliefs do not compromise their patients' right to choose an abortion. In addition to providing every patient full information, the physician should arrange an easy referral system so that a patient who chooses an abortion can obtain it without unnecessary delay or expense. Conversely, physicians who support abortion as a valid therapeutic technique must not force their views on their patients. They must be prepared to respect the wishes of a woman who, after being fully informed of the risks and benefits of pre- or postconception testing, chooses to bear her child without regard to potential genetic diseases.

Several states have recently passed laws restricting abortion. The provisions of the Utah law are representative:

> (2) An abortion may be performed in this state only under the following circumstances:
> (a) the pregnant woman's attending physician has certified that, in the physician's professional judgment, the abortion is necessary to save her life;
> (b) the pregnancy is the result of rape or rape of a child, as defined . . . that was reported by the victim to a law enforcement agency prior to the abortion;
> (c) the pregnancy is the result of incest, . . . and the incident was reported by the victim to a law enforcement agency prior to the abortion;
> (d) in the professional judgment of the pregnant woman's attending physician, to prevent grave damage to the pregnant woman's medical health; or
> (e) in the professional judgment of the pregnant woman's attending physician, to prevent the birth of a child that would be born with grave defects.
> (3) After 20 weeks gestational age, measured from the date of conception, an abortion may be performed only for those purposes and circumstances described in Subsections (2)(a), (d), and (e). (Utah 1991 Session Law Service, sec. 76-7-301 et seq.)

While it will be several years before the constitutionality of these laws is fully reviewed, it is expected that the Supreme Court will allow much greater restrictions on abortion than are currently enforced.

Some states may successfully outlaw abortions except in the most limited circumstances, but probably many will retain abortion on demand. As long as abortion remains a legal option in another state, it is arguable that physicians have a legal duty to continue to discuss abortion as an alternative. Even if a state that has outlawed abortion were also to prohibit wrongful birth and wrongful life lawsuits, physicians would continue to have an ethical duty to counsel patients about the role of abortion in managing genetic diseases and when otherwise medically indicated.

Record Keeping and Consent
Obstetric care demands special diligence in record keeping. Most of the lawsuits involving genetic counseling and fertility-related problems stem from claims concerning improper information rather that technical failures in medical procedures. The structured maternity record should incorporate entities for all of the relevant postconception recommendations for screening tests and the evaluation of their outcomes. There should also be a structured precounseling record to ensure that a proper genetic history is obtained from every woman and that she in turn receives complete information about potential problems and screening tests.

Genetic counseling should be done before conception. This is impossible for women who first seek medical care after conception but is simple for women who specifically seek preconception care. Physicians providing primary care for women with childbearing potential should discuss the importance of preconception counseling when they discuss contraception with their patients. Physicians should also consider obtaining a basic genetic disease history as part of the initial history when the woman begins her care. If this initial history demonstrates any risk factors, these can be discussed at the first patient visit. Bringing up a genetic disease history at the first visit also gives patients an opportunity to obtain information about their families' genetic history, if warranted.

It is critical to document the information given to the patient about her own specific risk factors: advanced maternal age, a history of genetic illness in her family, or an ancestor in a high-risk group for genetic illness. The physician must ensure that these risks are not lost in the boilerplate information that is provided to every patient. Patient information sheets on specific, identified risks should be differentiated from general information sheets. For example, they could have a place at the top to write in the patient's name and note that she has a special risk for the condition.

As with other medically indicated testing, it is as important to document the patient's informed refusal as to document the patient's informed consent to the test. Unless the test is hazardous, it is much more likely that a poorly documented refusal will result in litigation than will an equally poorly documented consent. The physician should periodically review the original recommendation with the patient to reinforce the importance of the test and to allow the woman to reevaluate her decision. It is not unusual for a woman's attitude toward testing for congenital disease to change as her personal situation and attitude toward pregnancy change with time.

ETHICAL QUESTIONS IN GENETIC COUNSELING

Three factors are combining to complicate the ethics and the law of genetic counseling. The first is the tightening of restrictions on abortion. Great advances have been made in postconception genetic testing, but the objective of most of these determinations is to allow the patient to make an informed choice of an abortion. The second is the publicity surrounding the human genome project. While this project only extends existing work on mapping and identifying the chromosomal basis for hereditary traits and diseases, it has gotten extensive publicity. This is partly because the federal research grant funding this project allocates several million dollars a year for legal and ethical research. This money has created an industry of conferences and articles on the potential societal problems of doing genetic research (Beckwith 1991).

The third factor is a backlash to the medicalization of pregnancy. A primary manifestation of this backlash is the willingness of women to sue their physicians if their baby is born with a defect. Many women interpret the marketing of obstetric services as a guarantee of a healthy baby, and physicians reinforce this message by implying that women who do not follow their recommendations have a greater chance of having a defective baby than women who do what their physicians recommend. This factor is complicated for genetic counseling because society is ambivalent about the proper goals of such counseling. In one author's view, there are three overlapping and conflicting models for genetic counseling: "1) as an assembly line approach to the products of conception, separating out those products we wish to develop from those we wish to discontinue; 2) as a way to give women control over their pregnancies, respecting (increasing) their autonomy to choose the kinds of children they will bear; or 3) as a means of reassuring women that enhances their experience of pregnancy" (Lippman 1991).

Conflicts over genetic counseling and obstetric care span the political spectrum. Conservative religious groups object to abortion, while some radical feminist groups decry high-technology obstetric care as a conspiracy against women. The stakes are high. Few states provide high-quality community care to reduce the burden on families with mentally handicapped children. Financial necessity requires that both parents work outside the home in most families, complicating the care of disabled children. The chance of these children's finding productive work and some level of independence becomes more problematic as American society shifts from a labor- to an information-based economy.

These factors combine to pressure women to strive for the perfect baby, while at the same time creating a sense of guilt for not treating pregnancy as a natural, nonmedical condition. This conflict can take the form of denial and the refusal of indicated testing or a hypersensitivity to risk and the aborting of fetuses with a fair probability of normal development. Physicians must be sensitive to both of these reactions, while carefully documenting the information provided and raising the issue at more than one encounter so that the woman has an opportunity to reconsider her decisions.

Duty to Counsel

All physicians who care for pregnant women or patients with genetic diseases have a duty to counsel their patients about the nature of the diseases, their probability of being passed on to children, and the diagnostic options available. A physician who does not offer genetic screening because he is opposed to abortion, or for any other reason, has a duty to refer the patient to another physician who can carry out the necessary counseling and testing. The physician has a duty to provide full information to the patient. There is no therapeutic exception to informing patients about potential risks to their children.

In some cases it may be necessary to give a patient medical information about another person. It is not possible to counsel the children of a patient with Huntington's disease without letting the children know about the parent's disease. Often the information will have been obtained with a release from the affected parent. If not, every effort should be made to protect the privacy of the other patient. Names and other identifying information should not be used, although it is probable that the patients can determine who is affected. There may also be situations in which the courts can help persons obtain necessary medical information about genetic diseases. In most states, adoption records are sealed, but the court that granted the adoption can order the records opened if there is a compelling reason for doing so.

Patient Privacy
When genetically counseling a pregnant or potentially pregnant woman, the physician should include her husband or other family members only at her request. Violating the patient's privacy can have devastating results. Legal and social paternity do not necessarily imply biologic paternity. Although it would be proper to discuss these matters with the patient, this type of information should not be disclosed to others.

If the patient is a child, the situation is somewhat different. A father and mother who are married to each other have equal authority over their children. If the legal father does not question his biologic paternity, there is usually no problem. If a father asks whether he is the child's biological father, a physician should be cautious. Both mutation and test variability can confound any genetic test of paternity. It is better to address the question of whether the child has a genetic disease than whether the disease came from the man asking the question.

Screening for Neural Tube Defects as a Model
The available tests and medical standards for detecting specific genetic diseases are changing rapidly. Rather than attempting to discuss each test and disease, this chapter identifies commonalties in counseling and testing through a discussion of a small number of diseases. Currently, maternal serum alpha-fetoprotein (MSAFP) is the only screening test for genetic diseases recommended for all women (ACOG 154). It provides a good model for genetic counseling because it is a disease with both a hereditary component and a random component that defies easy separations into risk groups. Neural tube defects are common, occurring in 1 or 2 per 1000 births among couples with no history. With one affected parent, the risk rises to 5 percent of births, rising further to 6 to 10 percent if the couple has two previous affected children. Despite this genetic link, 90 to 95 percent of the cases are in families with no previous history, prompting the recommendation that the screening test be offered to all pregnant women.

When first made, this recommendation was controversial because the test for MSAFP is quite sensitive but not very specific. There was concern that women would be frightened into aborting fetuses on the basis of the preliminary screening test. This led to specific standards of practice that stress the importance of the entire process of counseling and testing:

> The successful implementation of a screening program for MSAFP should include patient education, accurate and prompt laboratory testing, competent counseling

and support services, access to consultants for sonography, and complex prenatal diagnosis, as well as available options for pregnancy termination. Success is further dependent on the proper coordination of these components, all of which must function within a relatively short time span from screening to decision-making. Missing components or malfunctions could result in unnecessary anxiety for the patients, as well as improper diagnoses that could lead to unnecessary termination of pregnancy or other serious errors in judgment. (ACOG 154)

The coordination of the various components is critical because it is recommended that the test not be performed until 16 weeks of gestation. If the test indicates a sufficiently increased level of MSAFP, the patient should be offered a second test a week or two later, if time permits. Otherwise ultrasound should be used to correct the gestational age, check for multiple gestation, and, if possible, identify a neural tube defect. Among patients with two high MSAFP levels (or one low one) slightly over half will have a singleton fetus at the appropriate gestational age without an apparent anomaly. These patients should be offered amniocentesis. Of the patients undergoing amniocentesis, one to two will have significantly increased amniotic fluid AFP that indicates a high probability of a fetus with a serious abnormality (ACOG 154).

At this point further tests can be done to identify the specific defect, but this will be impossible in some cases. If a defect is confirmed, the patient must decide whether she wants an abortion. Many patients choose to abort the fetus. Some may be willing to accept a child with spina bifida but be unwilling to carry a fetus with anencephaly. The woman with an elevated amnionic AFP but no identifiable defect has the more difficult decision. She should be given full information and an opportunity to seek in-depth counseling before making her decision. Once the process of recommending the initial test begins, every following step must be planned carefully and executed. It is critical that the patient be carefully tracked to ensure that there are no delays that can push the abortion into the third trimester, with the attendant medical and legal complications.

MSAFP and Down Syndrome
The first widely available postconception test was for Down syndrome. This condition becomes more common with increasing age of the pregnant woman, reaching a level of 1 per 11 births at a maternal age of 48. Because testing for Down syndrome requires amniocentesis, with its attendant costs and risks, in women without specific risk factors the test is recommended only for those over 34 years of age. This is an arbitrary figure, however, because the risk rises relatively smoothly from the age of 21. As a result, approximately 80 percent of cases of Down syndrome occur in babies born to women under age 35. Once most pregnant women were being screened for MSAFP, it was found that an abnormally low level of MSAFP indicates an increased probability of Down syndrome. This information can be used to identify women under age 35 who should be offered amniocentesis for potential Down syndrome (ACOG 154).

The Genetic History
The indications for testing for MSAFP and Down syndrome depend more on epidemiologic information than patient-specific information. The proper management of other genetic diseases begins with a genetic history. Given that a

significant number of children will be born with unanticipated genetic diseases, this history should be carefully recorded and the significance of the questions explained to the patient. In a recent case, a couple sued when they gave birth to a child with Tay-Sachs disease. This couple had received genetic counseling, but no mention was made of testing for this disease because neither member of the couple met the traditional profile for persons at high risk for Tay-Sachs. After the birth of the child and the diagnosis of the disease, an exhaustive review of the parents' genealogy was done. The mother was found to be descended from a small, closed community of French Canadians who were at increased risk for Tay-Sachs.

The judge found that the physicians had asked the appropriate questions and that the plaintiffs had not given the physicians any information that would have indicated that either was at high risk for Tay-Sachs disease. The judge rejected the plaintiff's argument that they should have been offered testing for Tay-Sachs irrespective of the probability of their carrying the disease. In rejecting this claim, the judge noted that there were more than 70 tests that physicians would have had to offer to every patient to meet the plaintiff's requirements (*Munro v. Regents of the University of California*, 1989).

The American College of Obstetrics and Gynecology (ACOG) has established recommended procedures for taking genetic histories and diagnosing genetic diseases (ACOG 108). These are the starting point for all physicians providing general medical or obstetric care. The objective of this genetic history is to determine which women are at elevated risk for genetic disease. Once these women are identified, they can be referred to specialists in genetic diseases or managed by the treating physician if he or she has the necessary expertise.

Information about Specific Diseases

Physicians have an ethical duty to avoid reinforcing the belief of many women that all children with genetic disease are doomed to marginal lives. Legally, it is tempting to encourage a woman to abort. Even if she regrets the decision later, she cannot sue her physician for discussing too many risks. Women should be given enough information about the impact of the disease on an affected child to make an informed choice. The nature of the disease is important to most patients in making decisions about screening, conception, and abortion. The woman who has uncles, brothers, and sons who are healthy hemophiliacs may have no interest in prenatal diagnosis. The woman who has lost a child to Tay-Sachs disease may choose to avoid conception altogether or use donor sperm to avoid a recurrence.

An informed decision about genetic screening requires that the patient understand the treatment options available for the disease and whether they are curative or palliative. The prospect of having a child with a cleft lip that can be surgically corrected is not nearly so daunting as the prospect of a child with a biochemical defect that will result in a short life of illness and disability.

Knowing the likelihood of a particular fetus's having a genetic defect is also important for the patient's decision. A woman in her forties may find a 1 in 40 chance of Down syndrome an acceptable risk, particularly if she has amniocentesis and abortion as an option. A woman who has one child with Down syndrome and a chromosome attachment that gives her a 1 in 2 chance of conceiving another affected child may not be willing to accept the risk even if she has the same options for prenatal diagnosis.

Patient Characteristics
The personal concerns of the patient must be taken into consideration. A woman who has conceived and aborted several fetuses because of a genetic defect may decide not to try again even if her theoretical chances of bearing a healthy child are good. A defect that might seem difficult to one family may seem minor to another. There are many cases of women giving birth to child after child affected with the same genetic problem without creating family problems. There are also cases of women institutionalizing or relinquishing children with relatively minor problems because they were psychologically unprepared to cope with the child's needs. Patients receiving genetic counseling should be encouraged to consider their personal feelings about the anticipated disabilities the child could suffer.

Risks of the Diagnostic Procedures
There are risks to most of the prenatal diagnostic procedures, and these risks should be fully explained to patients considering this type of testing. The risk of the test's causing a miscarriage may be greater than the risk that the fetus is affected. This does not necessarily mean that the test should not be done. A 35-year-old woman who has finally conceived after three years of fertility treatment may feel that she would rather have a child with Down syndrome than no child at all. On the other hand, this woman may feel that it is morally reprehensible knowingly to bring a retarded child into the world. These decisions must be made by the patient. A physician who is asked for an opinion on what should be done should be sure that the patient understands what is medical opinion and what is personal belief.

Reliability of Testing
The reliability of various tests will also affect a patient's decision about genetic testing and abortion. The physician should try to give the patient a realistic understanding of what test results mean. No test is without false positives and false negatives. It is never wise to tell a patient that the amniocentesis was normal and therefore the fetus is normal. If the baby is born with a defect that was not detected on the amniocentesis, the family may have more trouble dealing with the problem and may be very angry with the physician who indicated the baby was healthy. On the other hand, a woman who appears to be carrying a defective fetus must understand that there is some possibility that there is no defect. It is difficult to tell a patient this without raising unreasonable hopes. If the decision to abort is made, patients should not be encouraged to ask for testing on the abortus unless this will provide useful medical information for future pregnancies. There is little to be gained from second-guessing an irrevocable decision.

Time Limitations
With prenatal diagnostic testing, there is a duty to schedule tests in a timely manner so that a patient is not deprived of choice by delays. If the only available abortion facility will not perform an abortion after 20 weeks, then amniocentesis cannot be scheduled for 17 weeks if the results may take 6 weeks to come back. The results must be available in time for the patient to abort a defective fetus if she chooses. A physician who refers patients out for such testing has the responsibility to ensure that the test results are available in a timely manner. There should be a system of flagging the calendar so that results that have not come

back in time are investigated. If the results are lost or the specimen destroyed, the physician must have left enough time to try again. The physician may have to work to find a laboratory that can handle a rush job or to arrange a late abortion. It is the physician's duty to do everything possible to preserve the patient's options. If a screening program routinely schedules such tests toward the end of the window of opportunity, the physicians should get this corrected or refer to another program. If the time is cut close on all the patients, eventually there will be a mistake in dates or a laboratory failure that will push a patient beyond the limit. The fact that the system endangered other patients in the same way will be a poor defense in a lawsuit.

THE TOUGH QUESTIONS

Some very tough questions arise in the process of genetic counseling or evaluation. The following is an attempt to guide physicians in answering these questions in ways that preserve the patients' rights without embroiling the physician in too many legal and social problems.

Am I the baby's father? Legally, a child's father is the mother's husband or a man who has been assigned paternity in a court proceeding. Biologic paternity is virtually irrelevant without legal recognition. Courts may choose to transfer legal paternity from one man to another, but they endeavor not to disturb paternity when it will render an otherwise legitimate child a bastard. Physicians should also avoid casting doubts on paternity when a family is already in crisis. While physicians should not lie to patients, there is enough uncertainty about paternity determinations to allow room for differing interpretations. Even tissue typing can be confused by mutation, the presence of related males among the candidates, or laboratory error.

It is best to avoid questions of paternity unless they are directly relevant to the patient's medical condition or care. If the father is concerned about possible genetic disease in his child, the information gathering should be directed to the disease, not the paternity. Physicians should decline to test a child to determine paternity unless it is a medical necessity. (This is usually an issue only for certain rare genetic diseases and as a side issue in tissue typing for organ transplantation.) If a court orders paternity testing, the physician must honor the order. But the physician acting as an expert witness in such a case should inform the court of the limitations of the tests and avoid making any unequivocal pronouncements of paternity.

Can I have a healthy baby with someone else? This is a very difficult question because the answer is so often yes. A woman who asks this question should be warned that choosing a father at random may be as risky as conceiving with her husband. Artificial insemination is a standard option that allows the woman to avoid genetic disease. But most programs will not inseminate a woman unless she is married and her husband consents. If the woman does not want her husband to know that he is not the genetic father, then she will have to seek help outside the traditional medical care system.

A physician who suspects that a patient is considering such private selection should be sure that she understands the risks. If she is the carrier, she must understand that another father will not alter the risk. If the problem is a recessive disease with a high gene prevalence, such as sickle cell disease or cystic fibrosis, she may have the bad luck to pick a father who is also a carrier. On the other hand, if her husband is the carrier and she is not, her idea is medically sound, if socially questionable. While it is reasonable to try to talk a woman out of seeking a surrogate father, it would violate her privacy to tell her husband. A physician who is uncomfortable with the situation should withdraw from the case. He or she should not try to control the actions of an independent adult.

Should we get married? Although this is not a medical question, it is one that a physician doing genetic counseling may be asked. The answer for a particular couple will depend on many things: How much do they want children? How great is their risk of genetic disease? How severe is the disease? What are their feelings about prenatal diagnosis and abortion? The birth of a handicapped child is a strain on any marriage and often contributes to divorce. If there are other potential problems, such as family objections or teenage partners, then the risk of divorce is fairly high.

Should we get divorced? The general understanding of genetic disease is not great. There are people who believe that there is a moral duty to dissolve a marriage if the parties are even distantly related or if there is genetic disease involved. One of the most widely publicized cases involved a biologic brother and sister who were adopted by different families as small children. They met in adulthood, married, and had three healthy children. Another person who knew of their earlier relationship tried to force them to divorce. They quite rightly refused.

Couples should understand the genetic problem they face and the likelihood that children will be affected. Once they understand their options, the parties to the marriage will have to make their own choices. Whatever a physician may advise, strong marriages will tend to survive; weak ones may not.

What should I tell my family? The best answer to this one is "Nothing." If a couple is considering alternative methods of conceiving a healthy child, such as artificial insemination, or if the couple is going to have prenatal diagnosis and abortion of a defective fetus, they are well advised to tell as few people as possible. If enough people are told, there is certain to be someone who will disagree with the decision out of ignorance or moral outrage. The child may also face ostracism in the family. A grandparent who has a number of biologic grandchildren may not care about a child of artificial insemination. The couple should be counseled to choose their confidants wisely.

If there are other members of the family who may be at risk or are concerned for themselves, they should be encouraged to come to the genetic counselor for their information. Even patients who understand their own problems fairly well can be a mine of misinformation for others. The birth of a child with a congenital defect can stop whole extended families from having children, a tragedy when these other couples may not be at risk.

FERTILITY TREATMENT

> Infertility is a condition with unique and profound psychological and emotional impacts. Infertility is experienced by most couples as a life crisis in which they feel isolated and powerless. Feelings of frustration, anger, depression, grief, guilt, and anxiety are common and should be anticipated and dealt with appropriately. (ACOG 125)

The treatment of infertility poses many controversial issues, ranging from religious objections to questions of fraudulent inducement by unscrupulous fertility clinics that misrepresent their actual success rate.

Infertility treatment has become a big business as the number of couples defined as infertile has increased. Some of this increase is related to the increased age at which many women attempt to conceive their first child. This delay shortens the period available to have children. Women who might have conceived by age 35 if they had begun trying to have children at age 20 are out of time if they start trying to conceive at age 35. Modern birth control methods allow women to be sexually active without becoming pregnant. This increases the probability that the woman will suffer complications of an STD that will impair her fertility. Perhaps the greatest increase in infertile couples has come from a more liberal definition of infertility.

Current statistics indicate that more than 14 percent of couples who desire a child are unable to conceive within a year (ACOG 125). It is recommended that fertility treatment not be started (in the absence of a specific problem) until the couple have tried to conceive without using birth control for one year (ACOG 142). This is considered a conservative time period and was recommended because some fertility clinics were beginning treatment after only a few months after a couple had begun to try to conceive. In earlier periods, however, a couple would not see themselves as having a medical problem until they had tried to conceive for several years at least. We do not know how many of the 14 percent who did not conceive in a year would eventually conceive without intervention. Thus, it is impossible to determine what component of the infertility epidemic represents changed expectations and the ready availability of fertility services for those able to pay for them.

Fitness

While treating infertility is undoubtedly a medical benefit in many cases, there are women who for physical or psychological reasons should not carry a pregnancy. For these woman, pregnancy becomes a threat to their own health and subjects the fetus to great risk of permanent injury or death. Fertility technology itself becomes a risk when it increases the probability of multiple births. Most fertility specialists are conscientious in counseling their patients about the risks and limitations of fertility treatment, but these physicians are reticent to deny a woman treatment if she is willing to assume the risks of the treatment.

The legal problems arise because a woman does not have an unfettered right to waive her injured baby's cause of action against the physician. The informed consent to fertility treatment must be complete and specific. Just reciting the risks is insufficient. The consequences of risks such as multiple births must be described in detail. Telling a woman that her baby may be premature does not give her the necessary information that a frequent complication of severe prematurity is brain damage. While it may be improper to deny women the right to risk their lives and the health of their potential offspring for the sake of becoming pregnant, they must be told exactly what risks they are assuming.

Medical Fitness

The first question that should be asked is whether the woman is medically fit to carry a pregnancy. There are many protective mechanisms within the body that reduce fertility if the woman is in poor condition to conceive. Hormone therapies can often overcome these protective mechanisms without correcting the underlying problem and increasing the risk that there will be a poor outcome for mother or baby. An obese woman who has ceased to ovulate may not want to hear that she must lose weight to become pregnant. It is much easier to give her pills to stimulate ovulation. This apparently simple solution can lead to respiratory compromise and weeks of hospitalization for which the physician may be held liable. The physician should exercise the same caution in recommending fertility treatment as any other hazardous procedure.

Studies on the products of spontaneous abortions point to a higher than normal rate of genetic problems. Given that the human body eliminates fetuses with genetic diseases in many cases, women who have had several unsuccessful pregnancies should be considered at risk for genetic disease. This is another situation in which medical science can sometimes overcome natural protective mechanisms. The couple who are disappointed at their lack of children may not realize that there could be a problem with the babies. They should have a careful evaluation to rule out the presence of a genetic disease that might be complicating their efforts to carry a baby to term.

Psychiatric Problems

It is important to rule out infertility caused by compulsive behavior that undermines a woman's health. A woman who cannot conceive because she has an eating disorder should not be helped to conceive by artificial means. The risk of turning a mild chronic psychiatric problem into an acute problem is substantial. If the woman continues to try to maintain a physiologically unreasonably low weight, the fetus may suffer substantial damage. Given the psychiatric basis of the problem, an informed consent to accept the risk of pregnancy would probably be invalid. If the woman had control of her behavior, she would have been able to conceive by gaining weight. The patient should be referred for psychological evaluation before any risky therapies are instituted.

Prospects for Successful Treatment

In spite of all the advances in infertility treatment, not every couple will be able to conceive and bear a child. Any couple asking for infertility treatment should be given a realistic idea of their chances. Adoption is a long process in the United States today, and there are age limits placed on adoptive parents. A physician who is treating an infertile couple should be sure that they are not offered false hope that limits or excludes the possibility of adoption. Patients should be reminded that they should preserve their options while the various therapies are tried.

Dealing with Multiple Gestation

Some fertility drugs substantially increase the probability of multiple births (ACOG 125). In vitro fertilization techniques can also result in multiple gestations if more than one embryo is introduced, with a rate of twins of 15 to 18 percent and of triplets of 1 to 2 percent with four preembryos (ACOG 140). Multiple gestation poses grave risks to both the fetuses and the mother (ACOG 120). These risks should be explained in detail. The woman must understand that the risk is not that she will have twins or triplets (or more) but that one or more of the babies may be severely disabled and that she may suffer medical complications. The physician should also discuss the possibility of pregnancy reduction and selective fetal termination. A woman with multiple gestation must be informed of her options:

1. Abort all fetuses
2. Attempt to carry all fetuses to term
3. Terminate some of the fetuses. (ACOG Committee 94)

The introduction of multiple preembryos is intended to increase the success rate of in vitro fertilization. This benefits the patients by reducing the cost and medical risks of multiple procedures, but it is also critical to the success of the fertility center's marketing. Few persons would be willing to undergo the risk and expense of in vitro fertilization if the success rate were only 3 to 4 percent. Physicians have a duty to ensure that patients understand this trade-off between success and the attendant risk of multiple births.

The physician should also discuss the possibility of amniocentesis on the individual fetuses and the termination of those with genetic diseases. This is a dangerous process, however, because it is usually done later in the term, and retained fetal tissue can cause disseminated intravascular coagulation, with fatal consequences for the mother (ACOG Committee 94).

Germinal Materials

While few states have laws that govern the storage of germinal material, there has been litigation over possession of fertilized eggs. (See Chapter 24.) Legal problems arise when the woman chooses to be inseminated at a point in time that is remote from when the germinal materials were stored. The husband has the legal and moral responsibility for the child who is born, but he loses the power to veto the conception that is implicit in the traditional way of being inseminated.

Given the politics of abortion, it is anticipated that some states will attempt to limit the disposal of preembryos. Some courts have already shown a reluctance to allow preembryos to be destroyed. Ideally, the physician would store ova and sperm separately and allow each person to control access to his or her respective germinal materials. This presents a problem because under current technology, the ova may not preserve as well as the preembryo and the sperm. This risk should be explained to the couple if they decide to keep the germinal materials separate. The couple must also be informed of the risk of third-party intervention and unwanted publicity if a dispute arises over the destruction of preembryos.

Outsider Involvement

Physicians should be cautious about participating in fertility treatments or conceptions that involve anyone but the couple under treatment. Many states have specific laws on artificial insemination that specify that the donor father has no legal rights. However, if a couple wants to choose their own donor or to arrange a contract pregnancy, the laws are not as clear. Custody fights and criminal charges of baby selling are known problems with these arrangements. The control of infectious and genetic diseases must also be considered. The use of any tissue from a third party requires that the physician have a complete genetic history and that the donor be tested for infectious diseases as would an anonymous donor.

Unmarried Couples

There is an ethical debate over whether fertility technology should be available to unmarried couples. This is not an issue for techniques that correct physiological or psychological conditions that impair fertility, when the patient then conceives through intercourse with a self-selected partner. While the physician may not approve of the behavior, just as he or she might disapprove of premarital sex in general, the physician has no right to impose his or her values on the patient. It does become an issue when physicians are asked to do procedures such as in vitro fertilization or artificial insemination.

While many physicians believe that marriage should not be a precondition to artificial insemination or in vitro fertilization, there is a societal policy, expressed through various laws, against having children outside of marriage. Most state laws on artificial insemination by donor (AID), which is the usual request, are written in terms of a married couple. It is not clear whether any of these laws forbids the artificial insemination of an unmarried woman. They do, however, leave a child born of AI outside of marriage in a legal limbo.

In some states, specific statutory authorization was necessary to permit AID. Without the statutory authorization, AID contravened state laws on adultery or fornication. If an authorizing law is written solely in terms of a married couple, then AID of an unmarried woman might violate fornication or adultery laws. Given that laws against fornication and adultery are constitutional, the constitutional right of reproductive freedom probably does not extend to unmarried couples. State civil rights laws requiring married and unmarried persons to be treated in the same way might imply that an unmarried person is entitled to AID or in vitro fertilization. Conversely, since in most states a married woman cannot be artificially inseminated without her husband's permission, equal treatment might also mean that AID is not available without a husband.

Physicians who choose to offer AID and in vitro fertilization to unmarried persons should seek legal advice to ensure that they do not violate any state laws. They should be meticulous in both infectious and genetic disease investigation. This is a controversial area. Physicians may be involved in highly publicized lawsuits if the couple decides to break up and the donor contests paternity.

ARTIFICIAL INSEMINATION

Artificial insemination has been widely practiced for decades, so many of the legal problems have been worked out. The issues of child custody are often covered by statute. There may be questions of malpractice involving either genetic disease or infection. There is also a societal problem because artificial insemination usually involves the rights of four people: the wife, the husband, the sperm donor, and the resulting child. Physicians should know and understand the laws of their states and the standard of care before working in this area.

As in any other area of medical practice, patients should not be given guarantees about the outcome of attempts at artificial insemination. If an unknown donor is used, the patient should understand that the donors are screened for disease, not for social desirability. Reasonable effort is made to ensure that the donor does not carry AIDS or Huntington's chorea; no effort will be made to ensure that the child will be smart or beautiful. Accepting artificial insemination carries most of the same risks as picking out a spouse.

Consent

This is a rare area of medical care in which the consent of the patient is not sufficient. The consent of the husband should be obtained before a married woman is impregnated by artificial insemination. Legal questions can arise when a married woman is artificially inseminated with donor sperm. In most states, this child is legally defined as legitimate to the husband. This presumption can be defeated if the physician fails to follow the statutory requirements. If the statute requires the permission of husband and wife, failing to obtain the husband's permission could allow him to deny paternity. The mother could then sue the physician for the child support that his negligence denied her from her (assumed to be divorced) husband.

The husband of a married woman is the legal father of the children she bears. In a natural conception, the consent of the man is implicit in the act. To conceive a child through artificial means with the sperm of another man would violate the terms of the marital contract. Unconsented artificial insemination can have the same legal consequences as adultery. Although the courts might view this as strictly between the husband and wife, they might honor a suit against the physician for any mental pain and suffering the unconsented insemination caused the husband.

Choosing a Donor

Choosing a sperm donor can be legally and medically risky. Even if the laws of the state cut off parental rights for a sperm donor, the donor might make a legal challenge if he knows who his biologic child is. These challenges can be very disruptive for the child and the legal parents. Friendships and family relationships are easily strained by conflicts that arise over custody and the raising of children. Artificial insemination may also be medically risky if the sperm donor is not rigorously screened for both genetic and communicable diseases. If the physician procures the sperm, it will be difficult to avoid liability if the mother or the child is harmed by a discoverable condition.

The Husband as Donor

If the husband is the source of the sperm, there are few legal problems. Custody and paternity are not at issue because the biologic father and the legal father are the same man. There may be problems if reasonable caution is not exercised in screening the couple for underlying problems. If there is genetic disease that is making it difficult for the woman to carry a pregnancy, this should be determined before steps are taken that might improve the chance of carrying a defective fetus.

Related Donors

Using the sperm of a relative of an infertile man may seem to be a good solution; the child will be genetically related to the legal father and will look like a member of the family. There are, however, some serious drawbacks. If a genetic problem is involved in the infertility, then the closer the relationship is to the father, the greater is the chance that the donor is also affected. Even if state law severs parental rights for a sperm donor, it will not sever the other relationship. If a brother is used as a donor, he is still the child's legal uncle. If the extended family is aware of the arrangement, they may treat the child as though the biologic father were the legal or social father. In case of divorce of the legal parents and/or infertility in the marriage of the donor, there may be a battle for custody of the child. An uncle has the right to go to court and challenge the fitness of a parent. If the uncle is also the biologic father of the child, this relationship may strengthen his case before the judge whatever the law on sperm donation may be.

The use of a relative of the mother carries the same legal risks plus the medical risks of consanguinity. In most cases, the risks of recessive genetic disease are not high, but using a maternal relative as donor carries a higher risk than using an unrelated donor. In addition, if custody questions do arise, the mother may face undue prejudice because of the cultural abhorrence of incest. Although artificial insemination with her brother's sperm is not the same as marrying her brother, the distinction may be irrelevant to a judge or a jury in a custody case.

Unrelated Donors

The legal aspects of accepting insemination from a known donor are discussed in the section on surrogate mothers. However, the donation of sperm by a friend or acquaintance for a baby to be kept by the mother creates some of the same problems. The presence of contracts or sperm donation laws may not prevent the parties from ending up in a court case or a custody battle. Even without legal entanglements, the social dislocations may be considerable. A man may believe that he can be indifferent when the child is only a theoretical possibility and find that he cannot keep away from the child when he or she is born. The mother and her husband may also have ambivalent feelings. It is very difficult to accept paternity as an abstraction or as a legal concept when all the people involved know one another well.

The use of banked sperm from an unidentified donor is legally safer than using a chosen donor. The anonymous donor has been screened for disease and has relinquished any right to the child conceived. The donor is unlikely to know who his biologic children are, and in general he is barred from making any legal claim to them. Conversely, the child is cut off from important information about the biologic parent's medical and psychiatric history.

Genetic Disease

Standard of care requires reasonable screening of any prospective sperm donor for genetic disease. This is true whether accepting donations to a sperm bank or accepting a donation for a specific woman. This screening should include testing when indicated. The availability of easy, inexpensive testing for sickle cell trait, for instance, makes this test mandatory for all prospective donors who are black. The fact that the woman has chosen the donor does not relieve the physician of the responsibility for using reasonable care. Many people are unaware of any genetic disease they may carry. The patient and the donor have a right to expect that proper precautions are taken.

Infection Control

The increase in severe sexually transmitted disease in the general population has made this a paramount consideration in artificial insemination. Virtually any venereal disease can be transmitted by fresh or processed semen. There have been cases of infection with HIV through artificial insemination. In such a case, there could be costly suits on behalf of the infected woman and on behalf of the baby if it is also infected.

There are medical standards for screening donors and treating specimens to prevent the spread of disease, and these should be followed carefully. The current recommendation on HIV control requires that the donor be tested for HIV when the semen is collected. The semen is then frozen for six months. The donor is tested again at the end of the six months. Only after this second test is negative can the semen be used (ACOG C.O. 109).

ACOG RECOMMENDATIONS ON SURROGACY

Surrogacy is fraught with legal risks. (See Chapter 24.) Medical opinion on surrogate parenting ranges from outright advocacy to harsh condemnation. As a legal matter, physicians have no duty to participate in surrogacy arrangements and may violate the law by doing so in some states. ACOG has published a thoughtful guide to physician participation in surrogacy arrangements (ACOG Committee 88). The core recommendations from this guide are reproduced here. Physicians who choose to participate in surrogacy should carefully consider these recommendations. If they choose to deviate from them, the reason for this deviation should be discussed in the medical record. While ACOG carefully declines to call these standards of care, it is clear that the courts will not be so reticent.

The ACOG recommendations first deal with decision making for the pregnant woman's medical care:

> In the committee's view, the genetic link between the commissioning parent(s) and the resulting infant, while important, is less weighty than the link between surrogate mother and fetus or infant that is created through gestation and birth. Thus, in the analysis and recommendations that follow no distinction will be drawn between the usual pattern of surrogate parenting and surrogate gestational motherhood.

This recommendation is at odds with many who advocate that pregnant women have a right to contract away their authority over their own medical decision making. It also accepts the legal notion that paternity is determined by societal convention rather than being rigidly bound to genetics. We support the treatment of the pregnant woman as the sole medical decision maker as being ethically and legally sound. To allow a woman to contract away the right to control her own health would be to institute contractual slavery. Preventing binding contracts to give up the infant after birth only reiterates the adoption laws in most states.

Public Policy Recommendations

Toward an Ethically Acceptable Public Policy on Surrogate Parenting Arrangements

An ethically acceptable public policy on surrogate parenthood will recognize that commissioning parents and surrogate mothers have divergent interests as well as interests in common. Because of the divergent interests, one professional person or agency should not attempt to represent the interests of both major parties to surrogate parenting arrangements. As in the case of organ donation and transplantation, public policy should require separation of roles to prevent apparent or real conflicts of interest. Further, because surrogate parenthood is in many respects analogous to adoption, the same kinds of safeguards that have been established for the practice of adoption should also be instituted for surrogate parenting arrangements.

In light of these general guidelines and the discussion above, the following specific policies are proposed:

1. Surrogate motherhood arrangements should be considered only in the case of infertility or other medical need, but not for reasons of convenience alone.
2. The surrogate mother and the commissioning couple should be regarded as distinct parties agreeing to cooperate for a defined purpose. Each party should be separately represented, both medically and legally.
3. Surrogate parenting arrangements should be viewed as preconception adoption agreements in which the surrogate mother is regarded as the mother for all medical and other purposes. After the birth of the infant, the surrogate mother can decide whether or not to place the child for adoption, in accordance with applicable local adoption rules and practices. This policy includes a specified period of time after birth during which the surrogate mother is free to depart from the preconception agreement and retain custody of the child. If she decides to place the child for adoption, the members of the commissioning couple will become the parents of the child.
4. While the committee is reluctant to propose a specific regulatory framework, it recommends that, for the near future, surrogate parenting arrangements be overseen by private nonprofit agencies with credentials similar to those of adoption agencies. Such agencies should seek to ensure that the interests of all involved parties are adequately protected. The agencies should conduct confidential counseling and screening of candidate surrogates and candidate commissioning parents. Their primary goal should be to promote the welfare of the future child, as well as the welfare of any existing children of the surrogate.
5. Plans for contingencies like the following should be carefully considered in advance by the commissioning couple, the surrogate mother, and the professionals involved in this reproductive arrangement: the prenatal diagnosis of a genetic or chromosomal abnormality; the inability or unwillingness of the surrogate to carry the pregnancy to term; the death of a member of the commissioning couple or the dissolution of the couple's marriage during the pregnancy; the birth of a handicapped infant; and a decision by the surrogate mother to retain custody of an infant conceived on behalf of, and typically with the aid of gametes from, the commissioning couple.
6. The contingency plans discussed by the parties to surrogate parenting arrangements should be written down to make explicit the intentions of the parties, to facilitate later recollection of these intentions, and to help promote the interests of the future child.
7. The surrogate mother, in consultation with her physician, should be the sole source of consent for medical decisions regarding pregnancy and delivery.
8. Whatever compensation is provided to the surrogate mother should be paid solely on the basis of her service in attempting to assist an infertile or otherwise medically handicapped couple; compensation should not be based on a successful delivery or on the health status of the child. (ACOG 88)

Implications for the Practice of Obstetrics-Gynecology

The physician who participates in surrogate motherhood arrangements, provides fertility services or obstetric services for a surrogate, or provides counseling services should carefully examine all relevant issues, including legal, psychological, societal, medical, and ethical aspects. Simple, clear answers cannot be anticipated.

The following recommendations are offered as guidance to physicians.

Avoidance of Conflict of Interest
The physician should not have as patients both the commissioning couple and the surrogate mother. Conflicts of interest may arise that would not allow the physician to serve both patients properly.

Initiation of Surrogate Arrangements
1. When approached by a patient interested in surrogate motherhood, the physician should, as in all other aspects of medical care, be certain that there is a full discussion of ethical and medical risks, benefits, and alternatives, many of which have been surveyed in this statement. In particular, the physician should be sure that contingencies like those outlined in item 5 (above) have been thoroughly considered.
2. A physician may justifiably decline to participate in initiating surrogate motherhood arrangements.
3. If a physician decides to become involved in surrogate motherhood arrangements, he or she should follow these guidelines:

   —The physician should be assured that appropriate procedures are utilized to screen the commissioning couple and the surrogate. Such screening should include appropriate fertility studies and infectious-disease and genetic screening.
   —The physician should receive only usual compensation for obstetric and gynecologic services. Referral fees and other arrangements for financial gain beyond usual fees for medical services are inappropriate.
   —The physician should not participate in a surrogate program in which the financial arrangements are likely to exploit any of the parties.

Care of Pregnant Surrogates
1. When a woman seeks medical care for an established pregnancy, regardless of the method of conception, she should be cared for as any other obstetric patient or referred to a qualified physician who will provide that care.
2. The surrogate mother should be considered the sole source of consent with respect to clinical intervention and management of the pregnancy. Confidentiality between the physician and patient should be maintained. (ACOG 88)

BIBLIOGRAPHY
Genetic Counseling
ACOG Committee Opinion 109: *Maximizing Pregnancy Rates Resulting from Donor Insemination with Frozen Semen*. April 1992.
ACOG Technical Bulletin 108: *Antenatal Diagnosis of Genetic Disorders*. September 1987.
ACOG Technical Bulletin 169: *Human Immune Deficiency Virus Infections*. June 1992.
ACOG Technical Bulletin 154: *Prenatal Detection of Neural Tube Defects*. April 1991.
Andrews LB; Jaeger AS: Confidentiality of genetic information in the workplace. Am JL Med 1991; 17:75.
Beckwith J: The Human genome initiative: Genetics' lightning rod. Am JL Med 1991; 17:1.
Cohen ME: *Park v. Chessin*: The continuing judicial development of the theory of "wrongful life." Am J Law Med 1978 Summer; 4(2):211–32.
Curtis D; Johnson M; Blank CE: An evaluation of reinforcement of genetic counselling on the consultand. Clin Genet 1988 Apr; 33(4):270–76.
Drugan A; Dvorin E; Koppitch FC III; Greb A; Krivchenia EL; Evans MI: Counseling for low maternal serum alpha-fetoprotein should emphasize all chromosome anomalies, not just Down syndrome. Obstet Gynecol 1989 Feb; 73(2):271–74.

Fletcher JC: Ethical and social aspects of risk predictions. Clin Genet 1984 Jan; 25(1):25–32.
Gostin L: Genetic discrimination: The use of genetically based diagnostic and prognostic tests by employers and insurers. Am JL Med 1991; 17:109.
Hollingsworth DR; Jones OW; Resnik R: Expanded care in obstetrics for the 1980s: Preconception and early postconception counseling. Am J Obstet Gynecol 1984 Aug 15; 149(8):811–14.
Humphreys P; Berkeley D: Representing risks: Supporting genetic counseling. Birth Defects 1987; 23(2):227–50.
Kessler S: Psychological aspects of genetic counseling: Analysis of a transcript. Am J Med Genet 1981; 8(2):137–53.
Kessler S; Jacopini AG: Psychological aspects of genetic counseling. II: Quantitative analysis of a transcript of a genetic counseling session. Am J Med Genet 1982 Aug; 12(4):421–35.
Kessler S; Kessler H; Ward P: Psychological aspects of genetic counseling. III. Management of guilt and shame. Am J Med Genet 1984 Mar; 17(3):673–97.
Kessler S; Levine EK: Psychological aspects of genetic counseling. IV. The subjective assessment of probability. Am J Med Genet 1987 Oct; 28(2):361–70.
King CR: Genetic counseling for teratogen exposure. Obstet Gynecol 1986 Jun; 67(6):843–46.
Lange K: Approximate confidence intervals for risk prediction in genetic counseling. Am J Hum Genet 1986 May; 38(5):681–87.
Lippman A: Prenatal genetic testing and screening: Constructing needs and reinforcing inequities. Am JL Med 1991; 17:15.
Lorenz RP; Botti JJ; Schmidt CM; Ladda RL: Encouraging patients to undergo prenatal genetic counseling before the day of amniocentesis. Its effect on the use of amniocentesis. J Reprod Med 1985 Dec; 30(12):933–35.
Lorenz RP; Kuhn MH: Multidisciplinary team counseling for fetal anomalies. Am J Obstet Gynecol 1989 Aug; 161(2):263–66.
Munro v. Regents of the University of California. 263 Cal Rptr 878 (1989).
Nelkin D; Tancredi L: Classify and control: The use of genetic screening information in the schools. Am JL Med 1991; 17:51.
Robertson GB: Civil liability arising from "wrongful birth" following an unsuccessful sterilization operation. Am J Law Med 1978 Summer; 4(2):131–56.
Rogers TD: Wrongful life and wrongful birth: Medical malpractice in genetic counseling and prenatal testing. S Cal L Rev 1982; 33:713.
Scott JA; Walker AP; Eunpu DL; Djurdjinovic L: Genetic counselor training: A review and considerations for the future. Am J Hum Genet 1988 Jan; 42(1):191–99.
Somer M; Mustonen H; Norio R: Evaluation of genetic counselling: Recall of information, post-counselling reproduction, and attitude of the counsellees. Clin Genet 1988 Dec; 34(6):352–65.
Sorenson JR; Scotch NA; Swazey JP; Wertz DC; Heeren TC: Reproductive plans of genetic counseling clients not eligible for prenatal diagnosis. Am J Med Genet 1987 Oct; 28(2):345–52.
Sorenson JR; Wertz DC: Couple agreement before and after genetic counseling. Am J Med Genet 1986 Nov; 25(3):549–55.
Taysi K: Preconceptional counseling. Obstet Gynecol Clin North Am 1988 Jun; 15(2):167–78.
Van Regemorter N; Dodion J; Druart C; Hayez F; Vamos E; Flament-Durand J; Perlmutter-Cremer N; Rodesch F: Congenital malformations in 10,000 consecutive births in a university hospital: Need for genetic counseling and prenatal diagnosis. J Pediatr 1984 Mar; 104(3):386–90.
Wassman ER; Cheyovich DL; Nakahara Y: "Possibly" de novo translocations: Prenatal risk counseling. Am J Obstet Gynecol 1989 Sep; 161(3):698–702.

Wertz DC; Sorenson JR; Heeren TC: Genetic counseling and reproductive uncertainty. Am J Med Genet 1984 May; 18(1):79–88.

West R: Ethical aspects of genetic disease and genetic counselling. J Med Ethics 1988 Dec; 14(4):194–97.

Yarborough M; Scott JA; Dixon LK: The role of beneficence in clinical genetics: Nondirective counseling reconsidered. Theor Med 1989 Jun; 10(2):139–49.

In Vitro Fertilization and Artificial Insemination

ACOG Committee Opinion 47: *Ethical Issues in Human In Vitro Fertilization and Embryo Placement*. Committee on Ethics, July 1986.

ACOG Committee Opinion 88: *Ethical Issues in Surrogate Motherhood*. Committee on Ethics, November 1990.

ACOG Committee Opinion 94: *Multifetal Pregnancy Reduction and Selective Fetal Termination*. Committee on Ethics, April 1991.

ACOG Technical Bulletin 120: *Medical Induction of Ovulation*. September 1988.

ACOG Technical Bulletin 125: *Infertility*. February 1989.

ACOG Technical Bulletin 140: *New Reproductive Technologies*. March 1990.

ACOG Technical Bulletin 142: *Male Infertility*. June 1990.

Annas GJ: Artificial insemination: Beyond the best interests of the donor. Hastings Cent Rep 1979 Aug; 9(4):14–15, 43.

Annas GJ: Redefining parenthood and protecting embryos: Why we need new laws. Hastings Cent Rep 1984 Oct; 14(5):50–52.

Bonnicksen AL: Embryo freezing: Ethical issues in the clinical setting. Hastings Cent Rep 1988 Dec; 18(6):26–30.

Capron AM: The new reproductive possibilities: Seeking a moral basis for concerted action in a pluralistic society. Law Med Health Care 1984 Oct; 12(5):192–98.

Davies I: Cryobanking and A.I.H. Med Leg J 1984; 52(Pt 4):242–47.

Fitzgerald JL: Rights and birth by artificial insemination. Med Leg Bull 1975 Oct; 24(10):1–11.

Flannery FT; Zimmerly JG: In vitro fertilization—sowing the seeds of liability? Leg Med 1982:227–37.

Gleitman v. Cosgrove. 227 A2d 689, 711 (1967).

Goldstein DP: Artificial insemination by donor—status and problems. In Milunsky A, Annas GJ, eds.: *Genetics and the Law*. 1976.

Grobstein C: The moral uses of "spare" embryos. Hastings Cent Rep 1982 Jun; 12(3):5–6.

Hubble GC: Liability of the physician for the defects of a child caused by in vitro fertilization. J Leg Med (Chic) 1981 Dec; 2(4):501–21.

Kirby MD: Medical technology and new frontiers of family law. Law Med Health Care 1986 Sep; 14(3–4):113–19, 128.

Levine RS: Artificial insemination donor: A constitutional model. Leg Med 1985;196–235.

McCormick RA: Bioethics in the public forum. Milbank Mem Fund Q Health Soc 1983 Winter; 61(1)113–26.

Marsh FH; Self DJ: In vitro fertilization: Moving from theory to therapy. Hastings Cent Rep 1980 Jun; 10(3):5–6.

Peckins DM: Artificial insemination and the law. J Leg Med 1976 May 1; 4(7):17–22.

Scott R: Experimenting and the new biology: "A consummation devoutly to be wished." Law Med Health Care 1986 Sep; 14(3–4):123–28.

Singer P: Making laws on making babies. Hastings Cent Rep 1985 Aug; 15(4):5–6.

Slovenko R: Sperm donation. Med Law 1986; 5(2):173–77.

Sweeney WJ III; Goldsmith LS: Test tube babies: Medical and legal considerations. J Leg Med (Chic) 1980 Apr; 1(4):1–17.

Wright GM; Zimmerly JG: The constitutional right to use in vitro fertilization. Leg Med 1982; 239–55.

27

Delivering Babies

CRITICAL POINTS

- Most negligent injuries in obstetrics are due to system failures.
- Unrealistic patient expectations underlie many obstetric legal problems.
- Obstetricians contribute to unrealistic patient expectations through inappropriate marketing and dependence on technology.
- Placental analysis and other scientific techniques promise to improve fetal health and reduce birth injury claims.

Obstetrics has the most critical medical malpractice problems. Routine prenatal care and delivery are the cornerstones of community health. These are imperiled by fears, both real and imagined, of litigation. Physicians in rural areas find it increasingly difficult to obtain affordable malpractice insurance coverage. Urban physicians turn away indigent patients in a mistaken belief that they pose an elevated risk of malpractice litigation. Under federal antidumping regulations, physicians will face these same patients as emergency admissions late in labor, when they may present a greater legal risk.

It is not possible to prevent every birth-related lawsuit. It is possible to limit systems failures and attendant negligent injuries, to correct patient and attorney misapprehensions about birth injuries, and to document better the nonnegligent basis of most birth injuries. Our belief, based on our experience with medical malpractice litigation and insurance claims management, is that such strategies will greatly reduce the incidence of birth-related lawsuits while providing excellent, cost-effective medical care.

MARKETING OBSTETRIC CARE

Marketing has a strong influence on obstetric services today. Many hospitals offer special facilities and services to compete for the lucrative market in delivering well-insured obstetrics patients. This is seen as a particularly attractive market because of the many ancillary services to be sold to affluent patients. These marketing strategies have varying impacts on patients' medical care. Providing comfortable waiting rooms or champagne for the family may attract patients, but it does not ensure quality medical care. Offering birthing rooms and one-day discharge can be beneficial to the patient but requires changing the practice habits of obstetricians and pediatricians.

Marketing obstetrics services becomes a legal problem when it reinforces the illusion that childbirth is a risk-free, enjoyable experience. Advertisements with pictures of healthy babies and smiling mothers may be accurate for most deliveries but not for all. For those who are not so lucky, those advertisements fuel the resentment and bitterness that lead to medical malpractice lawsuits. Obstetricians should be especially careful about associating with physician referral services that are coupled with public advertisements. These referral services often make explicit and implicit promises about the physician services, promises that can complicate the physician-patient relationship.

Both physicians and hospitals should be careful that their advertisements do not constitute a guarantee that patients will be delivered in whatever way they wish. The special facilities may not be available if there is a clustering of births on one day. In some cases, birthing chairs or natural childbirth may not be appropriate for a given patient. An obstetrician should know what the hospital offers and what his or her patients want. If the hospital has special programs that the physician does not participate in, every patient should be told of the nonparticipation. These matters must be addressed in the first prenatal visit. Seven months into the pregnancy is too late to find out that the patient has reserved the birthing room and the physician will not use it. This will anger the patient and could raise the issue of consumer fraud if the hospital's advertisements promise services that are not available.

A STRUCTURED APPROACH TO OBSTETRIC CARE

Most obstetric malpractice is due to medical system failures rather than intentionally made, incorrect decisions. System failures (more informally called "slipping through the cracks") occur when a patient receives, or fails to receive, needed care due to inadvertence. Patients are at the greatest risk for system failures when they have nonserious conditions that are routinely managed without ongoing evaluation. System failures usually involve overlooking unexpected data. This might be ignoring the third call back by the mother of a child with an infected throat, which should have triggered a reevaluation of the patient's treatment. This is not usually a problem because most children with infected throats have no major problem. It is the child with meningitis who is injured when the physician inadvertently continues routine treatment.

In obstetrics, common system failures include failing to diagnose existing systemic diseases, failing to offer screening tests at the appropriate time, failing to act on positive test results, and failing to respond quickly to threats to fetal or maternal health. System failures pose the major risk in obstetric care because most pregnant women are healthy and most pregnancies end in the birth of a healthy baby.

Since the medical component of prenatal care is a screening program, failures in the prenatal care system are irrelevant to most women because they do not have any of the conditions for which the screening is performed. As with the child with an infected throat, the system failure harms only the patient who does not have the usual condition. In obstetrics, the failure of the prenatal system does not matter for most women; it does matter for a woman who has a medical condition that requires nonroutine treatment to protect her health or the health of the baby.

To use the MSAFP example (see Chapter 26), assume the physician has all abnormal laboratory reports put on the front of the chart for review. The file clerk loses 2 percent of all laboratory reports. Since the physician depends on abnormal results being flagged, no flag is taken to be a normal result.

Assuming a rate of 1 neural tube defect per 500 births, the probability of a missed diagnosis is .02 × .002, or 1 per 25,000 births. The odds are that this practice could go on for years before resulting in an injury in any given physician's practice. That injury can be very expensive. A $1 million award would not be unusual in such a case. Assume further that an average obstetrician delivers 50 babies a year. (This is a low number for a full-time obstetrician but is used to include family-practitioners who deliver babies and physicians with substantial gynecology practices.) Then 25,000 births represent 500 obstetrician-years, for a risk of $2000 per obstetrician-year.

From a management perspective, delivering routine obstetrical services is more like flying an airliner than like treating an acute illness: small things matter, and mistakes are costly. As with flying the airliner, most of the things that matter are not done by the person in charge. The pilot does not service the engines, and most prenatal care is done by persons other than the supervising physician.

Zero-Defects Management

Zero-defects management is based on the premise that it is better to detect problems before they cause accidents or product defects. Airlines must use a zero-defects approach to maintaining and flying their planes. Everything is done and recorded by written protocol designed to identify problems before they become threats. Parts are replaced when they are worn but still safe rather than being allowed to fail. Judgment and art are critical in flying, but the objective is to recognize when they are necessary before it is too late for them to help. Medicine has the same problem. An obstetrician's skill in managing a complication of pregnancy can be exercised only if the complication is detected while still treatable.

The foundation for a zero-defects approach in obstetric practice is a highly structured medical record integrated with standardized patient education materials. This record system should be self-prompting and self-documenting. The simplest way to achieve this is with a preprinted medical record form. This form tracks the patient's care through time, with entries for every test and issue to be discussed with the patient. Most important, the patient educational materials are keyed to the protocol. For example, early in the pregnancy the patient receives information about the tests that will be performed during the pregnancy, including when they should be performed.

At 16 weeks, the record indicates that it is time for the MSAFP sample to be drawn, and a handout given to the patient. Even if the provider forgets to discuss the test and draw the sample, there is a high probability that the patient will remember the test and ask about it. The structured record both prompts the care provider and allows the patient to participate in the quality control for her own care.

Legal and Ethical Benefits of Structured Care
In a carefully designed structured prenatal care system, there are no second-class patients. Every woman is offered all appropriate care and is fully informed about the process of prenatal care. This does not resolve issues about who will pay for such care, but it is ethically preferable to rationing care by having different standards of prenatal care for different socioeconomic groups. To the extent that a substantial number of physicians use structured systems with the same core of services, these systems define the acceptable level of care. Such evidence of a standard of care should aid physicians in disputes with third-party payers over what is reimbursable care.

There have been no large-scale controlled studies of the legal benefits of structured prenatal care systems. Preliminary data and our experience with one of these systems in the malpractice insurance context are very suggestive. Physicians have used this system (Pre-Natal Care—A Systems Approach, developed by Arnold Greensher and his colleagues in Colorado Springs) for more than 100,000 births. Using the 50 births per year estimate, this would be 2000 obstetrician years.

The observed number of medical malpractice claims is much lower than would be expected for this number of deliveries. Analysis of the data is confounded by several potential biases:

1. Are high-risk or difficult births excluded from the system? This does not appear to be the case. Physicians who use the system generally use it for all deliveries.
2. Is it too soon to see the claims? In Colorado, the system has been used for approximately 50,000 births over a period of several years. Other data indicate that most birth injury claims in Colorado are filed within two years. This indicates that claims are not being filed rather than just being delayed.
3. Is there a bias in the selection of physicians using the system? This raises an intriguing question. If it is not the prenatal care system that protects these physicians from litigation, then what other physician characteristics correlate with an extremely low rate of birth injury claims? (Experience with communities where all the physicians use the system seem to mitigate physician selection as the sole basis for the system's effectiveness.)

Thinking Like a Plaintiff's Attorney
We suggest that these systems prevent litigation for three reasons. The first is that they prevent the systems failures that result in prenatal care-related injuries. The second is that they reduce the patient's incentive to sue. By making her a partner in her care and by providing full information about potential problems, the patient is less likely to be angry and surprised by things that happen in her care. Third, they present an unambiguous record of the care provided, the information given each woman, and the woman's choices based on that information. In this regard, the patient education handouts are as important as the record. Without the patient education component of the system, structured records are less credible because they are easy to alter. If the patient receives a handout, it helps prove the care was rendered. Perhaps most important for the psychology of litigation, they present this information in a well-organized, graphically attractive form. This is in stark contrast to the illegible notes or stream of consciousness

dictations that make up many medical records. Physicians and their attorneys see so many medical records that they do not appreciate that most laypersons assume that medical records are an important measure of a physician's skills. A skillful plaintiff's attorney can easily convince a juror that sloppy, incomplete medical records equate to sloppy incomplete care.

The combination of extensive patient handouts and a complete and well-structured record creates the impression that the physician was careful and competent. This makes the case much less attractive to a plaintiff's attorney whose strategy is to win on jury sympathy rather than on a showing of clear and unambiguous negligence. Conversely, a highly structured record used improperly is a litigation disaster. If the records are completed haphazardly and the patients are not given the proper information, the record is no longer self-auditing and will no longer prevent systems failures. Its elegant structure turns against the physician, making the record the plaintiff's best evidence of the physician's negligence. This has led some defense attorneys to recommend against the use of structured records, based on the correct analysis that physicians who do not use the system properly will be hard to defend. It ignores the probability that most physicians will use the system properly and thus not be sued.

THE BIRTH PLAN

Beyond a structured prenatal care system, physicians delivering babies should use birth plans to reduce conflicts and misunderstandings surrounding the delivery. Avoiding such conflicts can reduce the likelihood of litigation and improve the quality of medical care. The best way to reduce conflict is to make agreements in advance about what will be done in a normal delivery and what will be necessary if an emergency arises. A written birth plan provides a vehicle for exploring the expectations of patients who are either reticent to state their preferences or who have not yet considered the issues attendant upon delivery. The exercise of preparing the plan gives the physician an opportunity to determine the patient's level of sophistication and to educate her about the childbearing process. This avoids misunderstandings about which items are a matter of convenience or comfort and which are medically necessary.

Purpose of a Birth Plan

The birth plan serves three purposes. First, it structures the discussion between the physician and the patient. This ensures that all important issues are addressed with each patient. Second, it provides a framework for resolving inconsistencies between the patient's expectations and the risks of her particular pregnancy. Finally, it serves as documentation of the agreement between the physician and the patient. This will obviate questions about the information given the patient and any promises by the physician as to the management of the delivery. Legally most important, it will document the risks of pregnancy and the specific risks attendant on the delivery strategy chosen by the patient. This will not relieve the physician of liability for negligence. It will, however, bolster the physician's claim that certain injuries were foreseeable risks of pregnancy and not iatrogenic birth injuries.

Contraindications

The birth plan should detail all aspects of the individual patient's health that influence decisions about the management of the pregnancy: maternal diseases, habits such as smoking and drug use, medications that the woman must continue taking during pregnancy, and any other factors that might influence the course of the pregnancy. Discussing these factors with the patient will help her understand that her pregnancy must be managed differently from those of her friends. It will also help the physician remember that the patient has special needs. This can help avoid giving a patient medications that she cannot tolerate, or performing contraindicated procedures in the haste of an emergency delivery.

Authority to Consent

Except for certain fertility treatments, the patient has sole authority to make the decisions about her care. Paternalism in obstetric care is legally dangerous. An obstetrician who tells a patient not to worry because everything will be fine is making a guarantee on the outcome of a pregnancy with almost no ability to influence that outcome. Consent is a simple problem made complicated by misinformation. A pregnant woman is the only person who may consent to her medical care. This is always true for adults, and in most states a pregnant minor has the right to consent to her medical care. Neither husbands, lovers, prospective grandparents, prospective adoptive parents, nor adoption agencies have a right to consent to, or interfere in, the medical care of the pregnant woman. Any discussion of the woman's medical care with such third parties is a violation of the patient's rights unless she has given her explicit permission.

Participation of Others

While the pregnant woman has the right to exclude all third parties from consultation about her medical care, most women want to involve other persons in their decisions. The birth plan should include the names of any persons the patient designates to receive information about her pregnancy. The patient may also want to sign a durable power of attorney to delegate the right to consent to care to a third party if she becomes medically incompetent to consent to her own care. If the patient wants her husband or other person in the delivery room, this should be stated in the birth plan. The plan should discuss any restrictions on the presence of this third person (special training, a hospital orientation tour, etc.) and under what circumstances the person will be excluded. It is recommended that the husband or other person mentioned in the plan also be requested to read and sign the relevant portions of the plan.

Risk-Benefit Analysis

Although it is the patient who must consent to medical intervention, it is the physician who must provide the information necessary to make the decisions. Risk-benefit analysis in obstetrics is complicated because there are two patients and many social factors involved. The starting point for risk analysis in pregnancy is the risks of pregnancy itself. A woman must be warned that women die in childbirth, that 6 percent of children have some congenital abnormality, that things may happen in her pregnancy that will adversely affect the baby, and that some babies are inadvertently injured during birth. The woman must be warned about geographic risks such as high altitude and the limitation of local birth and emergency facilities.

The purpose of this background information is to establish the baseline risks of pregnancy. Understanding these risks is necessary to understanding the risks and benefits of various medical interventions. This is especially important for women who have been exposed to misinformation about the birth process. Some women believe that modern medicine is a conspiracy to subjugate women. While obstetric care could be made much more responsive to the needs of pregnant women, dispensing with medical attendance is not a proper response to this problem.

The Patient's Interests
The physician should learn as much as possible about social factors that affect a patient's decisions. The patient must consider the risks of losing the baby, the risks of a damaged infant, and the risks that she is willing to assume to carry the baby. The decisions of a married woman in her thirties who has taken years to conceive are likely to be very different from the decisions of a single woman in her teens who is considering adoption. A patient who does not tell her physician about her desires and expectations should be asked about them. Most women have a personal image of childbirth that the physician must understand. The further this image is from reality, the greater is the likelihood of conflict.

The physician should work to avoid exercising undue influence on the patient's decisions. If there are strong medical reasons for making a certain decision, the physician should make these reasons clear. The physician should realize that the social reasons may outweigh the medical reasons for a particular patient. The choices of a married male physician in his forties with six healthy children at home are not likely to match the decisions of either of our hypothetical patients.

Risks to the Baby
While pregnant women have great latitude in assuming the risk of various medical care options, they do not have an unlimited right to assume risks for the baby. Physicians should be careful not to agree to medical care that unnecessarily increases the risk to the baby. For example, a physician should not accept a patient who refuses consent to a cesarean section under all circumstances. The physician should not humor the patient with the intention of forcing care on her when an emergency arises. Physicians should be wary of situations that limit their options in an emergency. Conversely, physicians must tell their patients of the risks that are imposed by their practice styles. Physicians who practice at high altitudes or in facilities that cannot provide proper emergency services must document that the patient understands that she and her baby are at substantial additional risk because of these factors.

Emergencies

It is particularly important that the physician and patient discuss what will be done if an emergency arises or something does not work out as hoped. A woman who wants a large family may be very upset if a cesarean section becomes necessary during her first delivery. If she has not been prepared for the possibility, she may become angry with the physician who is doing the surgery. If the reason for the cesarean section leads to a birth injury, this family is primed to sue. In contrast, if the woman understands that cesarean delivery is necessary if the fetus is in trouble and that it does not necessarily lead to repeat surgery and limited family size, then she is better prepared for the surgery and the possible adverse outcome in the baby.

The physician should document how the birth plan will be modified for different emergencies to obviate the emotional turmoil that occurs when the patient's expectations are suddenly disappointed. The patient has time to consider and consent to different emergency options. While the patient retains her right to change her mind after the birth plan has been signed, the process of preparing and negotiating the plan should reduce the probability that she will become dissatisfied with her decisions.

Availability of Facilities and Personnel
The patient must be warned if there is a possibility that the hospital may not be able to supply expected facilities. For example, the birthing room may not be available if there is a cluster of births on the day the patient delivers. It is imperative that the patient be warned if the hospital cannot provide essential services such as an emergency cesarean section within a short period. If the patient is being delivered in a non-hospital-based birthing center, then provisions for emergency transfer and its risks must be documented. The patient must be informed of the potential consequences of such deficiencies and given the opportunity to seek care elsewhere.

The physician should explain the call system, identify who will attend the patient if her primary physician is not available, and be given an opportunity to meet the substitute physician. If the primary physician is a member of a multiphysician call system, the physician should make it clear to the patient that she may be seen by any member of the group. It is critical that every member of the group be aware of the existence of the patient's birth plan. A substitute physician should not be allowed to abandon the plan unless it is necessary because of unexpected medical complications. Any substitute physician who disagrees with the way the primary physician manages deliveries should not be in the same call system.

Custom versus Fashion
Both obstetricians and their patients are subject to fads and fashion. While there are no properly controlled studies indicating benefits for natural childbirth, LeBoyer deliveries, Lamaze, and other current fashions, there is also no evidence that they are harmful. The physician should accommodate the patient's wishes as much as possible without endangering the health of the mother or baby. Conversely, if the physician believes that certain procedures are medically necessary, they should not be bargainable issues. Physicians should be cautious, however, and consider whether the procedure or medication is medically necessary or just their usual practice.

EVALUATING THE MOTHER'S MEDICAL CONDITION

Several tests are required by law or medical standards for every pregnant woman. It is important that any physician who cares for a pregnant woman know the results of these tests and act upon them if necessary.

The first and most important test is for pregnancy. Any woman of childbearing age should be considered pregnant unless there is evidence to the contrary if any medical treatment might affect the pregnancy or the fetus. Most radiology departments are covered in signs that ask women if they might be pregnant. Many internists, however, do not ask a woman about pregnancy and contraception before prescribing a drug that is not accepted for use in pregnancy. The risks, both medical and legal, are much greater for some drugs than they are for a chest X ray.

On the other hand, there is no laboratory test that can establish pregnancy beyond doubt in the first trimester. A physician should never tell a woman that she is or is not pregnant on the basis of a laboratory test alone. A history and physical examination are as necessary to making this diagnosis as any other. A patient who is assured that she is not pregnant may expose herself to agents that can harm her fetus. Even if there are no expected problems, failure to diagnose the pregnancy can interfere with the patient's receiving proper prenatal care and will reduce her options about abortion or prenatal diagnosis.

Maternal Disease

Pregnant women should be tested for diseases that directly affect their health and thus secondarily affect the outcome of the pregnancy. Some of these tests are mandated by law or public health regulation. Others are widely accepted as the standard of care. Failing to diagnose or manage maternal illness properly is a major source of liability in obstetrics. The problem arises because most pregnant women are healthy. This makes it easy to attribute what would otherwise be symptomatic illness to the normal effects of pregnancy.

Once the tests are done, the physician must be very careful to evaluate the results in every patient and take action when necessary. In caring for a pregnant woman, a few days can make a tremendous difference in the outcome, so a physician should pay particular attention to the timely evaluation of test results. If a result has not been received, it should be treated as bad news until the result is available. If the syphilis serology or the blood type has been lost, it should be repeated promptly. The only true negative screening test is the one that has been reported by the laboratory and evaluated by the physician.

Tests should never be ordered simply as a defensive measure. It is legally more dangerous not to act on a test that indicates maternal illness than not to do the test. For example, if a patient has a negative rubella titer, her physician should be concerned if she develops a rash. What may be dismissed as an allergy in an immune patient should be worked up in a woman who may have rubella. In addition, this patient should be immunized as soon as she delivers. The obstetrician who failed to immunize a patient after her first pregnancy may be liable for a congenital rubella baby from her second pregnancy.

Legally Mandated Testing

Although congenital rubella has almost been conquered, the risk of congenital infection with herpes, hepatitis, syphilis, or HIV is increasing (ACOG 114). The laws requiring the reporting of such infections should be carefully followed to allow the health department to investigate the source of the disease. It does not help to treat a woman for syphilis in her first trimester if her consort remains infectious. If she contracts the disease again in the third trimester, the risk of fetal infection is greater than it was before. If the patient or the child is injured by the failure to comply with testing and reporting laws, the physician can be held liable for negligence per se. (See Chapter 6.)

It is imperative to consider the possibility of HIV infection in every pregnant woman (ACOG Committee 85). Ideally, women should be counseled and tested before becoming pregnant (ACOG 169). It is important to counsel and offer testing to every pregnant woman. In some urban centers, more than 1 percent of pregnant women are already HIV infected, and the rate appears to be increasing (Novick 1991). As HIV becomes more prevalent, it is anticipated that states will require prenatal testing for HIV. Until this happens, it is critical that physicians stress the medical necessity of knowing a patient's HIV status when managing maternal and child health problems.

HOME DELIVERIES

There is little legal experience with home deliveries because very few home deliveries in the United States are attended or supervised by physicians. While there is a small, visible group of middle-class and affluent women seeking home deliveries, most women delivered at home are poor and would prefer to be delivered in a hospital by a physician. Once these women are in labor, they can be brought into the hospital under the antidumping provisions of the Medicare/Medicaid laws, but they will still be responsible for their medical bills. These poor women pose a dilemma for physicians because of the conflict between their desire to help the woman avoid the hospital costs and the ethical and legal problems in engaging in potentially substandard care.

The Politics of Home Deliveries

Women who choose home deliveries because of political beliefs or involvement in quasi-religious antimedical groups are problematic because they usually have high expectations. Many believe that by avoiding the medicalization of birth, they will have a unique experience and a perfect baby. Physicians who might otherwise consider supervising a home delivery should be very cautious when working with a patient who has such unrealistic beliefs. The greatest threat posed by such patients is the refusal of necessary hospitalization should an emergency arise.

Even if the physician has discussed this possibility and documented the patient's agreement to hospitalization in the birth plan, the patient retains the right to refuse a transfer to the hospital. This can put the physician in the ethical and legal bind of a patient's refusing emergency medical care that is necessary to preserve her and her baby's health. There is no time for a court order for care, and, unlike the usual situation where the patient is in the emergency room, the patient must be transported against her will to make the care possible.

Participating in Home Deliveries

As long as a home delivery is successful, the physician is not at any special legal risk. If the mother or the baby is injured because of a complication that could have been successfully managed in the hospital, the physician must convince a jury that home deliveries constitute proper medical care. At this point the woman's attorney will pose the argument that the physician endorsed the safety of home deliveries by consenting to perform one. The woman's assumption of risk will evaporate if the jury agrees. Very few jurors are sympathetic to physicians who claim that the patient bullied them into agreeing to provide unsafe care. The defense that the woman could not afford to go to the hospital can be countered with the availability of emergency admissions. If the woman is in active labor and the physician is willing to fight with the hospital administrator, the woman will be admitted because of the laws governing emergency care of women in labor. The hospital may punish the physician for holding it to its legal duty, but that is not the pregnant woman's problem.

Legally, there is little to recommend participation in home deliveries. Analogies to the successful use of home deliveries in Europe have limited persuasion. The European countries have a structurally different medical and legal system that does not encourage a patient to sue her physician for any complications of a home birth. The ethics of home deliveries are more ambiguous. A woman in good health, without risk factors for birth complications, and with realistic expectations could reasonably consent to a home delivery. While the physician's legal risk might be great if any complications arose, it would not be unethical to participate in such a delivery.

Ethical problems arise when any of these preconditions is not met. If there are medical contraindications to a home delivery, the physician should hesitate before implicitly minimizing those risks by agreeing to deliver the woman at home. If the woman has unreasonable expectations, the physician should consider the possibility of not being able to render needed care in a crisis. A woman has a legal right to refuse necessary care, but physicians have an ethical duty not to encourage or support unreasonable medical care decisions. Physicians who choose to participate in home deliveries should carefully document the circumstances that make a home delivery necessary or appropriate. The informed consent must recite the added risks of the home delivery and why delivery in a hospital is undesirable or impossible.

MEDICAL INTERVENTIONS

There is evidence that induction of labor and cesarean sections have been overused in the United States. This overuse has been driven by nonmedical factors such as fear of legal liability, physician and patient convenience, and reimbursement policies that encourage medical procedures. Unlike most other forms of defensive medicine, however, there is a rational basis for the perception that performing a caesarean section makes it easier to defend a potential birth injury case. It is easier for a plaintiff's attorney to attack a physician's decision to do nothing or to operate too late than it is to prove technical errors in the performance of the caesarean section.

More fundamentally, while a medically unnecessary Caesarean section subjects the mother to operative risks and increased morbidity, these risks are inherent in the procedure. If a proper informed consent is obtained or the jury does not believe that the patient would have refused the operation had she been properly informed, it is difficult to convince a jury that a patient should recover for the consequences of a properly performed but unnecessary operation. Paradoxically, efforts to reduce unnecessary medical interventions may exacerbate this problem.

As patients become more reticent to consent to caesarean sections and induction of labor and insurance companies increase financial incentives not to perform these interventions, the probability increases that necessary interventions will be delayed or omitted. There is no evidence, however, that juries will accept cost containment as a defense. Juries are also skeptical about a patient's refusal to consent to needed treatment. As discussed in Chapter 11, when the question is refusal of necessary care, juries tend to believe that physicians ultimately can convince patients to consent. These factors require that decisions not to use medical interventions be well documented and the patient carefully educated.

Past-Term Pregnancies

Education about potential medical interventions should start at the first patient encounter and should be part of the birth plan. It is important to determine, at the earliest possible time, if the patient has unreasonable fears or expectations. The patient must understand that while induction of labor is medically necessary in many situations, it should not be done as a matter of physician or patient convenience. Patients should be discouraged from seeing induction of labor as a benign process, but they also must appreciate its usefulness in appropriate circumstances.

A patient's birth plan should detail the indications and risks of induced labor. These should include the medical reasons for what might otherwise appear to be an induction done merely for convenience. If the mother lives in a secluded area where emergency services are nonexistent, then induction at term may be safer than risking an unattended home delivery in a snowbound mountain cabin. If a mother is likely to need special care for herself or the infant and the entire area is under a hurricane warning, it may be better to deliver her than to leave her to compete for attention in a hospital on disaster status. These are valid indications for inducing labor and should be documented in the chart. This documentation will be important if the snow does not fall or the hurricane hits elsewhere and the delivery has an unfortunate outcome.

The patient should understand that babies that are well past dates may need to be delivered by induction or section. Physicians should enlist the aid of the woman in ensuring that the progress of the pregnancy is appreciated. If the physician is suspicious about the patient's reported dates, this should be investigated before the patient is grossly past term. The problem of past-dates babies has been exacerbated by the fragmentation of the medical care delivery system. It is easy for a woman to get lost in a group practice where all the prenatal care is delivered by nonphysician personnel. If no one physician is responsible for her care, there may be no one to notice if she misses an appointment or is several weeks overdue.

As changing health insurance plans force patients to move to new physicians, it is difficult for a physician to know if the patient has left the practice or is just not coming in for her appointments. Physicians must have tracking systems for pregnant patients. If the patient has been lost to follow-up as her due date approaches, the physician should attempt to contact her. If she is under the care of another physician, refuses to come in for an appointment, or cannot be located, this information should be documented in the chart.

Cesarean Sections

The possibility of a cesarean section should be discussed with every patient as part of the patient's birth plan, with contingent consent for a cesarean section obtained early in the woman's pregnancy. The woman must sign the consent form herself; her husband should not be asked to sign it. At the time the cesarean section becomes necessary, the woman should be asked to resign the original consent form, indicating that the conditions for needing a cesarean section have now occurred. The fact that the mother may have had some pain-relieving drugs does not render her legally incompetent to acknowledge the need for the procedure. Her husband has no authority to sign the consent to her surgery unless she has given him this right in a power of attorney. If the mother is medically unable to consent because she is psychotic or comatose, the surgery may go forward based on the consent signed as part of the birth plan.

The standard of care for pregnant women who have had a previous cesarean section has changed rapidly in the last few years. Many obstetricians encourage women to attempt labor if the reason for the original operation is not likely to be repeated. On the other hand, some highly respected obstetricians believe that vaginal delivery should never be attempted by these patients. Physicians should be careful to inform the patient of all her options. The consent to surgical delivery or to vaginal delivery must be well informed. If the patient wants a trial of labor and the physician does not believe that it is advisable, he or she should help the patient find another doctor who will accept her decision. The consent to a trial of labor should be discussed as part of the patient's birth plan.

Disagreements over the advisability of a trial of labor are different from a refusal of a cesarean section in all circumstances. A woman has a right to refuse surgical delivery without regard for the risk to the fetus. She may refuse a cesarean section for reasons that have no medical basis, even if her decision endangers the life or health of her fetus. Neither the pregnant woman's husband nor her physician has the right to force her compliance by physical force or chemical restraint. The only way to challenge a woman's refusal of a cesarean section is to obtain a court order. General medical-ethical thinking opposes the involuntary treatment of pregnant women who make a knowing decision to refuse medical care.

The strongest case for seeking to overturn a competent woman's decision is when the care is necessary for her own survival rather than the survival of the fetus. In analogous cases involving nonpregnant patients, the courts have expressed reluctance to allow an otherwise healthy person to refuse acute lifesaving care. The physician's ethical duty is difficult to determine in such situations. Ethicists who hold autonomy as the highest value argue that the patient should be allowed to die without attempts at legal intervention. Those who stress beneficience and the right of the state to act as parens patria for its citizens argue that the physician has an ethical duty to seek a judicial determination.

If this refusal is made during the first patient encounter, it presents the physician with the dilemma of whether to continue treating the woman. Most of the ethical debates have centered on the right of the state to force women to undergo unwanted medical care for the sake of the fetus. There has been much less attention to the right of the physician to refuse to treat a patient who prospectively refuses potentially lifesaving care. Many physicians ignore the refusal on the basis that the woman will change her mind if the section becomes necessary or in the hope that a section will not be required. This is a dangerous approach if an emergency section becomes necessary. Since there will be no time to obtain a court order, the physician must choose between respecting the woman's wishes or operating against her consent. Irrespective of the patient's expressed wishes, it will be difficult to defend allowing the patient and baby to die. The best that can be expected is a verdict based on the court's requiring the enforcement of a rigorously documented informed refusal of care. Conversely, operating against a patient's express refusal, without judicial authorization, is legally and ethically unacceptable.

BEHAVIORAL RISKS IN PREGNANCY

Many physiologic conditions make pregnancy dangerous to the mother and the baby. Most of these, such as diabetes, are intrinsic and, except for compliance issues, beyond the control of the woman. Some, such as alcoholism or cocaine use, are behavioral problems with substantial voluntary components. An unfortunate nexus of the medical efforts to improve prenatal health and the political debate on whether the fetus is a person deserving independent protection is the pregnant woman who engages in activities that might harm her fetus. Such women have been subjected to forced medical care, including cesarean sections, and to incarceration in prison.

Debates over the legality and even the usefulness of coercive policies aimed at pregnant women have obscured the issues in managing high-risk pregnancies. There is vast gulf between a physician seeking to have a woman treated against her will and the much more common problem of helping a patient understand the risks and benefits of various behaviors and medical care alternatives. In general, physicians providing personal health services should not attempt to force unwanted medical care on their pregnant patients. The AMA's position is illustrative.

The AMA Policy Statement
The AMA Board of Trustees recommends adoption of the following statement:

1. Judicial intervention is inappropriate when a woman has made an informed refusal of a medical treatment designed to benefit her fetus. If an exceptional circumstance could be found in which a medical treatment poses an insignificant or no health risk to the woman, entails a minimal invasion of her bodily integrity, and would clearly prevent substantial and irreversible harm to her fetus, it might be appropriate for a physician to seek judicial intervention. However, the fundamental principle against compelled medical procedures should control in all cases that do not present such exceptional circumstances.
2. The physician's duty is to provide appropriate information, such that the pregnant woman may make an informed and thoughtful decision, not to dictate the woman's decision.
3. A physician should not be liable for honoring a pregnant woman's informed refusal of medical treatment designed to benefit the fetus.
4. Criminal sanctions or civil liability for harmful behavior by the pregnant woman toward her fetus are inappropriate.
5. Pregnant substance abusers should be provided with rehabilitative treatment appropriate to their specific physiological and psychological needs.
6. To minimize the risk of legal action by a pregnant patient or an injured child or fetus, the physician should document medical recommendations made including the consequences of failure to comply with the physician's recommendations. (AMA Trustees Report, 1990)

Implications of the AMA Policy
The use of judicial process to force medical care on an unwilling patient has a long and checkered history. It is a power that has been abused in the past and will continue to be abused in the future. It is also a necessary power in the management of persons who are not able to make rational decisions about medical treatment. Most of these are chronically mentally ill, although some are suffering from acute toxic or psychiatric conditions that render them temporarily incompetent. The forced care of pregnant women is controversial because it is being applied to women who are mentally competent. These women may have made

self-destructive decisions, but they are rational decisions. The forced care is rationalized on the need to protect the fetus, not the health of a woman who is unable to make rational medical care decisions.

The AMA policy emphasizes that the duty of private physicians is to inform and educate their patients, not to make their decisions for them. (The duty of certain public health and mental health physicians is to protect the public, even at the derogation of an individual's right to determine his or her own medical care.) It is important to note that this presumes an informed refusal of medical care. Patients who are not able to make rational decisions are not able to make an informed refusal of medical care. In these cases, it is proper for the court to intervene and ensure that the person receives proper medical care. Physicians have the same duty to seek appropriate judicial intervention for a mentally incompetent pregnant woman as for a mentally incompetent diabetic man. They do not have the right to intervene to protect the health of the fetus if the woman is otherwise competent to make her own health decisions.

Consent in High-Risk Pregnancies

The physician's duty to inform and educate is the same whether the factor complicating the pregnancy is intrinsic or behavioral. This duty is complicated by the legal dilemma that the woman is the proper arbitrator of her medical care, but she is not the only person who can sue the physician for the consequences of that care. The patient's husband or surviving children can sue the physician if the patient dies or is gravely injured. (See Chapter 4.) If the woman knowingly assumes the risk of the pregnancy and her medical decisions, then she can waive her right to sue. This waiver will bar others who might sue on her behalf or on their own behalf because of their suffering occasioned by her injuries.

The patient's assumption of risk (or informed consent) is effective only if it is carefully obtained and documented. The risks to the patient and to the baby must be fully explained and the explanation documented. This is best done with a structured prenatal care system, tailored to the patient's special needs. Dilemmas arise because the law is ambiguous about a woman's right to assume the risk of injury for her fetus. While it is expected that the courts will not hold a physician liable when a woman clearly refuses care, the burden will be on the physician to convince the jury that the refusal was both knowing and unshakable. Juries assume that patients are rational and refuse care only if they are insufficiently informed of the risks. Juries will have a stronger prejudice that a pregnant woman would not knowingly have put her baby at risk. While it may be easy to convince a jury that a woman who uses crack does not care about her baby's well-being, it will be much harder to convince them that refusing medical care evidences the same level of disregard.

The Self-Destructive Pregnant Woman

Self-destructive behavior poses different legal and ethical problems depending on whether it is legal behavior, such as alcoholism, or illegal behavior, such as cocaine use. The AMA policy statement suggests that the physician should provide information and document consent. Beyond this, physicians must decide how far they are willing to accommodate a patient who is unwilling to modify medically destructive behavior. Is there a point where the physician's continued treatment of complications of self-destructive behavior becomes an impediment to the patient's commitment to changing the behavior? Is refusing to continue to treat the patient ethically justifiable if the patient does not have access to appropriate treatment programs? Should the physician's role differ for illegal activities such as cocaine use?

Every self-destructive patient poses these questions. They are more urgent when the patient is pregnant and her behavior threatens to injure her fetus. Absent a state law requiring the reporting of the behavior in question, the physician has no duty to report a patient's illegal drug use to the police or public health authorities. If the state offers only jail to illegal drug users, it is difficult to argue that reporting such a patient is in the patient's interest. A physician's ethical duty is more difficult to determine if the state offers appropriate rehabilitation services. Given the current knowledge of addictive behavior and the effects of drugs such as cocaine, it is difficult to speak of a knowing and voluntary refusal of care by an addicted patient. If the patient cannot make an informed choice, the physician's duty may be to seek judicial intervention to determine the patient's best interests.

THE BIRTH-INJURED INFANT

The first priority with a potential birth injury is to manage the infant's medical condition. Under no circumstances should concerns about possible litigation be allowed to interfere with the infant's medical care. The second priority is to make a definitive diagnosis. Determining what caused the problem may guide the treatment of the child and may help avoid similar problems in future children. It is also critical to the defense of any subsequent litigation.

The careless use of diagnoses such as cerebral palsy or anoxic birth injury has exacerbated the problem of obstetric malpractice litigation (ACOG 163). The pediatrician and the obstetrician should work together to obtain a good etiologic diagnosis for the child. There is a general assumption among laypersons and plaintiffs' attorneys that all nonspecific central nervous system damage is due to birth hypoxia and is therefore the physician's fault. Obstetricians have fostered this belief by failing to investigate the underlying causes of seeming birth injuries.

One promising avenue of investigation is placental analysis. Historically physicians have either discarded placentas or sold them to drug companies. Only recently have obstetricians realized that the placenta is an invaluable research tool and forensic pathology specimen. Placental research is documenting chronic placental insufficiency diseases that may account for 50 percent of what have traditionally been termed birth injuries. Placental pathology studies showing placental insufficiency have been used to defend physicians from charges of negligently injuring a child at birth.

Placental examination should be considered whenever these risk factors are present:

Maternal
- Diabetes Mellitus
- Pregnancy-Induced Hypertension (PIH)
- Premature Rupture of the Membranes (PROM)
- Pre-term Delivery (prior to 36 weeks)
- Post-term Delivery (4q weeks or beyond)
- Unexplained Fever
- Poor Previous Obstetrical History

Fetus/Newborn
- Stillborn
- Neonatal Death
- Multiple Gestation
- Intrauterine Growth Retardation (IUGR)
- Congenital Anomalies
- Erythroblastosis Fetalis
- Transfer to Neonatal Intensive Care Unit
- Ominous Fetal Heart Tracing
- Presence of Meconium
- Apgar Score Below 5 at 1 Minute, or Below

Placental/Umbilical Cord
- Infarction
- Abruptio Placentae
- Vasa Previa
- Placenta Previa
- Abnormal Calcification
- Abnormal Appearance of Placenta or Cord (Ward 1989)

In cases of suspected birth injury, the entire placenta and umbilical cord should be weighted and appropriately preserved. The placenta may be stored until it is determined that the baby does not have any residual damage. If the baby is injured, the placenta should be examined by a pathologist who is skilled in placental pathology. This is not a routine skill and must be specifically sought out. If an unskilled pathologist records that the placenta looks normal, this opinion will only bolster the plaintiff's case. Since these examinations are expensive and usually cannot be billed to the patient, physicians and their malpractice insurance companies must cooperate to pay for the pathologist's services.

BIBLIOGRAPHY
ACOG
ACOG Committee Opinion 49: *Use and Misuse of the Apgar Score*. Committee on Obstetrics: Maternal and Fetal Medicine (ACOG) and Committee on Fetus and Newborn (AAP). November 1986; reaffirmed 1989.

ACOG Committee Opinion 52: *Vitamin A Supplementation During Pregnancy*. Committee on Obstetrics: Maternal and Fetal Medicine. July 1987; reaffirmed 1989.

ACOG Committee Opinion 74: *Strategies to Prevent Prematurity: Home Uterine-Activity Monitoring*. Committee on Obstetrics: Maternal and Fetal Medicine. November 1989.

ACOG Committee Opinion 78: *Guidelines for Hepatitis B Virus Screening and Vaccination During Pregnancy*. Committee on Obstetrics: Maternal and Fetal Medicine. January 1990.

ACOG Committee Opinion 85: *Human Immunodeficiency Virus Infection: Physicians' Responsibilities*. Committee on Ethics. September 1990.

ACOG Committee Opinion 91: *Umbilical Cord Blood Acid-Base Sampling*. Committee on Obstetrics: Maternal and Fetal Medicine. February 1991.

ACOG Technical Bulletin 107: *Antepartum Fetal Surveillance*. August 1987.

ACOG Technical Bulletin 110: *Induction and Augmentation of Labor*. November 1987.

ACOG Technical Bulletin 114: *Perinatal Viral and Parasitic Infections*. March 1988.

ACOG Technical Bulletin 116: *Ultrasound in Pregnancy*. May 1988.

ACOG Technical Bulletin 119: *Gynecologic Herpes Simplex Virus Infection*. August 1988.

ACOG Technical Bulletin 169: *Human Immune Deficiency Virus Infections*. December 1988.

ACOG Technical Bulletin 163: *Fetal and Neonatal Neurologic Injury.* January 1992.

ACOG Technical Bulletin 130: *Diagnosis and Management of Postterm Pregnancy.* July 1989.

ACOG Technical Bulletin 131: *Multiple Gestation.* August 1989.

ACOG Technical Bulletin 147: *Prevention of D Isoimmunization.* October 1990.

ACOG Technical Bulletin 148: *Management of Isoimmunization in Pregnancy.* October 1990.

ACOG Technical Bulletin 149: *Stress in the Practice of Obstetrics and Gynecology.* November 1990.

General Obstetrics

AMA Board of Trustees Report: Legal interventions during pregnancy: Court-ordered medical treatments and legal penalties for potentially harmful behavior by pregnant women. JAMA 1990; 264:2663–70.

Blank RH: Emerging notions of women's rights and responsibilities during gestation. J Leg Med (Chic) 1986 Dec; 7(4):441–69.

Bundy AL; James AE Jr: The lawyer's perspective on the use of ultrasound in obstetrics and gynecology. Law Med Health Care 1985 Oct; 13(5):219–24.

Ellis TS III: Letting defective babies die: Who decides? Am J Law Med 1982 Winter; 7(4):393–423.

Field MA: Controlling the woman to protect the fetus. Law Med Health Care 1989 Summer; 17(2):114–29.

Finamore EP: Jefferson v. Griffin Spalding County Hospital Authority: Court-ordered surgery to protect the life of an unborn child. Am J Law Med 1983 Spring; 9(1):83–101.

Freeman JM: Making decisions for the severely handicapped newborn. J Health Polit Policy Law 1986 Summer; 11(2):285–96.

Greenlaw J: Delivery rooms: For women only? Law Med Health Care 1981 Dec; 9(6):28–29, 40.

Guillemin J: Increasing incidence and medical "necessity" babies by Cesarean: Who chooses, who controls? Hastings Cent Rep 1981 Jun; 11(3):15–18.

Huefner DS: Severely handicapped infants with life-threatening conditions: Federal intrusions into the decision not to treat. Am J Law Med 1986; 12(2):171–205.

Mackenzie TB; Nagel TC: When a pregnant woman endangers her fetus. Hastings Cent Rep 1986 Feb; 16(1):24–25.

Novick LF et al.: New York State HIV Seroprevalence Project, Chapter II Newborn Seroprevalence Study: Methods and results. Am J Pub Health Supp. 1991; 81:15–21.

Richardson D; Rosoff A; McMenamin JP: Referral practices and health care costs. The dilemma of high risk obstetrics. J Leg Med (Chic) 1985 Dec; 6(4):427–64.

Rosenbaum S; Hughes D; Butler E; Howard D: Incantations in the dark: Medicaid, managed care, and maternity care. Milbank Q 1988; 66(4):661–93.

Schifrin BS; Weissman H; Wiley J: Electronic fetal monitoring and obstetrical malpractice. Law Med Health Care 1985 Jun; 13(3):100–5.

Wachsman HF: Doctor and hospital sued successfully by child born eight years after injury to mother. Leg Aspects Med Pract 1978 Jul; 6(7):41–43.

Midwives and Home Births

Buhler L; Glick N; Sheps SB: Prenatal care: A comparative evaluation of nurse-midwives and family physicians. Can Med Assoc J 1988 Sep 1; 139(5):397–403.

Butter IH; Kay BJ: State laws and the practice of lay midwifery. Am J Public Health 1988 Sep; 78(9):1161–69.

Green W: So you want to have the baby at home? Can Med Assoc J 1989 Aug 1; 141(3):248.

Hinds MW; Bergeisen GH; Allen DT: Neonatal outcome in planned v. unplanned out-of-hospital births in Kentucky. JAMA 1985 Mar 15; 253(11):1578–82.

Hoff GA; Schneiderman LJ: Having babies at home: Is it safe? Is it ethical? Hastings Cent Rep 1985 Dec; 15(6):19–27.
Lecky-Thompson M: Homebirth midwives: Powerful pioneers or ratbag radicals? Lamp 1988 Mar; 45(2):10–14.
McClain CS: Perceived risk and choice of childbirth service. Soc Sci Med 1983; 17(23):1857–65.
Macdonald RR: In defense of the obstetrician. Br J Obstet Gynaecol 1987 Sep; 94(9):833–35.
Mann RJ: San Francisco General Hospital nurse-midwifery practice: The first thousand births. Am J Obstet Gynecol 1981 Jul 15; 140(6):676–82.
Pearse WH: Parturition: Places and priorities (editorial). Am J Public Health 1987 Aug; 77(8):923–24.
Purdy RJ; Lasnover AL; Harer WB Jr: Alternative birth practices and settings—indications of prevalence and use among California obstetricians. West J Med 1986 Jul; 145(1):124–27.
Saldana LR; Rivera-Alsina ME; Arias JW; Ross PJ; Pokorny SF: Home birth: Negative implications derived from a hospital-based birthing suite. South Med J 1983 Feb; 76(2):170–73.
Schneider D: Planned out-of-hospital births, New Jersey, 1978–1980. Soc Sci Med 1986; 23(10):1011–15.
Schramm WF; Barnes DE; Bakewell JM: Neonatal mortality in Missouri home births, 1978–84. Am J Public Health 1987 Aug; 77(8):930–35.
Sullivan DA; Beeman R: Four years' experience with home birth by licensed midwives in Arizona. Am J Public Health 1983 Jun; 73(6):641–45.
Tew M: Home, hospital, or birthroom. Lancet 1986 Sep 27; 2(8509):749.
Weatherston L: Midwifery in the hospital: Team approach to perinatal care. Dimens Health Serv 1985 Apr; 62(4):15–16, 22.

Placental Pathology

Altshuler G: Diseases of the placenta and their effect on transport. Mead Johnson Symp Perinat Dev Med 1981; 18:35–43.
Benirschke K; Driscoll SG: *The Pathology of the Placenta.* 1967.
Bjoro K Jr; Myhre E: The role of chronic non-specific inflammatory lesions of the placenta in intra-uterine growth retardation. Acta Pathol Microbiol Immunol Scand (A) 1984 Mar; 92(2):133–37.
Bracero LA; Beneck D; Kirshenbaum N; Peiffer M; Stalter P; Schulman H: Doppler velocimetry and placental disease. Am J Obstet Gynecol 1989 Aug; 161(2):388–93.
Crane J; Anderson B; Marshall R; Harvey P: Subsequent physical and mental development in infants with positive contraction stress tests. J Reprod Med 1981 Mar; 26(3):113–18.
Fox H: Pathology of the placenta. Clin Obstet Gynaecol 1986 Sep; 13(3):501–19.
Garcia AG: Placental morphology of low-birth-weight infants born at term. Contrib Gynecol Obstet 1982; 9:100–12.
Hills D; Irwin GA; Tuck S; Baim R: Distribution of placental grade in high-risk gravidas. AJR 1984 Nov; 143(5):1011–13.
Kazzi GM; Gross TL; Rosen MG; Jaatoul-Kazzi NY: The relationship of placental grade, fetal lung maturity, and neonatal outcome in normal and complicated pregnancies. Am J Obstet Gynecol 1984 Jan 1; 148(1):54–58.
Naeye RL: Functionally important disorders of the placenta, umbilical cord, and fetal membranes. Hum Pathol 1987; 18:680.
Salafia CM; Weigl C; Silberman L: The prevalence and distribution of acute placental inflammation in uncomplicated term pregnancies. Obstet Gynecol 1989 Mar; 73(3 Pt 1):383–89.
Sander CH; Kinnane L; Stevens NG; et al.: Haemorrhagic endovasculitis of the placenta: A review with clinical correlation. Placenta 1986; 7:551.

Shen-Schwarz S; Macpherson TA; Mueller-Heubach E: The clinical significance of hemorrhagic endovasculitis of the placenta. Am J Obstet Gynecol 1988 Jul; 159(1):48–51.

Sheppard BL; Bonnar J: The ultrastructure of the arterial supply of the human placenta in pregnancy complicated by fetal growth retardation. Br J Obstet Gynaecol 1976 Dec; 83(12):948–59.

Vorherr H: Placental insufficiency in relation to postterm pregnancy and fetal postmaturity: Evaluation of fetoplacental function; management of the postterm gravida. Am J Obstet Gynecol 1975 Sep 1; 123(1):67–103.

Ward CJ: The case for placental examination. The Digest: A Medical Liability and Risk Management News Letter (St. Paul Fire and Insurance Company, Fall) 1989:1.

28

Taking Care of Children

CRITICAL POINTS
- Inadequate immunizations are a critical childhood problem in the United States.
- Persons who provide medical care for children must understand the Vaccine Compensation Act.
- Pediatric record keeping must include the recording and analysis of growth and development data.
- Physicians must recognize and report child neglect as well as child abuse.

Pediatrics, or more specifically, the medical care of children, is the most legally distinct of the medical specialties. This legal uniqueness has three threads. The first is consent to care. Children may not legally determine their own care, but neither are parents fully empowered to control their child's medical care. The second is communication with the physician. Very young patients are unable to communicate their medical needs to a physician effectively. Finally, childhood immunizations are the frontline in protecting society from epidemic communicable diseases. Immunization, with the potential risk of serious sequellae, creates a conflict between the child's individual medical care needs and the protection of society.

With the exception of intensivists treating neonates, the care of children is a legally low-risk endeavor. General pediatricians tend to get in trouble more for what they do not do than for what they do. This is to be expected in any area of medicine in which the vast majority of patient encounters are either preventive in nature or are for minor illnesses. Many of the cases in which pediatricians are charged with failure to diagnose a condition actually involve a systems failure in the physician's office routine rather than an error in medical judgment. As with all other physicians who have highly routinized practices, pediatricians must take special care to document all findings and ensure that atypical events are identified.

IMMUNIZATIONS

Over the last 20 years, the American political system has handled immunization policy poorly. This reflects profound ignorance of disease control among elected officials and lawyers. These individuals see immunization as a personal health problem rather than a public health and safety issue. As a result of this narrow view of the role of immunization in protecting the community's health, litigation has been allowed to drive the cost of routine immunizations beyond the means of many poor families. At the same time, governmental agencies have reduced their commitment to a fully immunized population, and private individuals are encouraged in unfounded fears of the risks of immunization.

Herd Immunity and Community Health

Immunization protects community health in two ways. The more obvious is through protecting individuals from communicable diseases. The second is the promotion of herd immunity. If an immunization were 100 percent effective (an immunized person had a zero probability of becoming infected with the target disease), then immunizing every person in a community would eradicate the target disease in that community. In this situation, personal protection and community protection are the same.

If everyone in the community were immunized save one, that one unimmunized person would also be protected from infection. Assuming that the community is isolated from other, unimmunized communities, the single unimmunized individual is protected because the disease has been eradicated. The problem is that immunizations have risks, so every person wants to be the one unimmunized individual protected by the herd.

Herd immunity is critical to the control of immunizable diseases. It is difficult, however, to predict the precise level of community immunity that is necessary to prevent the spread of a disease. Herd immunity is dependent on the communicability of the disease, the nature of transmission, the effectiveness of the immunization, the duration of period that an infected person may communicate the disease, whether the disease is treatable, whether the disease has a silent period when it is communicable, the general health of the community, and the health of the infected individuals.

Herd immunity is also dependent on the dynamics of a given epidemic. What might be an acceptable level of immunity to prevent spread from random, single cases of the disease could be insufficient to stop a major inoculation such as the arrival of a planeload of infected refugees. Most critically, herd immunity depends on the unimmunized individuals' being randomly distributed in the community. If unimmunized persons cluster, then it is the percentage of immunization in the cluster that determines the spread of the disease. This is frequently the case with religious groups that refuse immunization. One hundred unimmunized persons in a large city will not be a problem until they all meet at church.

The inherent uncertainty in herd immunity limits its use as an explicit disease control strategy. A community must attempt to immunize every susceptible individual. Herd immunity will then cover the small number of susceptible persons who are inadvertently missed or who are not candidates for immunization. (Herd immunity is the only realistic defense for many immunocompromised individuals.) A community immunization plan must target the two main groups of individuals who are weak links in a herd immunity system. The largest group is the poor, especially the medically indigent. These individuals are both less likely to be immunized and more susceptible to infection.

Compulsory Immunization

The more difficult problem is religious or cultural groups that oppose immunizations. These groups tend to cluster, reducing the effective immunization level in their neighborhoods, schools, and churches. In addition to endangering their own children, such groups pose a substantial risk to the larger community. By providing a reservoir of infection, a cluster of unimmunized persons can defeat the general herd immunity of a community. As these infected persons mix with members of the larger community, they will expose those who are susceptible to contagion.

Many physicians, lawyers, and judges believe that the constitutional protection for freedom of religion includes freedom from immunizations. This is not the law today, nor has it ever been the law in the United States. The U.S. Supreme Court, in *Jacobson v. Massachusetts* (1905), held that an individual could not refuse smallpox vaccination: "We are not prepared to hold that a minority, residing or remaining in any city or town where smallpox is prevalent, and enjoying the general protection afforded by an organized local government, may thus defy the will of its constituted authorities, acting in good faith for all, under the legislative sanction of the State" (p. 37).

In the later case of *Prince v. Massachusetts* (1944), the U.S. Supreme Court spoke directly to the issue of religious objections to vaccination:

> But the family itself is not beyond regulation in the public interest, as against a claim of religious liberty. And neither rights of religion nor rights of parenthood are beyond limitation. Acting to guard the general interest in youth's well being, the state as parens patriae may restrict the parent's control by requiring school attendance, regulating or prohibiting the child's labor and in many other ways. Its authority is not nullified merely because the parent grounds his claim to control the child's course of conduct on religion or conscience. Thus, he cannot claim freedom from compulsory vaccination for the child more than for himself on religious grounds. The right to practice religion freely does not include liberty to expose the community or the child to communicable disease or the latter to ill health or death.

Despite the clear language of the U.S. Supreme Court, nearly all state immunization laws provide an exemption for persons with religious objections to immunization. This creates a large loophole because the Constitution will not allow laws that favor one religion over another. Christian Scientists are exempt if they choose to be, but so are individuals who have their own unique religious beliefs. If a state provides a religious exemption, the state may not question the validity of the religious beliefs of those who invoke the exception.

State compulsory immunization laws contain these exemptions because few legislators understand the public health and safety implications of immunization. No states exempt religious groups from child abuse laws or other criminal laws intended to protect either children or the general public. Physicians should make a concerted effort to educate their legislators to the risks of allowing children to remain unimmunized.

Consent for Immunizations

All states require that children be immunized for certain diseases before entering school. Since school attendance is mandatory, the law makes immunization mandatory. Philosophically, it is absurd to speak of informed consent to a mandatory treatment. Nonetheless, physicians are expected to obtain informed consent for these immunizations. There is only one acceptable way to obtain this consent: using the federally promulgated vaccine information pamphlets (Goldsmith 1992). These are often referred to as the IMPORTANT INFORMATION forms because of their introductory header. They are available from the vaccine distributors, state health departments, and the CDC. The forms have a section to document the consent, including the manufacturer and lot number for the biological, and the date of the immunization. While not part of the mandatory information, it is also useful to record the name of the person administering the immunization.

It is imperative that every patient or person authorizing the immunization (parent or guardian) be given the information in the federal form and a copy to keep. The federal information form should be incorporated into the child's medical record. The consent can be further documented in a more conventional immunization record such as those provided by the World Health Organization. These formal immunization records are useful to show that the child's immunization status is current.

Medical Exemptions

All state immunization laws contain an exemption for individuals with medical contraindications to immunization. It is beyond the scope of this book to list all the contraindications to immunization. Every physician who cares for children or authorizes immunizations should have a current copy of the *Report of the Committee on Infectious Disease* published by the American Academy of Pediatrics (the "Red Book"). This book is a storehouse of invaluable information about immunizations and the management of communicable diseases. It sets the legal standard of care for this branch of medical practice.

The general medical concern is that persons with suppressed immune systems should not be given live vaccine preparations. These include oral polio, oral typhoid, measles, mumps, rubella, and BCG vaccines. Persons with normal immune function develop antibodies to these agents and suffer a mild or subclinical infection. Persons with suppressed immune systems frequently develop full symptomatic disease, including adverse sequellae. Immunosuppressed persons, or patients who live with immunosuppressed persons, should receive live vaccines only under controlled circumstances.

Physicians must be careful to ensure that patients do not receive contraindicated immunizations. As discussed in the Red Book, there are several short-term contraindications to immunization, as well as the long-term contraindication of immunosuppression. All patients must be questioned or examined to identify the existence of medical contraindications. If these are present, they should be documented in the patient's medical record. Such patients should also be given a medical exemption form to allow them to enter school without the requisite immunizations. Unless required by state law, this exemption need not detail the patient's personal medical condition, only that the patient is not a candidate for immunization. If the exemption is based on a short-term contraindication, this should be reviewed on a subsequent visit and the child immunized as soon as medically advisable.

Physicians should never grant medical exemptions that are not based on objective medical findings. There are parents who are unwilling to claim a religious objection for their children but do not want their children immunized. A physician who grants such a child an exemption from immunization will be legally liable if the child contracts a disease that could be prevented through immunization. Physicians who exempt a child from immunization improperly may also be a party to child neglect. This could result in a legal prosecution if the child were to suffer a permanent injury from a preventable disease.

The Vaccine Compensation Act

Products liability losses by vaccine manufacturers have driven the cost of vaccines beyond the reach of indigent patients and many health departments. In an effort to control these losses, Congress passed the Vaccine Injury Compensation Act to compensate persons injured by vaccines. This compensation program is funded by a combination of tax revenues on vaccine sales and general tax revenues. This law has two major flaws. One is that the tax on vaccine sales is very high, exceeding four dollars a dose for some common vaccines. The more important is that it is not an exclusive remedy.

While the plaintiff is required to file a claim for review under the act, the plaintiff may reject the award offered under the act and sue the vaccine manufacturer. This is most likely to happen in cases involving brain-injured children. These are the cases that are sympathetic to jurors and thus are most likely to result in huge damage awards. Allowing these plaintiffs to opt out of the compensation system leaves vaccine manufacturers subject to the same high products liability costs that have driven up the price of vaccinations. It is possible that the net result of the law will be to increase vaccine costs, further crippling immunization efforts in the United States.

Recording Duties

Section 300aa-25 of Title 42 of the U.S. Code requires:

> Each health care provider who administers a vaccine set forth in the Vaccine Injury Table to any person shall record, or ensure that there is recorded, in such person's permanent medical record (or in a permanent office log or file to which a legal representative shall have access upon request) with respect to each such vaccine—
>
> (1) the date of administration of the vaccine,
> (2) the vaccine manufacturer and lot number of the vaccine,
> (3) the name and address and, if appropriate, the title of the health care provider administering the vaccine, and
> (4) any other identifying information on the vaccine required pursuant to regulations promulgated by the Secretary.

Reporting Duties

> Each health care provider and vaccine manufacturer shall report to the Secretary—
>
> (A) the occurrence of any event set forth in the Vaccine Injury Table, including the events . . . which occur within 7 days of the administration of any vaccine set forth in the Table or within such longer period as is specified in the Table or section, [and]
> (B) the occurrence of any contraindicating reaction to a vaccine which is specified in the manufacturer's package insert. . . .
>
> A report . . . respecting a vaccine shall include the time periods after the administration of such vaccine within which vaccine-related illnesses, disabilities, injuries,

or conditions, the symptoms and manifestations of such illnesses, disabilities, injuries, or conditions, or deaths occur, and the manufacturer and lot number of the vaccine.

Attorney's Duty

It shall be the ethical obligation of any attorney who is consulted by an individual with respect to a vaccine-related injury or death to advise such individual that compensation may be available under the program for such injury or death.

Physicians probably have an ethical duty to counsel vaccine-injured patients about the availability of compensation under the Vaccine Compensation Act. If the physician assists the patient in obtaining compensation, the patient may be more likely to accept the award under the act and forgo a lawsuit. The problem is that the vaccine injury table (see Table 28-1) and the vaccine pack inserts list many events that have not been proven to be related to vaccine administration

Table 28-1. Reportable Events Following Vaccination

Vaccine/Toxoid	Event	Interval from Vaccination
DTP, P, DTP/Polio Combined	A. Anaphylaxis or anaphylactic shock	24 hours
	B. Encephalopathy (or encephalitis)*	7 days
	C. Shock-collapse or hypotonic-hyporesponsive collapse*	7 days
	D. Residual seizure disorder*	(See Aids to Interpretation*)
	E. Any acute complication or sequela (including death) of above events	No limit
	F. Events in vaccinees described in manufacturer's package insert as contraindications to additional doses of vaccine† (such as convulsions)	(See package insert)
Measles, Mumps, and Rubella; DT, Td, Tetanus Toxoid	A. Anaphylaxis or anaphylactic shock	24 hours
	B. Encephalopathy (or encephalitis)*	15 days for measles, mumps and rubella vaccines; 7 days for DT, Td, and T toxoids
	C. Residual seizure disorder*	(See Aids to Interpretation*)
	D. Any acute complication or sequela (including death) of above events	No limit
	E. Events in vaccinees described in manufacturer's package insert as contraindications to additional doses of vaccine†	(See package insert)
Oral Polio Vaccine	A. Paralytic poliomyelitis	
	-in a non-immunodeficient recipient	30 days
	-in an immunodeficient recipient	6 months
	-in a vaccine-associated community case	No limit
	B. Any acute complication or sequela (including death) of above events	No limit
	C. Events in vaccinees described in manufacturer's package insert as contraindications to additional doses of vaccine†	(See package insert)

Table 28-1. (Continued)

Vaccine/Toxoid	Event	Interval from Vaccination
Inactivated Polio Vaccine	A. Anaphylaxis or anaphylactic shock	24 hours
	B. Any acute complication or sequela (including death) of above event	No limit
	C. Events in vaccinees described in manufacturer's package insert as contraindications to additional doses of vaccine†	(See package insert)

*Aids to Interpretation:

Shock-collapse or hypotonic-hyporesponsive collapse may be evidenced by signs or symptoms such as decrease in or loss of muscle tone, paralysis (partial or complete), hemiplegia, hemiparesis, loss of color or turning pale white or blue, unresponsiveness to environmental stimuli, depression of or loss of consciousness, prolonged sleeping with difficulty arousing, or cardiovascular or respiratory arrest.

Residual seizure disorder may be considered to have occurred if no other seizure or convulsion unaccompanied by fever or accompanied by a fever of less than 102° F occurred before the first seizure or convulsion after the administration of the vaccine involved,

AND, if in the case of measles-, mumps-, or rubella-containing vaccines, the first seizure or convulsion occurred within 15 days after vaccination OR in the case of any other vaccine, the first seizure or convulsion occurred within 3 days after vaccination,

AND, if two or more seizures or convulsions unaccompanied by fever or accompanied by a fever of less than 102° F occurred within 1 year after vaccination.

The terms seizure and convulsion include grand mal, petit mal, absence, myoclonic, tonic-clonic, and focal motor seizures and signs. Encephalopathy means any significant acquired abnormality of, injury to, or impairment of function of the brain. Among the frequent manifestations of encephalopathy are focal and diffuse neurologic signs, increased intracranial pressure, or changes lasting at least 6 hours in level of consciousness, with or without convulsions. The neurologic signs and symptoms of encephalopathy may be temporary with complete recovery, or they may result in various degrees of permanent impairment. Signs and symptoms such as high-pitched and unusual screaming, persistent unconsolable crying, and bulging fontanel are compatible with an encephalopathy, but in and of themselves are not conclusive evidence of encephalopathy. Encephalopathy usually con be documented by slow wave activity on an electroencephalogram.

†The health-care provider must refer to the CONTRAINDICATION section of the manufacturer's package insert for each vaccine.

(Fulginiti 1992). In addition to encouraging unfounded claims, the listing of these unproven risks fuels the myth that vaccines are dangerous (Lynch 1991).

PEDIATRIC RECORDS

Pediatric record keeping has two complicating aspects. First, most visits are for minor illnesses. Second, the records must track growth and development, which is not an issue in adult medical practice. The difficulty with a practice that is overwhelmingly devoted to minor illnesses and well-child care is that it is easy to miss subtle developmental problems and rare, fast-evolving illnesses such as meningitis. This is particularly a problem in children with atypical presentations. It can be impossible to tell the early onset of meningitis from an upper respiratory infection. If the disease progresses very quickly, the child may be permanently injured before the physician could reasonably have expected to make the proper diagnosis.

Juries will be unsympathetic to a physician's claims unless the medical record carefully documents the child's condition and the physician's plans. The problem is that many physicians keep sketchy records on children with minor illnesses. These records are adequate for the vast majority of patients who are not seriously ill, but they may mask the progress of a severe illness. This increases both the chance of prolonging the misdiagnosis and the probability that a jury will rule against the physician. Physicians caring for children must make a special effort to record the presence and absence of diagnostic signs that indicate serious illness.

Acute Illness Observation Scale

P. L. McCarthy's technique of evaluating pediatric patients focuses on six easily observed factors that, taken together, are a sensitive indicator of serious illness in an infant. Ideally, each of these factors would be noted on every pediatric patient seen for an illness. This could be accomplished by using a rubber stamp to enter the list into the medical record. Even if the individual factors are not recorded for each visit, they should always be recorded for patients in whom they are abnormal:

Quality of Cry
1—strong cry with normal tone or contented and not crying
2—whimpering or sobbing
3—weak cry, moaning, or high-pitched cry

Reaction to Parental Stimulation
1—cries briefly and then stops, or is contented and not crying
2—cries off and on
3—cries continually or hardly responds

State Variation
1—if awake, stays awake, or if asleep and then stimulated, awakens quickly
2—closes eyes briefly when awake, or awakens with prolonged stimulation
3—falls asleep or will not arouse

Color
1—pink
2—pale extremities or acrocyanosis
3—pale, cyanotic, mottled or ashen

Hydration
1—normal skin and eyes, moist mucous membranes
2—normal skin and eyes, slightly dry mouth
3—doughy or tented skin, dry mucous membranes and/or sunken eyes

Response (Talk, Smile) to Social Overtures, Over 2 Months
1—smiles or alerts
2—smiles briefly or alerts briefly
3—no smile, anxious face, dull expression, or does not alert

Recording Physical Growth and Development

Carefully recorded charts of a child's growth and development are critical to detecting long-term developmental problems and chronic illnesses with gradual onset. The child's physical development should be recorded on height and weight charts. Height and weight should be recorded at regular intervals, and weights should be taken at every visit. Weights should be measured at every pediatric visit for acute illness. A physician cannot access hydration or weight loss in a small child if there is no record of the child's weight before the onset of the illness.

The data should be plotted at the time they are taken. The most legally damaging situation is to have height and weight information recorded in the child's chart but not plotted. It is impossible to evaluate changes in these data without comparing them to previous measurements and the norms on the charts. When the physician's care is questioned, the plaintiff's attorney will plot the data to demonstrate to the jury that the physician should have seen problems.

Recording Neuromuscular Development

The child's neuromuscular development should be tracked with a standard assessment tool such as the Denver Developmental Screening Test. If these tools are used conscientiously, they can illustrate subtle developmental problems that might otherwise go unnoticed. They also allow the early detection of medical problems, such as hearing impairment, that must be treated promptly to prevent disruption of the child's development.

The standards of care for pediatric preventive medicine are stringent. The federal maternal and child health programs set explicit standards for developmental screening. A physician in private practice cannot justify a lower standard of care for health assessment than the child would receive in a community health center or from the local health department.

TELEPHONE ENCOUNTERS

Pediatric practice is telephone intensive. This is consistent with the minor nature of most pediatric illnesses. Most calls to the pediatrician are for reassurance that the child is not seriously ill. More problematically, most calls are handled by office personnel other than the physician in charge. These calls are seldom recorded in the patient's chart, and calls are often answered without reference to the chart. This leads to the most common telephone-related legal problem: misunderstanding about the severity or progression of the child's illness.

One of the most important diagnostic indicators for children is the parent's level of concern. If a parent calls the physician's office repeatedly over a period of hours or days, this should alert the physician that the child should be seen immediately. Legally, it is very difficult to defend cases in which the parents have repeatedly called the physician's office. If the child is injured due to a missed diagnosis or treatment failure, the jury will assume that the problem could have been managed if the child had been seen.

Physicians must know what their office personnel tell patients who call with medical questions. There must also be a protocol to identify the cases that must be handled by the physician and potential emergencies. In addition to the general telephone problems discussed in Chapter 9, pediatric telephone advice poses special problems that are beyond the scope of this book. (See Schmitt 1980.)

When the physician on call has not had an uninterrupted meal or night's sleep in a week, it is easy to forget that one cannot look at a rash, listen to a chest, or palpate an abdomen over the telephone. The mother's description is not a substitute for a physical examination. If the child potentially has any condition where proper care decisions would require a physical examination, the child should be sent to the office or the emergency room immediately. If the mother is unreliable, then her descriptions over the telephone are also suspect. If the mother is reliable, then she would not call late at night unless she has a serious concern.

The same basic information must be recorded for every telephone call: date; time; name and age of the patient; telephone number; symptoms; disposition of the call; whether it is a repeat call; and the person handling the call. In most offices, the only practical way to record this information is in a telephone log. It is too difficult to pull patient charts for every call. Using a central telephone log also allows the supervising physician to monitor the management of calls in the office. The problem with telephone logs is that they can prevent important medical information from being incorporated into the patient's chart.

There must be a protocol to determine what information should be transcribed from the telephone log into the patient's chart. This problem will be eased considerably if the physician uses a telephone log with a preprinted information form on 2-part carbonless paper. Ideally, the copy of every call slip will be filed into the patient's chart. If this is impossible, it is critical to transfer all treatment recommendations, prescriptions, refill call-ins, referrals to the emergency room, and repeat calls for the same problem.

CONSENT TO TREATMENT

The legal requirements for consent to a minor's medical care are discussed in Chapters 11 and 12. In addition to these legal requirements, physicians must contend with the special logistics problems of caring for children. One common problem is that pediatric patients are often brought to the office by someone other than the parent or legal guardian. In a busy pediatrics practice, it is easy to lose track of who has the legal right to consent to medical care for a child. As the divorce rate increases, more children have multiple parents with varying rights to consent to medical care.

The first time children are brought to the office, they should be accompanied by the parent or guardian who has full authority to consent to care. At that time, the physician should obtain written consent to care, including written authorization for any other persons who will be bringing the child in for care. This authorization should list who may consent to the child's care and whether there are any restrictions on what kind of care they may authorize. While it sometimes cannot be avoided, the physician should check with the parents or guardian before accepting this proxy consent for surgical procedures or extensive nonemergency care. If there is disagreement between divorced parents over a child's medical care, it is important to find out which parent has the legal right to consent to the child's care. This can usually be determined by a call to the clerk of the court that has jurisdiction over the divorce. Child welfare services can also help in determining this information.

CHILD ABUSE

Child abuse and neglect is a common problem in our society, prevalent in all races, religions, and socioeconomic groups. All states have laws requiring that physicians report suspected child abuse to a government agency in charge of protecting children. This is sometimes a frustrating experience for the physician.

These agencies are overworked and have limited resources. All physicians who care for children should know which local agency enforces the child welfare laws in their state.

Child abuse is not a diagnosis; it is a legal determination. A physician who suspects that a child is abused or neglected or is in danger of being abused or neglected has a duty to report that suspicion. Physicians should not try to investigate the potential abuse on their own. This may endanger the child, confuse the legal issues, and subject the physician to prosecution for failing to report the suspected abuse. Many physicians are slow to report suspicions of child abuse because they are concerned that they may be making an unfounded judgment about the parents or the family. Physicians must also guard against parents' rationalizations about why their behavior should not be considered child abuse. The physician's obligation is to evaluate the effect of the behavior on the child. The child protection agency will investigate the parents' explanations before taking any legal action. Physicians must not second-guess the child protection agency or attempt private resolutions of possible abuse.

Child Neglect

Child abuse includes acts of omission as well as commission. Parents must provide a child with food, shelter, clothing, education, medical care, and reasonable emotional support within the limits of their ability. If a child appears to lack any of these necessities, the physician should be involved in finding out why. If the family is in crisis and lacks the resources to provide for the children, local social service agencies should be contacted to assist. A church food bank may be able to provide food until the family is eligible for food stamps, or a shelter for the homeless may be able to take them in until housing becomes available. Most public hospitals have social workers on staff who can help with such problems.

If the parents have the resources to care for a child properly but choose not to, they are neglecting that child. This includes parents who do not have adequate resources but refuse necessary social services for personal reasons. Parents who are disabled or emotionally disturbed may be incapable of caring for a child properly. In such situations, a report should be made to the child protection agency. If the parents have good intentions but difficulty coping, then protective services may be able to help them find the necessary community support. If the parents are not willing or able to meet the needs of the child, the protection agency may have to remove the child from the home.

Defending the Child

Because a parent or guardian is the one who consents to medical care for a child and pays for the care, it is easy to forget that the physician-patient relationship runs to the child rather than to the parents. Physicians who have reason to think that a child is in danger should pursue all avenues of protection for that child. Physicians should be prepared to testify in court proceedings and to work with protective services. If the child is returned to the custody of an abusive parent under a restrictive order, the child's physician should know the conditions and should contact protective services if there is any indication that the order is being violated.

If the child protection agency does not intend to pursue the case, a reporting physician should ask for a reasonable explanation of the injuries or conditions that led to the suspicion of child abuse. If the explanation is unsatisfactory or incomplete, the physician should discuss this fully with the person in charge of the agency. Clearing up misunderstandings may save a child's life. The agency may also give more attention to a case in which a physician has serious concerns. Since the agency is not a court and must ask for court orders in serious cases, the support of the child's physician may help them to convince the judge that legal actions are needed.

INTERESTS OF THE CHILD VERSUS THE PARENTS

Parents are presumed to have the best interests of their children at heart. In many cases, however, the values and interests of the child are not the same as those of the parents. This problem becomes more common as children enter adolescence. Physicians who care for adolescent boys often see families in which the boy feels compelled to compete in sports to retain his father's affection. As long as this does not interfere with the child's growth and development, it is not a problem for the physician. However, parental enthusiasm becomes detrimental to the child if decisions about the care of injuries are made on the basis of ability to play rather than what is best for the long-term health of the child.

Physicians are increasingly pressured by parents to use medical treatments to alter characteristics of normal healthy children. One of the most controversial therapies is the use of human growth hormone to stimulate growth in children without intrinsic growth hormone deficiency. In most cases, the child is short for his or her age.

Questions are being raised, however, about using growth hormone to help already tall children gain the extra height and size that is a critical edge in professional sports. Unlike the analogous problem of vanity surgery, the patient is not able to give an informed, legally binding consent to the treatment. This raises profound ethical questions about the role of the physician and the definition of health (Lantos 1989).

Religious Objections to Medical Care

This is one of the most important areas of change in the law governing medical care for minors. Where the religious beliefs of the parents once were paramount, the child's right to life and health now takes precedence over the parents' right to freedom of religion. An adult Jehovah's Witness, for instance, may have the right to refuse transfusion, even if it means certain death. That same person does not have the right to refuse transfusion for a child who will likely die. If parents refuse necessary care for a child, the physician or hospital administrator should immediately seek a court order for the care. If the care is needed urgently and cannot await the court order, then the physician should proceed with the care regardless of the parents' objections. The court order should be sought at the same time. The justification for this is the same as the emergency exception to consent. It is reasonable to assume that the court will uphold the child's right to life and health and grant the order for care. If the court cannot be contacted in time, the physician should go ahead with the care just as if it were the parents who are unavailable (Holder 1987).

Specific Types of Care

Parents may have many reasons for refusing specific types of care. Refusing the care offered by a particular physician or institution is not the same as neglecting the medical needs of the child. Parents may refuse a particular type of care because they do not believe it is in the child's best interests. Courts generally defer to the parents as the most appropriate judge of the child's interests; however, if the physician believes that the parents are not acting in the child's best interest, this should be reported to the child protection agency.

Physicians should be careful about the claims they make for the offered care. It is not unreasonable for parents to refuse medical care that is difficult or painful if it does not offer a substantial benefit to the child. Parents who refuse supportive care when there is little or no hope of cure are properly asserting the child's right to refuse unnecessary care. This is also true for discontinuing care. If parents refuse treatment for the first presentation of acute lymphocytic leukemia because they do not believe in treating cancer, the physician should seek court intervention. If the parents refuse a repeat course of chemotherapy when there is little hope of remission because they want the child to die at home in comfortable surroundings, the physician should probably do what he or she can to assist them. Physicians should not try to enforce their personal beliefs about hope or dying on the parents or the afflicted child.

SPECIAL LEGAL CONSIDERATIONS

For the most part, malpractice cases involving children are handled the same as cases that involve adults. Discovery, standards, and expert testimony are not substantially different; however, there are some differences that are important to anyone who cares for children. The most fundamental of these is that juries like children. The child may have been injured by the parents' neglect and refusal to follow the physician's orders, but the jury gives the money to the child. If the physician is concerned about liability secondary to parental neglect, then the proper course of action is to contact child protection services.

Acute Medical Care

Physicians have an obligation to ensure that children are not deprived of medical care for financial reasons. Ethically, children are entitled to special consideration because of their dependent status. Legally, it is risky to turn away a child in need of care because of the volatility of childhood diseases. A simple case of diarrhea can prove fatal quickly in an infant. The delay that is attendant upon being refused care without a proper referral to a physician willing to care for the child may prove fatal. A physician must never allow a child to be turned away from a hospital or emergency room because the parents do not have money or insurance. If there is an ongoing physician-patient relationship, the physician must be the child's advocate and demand care. Payment issues between the parents and the hospital should not be allowed to interfere with medical care. A physician who is not willing to insist on proper hospital care may violate federal laws governing the provision of emergency medical care. (see Chapter 32.)

Long Statutes of Limitation

The period of time that a physician may be sued for malpractice by or for a child is much longer than it is for an adult. Most states have a statute of limitations that starts when the injury occurs or when it is discovered by the patient. It is common practice to toll the statute of limitations on children until the child reaches the age of majority. For instance, an adult patient might have two years to bring suit. A 3-year-old child may have until age 18 plus 2 more years to bring a malpractice suit, a total of 17 years. This prevents the child's rights from being compromised if the parents fail to pursue the action.

The functional statute of limitations may also be quite long if the statutory period does not begin to run until the injury is discovered. Assume that the uterus of a 5-year-old child is negligently damaged during bladder surgery. As the child grows, her sexual development is normal, and no problem is suspected. The girl reaches adulthood, marries, and uses contraceptives to postpone childbearing until she is ready for children. At age 30, she attempts to conceive and is unable to do so. After two years of infertility, she has a surgical procedure that reveals that the damage from the first surgery is the reason for her infertility. If the statute of limitations runs until two years after the injury is discovered, this patient may be age 34 when she sues the surgeon for an operation done 29 years before.

Despite the long-term potential liability and the uncertainty it generates in malpractice insurance rate setting, general pediatricians still pay relatively low rates. Nonetheless, all physicians who care for children should be careful to preserve medical records until at least a few years past the child's maturity. As with other medical records, the physician should attempt to provide the patient with a copy before destroying the old record. (See Chapter 8.) While this is difficult with records of now-adult pediatric patients, these records can be especially valuable. Unlike adults who are informed of the nature of their illness at the time the care is rendered, pediatric patients have no personal memory of their early medical history. This history can be important for their adult medical care and for determining the presence of inherited conditions that may afflict their own children.

BIBLIOGRAPHY

Child Abuse

Berger DK; Rolon Y; Sachs J; Wilson B: Child abuse and neglect: An instrument to assist with case referral decision making. Health Soc Work 1989 Feb; 14(1):60–73.

Besharov DJ: Reporting out-of-home maltreatment: Penalties and protections. Child Welfare 1987 Sep–Oct; 66(5):399–408.

Eckenrode J; Powers J; Doris J; Munsch J; Bolger N: Substantiation of child abuse and neglect reports. J Consult Clin Psychol 1988 Feb; 56(1):9–16.

Kaplan JM: The misdiagnosis of child abuse. Am Fam Physician 1984 Sep; 30(3):197–200.

Lantos J; Siegler M; Cuttler L: Ethical issues in growth hormone therapy. JAMA 1989; 261:1020–24.

Racusin RJ; Felsman JK: Reporting child abuse: The ethical obligation to inform parents. J Am Acad Child Psychiatry 1986 Jul; 25(4):485–89.

Reece RM; Grodin MA: Recognition of nonaccidental injury. Pediatr Clin North Am 1985 Feb; 32(1):41–60.

Saulsbury FT; Hayden GF: Child abuse reporting by physicians. South Med J 1986 May; 79(5):585–87.

Steiner H; Taylor M: Description and recording physical signs in suspected child sexual abuse. Br J Hosp Med 1988 Nov; 40(5):346–51.

Tammelleo AD: Report suspected child abuse immediately. Case in point. *Milburn v. Anne Arundel County DSS* (871 F. 2d 474—MD (1989)). Regan Rep Nurs Law 1989 Jun; 30(1):4.

Woolf A; Taylor L; Melnicoe L; Andolsek K; Dubowitz H; De Vos E; Newberger E: What residents know about child abuse. Implications of a survey of knowledge and attitudes. Am J Dis Child 1988 Jun; 142(6):668–72.

Immunizations

Anderson RM; Grenfell BT; May RM: Oscillatory fluctuations in the incidence of infectious disease and the impact of vaccination: Time series analysis. J Hyg (Lond) 1984 Dec; 93(3):587–608.

David AB; Jalilian-Marian A: DTP: Drug manufacturers' liability in vaccine-related injuries. J Leg Med (Chic) 1986 Jun; 7(2):187–233.

DeWitt DE; Ostergaard D: Immunization: A shot in the arm for travelers. Postgrad Med 1984 Oct; 76(5):243–45.

Fulginiti VA: How safe are the pertussis and rubella vaccines? A commentary on the Institute of Medicine Report. Ped 1992 Feb; 89:334–36.

Gillum JE; Garrison MW; Crossley KB; Rotschafer JC: Current immunization practices. 1. Polio, diphtheria, tetanus, pertussis, measles, mumps, rubella, and influenza. Postgrad Med 1989 Feb 1; 85(2):183–86, 188–90, 195–98.

Gillum JE; Garrison MW; Crossley KB; Rotschafer JC: Current immunization practices. 2. Hemophilus influenzae, pneumococcal, and meningococcal infections, rabies, and hepatitis. Postgrad Med 1989 Feb 1; 85(2):199–202, 207–10.

Goldsmith MF: Vaccine information pamphlets here but some physicians react strongly. JAMA 1992 Apr 15; 267:2005–7.

Hinman AR: Vaccine-preventable diseases and child day care. Rev Infect Dis 1986 Jul–Aug; 8(4):573–83.

Hirayama M: Surveillance of communicable diseases and immunization program. Acta Paediatr Jpn Overseas Ed 1988 Apr; 30(2):127–35.

Hughes WT; Townsend TR: Nosocomial infections in immunocompromised children. Am J Med 1981 Feb; 70(2):412–16.

Jacobson v. Massachusetts. 197 US 11 (1905).

Katz SL: Controversies in immunization. Pediatr Infect Dis J 1987 Jun; 6(6):607–13.

Klein JO: Infectious diseases and day care. Rev Infect Dis 1986 Jul–Aug; 8(4):521–26.

Leenders F: Immunisation: Vital jabs. Community Outlook 1987 Oct 14:20–22.

Lynch TP: Vaccine myth and physician handouts. Am J Dis Child 1991; 145:426–27.

Marcati P; Pozio MA: Global asymptotic stability for a vector disease model with spatial spread. J Math Biol 1980 Apr; 9(2):179–87.

Parkman PD; Hopps HE: Viral vaccines and antivirals: Current use and future prospects. Annu Rev Public Health 1988; 9:203–21.

Prince v. Massachusetts. 321 U.S. 158 (1944).

Sokhey J; Kim-Farley RJ: Evaluation of vaccination coverage through sample surveys. J Commun Dis 1987 Dec; 19(4):341–48.

Stanger L: "Immunization mobile" brings protection to children in southeastern Idaho. Public Health Rep 1987 Sep–Oct; 102(5):543–45.

Malpractice Issues

Andrews LB: Newborn screening for sickle cell disease and other hemoglobinopathies. Overview of legal issues. Pediatrics 1989 May; 83(5 Pt 2):886–90.

Avery JK: Loss prevention case of the month. Where is that prenatal record? J Tenn Med Assoc 1988 Oct; 81(10):640.

Brahams D: Pertussis vaccine and brain damage: Two claims before the courts. Lancet 1985 Nov 16; 2(8464):1137–38.

Britton RM; Magen BS: Preventive measures to limit legal liability in pediatric emergencies: An analysis through cases concerning failure to diagnose meningitis. Pediatr Emerg Care 1986 Jun; 2(2):109–12.

Garson A Jr: Medicolegal problems in the management of cardiac arrhythmias in children. Pediatrics 1987 Jan; 79(1):84–88.

Giacoia GP: Low Apgar scores and birth asphyxia. Misconceptions that promote underserved negligence suits. Postgrad Med 1988 Aug; 84(2):77–82.

Holder AR: Minors' rights to consent to medical care. JAMA 1987 Jun 26; 257(24):3400–2.

Markham BF: Legal issues for the practicing pediatrician. Pediatr Clin North Am 1981 Aug; 28(3):617–25.

McCarthy PL: Observation scales to identify serious illness in febrile children. Pediatrics 1982 Nov; 70:802–9.

Nazarian LF: The pediatrician and the under toad. Pediatr Rev 1988 Oct; 10(4):99–100.

Ricci JA; Lambert RL; Steffes DG: Pediatrics and professional liability. Pediatr Emerg Care 1986 Jun; 2(2):106–8.

Schifrin BS: Polemics in perinatology: Justice and the medical expert witness. J Perinatol 1989 Jun; 9(2):207–10.

Schmitt BD: *Pediatric Telephone Advice.* 1980.

Selbst SM: Treating minors without their parents. Pediatr Emerg Care 1985 Sep; 1(3):168–73.

Silber TJ: Ethical considerations in the medical care of adolescents and their parents. Pediatr Ann 1981 Oct; 10(10):46–48.

Stanley-Brown EG: Preventing medical negligence in caring for infants and children. N Y State J Med 1986 Jul; 86(7):396–97.

VI Physicians and Special Practice Areas

29

Institutional Practice: Teams, Schools, and Prisons

CRITICAL POINTS

- School and team physicians must resist pressures to compromise the care of individual patients for the good of the institution.
- Appropriate practice in sports medicine differs dramatically between professional and recreational athletes.
- Team physicians must resist parental demands for performance-enhancing treatments and drugs for minors.
- The physician-prisoner relationship is a more limited relationship than the usual physician-patient relationship.
- Unlike the team and school physicians, physicians treating prisoners must often put the institution's needs above those of the prisoner.

Institutional practitioners are physicians who work for an entity whose interests are sometimes adverse to their patients' interests. The most common institutional practice is occupational medicine, which is reviewed in Chapter 30. This chapter discusses prisons, sports teams, and schools. These represent a continuum, with prisons having the greatest conflict between the institution and the patients, and schools having the least. When physicians practicing in these environments balance their duty to the patient against their duty to the institution and the community, they must not confuse public safety issues with institutional convenience. For example, prison physicians should not drug patients just to keep them quiet but must not hesitate in diagnosing and treating communicable diseases that may spread in the prison setting. School physicians face the same dilemma when requested to recommend Ritalin to quiet an unruly student.

The team and school physicians share the conflict between institutional obligations and the fiduciary duty to the individual patient. This conflict is exacerbated because many patients are unable to make knowing choices of treatment. Often the patients are minors. In others, the coercive atmosphere of team sports makes it difficult for individual athletes to resist the pressure to compete when it is medically contraindicated. School and team physicians must be careful to protect their adult patients' autonomy. When the patient is a minor, the physician may have to intercede to protect the child from the pressure of overly competitive parents and coaches.

THE TEAM DOCTOR

Sports medicine was once the province of a few physicians serving professional sports teams. It has spread as a specialty through the professionalization of college and high school athletics and through the popularization of high-performance athletics for personal fitness. The sports medicine physician must balance the issues of long-term health with short-term performance. This compromise is not new to sports medicine, but it has become controversial as questionable practices such as the use of steroids and local anesthetics have come to the attention of the public. Sports medicine poses substantial legal problems, particularly when it is practiced on children.

The team physician has a more ambiguous role than the sports medicine physician who treats individual athletes but has no involvement with organized sports teams. The team physician's job has become more difficult as the notion of amateur athletics has been displaced by professionalism in all but name. College football is run as a farm club for professional teams. In large high schools, the coach who in the past might have been an ex-football player and taught in the school system has been replaced by highly specialized coaching staffs with trainers and big budgets. The responsibilities of the team doctor have changed from being available to treat injuries at the weekly game to an ongoing responsibility for the development and care of the athletes. These coaches train their players for professional-style play and expect team physicians to minister to them as if they were professional athletes. This situation creates a conflict of interest for the physician when the athletes are legally and physiologically children.

The Physician-Player Relationship

Team physicians' duties are to their patients as individuals, not to the team or to the school. The physician must have proper consent to provide medical care and must respect patient confidentiality. No matter how interested the coach may be in a star athlete, he or she has no right to participate in the medical care. Medical decisions must be made on medical grounds by the physician responsible for the care.

The most difficult decision in sports medicine is determining when to allow injured athletes to play. The football player with a sprained ankle may miss the entire season if his activities are limited for as long as is usual in nonathletes. If he is allowed to play too soon, he has a greater chance of reinjuring the ankle and being disabled for a longer time. Blanket prohibitions on play for an extended period may encourage the athlete to ignore the physician's advice altogether. If the athlete is an adult who can understand the risks of playing while injured, the physician must consider patient compliance. The patient needs accurate information on the risks of continued play.

When sports medicine physicians are dealing with athletes with less information and support than are available to professionals, they should be more conservative in balancing the need to get back to play against the probability of impairing permanent healing. For example, if a sprain can be adequately supported by tape, the athlete should be taught to tape and be allowed to play. If an injury would heal without surgery but surgery will speed the process, the athlete may choose to be operated on. While a physician may aid a professional athlete in a calculated decision to compromise future healing for short-term gain, this should not be done for college and high school players. Using pain killers or steroids to get the player back on the field when this endangers permanent recovery is bad medicine and legally risky. The promising player who wants to be in the game when the pro scout is there will not be grateful if that game is his last because his injury becomes permanent.

Team versus Player
Team physicians face the ethical problem of determining when it is appropriate to compromise an athlete's long-term health for short-term performance. Informed consent is at the heart of this problem. A physician must be sure that the athlete understands the long-term consequences of the recommended medical treatment. Physicians who do not tell patients the risks of treatments that allow an athlete to compete when it is medically contraindicated face substantial malpractice liability. If there is evidence that the coach encouraged the physician to withhold information about the risks of treatment, the physician may face punitive damages for fraud.

An equally difficult problem is the degree to which players exercise the free choice that is necessary for an informed consent. There is pressure to maintain team performance, irrespective of the risk to the individual. Players who will not take risks for the team do not last long in the starting lineup. It is arguable whether consent given out of the fear of ending one's career is uncoerced. Conversely, physicians are limited in their right to impose their values on patients. The decision to risk disability by continuing play is the reasoned choice of some athletes.

Athletes in highly competitive, commercialized sports such as football are under constant pressure to play when injured and to submit to risky surgery rather than prolonged convalescence. The risks posed by these actions are much the same for all athletes. The benefits, however, are vastly different, depending on the athlete's status. A veteran professional football player is protected by a pension system and extensive knowledge of the consequences of various injuries. Such a player is paid very well to accept the risk of permanent injury.

Moving back in the athletic hierarchy to college teams, players have little protection if their injuries are permanently disabling. The college athlete faces the pressure to play but with limited benefit as compared with the risk. This is a special problem for athletes who are attending college only because of athletics. If they aggravate an injury and are unable to play, few will stay in college as regular students. Since the probability of a given college athlete's entering professional athletics is small, it is difficult to justify the risk of aggravating an injury to play an extra few games in a season.

The Child Athlete
College and high school athletes pose additional problems. Persons under the age of 18 are legally able to make their own medical decisions in only certain situations established by state law. Most states allow minors to consent to treatment for substance abuse, communicable diseases, pregnancy, and other conditions that pose a threat to persons other than the minor. No state specifically authorizes minors to consent to treatment for sports injuries. Sports medicine may not be practiced on minors without parental consent. This parental consent is constrained by the child welfare laws.

Parents may consent only to medical care that is in the child's best interest. If a physician believes that a medical regime chosen by the parents is not in the child's best interest, the physician must report this to the child welfare authorities. Children themselves are unable to balance the desire to get back in the game against the risk of permanent injury. A child who is later unable to continue in athletics or is otherwise disabled may sue the physician for malpractice. Physicians should not allow the enthusiasm of child athletes or their parents to weigh in medical decisions that will affect the long-term health of the child. Most parents will not persist if they are fully informed as to the risks of continued participation by an injured child. If the parents continue to pressure the child to engage in unsafe activity, then this becomes a matter of child abuse.

Supervision of Nonphysician Personnel
In most cases, the physician is not a full-time employee for the team. Most routine first aid and training programs are carried out by nonphysician personnel. This creates the same liability issues as supervision of nonphysician personnel in other medical settings.

Trainers were once a luxury reserved for professional athletes and world-class amateurs. Today large high schools often employ trainers on their coaching staffs, and professional coaches are also taught these skills. The trainer is both an athletic coach and a medical assistant. Treating minor injuries, doing physical therapy, and overseeing such preventive measures as taping and reconditioning are all part of the trainer's job. Consequently, the team physician must oversee the activities of the trainer in the same way that the physician would supervise a nurse or a physical therapist. This is a politically sensitive issue because trainers are usually given a free hand in both diagnosing and treating medical conditions. That trainers violate the medical practice act in many states is usually ignored by the state boards of medical examiners. When a physician is involved, however, infractions by the trainer are grounds to discipline the supervising physician, and they subject the physician to medical malpractice liability. Physicians must ensure that trainers comply with applicable scope-of-practice laws.

The team physician may not delegate control of prescription medications to a nonphysician. Providing the trainer with a bottle of codeine tablets to use when someone gets hurt is illegal. As with other drug law violations, there is a high probability that the physician will face criminal charges if the practice is discovered. Although narcotics are the most likely to lead to trouble, there is increasing scrutiny of prescriptions for other drugs, such as anti-inflammatory agents and hormones. Prescriptions can be written for direct use by only the affected individual. If a physician wishes to stock and dispense medication, it must be done in compliance with the pharmacy laws of the state. Writing a prescription for office use and letting the trainer dispense the drugs is no longer acceptable practice, nor is allowing nonphysicians to distribute samples of prescription drugs.

Performance Enhancement
The most controversial issue in sports medicine is performance enhancement beyond what can be achieved by proper nutrition and general conditioning. The publicity has focused on drugs: first amphetamines, now steroids, next human growth hormone (HGH) and other genetic engineering products. The problems are not limited to drugs. Biomechanics and the use of direct muscle stimulation tools are changing the nature of training and allowing the selective overdevelopment of muscle groups. Improperly used, these techniques can increase the probability of injury and disability.

Taking drugs to improve athletic performance has been publicly deplored but also privately practiced for years. It has become a risky practice for both the athlete and the physician. Most competitive athletic organizations have rules against any use of drugs or doping to enhance performance. Urine testing has become cheap, quick, and easy. The athlete who gets caught is likely to be excluded from participation for some time. Blood doping is less easily detected but may be more dangerous. Even the use of the patient's own blood can be risky. Physicians should remember that it is unethical and usually illegal to prescribe for nontherapeutic purposes. As drug enforcement programs adopt zero-tolerance policies, physicians with questionable prescribing habits can expect to face investigation and prosecution.

Engineering People

Medicine has a history of bad therapies that failed because they tried to subvert the natural human growth or healing processes. We are appalled by the practices of societies that produce physical deformity for a perceived social good. We would not allow the castrating of young boys who sing well so that they can continue to sing soprano. We would not allow parents to bind the feet of infant girls to produce a lotus foot. Yet it is not clear how far this society will go to prevent the use of medical and hormonal techniques to alter normal development to produce a better athlete.

Physicians who practice sports medicine on children should be very careful about interfering with natural development. Modern training techniques and machines have made it possible to alter the balance of muscle function in a way that natural exercise cannot. Drugs and hormones can be used to change the very processes of growth. These changes can have unexpected and undesirable side effects. What seems reasonable during training or performance may appear unreasonable in later years if it results in permanent deformity or disability. The engineering of people to improve athletic performance may appear to the adult athlete or the jury as abhorrent as castrating boy sopranos. Physicians should be cautious about recommending any nontherapeutic interventions in athletes who are not fully grown.

THE SCHOOL DOCTOR

There are two distinct types of school medicine practice. The more common is practiced in nonresidential elementary and secondary schools. This practice is a combination of pediatrics, emergency medicine, and public health. Large school districts usually employ a physician to direct the school health programs and oversee the nursing staff. Smaller districts rely on physicians in the community to provide these services as paid consultants or as unpaid volunteers. The second practice type is school medicine programs in residential schools—usually in colleges but in some elementary and secondary boarding schools. The basic problems are the same in both settings, but the physician's responsibilities are greater in the residential settings.

Supervisory Responsibilities

Only the largest school health programs employ physicians to deliver direct patient care. In most programs, the primary role of the school physician is to supervise nonphysician personnel: school nurses, dietitians, coaches, and trainers.

In some smaller districts, the school physician also may need to oversee food sanitation in the lunch room and zoonosis problems in vocational agriculture classes.

Most states require nurses, child health associates, physicians' assistants, and other such personnel to be supervised by a physician. If the school employs personnel (or uses volunteers) who may not practice without physician supervision, the duty to supervise these personnel will flow to any physician who is nearby. The legal theory for this responsibility by proximity is called *ostensible agency*. This means that if, from the patient's point of view, it appears that the physician is supervising the personnel, the law will hold that physician responsible. Since ostensible agency is judged from the patient's perspective, a contract between the physician and the school to exclude such supervision will not obviate the physician's responsibility if the physician appears to be supervising the personnel.

All school physicians should insist that their supervisory responsibilities be listed and described in a contract with the individual school or the district. This delineation of responsibilities is necessary whether the physician is an employee or a volunteer. The problem of apparent agency is greatest when there is no other physician supervising activities that should be physician supervised. Unless the physician has explicitly declined to supervise such activities, he or she will be held liable as the supervising physician. Explicitly declining to supervise a given activity is not enough. The physician must not become involved with the activity in such a way as to appear to supervise it.

The school physician has a duty to ensure that all the medical professionals that he or she supervises are competent, adequately trained, and practicing within the limits of the law. Disciplining a nurse may be difficult if the nurse reports to a nursing supervisor or other administrator who is not responsible to the physician. If a supervising physician has reason to believe that a nurse is practicing in an incompetent or illegal manner, the physician must stop the practices or resign. The physician cannot defend improper supervision by blaming nonphysician administrators.

School Clinics

Increasingly, acute care clinics, which provide preventive services and care for minor illnesses, are being placed in nonresidential school facilities. Unlike the nurse's office, where students are sent so the nurse can call home, these clinics establish a provider-patient relationship with the students. The physicians and nurses in the clinic have the same legal responsibilities that they would have in a private office. If the clinic is part of the school health program, it is the school doctor's responsibility. If the clinic is a separate entity, it must have its own supervising physician.

Physicians overseeing a school clinic should ensure that there are proper protocols, policies, and procedures for the staff of the clinic just as they would for any other outreach clinic or physician extender. There should be formal agreements on the scope of practice within the clinic and provision for appropriate follow-up for problems that go beyond this scope of practice. The physician should not lose sight of the fact that he or she is assuming all the responsibilities of the physician-patient relationship for the patients who use the clinic. This includes the duties of continued treatment and proper referral.

Consent to Care

The general rules of consent to care for minors apply to school children. The emergency exception, legally mandated care, proxy consent, and prior consent of parents all apply in various school situations.

Parents may sign a proxy consent for medical care if it is required when the child is at school. These often ask for information on preferred physicians and hospitals. All residential schools with students under the age of 18 should require that a proxy consent be part of the student's admission materials. The extent to which the proxy consent should be relied upon depends on the circumstances and the difficulty of contacting the parents. A physician treating children in a neighborhood public school should rely on proxy consent only to deliver urgent care until the children's parents can be contacted. (This type of care is sheltered under the emergency exception.) If the children are in a residential school and their parents are out of the country, the proxy consent will have to cover all routine and emergency medical care. Such extensive consent is best documented by a power of attorney to consent to the child's medical care.

If a child is seriously ill or injured, the emergency exception to the need for consent generally applies. Reasonable attempts should be made to contact the child's parents and to follow their wishes in selecting caregivers, but these should not interfere with getting the child prompt emergency care.

The school system should have a formal policy, and preferably a written contract, for ambulance services for children who are seriously ill or injured. Schools need not wait for parental permission to call an ambulance. Paying the ambulance fee is much less expensive than settling the claim on the broken neck that became a spinal cord injury when the teacher carried the child into the office.

Medicines at School

School health programs should be cautious about inserting themselves between physician and patient or between parent and child when providing medical care for children. It has become common practice to take medicines away from the children and insist that the child come to the office or the nurse for treatment. If the school is prepared to take responsibility for administering the medicine properly and on time and if the teacher or nurse can be sure that the child leaves with the medicine so that nighttime doses can be given, the school may not increase its legal risks by doing this. It also does not reduce the risks.

This policy can lead to major problems for the school in two situations. If the school nurse or physician does not agree with the prescriptions of the attending physician and prevents the child from following the physician's orders, then the school personnel would be liable for any harm that came to the child because of the lack of medical care. A school nurse or doctor who substituted other medical care for that prescribed by the attending physician would be liable for rendering care without legal consent. It is wise to remember that for a physician or a nurse, telling a patient not to do something is an act of medical judgment.

The other serious problem involves situations when it is medically important that the patient control his or her own medications. The asthmatic child cannot use inhalers on demand if the inhalers are in the nurse's office. The attack that could have been aborted by the inhaler in the pocket may require emergency care in the time it takes to find the person with the key to the medicine locker.

If responsibility is a central issue in the patient's care, then no amount of planning by the school nurse can make up for the harm done by removing medications. Adolescents with diabetes are typically very hard to maintain in control. They shift from denial to dependence very quickly. They must cooperate with their physicians and their parents and a host of others. If the school officials are not active participants in this child's care program, they should not interject themselves into the care.

Athletics

The information earlier in this chapter about being a team doctor applies whether the physician takes on the team separately or as part of the work of the school doctor. Physicians who are considering accepting a position as a school physician should find out whether they are expected to care for athletes. If the school engages in any form of athletic activity and does not have a separate sports medicine system, the school health physician will be assumed to be supervising the sports medicine program.

Medical and Public Health Responsibilities

The federal and state governments use schools as the vehicle to enforce various public health laws directed at children. States have customarily required proof of immunization for childhood diseases for school admission. Some states are mandating that schools screen children for personal health problems. State laws also provide schools with the authority to screen and exclude students to prevent the spread of communicable diseases. The controversies over school children with HIV have sensitized the public to communicable diseases in schools. While HIV in young school children is diminishing (most HIV babies die before school age), HIV is an increasing problem in adolescents. This will force school physicians to become a front line force in community disease control.

A variety of screening programs are carried out in schools. Some of these, such as scoliosis screening, are of questionable medical importance. Others, such as vision and hearing testing, are very important but overinclusive. These programs must be combined with reliable follow-up systems for all positive findings. The follow-up examination may be done by the school physician, but it is preferable to refer the child to a personal physician or clinic that can oversee treatment and continued evaluation.

Physicians who receive these referrals should make a careful evaluation of any abnormalities detected on screening and notify the school physician of the disposition of the referral unless the child's parents object. School physicians must ensure that the child keeps the referral appointment and is properly evaluated. The school physician has a duty to ensure adequate care for problems detected on school screenings just as for problems he or she detects personally in private office.

All states require that physicians report communicable diseases to the public health department. Most also require reporting of outbreaks of any disease that may be caused by infection, infestation, or environmental hazards, particularly if they occur in a school. School physicians have personal responsibility for seeing that the reports are made. Normally, the school nurses will do the actual tallying and reporting of routine cases such as influenza or chicken pox. They should report unusual disease problems to the school physician immediately.

Every school needs a detailed, written policy on the management of students with communicable diseases. Schools have the right and duty to screen and restrict students infected with diseases that pose a risk to other students, but they cannot use this power to remove students who pose a political problem rather than a communicable disease problem. For example, a student with asymptomatic HIV infection does not pose a risk to other students. This student must be allowed to stay in school without restrictions unless the student is violent due to dementia, or has infectious tuberculosis. (See Chapter 21.)

Handicapped Children

Handicapped children have special rights under federal law. School physicians are often caught between the needs of the handicapped child and the limited resources of the school district. Special education programs and facilities for the handicapped are expensive. If the school district employs only one speech therapist, the physician will be pressured to limit the diagnosis of significant speech defect to the number of children this therapist can treat. Since handicapped children are protected by federal law and seldom pose a threat to other students, the school physician's duty is clearly to the student rather than to the school. The diagnosis of articulation defect must be based on an objective evaluation of the speech performance of the individual child.

Physicians must not compare one child with another to determine which will be referred for special help or care. If both children require therapy, that should be the physician's recommendation. If there are not sufficient resources to provide for all the handicapped children, then it is the duty of the school district to find the resources. The physician cannot legally or morally withhold a diagnosis to withhold special care. Irrespective of state law immunity for schools, a physician who did so as a matter of routine may be sued under the federal civil rights act for violating the child's rights.

College Health Programs

College students face many of the same health problems as younger students, but the legal problems are more complicated. The college student is often away from home and without the usual support system in times of illness. Dormitories do not provide chicken broth and dry toast to every student with the flu. They may even be the source of food poisoning, measles, and epidemic respiratory disease.

As in other school settings, the physician's duty is to the patient, not the institution. If the college food service is a frequent source of food poisoning, the college physician should insist that something be done to correct the problem. Physicians must not change the diagnosis from food poisoning to gastroenteritis to avoid political problems. They should work with the college administration to address particular health problems, but medical judgments should not be compromised for administrative convenience.

Issues of consent and confidentiality do not change when the patient is a college student. All residential schools should have a power of attorney to consent to medical care for students who are still minors. It is risky to assume that they will all stay healthy until they reach their majority. This is especially important for minors who are far from home, particularly international students. It is also useful for students who are not minors to consider a power of attorney to consent to medical care if their parents are not readily available or if they do not want their parents involved in their medical care decisions.

College physicians must respect the students' confidentiality. The fact that a parent may be paying the tuition or medical bills does not give the parent the right to medical information about a child who is not a minor. At the same time, the parents of a college student have the reasonable expectation that they will be contacted if the student is in trouble or requires significant medical care. The university should require students to sign a waiver that allows it to contact the student's parents in such circumstances. (The university should allow exceptions for students who are estranged from their parents.) For certain kinds of care, such as treatment for drug abuse or venereal disease, the information should be protected unless the student requests that parents be notified. However, students must understand that they may have to pay for the care if they want to keep it confidential. The physician should explain to students who ask that something not appear in a bill that few parents and no insurance company will pay for unspecified services.

Comprehensive Care
Many college physicians are caught in the dilemma between the medical needs and financial problems of students. With rising tuition and fees for education, many administrators are loath to require all students to show that they are covered by health insurance. The expectation of both students and administrators is that the student health service will take care of most health problems. The student's failure to buy insurance does not relieve the physician of responsibility for providing quality medical care. The student health service and the individual physicians should set policies for dealing with students who are unable to pay for necessary medical care.

For residential students with major medical problems, physicians must consider whether the student can stay in school. If the student is hospitalized or otherwise completely unable to attend school, the decision is obvious. The issue becomes one of where and when to transfer the patient for ongoing care.

For students with less severe problems, the decision is more difficult. Most people do not choose a school based on the availability of medical care. However, if the student has a major disease requiring care that is unavailable at or near the school, the potential for crisis is great. Student health physicians should be cautious about accepting responsibility for caring for students with problems that they would consider beyond their skills in another setting. The presence of such disease in a student constitutes a federally protected handicap. The school must make proper accommodation for the student's handicap, including arrangements for medical care.

THE PRISON DOCTOR
Over the last 30 years, the role of prison physicians has changed dramatically. Being the doctor for the county jail used to be a relatively easy job. The position was frequently filled by a physician who had retired from private practice. Prisoners were viewed as having little right to medical care, and there was not much concern about its quality. Even incompetent physicians were usually immune from suits for medical malpractice.

Prisons are now highly regulated. (This chapter will use *prison* as a generic term for all correctional and detention facilities.) State and federal court cases, combined with legislation, set minimum standards for prisons and jails. The first effect of these standards was to end most medical experiments on prisoners. (See Chapter 14.) In addition, the standards ensure that inmates receive adequate medical care and create a federal cause of action against physicians and others involved in improperly run prison medical programs. Despite these regulations, prison conditions are deteriorating in many parts of the country. Prisons are overcrowded, and inmates are increasingly HIV infected secondary to the drug abuse that may have led to their incarceration.

Prison Medical Care

Our most fundamental constitutional right is that no person may be deprived of life, liberty, or property without due process of law. When an individual is deprived of liberty by the state, the state assumes the responsibility for caring for the basic needs of that individual. A prisoner is unable to go out and get food and water, so the state must provide it. If the state did not provide it, the prisoner would be deprived of life. This is also the basis for a prisoner's right to medical care: a prisoner deprived of necessary medical care may be deprived of life or health. It is the extent of this constitutional right to care that is at issue.

The legal standard for judging the adequacy of prison medical care is whether it evidences a deliberate indifference to the prisoners' welfare. The prisoner need not show that the prison officials intend harm through inadequate or improper medical care. A mere showing of malpractice is not enough, however. Thus, the legal standard for prison medical care is much lower than the standard for free persons. This poses an ethical dilemma for prison physicians: when is it ethically permissible to provide lower quality of medical care for prisoners? While the easy answer is "never," there are few prisons that will fund community standard medical care for prisoners. Is it unethical for physicians to work for these institutions, or is it better to provide the care that is possible under the limited circumstances?

Physician-Prisoner Relationship

The physician-prisoner relationship is different from the traditional physician-patient relationship. The physician-prisoner relationship is not a fiduciary relationship. Legally, it most closely resembles the relationship between a public health physician and a patient. In both cases, the physician's first duty is to the health and safety of the community rather than to the patient. Prison officials have broad discretion to preserve order in the prison. Prisoners lose most of their rights to privacy along with their liberty. Prison officials have a right to any information a physician may obtain that would affect the health and safety of the prison community. Reportable diseases and conditions should also be reported to the health department with jurisdiction over the community where the facility is located.

While prisoners have little expectation of privacy, they do have an expectation that their physician will exercise independent medical judgment regarding the diagnosis and treatment of their medical conditions. The correctional staff should not be in the position of influencing medical care decisions. Under no circumstances should access to proper medical care be used as a disciplinary tool. The prison officials do have the right to establish policies that ensure that prisoners do not use untreated illness to avoid prison discipline and that prisoners' medical conditions do not interfere with prison order.

Right to Refuse Medical Care

Prisoners have a liberty interest, protected by the Fourteenth Amendment, in not being treated against their will. The extent of this liberty interest was defined in *Washington v. Harper* (1990), a case arising from a prisoner's objection to being given antipsychotic medications. The Washington prison system provided elaborate administrative protections before an inmate could be medicated against his will. The Washington Supreme Court rejected these administrative protections as inadequate and required that an inmate be given a full adversarial hearing before being treated against his will:

> The [Washington Supreme] Court concluded that the "highly intrusive nature" of treatment with antipsychotic medications warranted greater procedural protections.... It held that, under the Due Process Clause, the State could administer antipsychotic medication to a competent, non-consenting inmate only if, in a judicial hearing at which the inmate had the full panoply of adversarial procedural protections, the State proved by "clear, cogent, and convincing" evidence that the administration of antipsychotic medication was both necessary and effective for furthering a compelling state interest. (p. 1035)

Mr. Harper, the prisoner who brought this action, claimed that the prison authorities could not medicate him unless he was found to be mentally incompetent in an adversarial hearing. He further alleged that even if he was found to be incompetent, he could be medicated only if the fact finder determined that he would have consented to the medication had he been competent. The U.S. Supreme Court rejected these claims, finding that the prison's policy was constitutionally adequate. The Court's rationale for endorsing the prison's policy is relevant to the general problem of prison health because it accepts expert decision making as a substitute for adversarial decision making.

The Court reviewed the Washington Supreme Court's decision to determine what facts would support a decision to force antipsychotic medication on a prisoner and what procedural protections were necessary to determine those facts. It agreed that Harper had a liberty interest in not being medicated against his will. However, the Court held that this liberty interest was sufficiently protected by the prison's administrative proceeding, which required that a psychiatrist certify the treatment's appropriateness.

The Court's acceptance of expert decision making as a substitute for an adversary hearing seems to be rooted in the limited autonomy granted to prisoners. The Court found that a prisoner's right to refuse antipsychotic medication was limited by the conditions of his confinement. In particular, the Court found that the purpose of the prison's medication policy was "to diagnose and treat convicted felons, with the desired goal being that they will recover to the point where they can function in a normal prison environment."

The Court in *Harper* balanced the prisoner's best interests against the prison's interest in returning him to the general prisoner population and his punishment. The role of the expert decision maker, the prison psychiatrist, was to ensure that the prisoner was mentally ill and dangerous and that medication was appropriate to remedying these conditions. The protection of the prisoner's interests was left to the integrity of the prison psychiatrist. The Court's finding that expert decision making satisfied the prisoner's due process interests reflects the Court's general reticence to interfere in matters of prison safety and security.

Prisoners retain some right to refuse medical care after *Harper*, but this is severely circumscribed as compared with the rights of a nonprisoner patient. Prisoners may not refuse testing or treatment for a condition that would threaten the health and safety of the prison community, these including communicable diseases and treatable psychiatric conditions. Prisoners may also be forced to accept treatment that is necessary to protect their health from permanent injury. Prisoners with religious objections to medical treatment may be treated against these objections if the treatment is necessary to preserve prison discipline.

Emergency Medical Care

The weakest part of most prison medical programs, especially small programs without full-time physician supervision, is the evaluation and treatment of acute injuries and illnesses. These are most common in the drunk tank: a large room where those who are intoxicated and other prisoners are held until they post bond. The drunk tank is an ongoing source of unnecessary deaths and accompanying liability suits against local governments and physicians. Neither police officers nor physicians can visually distinguish an intoxicated prisoner with a mild bump on his head from a severe head injury patient who has had a couple of drinks. Diabetic coma and a drunken stupor look and smell very much alike. Most physicians know this; most police officers do not.

Considering the extent to which alcohol is involved in traffic accidents and crimes of violence, it is hard to think of any profession with more experience with drunkenness than law enforcement. The vast majority of those who are intoxicated have no acute medical problems, so it is not reasonable to expect police officers to learn to do a medical evaluation of every intoxicated person they arrest. No one, however, should be locked up without such an evaluation. This means that every prisoner who appears intoxicated at the time of arrest should be taken to the jail physician or practitioner on duty before being put in a cell. The jail physician should review the protocols for treating intoxication frequently and should be sure that they are being followed carefully. Evaluating a lot of prisoners is the price for preventing jail cell deaths from, say, diabetes. Picking up the head injuries early may protect the officers from accusations of brutality in the jails.

Experimentation

For most purposes, the use of healthy prisoners as medical research subjects has stopped in this country. The reason is that a prisoner cannot freely consent to being a research subject; the situation is coercive by its nature. If prisoners are good research subjects for a particular experiment, they will assume that participating will bring favors from the jailers and refusing to participate will bring retribution. Research on prisoners is highly regulated by HHS. Prisoners should never be used as research subjects without the appropriate IRB approval. (See Chapter 14.)

Public Health and Safety in Prisons

Prisons pose unique public and mental health problems. Many prisoners are poorly educated, of limited intelligence, behaviorally impaired, and, increasingly, drug addicted. They are crowded together in communal facilities with marginal provisions for sanitation. In some systems, nearly 20 percent of newly incarcerated prisoners are HIV infected, posing a direct risk to other prisoners through sexual assault. Indirectly, HIV infection poses a risk through its suppression of normal immune system function. Immunosuppressed patients are also of susceptible to diseases such as tuberculosis. More critically, providing humane care for

HIV-infected prisoners will outstrip the prison health resources in the states with substantial HIV-infected prisoner populations.

Disease Control in Prisons

Every prisoner who will be incarcerated for longer than a few hours should be screened for communicable diseases, including tuberculosis, because transmission is common in prison populations. Venereal disease screening should be included because the prison population is predominantly young, single males who have a high prevalence of venereal infections. These infections should be identified and treated to protect the health of the infected prisoner and to prevent spread in the prison. Prisoners should be screened for HIV and hepatitis because of the high infection rates among drug addicts.

Beyond these common diseases, prison physicians should work with local health authorities to determine which other communicable diseases are probable in the prison population. Ideally, prisoners with inadequate immunization histories would be immunized against tetanus, measles, and other childhood diseases.

An admission physical should screen for chronic diseases or conditions that might cause problems if they remain untreated. Since work will be part of prison life in most cases, the prison physician should look for any disabling conditions that might require special consideration. Just as prisoners are entitled to expect reasonable care for acute problems, they are entitled to expect that their prison regime will not endanger their health.

It is wise for any jail or prison to have comprehensive policies for control of certain communicable diseases, particularly tuberculosis, hepatitis, and AIDS. Without formal policies, decisions tend to be made in the heat of the moment on nonmedical grounds. This ad hoc disease control is usually ineffective and can be expensive. For instance, if there is no policy for immunizing staff against hepatitis B and no determination of who is at risk for contracting hepatitis A, then there is likely to be a large demand for gamma globulin shots every time a prisoner develops jaundice. In addition to the cost of the shots, the institution that perpetuates the myth that hepatitis can be spread by casual contact may find itself paying for every case of community-acquired hepatitis among its employees as a worker's compensation claim.

Prison communicable disease policies should be developed in conjunction with state and local public health authorities. The policies must protect inmates from infection while not unduly interfering with the rights of the infected prisoners. HIV-infected prisoners must be identified to ensure that they receive proper preventive medical care, but there are no disease control justifications for isolating them. In contrast to HIV, tuberculosis is a severe problem in prisons and demands both aggressive investigation of outbreaks and the isolation of infectious prisoners. The federal courts have found that failing to protect prisoners from tuberculosis violates the requirements of the U.S. Constitution.

The Physician's Obligations to the Jailers

As with other institutional settings, physicians should request a written description of their duties. This is especially important for independent contractor physicians who may not enjoy governmental immunity for their actions. For example, some jurisdictions have specific arrangements in the jail health system or with the county hospital system to take blood samples and other specimens from criminal suspects. Physicians accepting a position in prison health should know whether they will be called upon to obtain such biologic evidence and to provide court-ordered medical testing and involuntary treatment.

Independent contractor physicians should be careful not to compromise their professional standards when caring for prisoners. Care that would be protected from suit if performed by an employee of the prison system may be actionable if performed by an independent physician. Such physicians should also ask the prison authorities to indemnify them for legal expenses and lost time if they are named as parties in civil rights litigation against the prison medical care system. Without such an agreement, a private physician may have to spend tens of thousands of dollars and hundreds of hours of uncompensated time defending actions taken on behalf of the prison.

BIBLIOGRAPHY

Team Physicians

Albright JP; Noyes FR: Role of the team physician in sports injury studies. Am J Sports Med 1988; 16 Suppl 1:S1–4.

Anderson V: School physician: Crucial role in secondary school athletics. N Y State J Med 1977 Apr; 77(5):776–78.

Dick AD: Chalktalk for the team physician. Am Fam Physician 1983 Sep; 28(3):231–36.

Hopkins JR; Parker CE: Experience of family practice residents as athletic team physicians. J Fam Pract 1978 Sep; 7(3):519–25.

Kappelman M; Roberts P; Rinaldi R; Cornblath M: The school health team and school health physician: New role and operation. Am J Dis Child 1975 Feb; 129(2):191–95.

Kujala UM; Heinonen OJ; Lehto M; Jarvinen M; Bergfeld JA: Equipment, drugs and problems of the competition and team physician. Sports Med 1988 Oct; 6(4):197–209.

Luckstead EF: Pediatric team physicians. Pediatrics 1986 Nov; 78(5):941–42.

McLain LG; Reynolds S: Sports injuries in a high school. Pediatrics 1989 Sep; 84(3):446–50.

Menna VJ: The pediatrician as team physician. Pediatr Rev 1987 Aug; 9(2):35.

Oseid S: Doping and athletes—prevention and counseling. J Allergy Clin Immunol 1984 May; 73(5 Pt 2):735–39.

Ray RL; Feld FX: The team physician's medical bag. Clin Sports Med 1989 Jan; 8(1):139–46.

Savastano AA: The team physician, trainer, instructor, coach, and the law. Good medical judgment and adequate malpractice insurance are important components of protection. R I Med J 1979 Sep; 62(9):367–72.

Shaffer TE: The physician's role in sports medicine. Serving the athlete, school, and team. J Adolesc Health Care 1983 Jan; 3(4):227–30.

Schools

Boyce WT; Sprunger LW; Duncan B; Sobolewski S: A survey of physician consultations in an urban school district. J Sch Health 1983 May; 53(5):308–11.

Chilton LA: Informal provision of school health services by a physician. J Sch Health 1982 Mar; 52(3):159–61.

Crouchman MR: The role of the school medical officer in secondary schools. J R Coll Gen Pract 1986 Jul; 36(288):322–24.

Davis JM; Strenecky BJ: Physician in the community school. Fam Med 1987 Jan–Feb; 19(1):46–47.

De Bec Turtle P: The medical officer in the independent boarding school. Public Health 1972 Jan; 86(2):89–95.

Farley WJ: The expanded role of the school physician. J Med Soc N J 1979 Nov; 76(12):821–24.

Francis HW: The school physician and the emotional hazards of the school. Public Health 1971 Sep; 85(6):286–94.
Goldberg ES: School physicians: What do they do and why are they needed? J Dev Behav Pediatr 1982 Sep; 3(3):179–81.
Katcher AL: Learning-disabled children, schools, and doctors. J Med Soc N J 1983 Nov; 80(11):902–3.
Menkes JH: A new role for the school physician. Pediatrics 1972 Jun; 49(6):803–4.
Poole SR; Schmitt BD; Sophocles A; Cullen J; Kharas A; Updike J: The family physician's role in school health. J Fam Pract 1984 Jun; 18(6):843–48, 851, 854–56.
Wright GF; Vanderpool N: Schools and the pediatrician. Pediatr Clin North Am 1981 Aug; 28(3):643–62.

Prison Health

Braun MM; Truman BI; Maguire B; DiFerdinando GT Jr; Wormser G; Broaddus R; Morse DL: Increasing incidence of tuberculosis in a prison inmate population. Association with HIV infection. JAMA 1989 Jan 20; 261(3):393–97.
Costello JC; Jameson EJ: Legal and ethical duties of health care professionals to incarcerated children. J Leg Med (Chic) 1987 Jun; 8(2):191–263.
Demers R; Walsh K: Use of medical services during a 2-month period in the Seattle-King County (Washington) jail. Public Health Rep 1981 Sep–Oct; 96(5):452–57.
Elton PJ: Mothers and babies in prison. Lancet 1987 Aug 29; 2(8557):501–2.
Greenberg MJ: Prison medicine. Am Fam Physician 1988 Jul; 38(1):167–70.
Guzzardi LJ: Health care for prisoners (editorial). Ann Emerg Med 1985 Feb; 14(2):185.
Kutch JM Jr: Prison medical services. Milit Med 1984 Feb; 149(2):70–72.
Lamb HR; Schock R; Chen PW; Gross B: Psychiatric needs in local jails: Emergency issues. Am J Psychiatry 1984 Jun; 141(6):774–77.
Lessenger JE: Health care in jails: A unique challenge in medical practice. Postgrad Med 1982 Sep; 72(3):131–34, 137, 141–44.
Marcus G: Liability for the health of detainees. S Afr Med J 1988 Nov 5; 74(9):456–59.
Safyer SM; Alcabes P; Chisolm S: Protecting public health in U.S. jails: A call for the development of guidelines for managing communicable disease outbreaks. Am J Infect Control 1988 Dec; 16(6):267–71.
Segest E: Police custody: deaths and medical attention. J Forensic Sci 1987 Nov; 32(6):1694–1703.
Shapiro S; Shapiro MF: Identification of health care problems in a county jail. J Community Health 1987 Spring; 12(1):23–30.
Sheps SB; Schechter MT; Prefontaine RG: Prison health services: A utilization study. J Community Health 1987 Spring; 12(1):4–22.
Washington v. Harper. 110 S Ct 1028 (1990).

30

General Occupational Medicine Practice

CRITICAL POINTS
- The Americans with Disabilities Act has changed the nature of occupational medicine practice.
- Preemployment inquiries are much more limited under the new law.
- The occupational medicine physician must become a partner in ensuring that workers with disabilities are properly accommodated in the workplace.
- Improperly trained or qualified private contractor occupational medicine physicians face substantial legal liability.

LEGAL AND ETHICAL PROBLEMS IN OCCUPATIONAL MEDICINE

Occupational medicine is one of the three subspecialties certified by the Board of Preventive Medicine. It is a subspecialty of preventive medicine because occupational medicine physicians must practice primary prevention, evaluating the short-term and long-term hazards of the workplace as they relate to people and disease. In the 40-year history of the board, only a few thousand physicians have become board certified in occupational medicine. This certification assumes competence in general medicine and minor emergency care, toxicology, environmental medicine (heat, physical stress, etc.), ergonomics, and job fitness evaluations.

In general, it is ethically questionable for physicians to offer services they are not properly qualified to perform. Occupational medicine poses a particular problem because the employee usually has no right to refuse the physician's services or seek alternative care. There is a special duty to protect patients who are in coercive environments. Employees are peculiarly dependent on the occupational medicine physician's expertise to protect them from toxic exposures. As discussed in Chapter 31, it is anticipated that occupational medicine physicians will seek information about toxic exposures, even if that information is a trade secret. Independent contractor physicians with limited access to the workplace and no detailed knowledge of workplace toxicology cannot effectively protect their employee patients from toxic exposures.

In several specific situations, state or federal regulations mandate special training or certification for physicians performing the regulated activity. The most widely known are the Department of Transportation regulations on who may do physical examinations of pilots. Only a Federal Aviation Administration–approved flight surgeon is allow to perform these on licensed pilots. Yet even simple activities such as reading routine X rays of industrial employees may require a special certification. Physicians who read chest X rays on workers exposed to asbestos must be certified for the readings to satisfy OSHA surveillance requirements. In some instances, the OSHA regulations require occupational medicine physicians to refer workers to specialists. If the white blood cell count on a benzene-exposed worker falls below a certain level, the occupational medicine physician must refer the patient to a hematologist for further evaluation.

Despite the special nature of occupational medicine practice, most ambulatory care centers, minor emergency clinics, and group practices hold themselves out as offering occupational medicine services. Until recently this meant preemployment physical examinations and treatment for acute workplace injuries. Increasingly, however, these entities are contracting with employers to provide services that are expected to be professionally comparable to inhouse occupational medical services provided by experienced occupational medicine professionals. These contracts subject such providers to the full panoply of state and federal regulations.

Independent contractor occupational medicine providers are handicapped by their isolation from the workplace. They are generally limited to second-hand, fragmented information about working conditions and workplace exposures, yet determining job fitness requires detailed information about both the job and the workplace. If they also provide the employee's general medical care, they are faced with significant questions about the segregation of job-related and personal medical information. Moreover, the checks and balances inherent in having general medical care rendered by a physician who is independent of the company are lost in these hybrid practices. This raises ethical issues when the physician is asked to determine whether an injury such as a heart attack is work related, triggering worker's compensation coverage, or not work related, perhaps denying the employee compensation but reducing costs for the employer. These conflicts are greatly exacerbated when the employee lacks insurance for general health problems.

Independent contractor occupational medicine providers are subject to medical malpractice litigation for the services they provide to employees. While corporate employee physicians may also be sued under the dual-capacity doctrine, employers usually indemnify their physicians for any losses that result from actions within the course and scope of their employment. Unless contractually indemnified by the employer, physicians are also liable for the cost of complying with state and regulatory agency actions. Such actions can be very expensive in terms of legal costs and lost time for the providers involved. Unlike lawsuits that allege medical negligence, these costs will not be paid by the physician's malpractice insurer. In contrast, if the occupational medicine provider is an employee of the company, these actions will be brought against the employer rather than the physician. Even if the physician is individually joined, the company will remain liable for the incurred costs. Physicians who contract with employers to deliver occupational medical services must ensure that their contracts require the employer to pay for the costs of agency enforcement actions that arise from treating its employees. Private physicians without special training or experience in occupational medicine should consult an attorney about their allowable scope of practice and legal obligations before agreeing to provide occupational medical services.

OCCUPATIONAL PHYSICIAN-PATIENT RELATIONSHIP

The central problem in occupational medicine is the artificial distinction between work-related and non-work-related injuries and illnesses. From a medical perspective, there is no need to maintain a separate system of care and compensation for work-related medical problems. While special expertise may be be necessary to evaluate and treat the special risks of workplace toxic exposures, hair-splitting over the contribution of the workplace stress to a patient's heart attack is a legal rather than a medical issue. This arbitrary separation affects all occupational medical practice. It poses serious legal and ethical problems when the employee-patient does not have adequate health care and disability coverage for general injuries and illnesses.

Employers must pay the medical and disability costs of all work-related injuries and illnesses. Medical services are provided either directly by employee or contract physicians or indirectly through worker's compensation claims for care provided by independent physicians. In most states, employers are not required to pay for or offer group health insurance. If the employer does not offer coverage for the employee's general medical needs, the employee may be able to pay for care only for work-related illnesses and injuries. This presents a problem because the law expects a physician to manage all of the patient's medical needs, consistent with that physician's specialty practice limitations. (See Chapter 9.) Even when these needs are beyond the physician's area of practice, there remains the duty to refer the patient to an appropriate specialist. This usually does not present a problem for a company-based occupational medicine specialist. Such specialists are in a clearly limited practice situation and may justifiably request that their patients go to a community physician for general medical care. More important, most companies that have in-house medical departments also provide their employees with group health insurance, making it possible for the employees to afford private general medical care.

Family practitioners or internists who offer occupational medical services in addition to a general office practice will not be able to assert that an employee-patient's general medical needs are beyond the scope of their practice. When such physicians detect general medical problems while providing occupational medicine services, they may refer the patient to an appropriate indigent care provider. The problem arises when there is no other provider willing to accept the patient for general medical care. Ethically, contract occupational medicine physicians cannot continue to see patients for work-related conditions while ignoring the patients' general medical problems. Legally, it will be difficult to convince a jury that it was reasonable to fit the patient's medical care to the contract with the employer. Even company-based occupational medicine providers must care for general medical problems if proper referrals are impossible. A private physician should be cautious about agreements to provide occupational medicine services for an employer that will not pay for necessary general medical services that will otherwise be unavailable to the employees. A physician who agrees to provide care in such a situation should be prepared to provide such other care as is necessary without payment.

Confidentiality
Traditionally, employees had little expectation of privacy in their occupational medical information. While the Code of Ethics for occupational medicine practitioners requires that employee medical information be kept confidential, this could be waived by the employee and thus provided only limited protection. OSHA regulations and the Americans with Disabilities Act of 1990 (ADA) have greatly limited the employer's access to an employee's medical information. The ADA will have a great impact on occupational medicine practice because, among other provisions, it greatly restricts preemployment fitness evaluations. Employers continue to have access to data concerning workplace injuries and illnesses and other data that must be collected to comply with governmental regulations. They also retain the right to information about the use of alcohol and illegal drugs. Except as it is related to the workplace, the employer does not have a right to the employee's general medical and personal information. Occupational medicine physicians are also required to report work-related conditions or exposures to OSHA and the state health department.

Since OSHA rules require that the entire employee occupational medical record be disclosed in several situations, it is important that nonworkplace information be maintained separate from workplace information when possible. Physicians who treat patients for both general medical conditions and occupational health problems often keep the work-related information in the same chart as the patient's other medical information. If the physician has treated the patient for non-work-related problems such as marital conflict or pregnancy termination and that information is in the same file as workplace information, it may be available to OSHA and other entities that are authorized to have access to the employee's occupational medical information.

If the employee files a claim for worker's compensation, the worker's compensation insurer or state agency will be entitled to the information necessary to evaluate the claim. In general, when employees file a worker's compensation claim, they waive their rights to confidentiality for any medical information involved in the claim. The physician may also be required to file special reports or give testimony as the agency investigates the worker's claim. This waiver of confidentiality does not include information that is protected by federal laws protecting substance abuse and psychiatric information. Physicians handling worker's compensation should investigate their state's rules on filing and investigating such claims so that they may help their patients obtain appropriate compensation. Physicians who do not want to participate in filing worker's compensation claims should inform their patients before treating them for work-related conditions.

Duty to Evaluate Fully
While the law has separated the compensation systems for work-related and general medical conditions, human maladies are less accommodating. It is ethically and legally questionable for a physician to ignore a patient's general medical condition while evaluating the symptoms of the work-related condition. For example, assume an otherwise healthy-appearing patient presents with an injured foot. It is tempting to treat the injury without inquiring into the patient's general medical condition. To do so could prove disastrous if the patient is an

insulin-dependent diabetic. If the physician does not inquire about potentially complicating conditions such as diabetes, the employer could be liable for the loss of the foot, and the physician could be sued for medical malpractice.

Occupational medicine physicians should evaluate the patient's acute medical problems, even if they do not bear directly on the treatment of the work-related condition. If a patient walks into the physician's office with swollen ankles, blue lips, and respiratory distress, the physician must evaluate the patient's cardiac function. A patient in acute distress must be managed until a proper referral—emergency transport to a hospital or transfer to the care of an appropriate specialist—is made. The patient cannot be left to make arrangements for care if his or her medical condition requires prompt attention. If the patient is referred to an outside physician, the occupational medicine physician should ensure that the patient receives the needed care. When the condition prompting the referral is work related, the occupational medicine physician will retain primary responsibility for coordinating the patient's care.

A common problem is ensuring that all medical tests are fully evaluated. Irrespective of the reason that laboratory tests are ordered or X rays taken, the physician is charged with evaluating all detected pathologies. Even tests taken as baseline indicators must be evaluated before being filed for future reference. In one case, a physician was found liable for not detecting the shadow of a lung tumor in X rays taken to detect spinal injuries. In another case, a physician was successfully sued for not noting an abnormal white blood cell count in a test taken for unrelated purposes. If blood and urine screening tests for substance abuse report other medical information, that information must be evaluated. This can pose a problem if the tests are part of a more general panel whose other results are discarded. Yet not discarding such results can subject the company to liability for violating confidentiality provisions of the ADA.

Duty to Inform

Occupational medicine physicians must inform patients fully about their medical conditions. While it is debatable whether a therapeutic exception (see Chapter 11) exists in general medical practice, there is no legal or ethical justification for withholding occupational medical information from an employee. This includes informing patients when they are being monitored for possible long-term toxic effects of known workplace exposures. Sharing information about monitoring with the patient will prevent allegations of cover-ups. It also allows an employee who retires or changes employers to ensure that necessary follow-up examinations or tests are performed. Although departing employees have a right to a copy of their medical records, few actually request the record and carry it to their next physician.

Occupational physicians should consider giving all departing employees a brief summary of information that they should provide to their next physician. Preemployment evaluations pose special problems because the patient may not be available for follow-up if they are not hired. Physicians must ensure they have enough information on each person they examine to allow them to contact the person later when test results become available.

Return to Work Certifications

All physicians engaged in clinical practice face the problem of certifying that a patient was legitimately absent from work because of an acute illness or injury. (Also see Chapter 29.) Most employees who are covered by the ADA because of long-term disabilities have periods of acute illness. Acute problems are not covered by the ADA. The same medical standards for work fitness apply to disabled employees covered by the ADA as to other employees. It is not certain, however, whether the ADA's limitations on information to be provided to employers prevents the employer from inquiring into the cause of a disabled employee's absence.

Return-to-work evaluations fall into two classes, depending on whether the employee is seeking to avoid returning or wishes to return to work. Situations in which the patient wishes to return to work pose fewer ethical problems because the patient and the employer have the same interest. Nevertheless, the physician must still determine the employee's medical fitness to return to prevent possible injuries to the employee and potential legal liability for the physician. Except for company-employed occupational medicine physicians, the decision about return to work will usually involve both the physician and the employer. The physician can describe the medical limitations on the worker, but without special knowledge (of OSHA rules, the nature of certain jobs, etc.), he or she cannot decide that a patient can do the job adequately and safely. When evaluating patients' ability to return to work, the environment in which they work must be given careful consideration. A painter with a broken leg may be able to paint walls while wearing a cast but could not work on scaffolding high above the ground. Cardiac patients who want to go back to work may tell their physicians that they sit at a desk or walk around slowly for the entire workday. What the physician may not know is that the patient works in an area of the plant with an ambient temperature of 120 degrees. On the other hand, the section foreman is not likely to be able to judge how much weight a postoperative patient may lift without danger. These questions should be worked out cooperatively among the worker, the employer, and the physician.

Physicians should be cautious about accepting the patient's evaluation of the work environment. Patients may not know company policies on light work or the availability of special positions for temporarily disabled employees. Private physicians should get their patients' permission to talk to their supervisors for an accurate description of the work available for the patient and the environmental conditions under which the work is to be done. In many cases, the only way to determine if patients are fit to return to work is to allow them to try but with instructions to both the patient and the supervisor to watch for signs of fatigue or reoccurrence of the medical problem.

Release from Work Certifications

Employees seeking off-work slips pose more difficult problems. Although most have legitimate illness, some do not. There are also employees with valid reasons for missing work, such as caring for a sick child, who seek medical excuses for missing work because personal illness is the only approved reason for absence from their workplace. Employers argue that unnecessary absences hurt all employees by reducing the productivity of the company. This can result in reduced benefits for employees with legitimate medical needs and in lost jobs or even bankruptcy. Disputes over time off from work pose the recurring dilemma of occupational medical practice: how are physicians to resolve the conflict between the patient's interests and the employer's interests?

This conflict is greatest when the patient sees the physician after recovering from the putative illness, requesting an excuse for time already taken. Assuming that there is no objective evidence to corroborate the patient's claims, the physician is put in the position of an investigator for the employer. Some physicians believe that employees do not have a duty to tell the truth to a physician who is acting in this investigatory role. (See Holleman and Holleman 1988.) These physicians may accept the patient's assertions unquestioningly because they see their role as one of patient advocate. This may benefit the patient, but it misrepresents the physician's role to the employer. In extreme circumstances, it may even constitute a fraud against the employer. It is also detrimental to the physician's professional reputation. Physicians who become known as an easy source of time off will find that they have the same unsavory reputation as those who dispense drugs too readily.

Another approach is to refuse to participate in off-work certifications. This position injures the employee because many employers punish unexcused absences. The best approach may be to limit off-work certifications to patients whom the physician has treated or diagnoses with an injury or illness. This does not put the physician into the position of an investigator, while still allowing legitimately ill employees to be excused from work. As a work policy matter, this may unnecessarily increase health care costs by forcing employees to see a physician for every minor illness. It also fails to deal with problems such as the illness of other family members for whom the employee must care.

Many employers are adopting no-fault absence plans. Employees are given a certain number of personal days that can be used for illness, vacations, or other personal business. This eliminates the incentive to fake illness to get time off from work. It has benefits in dealing with ADA-covered disabled employees because it does not require the employer to inquire into the employee's reason for missing work. Such plans have disadvantages too. If employees do not need to see a physician to get a back-to-work slip, they may return to work before it is medically wise. Treating all absences alike may also put the employer in conflict with the ADA. While the ADA does not require disabled employees to be given more sick days than those who are not disabled, the rules interpreting the ADA indicate that part-time work may be part of a reasonable accommodation to the employee's disability.

Worker's Compensation

Worker's compensation is not discussed in detail because it is a state program whose rules vary substantially by state. The basic structure of these programs guarantees compensation for work-related injuries and illness without the need to prove fault on the employer's part. The amount of compensation is fixed for each injury, and the employee has a very limited right to sue the employer for additional compensation. Because this compensation is much lower than the employee could recover in the courts, worker's compensation laws are often criticized for not creating a sufficient incentive to protect workers. The courts have allowed this limitation of liability because all injured workers receive medical care and some compensation. In contrast, private civil litigation (see Chapter 4) is available only to the small number of workers who are severely injured or killed.

All physicians who treat work-related injuries and illnesses should understand their state worker's compensation system. Failing to comply with reporting requirements and claims filing procedures can deny the patient needed care and delay payment of physician charges. Physicians should be prepared to provide reports to worker's compensation hearing examiners. They should also realize that worker's compensation laws have not eliminated litigation over workplace injuries. Employees must still litigate whether their injury was workplace related and the extent of their incapacitation. Physicians should contact the agency that regulates worker's compensation in their state for specific information about complying with its claims procedures.

Government Benefits for Disabled Workers
The social security insurance that covers most private workers includes a component that covers most kinds of disability, whatever the origin of the problem and whatever the age of the worker. Unlike most forms of private disability insurance, the spouse and children of a disabled worker may be entitled to benefits such as educational stipends. The disabled worker must apply to the Social Security Administration for benefits. There are specific forms that must be filled out by the health care providers, and the claimant's medical records must be made available. A worker denied benefits can follow a standard appeals process. It is important for the physician to work with the patient in getting through this system. Patients have the right to expect that their physicians will not add to the burden of dealing with the social security system.

Occupational physicians should be aware of the state and federal programs for injured or disabled workers in certain industries. The black lung program for miners is an example. In general, these programs require special evaluations for an individual to become eligible for benefits. If physicians must evaluate patients with a problem covered by one of these programs, they should consult with an attorney or occupational medicine physician who is experienced with the program.

THE AMERICANS WITH DISABILITIES ACT

The ADA attempts a comprehensive solution to discrimination against the disabled. This chapter examines only the provision of it dealing with the hiring and retention of disabled employees. This is not a comprehensive guide to the ADA and its restrictions on discrimination against disabled persons. These materials are intended to help occupational medicine physicians recognize the issues posed by the ADA in their practice. A physician who is charged with establishing an employer's policies and procedures for complying with the requirements of the ADA must seek the advice of counsel.

By July 1994, the ADA will cover all workplaces with 15 or more employees. This includes governmental entities, making its coverage broader than OSHA, which exempts governmental workplaces. Most private employers will be covered by both the ADA and OSHA regulations. The ADA will require all covered workplaces to restructure their handling of employee health programs.

The Purpose of the ADA
The purpose of the ADA is "to provide a clear and comprehensive national mandate for the elimination of discrimination against individuals with disabilities ... the Nation's proper goals regarding individuals with disabilities are to assure equality of opportunity, full participation, independent living, and economic self-sufficiency for such individuals." The ADA also is intended to reduce

federal payments for social security income and other federal tax-funded disability programs.

The Justice Department and the Equal Employment Opportunity Commission's final rules on the hiring and retention of disabled employees went into effect in July 1992 for workplaces with more 25 or more employees; they will apply in July 1994 for workplaces with fewer than 25 but more than 14 employees. Both employer organizations and groups representing disabled individuals had substantial input into the final rules. Consistent with the restrictions of the original legislation, these rules represent an attempt to balance the needs of employers and disabled individuals.

The employment provisions of the ADA mirror the requirements of section 504 of the Rehabilitation Act. The ADA covers more employers, however, because section 504 was limited to employers who did business with the government. While these included most large employers—universities, medical institutions, and governmental entities themselves—many small businesses were exempt. The major difference between section 504 and the ADA is the ADA's underlying presumption that there is widespread and systematic workplace discrimination against disabled individuals.

Section 504 was a remedial statute that provided standards to judge whether a given individual was the victim of discrimination. It allowed employers to use medical examinations and inquiries to determine the status of a potential or current employee's medical condition, including disabilities. The ADA presumes that employers will discriminate against disabled individuals. It seeks to prevent discrimination by limiting the employer's access to information, as well as providing legal remedies for victims of discrimination. It is this shift from nondiscrimination to noninquiry into disability that changes traditional occupational medicine practice.

ADA-Defined Disability
Disability as used in the ADA is much more expansive than the accepted medical usage. In the congressional findings supporting the ADA, it was estimated that approximately 43 million persons were disabled by the standards of the ADA. While traditional definitions of disability would hardly include one-fifth of the population, the ADA defines disability, with respect to an individual, as

- a physical or mental impairment that substantially limits one or more of the major life activities of such individual;
- a record of such an impairment; or
- being regarded as having such an impairment.

The ADA covers only long-term disabilities, not those from acute illnesses or injuries that affect the worker for less than six months. The ADA specifically exempts illegal drug use, drunkenness, sexual preference (homosexuality, bisexuality, and transvestism), and pregnancy from the definition of disability. Beyond these specific exemptions, it provides that the employee's physical or mental condition cannot be considered except as directly relevant to job performance. This follows the existing law that limits educational testing to qualifications that are directly related to job performance. Employers may not use a calculus test to screen applicants for janitorial jobs, and they may not use blood sugar testing to screen potential secretaries.

Preemployment Medical Examinations
The ADA bifurcates the hiring process into preoffer or appointment and post-offer of employment. At the preoffer stage, with certain exceptions for mandated affirmative action record keeping, "It is unlawful for a covered entity to conduct a medical examination of an applicant or to make inquiries as to whether an applicant is an individual with a disability or as to the nature or severity of such disability" (sec. 1630.13(a)).

The employer may ask the applicant if he or she is able to do the job and may require job-oriented skills tests. The employer must provide any reasonable accommodations that the applicant requires to complete these tests.

Allowable Examinations
A covered entity may require a medical examination after an offer of employment has been made to a job applicant and prior to the commencement of the employment duties of such applicant, and may condition an offer of employment on the results of such examination, if—

—all entering employees are subjected to such an examination regardless of disability;
—information obtained regarding the medical condition or history of the applicant is collected and maintained on separate forms and in separate medical files and is treated as a confidential medical record.

Preemployment Examination Records
Maintaining employee medical examination records as separate, confidential medical records is a fundamental change from the practices in most workplaces. This appears to preempt directly the OSHA requirement that medical information from preemployment evaluations be maintained with the occupational medical record. The employer and its agents have only limited access to such information:

supervisors and managers may be informed regarding necessary restrictions on the work or duties of the employee and necessary accommodations;
first aid and safety personnel may be informed, when appropriate, if the disability might require emergency treatment;
government officials investigating compliance with this Act shall be provided relevant information on request.

State workers' compensation laws are not preempted by the ADA or this part....
Consequently, employers or other covered entities may submit information to state workers' compensation offices or second injury funds in accordance with state workers' compensation laws without violating this part.

These restrictions also apply to routine medical examinations of employees made in the regular course of their employment, creating a dilemma for employers who process employee medical examination data through their personnel. The intent of the ADA is to deny information about disabilities to persons involved in employee hiring and retention. This would seem to require that the occupational medicine department, or the examining physician, maintain and disperse this information in accordance with restrictions in the ADA and its regulations.

New Duties for Occupational Medicine Physicians
Shifting the burden of compliance with the ADA medical examination restrictions to the medical department or the examining physicians creates new risks

that must be addressed by corporate counsel. The occupational medicine physician will now have the burden of determining employee fitness, with the attendant risk of error. The greatest risk is that the physician improperly withholds information that results in the employee's being injured. Conversely, if the employee's confidential medical information is available to unauthorized persons, there will be a presumption that any disciplinary action against the employee was due to his or her disability.

The best way to deal with this dilemma is to obtain the patient's authorization to release information to persons outside the medical department. This should not be a blanket authorization to release all medical information. The employee should be given a copy of the report the physician proposes to send to supervisors and first aid personnel authorized to receive such information. If the examinee refuses to authorize the release of the information, the physician should give the examinee a written description of the potential risks to the patient's health by withholding the information. If an incomplete report will improperly mislead the examinee, the physician may be ethically bound to refuse to provide any report on the examinee.

The ADA is not intended to affect group and individual health insurance plans, even if the restrictions of these plans on matters such as sick leave and coverage of preexisting conditions have an adverse impact on disabled persons. While not clearly defined in the proposed rules, an employer may offer "voluntary medical examinations, including voluntary medical histories, which are part of an employee health program available to employees at that work site." It is assumed that these include various wellness programs, as well as group medical insurance plans.

Persons with Known Disabilities

The ADA allows employers to hold all employees to the same workplace productivity standards, as long as these standards are a fair measure of the core functions of the job. Employers are prevented from discriminating against qualified individuals with a disability:

> The term "qualified individual with a disability" means an individual with a disability who, with or without reasonable accommodation, can perform the essential functions of the employment position that such individual holds or desires.
> ... Consideration shall be given to the employer's judgment as to what functions of a job are essential, and if an employer has prepared a written description before advertising or interviewing applicants for the job, this description shall be considered evidence of the essential functions of the job.
> The term "reasonable accommodation" may include—
>
> > making existing facilities used by employees readily accessible to and usable by individuals with disabilities; and
> > job restructuring, part-time or modified work schedules, reassignment to a vacant position, acquisition or modification of equipment or devices, appropriate adjustment or modifications of examinations, training materials or policies, the provision of qualified readers or interpreters, and other similar accommodations for individuals with disabilities.

The occupational medicine physician, in consultation with appropriate experts and the employee, must determine the appropriate accommodation. The employer must then decide if the person is otherwise qualified. Can the employee do the job with the accommodation, and is the accommodation reasonable? These decisions are legally contentious because they reflect economic and policy questions about the workplace. For example, is it reasonable to employ a sign-language interpreter for a manual laborer when the cost of the interpreter may double the cost of employing the laborer? While the employer may consult with the occupational medicine physician about the accommodation, the physician should avoid making the determination of reasonability. Making such decisions will impair neutrality that the ADA seeks to preserve for the examining physician.

Direct Threats to Health and Safety

The ADA does allow an employer to refuse to hire persons whose employment in the proposed job would pose a direct threat to themselves or others. This recognizes the existing rule that employers may choose to protect employees from harm and protect themselves from worker's compensation claims. The primary difference under the ADA is a greatly strengthened presumption that the employee is fit for work.

> Direct Threat means a significant risk of substantial harm to the health or safety of the individual or others that cannot be eliminated or reduced by reasonable accommodation. The determination that an individual poses a "direct threat" shall be based on an individualized assessment of the individual's present ability to safely perform the essential functions of the job. This assessment shall be based on a reasonable medical judgment that relies on the most current medical knowledge and/or on the best available objective evidence. In determining whether an individual would pose a direct threat, the factors to be considered include:
>
> (1) The duration of the risk;
> (2) The nature and severity of the potential harm;
> (3) The likelihood that the potential harm will occur; and
> (4) The imminence of the potential harm.

Most critically, the determination must be made on a case-by-case basis. Employers must be prepared to prove a "high probability, of substantial harm; a speculative or remote risk is insufficient." For example, if the threat is due to a behavioral disorder, the employer must identify the specific behavior that would pose a threat and the likelihood of occurrence. If the behavior is quasi-voluntary, such as sexual assault, an assurance by the employee that he is reformed would probably defeat the employer's attempt to prove him unfit. Compliance with the ADA provides no defense, however, if the employee assaults a customer. The injured customer may sue the employer for negligently hiring a known rapist.

Drug and Alcohol Testing

Congress intended the ADA to be neutral on testing for substance abuse. Persons using drugs or alcohol are specifically exempted from the coverage of the ADA, and tests for substance abuse are not regulated by the ADA. This means that employers can do preemployment drug screening and refuse to hire persons testing positive (as allowed by other laws and union agreements) without violating the ADA. Persons in the workplace may also be screened and disciplined without violating the ADA. The ADA does apply to a person who has "successfully completed a supervised drug rehabilitation program and is no longer engaging in the illegal use of drugs, or has otherwise been rehabilitated successfully and is no longer engaging in such use" or "is participating in a supervised rehabilitation program and is no longer engaging in such use."

The employer may adopt reasonable policies, including periodic drug testing, to ensure that such persons are not engaging in substance abuse. The employer may prohibit the use of alcohol and illegal drugs at the workplace, may require that employees not be under the influence of illegal drugs or alcohol while at work, and may hold "an employee who engages in the illegal use of drugs or who is an alcoholic to the same qualification standards for employment or job performance and behavior that such entity holds other employees, even if any unsatisfactory performance or behavior is related to the drug use or alcoholism of such employee." The employer may also regulate or ban smoking in the workplace without violating the ADA.

Physicians involved in drug and alcohol screening programs should appreciate that alcohol remains the most serious drug problem in most workplaces. It is medically (though perhaps not legally) unjustifiable to screen for illegal drug use and not screen for alcohol use. While the legislatures and the courts are increasingly allowing and encouraging random drug testing, there are arguments that such policies are unnecessarily intrusive. They present ethical problems for the supervising physician who is put in an adversary position with the employee. Moreover, the evidence is not conclusive that such programs substantially improve workplace safety or productivity. Physicians advising on such programs should consider behavior-related testing as an alternative to random screening. Behavior-related testing is less intrusive to innocent workers. Most important, it may identify workers with dangerous personality problems who are not drug users but need medical or psychiatric attention.

The Legal Risks of the ADA

While not specifically addressed in the law, the presumption that it is improper for employers to inquire into potential and current employees' disability status could be used in litigation against occupational medicine physicians. Prior to the ADA, the employer could not discriminate based on disability status, but it was proper for the examining physician to provide the employer with such information. Under the ADA, the inquiry itself is suspect. Even when such inquiries are permitted, the employer has only limited access to the information. The courts may find that the occupational medicine physician has a duty to refuse to make improper inquiries and examinations. This policy of noninquiry poses new ethical problems for occupational medicine physicians.

If failing to inquire into disabilities only subjects the employee and employer to the risk that the employee will not be able to do the job, there is no medical reason for the inquiry. In some situations, however, the risk is that the employee or others will be injured if the employee is medically unfit for the job. This problem arises with silent disabilities such as cardiac conditions. Without a potentially illegal inquiry, the employer will not know that the employee is disabled. The employer is allowed to inquire into potential employees' ability to perform the job, but such employees may not know which medical conditions pose a risk on the job and which are irrelevant to the workplace. This becomes an occupational medicine problem if the physician is asked to examine the employee but not to inquire into disabilities.

The problem posed by the ADA is that it encourages employees and employers to make decisions without information rather than to make informed choices about the risks of employment. This can create ethical conflicts for physicians, whose usual role is to ensure that patients have enough information to make an informed choice. Concomitant with that duty to provide full information is the duty to evaluate the patient's full medical status. Legally, the ADA does not provide any immunity for certifying physicians or employers. Employers remain strictly liable under worker's compensation for any injuries the employee suffers due to workplace conditions. If the occupational medicine physician is an independent contractor (or in states that recognize the dual-capacity doctrine), the injured employee will also sue the examining physician for malpractice for improperly certifying the employee as fit for the job. These legal and ethical problems make it questionable to agree to undertake preemployment and job placement examinations that do not fully explore the examinee's medical condition.

Pregnant Workers

The ADA does not apply to pregnant women. Workplace discrimination against pregnant women is prohibited by Title VII of the Civil Rights Act of 1964, as amended by the Pregnancy Discrimination Act (PDA). This law was recently construed by the U.S. Supreme Court in the landmark case of *International Union v. Johnson Controls* (1991). The decision held that fetal protection policies are against federal law. More generally, the Court found that employers cannot treat women differently because they may become pregnant, nor may they treat pregnant women differently solely because of their pregnancy. Under federal law, pregnancy must be handled like any other illness or disability. This applies to medical and disability insurance, leave policies, and fitness-for-work decisions. As with the ADA, the employer's only appropriate criterion is whether the pregnancy affects the woman's ability to do the job.

The *Johnson Controls* case was highly controversial because it pitted the job rights of the pregnant worker against the health of the fetus. Irrespective of an employer's emotional or religious views on protecting a fetus, injuring a fetus can be catastrophically expensive. Under current law, a fetus is a third person for worker's compensation purposes. This means that there is no cap on the damages that may be recovered from the employer. A woman may not absolve the employer of this liability by signing a waiver because the right to compensation belongs to the baby, not to the mother. The most difficult problem is that many women do not realize that they are pregnant quickly enough to prevent exposure during the critical first trimester. This led employers to deny women with reproductive capacity the right to work in certain jobs, although there has been little objective evidence of work-related fetal injuries.

Johnson Controls found that the employer had no independent right to protect the fetus. If a woman chooses to expose her fetus to workplace toxins, the employer cannot interfere. The majority opinion asserted that federal workplace safety laws might prevent lawsuits against the employer if the fetus was injured in such a situation, but this has not been the case for other workplace safety problems. The Court also reiterated the popular misconception that workplace toxins pose the same reproductive risks to men as to women. This ignores the issue that most of the known risks are due to interutero exposure.

Companies who employ women in positions that might endanger a fetus must warn women of the risk and provide alternative employment opportunities if the woman becomes pregnant. A physician who believes that a patient might be endangering her fetus by the work she does has the responsibility to warn her. This belief must be based on the scientific evidence. Physicians who care for women in their childbearing years should realize that not all chemicals are dangerous to a fetus. The current tendency to worry pregnant women with potential but minimal risks has the effect of discrediting warnings of real risks such as smoking. While there are occupational exposures that endanger a fetus, the more common risk is to the mother because of her reduced agility and shifting center of gravity.

A woman may be put on leave or alternative duties if the pregnancy makes her physically unable to fulfill her regular duties or if the work might endanger her health or the public safety. An airline was allowed to limit flights by pregnant women because their condition impaired their ability to function effectively in an emergency. Such decisions must be made on sound medical and workplace safety grounds. In the rare circumstances where such restrictions would be appropriate, employers should find alternative employment when possible. A pregnant telephone company employee may not be able to climb poles safely by the time she is 15 weeks pregnant, but she can do indoor installations until she goes into labor.

Physicians involved in obstetric care of women in the work force should make a clear distinction between social issues and medical decisions. A healthy woman with an uncomplicated pregnancy may want a maternity leave that extends for three months after the baby is born. Her company may offer a six-week leave. It is generally accepted that the normal disability associated with pregnancy and delivery has resolved by six weeks. It would not be legitimate to give this woman a medical excuse from work for the second six weeks postpartum unless she had a specific medical indication for such leave. No matter how strongly a physician feels about issues like bonding and breast-feeding, these are social issues that do not bear on the woman's physical fitness for work.

Determining Disability: Worker's Compensation versus ADA

The ADA blurs the traditional distinction between the medical determination of a functional impairment and the legal determination of the disability resulting from that impairment. In addition to disability determinations under the ADA, physicians are routinely asked to make functional impairment determinations for worker's compensation claims and for civil litigation arising from nonworkplace injuries. The physician's role is to determine the patient's loss of function in the affected organ system. The insurance company, court, or administrative agency providing the compensation decides how much of a disability this limitation of function constitutes. A disability may be caused by either illness or injury. The etiology of the illness or injury may determine how the patient will be compensated for the disability but is not important to the evaluation of the extent of the disability. For the purpose of the medical evaluation, it does not matter whether the patient is injured on the job or playing football on the weekend.

For instance, a physician may determine that a patient has lost 20 percent of the range of motion in his right hand. This determination is unrelated to the patient's occupation. The extent of disability caused by a functional impairment is a job-specific determination. For a manual laborer or an attorney, this loss of range of motion may not constitute a disability. The patient is able to pursue his usual occupation with little or no difficulty, and there is no substantial limitation on household tasks. If the patient is a concert pianist or a surgeon, this 20 percent loss of range of motion may constitute a total disability from his chosen work.

The severity of the workplace disability is not directly related to the extent of functional impairment or disability in personal living. A telephone operator who is blinded is severely disabled in his or her personal life but may not be occupationally disabled. A stevedore with a back injury may have little handicap in day-to-day living but be totally and permanently disabled regarding this work. In an evaluation of disability under the ADA, the focus is on alternative related employment. The proposed rules discuss the example of a surgeon with a mild palsy. While the surgeon may be disqualified from performing surgery, he or she may be employed in other medical activities and is thus not disabled. This is consistent with a policy that encourages full employment. Conflicts arise because a person making a tort or worker's compensation claim wants to be found maximally disabled, while a person claiming under ADA does not want to be found to be unqualified for a given job.

Food Handlers

There is a specific requirement that the secretary of health and human services develop regulations on allowable restrictions on food handlers with communicable diseases. Like all other communicable disease problems, when faced with determining whether a person poses a threat of contagion, a physician should contact the state or local health department. (See Chapter 23.)

These provisions do not preempt specific federal laws and regulations on evaluating persons in certain public safety positions such as aviation and transportation. In general, however, the proposed regulations make it difficult for an employer to disqualify a person based on a threat of personal harm or harm to others. This conflicts with the increasing pressure on employers to protect fellow employees and the public from dangerous employees. The ADA does not give employers immunity for liability for injuries caused by a dangerous employee. The ADA's limitations on preemployment inquiries on behavioral problems also conflict with efforts to encourage employers in businesses such as child care and delivery services to protect the public by screening for sexual offenders and other dangerous individuals.

BIBLIOGRAPHY

Reproductive Hazards

Bayer R: Women, work, and reproductive hazards. Hastings Cent Rep 1982 Oct; 12(5):14–19.

Carlo GL: Systematic account and critical appraisal of current epidemiological approaches for monitoring reproductive outcome in industry. Prog Clin Biol Res 1984; 160:139–45.

Erickson JD: Assessing occupational hazards to reproduction: Uses of existing data sets. Prog Clin Biol Res 1984; 160:99–107.

International Union v. Johnson Controls. 111 S Ct 1196(1991).

Johnson DG: Health risks and equal opportunity. Hastings Cent Rep 1980 Dec; 10(6):25–26.

Reilly P: Adverse reproductive outcome: Legal viewpoint. Prog Clin Biol Res 1984; 160:157–61.
Rosenberg MJ: Practical aspects of reproductive surveillance. Prog Clin Biol Res 1984; 160:147–56.
Sever LE; Hessol NA: Overall design considerations in male and female occupational reproductive studies. Prog Clin Biol Res 1984; 160:15–47.
Valentine JM; Plough AL: Protecting the reproductive health of workers: Problems in science and public policy. J Health Polit Policy Law 1983 Spring; 8(1):144–63.

General

Bowyer EA: The liability of the occupational health nurse. Law Med Health Care 1983 Oct; 11(5):224–26, 238.
Brandt-Rauf SI; Brandt-Rauf PW: Occupational health ethics: OSHA and the courts. J Health Polit Policy Law 1980 Fall; 5(3):523–34.
Canter EF: Employment discrimination implications of genetic screening in the workplace under Title VII and the Rehabilitation Act. Am J Law Med 1984 Fall; 10(3):323–47.
Cone JE: Public health—theory and practice in occupational medicine programs. Toxicol Ind Health 1989 Jul; 5(4):49–55; discussion 79–84.
Gold J: Epidemiology in occupational health. Med J Aust 1984 May 12; 140(10):588–90.
Lewy R: Preplacement examination of temporary hospital workers. J Occup Med 1985 Feb; 27(2):122–24.
Holleman WL; Holleman MC: School and work release evaluations. JAMA 1988 Dec 23/30 260:3629–3640.
Richards EP; Rathbun KC: Does the ADA mean no more medical examinations for disabled workers? Prev L Rptr 1991; 10(3):14.
Rothbart PL: Liability of corporate physicians in conducting preemployment and annual physical examinations. J Leg Med (Chic) 1985 Dec; 6(4):477–87.
Stein ZA: Surveillance: Symptoms, exposure, and trust. Prog Clin Biol Res 1984; 160:131–38.
Wong O: A practical guide for non-epidemiologists. Occup Health Saf 1981 Oct; 50(10):31–39.
Wong O: A practical guide for non-epidemiologists: Part II. Occup Health Saf 1981 Nov; 50(11):21–26.

31

Occupational Safety and Health Administration Rules on Occupational Medicine Practice

CRITICAL POINTS

- Occupational Safety and Health Administration (OSHA) rules apply to all physicians and clinics providing occupational medicine services, not just to company physicians.
- Contract physicians providing occupational medicine services can incur liability for violating OSHA rules.
- OSHA rules on access to medical records can pose problems for private medical practices.
- Regulated industries such as transportation impose additional restrictions on occupational medicine practice.
- Contract physicians should address OSHA requirements in their agreements with employers.

Occupational medicine physicians face a conflict between the interests of the patient and those of the employer. The physician's ethical duty to the patient has always been primary. Corporate pressures have sometimes prevailed over patient interests, leading employees and unions to distrust occupational medicine physicians. In highly regulated industries such as transportation, employers and employees may jointly pressure occupational medicine physicians to ignore individual health conditions that might endanger the public safety. These conflicts have resulted in the extensive regulation of occupational medicine practice to ensure that both employee health and the public's interests are properly protected.

The Occupational Safety and Health Administration (OSHA) is the basic source of regulations governing workplace safety and occupational medicine practice. OSHA regulations are supplemented by the ADA and specific workplace monitoring and employee certification rules from other agencies, such as the Department of Transportation (DOT). Most states have their own regulations that complement the federal regulations and, in some cases, substantially extend their requirements. These regulations were originally targeted at large employers with internal occupational medicine departments and corporate legal counsel. As small employers have been pressured to comply with the rules and as large employers contract out occupational medicine services, many private physicians and clinics are providing occupational medical services. These providers are predominantly family physicians and general internists without specialty certification in occupational medicine.

This chapter discusses the OSHA rules that company and contract physicians must follow in their occupational medicine practice. Chapter 30 discusses the special problems of the physician-patient relationship in occupational medicine and the impact of laws those governing employment discrimination.

EMPLOYEE MEDICAL INFORMATION

In 1980 OSHA promulgated rules governing access to and maintenance of employee medical records (29 C.F.R sec. 1910.20, Access to employee exposure and medical records). (The following discussion omits citations to specific statutory language.) While directed at managing medical information, these regulations define the scope of occupational medicine practice through their expansive definition of workplace-related medical information. These rules were written for records maintained in a company-based occupational medicine department, but they specifically include nonemployee physicians and clinics that provide occupational medical services. Any physician who treats workplace-related injuries or illnesses or does preemployment or work fitness evaluations is subject to these regulations.

OSHA promulgated these rules to:

1. Ensure employees, their representatives, and OSHA access to the employees' medical records.
2. To require employers to supply medical care providers sufficient information about toxic exposures to allow the treatment and long-term evaluation of exposed employees.
3. To create a way for medical care providers to report potential hazardous exposures to OSHA without violating the employer's trade secrets.
4. To ensure that employee medical records are maintained for a sufficient period (30 years after the termination of employment) to allow the monitoring of conditions with long latency.

These rules are directed at employers rather than medical care providers. The employer is expected to see that the medical care personnel follow the rules, and it is the employer that is subject to administrative sanctions if the rules are not followed. Physicians employed in a company occupational medicine department that does not comply with the rules may be subject to sanctions as company representatives. Nonemployee physicians may be subject to sanctions if they contractually accept the responsibility for maintaining employee medical information. This can become a problem if the employer goes out of business without arranging for an orderly transition in responsibility for the employees' medical information. An abrupt termination of business may leave the physician with the duty and financial responsibility to maintain the records or transfer them properly.

OSHA clearly intended these rules to supplement, rather than replace, traditional practices: "Except as expressly provided, the rules do not affect existing legal and ethical obligations concerning the maintenance and confidentiality of employee medical information, the duty to disclose information to a patient/employee or any other aspect of the medical-care relationship, or affect existing legal obligations concerning the protection of trade secret information." The rules do not pose any ethical problems beyond those already inherent in occupational medicine practice. In the case of providing access to trade secret information, they help resolve an existing ethical dilemma.

DEFINING OSHA REGULATED OCCUPATIONAL MEDICINE

The OSHA regulations indirectly define occupational medical practice by establishing what constitutes OSHA occupational medical information. By inference, physicians generating such regulated medical information are practicing occupational medicine as regulated by OSHA. The regulations apply to any employer "who makes, maintains, contracts for, or has access to employee... medical records... pertaining to employees exposed to toxic substances or harmful physical agents." The rules include all medical records maintained on a covered employee—not just those mandated by "specific occupational safety and health standards." The rules specifically include records maintained by physicians who are not employees of the covered employer but provide medical services on a contractual or fee-for-service basis. There are additional regulations that require monitoring of exposure to specific toxic substances. These regulations prevent employers from avoiding the rules on employee medical records by ignoring employee health entirely.

It is the definitions of exposure and toxic agents that account for the broad reach of these rules:

- —"Exposure" or "exposed" means that an employee is subjected to a toxic substance or harmful physical agent in the course of employment through any route of entry (inhalation, ingestion, skin contact or absorption, etc.), and includes past exposure and potential (e.g., accidental or possible) exposure.
- —"Toxic substance or harmful physical agent" means any chemical substance, biological agent (bacteria, virus, fungus, etc.), or physical stress (noise, heat, cold, vibration, repetitive motion, ionizing and non-ionizing radiation, hypo- or hyperbaric pressure, etc.) which: (i) Is listed in the latest printed edition of the National Institute for Occupational Safety and Health (NIOSH) Registry of Toxic Effects of Chemical Substances (RTECS); (ii) Has yielded positive evidence of an acute or chronic health hazard in testing conducted by, or known to, the employer; or (iii) Is the subject of a material safety data sheet kept by or known to the employer indicating that the material may pose a hazard to human health.

Given that the current edition of the RTECS contains over 45,000 chemicals, including nearly 6,000 that have been added in the past ten years, it is hard to imagine an industrial employee who is not covered by these regulations. The addition of biological agents expands coverage to most health care workers. The inclusion of repetitive motion and nonionizing radiation adds every office worker who touches or sits near a computer. There are exceptions for situations where the employer can "demonstrate that the toxic substance or harmful physical agent is not used, handled, stored, generated, or present in the workplace in any manner different from typical non-occupational situations," but these exceptions are construed strictly.

EMPLOYEE MEDICAL RECORDS

The OSHA rules govern information rather than just traditional paper records and several types of records in addition to medical records. For the purposes of these rules, a record includes "any item, collection, or grouping of information regardless of the form or process by which it is maintained (e.g., paper document, microfiche, microfilm, X-ray film, or automated data processing)." A medical record means "a record concerning the health status of an employee which is made or maintained by a physician, nurse, or other health care personnel or technician," including:

Medical and employment questionnaires or histories (including job description and occupational exposures).
The results of medical examinations (preemployment, preassignment, periodic, or episodic) and laboratory tests, including chest and other X-ray examinations taken for the purposes of establishing a baseline or detecting occupational illness, and all biological monitoring not defined as an "employee exposure record." (Under the ADA, information obtained from preemployment physicals may need to be kept separate from the remainder of the employee medical record.)
Medical opinions, diagnoses, progress notes, and recommendations.
First-aid records.
Descriptions of treatments and prescriptions.
Employee medical complaints.

Information that is not covered by these rules (and thus not subject to the access and retention provisions) includes:

Physical specimens (e.g., blood or urine samples) that are routinely discarded as a part of normal medical practice.
Records concerning health insurance claims if maintained separately from the employer's medical program and its records and not accessible to the employer by employee name or other direct personal identifier (e.g., social security number, payroll number).
Records created solely in preparation for litigation, which are privileged from discovery under the applicable rules of procedure or evidence.
Records concerning voluntary employee assistance programs (alcohol, drug abuse, or personal counseling programs) if maintained separately from the employer's medical program and its records.

It would seem that records of employee assistance programs that are mandated for employees with identified problems would be subject to the rules. It is usually argued, however, that these programs are voluntary in that the employee can always choose to lose his or her job.

In all cases information will be subject to the provisions of these rules if it is maintained in the same record as covered information. Even information prepared for litigation would lose its privilege if kept in the patient's medical record. This is a general rule of evidence and is not specific to the OSHA-regulated information. Given the potentially broad access to covered records, it is especially important that information on voluntary employee assistance programs be kept separate from covered medical information. Ideally this means separate folders in separate filing systems. This level of physical separation is not legally mandated, but it prevents the inadvertent release of information when OSHA or the union inspects a large number of records.

AUTHORIZATION TO RELEASE COVERED RECORDS

These rules provide that employees, their designated representatives, and OSHA will have access to covered employee medical records. Access means the right to examine and copy the records. If the employee is dead or legally incapacitated, the employee's legal representative may exercise all the employee's rights under the rules. A designated representative is any individual or organization to whom the employee gives written authorization for access to his or her medical records. A recognized or certified collective bargaining agent is automatically treated as a designated representative without regard to written employee authorization for access to certain other records covered under these rules. This implied authorization does not extend to employee medical records.

A designated representative must have the employee's specific written consent to have access to the employee's medical records. This written authorization must include:

The name and signature of the employee authorizing the release of medical information.
The date of the written authorization.
The name of the individual or organization that is authorized to release the medical information.
The name of the designated representative (individual or organization) that is authorized to receive the released information.
A general description of the medical information that is authorized to be released.
A general description of the purpose for the release of the medical information.
A date or condition upon which the written authorization will expire (if less than one year).

A written authorization [Figure 31.1] does not operate to authorize the release of medical information not in existence on the date of written authorization, unless the release of future information is expressly authorized, and does not operate for more than one year from the date of written authorization." A written authorization may be revoked in writing at any time.

While OSHA has the right to have access to employee medical information without the employee's written permission, the employer must notify its employees when OSHA seeks access to their medical records:

Each employer shall, upon request, and without derogation of any rights under the Constitution or the Occupational Safety and Health Act of 1970, 29 U.S.C. 651 et seq., that the employer chooses to exercise, assure the prompt access of representatives of the Assistant Secretary of Labor for Occupational Safety and Health to employee exposure and medical records and to analyses using exposure or medical records.... Whenever OSHA seeks access to personally identifiable employee medical information ... the employer shall prominently post a copy of the written access order and its accompanying cover letter for at least fifteen (15) working days.

```
┌─────────────────────────────────────────────────────────────────────┐
│                                                                     │
│  I, _____ (full name of worker/patient), hereby authorize│
│  _____ (individual or organization holding the medical records)│
│  to release to _____ (individual or organization authorized to│
│  receive the medical information), the following medical information from my│
│  personal medical records:                                          │
│  _____│
│  _____│
│  (Describe generally the information desired to be released)        │
│  I give my permission for this medical information to be used for the following│
│  purpose:                                                           │
│  _____│
│  _____│
│  but I do not give permission for any other use or re-disclosure of this informa-│
│  tion.                                                              │
│                                                                     │
│  (Note: several extra lines are provided below so that you can place additional re-│
│  strictions on this authorization letter if you want to. You may, however, leave these│
│  lines blank. On the other hand, you may want to (1) specify a particular expiration│
│  date for this letter (if less than one year); (2) describe medical information to be│
│  created in the future that you intend to be covered by this authorization letter; or│
│  (3) describe portions of the medical information in your records which you do not│
│  intend to be released as a result of this letter.)                 │
│                                                                     │
│  _____│
│  _____│
│  _____│
│  _____│
│                                                                     │
│  _____ Full name of Employee or Legal Representative    │
│  _____ Signature of Employee or Legal Representative    │
│                                                                     │
│  _____│
│  _____ Date of Signature        │
│                                                                     │
└─────────────────────────────────────────────────────────────────────┘
```

Figure 31-1. Sample Authorization Letter for the Release of Employees Medical Record Information to a Designated Representative

PHYSICAL ACCESS TO RECORDS

The OSHA rules provide that employees and their designated representatives have access to their medical records and the allowable conditions on that access. Although these rules were drafted for employer-based medical departments, they also apply to private physicians' offices and clinics. The rules can be problematic for private physicians and clinics since some of their requirements differ from customary private medical practice. The most fundamental of these differences is that OSHA grants the employee or representative the right to examine the original medical record.

This right differs from the usual practice of limiting the patient to a copy of his or her original medical record. This practice reflects state laws that are concerned with ensuring patients access to their medical information rather than the record itself. The state laws assume that physicians maintain records in a proper manner. The OSHA rule allowing inspection of the original record arises from the suspicion that company physicians may try to cover up occupationally related health conditions. OSHA does allow the medical records custodian to "delete from requested medical records the identity of a family member, personal friend, or fellow employee who has provided confidential information concerning an employee's health status." In the absence of specific authorization by the patient, however, this provision does not give medical care providers the right to discuss the patient's medical condition with third parties.

A demand to examine the original record should not disrupt office routines in the individual case, but it can become a problem when a designated representative requests access to the records of all the employees of a company. The physician or clinic is required to provide proper facilities for reviewing the records, which can take weeks or months, or to loan the records to the requesting organization. In either case, the physician or clinic may find it necessary to make and retain a copy of the records to provide ongoing care for the employees during the period when the records are unavailable. This can be very expensive and should be addressed in the contract between a company and a contract provider of occupational medical services.

Whenever an employee or designated representative requests a copy of a record, the employer (or contracting occupational medicine provider) must provide a copy of the record without charge, provide free access to a copying machine, or loan the record to the requesting employee or representative for a reasonable period of time to allow copying. "In the case of an original X-ray, the employer may restrict access to on-site examination or make other suitable arrangements for the temporary loan of the X-ray." If the record has been previously provided without cost to an employee or designated representative, the employer may charge reasonable, nondiscriminatory administrative costs (search and copying expenses but not including overhead expenses) for additional copies of the record. The employer shall not charge for an initial request for a copy of information that has been added to a record since it was previously provided.

LIMITATIONS ON ACCESS TO MEDICAL RECORDS

When an employee requests access to his or her medical records, the physician may recommend that the employee discuss the records with the physician, accept a summary of material facts and opinions in lieu of the records requested, or accept release of the requested records only to a physician or other designated representative. If the employee persists in his or her request to see the complete record the rules provide that release may be made to a designated representative rather than to the employee:

> Whenever an employee requests access to his or her employee medical records, and a physician representing the employer believes that direct employee access to information contained in the records regarding a specific diagnosis of a terminal illness or a psychiatric condition could be detrimental to the employee's health, the employer may inform the employee that access will only be provided to a designated

representative of the employee having specific written consent, and deny the employee's request for direct access to this information only. Where a designated representative with specific written consent requests access to information so withheld, the employer shall assure the access of the designated representative to this information, even when it is known that the designated representative will give the information to the employee.

This provision presupposes that an employee's medical records may contain information that has not been provided to the employee. Case law, and related OSHA regulations on informing employees of medically significant information, would seem to mitigate against the right of an occupational medicine physician to withhold information from a patient. While some state laws allow withholding potentially damaging information from patients, OSHA allows the physician only to impede, not prevent, a patient's access to his or her records. Ethical questions aside, requiring a patient to get his or her records indirectly and then having those records contain an unpleasant surprise would certainly increase the chance that the patient will see an attorney.

PRESERVATION OF RECORDS

Unless a specific occupational safety and health standard provides a different period of time, . . . the medical record for each employee shall be preserved and maintained for at least the duration of employment plus thirty (30) years. This requirement does not apply to health insurance claims records maintained separately and to first aid records (not including medical histories) of one-time treatment and subsequent observation . . . if made on-site by a non-physician and if maintained separately from the employer's medical program and its records.

The medical records of employees who have worked for less than (1) year for the employer need not be retained beyond the term of employment if they are provided to the employee upon the termination of employment.

Nothing in this section is intended to mandate the form, manner, or process by which an employer preserves a record as long as the information contained in the record is preserved and retrievable, except that chest X-ray films shall be preserved in their original state.

The OSHA rules also provide for the maintenance of records on employees whose employer is no longer in business. If an employer goes out of business, its employee's medical records shall be transferred to the successor employer, who must receive and maintain the records. This can pose problems if the successor employer chooses to sever the relationship with the private physician or clinic and take possession of the records. The records must be surrendered, but it is important, as much as possible, to comply with state laws governing the transfer or release of medical information. It may be advisable to notify the employees that their records will be transferred and that they should contact the new employer if they have questions or objections. Since the successor employer has the right to the records of all previous employees, not just those whom it rehires, there may be employees who would want the physician to retain a copy of the records and continue providing medical care. The physician or clinic may also want to retain copies of the records for medical-legal concerns.

When there is no successor employer, the employees must be notified of their rights of access to the records at least three months prior to the cessation of the employer's business. The employer must also transfer "the records to the Director of the National Institute for Occupational Safety and Health (NIOSH) if so required by a specific occupational safety and health standard" or "notify the Director of NIOSH in writing of the impending disposal of records at least three (3) months prior to the disposal of the records." The physician or clinic maintaining the records should assure that these obligations have been carried out.

MATERIAL SAFETY DATA SHEETS

Workers in modern industrial workplaces are exposed to myriad toxic chemicals. In an effort to inform employees and persons in the community about the risks of toxic chemicals in the workplace, OSHA requires that employers make material safety data sheets (MSDS) available to employees, health care providers, local fire departments, and other community organizations with an interest in toxic exposures. (See Lerman and Kipen 1990 for a detailed discussion of MSDS.)

MSDSs are the starting point for determining if an employee has been exposed to a toxic substance. Occupational medicine physicians should obtain appropriate MSDSs from each employer for whom they provide occupational medical services. MSDSs can also be useful for general medicine physicians who suspect that a patient is suffering from an occupational exposure.

> Each material safety data sheet shall be in English and shall contain at least the following information:
>
> —The identity used on the label, and, except as provided for . . . trade secrets;
> —If the hazardous chemical is a single substance, its chemical and common name(s);
> —If the hazardous chemical is a mixture which has been tested as a whole to determine its hazards, the chemical and common name(s) of the ingredients which contribute to these known hazards, and the common name(s) of the mixture itself; or,
> —If the hazardous chemical is a mixture which has not been tested as a whole:
> —The chemical and common name(s) of all ingredients which have been determined to be health hazards, and which comprise 1% or greater of the composition, except that chemicals identified as carcinogens under paragraph (d)(4) of this section shall be listed if the concentrations are 0.1% or greater; and,
> —The chemical and common name(s) of all ingredients which have been determined to be health hazards, and which comprise less than 1% (0.1% for carcinogens) of the mixture, if there is evidence that the ingredient(s) could be released from the mixture in concentrations which would exceed an established OSHA permissible exposure limit or American Conference of Governmental Industrial Hygienists (ACGIH) Threshold Limit Value, or could present a health hazard to employees; and,
> —The health hazards of the hazardous chemical, including signs and symptoms of exposure, and any medical conditions which are generally recognized as being aggravated by exposure to the chemical;
> —The primary route(s) of entry;
> —Emergency and first aid procedures;
> —The name, address and telephone number of the chemical manufacturer, importer, employer or other responsible party preparing or distributing the material safety data sheet, who can provide additional information on the hazardous chemical and appropriate emergency procedures, if necessary.

There are several important limitations that may make the data on MSDS misleading. Within certain limitations, the manufacturer is not required to perform toxicity testing on the mixture or its constituents. The MSDS need only be based on a review of the literature. Even this review is subject to question because there are no standards to define an adequate search or to resolve conflicting research reports. It is not unusual to find manufacturers of the same chemical with different health risks on their MSDS. In addition, manufacturers sometimes ignore chemicals that they use as vehicles but do not manufacture themselves. While these are generically described as inert ingredients, they sometimes include highly toxic aromatic hydrocarbons or complex organic resins.

If the MSDS does not provide enough information, either because trade secret information has been left out or because the physician suspects that an ingredient is toxic, the physician can obtain more detailed information directly from the manufacturer identified on the MSDS. This may require several inquiries, however; only the original manufacturer of the substance is responsible for keeping full information on health hazards. Thus the physician may need to call the manufacturer of each substance that has been mixed into a product.

TRADE SECRETS

While keeping track of exposures to known chemicals can be a daunting problem, the exact constituents in some chemical processes are trade secrets: "Any confidential formula, pattern, process, device, or information or compilation of information that is used in an employer's business and that gives the employer an opportunity to obtain an advantage over competitors who do not know or use it." With certain exceptions, employers and manufacturers of chemicals are allowed to withhold trade secret information if they warn the health care provider, employee, or designated representative that the information has been deleted. When information is withheld, the employer or manufacturer must provide an MSDS with "all other available information on the properties and effects of the toxic substance."

There are circumstances when medical care providers need to know the specific chemical and concentration to which an employee has been exposed. If there is a medical emergency and the "specific chemical identity of a toxic substance is necessary for emergency or first-aid treatment," the employer or manufacturer must provide the needed information. The medical care providers obtaining this information must not disclose it except as necessary to provide the needed medical care. The employer or manufacturer may not withhold the information in an emergency but may require that the medical providers sign a confidentiality agreement as soon as circumstances permit. Irrespective of the existence of such a written agreement, disclosing such information is illegal in most states and can subject the violator to substantial civil damages.

The OSHA rules also allow access to trade secret information in nonemergency situations if the request is in writing and describes with reasonable detail one or more of the following occupational health needs for the information:

—To assess the hazards of the chemicals to which employees will be exposed;
—To conduct or assess sampling of the workplace atmosphere to determine employee exposure levels;

—To conduct pre-assignment or periodic medical surveillance of exposed employees;
—To provide medical treatment to exposed employees;
—To select or assess appropriate personal protective equipment for exposed employees;
—To design or assess engineering controls or other protective measures for exposed employees; and
—To conduct studies to determine the health effects of exposure.

The request must explain in detail why the disclosure of the specific chemical identity is essential. This explanation must include the reasons that the disclosure of the properties and effects of the chemical, the means of controlling exposure, the methods of analyzing exposure, and the methods of diagnosing and treating exposure to the chemical are not sufficient. The request should describe the procedures for maintaining the confidentiality of the disclosed information. The person receiving the information must agree, in a written confidentiality agreement, not to use the trade secret information for any purpose other than the health needs asserted and not to release the information except to OSHA. If the employer or manufacturer refuses to disclose the requested information, the requesting person may request OSHA to force the employer to disclose the needed information.

Irrespective of the contents of any confidentiality agreements, trade secret information may be disclosed to OSHA if the person receiving the information believes that such a disclosure is necessary to workplace safety. The physician or other person disclosing such information to OSHA must inform the employer or manufacturer that supplied the information that it will be given to OSHA. This warning may be given before disclosure to allow the employer or manufacturer time to request that OSHA determine if such disclosure is warranted. The employer or manufacturer may also be informed at the same time that the disclosure is made to OSHA. The employer or manufacturer may still object to OSHA's use of the information, but this will ensure that an OSHA official learns of the toxic exposure.

Physicians in occupational medicine practice have a duty to inquire into the cause of toxic symptoms observed in their patients. Such physicians must also respect the employer's need to protect its trade secrets. Many chemical processes are not patented, either because the disclosures necessary to obtain a patent would give away the company's competitive edge or because the process is not sufficiently different from known processes to qualify for patent protection. In most cases, this is not a problem because it is not the identity of the chemicals that matters as much as the way they are used. In some circumstances, however, the identity of the chemical itself would be enough to allow competitors to copy the process. An occupational medicine physician should inquire about potential trade secret problems before agreeing to provide services to an employer. Any necessary confidentiality agreements should be part of the contract between the physician and the employer. This will avoid misunderstandings if the physician should inadvertently identify a chemical that the employer considers a trade secret. Such an agreement should make clear that the employer understands that under some circumstances the physician may be required to disclose trade secret information to OSHA.

BIBLIOGRAPHY

Beebe GW: Chronic disease in the workplace and the environment. Record linkage: Methodologic and legal issues. Arch Environ Health 1984 May–Jun; 39(3):169–72.

Gill FS: Occupational health record systems—an ideal approach. J Soc Occup Med 1987 Summer; 37(2):55–58.

Karrh BW: The confidentiality of occupational medical data. Del Med J 1983 May; 55(5):287–88, 291–93.

Lerman SE; Kipen HM: Material safety data sheets: Caveat emptor. Arch Intern Med 1990; 150:981–84.

McGarity TO: The new OSHA rules and the worker's right to know. Hastings Cent Rep 1984 Aug; 14(4):38–45.

Miller FH: Biological monitoring: The employer's dilemma. Am J Law Med 1984 Winter; 9(4):387–426.

Munn A: Records and the occupational physician. J Soc Occup Med 1984 Nov; 34(4):105–7.

Richter ED: The worker's right-to-know: Obstacles, ambiguities and loopholes. J Health Polit Policy Law 1981 Summer; 6(2):339–46.

32

Access to Emergency Care

CRITICAL POINTS
- Physicians have an ethical duty to render emergency medical care.
- Common law tradition and Good Samaritan laws protect physicians rendering volunteer emergency care.
- Federal law requires emergency rooms to evaluate and manage all patients who request treatment.
- Physicians who violate the federal access to emergency care law can be fined $50,000.

Emergency care is often thought of as care for accident victims. It is as frequently required for emergent medical conditions such as heart attacks. Emergency care can be provided in emergency rooms, in physicians' offices, and at the scene of accidents or sudden illnesses.

The law assumes that a person in need of emergency care would consent to the care if able. This assumption makes consent for emergency care a low-priority issue. There are no cases known to us in which a physician was successfully sued for failure of informed consent in an emergency situation.

Contrary to medical-legal mythology, few physicians have been sued for rendering emergency care. Most of the litigation, and the legal risk, in emergency medicine arises from denying patients care. This should not be surprising. The juror who will not rule against a physician who volunteers help may decide against a physician for refusing to help when required by law. This belief that no one should be denied emergency care has recently been incorporated into the federal law. Essentially all emergency rooms are now required to provide emergency care without regard to the patient's ability to pay. Every physician must understand the provisions of this law because it carries a potential $50,000 fine, not payable by insurance, for physicians who violate its requirements.

ASSISTING AT ACCIDENTS

A physician has no duty to help an injured or sick individual unless there is a preexisting physician-patient relationship or other statutory or contractual relationship. While morally reprehensible, it is not illegal for a physician to drive past the scene of an accident where his or her services could be lifesaving or to refuse to provide cardiopulmonary resuscitation (CPR) to a fellow diner at a restaurant.

If the physician does choose to help, there is one central rule for volunteers: do not make the victim worse off.

The classic legal example is the person drowning in a lake. There are several boats within sight of the victim, and one of them heads toward the victim. The others stay away so as not to complicate the rescue. The original rescuing boat now has a duty to continue the rescue because it has interfered with the victim's chance to get other help. In the same way, once a physician stops to help at an accident, the help must be continued until the patient may be safely transferred to another medical care provider or until the patient is no longer in need of medical attention.

Physicians should be careful not to interfere with other persons who have superior skills for the task at hand. If there is ambulance service available, it should be summoned. The paramedic on the ambulance may be much better at resuscitation than the physician. And a veterinarian with an active farm practice may be a much better candidate for delivering a baby than an internist who has not seen a delivery in 20 years. The internist should stand by, however, in case the veterinarian needs advice or assistance in the care of a human.

Physicians should not be offended if they are asked to provide identification at the scene of an accident. All emergency professionals are plagued by people who join in the excitement. Following the fire brigade is as old as organized fire fighting; impersonating a police officer has been criminalized because it is common and dangerous to society. There are also people who impersonate physicians in hospitals and at the scenes of accidents. Many states provide wallet-sized copies of the medical license to use as identification in such a case. Physicians should understand the need for such identification and be willing to provide it.

While physicians do not have a duty to carry medical equipment with them, it is recommended that they carry basic equipment when traveling. If the physician does volunteer help in an emergency, it is extremely disconcerting not to have the necessary tools available. Many emergency medical technicians, nurses, and doctors keep first-aid equipment in their cars or at home because they do not want to be in an emergency situation without the equipment necessary to save a life. This is especially important for physicians who practice in small towns where there are no paramedics and a readily available and fully equipped ambulance.

Once a physician has assumed the care of a patient in an emergency, there is a duty not to be negligent in treating the patient. This duty does not end until the patient is assured of proper follow-up care. If the patient is taken away by ambulance, it is wise to notify the hospital that the patient is coming and to pass on medical information. A follow-up call to make sure the patient arrived is also a good idea. Unless there is no question of undetected injury, the patient should not be allowed to assume that the roadside care is all that is required. An emergency room record with notations from the physician at the scene will improve the quality of care a patient receives if late complications develop.

Physicians may be faced with rendering emergency care in a state where they are not licensed. The drowning on the beach, the car accident, or the call for a physician in the air terminal may expose the vacationing physician to the need to practice medicine without a license. Considerations of licensure should not stop a physician from saving a life. The physician should make a good-faith effort to help and should turn the case over to qualified medical personnel as soon as possible. The same rules on relinquishing care and follow-up should be followed as if the physician were licensed. Most state licensing laws explicitly allow for emergency care by nonlicensed physicians, and no state would prosecute a physician for volunteering emergency medical care.

GOOD SAMARITAN LAWS

There is a widespread myth that physicians will be sued for a poor outcome if they stop to help a stranger in need. Nevertheless, no physician has ever lost a suit over a Good Samaritan act. It is hard for most physicians and nurses to believe that physicians do not get sued for volunteering medical care. Millions of people watched Dr. Kildare lose a suit for helping at the scene of an accident. Every physician has heard a story over coffee about some other physician who got sued. It may have happened to Dr. Kildare, but it has not happened to any real doctors. There have been many cases in which poor care was rendered in an emergency, but they were cases where the physician had a duty to treat that patient, not cases of volunteer care. Even before the enactment of Good Samaritan laws, there was a common law protection and a social policy against such suits. Unfortunately, the myth persists because it is an excuse for some physicians who refuse to inconvenience themselves by helping others in emergencies.

Because of the pervasive myth of liability in the medical professions, most states have enacted some form of Good Samaritan law prohibiting a patient from suing a physician or other health care professional for injuries from a Good Samaritan act. To trigger the protection of such an act, two conditions must be satisfied: it must be a volunteer act, and the actions must be a good-faith effort to help. Displacing a neck fracture in an effort to do rescue breathing might be malpractice in the emergency room, but it is not bad faith on the roadside. Trying an unnecessary tracheostomy just for the practice would be bad faith.

In the medical sense, a Good Samaritan is a medical care professional who volunteers to help someone in need of emergency medical care. The act must be done without there being any duty to care for the patient and without any expectation of compensation. The classic case is the physician who comes upon the scene of a car accident. A physician who stops and renders aid to the victims of the accident has acted as a Good Samaritan. If the physician later sends a bill for the emergency services, this is no longer a Good Samaritan action. If the victims spontaneously send the physician a dozen roses as a thank-you gift, this does not affect the voluntary nature of the act.

Most of the stories about physicians who are sued for Good Samaritan acts involve a physician who has a duty to treat the patient in question. It is not a Good Samaritan act to take care of one's own patients. The physician-patient relationship is a 24-hour-a-day relationship. A physician at a wedding reception who watches his own diabetic patient eat three pieces of wedding cake and drink a bottle of champagne has a duty to handle the ensuing diabetic coma. The fact that the patient was acting foolishly or that the physician is the bridegroom and is not taking calls does not alter the duty of the physician to provide medical care to his patients when and where they need it.

The legal problem with Good Samaritan laws is that they were unnecessary. If the common law was a perfect protection against a Good Samaritan lawsuit, then specific Good Samaritan legislation cannot improve the situation. Conversely, by passing statutes, legislatures encourage attorneys to look for loopholes. An attorney who can find a way to convince a jury that a physician was not covered by the Good Samaritan law may be tempted to sue.

EMERGENCY CARE IN THE OFFICE

Emergencies occur in every type of medical practice. The dermatologist may not treat anaphylaxis as often as the emergency physician, but there is always the chance that a patient will react to a drug. All physicians must consider the types of emergencies that may arise in their practices and be prepared to deal with them. Some minimum standards for all physicians are set by professional organizations and hospital staff rules. Proficiency in basic life support at the level necessary to maintain certification with the American Heart Association or the American Red Cross has become such a common requirement for employment or staff privileges that it is arguably a standard of care for all practicing physicians.

The same general standards of care apply for emergencies as for routine care in the office or the hospital. Specialists are expected to work to the standards of their specialty and to have general competence in other areas of medicine. This can be a problem for subspecialists who were not trained as general practitioners before they did their specialty training. The law assumes that there is a core body of medical knowledge shared by all physicians. This includes the management of basic emergency conditions such as heart attacks and the management of iatrogenic complications of specialty practice, such as anaphylactic shock from a drug administered in the physician's office.

Physicians should have appropriate emergency equipment available where they practice, with the specific equipment needed tailored to the practice and the patient panel. For example, physicians who give injectable drugs should have all the equipment necessary to treat anaphylaxis. If the physician does not treat anyone under the age of 16, pediatric-sized airways are not necessary. If the physician does not treat anyone over the age of 10, a kit full of 18-gauge needles and liter bottles of fluid would not be appropriate. Physicians whose practices include older individuals should have the equipment and training to deal with a myocardial infarction. While the physician may not cause the patient's heart attack, heart attacks are an expected occurrence in the patient group.

The manufacturers of emergency kits are working to raise the standard of care for office emergency equipment. A bite block made from a tongue depressor and a syringe full of epinephrine taped to the wall is no longer acceptable emergency preparation. Oxygen, intravenous fluids, and steroids may be lifesaving. They are readily available in a suitcase kit that contains protocols for the use of all the equipment. Appropriate drugs and equipment should be readily available in usable form to treat a patient in a foreseeable emergency. Losing a patient to anaphylaxis because there is no oxygen available or the epinephrine is out of date is inexcusable.

Physicians should accompany patients to the hospital in the emergency transport vehicle if there is no proper paramedic service. Many helicopter transport systems, however, will not allow the attending physician to ride in the helicopter. These systems usually have a physician on the helicopter when it is sent out. The attending physician should call ahead while the helicopter is en route and talk to the staff physician at the receiving hospital.

Physicians rendering emergency medical care should recognize the limitations of the situation and of their skills. This is especially true of emergencies in the physician's office. Physicians should not hesitate to call an ambulance to transport a patient to an emergency room. If the physician cannot manage the emergency, it is negligent not to transport the patient to a proper emergency facility.

The physician should never send a patient with a serious condition to an emergency room in private transportation. If the condition requires emergency care, the patient should be transported in an ambulance. (This may not hold true in rural areas without available ambulance service. In this case, the physician may need to accompany the patient.) The ambulance personnel may not be able to keep the asthmatic patient from dying, but a jury would never believe that the ambulance would not have helped.

EMERGENCY ROOM STAFFING

The presence of an emergency room in a hospital gives the members of the medical staff of that hospital many legal duties. The accreditation requirements for hospitals include extensive regulations for emergency services. The medical staff as a group have responsibilities to provide certain services to the hospital and its patients. These responsibilities go beyond the care of the patients whom the individual physician has admitted. If being a staff member in the internal medicine section requires taking referrals from the emergency room, then internists have relinquished the right to choose not to accept such referrals. They have a duty to accept and care for the ER patient as though that patient was their own.

The duty to accept ER referrals is sometimes ignored by physicians who do not wish to accept emergency calls or who are on the staff of too many hospitals. A staff physician cannot refuse a call or deny care to emergency patients if this is required as a condition of medical staff privileges. If a patient with head trauma is brought to the hospital and the emergency room physician determines that a neurosurgeon is needed, the staff neurosurgeon must provide care for the patient. If the neurosurgeon refuses to attend the patient, he or she is liable for any injury to the patient that results from the delay or lack of care. If the emergency physicians and the hospital staff committees do not discipline medical staff members for refusing ER referrals, they too are liable for any resulting patient injuries. Physicians who violate their obligations to treat emergency patients also are subject to fines under federal law.

Residents who are moonlighting in an emergency room must be independently licensed and evaluated for privileges through the regular medical staff process. Their status as residents is irrelevant to their private, unsupervised practice. If residents are working in the emergency room as part of their training, they must be properly supervised. No matter how long the residency or how great the skills of a particular resident, a resident in training may not be given primary responsibility for the care of patients. There must be a qualified physician who is responsible for both the resident and the patient care. (See Chapter 15.) Supervising physicians do not have to be with the resident all the time, but they should be cautious about how much authority they delegate to the resident. A telephone consultation in the middle of the night may be adequate, but in serious situations, the supervising physician should be with the patient.

Many hospitals now contract with physician groups to provide emergency medical services. These services may be limited to the emergency room, or they may include some intensive care or resuscitation duties. Usually the contracts specify financial arrangements, confer staff appointments on the members of the group, and specify the responsibilities of the rest of the medical staff in providing specialty services and follow-up for patients seen by the emergency medicine physicians. Such contracts do not relieve the hospital or the remainder of the medical staff of responsibility for the amount or quality of care provided in the emergency room.

ACCESS TO EMERGENCY CARE UNDER THE FEDERAL LAW

Emergency rooms have always tested the common law rule of no duty to strangers. There are legions of cases in which blacks have been turned away from all-white hospitals and poor people of all colors have been refused emergency care. Fortunately, these cases are rarer each year, yet abuses are common enough that Congress has created uniform standards for the provision of emergency care and the transfer of emergency patients to other facilities. These are embodied in Examination and Treatment for Emergency Medical Conditions and Women in Labor (the act). The act sweeps away the traditional common law rules for access to emergency care. It applies uniformly in all states and so will make up the remainder of this chapter. The following discussion includes the relevant statutory provisions. Understanding the language of the law will help physicians work with their counsel to ensure that they comply with its provisions.

Medical Screening

The key provision of this statute is the medical screening requirement.

> In the case of a hospital that has a hospital emergency department, including ancillary services routinely available to the emergency department if any individual (whether or not eligible for benefits under this subchapter) comes to the emergency department and a request is made on the individual's behalf for examination or treatment for a medical condition, the hospital must provide for an appropriate medical screening examination within the capability of the hospital's emergency department to determine whether or not an emergency medical condition (within the meaning of subsection (e)(1) of this section) exists. (1395dd(a))

The statute defines emergency condition much more broadly than the traditional common law definition of care necessary to save life or limb:

(A) a medical condition manifesting itself by acute symptoms of sufficient severity (including severe pain) such that the absence of immediate medical attention could reasonably be expected to result in—
  (i) placing the health of the individual (or, with respect to a pregnant woman, the health of the woman or her unborn child) in serious jeopardy,
  (ii) serious impairment to bodily functions, or
  (iii) serious dysfunction of any bodily organ or part; or
(B) with respect to a pregnant woman who is having contractions—
  (i) that there is inadequate time to effect a safe transfer to another hospital before delivery, or
  (ii) that transfer may pose a threat to the health or safety of the woman or the unborn child.

If the person has a condition that meets this definition of emergency, the hospital must either stabilize the patient's condition or transfer the patient to another facility. It is the act's definitions of stabilization and appropriate transfer that ensure that the patient receives proper medical treatment.

Stabilization

> The term "to stabilize" means, with respect to an emergency medical condition [other than active labor] to provide such medical treatment of the condition as may be necessary to assure, within reasonable medical probability, that no material deterioration of the condition is likely to result from or occur during the transfer of the individual from a facility, or, with respect to [a woman having contractions] to deliver (including the placenta).
>
> The term "stabilized" means, with respect to an emergency medical condition [other than active labor] that no material deterioration of the condition is likely, within reasonable medical probability, to result from or occur during the transfer of the individual from a facility, or, with respect to [a woman having contractions] that the woman has delivered (including the placenta).

Under these definitions, a stabilized patient is no longer in need of emergency medical care. This definition is important because a patient who is stabilized may be transferred without meeting the strict requirements of the act.

Definition of Transfer

The law speaks in terms of transferring patients, but it uses an unusual definition of transfer that also includes discharging the patient or just turning the patient away:

> The term "transfer" means the movement (including the discharge) of an individual outside a hospital's facilities at the direction of any person employed by (or affiliated or associated, directly or indirectly, with) the hospital, but does not include such a movement of an individual who (A) has been declared dead, or (B) leaves the facility without the permission of any such person.

If a patient is transferred—sent from the emergency room in any fashion without having been stabilized—the emergency room personnel must satisfy the statutory requirements for a proper transfer:

> An appropriate transfer to a medical facility is a transfer—
> (A) in which the transferring hospital provides the medical treatment within its capacity which minimizes the risks to the individual's health and, in the case of a woman in labor, the health of the unborn child;
> (B) in which the receiving facility—
>   (i) has available space and qualified personnel for the treatment of the individual, and
>   (ii) has agreed to accept transfer of the individual and to provide appropriate medical treatment.

The act requires that the patient be accompanied with all available medical information and the documents establishing compliance with the act. Requiring the inclusion of these records, including the name of any physicians who do not comply with the act, ensures that they will be incorporated in the patient's medical record. This makes them available to federal inspectors and to interested plaintiffs' attorneys:

The transferring hospital sends to the receiving facility all medical records (or copies thereof), related to the emergency condition for which the individual has presented, available at the time of the transfer, including records related to the individual's emergency medical condition, observations of signs or symptoms, preliminary diagnosis, treatment provided, results of any tests and the informed written consent [requesting transfer] or certification [of the medical necessity of transfer] and the name and address of any on-call physician . . . who has refused or failed to appear within a reasonable time to provide necessary stabilizing treatment.

It is critical that these materials establish the medical facts to support the medical necessity of the transfer. In the case upholding a $20,000 fine against a physician who violated the act, the court stressed the importance of documenting the medical basis of the transfer (*Burditt v. U.S. Department of Health and Human Services*, 1991).

Restriction on Transfers

Before a patient may be transferred to another medical facility, a physician must certify that the transfer is in the patient's best medical interests:

(ii) a physician (within the meaning of section 1395x(r)(1) of this title) has signed a certification that, based upon the reasonable risks and benefits to the individual, and based upon the information available at the time of transfer, the medical benefits reasonably expected from the provision of appropriate medical treatment at another medical facility outweigh the increased risks to the individual and, in the case of labor, to the unborn child from effecting the transfer, or

(iii) if a physician is not physically present in the emergency department at the time an individual is transferred, a qualified medical person . . . has signed a certification described in clause (ii) after a physician . . . in consultation with the person, has made the determination described in such clause, and subsequently countersigns the certification; and

. . . A certification . . . shall include a summary of the risks and benefits upon which the certification is based.

This requirement is intended to ensure that a physician evaluates the patient's condition. As discussed in Chapter 9, such an evaluation creates a legal duty for the physician to care for the patient. Triggering this duty was a prime goal of the act. The drafters wanted to discourage the common practice of doing the financial screening before the patient was allowed to see the physician. The courts allow patients to sue for failing to screen, irrespective of whether there was also an inappropriate transfer (*Thompson v. St. Ann's Hosp.* 1989).

This allows a patient to refuse a transfer if this is a knowing refusal made after being apprised of the risks and benefits of transfer. Since a formal transfer is unnecessary if the patient is stabilized, this implies that a patient refusing transfer still requires medical care either to prevent deterioration of the patient's condition or the delivery of her baby. Such a patient cannot be discharged from the hospital until he or she is stabilized.

Appropriate Transfers

A transfer is appropriate only as defined in (c)(2) if the patient will be medically better off in the receiving institution and the receiving institution consents to the transfer. Section (g) limits the ability of regional or specialized facilities to refuse transfers for reasons other than not having a bed available.

Labor and Delivery

Previously, these regulations, and many state emergency care laws, referred to women in labor or active labor. Hospitals and physicians who did not want to care for pregnant women who presented in the emergency room set up elaborate requirements around the definition of labor. A woman with premature rupture of membranes is at high risk for a bad outcome, but she might be turned away because she was not in labor. Neither Congress nor the regulatory authorities were tolerant of these subterfuges. The regulations are now clear and explicit. If a pregnant woman presents for care, she must receive any care needed to protect her health or the health of the unborn child. If she is having contractions, she must be delivered unless there is compelling medical indication for a transfer. If she refuses transfer, she must be delivered at the original hospital.

Enforcement

This statute provides for several enforcement mechanisms. The government can fine a hospital or physician up to $50,000 for each violation of the statute. The hospital or physician can be excluded from participation in all health programs that receive state or federal money. The hospital can lose not-for-profit status (Pizza 1992). Perhaps most important, the statute creates a federal cause of action, essentially a federal malpractice lawsuit, against hospitals that do not comply with the statute (*Reid v. Indianapolis Osteopathic Medical Hosp., Inc.*, 1989). This action is predicated on a failure to comply with the law's requirements for screening and transfer. It does not include malpractice claims based on incorrect diagnosis or treatment (*Cleland v. Bronson Health Care Group*, 1990). Interestingly, both patients and other health care institutions may sue for injuries. This would allow a receiving hospital to sue a transferring hospital that misrepresented a patient's condition in order to dump the patient for financial reasons.

At least one court (*Sorrels v. Babcock* 1990) has found that the statute does not create a federal cause of action against physicians, in addition to allowing physicians to be sued under state law for malpractice. At least one federal district court has held that such lawsuits are not subject to tort reform caps on damages (*Reid v. Indianapolis Osteopathic Medical Hosp., Inc.* 1989). As discussed in Chapter 6, this statute sets the standard of care for access to emergency care. A physician who violates the provisions of this statute could be sued for negligence per se.

LIVING WILLS IN THE EMERGENCY ROOM

A patient who presents in an emergency room is presumed to be there for all necessary medical care. Patients who are conscious and able to make their wishes known may refuse unwanted medical care. (See Chapter 13.) But a living will should not be taken to forbid resuscitation efforts in the emergency room. Without prior knowledge of the patient, the physician should not assume that the document belongs to that patient or that it reflects the patient's wishes in that situation. However, at the same time that the resuscitation is being attempted, someone should try to clarify the status of the living will. The CPR must be stopped at the point that it is reasonably certain that the living will is authentic. Once a terminally ill patient's wishes are known, there is no justification for rendering unwanted treatment.

Emergency room personnel should not circumvent living wills by demanding unreasonable proof that the living will is valid. It must be remembered that the burden is on medical personnel to disprove the will if it appears valid on its face. If the will is not over a few years old, is clearly written, is signed and witnessed (many states make notarization optional), and the identity of the patient is well known, the living will is facially valid. Yet even if the will is valid, it is not an absolute bar to the forbidden care. If there is a reasonable probability that CPR or other lifesaving care will be successful, then it should not be withheld if there is an indication that the patient would have wanted the care. For example, an elderly patient in currently good health may have signed a living will out of fear of a lingering cancer death. This patient might very well want to be given emergency treatment and CPR after an automobile accident.

BIBLIOGRAPHY

Brenner BE; Simon RR: The specialty of emergency medicine. J Emerg Med 1984; 1(4):349–52.

Burditt v. United States Dept. of Health and Human Services. 934 F2d 1362 (5th Cir, Jul 9, 1991).

Cleland v. Bronson Health Care Group, Inc. 917 F2d 266 (CA6 Mich 1990).

George JE: A prescription for avoiding malpractice suits in the E.D. Enlb 1980 Winter; 6(1):2–11.

Hoge MA; Hirschman R: Psychological training of emergency medical technicians: An evaluation. Am J Community Psychol 1984 Feb; 12(1):127–31.

Hudson T: Risk managers see new regulations as boon and burden. Hospitals 1990; 64(18):44.

Laddaga LA; Haynes JA: Anti-dumping law flashes a yellow light on emergency cases. Healthcare Fin Manage 1991; 45(3):84.

Lane DS; Evans D: Study measures impact of emergency department ombudsman. Hospitals 1978 Feb 1; 52(3):99–100, 102, 104.

McMillan JR; Younger MS; DeWine LC: Satisfaction with hospital emergency department as a function of patient triage. Health Care Manage Rev 1986 Summer; 11(3):21–27.

Makadon HJ; Gerson S; Ryback R: Managing the care of the difficult patient in the emergency unit. JAMA 1984 Nov 9; 252(18):2585–88.

Mannon JM: Defining and treating "problem patients" in a hospital emergency room. Med Care 1976 Dec; 14(12):1004–13.

Mayer TA: The emergency department medical director. Emerg Med Clin North Am 1987 Feb; 5(1):1–29.

Newhouse JP: Do unprofitable patients face access problems? Health Care Fin Rev 1989; 11(2):33.

Pizza NF: Patient transfers—COBRA as amended. The Health Lawyer 1992; 6(2):1–10.

Reid v. Indianapolis Osteopathic Medical Hosp., Inc. 709 F Supp 853 (SD Ind 1989).

Schwartz LR; Overton DT: Emergency department complaints: A one-year analysis. Ann Emerg Med 1987 Aug; 16(8):857–61.

Shesser R; Smith M; Adams S; Walls R; Paxton M: The effectiveness of an organized emergency department follow-up system. Ann Emerg Med 1986 Aug; 15(8):911–15.

Silverman GK; Silverman HM: Efficacy of the follow-up system in the community hospital emergency department. Am J Emerg Med 1984 Mar; 2(2):119–22.

Sorrels v. Babcock. 773 F Supp 1189 (1990).
Soskis CW: Emergency room on weekends: The only game in town. Health Soc Work 1980 Aug; 5(3):37–43.
Suokas J; Lonnqvist J: Work stress has negative effects on the attitudes of emergency personnel towards patients who attempt suicide. Acta Psychiatr Scand 1989 May; 79(5):474–80.
Thompson v. St. Ann's Hosp. 716 F Supp 8 (Ill. 1989).

33

High-Technology Medicine and Critical Care

CRITICAL POINTS

- The improper use of safety devices can increase medical malpractice litigation.
- Physicians must understand the limitations of physiologic monitoring if they are to use medical devices appropriately.
- Cost containment is exacerbating the problems of critical care medicine and will increase litigation against critical care physicians.
- The best protection against arbitrary limitations on the availability of critical care is good data on the cost-effectiveness of critical care.

High-technology devices have had a profound impact on the evolution of modern medical practice. Many of the medical subspecialties are defined as much by technology as pathology or physiology. Yet physicians are ambivalent about technology. They receive extensive training in the biochemistry and physiology of drugs, followed by clinical training in therapeutics, and they regard themselves as experts in the use of drugs. This is reflected in the legal theory of the learned intermediary. Given the pervasive role that devices play in medical practice, it seems reasonable that physicians would receive comparable training in the theory and application of biomedical engineering.

This is not the case. Physicians are not routinely taught biomedical engineering and electronics. As discussed in Chapter 34, the legal standard for physicians' knowledge of medical devices is little more than that of the average lawnmower user. This leads to the misuse of devices, the inappropriate substitution of instruments for human judgment, and an uncritical acceptance of machine-generated data as accurate and objective. This chapter discusses the problems posed by medical instrumentation and special problems of critical care medicine.

THE LEGAL RISKS OF SAFETY DEVICES

Paradoxically, medical instrumentation poses the greatest challenges in critical care units (CCUs) but generates the most litigation in areas such as obstetrics and anesthesia. CCUs are the subject of legal debate far in excess of the medical malpractice cases they spawn. Most of the legal attention has been focused on the right of patients to refuse life support rather than on medical malpractice issues. As financial considerations reduce the availability of CCU care, it is expected that the legal controversies will shift from refusal of care to denial of care and conventional malpractice claims. Before discussing the expected increase in CCU-related litigation, it is important to understand why a relatively simple problem such as obstetric monitoring has generated much more litigation than the difficult problem of CCU monitoring.*

When physicians think of medical device litigation, it usually brings to mind products liability claims against the device's manufacturer. Such primary litigation is a problem for device manufacturers but not a direct threat to physicians using the devices. The problem for physicians is secondary litigation. Secondary litigation arises from medical devices that perform properly but increase litigation against the physicians who use them. Safety devices such as monitors have generated most secondary litigation, although it can occur with life-supporting devices as well. The best-documented example of secondary litigation is that due to obstetric fetal monitors. The problems that arose from fetal monitors have implications for selection of new technologies by physicians and hospitals.

Electronic fetal heart monitors and pulse oximeters illustrate a continuum from devices that increase secondary litigation to those that decrease it. The widespread use of fetal heart monitors was accompanied by a dramatic increase in obstetric malpractice litigation. It is certain that factors other than fetal heart monitors were primarily responsible for this increase. It is also certain, however, that the use of these monitors did not decrease litigation and, in the cases where fetal heart monitor records are available, these records increase the probability of litigation when a baby is born damaged. Conversely, the widespread adoption of pulse oximetry in the operating room was accompanied by a dramatic reduction in malpractice claims against anesthesiologists. These monitors appear to be among the primary causes of this reduction in claims. They clearly are not being used against anesthesiologists in the way that fetal heart monitors have been used against obstetricians.

Secondary litigation does not imply a defectively designed product, at least not in the traditional sense. Fetal heart monitors perform accurately and reliably within the constraints of what they measure. Devices that are unreliable or otherwise directly dangerous to patients will be the target of primary litigation against the device manufacturer. Pure secondary liability is an issue for otherwise safe and well-engineered devices. Secondary liability becomes a problem when the device in question documents previously undocumented behavior indicating negligence on the part of the medical care providers, records data with ambiguous interpretations, and/or inappropriately leads to changes in medical care supervision, staffing, or patient contact because of reliance on the device.

Filtering Data

The first problem, documentation of previously undocumented behavior, is common to all recording instruments. Medical record systems that depend on people to record events, either on paper or computer, are highly filtered. Sometimes this filtering is conscious and intentional, as when personnel attempt to cover up an error by not entering incriminating information into the medical chart. In the

---

*The following material is adapted from Richards 1990 and Richards and Walter 1991.

worst case, there may even be attempts to change previous entries. This intentional distortion of data, however, is assumed to be relatively infrequent. Most commonly the filtering is unconscious and unintentional. It may occur because the recorder's memory fades between rendering the care or making the observations and recording them in the medical record. In many situations, it occurs because the nurses do not make their primary entries into the medical record.

While generally forbidden by protocols on medical records management, off-chart records are commonly used by nurses to keep track of things to do, medications given, and patient observations. These temporary records allow the nurses to batch-enter data into medical records rather than keep contemporaneous records. This allows two stages of filtering: first the information is compressed into a minimal temporary record, and then that minimal record is expanded into the permanent chart record. Such filtering makes it easy to transform an item accidentally from the to-do list to the done list without the task's actually being performed. It also gives the filter an extra chance to remove nonconforming information.

Filters are defined by what they exclude. Human clinical filters tend to exclude things that do not easily fit into the expectations associated with the care of a given patient. This should not be seen as an act of deception or even of carelessness. It is more a smoothing of data that tends to obscure anomalies. The smoothing is aided by the limited amount of information that can be recorded by periodic observations recorded in essentially narrative format. The end result of this process of smoothing and filtering is a medical record that is more often characterized by what it does not contain than by what it does document. This is borne out in litigation where records are usually incriminating because they fail to record what was allegedly done.

Fetal Monitors

When a real-time recording technology is introduced into a situation that previously depended on manual records, the amount of data recorded increases dramatically. A record that displayed fetal heart rates taken at 15- to 30-minute intervals and recorded at some later time by a nurse is suddenly displaced with a fetal heart monitor that generates a paper tape with a continuously recorded fetal rate. Previously unnoted short-term irregularities are now carefully preserved. Whenever an injured child is born, the fetal heart rate record will be scanned by plaintiff's counsel in the hope of finding some deviation from normal that can be used to build a case against the delivering physician. This search is seldom in vain because of the second problem that leads to secondary liability: data with ambiguous interpretations.

Fetal heart rate is monitored in women in labor to determine if the fetus's well-being is compromised. If the fetus is in trouble, the usual response is an emergency cesarean section. Fetal heart monitors provide a reasonably accurate record of fetal heart rate. The problem is in interpreting these records. Dramatic, prolonged slowing of the fetal heart rate clearly means trouble. But many other patterns of fetal heart rate irregularities do not so clearly point to trouble that they unambiguously call for an emergency cesarean section with its attendant risks and costs. On the other hand, if the baby is born damaged, such irregularities will seem very important in hindsight. In a strict sense, much of what a fetal heart monitor records is not information: it does not reduce the physician's uncertainty over the selection and timing of cesarean sections.

In retrospect, the major factor in secondary litigation from fetal heart monitors may be the third factor: the shift in patient care patterns that accompanied the routine use of the devices. The traditional method of determining fetal fitness was to auscultate the fetal heart with a stethoscope. This requires that someone closely observe the laboring woman at frequent intervals. The premise of electronic fetal monitoring was that the heart rate itself was the critical parameter in this evaluation. It may be that other observations that accompanied this direct and intimate contact with the patient provided a necessary context for interpreting the significance of changes in the heart rate. As physicians and nurses came to rely on fetal heart monitors, they could evaluate the fetus by looking at the monitor strip and ignore the patient entirely. It is also likely that these cursory evaluations decreased in frequency because the monitor allowed the retrospective review of the heart rate. While it is difficult to sort out the causal factors, the most recent research indicates that the use of fetal monitors increases the probability of adverse fetal outcomes.

Pulse Oximeters

Pulse oximetry is a relatively simple technology that measures arterial oxygen saturation in real time. The oximeters that are routinely used in clinical care are display-only instruments; they do not produce a continuous historical record of oxygen saturation. When saturation falls below a certain threshold, an alarm is sounded, unambiguously signaling that the patient needs more oxygen or that the instrument has become detached or dysfunctional. In either case, definitive action can be taken at once. These factors make oximetry an ideal safety technology. It helps prevent injuries while not otherwise affecting record keeping or staffing practices. This is not entirely due to special virtues of oximetry.

It is rare that the patient is left completely alone in the operating room. The genius of oximetry is that it is an easily understandable monitor. When the alarm goes off, the surgeon can call for help if the anesthesiologist has drifted away. It can be assumed that oximetry used as a remote-sensing, continuous-recording technology will pose the same documentation and staffing problems as fetal heart monitors. These may be outweighed by the clear intervention signal provided by oximetry. If, however, hospitals use recording-remote oximeters in situations where this clear signal is ignored, they will suddenly find oximetry to be a fertile source of litigation.

Lessons for Technology Assessment

Continuous recording instruments are invaluable research tools. If there is a central criticism of fetal heart monitor usage, it is that the monitors were adopted for routine use without the research background necessary to understand their limitations. Fetal heart monitors illustrate that data, as opposed to information, increase the risk of litigation. This happens because plaintiffs' attorneys thrive on ambiguity. If a patient is injured, the plaintiff's attorney will comb the records for anything that cannot be clearly explained to portray as the cause of the injury. This is countered to some extent by the highly filtered nature of traditional medical records. Continuously recorded streams of ambiguous instrument output, in contrast, provide a gold mine of exploitable ambiguity.

It is critical that new instruments be evaluated for the reliability of their intrinsic measurements and for the clinical significance of those measurements. Do the data resolve clinical questions or merely complicate them? This question becomes more interesting as hospitals purchase clinical information systems that feed the outputs of various monitors into a computer-based continuous-recording system. The assumption is that since these instruments are already in place, their output must be useful. It is possible, however, that many existing measurements are useful only in the larger context of patient care. Like a fetal heart rate observed without the context of the mother, their readings may be much less valuable as retrospective records. Given that efficacy testing is a recent innovation for medical devices, it is also possible that some existing measurements are clinically irrelevant. This means that their outputs will be randomly related to the patient's condition, creating that ambiguity so valuable to plaintiffs' attorneys.

Clinical instruments provide data, not necessarily information that aids in clinical decision making. The data create noise that can obscure significant clinical information while providing clear hindsight to those who would second-guess the physician's actions. Real-time clinical information systems take this to the extreme. Some of these systems carefully log the output of every monitor in the CCU, allow free text comments by CCU personnel who have not necessarily seen all the recorded data, and create the expectation that all data will be recorded. This last expectation may be the most damaging, given the traditional presumption that missing information is assumed to support the plaintiff's case. Unless these systems are carefully thought through and tested, it may be that the connector that is used to connect most real-time recording systems will someday be renamed the plaintiff's best friend.

INFORMATION THEORY IN THE CCU

Information theory is the mathematical study of the transmission and coding of signals (Richards 1990). Originally developed to understand radio and telephone signals better, it is directly relevant to some of the problems of instrument use in the CCU. CCU practice is characterized by large amounts of constantly changing data. This data-rich environment pushes the dominant paradigms for clinical decision making to the breaking point. One thoughtful article that reviewed the theories of clinical decision making and their relevance to critical care medicine stressed the importance of examining CCU practice patterns for pitfalls and blind alleys that compromise patient care (Goldman 1990).

Introspection about critical care decision making is not a hollow academic exercise. It is practiced on a daily basis by quality assurance committees, at morbidity and mortality conferences, and in medical negligence litigation. A physician who does not think about "thinking about" decision making (meta decision making) is in a poor position to document and explain that decision making when it is retrospectively reviewed.

Critical care medicine can be distinguished from other practice situations by the information flow in the CCU. This is useful because information theory is concerned with the basic problem of CCU medicine: decision making under uncertainty. An intensivist must cope with costly information in a high noise environment. By explicitly recognizing the cost of information and its inherent uncertainty, intensivists may be better able to make and defend decisions made in the "fog of war" that typifies critical care medicine.

Information is frequently confused with data. *Information* is a datum that allows a decision to be made. The results of laboratory tests are not information unless they aid in the clinical decision-making process. Data that are not information are noise. The intensive care environment is extremely noisy because it is saturated with data that do not contribute to clinical decision making. Sorting the information from this data stream is costly in both the economic sense and in other measures of value, such as delay and physical risk to the patient. What separates the noise problem in critical care decision making from that in other data-intensive medical environments is the time domain.

THE PROBLEM OF SAMPLING

Events happen quickly in critical care medicine. This can be beneficial in that it forces thoughtful practitioners to reevaluate their diagnostic hypotheses constantly. In general, however, it is destructive because of a problem described by an area of information theory called the sampling theorem (Pierce 1980). The sampling theorem says that monitoring a process requires that the process be sampled twice as fast as the measured variable changes. For example, assume that a 1 cycle per second (hertz) wave is being sampled. If the wave is sampled once a second, every sample might be a peak. To the experimenter, the 1 hertz cycle looks like a steady pressure. If the wave is sampled every 30 seconds or less, then its wave nature will be obvious.

The sampling theorem haunts critical care medicine in two ways. The more obvious is in serial measurements of physiologic variables. It is not unusual to monitor a dozen variables on a patient in the CCU. These variables may have vastly different periods, ranging from minutes to days. It is also not unusual to follow these variables with isolated snapshots. This hides the periodicity of the variables and can lead the physician to miss important phenomena that are driven by the transient extremes of a variable rather than its average or randomly chosen value. Thus, it is more important to know that a patient's blood pressure has transients of 300/120 than to know that at 10:00 P.M. the pressure was 130/80.

The problem of sampling is exacerbated by the continuity heuristic: once a therapy has been chosen, it biases the decision maker in favor of continuing that treatment rather than trying another. This bias can be profound when a CCU patient's therapy is constantly modified based on measurements of a physiologic variable. If this variable is measured less frequently than twice the rate at which it is affected by the intervention, the intervention can appear to have a paradoxical effect.

For example, assume that a severely hypotensive patient is treated with a very short-acting pressor agent. This hypothetical pressor agent is given in a bolus. It takes 1 hour to act and wears off in 4 hours. The patient's blood pressure is taken every 4 hours. The first measurement is taken 30 minutes after injection and shows the pressure to be low. Four hours later (30 minutes after the second dose), the pressure is again measured as low. The dose is now increased. The third measurement, taken 4 hours later (30 minutes after the increased dose has been given), is now normal. The patient, however, is severely hypertensive in the intervals between the measurements.

Few physicians would make this simple mistake. However, as the number of drugs and variables increases and the drugs interact with each other, it becomes difficult to ensure that a measured variable truly represents the effect of a given drug or the indirect effect of a drug given to affect a different organ system.

Unlike office practice internal medicine, the intensivist cannot tell the patient to add one new drug each week and see what happens.

THE TECHNOLOGICAL IMPERATIVE VERSUS COST CONTAINMENT

The underlying paradigm of critical care medicine is the technological imperative: "the desire of physicians to do everything that they have been trained to do, regardless of the benefit cost ratio" (Fuchs 1974). This approach evolved during the period of fee-for-service reimbursement when there was no reason to contain costs. Since CCU care is disproportionately expensive, reducing its cost is central to all managed care schemes.

The Office of Technology Assessment case study on intensive care units listed the following as factors that led to a treatment imperative in intensive care medicine:

1) The focus on high technology, which obscures the underlying rational for treatment;
2) The nature of ICU illnesses, which often require technologically oriented treatment just to keep the patient comfortable. This blurs the distinction between palliative treatment and definitive treatment;
3) The moral climate which stresses erring on the side of more treatment, rather than less;
4) Diffusion of decision making responsibility;
5) The problem that many patients are not able to make their wishes known;
6) The practice of so called "defensive medicine";
7) A payment environment which encouraged ICU care in general and procedure oriented care in specific; and
8) The difficulty of projecting the probability of recovery for specific ICU patients. (Berenson 1984)

COST CONTAINMENT IN THE CCU

CCU care is expensive because it is staff and equipment intensive. Its cost-effectiveness is controversial because it has been difficult to show that CCU care is more effective than routine nursing care for most patients. While the negative studies are probably due to the difficulty in carrying out a proper randomized study, they also reflect that the effectiveness of many CCU procedures remains unproved. Since CCU care is very stressful for patients and their families, reducing unnecessary CCU care would save money and improve patent well-being. This makes reducing CCU use a prime target of managed care plans and other third-party payers. Unfortunately, this sometimes results in an arbitrary pressure to reduce CCU use without regard to the needs of individual patients.

As a practical matter, doing too much for a patient poses fewer legal risks than doing too little. It is difficult to show that any specific treatment out of the many performed on a very sick patient made him worse or killed him. It is much easier for a jury to believe that denying a patient entry to the CCU was the cause of his demise. Denial of care will be particularly difficult to defend when the plaintiff can show that it was motivated by financial considerations. This has the potential for dramatically increasing the traditionally low levels of litigation against adult-patient CCU practitioners. Adult CCU care has had little litigation because of the demographics of the patients.

In most cases, patients in the CCU perceive their condition to be serious, and thus they are more understanding of an adverse outcome. Debates over the right to die reinforced the belief that if the intensivist could not save the patient, the patient could not have been saved. Public concern about DRGs (diagnosis-related groups) has now highlighted the hospital's economic interest in a patient's early demise. This will result in intensivists increasingly being sued in the belief that they would have done more had they not bowed to financial pressures.

DEFINING THE CCU

The central legal problem with CCU care is the absence of well-defined standards for staffing and facilities. Critical care medicine has been defined more by the name of the place it is practiced in than by the qualifications of the persons delivering it. While there is a nationally recognized certification in critical care medicine, very few physicians practicing in CCUs have formal training in critical care medicine.

Ideally, CCUs would have 24-hour staffing by physicians with expertise in critical care medicine, which would limit CCUs to teaching hospitals and large, wealthy private facilities. Such a standard was politically unthinkable in the 1970s, when patient-days in the CCU translated into profits for hospitals. Even in an era of DRGs and other limits on reimbursement for CCU care, maintaining a CCU is critical to supporting certain highly profitable surgeries.

The data on surgical morbidity and mortality indicate that complicated surgery should be centralized for the best patient care. Small community hospitals downplay morbidity and mortality in favor of the convenience of local care. Such hospitals typically cannot meet proper standards for CCU staffing. Financial difficulties have forced many large urban hospitals to reduce CCU staffing and not to maintain CCU equipment properly. Physicians practicing in hospitals with inadequate CCU facilities must consider whether they can justify admitting patients needing critical care. While there may be no alternative for emergency admissions, many CCU patients are elective admissions. As it becomes increasingly difficult to transfer patients, physicians must ensure that patients are admitted to the facilities best able to care for them.

RATIONING CARE

Critical care medicine has engendered much medical-legal scholarship over the past several years, almost all of it dealing with the termination of treatment for patients who are either terminally ill or irreversibly comatose. While this is an important subject, it pales in comparison to the legal question posed by the shifting reimbursement climate in health care: when must we withdraw or deny treatment to patients whose treatment would consume a disproportionate share of resources (Zoloth-Dorfman 1991)?

Such decisions are complicated by financial incentives to care for patients who are well insured or have a favorable DRG. Likewise, there are pressures not to admit poorly insured patients to the CCU. Physicians who care for patients in the CCU must resist the pressure to make medical decisions on billing criteria. When financial considerations enter into these decisions, physicians are more susceptible to malpractice litigation and punitive damage awards for violating the fiduciary duty owed to their patients.

Effectiveness of CCUs

All rational approaches to rationing CCU care stumble over the problem that CCU care has not been proved to improve patient survival for many classes of patients. This makes it difficult to calculate the cost-benefit ratios that are necessary to make rationing decisions. The one class of patients for whom CCU care is clearly effective are those who are fundamentally healthy but have an acute, curable condition that requires life support. While these patients are easy to identify, they are a small percentage of CCU patients. Other than accident victims, persons who have overdosed on drugs, and the victims of certain rare illnesses, many persons who have traditionally been treated in the CCU suffer conditions from which there is little probability of recovery.

There are three classes of patients who may benefit from treatment in an intensive care unit but for whom the benefits are marginal: (1) those with chronic conditions who may survive the acute exacerbation of their underlying illness but have no prospect of returning to health; (2) those with acute illnesses or injuries who require extensive treatment and have a low probability of recovery; and (3) those with nonserious conditions who are admitted to the CCU for monitoring because they have a small probability of developing a more severe problem. These patients mask the benefits of CCU care and provide the greatest argument for limiting the availability of CCU care.

The lack of litigation over CCU care has created a false sense of security about the robustness of the therapeutic imperative. Rather than leading to ever more effective care, the complexity of high-technology medicine has created a therapeutic parallel to Heisenburg's uncertainty principle: the more you do to the patient, the greater is the chance of iatrogenic injury. The increased risk of infection, stress, and equipment-related problems becomes a significant limit on the effectiveness of CCU care.

Explicit Rules

Every intensive care unit should have written protocols for admitting and discharging patients. A patient should not be accepted just because there is a bed available. This leads to problems in quality of care and accusations that the physicians are more concerned about money than care. An example might be the terminal patient who has decided that she does not want invasive therapy to postpone the time of death. This patient should have been given the opportunity to sign a living will and to ask that CPR not be performed. It is hard to see what benefit such a patient would derive from intensive care. But if the patient is well insured and the floor nurses are unable or unwilling to provide good supportive care, this patient is likely to end up in the CCU. Unfortunately for the patient, being in the CCU may hasten her death and will certainly make the process of dying less pleasant. In many CCUs she will be surrounded by lights and noisy machines day and night and will have limited opportunities to see family and friends.

A corollary problem to rationing care is the necessity for triage. As the availability of properly staffed and equipped CCU beds declines, it will become imperative to ensure that these beds are reserved for persons who can best benefit from CCU care. This is problematic, however, because of the lack of scientific evidence as to the relative benefits of CCU care. Triage becomes especially difficult when it involves moving a patient out of the CCU when a patient with better prospects for recovery requires care. While displacing less ill patients was once a common procedure, it has fallen out of use in the last 20 to 30 years. This may have to be reinstated in CCU protocols as ever more patients, especially AIDS and elderly patients, compete for limited CCU resources.

AUTHORITY IN THE CCU

A common problem in CCU care is determining who has the duty to care for a patient and who has the authority to direct the patient's care. The admitting physicians and their associates may write orders and make care decisions, the CCU nurses make many medical decisions using standing orders, residents and fellows may be responsible for the patient's care between visits by the attending physician, and specialty consultants may write orders for specific problems. In some CCUs there is no single person with the sole responsibility for the patient's care or the authority to coordinate all of the care rendered to the patient.

Unlike this medical model of "the more the merrier," the law uses the "too many cooks spoil the broth" model. The basic premise of tort law is that legal liability must be vested in specific individuals in relation to their duty to the patient. When a patient is injured, the patient's attorney will sue all of the persons involved with the aspect of the patient's care that went wrong.

The court must sort out the tangle of overlapping authority and hold one or more persons liable for the patient's injuries. The problem is that the court may see responsibility for the patient's care in different terms than the CCU team. For example, members of the medical staff committee who approve CCU standing orders could be liable for patient injuries caused by the nursing staff's inability to apply the protocols properly.

The CCU Director

While it is desirable for the CCU director to be a critical care medicine specialist, this is seldom the case. The NIH Conference Statement on Critical Care Medicine found that "the ICU should be directed by a physician with demonstrated competence in the areas necessary for provision of critical care. These areas generally include a broad base in physiology, pharmacology, the continuum of disease, cardiopulmonary function, and the associated intervention skills."

There should be one physician in charge of each CCU patient's care. This need not be the same physician throughout the patient's stay, but there should never be a time when the patient's care is being managed by a group rather than a single individual. The responsible physician may be part of a group, but he or she must have full responsibility for the patient's care. If the responsibility for the care is shared, conflicting orders may be given or situations may occur when care will not be rendered because each person assumed that the other took care of it.

The CCU attending physicians should have demonstrated skills in CCU practice and should regularly practice in the CCU. The attending must limit his or her practice (when on CCU duty) to one hospital. This physician must also have the authority to commit whatever resources are necessary for the patient's care. It is critical to avoid the teaching hospital problem where a resident is in charge of the patient's care but must have permission or a counter-signature to order needed care.

Many hospitals attempt to run their CCUs without sufficient physician coverage. Since CCU decisions must be made quickly, this means that the nursing staff is forced to make medical decisions. This is hidden by standing orders, whereby the fiction is created that the nurse is following a set protocol rather than making medical decisions. If a patient is injured, the jury will see the standing orders as a sham to allow nurses to substitute for physicians. If an institution cannot arrange for proper physician coverage in the CCU, it should reexamine whether it can justify having the CCU.

The physician coverage must also be arranged to ensure that there is a smooth transition between the different physicians who accept responsibility for a patient's care. This shifting of authority must be done in a formal manner, and it must ensure that there is reasonable continuity of care. At all times, the physician responsible for an individual patient should know the history of the patient's illness and all the care the patient has received. It is difficult to explain to a jury how a patient can walk into a hospital with an acute problem and end up viewed by the CCU staff as a long-term case with no hope of recovery.

The physician director of the CCU is often a member of the medical staff rather than a salaried administrative employee of the hospital. If this is the case, there should also be a single high-level administrator assigned to oversee the CCU. This administrator must act as a buffer between the CCU and the hospital, protecting the CCU from policies that would jeopardize patient care and monitoring the CCU to prevent it from becoming a financial burden on the hospital. To carry out these duties effectively, the administrator must be familiar with CCU activities and be available at all times to manage emergent situations. Most important, the administrator should have enough authority to act unilaterally if an administrative crisis develops. This authority must include hiring temporary personnel, bringing in outside equipment and technicians, and, in cooperation with the physician director, suspending personnel, both physician and nonphysician, from duty in the CCU until the normal hospital grievance or disciplinary process can review any questionable conduct.

Cardiopulmonary Resuscitation

Cardiopulmonary resuscitation presents interesting legal questions. Although training and practice are required to be proficient at CPR, it has become a first-aid skill expected of all medical care providers. It is expected that every patient who suffers a cardiac or respiratory arrest will receive CPR unless there are specific written orders to the contrary. Hospitals may face litigation if they do not have a capable CPR team available at all times, yet the benefits of CPR in a hospital setting are unproved. In many cases it is simply delaying death and adds thousands of dollars to the bill.

The standard of care is that anyone who discovers a patient who is not breathing or has no pulse should call the CPR team. There should never be limitations on who may call a code. Since seconds can mean the difference between life and death, there is no justification for requiring that the call be verified by a physician or nurse. It is better to send the team away than not to have them when needed.

Identifying Who Is in Charge

All CPR teams should have well-understood protocols about who is in charge. This should be based on skill and availability. In addition to the usual members of the team, there should be a person with the sole duty of documenting every action taken by the team. This should be a chronologic record and should be kept to the second. This record keeper need not be a physician or RN but must understand the procedures of a CPR and the drugs that are used. This record will document the CPR for the medical record. More important, it will allow the physician in charge to determine what drugs were given and when. Since 2 minutes can seem like 20 in an emergency, this is critical information when assessing the effect of drugs that have been given.

If the patient's attending physician is present, this physician should defer to the head of the CPR team. In teaching hospitals, this may mean that a professor is deferring to a resident. But the resident who has spent every third day for the last three years on CPR duty is likely to be more skilled than an attending physician who participates in a CPR a few times a year. The physician who is there must be in charge. No one can do CPR over the telephone.

Attending physicians do not give up their responsibility for their patients. They should monitor the progress of the resuscitation and make decisions about the types of supportive therapy that are appropriate. For example, a CPR team will normally put a patient on a respirator if the patient is unable to breathe without external support. If the attending physician considers a patient not a candidate for a respirator, this should be in the orders. Decisions about the conduct of the CPR are made by the team leader. Decisions about the advisability of CPR and the extent of ongoing care should be made by the attending physician.

Drawing the line between life and death is a medical decision. Anyone who undertakes to do CPR should make a good-faith effort to revive the patient. This does not mean that every possible procedure must be done or drug given. When there is little hope of response and the patient appears to be dead, the physician in charge or the attending physician should stop the resuscitation, document the absence of vital signs, and pronounce the patient dead. The record of the resuscitation efforts should be completed and the reason for pronouncing the death recorded immediately by the physician.

Special Orders

There has been a great deal of debate over the ethics of resuscitation orders. Too often this debate is put in terms of ethics, ignoring the laws that govern consent to treatment and the rights of patients. Family members without the right to consent to trivial medical care are not suddenly enfranchised to consent to critical care for a patient. Difficult as it is for physicians to face a dying patient, this is a necessary part of providing medical care.

If a patient has a living will, a copy of the document should be placed in the chart at the time of hospitalization. Specific orders should be written to reflect the terms of the living will. For instance, if the patient will accept CPR but not accept respirator therapy, there should be a limited code order in the chart that conforms to the policies and procedures of the hospital. If the patient is not hospitalized and is expected to die at home, the family and caretakers should be aware of the procedure to be followed at the time of death. Everyone should realize that if the patient is brought to an emergency room, there will be attempts made to resuscitate the patient.

Every time a physician admits an elderly or critically ill patient to a hospital, the question of CPR should be discussed. (See Chapter 13.) The hospital should let every patient know the CPR policies of the hospital and provide an opportunity for the patient to refuse such services. Far too many patients undergo one resuscitation only to request that it not be done again. Such decisions should not be left until the patient is unconscious, and there is no one with the legal right to authorize or refuse care.

Code Orders

If patients indicate, either verbally or in writing, that they do not want CPR, their attending physicians should indicate this as an order in the chart. Every hospital should have a system of marking charts so that it will be obvious when there is a no-code order. Frequently, a code will be called before anyone realizes that there is an order to the contrary. As soon as the chart is found and the order noted, the resuscitation is stopped. This is not the same as stopping the resuscitation because the patient is dead. The fact that there may be respiratory efforts in the absence of a pulse, or vice versa, is not justification for countermanding a no-code order.

All no-code orders should be in writing, and the consent of the patient or guardian should be documented. Ideally, the patient or guardian will sign the order for no CPR. As with other consent to medical care, the family should not be involved without the patient's permission. In reality, this may not be possible. Patients who are no longer mentally competent cannot make their wishes known. (See Chapter 11.) If the care of an incompetent patient must continue over a period of days or weeks, then a court-appointed guardian should be obtained to make consent decisions.

Resuscitation is not always an all-or-none action. Both a patient and a physician may limit the extent of a code. A patient may want to be revived if independent existence is possible but not if a respirator would be required. A physician may make the same decision based on whether the patient is medically a candidate for a respirator. The prescribing of respirator support is a medical decision. There is no requirement that a patient be put on a respirator, and it is poor practice to prescribe a respirator for a patient who is unlikely to be weanable. Like a no-code order, any limitations on resuscitation should be well documented in the chart and well known to the caretakers.

There is no such thing as a slow code. Physicians must not use informal mechanisms to deny patients medical care. If there is not a no-code or limited-code order in the chart, every reasonable effort must be made to revive the patient. A nurse or resident should never accept an order or a hint to take it slow on a particular patient. If the attending physician thinks that the patient is not a good candidate for CPR or other support measures, the physician should discuss this with the patient and write the appropriate orders. Physicians who will not properly document limited code orders must be reported to the appropriate hospital review committee.

ILLEGAL USE OF CODE

Medical care institutions need to be alert to people who get an inordinate thrill out of emergency situations. There have been several notorious cases of nurses who injected patients with paralyzing drugs for the thrill of the resuscitation. Not all the resuscitations were successful. This is an extreme example, but many hospitals have physicians or nurses who cannot stay away from the excitement. While they may be very capable members of the CPR team, they may consciously or unconsciously precipitate emergency situations. A patient's family, who has been watching the patient for weeks, may be more sensitive to this problem than other health care personnel, which increases the risk of litigation over a resuscitation that goes wrong. Anyone not involved with the resuscitation should be firmly excluded from the scene. Disciplinary action should be taken against personnel who act inappropriately.

BIBLIOGRAPHY

Bedell SE; Delbanco TL: Choices about cardiopulmonary resuscitation in the hospital. When do physicians talk with patients? N Engl J Med 1984 Apr 26; 310(17):1089–93.

Berenson RA: Intensive care units (ICUs): Clinical outcomes, costs, and decision making. (Health Technology Case Study 28) prepared for the Office of Technology Assessment, U.S. Congress, OTA-HCS-28, Washington, DC, Nov 1984 at 12.

Carlson RW; Haupt MT; Kruse JA: Comparison of critical care by family physicians and general internists. JAMA 1989; 261:243–44.

Eagle KA et al.: Length of stay in the intensive care unit; effects of practice guidelines and feedback. JAMA 1990; 264:992–97.

Escarce JJ; Kelley MA: Admission source to the medical intensive care unit predicts hospital death independent of APACHE II score. JAMA 1990; 264:2389–94.

Frankl D; Oye RK; Bellamy PE: Attitudes of hospitalized patients toward life support: A survey of 200 medical inpatients. Am J Med 1989 Jun; 86 (6 Pt 1):645–48.

Fuchs VR: *Who Shall Live? Health, Economics and Social Choice.* 1974.

Goldman GM: Judgmental error in intensive care practice. J Intensive Care Med 1990; 5(3):93–103.

Green J; Wintfeld N; Sharkey P; Passman LJ: The importance of severity of illness in assessing hospital mortality. JAMA 1990; 263:241–46.

JCAHO: Heart, cancer, and trauma indicators refined for beta testing. JCAH Perspectives 1991; 11(3):1, 8.

Kalb PE; Miller DH: Utilization strategies for intensive care units. JAMA 1989; 261:2389–95.

Keeler EB et al.: Changes in sickness at admission following the introduction of the prospective payment system. JAMA 1990; 264:1962–68.

Kiely WF: Psychiatric aspects of critical care. Crit Care Med 1974 May–Jun; 2(3):139–42.

Krieger BP; Ershowsky P; Spivack D: One year's experience with a noninvasively monitored intermediate care unit for pulmonary patients. JAMA 1990; 264:1143–46.

Kruse JA; Thill-Baharozian MC; Carlson RW: Comparison of clinical assessment with APACHE II for predicting mortality risk in patients admitted to a medical intensive care unit. JAMA 1988; 260:1739–42.

La Puma J; Lawlor EF: Quality-adjusted life-years; ethical implications for physicians and policymakers. JAMA 1990; 263:2917–21.

Lipton HL: Physicians' do-not-resuscitate decisions and documentation in a community hospital. QRB 1989; 15(4):108–13.

Luce JM: Improving the quality and utilization of critical care. QRB 1991; 17:42–47.

Luce JM et al.: Ethical principles in critical care. JAMA 1990; 263:696–700.

Pierce JR: *An Introduction to Information Theory: Symbols, Signals, and Noise.* 2d ed. 1980.

Redelmeier DA: Who will die in the ICU? APACHE II, ROC curve analysis, and, of course, cleone (letter). JAMA 1989; 261:1279–80.

Richards EP: Living with uncertainty: Information theory and critical care decisionmaking. J Intensive Care Med 1990; 5:91–92.

Richards EP, Walter CW: How effective safety devices lead to secondary litigation. IEEE Engineering in Medicine and Biology 1991; 10(2):66–68.

Schwartz S; Griffin T: *Medical Thinking.* 1986.

Silverstein MD: Prediction instruments and clinical judgment in critical care. JAMA 1988; 260:1758–59.

Speedling EJ: Social structure and social behaviour in an intensive care unit: Patient-family perspectives. Soc Work Health Care 1980 Winter; 6(2):1–15.

Stolman CJ; Gregory JJ; Dunn D; Ripley B: Evaluation of the do not resuscitate orders at a community hospital. Arch Intern Med 1989 Aug; 149(8):1851–56.

Weiner JP; Steinwachs DM; Steinwachs GM; Dent G: Applying insurance claims data to assess quality of care: A compilation of potential indicators. QRB 1990; 16:424–38.

Zoloth-Dorfman L; Carney B: The AIDS patient and the last ICU bed: Scarcity, medical futility, and ethics. QRB 1991; 17:175–81.

34

Surgery and Anesthesia

CRITICAL POINTS

- Surgeons must take special care when documenting surgical procedures.
- Surgeons and their assistants must be properly qualified when they perform procedures such as endoscopy that require new technology and new skills.
- Day surgery requires special diligence to ensure that patients' general medical conditions are properly evaluated.
- Surgeons and anesthesiologists must work together to obtain a proper consent for surgical treatment.

With the exception of obstetrics, surgical specialties and anesthesia have historically had the largest medical malpractice losses. This is due to both the increased opportunities for problems implicit in surgery and to the psychology of surgical practice. The confidence and decisiveness that are basic requirements for a good surgeon tend to encourage patients to have unreasonable expectations for the results of surgery. Anesthesiologists have the special problem of bearing full responsibility for injuries but limited authority to control the care of the patient. Despite this dilemma, anesthesia practice has been the only real preventive law success story. Through a combination of improved technology, tighter standards for practice, and the elimination of many marginal practitioners, anesthesia-related medical malpractice losses have declined for the past several years.

SURGERY

Surgical complications tend to be obvious. Unlike the complications of medical therapy, which often mimic underlying disease processes, surgical complications are usually different from the patient's presenting condition. Surgery is frequently performed on persons who are basically in good health and in whom death or permanent injury is unanticipated. The errors of surgeons are often the sins of commission, which are more difficult to defend than errors of omission. The inherent risks of surgery are exacerbated by the weak physician-patient relationship between surgeons and their patients. Patients who have been referred to a surgeon for the correction of a specific problem may see the surgeon for only a single visit before the surgery. In some cases, such as trauma, the patient may never have met the surgeon.

STANDARDS FOR SURGERY

Although there is no fundamental reason that surgeons should be held to stricter standards than other practitioners, the nature of their errors makes it easier to convince a jury that a surgeon was negligent. Surgeons tend to present their treatments as curative, encouraging patients to have high expectations about their prognosis. There is also a tendency for laypeople to view surgery as a technical skill, such as carpentry or plumbing. While this may be true of the actual cutting and sewing, it ignores the judgment that is necessary to decide when and what to cut. Surgical consents are too often explained in mechanical terms that oversimplify the patient's problem and the surgeon's remedy.

Documenting Surgical Procedures

Once a patient is closed, it is impossible to determine what the surgeon did during the operation. Juries are very skeptical about surgeons' recollections. Major malpractice cases have turned on points as simple as whether a surgeon checked the integrity of a screw on an orthopedic appliance (*Burkhardt v. Houston Orthopedic Associates*, 1990). In that case, which involved osteomyelitis associated with a fixture plate on a compound fracture, the argument for leaving the plate in place was weakened because there was evidence when the plate was eventually removed that the screws were loose and providing no support to the fracture.

On exploratory surgery to determine the status of the plate, the surgeon recorded that several screws were loose but did not record the status of the other screws holding the plate. The plate was left in place, and the osteomyelitis spread. At trial there was evidence that the size and position of the surgical incision precluded checking the status of the unmentioned screws. While the surgeon recalled that the screws had been checked and found solid, it was difficult to convince the jury that all the screws were checked but that only the loose ones had been recorded. Had the procedure been carefully documented (assuming that the screws had been checked), the case would have been much easier to defend.

The traditional surgical note, dictated after the operation, can be effective documentation for short or routine operations. (Preprinted or word-processed standard operative notes are never credible in legal proceedings and should not be allowed in hospital charts.) Postsurgical recollections become questionable for long, complex procedures and those with unexpected findings. These procedures should be documented while in progress by dictation to a nurse, by a tape recorder that is activated on demand, or by videotape. Unlike a tape for a teaching film, a video surgical note need not be of high quality, nor need it follow the surgeon's hands in close-up. It serves as the visual context for the surgeon's description of the operation, not an independent visual audit of the procedures. Supplemented with a dictated chart note, these provide an inexpensive record of risky operations.

Operating on Bilateral Organs

Operations on bilateral organs pose special documentation problems. While it is impossible to defend operating on the wrong side, it does happen. The risk managers for the Copic insurance company have developed a six-step procedure for ensuring that the operation is carried out on the correct side:

1. The physician should record the correct side in the admission note to the hospital;
2. The nurse's admission note should list the correct side;
3. If applicable, the radiology report or x-rays themselves should be available in the operating room;
4. The anesthesiologist should be asked to record the proper side in the anesthesia note;
5. The circulating nurse should ask the patient before induction and record the results in the operative log; and
6. The patient's consent form should list the correct side for the procedure.

If any of the six does not agree, then stop the surgery.

Sponge and Instrument Counts
In most hospitals, the operating room nursing personnel are responsible for ensuring that sponge and instrument counts are correctly carried out and documented. The surgeon should always ask the operating room nurse the count and whether it is correct. This verification should be included in the operative note, including the name of the nurse certifying the count. Under no circumstances should a surgeon pressure the nursing staff to ignore an incorrect count. If the count is incorrect, the appropriate steps should be taken to find what is missing. If the missing item does not turn up with a properly conducted search, every detail of the search should be documented and the surgery completed. The patient should be fully informed as soon as feasible. Under no circumstances should the information be withheld from the patient.

Medical Consultations
Patients with coexistent medical problems should have a presurgical consultation with an appropriate specialist. This has become more complicated with the increase in day and outpatient surgery. It is much easier for a patient to be referred for the surgical correction of a problem without a general medical evaluation. Such patients require the surgeon to exercise special diligence to detect silent medical conditions that may complicate surgery or recovery. These patients should be seen by an appropriate specialty consultant before the surgery. This consultant must write a presurgical note detailing the patient's medical status and any special considerations in the surgical and postsurgical care. The consultant should personally follow the patient's care after surgery or detail the circumstances in which further consultation is necessary. If the patient may require substantial critical care after surgery, either as a usual consequence of the surgery or as a common complication, it is valuable for the critical care medicine service to see the patient before surgery.

Surgical Assistants
Surgical assistants range in training from fully licensed board-certified surgeons to high school students trained by the surgeon whom they assist. The appropriate training for a surgical assistant depends on the the assistant's role and the laws of the state. The liability for the surgeon and the hospital in allowing untrained or inappropriate surgical assistants is tremendous.

If the surgical assistant is expected to assist in cutting and sewing, he or she should be a licensed physician. If the assistant might have to take over the surgery, he or she must be a fully qualified and licensed surgeon. Complex surgery also requires a qualified surgeon as the surgical assistant. Procedures that involve equipment with special training requirements, such as endoscopic gall bladder removal, require an assistant who is qualified to use the equipment. If there is any possibility that the patient may have problems outside the surgeon's scope of practice, the assistant should be an appropriate specialty surgeon, unless such a surgeon is immediately available in the operating suite. A gynecologist who is not prepared to do bowel surgery should not discover that the suspected tubal abscess is actually an appendiceal abscess when there is no general surgeon available to take over. Surgery should not be started without adequate preparation and personnel to handle foreseeable complications.

Family practitioners should avoid acting as surgical assistants in situations in which they are not trained in the procedures to be carried out. If the patient is undergoing a simple procedure and the family physician could take over in an emergency, the family physician may be an appropriate assistant. If the family physician simply wishes to observe a major surgery, then he or she should not be the primary assistant.

Hospitals should monitor and credential surgical assistants just as they do all other professional personnel. A surgical assistant should be at least a licensed registered nurse. There is little justification for allowing persons without proper medical training and licensure to assist in surgery. Under no circumstances should unlicensed physicians be allowed to act as surgical assistants. Most boards of medical examiners view such practices as an attempt to circumvent the licensing laws. If a physician is needed, it must be a licensed physician.

ANESTHESIOLOGY

Anesthesiology is the most legally curious of the medical specialties. It is a medical specialty with full residency training and formal board certification, yet it is openly practiced by nurses, often in violation of state law and sometimes in violation of the federal laws governing the administration of narcotics. Until recently, it was one of the most costly specialties to insure. The cost of medical malpractice insurance for anesthesiologists has now moderated, due to several factors intrinsic and extrinsic to the specialty.

Anesthesiologists often practice on generally healthy individuals whose next of kin tend to file lawsuits if something goes wrong. Complications of anesthesia delivery are obvious in these patients; they either die or suffer serious brain injuries. If a healthy person dies during surgery or immediately after, the anesthesiologist is suspect. In the 1970s anesthesiologists increasingly became the targets of medical malpractice litigation. Since there are no reliable data on anesthesia deaths, it is impossible to determine if the increase in litigation was secondary to increased bad outcomes or a reflection of increased sophistication on the part of plaintiffs' attorneys. The result was a dramatic increase in medical malpractice insurance rates.

Patient Selection

Anesthesiologists do not select the patients they practice on. Surgeons determine if a patient needs surgery and obtain the consent for the surgery. Once the patient has been convinced that surgery is necessary and has been admitted to the hospital, the anesthesiologist determines if the patient is a candidate for anesthesia. While the anesthesiologist should obtain an independent informed consent for anesthesia, this is impossible once the patient has been convinced the surgery is necessary. If the anesthesiologist determines that the patient is not a candidate for anesthesia, the anesthesiologist must cancel the surgery, a situation almost certain to displease the surgeon and the patient.

As independently licensed physicians, anesthesiologists cannot blame the surgeon if the patient expires because of a contraindication to anesthesia. The law expects anesthesiologists to exercise independent judgment in the evaluation of patients. While anesthesiologists were once sheltered by the captain-of-the-ship doctrine (see Chapter 6), this has been abolished in most states. The surgeon and the anesthesiologist are co-captains under modern law. Each has the right and the duty to cancel or stop surgery if that is necessary to protect the patient.

The Problems of Certified Registered Nurse Anesthetists

More than any other specialty, anesthesiology in the United States has blurred the distinction between physicians and nurse-practitioners. This confusion of roles has its roots in the late differentiation of anesthesiology as a specialty. There was a considerable period during which anesthesia delivery consisted of a paper cone and a container of ether, both held by a nurse. This created a perception that anesthesia was a nursing task. With the certification of registered nurse anesthetists (CRNAs), surgeons explicitly accepted that anesthesia could be practiced by a nurse, albeit under the supervision of a surgeon. This pattern of allowing nurses to practice a medical specialty did not pose a problem until anesthesia practice began to become much more sophisticated and technologically oriented.

Board certification in anesthesia now requires a medical degree, training in a formal residency, and passing a certification examination. This creates an enormous gulf between the knowledge base of CRNAs and physician anesthesiologists. It also creates a knowledge gap between board-certified anesthesiologists and physicians who practice anesthesia without formal training. Such physicians include family practitioners who provide anesthesia in rural hospitals, noncertified physicians who hold themselves out as anesthesiologists, and most surgeons who supervise CRNAs.

A major controversy between surgeons and anesthesiologists is the proper role of CRNAs. Few, if any, states allow the independent practice of anesthesia by nurses. The legal expectation is that the CRNA will be supervised by a properly qualified anesthesiologist. If the CRNA is not under the supervision of an anesthesiologist or if this supervision is too attenuated, the law will assign the surgeon legal responsibility for the CRNAs' actions. (See Chapter 15.)

Medical malpractice insurance rates for CRNAs are artificially low because the nurses do not bear primary responsibility for any negligent actions. When a CRNA injures a patient, the legal liability for that injury flows directly to the supervising physician—either the surgeon or the anesthesiologist. In some cases, the nurse is not even sued. In cases where the CRNA is not supervised by an anesthesiologist, the plaintiff's attorney focuses on the surgeon rather than the CRNA. The surgeon is a much less sympathetic target in front of a jury. As the licensed physician in charge, the surgeon is expected to know all aspects of anesthesiology practice. Plaintiffs' attorneys are able to make supervising surgeons appear negligent by forcing them to admit that they relied on the nurse's knowledge of anesthesia. This is ethically questionable and violates the medical practice act in most states because it is impossible to supervise care that one does not understand.

The Malpractice Crisis
The wide variety of anesthesia practitioners was a major factor in the explosive rise in anesthesia medical malpractice insurance rates in the late 1970s and early 1980s. Medical malpractice insurance companies rate insurance on the procedures that the physician performs, not the physician's training. Board-certified anesthesiologists pay the same rates as untrained practitioners who hold themselves out as anesthesiologists. These unqualified practitioners increased the losses in the pool, which raised the rates for every insured in the pool.

The diversity in anesthesia practice styles and training made it impossible for any accrediting body to establish basic standards for anesthesia practice. The absence of such basic standards allowed marginal practices to continue, greatly increasing the risks to patients. Perhaps the best example of such practices was the debate over whether the person delivering anesthesia needed to stay in the operating room with the patient. In a number of cases in which the patient suffered a sudden anesthesia death, there was an indication that the patient did not die suddenly but was discovered to be dead only when the anesthesiologist returned to the room. Even if the death in such a case might have been unpreventable, the case becomes impossible to defend as soon as the plaintiff's attorney finds out that the anesthesiologist was not in the room.

Technology and Anesthesia Practice
The increase in medical malpractice litigation was difficult for physicians and devastating for anesthesia machine manufacturers. In the late 1970s, products liability claims against anesthesia machine manufacturers threatened to destroy the industry. The impact of these claims was harsh because the industry is very small and machines are relatively inexpensive. Since the industry did not have the capacity to absorb multimillion-dollar losses, it became impossible for the manufacturers to afford products liability insurance.

Ironically, few claims actually involved defective equipment. Most of the claims were based on the equipment manufacturer's failure to make their machines error-proof. The manufacturers complained that they never intended their machines to be used by nonprofessionals, but the lack of standards in pre-1986 anesthesia practice prevented the courts from finding that anesthesiologists were learned intermediaries.*

Learned Intermediaries
Products are designed for specific uses and users. Some products, such as can openers and lawn mowers, are designed for unsophisticated users. Others, such as airplanes, are designed for highly trained users. The learned intermediary problem arises when engineers and lawyers disagree over whether a device is designed for a sophisticated or an unsophisticated user. For example, both engineers and lawyers agree that airplanes should only be operated by trained pilots. They also agree that lawnmowers are usually operated by untrained users. However, they

---
*The following discussion has been adapted from Richards and Walter (1989).

disagree over complex medical equipment such as anesthesia machines. Engineers assume that complex medical devices will be used by trained, competent users, analogous to pilots. The law frequently assumes that they will be used by persons more analogous to lawnmower users.

Determining Who Should Use a Medical Device

The courts have not established criteria for classifying machines as to the necessary competence of the user. The critical parameters for such a classification may be grouped under the heading of indeterminacy. If indeterminacy is measured from 0 to 1, a completely understood machine with a limited number of fixed behaviors would have an indeterminacy index approaching 0. A machine with an unlimited repertoire of behaviors would have an indeterminacy index of 1. The more indeterminate a machine, the more the designer must rely on the user to control the behavior of the machine. A lawnmower has a low indeterminacy because it has a limited purpose and well-defined operational modes. Conversely, personal computers and airplanes are highly indeterminate.

The indeterminacy index must be coupled with a dangerousness index to predict legal liability properly. An unprogrammed personal computer is highly indeterminate, but its potential for injuring people is limited. An airplane is also indeterminate, but it has great potential for causing injury. Using the 0 to 1 scale for dangerousness, a computer might be 0.05 and an airplane 0.9. The legal risk associated with the use of a machine by an incompetent user will be a function of the indeterminacy and the dangerousness of the machine. Applying this analysis to a lawnmower, one finds that although a lawnmower is dangerous, it is dangerous in a limited number of manageable ways. Through proper engineering, a lawnmower can be made relatively safe for an inexperienced user. An airplane, however, combines both high indeterminacy and high dangerousness and cannot be made safe for an inexperienced user.

Some medical devices, such as a tongue depressor, have a low indeterminacy index and a low dangerousness index. Others, such as a pulse oximeter, have low indeterminacy but high dangerousness. Anesthesia machines combine high indeterminacy and high dangerousness, creating a high legal risk when in the hands of an unsophisticated user. Legally, anesthesia machines should be treated like airplanes, not lawnmowers. Because they combine high indeterminacy and high dangerousness indexes, they cannot be rendered safe for incompetent users.

Unlike the Federal Aviation Authority, boards of medical examiners do not require physicians or other persons to be trained and certified to operate medical devices. Since there is no legal requirement of proved competence for anesthesia machine users, the courts have adopted a lawnmower standard rather than an airplane standard to judge the design of anesthesia machines. From an engineering perspective, requiring complex devices to be error proof is absurd. Legally, however, it is a reasonable response to the real-world operating environment for medical devices.

Real Users versus Ideal Users

Products liability law is largely judge-made law derived from cases involving real product users, not idealized users who read manuals and follow instructions. Most products liability cases involve either mass market devices such as power saws and lawnmowers or industrial machine tools such as lathes. These cases have shaped the definition of a reasonable product user in a very contentious way. As an illustration, reasonable lawnmower users have used lawnmowers as hedge trimmers, given children rides while cutting the grass, and used their hands to remove debris from the turning blade. Lawnmower manufacturers have been found liable for not engineering protection to prevent these reasonable misuses.

It is important to understand how the law reaches the conclusion that a manufacturer should foresee that people will stick their hands in running lawnmowers. People do not always use machines wisely. Physicians, attorneys, and even engineers stick their hands in lawnmowers because they are unskilled in the use of these machines. When otherwise reasonable people have these sorts of accidents, jurors assume that the accident should have been prevented by the manufacturer. In contrast, the law does not require that airplanes be error proof because airplanes are used only by trained pilots. If airplanes were flown by untrained users, they would have to be designed like lawnmowers. Since it would be impossible to design an airplane for these users, the airplane industry exists only because various legal restrictions prevent untrained or incompetent pilots from flying airplanes.

The vast majority of states do not require medical device users to be licensed, trained, or tested for competence. It is not unheard of for a general practitioner to perform surgery while supervising a nurse's aide delivering anesthesia. Even board certification is no guarantee of a competent user of an anesthesia machine. Certified anesthesiologists are not retested for competence in the rapidly changing field of anesthesia technology. Anesthesia machine manufacturers, like most other medical device manufacturers, have not attempted to restrict the sale or use of their machines to trained users. They have delegated the assessment of user skills to the medical profession.

Physicians, however, treat medical devices like lawnmowers: they use them without training and sometimes figuratively stick their hands (or the patient's hand) into the blade. Faced with this user group and the failure of anesthesia machine manufacturers to attempt to control the use of their machines, the courts have rationally concluded that medical devices are like lawnmowers rather than airplanes. This caused a crisis in anesthesia machine manufacture but one that has abated because of increased pressure to ensure the competence of persons providing anesthesia services. Physicians in other specialties that are technology dependent should heed the lesson from anesthesia and demand that complex devices be used only by properly qualified personnel.

The End of the Crisis

Several events in the mid-1980s changed the course of anesthesia practice. The first was a direct selective effect of dramatically higher insurance rates. These higher rates, combined with a requirement that part-time practitioners pay full rates, forced many marginal physicians out of anesthesia practice. The second event was the development of cheap, easy-to-use monitors for oxygen tension in the blood and end-tidal carbon dioxide. The inseparable role of oximetry and capnography in reducing anesthesia claims highlights the interdependence of medical practice and technical innovation. The most important factor was that the higher rates motivated anesthesia professional societies to propose basic standards of practice. These standards reflected the consensus of most certified anesthesiologists that someone should stay with the patient and that patient ventilation should be continually monitored.

It is impossible to sort out the contributions of each of these events to the reduction of medical malpractice awards against anesthesiologists. It is clear that these awards have declined, resulting in lowered insurance premiums for anesthesiologists. What is particularly problematic is that it is not possible to prove that anesthesia deaths and injuries have declined. While anecdotal evidence indicates that deaths have decreased, there is no reliable statistical evidence to support this belief. It is possible that staying with the patient and using proper monitoring has merely made it more difficult to prove anesthesia negligence. The presumption that an anesthesia death in a healthy patient must be due to negligence is destroyed if the patient was properly monitored. The plaintiff is left with the often impossible task of proving what really happened.

WORKING TOGETHER TO AVOID PROBLEMS

Surgeons and anesthesiologists have a common interest in avoiding patient injuries and medical malpractice litigation. The central dilemma is that the evaluation and informed consent for surgery is generally done separately from the evaluation and informed consent for anesthesia. In most cases, this poses no problem because the patient is either too healthy or too sick for the anesthesia evaluation to change the decision to perform the surgery. The conflict arises when the patient is sufficiently unhealthy to pose an anesthesia risk but not in need of urgent surgery. In these cases, the patient's anesthesia fitness should be determined before the consent is obtained for surgery.

Evaluating the Patient

Until the operation begins, the anesthesiologist has the right and the duty to refuse to participate in the surgery if the risks of anesthesia outweigh the benefits of the surgery. Once the operation begins, the anesthesiologist still retains the duty to ask that the surgery be stopped, but there is little that can be done if the surgeon refuses. The anesthesiologist cannot abandon the patient once the operation has begun.

The surgeon is entitled to rely on the anesthesiologist's expertise in determining if the patient is a candidate for anesthesia. Surgeons should demand that the anesthesiologist interview and examine the patient before the patient has been premedicated for surgery. The increasingly common practice of skipping the independent anesthesia evaluation is legally indefensible. The surgeon should make sure that the anesthesia note is written before the surgery begins.

Surgeons should also be careful that an anesthesiologist performs the preanesthesia evaluation. A surgeon may not legally rely on a nurse's evaluation of a patient's medical condition; if the patient is not a candidate for anesthesia, the surgeon will be liable unless the determination of fitness was made by a properly qualified physician. If the CRNA evaluating the patient is ostensibly supervised by an anesthesiologist, then the anesthesiologist must countersign the anesthesia note before surgery.

Consent

While the general topic of consent to treatment is discussed in Chapters 12 and 13, surgical consents pose certain special problems. Primary among these is that it involves two procedures by independent physicians. The purpose of informed consent to surgery, as with all other informed consents, is to obviate misunderstandings between the physician and the patient. Through a thorough discussion of the procedure, its risks, and the alternatives, the patient is given a chance to accept the procedure and its possible complications emotionally as well as intellectually. Patients may decline the surgery because the risk-to-benefit ratio is too high for their personal risk-taking profile.

The informed consent process is also a time for the patient and the surgeon to discuss nonmedical considerations that may affect the decision to have surgery, or at least its timing. A patient may want to postpone elective surgery to attend a wedding or other special event. If the surgeon does not know this and forces the patient to miss the event, the patient will be much less tolerant of complications of surgery. Surgeons should also explain any special considerations in their own schedules. Patients should be told if the surgeon is going out of town after the surgery. In this case, the patient should be told who will be handling any postsurgical care. If the planned surgery is elective, the patient may choose to wait until the surgeon returns. It may also be to the surgeon's benefit not to schedule elective surgery for the week before leaving town. Patients and family are always angry if something unexpected happens and the surgeon is unavailable.

The Surgical Consent Form
Surgical consent forms should include the general risks of surgery and the specific risks of the proposed treatment. The form should mention that there is always a small chance of death and brain injury from anesthesia. The consent form should present an accurate picture of the risks of the procedure. While there is no foolproof way to determine which risks to list, a starting point is the risks that the surgeon would worry about if undergoing the proposed operation. In almost all cases, a specific risk should be that the surgery will not cure the underlying problem: vasectomies fail, laminectomies sometimes make the pain worse, and facelifts sometimes fall. There should be no guarantees, either implicit or explicit.

Most surgical consent forms include a brief note on the risks of anesthesia. Ideally the consent form will separate the consent to surgery from the consent to anesthesia. The risks will be separately delineated, as will possible alternatives. The anesthesiologist should be named, just as the surgeon is named. Since patients expected anesthesia to be delivered by an anesthesiologist, there should be specific consent for a CRNA to deliver or monitor the anesthesia. This should include information about the limited training of a CRNA as compared with an anesthesiologist and the person with the legal liability for supervising the CRNA. Such information is necessary for a patient to make an informed consent. It will also prevent misunderstandings with the surgeon in situations where there is not a supervising anesthesiologist.

The advent of new procedures such as laser surgery and endoscopic gall bladder removal has raised new issues for informed consent. The first problem is whether patients are properly informed when they are undergoing what should be considered experimental treatments. The explosive growth of laparoscopic cholecystectomy occurred before the risks were well understood (Cole 1991). Many patients did not appreciate the experimental nature of the procedure. During this growth phase, death was more common with endoscopic procedures than in open procedures. This was not explained to the patients undergoing the procedure, creating a classic failure of informed consent. Patients are also entitled to information about the surgeon's experience with the procedure. This is especially relevant if the surgeon does not meet the generally accepted standards for training and experience with the procedure (SAGES 1991).

Getting the Form Signed

There is only one acceptable time to get a surgical consent form signed: when the consent is obtained. In most cases the consent for surgery is obtained in the physician's office before the patient is admitted to the hospital. The consent form should be filled out and signed while the physician is talking to the patient. Obtaining the consent should not be delegated to a nurse or other assistant.

Except in emergency circumstances, consent for surgery should always be obtained by the surgeon who will be performing the operation. The surgeon should review the consent form with the patient. It is useful to have the patient initial the section of the form listing the risks, as well as signing the form in the presence of the surgeon. The surgeon should also sign and date the form. The patient should be given a copy of the form to keep. When the surgeon sees the patient in the hospital before the surgery, the patient should be asked if there are any additional questions that the surgeon can answer. In states that have laws requiring specific consent forms, the surgeon must have the forms available and use them appropriately. No judge or jury would accept that a surgeon had a fully equipped operating room available but could not obtain the statutory forms.

Ghost Surgery

Surgery is unusual among medical treatments in that it is performed on voluntarily unconscious patients. This makes it possible to substitute surgeons without the patient's knowledge and permission. Surgical ghosts are ethically questionable and legally dangerous. Laypeople, including patients and jurors, do not believe that surgeons are interchangeable (fungible, in legal terms). They believe, rightly, that a patient's choice of surgeons is as important as the informed consent to the surgery. Intentionally misleading the patient about the surgeon's identity is fraud. Unintentionally misleading the patient could defeat the informed consent to the surgery. As one court found:

> No "malice" or intent to injure, however, is required to establish battery in general or specifically, "ghost surgery." In Perna v. Pirozzi, 92 N.J. 446, 457 A.2d 431 (1983), the Supreme Court held that such a battery results when a medical procedure is performed by a "substitute" doctor regardless of good intentions. The Court there took notice of standards published by the Judicial Council of the American Medical Association, which read: To have another physician operate on one's patient without the patient's knowledge and consent is a deceit. The patient is entitled to choose his own physician and he should be permitted to acquiesce in or refuse to accept the substitution. The surgeon's obligation to the patient requires him to perform the surgical operation: (1) within the scope of authority granted by the consent to the operation; (2) in accordance with the terms of the contractual relationship; (3) with complete disclosure of all facts relevant to the need and the performance of the operation; and (4) to utilize his best skill in performing the operation. It should be noted that it is the operating surgeon to whom the patient grants consent to perform the operation. The patient is entitled to the services of the particular surgeon with whom he or she contracts. The surgeon, in accepting the patient is obligated to utilize his personal talents in the performance of the operation to the extent required by the agreement creating the physician-patient relationship. He cannot properly

delegate to another the duties which he is required to perform personally. Under the normal and customary arrangement with private patients, and with reference to the usual form of consent to operation, the surgeon is obligated to perform the operation, and may use the services of assisting residents or other assisting surgeons to the extent that the operation reasonably requires the employment of such assistance. If a resident or other physician is to perform the operation under the guidance of the surgeon, it is necessary to make a full disclosure of this fact to the patient, and this should be evidenced by an appropriate statement contained in the consent. If the surgeon employed merely assists the resident or other physician in performing the operation, it is the resident or other physician who becomes the operating surgeon. If the patient is not informed as to the identity of the operating surgeon, the situation is "ghost surgery." Ghost surgery "remains a battery even if performed skillfully and to the benefit of the patient." Thus, the Court concluded that, [i]f an operation is properly performed, albeit by a surgeon operating without the consent of the patient, and the patient suffers no injuries except those which foreseeably follow from the operation, then a jury could find the substitution of surgeons did not cause any compensable injury. Even there, however, a jury could award damages for mental anguish resulting from the belated knowledge that the operation was performed by a doctor to whom the patient had not given consent. Furthermore, because battery connotes an intentional invasion of another's rights, punitive damages may be assessed in an appropriate case. (*Monturi v. Englewood Hospital*, 1991)

BIBLIOGRAPHY

Block FE Jr: A proposed standard for monitoring equipment: What equipment should be included? J Clin Monit 1988 Jan; 4(1):1–4.

Block FE Jr: Do we monitor enough? We don't monitor enough. J Clin Monit 1986 Oct; 2(4):267–69.

Blumenreich GA: The impact of professional liability insurance on nurse anesthesia practice. AANA J 1987 Jun; 55(3):203–4.

Brunner EA: Analysis of anesthetic mishaps. The National Association of Insurance Commissioners' closed claim study. Int Anesthesiol Clin 1984 Summer; 22(2):17–30.

Brunner EA: Monitoring anesthetic care: New directions (editorial). JAMA 1989 Mar 17; 261(11):1633.

Burkhardt v. Houston Orthopedic Associates. 795 SW2d 221, (Tex App—Hous [14 Dist.], 1990).

Cheney FW; Posner K; Caplan RA; Ward RJ: Standard of care and anesthesia liability. JAMA 1989 Mar 17; 261(11):1599–1603.

Choi JJ: An anesthesiologist's philosophy on "medical clearance" for surgical patients (editorial). Arch Intern Med 1987 Dec; 147(12):2090–92.

Cole HM: Diagnostic and therapeutic technology assessment (DATTA). JAMA 1991; 265:1585–87.

Eichhorn JH: Prevention of intraoperative anesthesia accidents and related severe injury through safety monitoring. Anesthesiology 1989 Apr; 70(4):572–77.

Eichhorn JH; Cooper JB; Cullen DJ; Maier WR; Philip JH; Seeman RG: Standards for patient monitoring during anesthesia at Harvard Medical School. JAMA 1986 Aug 22–29; 256(8):1017–20.

Ficarra BJ; Corso FM: Iatrogenic surgical liability. Leg Med 1985:236–57.

Monturi v. Englewood Hospital. 588 A2d 408 (NJ Super AD 1991).

Nemiroff MS: Preoperative medical consultation and treatment—an anesthesiologist's view. J Med Soc N J 1985 Aug; 82(8):675–76.

Price SH: The sinking of the "captain of the ship": Reexamining the vicarious liability of an operating surgeon for the negligence of assisting hospital personnel. J Leg Med 1989 Jun; 10(2):323–56.

Richards EP; Walter C: How is an anesthesia machine like a lawnmower? The problem of the learned intermediary. IEEE Engin Med Biol 1989; 8(2):55.

Rosenbach ML; Cromwell J: When do anesthesiologists delegate? Med Care 1989 May; 27(5):453–65.

Society of American Gastrointestinal Endoscopic Surgeons (SAGES): Guidelines on privileging and credentialling: Standards of practice and continuing medical education of laparoscopic cholecystectomy. Am J Surg 1991; 161:324–25.

Tammelleo AD: Nurse-anesthetist negligence: Vicarious liability. Case in point: *Thomas v. Raleigh General Hospital* (358 S.E. 2d 222-WV). Regan Rep Nurs Law 1987 Sep; 28(4):4.

Zeitlin GL: Possible decrease in mortality associated with anaesthesia. A comparison of two time periods in Massachusetts, USA. Closed Claims Study Committee. Anaesthesia 1989 May; 44(5):432–33.

Glossary

Note: **Bold** terms are referenced in other parts of the glossary.

Abandonment As a general legal term, abandonment is the surrender, relinquishment, disclaimer, or cession of property or rights. In medical law, abandonment is the physician's unilateral refusal to continue treating a patient with whom the physician has a physician-patient relationship.

Action A civil or criminal proceeding in a court of law, a lawsuit.

ACOG American College of Obstetrics and Gynecology.

ADA The Americans with Disabilities Act of 1990.

Adjudication A decision by a court of law or an administrative law judge.

Ad litem (Usually attorney or guardian ad litem.) A person, usually an attorney, appointed to protect the rights of a minor or an incompetent who is involved in a legal proceeding. An attorney or guardian ad litem's duty is limited to issues that arise in the legal proceeding. The usual role of the attorney or guardian ad litem is to ensure that the parents or legal **guardian** do not put their interests before the child or incompetent. See Guardian.

Administrative Agency An executive branch department of the state or federal government arm which administers or carries out legislation. The **FDA, DHHS, HCFA,** and state **BOMEs** are administrative agencies.

Admissible Facts or testimony that the judge in a lawsuit allows the jury to consider. For example, the judge in a medical malpractice lawsuit must decide if the **expert witnesses** presented by the plaintiff are properly qualified to give evidence to the jury. If they are not, the judge can declare their testimony to be inadmissible and they cannot testify to the jury.

ADR Alternate Dispute Resolution: The resolution of conflicts using means other than litigation; chiefly by **arbitration, mediation,** or facilitated settlement conferences.

Affiant A person who makes an **affidavit**.

Affidavit A voluntary, sworn statement of facts or a declaration in writing made before a person with the authority to administer an oath. These are usually prepared by an attorney in consultation with the affiant, then signed before a **notary public.**

Affirmative defenses Arguments raised by a defendant in a civil lawsuit that indicate extenuating circumstances that negate the plaintiff's claim. A physician sued for failure to attend a patient in a hospital could plead the affirmative defense that he or she had not admitted the patient, previously treated the patient during the hospital admission, or been consulted by the patient's admitting physician. If the judge accepts this evidence as true, then the plaintiff's case would be dismissed.

Affirmed Action of an appellate court in which it declares that a judgment, decree, or order of a lower court is valid and correct and must stand.

Agency The legal term for the relationship in which one person either acts for or represents another. The person acting is the agent and the person for whom the agent acts is called the principle. Lawyers act as agents for their clients when they negotiate leases and other contracts with a **third-party** for their client. Physicians act as agents for their patients when they order medical tests for which a patient is legally obliged to pay a hospital.

AI Artificial Insemination. (Confusion sometimes arises because in medical computing AI means artificial intelligence.)

AID Artificial Insemination by Donor.

Amicus Curiae "A friend of the court." A person who has no right to appear in a suit (no **standing**), but is allowed, at the court's discretion, to present legal arguments or evidence to the judge. Medical professional organizations often file **briefs** as amicus curiae in cases such as *Cruzan v. Director, Missouri Dept. of Health* (1990) that affect medical practice.

Answer The defendant's response to the plaintiff's **complaint** or **original petition**.

Antitrust Laws State and federal laws intended to prevent businesses from using their market power to injure their competitors.

Appeal A complaint to a superior court to reverse or correct an alleged error committed by a lower court.

Appellant The party who appeals the decision of a lower court to a higher, appellant court.

Appellate Court A court which has the power to review the actions and decisions of a lower court. The U.S. Supreme Court has final appellate jurisdiction over all the courts in the United States.

Appellee The party against whom an appeal to a higher court is taken.

Arbitration A private, nonjudicial proceeding in which two or more parties agree to allow one or more arbitrators to decide disputed issues. This agreement may be made before there is a dispute, as when patients insured by an **HMO** agree to arbitrate medical malpractice disputes. Arbitration is binding if the parties agree that neither can bring a legal action on the same facts that are subject to the arbitration agreement. Arbitrators are persons who have no interest in the dispute. They may be attorneys, but are often lay specialists in the area being arbitrated. Each party chooses one or more arbitrators. The parties often agree to abide by the American Arbitration Association (AAA) established rules for arbitration. They may also agree to choose arbitrators from a list of persons certified by the AAA.

Assault Legally, an assault is the act of putting a person in apprehension of immediate harm. (Battery is actually inflicting the threatened harm.) In general usage, and even in many legal proceedings, assault is used to denote both the threat and the action. Threatening a person with a gun is an assault, and an unwanted sexual touching is also an assault. Since assault is a threat of immediate action, upsetting a person by threatening to do something in the future is **intentional infliction of mental distress** rather than assault.

Assignment The transfer of rights or property to another. This is commonly done by physicians when assigning their delinquent accounts to a collection agency.

Assumption of Duty The process of agreeing to accept legal obligations. A physician has the legal right in most circumstances to drive by a roadside accident without stopping to render aid. A physician who does stop to render aid assumes certain obligations to care for the patient in a professional manner.

Assumption of Risk An important legal doctrine whereby a person agrees to accept the consequences of certain behavior. Assumption of risk is effective only if the person makes a free, uncoerced choice and understands the risk being assumed. Informed consent is the assumption of the risks of the medical treatment that the patient agrees to undergo.

Attestation Signing a written statement that a document is correct or that you have witnessed the document being signed. The witnesses to a living will may attest that the patient making the will was of sound mind and made the will of his own volition.

Award The amount of money a court orders a party in a legal proceeding to pay.

Battery An unconsented, harmful or offensive touching. A patient who is restrained without permission, or properly documented medical indications, could bring an action for battery. A patient who is sexually assaulted will bring a legal action for battery, with the sexual touching being the offensive contact. Since a battery is considered an injury to the person's dignity as well as to their person, the court can find large **damages** even if the person suffered no physical harm.

Best Evidence Rule A legal doctrine that requires the primary evidence of a fact should be found, or its absence explained, before a copy or oral evidence on the same matter can be introduced. This is often at issue in medical records. A physician may not testify about the contents of medical records unless the record is in evidence. If the defendant can show that the medical record was lost in a fire, then the court will allow the testimony. If, however, a party intentionally destroys a record, the court may not allow that party to testify about the contents of that record.

Boilerplate A disparaging term for generic paragraphs that are inserted in legal documents without reference to the specific subject of the contract. A common example is the endless pages of fine print that fills commercial leases. A certain amount of boilerplate is necessary in most legal documents to establish the assumptions underlying the agreement. Boilerplate becomes a problem when it is inserted as a matter of course without determining its effect on the document. This is a special problem for physicians because of the special laws that govern medical practice. A standard commercial lease often has terms that base part of the rent on the tenant's net sales. While acceptable for a clothing store, such terms violate the medical practice acts of many states when applied to a physician's office.

BOME Board of Medical Examiners.

Bona fide In good faith; openly, honestly, or innocently; without knowledge of fraud; without fraudulent intent.

Borrowed Servant An employee temporarily under the control of another. The temporary employer of the borrowed servant will be held responsible for the negligent acts of the borrowed servant. Hospital employees were once considered to be the physician's borrowed employees for all medical care. See **Captain-of-the-Ship Doctrine.**

Breach of Contract Failing to comply with the terms of a contract. A breach can occur through failing to comply at all, through incomplete compliance, or through untimely compliance. A breach can be excused if the court finds that either the contract contained an applicable exclusion, such as a physician not being able to fulfill an employment contract requiring a medical license because he lost his license, or that the contract was breached because of the occurrence of an event, such as an act of war, beyond the control of the contracting parties.

Briefs Written arguments on questions of law or facts to assist the judge in making a decision. May be filed by the parties to the lawsuit or by **amicus curia.**

Captain-of-the-Ship Doctrine A legal doctrine holding a surgeon liable for the acts of the entire operating room personnel. This is an old doctrine, predating physician anesthesiologists and nurses with independent duties to the hospital. It has been overruled in most jurisdictions, at least as regards the actions of other physicians.

Causation The legal test for whether a given action lead to the plaintiff's claimed injury. It is not enough to be negligent: the negligence must cause the injury. Causation is often at issue in claims of malpractice associated with the treatment of severe illness. In most states, plaintiffs must prove they had a more than 50 percent probability of recovering from their medical condition before they can sue a physician for allegedly reducing their change of recovery.

Cause of Action A set of facts or legal circumstances which can support a claim for relief in the courts.

CCU Critical Care Unit.

Certification A designation by a private or governmental body that a person or entity has satisfied a pre-established set of standards or requirements. In medicine, it is common for governmental agencies to defer to certifications by private, voluntary organizations such as **JCAHO.**

Certiorari A legal order directing a lower court to transmit the record of a proceeding to an appellate court for review.

CFR Code of Federal Regulations. A listing of federal regulations arranged by subject matter into fifty different titles. Regulations are first published in the ***Federal Register.***

Charge The final address by a judge to the jury in which the judge instructs the jury how to apply the law to the facts in the case before them. Since the slant of the jury charge has a great impact on the jury's final decision, many appeals cases are based on the errors in the charge.

Charitable Immunity A disappearing legal doctrine that gives a charitable hospital immunity from the negligent acts of its employees.

Civil Law In the United States, legal actions that cannot result in a person being punished by imprisonment. In most of Europe, and Louisiana, civil law refers to a system of law based on statutes rather than court decisions. See **common law.**

Claim A demand for compensation, benefits or relief.

COBRA Congressional Omnibus Budget Reconciliation Act. The massive bill passed at the end of a term of Congress that approves the spending for all areas not previously authorized in specific bills.

Common Law Law made by judges in the context of particular cases, and based on decisions made in previous cases involving related facts and laws. In the United States, the Constitution provides a limit on the reach of judges making common law. (Most of constitutional law, however, deals with disputes over the extent of these limits.) The United States has a combination of common and **civil law** because the legislatures can overturn the common law made by judges.

Comparative Negligence The legal theory that allows the jury to consider the plaintiff's negligence in determining whether the defendant's actions caused the plaintiff's injuries. In most states, negligent plaintiffs can still recover, provided that they were not more than 50 percent negligent. See **contributory negligence.**

Compensatory Damages Money paid to an injured or wronged plaintiff based on their proven losses.

Complaint The written statement in a civil case setting forth the plaintiff's claims and the legal basis for the lawsuit.

CON Certificate of Need.

Confidential Communication Communications between persons in fiduciary or confidential relationships. The right of confidentiality belongs to the client or patient, not to the fiduciary. A patient can freely discuss his physician's advice, but the physician cannot freely discuss the patient's condition or the advice given the patient.

Consent A voluntary choice based on appropriate information. Informed consent to medical treatment is a special case of the general laws governing consent. The legal effect of consent is the **assumption of the risks** of the acts consented to.

Contingent Fee When attorneys base their fees on a percentage of their client's recovery. This allows clients to secure representation without having to pay the costs of the litigation. Most medical malpractice litigation is done on a contingent fee, as is some medical business litigation.

Contributory Negligence A legal theory that prevented plaintiffs from recovering damages if they were even one percent at fault. This has been supplanted in most states by **comparative negligence.**

Conversion Any unauthorized interference in a person's or legal entity's right to goods or personal possessions, usually the conversion of those goods to another's use or possession. Keeping an insurance payment intended for a patient but mistakenly sent to the physician's office would be conversion.

Coroner's Jury A special jury called by the coroner to determine whether a person died because of criminal action.

CPT Current Procedural Terminology. A standard system for describing medical procedures.

Criminal Law Laws dealing with individuals and society as defined by acts that are prohibited by statute or regulation and punishable by fine or imprisonment.

CRNA Certified Registered Nurse Anesthetist.

Cross-Examination Witnesses who testify in a legal proceeding may be questioned by the opposing counsel to test the truth and credibility of their character and testimony.

Damages The amount of money necessary to compensate a plaintiff for injuries caused by the defendant's conduct.

Declaratory Judgment A court decision that interprets a law without a trial on the merits of a particular dispute. In some states, the State Supreme Court can give declaratory judgments about the constitutionality of proposed state laws.

De Facto A right or obligation that is recognized because of existing custom, rather than by a statute or court decision. Many physicians believed that joint ventures in health businesses were de facto legal because they were so widely practiced. See **de jure.**

Defamation The injury of a person's reputation or character by untrue statements made (published) to a third person. Defamation includes both **libel** and **slander.**

Defendant The person accused of committing a crime in a criminal case; or the party against whom suit is brought seeking either damages or relief in a civil case.

Defense The defendant's answer to the **plaintiff's complaint.** A defense may contest the truth of the plaintiff's allegations, or claim a legal **privilege** to commit the act complained of.

De Jure Status of a right or obligation that exists by an act of law. See **de facto.**

Depositions Oral or written testimony taken under oath but outside of a courtroom. A verbatim transcript is made and can be used as evidence in a trial.

Dicta The writings of a judge in an opinion that do not specifically affect the resolution or determination of the case and are not part of the common law resulting from the decision. Dicta are important when used to indicate how the court might rule in future cases with related facts.

Directed Verdict When a trial judge decides that the evidence or law is so clearly in favor of one party that it is pointless for the trial to proceed, the judge may direct the jury to return a verdict for that party.

Discovery The pretrial investigation by an attorney to determine the relevant facts of a case.

Discovery Rule A rule **tolling** the **statute of limitations** until the plaintiff knew or should have known of the injury. This is important for conditions such as cancer due to a toxic exposure that take years to become manifest.

DHHS Department of Health and Human Services.

Doe or Roe Fictitious names used in test cases brought on behalf of many parties by representative plaintiffs who, although they may also have a personal interest and standing to bring to the case, prefer to remain unnamed. The best known example is *Roe v. Wade*, where Roe was a pseudonym and Wade was the District Attorney in Dallas, Texas.

Donee One who receives a gift.

Donor One who makes a gift.

DRG Diagnosis Related Groups. A prospective payment system based on diagnoses rather than on the medical services provided to the patient.

Due Care The degree of care that would or should be exercised by an ordinary person in the same position.

Due Process Procedural Due Process: The assurance of fundamental fairness in the legal procedure used. A physician who has his or her hospital privileges terminated has a right to a hearing before an impartial party to assure the fairness of the termination proceeding.

Substantive Due Process: The assurance of fundamental fairness in the result reached. Terminating a physician's hospital privileges because of his or her religious beliefs (independent of actions taken to further those beliefs) would be unfair, irrespective of the procedural due process afforded him or her.

Durable Power of Attorney The written authorization of one person to act for another should they become disabled. A recent variation would be living wills or termination of care provisions.

ELISA Enzyme Linked Immunosorbent Assay. This acronym is commonly used to refer to the screening test for HIV infection.

Emancipated Minor A person who, although they haven't reached the statutory age of majority, is granted the legal status of an adult. This may be done through a legal proceeding where the minor proves that he or she is not living with his or her parents and is self-supporting. Marriage and joining the military also convey adult status in most states.

Equity A historic term for courts dealing with situations where there was no specific legal remedy.

Evidentiary Standards The level of evidence required by a court to reach a finding differs depending on the nature of the claim. Criminal actions must be proven beyond a **reasonable** doubt, while civil actions must only be proven by a preponderance of the evidence. The legal question in the Cruzan right to die case was whether Missouri could require an incompetent patient's wishes to be proven by clear and convincing evidence, a standard more strict than a preponderance of the evidence.

Exculpatory Tending to disprove or excuse a charge of fault or guilt.

Execute To sign, seal, and deliver a written legal instrument.

Expert Witness One who has special training, experience, skill, and knowledge in a relevant area, and is allowed to offer their personal opinion as testimony in court.

Express Manifestation using direct, clear language, either spoken or written.

FDA Food and Drug Administration.

Federal Question Legal question involving the U.S. Constitution or a statute enacted by Congress.

Federal Register A daily journal (running to hundreds of pages) that contains all the official announcements by federal agencies. Agency regulations must be published in the *Federal Register* before they are accepted as legally binding.

Felony A serious crime usually punishable by imprisonment for a period of more than one year or death.

Fiduciary Duty A class of legal duties that arise when one party in a legal relationship has greater power than the person seeking the party's aid. The attorney-client relationship is a fiduciary relationship, as is the relationship of trustee to the beneficiary of a trust. Most states hold that the physician-patient *relationship is a fiduciary relationship. A fiduciary is bound to act in the client/patient's best interests even if it is against the fiduciary's interests. Most importantly, the fiduciary must avoid conflicts of interest. The **Safe Harbor Regulations**, while viewed as overly restrictive by some physicians, merely reflect traditional fiduciary law.*

First Impression A case that presents issues in controversy for which there is no prior judicial precedent.

Forensic The investigation, preparation, preservation, and presentation of medical evidence and opinion in court.

Foreseeability The degree to which a reasonable person would expect a given injury to follow from a specific action. While defendants are liable for unexpectedly severe injuries (**thin skull rule**), they are not necessarily liable for injuries that are too remote from the negligent action. The classic example is the physician who saves the life of a baby who later becomes a bank robber. While it is logically correct that, had the physician not saved the baby's life, there would have not been a bank robbery, the physician is not liable for the bank robbery.

Fraudulent Concealment Hiding or suppressing a material fact or circumstance that the party is legally or morally bound to disclose.

Fungible Items that are so similar to one another that a consumer does not care if they are interchanged. Most produce is fungible; personal computers are becoming fungible. Many health insurance plans assume that physicians are fungible.

Good Faith Honesty in intentional acts toward others. Part of a physician's fiduciary duty is to act in good faith to further the interests and well-being of the patient.

Good Samaritan Laws Laws designed to protect those who stop to render aid in an emergency. These laws generally provide immunity for specified persons from any civil suit arising out of care rendered at the scene of an emergency, provided that the one rendering assistance has not done so in a grossly negligent manner.

Guardian A person appointed by the court to protect the interests of a **ward**: a minor or legal incompetent. The guardian has the rights of a parent for minors. A guardian may have full powers over an incompetent, or the court may limit the guardian's powers to a specific task such as managing the finances of the incompetent. A guardian has a right to full informed consent before making medical decisions for a ward.

Habeas Corpus Literally, bring me the body. A petition to the court requesting the release of an individual who claims to be unjustly or illegally confined. The traditional remedy for a person who claims to have been improperly quarantined is to seek habeas corpus.

HBV Hepatitis B virus.

HCFA Health Care Finance Administration.

Hearsay Rule Testimony of what another person witnessed or said is inadmissible in a trial as being hearsay. A nurse who was present in an examining room could not testify as to what the physician told a patient during diagnosis. She can testify as to whether the physician's testimony reflects what she remembers.

HEPA A high efficiency particulate filter that can remove bacteria and some virus from air.

HMO Health Maintenance Organization.

Iatrogenic Injury Injury or sickness caused by medical treatment.

Immunity Society has decided that certain endeavors or institutions provide such a vital service that they should be protected from attack in the courts should injuries result from the providing of the service. Some types of immunity are codified as law. Governmental or sovereign immunity protects governmental units from some types of lawsuits. At one time hospitals were granted immunity because they were charities serving the public good.

Incident Reports Reports, usually filed by nurses, describing any unexpected events. These are used to identify quality of care and potential legal problems.

Indemnity A contractual agreement in which one party agrees to reimburse another for losses of a particular type. Many insurance policies have indemnity clauses that allow them to recover money paid to an insured who later recovers damages in court for the same injury.

Independent Contractors Persons with special expertise hired for a specific job. Independent contractors control the details of their own work. The person or entity contracting for the work of the independent contract is not legally responsible for the negligent actions of the contractor. The contracting party can be liable if the independent contractor was negligently chosen or retained. The medical staff members of a hospital are independent contractors. The hospital is only liable for their actions if it was negligent in giving or continuing their medical staff privileges.

Indictment A formal written accusation of crime brought by the prosecuting attorney against a person charged with criminal conduct.

Informed Consent A physician cannot perform any procedure upon a patient without ensuring that the patient understands the purpose of the procedure including its potential benefits and dangers. The physician must make certain the patient has all the information needed to make a knowledgeable decision to accept or reject a given treatment or to choose an alternative treatment. See **assumption of risk** and **consent.**

Injunction A court order preventing a person or entity from performing a certain act. A preliminary injunction is temporary and awarded prior to a trial on the merits of the case. A permanent injunction is awarded after the trial and is a final order.

In Loco Parentis Literally, in the place of the parents. At one time colleges and universities acted as the parents of their students, but this ended in the 1960s. The state has the right to act in loco parentis in child welfare cases. See **parens patria.**

Intentional The law punishes intentional acts more severely than negligent acts. A physician who negligently fails to obtain an informed consent may be sued only if an injured patient can establish that he or she would have refused the surgery had he or she been given sufficient information. A physician who intentionally deceives a patient about surgery can be sued for battery even if the surgery is a success.

Intentional Infliction of Mental Distress A cause of action for intentionally causing emotional suffering. The defendant must intend to cause the suffering, the defendant's conduct must be outrageous, and the suffering must be more than just the ordinary distress of daily living.

Interrogatory Written questions used to investigate a lawsuit or establish facts for a trial. These are answered in writing and under oath. The most common interrogatories are those that are used to establish that a copy of a medical record is complete and that the original record was properly created and maintained.

IRB Institutional Review Board.

IVDU Intervenous Drug User.

JCAHO Joint Commission on Accreditation of Healthcare Organizations.

JNOV Judgment Non Obstante Veredicto (not withstanding the verdict). A judgment entered by order of the court in favor of one party, notwithstanding the verdict by the jury in favor of the other party. A court only orders a JNOV when the jury's findings contradict the clear evidence in the case.

Joint and Several Liability When several persons share responsibility for another's injury, they are each liable for the full amount of the damages, irrespective of their percentage of fault. This becomes a problem when one or more of the defendants are underinsured or are insolvent. Many states have abolished joint and several liability in medical malpractice lawsuits. This increases the pressure on plaintiffs to sue everyone who had any part in the patient's care.

Judgment The court's official decision in a legal case. The judgment in a case establishes what damages, if any, must be paid, and the legal responsibilities of all the parties in the lawsuit.

Jurisdiction Jurisdiction over the subject matter of a claim is the power of a court to hear the case and bind the parties. There are monetary, geographic, and political limits on jurisdiction.

Laches A defense in which the defendant claims that the plaintiff waited so long in bringing the complaint that it would be unjust to allow the case to go to trial. The laches defense is important in claims that have no clear **statute of limitations.**

Learned Intermediary This is a doctrine that modifies the **strict liability** (**products liability**) that usually accompanies injuries due to dangerous products such as drugs. In general, the manufacturer of a product has a duty to warn the consumer about the dangers posed by the product. Since patients cannot purchase prescription drugs without a physician's order, the law holds the drug manufacturer must warn the physician. If the physician is provided proper warnings, the drug company is not liable if the patient is injured because the physician improperly prescribed the drug.

Liability A legally enforceable obligation.

Libel **Defamation** by written or printed materials, including pictures.

Litigation Trial of a dispute in a court of law or other legal forum to determine factual and legal issues, rights, and duties between the parties.

Living Wills A legal document that outlines the patient's wishes for refusing or discontinuing lifesaving medical treatment if the patient becomes incompetent.

Malpractice Professional negligence resulting from improper discharge of professional duties or failure to meet the standard of care of a professional, resulting in harm to another.

Mandamus A court order compelling public officers to do their legally mandated duties.

Mediation A process in which the parties to a dispute ask a neutral person to help them come to a mutually beneficial settlement.

Misdemeanor An unlawful act of a less serious nature than a felony, usually punishable by fine or imprisonment for a term of less than one year.

MSAFP Maternal Serum Alpha-fetoprotein. Used in the prenatal diagnosis of neural tube defects and Down's syndrome.

MSDS Material Safety Data Sheets.

Negligence The failure to exercise the degree of diligence and care that a reasonable and ordinarily prudent person would exercise under the same or similar circumstances.

Negligence Per Se Violation of a law or statute that leads to an injury. The law or statute provides the proof of the proper standard of care. The harm complained of must be the kind the statute was intended to prevent, and the plaintiff must be in the class of persons that the law was intended to protect. If a person catches a communicable disease because the physician does not comply with a state disease reporting law, then the physician can be liable for negligence per se.

Nonfeasance Failure to do an act that should have been done.

Notary Public Historically, a notary was a powerful public official who approved the filing of all official documents. In the United States (outside of Louisiana) a notary, or notary public, is a public officer, usually bonded, who may attest to the signing of legal documents. In most states the notary must affix a seal or stamp to the document and must keep a record book of all witnessed documents. Since the notary only attests that he or she saw the document signed, not the content of the document, notarization adds little but pomp to a legal document.

Notice Knowledge of the existence of a fact by a party such that they can be held accountable for any ramifications resulting from the receipt of that knowledge. Notice may be either actual or constructive. If a hospital administrator knows that a physician has a drinking problem, the hospital has actual notice that the physician is impaired even if the medical staff committee never disciplines the physician. The hospital will then be liable for negligent continuation of medical staff privileges. If the National Practitioner Data Bank of the Department of Health and Human Services contains the information that the physician is an alcoholic, the hospital is charged with knowledge of this information even if it never checks the database. This is constructive notice.

Nuncupative Will Oral statement intended as a last will made in anticipation of death.

Opinion The judicial reasons given for an appellate court's decision.

Ordinance A law passed by a municipal legislative body such as a city council.

Original Petition The **pleading** that begins a lawsuit. Also called the **complaint**.

Parens Patria The power of the state to act as parent to protect an individual for the individual's own good. This is different from the **police power,** in that the individual is protected because of the state's interest in not having to bear the burden of injured citizens. Motorcycle helmet laws are enacted under parens patria.

Parol Evidence Oral evidence rather than written evidence. The parol evidence rule says that a written contract is presumed to be the final expression of agreement between the parties and other oral testimony cannot be used to vary the terms of the contract.

Party Any direct, named litigant in a legal proceeding.

Patient Dumping The slang term for transferring a patient because the patient is unable to pay for the needed care.

Peer Review The process whereby a group of physicians determines the medical competence and general professionalism of a physician.

Per Curiam A court opinion made by all members of the court.

Perjury The willful act of giving false testimony under oath.

Physician Extenders Nonphysician personnel who are limited to practicing under the direction and supervision of the attending physician. Physicians are personally liable for the actions of such personnel.

Plaintiff The party to a civil suit who brings the suit seeking damages or other legal relief.

Pleadings A formal statement made to the court setting out a party's claims. The plaintiff initiates a lawsuit by a pleading called a "**complaint.**" The defendant responds to the plaintiff's complaint by filing an "**answer.**"

Police Power The power of the state to protect the health, safety, morals, and general welfare of the people. The police power is the power to restrict the liberty of individuals to protect other individuals. Communicable disease laws are enacted under the police power.

Prima Facie When all the necessary elements of a valid cause of action are alleged to exist. Once the plaintiff has established a prima facie case, the defendant will lose unless he can rebut one or more elements of the case.

Privilege A special legal status that prevents the privileged actor from being held legally liable for actions that would otherwise trigger liability. The state and federal governments are privileged to do actions, such as exposing a population to atomic radiation, that would be torts if done by a private individual. The physician-patient relationship is privileged in most states, allowing the physician to refuse most requests for information about the patient's medical condition.

Privileges Business relationship between a physician and a health care facility, in which the physician remains an independent contractor but has the right to be part of the medical staff and to admit and treat patients in the facility, in return for meeting certain standards set by the facility.

Probate The judicial proceeding that determines the existence and validity of a will in the Probate Court.

Production To bring (produce) documents or physical objects during the **discovery** phase of a lawsuit.

Products Liability Manufacturers are liable for injuries caused by their products, regardless of whether they were negligent in designing or manufacturing the product. This **strict liability** is based on the policy that the manufacturer is better able to bear the cost of injuries, and that strict liability for injuries will encourage the manufacturers to be more careful in product manufacture and design. There is an exception for inherently dangerous products such as guns and tobacco, and for products such as drugs that are controlled by a **learned intermediary.**

Punitive Damages Money awarded to a plaintiff to punish a defendant for intentional or grossly negligent conduct.

Reasonable-Person Standard The vaguest of all legal terms of art. Typically used to describe an objective standard of behavior, for example, one that is based on what a reasonable person would have done, had that reasonable person been in the defendant's position. For physicians, this is a reasonable physician familiar with the standards of practice that would apply to the defendant physician.

Rebuttal Answering the allegations of an adverse party in a legal proceeding. If a charge is not rebutted, the court must accept it as true.

Regulation A standard published by a governmental administrative agency under legal authority delegated to it by the legislature. Regulations have the force of law in both civil and criminal proceedings. Much of medical practice is governed by regulations rather than by statutes.

Regulatory Agency An executive branch department such as the FDA or HCFA which enforces legislation regulating an act or activity in a particular area.

Reliance The legal requirement that persons making claims based on representations made to them prove that they actually relied on the representations. In cases alleging failure of **informed consent,** patients must show that they relied on the physician's representations, for example, that they would not have undergone the treatment had they been given correct information.

Remand When an appellate court reverses the decision of a lower court and sends the case back to the lower court for retrial or other action in accordance with the appellate court's ruling in the case.

Remedies The means by which a court will enforce a party's rights or redress a wrong. These include payment of damages, injunctions, and ordering the parties to carry out specific actions.

Remittitur A judge may decrease the amount of a jury award if the amount is clearly unjust. Many of the large jury verdicts reported in the news and in jury verdict reports are reduced, often substantially. The plaintiff may either accept the reduced award or retry the case.

Res Ipsa Loquitur A legal presumption against a defendant who had exclusive control of the instrument causing the harm when the harm suffered would not ordinarily occur without negligence. Res ipsa loquitur allows a plaintiff to make a claim when no one knows how the injury occurred. A surgery patient who wakes up with a dislocated shoulder can claim that although no one knows how the injury occurred, it must have been due to someone's negligence. Many states have limited the use of res ipsa loquitur in medical malpractice litigation.

Res Judicata A rule that a final judgment on the merits of a case precludes any further litigation on the issues decided.

Respondeat Superior An employer or supervisor of a person who is not an **independent contractor** is liable for the actions of that person. In some cases this **vicarious liability** extends to intentional acts such as sexual assault.

Respondent The party who argues against a petition or appeal.

Restraining Order A court order forbidding a threatened or imminent act until a hearing on the proposed act can be held.

RICO The common abbreviation for state or federal racketeering laws.

Safe Harbor Regulations The legal regulations governing the involvement of physicians in medical businesses. They are termed "safe harbor regulations" because they describe what practices are legal under laws prohibiting **self-referral** arrangements.

Self-referral The practice of sending patients to a medical business because the physician referring the patient has an interest in the business or is given a benefit by the business for patient referrals. Self-referrals create a conflict of interest, violating the physicians **fiduciary duty** to the patient. Self-referrals are also criminal conduct under federal and some state laws.

Service of Process Notification to persons named as defendants in a lawsuit that a suit has been filed against them. Made by an agent of the court, either in person or by mail.

Slander **Defamation** by spoken words.

Standing The required status, based on a party having a personal stake in the outcome of a suit, to raise a particular issue in court. The critical issue in many constitutional law cases is who has standing to bring an issue before the court. Standing is always at issue when physicians bring lawsuits over issues such as medicare funding where patients are the intended beneficiary of the litigation.

Stare Decisis "Let the decision stand." The legal doctrine stating that courts should follow previous decisions and apply them to subsequent cases involving similar facts and questions.

Statute of Frauds The requirement that contracts governing certain transactions be in writing. This is intended to prevent fraudulent lawsuits based on allegations that the parties had entered into an oral contract.

Statute of Limitation A statutory deadline for filing lawsuits. Unless the statute is **tolled,** the plaintiff cannot bring an action after the statute of limitation has run. The statute of limitation is typically two to four years for medical malpractice actions. See **discovery rule.**

STD Sexually transmitted disease.

Stipulate Where the parties to a lawsuit agree to a particular statement of facts and dispense with the need to produce evidence to formally prove those facts.

Strict Liability Liability without fault. Traditionally, strict liability has been limited to ultrahazardous activities such as blasting. **Products liability** is a modified form of strict liability, as is **vicarious liability.**

Subpoena A command to an individual by a court that the individual must obey or face discipline from the court. A *subpoena ad testificandum* is a command to appear at a certain time and place to testify on a matter. A *subpoena duces tecum* is a command to produce specific documents needed in a trial or court proceeding.

Suit Civil court proceeding where one person seeks damages or other legal remedies from another.

Summary Judgment A judgment that decides a case based on affidavits or depositions. Requests for summary judgment are made before trial. A summary judgment is desirable because it saves the time and expense of a trial.

Survivorship Clause A contractual agreement between joint owners of property that, should one of the owners die, the surviving owner is entitled to the decedent's ownership rights in the property.

Testimony Statements made at a hearing or trial by a witness under oath.

"Thin Skull Rule" The legal principle that a defendant must take the plaintiff as he finds him. For example, the defendant cannot complain that the plaintiff's injuries were unusually severe because the plaintiff has an unusual physical condition. The term comes from an apocryphal case involving a plaintiff with a thin skull who suffers a serious head injury in a very minor accident.

Third Party A third party, sometimes abbreviated TP, is a person who is not a party to a legal relationship or transaction, but is affected by the transaction.

Third-Party Liability A defendant in a civil case can compel a third party to join the suit as their co-defendant and share in the liability if the third party is also liable to the plaintiff. A surgeon who is named in a wrongful death suit may implead an anesthetist who is partially or completely at fault.

Toll Under some circumstances the **statute of limitations** is suspended, allowing an action to be brought after the usual deadline. These include the plaintiff's minority, which tolls the statute until the plaintiff reaches eighteen, and periods when the defendant is out of the United States and thus unavailable for service of process. The **discovery rule** also gives a plaintiff additional time to file a lawsuit.

Tort A civil wrong done to an individual by a private individual or private legal entity. Torts usually involve personal injuries. A criminal wrong done to an individual becomes a matter of state interest with prosecution and punishment being handled by the state on behalf of the people of the state. Accidentally injuring someone in a car crash is a civil matter; attempted murder using a car is a criminal matter.

Tortfeasor A person who commits a tort.

Uniform Act A model act concerning a particular area of the law created by a nongovernmental body in the hope that it will be enacted in all states to achieve uniformity in that area of the law.

USCA United States Code, Annotated. A collection of all the federal laws, arranged by topic under fifty broad headings and cross-referenced to specific case law that has arisen concerning the law in question.

Utilization Review The review of the medical care rendered a patient to determine its medical and financial appropriateness.

Vacate When a court sets aside a previously entered order or judgment.

Verdict The formal declaration of the jury of its findings of fact.

Vicarious Liability Liability for the actions of another. This is a special case of **strict liability.** Vicarious liability arises from a special legal relationship between the parties. This may be the employer-employee relationship, parent-child relationship, or relationships created by licensing and certification laws, such as the medical licensing laws. The **borrowed-servant** rule made physicians vicariously liable for the actions of nurses taking care of their patient, even though the nurses were employees of a hospital. See **Respondeat Superior.**

Waiver The voluntary, informed relinquishment of a legal claim or right.

Ward A minor or legal incompetent who has a legally appointed guardian.

Work Product Attorneys preparing for litigation enjoy protection from **discovery** for their work product, for example, their writings, documents, and impressions of the case. This is a limited immunity. A physician's confidential interview with his or her attorney concerning pending malpractice litigation is protected. Giving otherwise discoverable materials such as personal diaries to one's attorney will not protect them from discovery. The privilege applies only to the attorney's own work. A court may order the **production** of work product if it is the only way to obtain critical facts.

Written Authorization Consent given in writing specifically empowering someone to do or assume a duty for another.

Wrongful Birth A legal cause of action by the parents for the extra medical costs of raising a baby with birth defects. The legal claim is a form of failure of informed consent: had the physician properly informed the parents about the risk of a defective baby, the woman would either have not become pregnant or would have aborted the fetus. A wrongful birth claim is different than a claim that the physician's actions injured the baby.

Wrongful Life A legal cause of action brought on behalf of a child with birth defects claiming damages for being alive. Since the essence of these claims is that the child would have been better off dead, most courts reject wrongful life claims.

Index

Abandonment
  of child, 354
  of patient, 122–123, 257
Abortion, 67, 141, 177, 383–387
  adoption alternatives to, 387
  consent to, 386
  controversies about, 368, 383, 387
  counseling on, 385–386, 391
  government support for, 384–386
  minors and, 187
  parental information on, 386
  personal beliefs and, 358, 384, 392–393
  politics of, 383
  privacy rights and, 383–384
  RU 486 and changes to, 387
Academy of Pediatrics, 260
Accidents, 42, 44, 177, 294, 463, 496–498
Accreditation Council for Graduate Medical Education (ACGME), 370
Acquired immunodeficiency syndrome (AIDS), 312, 315–330, 332, 404
  contraception counseling and, 376–377
  critical points about, 315
  definition of, 318
  fear of, 320, 343–344
  historical overview of, 316–319
  medical records in, 103
  mothers with, 354
  parallels between other diseases and, 319–321
  prison doctor and, 464
  treatment of, 82, 208–209
Acute illness observation scale, 439
Administrative law, 14
Adoption, 355–358
  as abortion alternative, 387
  Baby M surrogacy case and, 361–365
  evaluating children for, 356–357
  fertility procedures and, 356
  matchmaking in, 356
  parental rights and, 349, 355–356
  payments in, 355, 362, 364
  private placement in, 350, 356
  proceedings in, 354, 355
  records in, 357–358

state restrictions on, 349, 350–351
Advertising, 130, 156, 413
Affidavit, 31
Affirmative defense, 20–21
AIDS. *See* Acquired immunodeficiency syndrome (AIDS)
AIDS-related complex (ARC), 316, 318
Alcoholism, 425, 478–479
Alternative dispute resolution (ADR), 26–28
Alternative treatments, 152
AMA. *See* American Medical Association (AMA)
Ambulance services, 457
Ambulatory care centers, 118, 121, 468
American Academy of Pediatrics, 357, 435
American Arbitration Association (AAA), 27
American College of Obstetrics and Gynecology (ACOG), 397, 407–409
American Medical Association (AMA), 52, 185, 186, 425–426
Americans with Disabilities Act (ADA), 14, 474–475
  communicable diseases in workplace and, 332, 336–337, 342
  confidentiality under, 470, 471
  legal risks of, 479–481
  occupational health and, 467, 473, 474–482
  return to work certification and, 471–472
Amniocentesis, 396, 398, 403
Anesthesia, 525–530
  certified registered nurse anesthetists (CRNA) in, 526–527, 531
  critical points about, 522
  malpractice and, 79, 522, 525, 527
  patient selection for, 525–526
  surgeons and, 530–533
  technology and, 527–529
Antitrust laws, 9, 87, 128, 261–262, 263, 264, 266, 267
Appellate process, 6–7, 8, 9, 26
Appointments
  abandonment of patient and, 123

551

552 Index

Appointments—*Continued*
  delegation of authority to staff to make, 221
  follow-up after missing, 123, 125–126
  physician-patient relationship and, 114, 120
Arbitration, 26–27
Articles of Confederation, 5, 8
Artificial insemination (AI), 390, 404–407
  choosing donor in, 399–400, 405–406
  consent in, 405
  infection control in, 406–407
  restrictions on, 351
  surrogacy and, 360
  See also Fertility treatment
Athletics. *See* Team doctor
Attending physicians, 74–75, 243–244, 246
Attorney-client privilege, 37–38
Attorney fees, 15–16
  billing systems for, 52, 54–57, 62
  caps on, 17
  contingency and, 16–17, 18, 40
  malpractice litigation and, 57
  padding of, 57–58
  peer review of, 278
  structured settlements and, 48
Attorneys, 50–62
  autonomy of, 51–52
  billing system of, 52, 54–57, 62
  business ventures between physician and, 58–59
  choosing, 60
  conflict of cultures between physicians and, 50–52
  conflicts of interest with, 58–59
  critical points concerning, 50
  delegation of work to others by, 56–57, 62
  limited engagement doctrine and, 51–52
  physician as effective client of, 59–62
  physician-patient relationship different from relationship with, 50–51
  physician refusal to treat, 119
  preparing for trial and, 18–22, 25
  preventive law audit by, 60–62
  structure of legal work by, 52–54
Attorney work product, 37–38
Audit, preventive law, 60–62
Authority of physician
  critical care unit (CCU) and, 516–519
  delegation of. *See* Delegation of authority
  medical judgment and, 216–217
  medical records and, 98
  nonphysician employees and, 73
Automobile accidents, 42, 44, 177, 294, 463, 496–498

Autopsies, 294–295
Awards. *See* Damages

Baby M case, 358, 361–365
Baby-selling, and adoption, 356
Backup coverage, 122, 123
Bankruptcy, 26
Basic life support, 499
Bastardy, 352
Battery, legal standard for, 67, 146
Beyond a reasonable doubt standard, 10
Bias, and peer review, 280
Birth certificates
  filing of, 292
  information on, 292
  naming child on, 292–293
  public health statistics and, 291, 292
Birth control. *See* Contraception; Oral contraceptives
Birthing rooms, 413, 419
Birth-injured infants
  malpractice litigation over, 82, 391
  pregnancy risks and, 417, 427–428
Birth plan, 416–419, 423
Birth records, 291, 293, 357
Blood doping, and sports, 455
Blood tests, and paternity, 353
Blood transfusions, refusal of, 443
Board of Preventive Medicine, 467
Boards of medical examiners, 14, 80, 216, 217, 245, 251–252, 253, 275, 308
Boards of nursing examiners, 246
Boards of pharmacy, 216, 219
Borrowed-servant doctrine, 74
Breach of contract, 65, 71
Bribery, 139, 268
Business records, hearsay rule exception for, 34–36, 98
Business ventures
  medical research and, 189, 208
  physician-attorney partnership in, 58–59
  possible criminal activities in, 141–142
  RICO litigation over failure of, 141
  settlement of disputes in, 27

Captain-of-the-ship doctrine, 74, 75
Cardiology, 244
Cardiopulmonary resuscitation (CPR), 496, 504–505, 517–518
Carrier state
  disease control and, 303–304, 309, 312
  HIV infection and, 321, 322, 344
Causation, 63, 71–72
Cause of death, 293
CCU. *See* Critical care unit (CCU)
Centers for Disease Control (CDC), 295, 303, 304–305, 318, 321, 325, 341, 344, 435
Certification
  basic life support and, 499

Index 553

locality rule and, 70
occupational medicine and, 468
Certified registered nurse anesthetists (CRNA), 526–527, 531
Cesarean section, 422, 423–424
  consent in, 423, 424
  emergency care with, 418
Charts
  consultations documented in, 235, 242
  physician's orders in, 222, 223
  physician extenders (PEs) and, 229
  readability of, 99
  telephone calls documented in, 116, 440
  test evaluations in, 221
  transcription of notes into, 35, 99
  See also Medical records
Child abuse
  as legal finding, 295, 442
  investigation of, 350
  pediatric care and, 441–442
  reporting of, 169, 242, 295–296, 355, 441–442
  treatment for, 171
Children
  abandonment of, 354
  athletics and injuries to, 453–454
  conflict between parents and, 170
  custody after divorce and, 168–169, 354–355
  development and hormonal techniques for, 455
  guardianship and, 165–167
  HIV infection in, 356, 357
  informed consent and emergency care for, 147
  injunctions for, 13
  litigation over injuries to, 391
  medical research and, 195, 204–206
  parental refusal of medical care to, 166, 167–168
  school doctor and, 455–460
  See also Minors; Pediatric care
Child welfare agency, 169, 171, 355
Civil law, 12
  administrative regulations and, 14
  civil remedies in, 12–13
  nonmonetary remedies in, 13
  origins of, 5
  peacekeeping function of, 12
  privileged communication under, 37–38
Civil litigation. *See* Litigation
Civil rights legislation, 8, 260, 280, 404, 465
Civil rights movement, and quarantine, 7, 312
Claims-made insurance policy, 90
Clayton Act, 266
Clear-and-convincing-evidence standard, 178, 179
Closed claim studies, 80–81
Cocaine abuse, and pregnancy, 425, 427

Code of Ethics for occupational medicine, 470
Code orders, in critical care unit (CCU), 519
Collateral source rule, 46–47
College students
  health programs for, 459–460
  sports and, 453
  See also Universities
Commercial law, and medical research, 209, 210
Common law, 501
  democratic traditions and, 7
  emergency care under, 496, 498
  legitimacy of children under, 352–353
  origins of law within, 5–6
  physician-patient relationship in, 4
  pleading under, 20
  public health authority under, 287–288
Communicable diseases
  Americans with Disabilities Act (ADA) concerning, 336–337
  critical points about, 332
  direct threat from, 336–337
  as disabilities, 336
  fear of, 320, 343–344
  immunosuppression and, 342–343
  legal risks of, 334–335
  of minors, 170, 171
  policy regarding, 337–343
  prison doctor and, 463, 464
  reporting of, 171, 290, 305–308, 458
  school doctor and, 458–459
  significant risk from, 336, 337
  third-party liability in, 334–335
  transmission methods for, 338–339
  treatment of, 171
  workplace and, 332–345
  See also Disease control
Community
  HIV infection control and, 323–324
  immunization programs and, 433
  informed consent and standards within, 150–151
  respect for physicians in, 24
Company doctor, 121
Competition, 5
  malpractice insurance companies and, 89–90
  peer review and, 264
  professional standards and, 77
Compliance, and termination of care, 125
Computers, and medical records, 99, 100
Condoms, and birth control, 376–377
Confidentiality
  adoption records and, 357
  college health programs and, 459–460
  disease control reporting and, 304, 305
  medical records and, 104
  occupational medicine and, 470, 494
  peer review and, 276–277

Confidentiality—*Continued*
  preemployment medical examination and, 476–477
  security law and, 208, 209
Conflicts of interest, 128–142
  attorneys and, 58–59
  critical points about, 128
  hospital ownership and, 131
  incentive plans and, 138–139
  informed consent and, 131
  laboratory ownership and, 131–132
  malpractice insurance companies and, 91
  medical research and, 189
  physician-patient relationship and criminal activity, 11
  proxy consent and, 163–164
  sexual relationships with patients and, 132
  surrogate parenthood and, 409
  team doctor and, 452
  treating family members and, 131
Congress, 279, 332, 436, 478
  contraception and, 373, 374
  legal system and, 6, 8, 10
  Medicare/Medicaid regulation by, 133, 137
  racketeering laws of, 137
Consent
  for autopsy, 295
  defining, 145–146
  documenting, 159–160, 170
  guardianship and, 165, 166–167, 169
  intoxication testing and, 296
  minors and, 167–171
  proxy, 162–165, 168, 170
  See also Informed consent; Substituted consent
Consortium, 44, 45
Conspiracy, and peer review, 262
Constitution, 8, 54, 182, 265, 311
  origins of law in, 5, 6
  public health authority and, 288, 290, 302
  right to counsel under, 11
  sovereignty determination under, 9–10
Consultations, 121, 232–235
  child abuse seen in, 242
  critical points about, 232
  documentation of, 235
  functions of, 233
  informal, 118, 234
  information on patient provided in, 241
  institutional, 242–244
  physician's duty to choose, 234–235
  record keeping in, 241–242
  referrals differentiated from, 232
  request for, 233–234
  tests and procedures and, 240–241
Contact effectiveness, 340
Contact tracing, 310, 326–327

Contagious disease. *See* Disease control
Contingent fees, 16–17, 18, 24, 40
Continuing care, 238
Contraception, 372–377
  balancing physician's and patients' rights in, 377
  choice in, 373
  HIV infection and, 322, 368, 376–377
  implantable contraceptives and, 375–376
  IUDs and, 375
  minor's access to, 170, 377–379
  natural family planning and, 376
  risk of pregnancy and, 373, 393
  sterilization and, 379
  See also Oral contraceptives
Contracts
  artificial insemination and, 403
  breach of, 65, 71
  civil law covering, 13
  emergency room staffing and, 500–501
  health maintenance organizations (HMOs) and, 119
  between hospitals and physicians, 119
  medical research and, 189, 210
  occupational medicine physicians and, 467, 468–469, 484
  peer review interference with, 264
  preferred provider organizations (PPOs) and, 120
  preventive law audit of, 61–62
  prison doctor and, 464–465
  school doctor and, 456
  surrogacy and, 358, 361–362
Coroner cases, 294–295
Correctional facilities. *See* Prisons
Costs
  critical care unit (CCU) and, 513–514
  lawyers' fees and, 15–16, 17, 40, 48, 57
  litigation and, 15–18, 40, 53
  peer review and, 263
  public health and, 290
  standard of care and, 76
  trial, 24–25
Counseling
  abortion, 141
  See also Genetic counseling
Court system
  administrative regulations enforced by, 14
  appellate process in, 6–7, 26
  definition of death by, 180
  guardianship in, 147
  life support system termination and, 183, 184–185
  litigation bias in, 7
  malpractice data from, 80
  role of judges in, 6
  treatment mandated by, 147, 298, 310–311
  See also Litigation; Trial

Criminal law, 6, 10–11
  citizen's duty under, 11
  decision to prosecute under, 11
  medical businesses and interpretation of, 141–142
  medical research and, 189
  physician-patient relationship protection under, 11
  privileged communication under, 36–38
  quarantine and, 328
  reporting duties under, 296
Critical care unit (CCU)
  authority in, 516–519
  cost containment issues in, 507, 513–514
  critical points concerning, 507
  defining standards in, 514
  effectiveness of, 515
  fetal monitors in, 508, 509–510
  information theory used in, 511–512
  legal risks with safety devices in, 507–511
  protocols used in, 515–516
  rationing care in, 514–516
  sampling issues in, 512–513
Cross-examination, 33–36
Cruzan case, 177–180, 185–187
Current procedural terminology (CPT) system, 52
Custody, and medical treatment of children, 168–169, 354–355

Dalkon shield, 375
Damages, 40–48, 65
  civil law mandating, 12–13
  collateral source rule and, 46–47
  costs of litigation and, 40
  critical points about, 40
  direct economic, 40–44
  in excess of policy, 92
  indirect economic, 44–45
  paying, 47–48
  peer review of settlements of, 274–276
  punitive, 45–46
Davis divorce case, 358–360
Death
  legal definition of, 180, 294
  public health records on, 291
Death certificates, 293–294
Decision making
  in contraception, sterilization, and abortion, 368
  nonphysician employees and, 73
  peer review of good faith, 278–279
  public health authority and, 289–290
Declaration of Geneva, 191
Declaration of Helsinki, 190, 191–192
Defamation, 264
Defensive medicine, 84–86
Delegation of authority
  classes of medical tasks in, 220

  critical points about, 215
  explicit, 220
  implicit, 220–222
  issues to consider in, 220
  legal and ethical issues regarding, 215–216
  limitations on, 217–220
  medical judgment and, 216–217
  midwives and, 246
  nonphysician employees and, 215
  physician's orders and, 222–223
  protocols and, 223–227
  supervision with, 227–230
Dementia, and AIDS, 315, 330, 343, 344
Denver Development Screening Test, 440
Department of Health and Human Services (HHS), 134, 192, 193–207
Department of Justice, 134, 140
Department of Transportation (DOT), 484
Deposition, 29, 30–32
Detention facilities. *See* Prisons
Development of child
  hormonal techniques for altering, 455
  medical records on, 439–440
Diagnosis
  birth injuries in, 427
  defensive medicine against malpractice and, 83, 85–86
  differential diagnosis list for, 218, 224
  HIV infection and, 330
  incentive plans and conflicts in, 138–139
  nursing, 228–229
  protocols for, 223–224, 225
Diagnosis-related groups (DRGs), 183
Direct damages, 40–44
Direct orders, 222–223
Direct threat, and communicable diseases, 336–337, 478
Disabled persons, 467
  Americans with Disabilities Act (ADA) definition of, 475
  communicable diseases and, 336–337
  damage award for expenses of, 43
  government benefits for, 474
  immunosuppression and, 333
  worker's compensation and, 481–482
Discovery, 29–38
  contesting orders for, 33
  critical points about, 29
  cross-examination for, 33–36
  definition of, 29
  forms of, 29–33
  latitude for, 36–38
  medical records and, 30, 32, 33
  privileged information in, 36–38
Discrimination, and HIV infection, 328–329
Disease control, 301–313
  carrier state in, 303–304

556 Index

Disease control—*Continued*
  coercive measures permitted in, 30–312
  critical points about, 301
  environmental health and, 313
  epidemics and plagues and, 303
  food sanitation and, 312–313
  HIV infection and, 321–328
  immunization laws and, 301–302, 432–433
  physician-patient relationship and, 304–305
  prison doctor and, 464
  quarantine and, 7, 311–312
  reportable diseases in, 305–308
  warning third parties in, 308–309, 322
Disease registries, 295
Divorce
  embryo custody after, 358–360
  genetic counseling and, 400
  medical treatment of children, 168–169, 354–355
  parental rights in, 354
  pregnancy and, 355
Domestic violence, 296
Down syndrome, 396, 397, 398
Drug abuse
  college students and, 460
  mothers and, 354
  preemployment medical examination and, 478–479
  prisoners and, 463
  rehabilitation program for, 479
  See also Substance abuse
Drug Enforcement Administration (DEA), 216, 219, 253
Drugs
  laws covering, 219
  prescription of. *See* Prescription practices
  samples of, 219
  testing of, 192–193, 297, 298
Due process
  peer review and, 265–266
  prison doctor and, 462
  public health and, 290
Durable power of attorney, 164, 179, 181, 417
Duration of risk, with communicable diseases, 338

Earnings, lost, 41–42, 46
Ecclesiastical law, 6
Electrocardiograms (EKGs), 244
ELISA test, 324–325
Emancipated minor, 171
Embryo transplantation
  divorce and custody of, 358–365
  donors in, 354
  See also Fertility treatment
Emergency care, 496–505
  abortion, sterilization, and contraception counseling and, 370–371
  accidents and, 496–498
  critical points about, 496
  death certificates and, 294
  definition of, 147
  federal law on access to, 501–504
  Good Samaritan laws on, 498
  guardianship and, 166
  informed consent and, 146–147
  intoxication and, 297
  medical office and, 499–500
  midwives and, 245
  minors and, 170
  negligence in, 67
  obstetric care and, 298, 418–419
  physician-patient relationship and, 114, 119
  prison doctor and, 463
  prisoner care in, 298
  right to refuse, 174
  school doctor and, 455, 457
  screening in, 501–502
Emergency rooms
  stabilization in, 502
  staffing of, 500–501
  transfer of patients from, 502–504
Emotional distress, damage awards for, 44–45
Employees. *See* Nonphysician employees; Physician-employee relationship; *and specific types of employees*
Employer, physician as, 5. *See also* Physician-employee relationship
English common law, 5, 6, 9, 287, 352
Entitlement programs, 8
Environmental health, 313
Epidemics, 303, 305, 318, 433
Epidemiology, protocols for, 227
Equal Employment Opportunity Act, 280
Ethical Advisory Boards, and medical research, 200–201
Euthanasia, 183
Evidence
  hearsay rule and, 34
  prison doctor and, 464–465
  standards for, 7
Examination of patient, standard of care on, 68
Exemplary damages, 46
Expenses. *See* Costs; Medical expenses
Experiments. *See* Medical research
Expert witnesses
  effective presentation by, 71
  locality rule and, 69–70
  malpractice litigation and, 21–22, 69, 83
  product liability and, 75
  qualifying, 70–71
  specialty qualifications of, 69
  standard of care and, 66, 70–71, 76
  trial and, 21–22, 25

Faith healers, 219–220

Family
  artificial insemination and, 405–406
  disease control reporting and, 309, 310
  fertility treatment and, 400–404
  genetic counseling and, 390–400
  guardianship and, 165
  life support system termination and, 7, 176, 180, 183–184, 186–187
  obstetric care and, 412–428
  parental rights in, 349–365
  pediatrics and, 432–445
  of physician, and treatment decisions, 131
  power of attorney to consent to medical care and, 163–164
  substituted consent and conflicts in, 186–187
  surrogacy and, 358–365, 407–409
  work-place acquired infection and, 334–335
Family law, 12
Family planning, and federal policy, 378, 384–385
Family practitioners, 120, 121–122, 469, 525
Fathers
  adoption and, 355
  artificial insemination and choice of, 399–400, 403, 405
  assuming legitimacy of children and, 352–353
  determination of legitimacy for, 349, 353
  genetic counseling and, 399
  medical care of mothers and, 351
Federal court system, 8–9
  administrative regulations enforced in, 14
  appellate process in, 6, 8
  medical malpractice in, 9
  sovereignty of, 9–10
Federalist system, 8–10
Federal laws
  abortion and, 368, 385–386
  communicable disease plan and, 341
  family planning and, 378, 384–385
  handicapped children and, 459
  immunization programs and, 435
  informed consent under, 153
  occupational medicine and, 468
  patient dumping under, 237, 501
  peer review under, 263, 264–268, 271–282
  regulation of medical practice under, 8
  sterilization and, 381–383
Federal taxes, 72–73
Federal Trade Commission (FTC), 77, 130, 260, 267
Fees. *See* Lawyer fees; Physician fees
Fertility treatment, 390, 400–404
  adoption and, 356
  embryo custody after divorce and, 358–360
  embryo storage in, 403
  fitness issues in, 401–402
  malpractice and, 82
  multiple gestation in, 402–403
  unmarried couples and, 404
  See also Artificial insemination (AI); Embryo transplantation; In vitro fertilization
Fetuses
  medical research on, 201–202
  monitors for, 509
Fiduciary physician-patient relationship, 128, 129–131
  incentive plans and, 138–139
  institutional practice and, 451
  market factors in choice of provider and, 130–131
  RICO fraud and, 138
First Amendment, 384
Follow-up care
  IUDs and, 375
  medical records and, 101
  missed appointments and, 123, 125–126
  protocols for, 226
Fomites, 338
Food and Drug Administration (FDA), 82, 182, 387
Food sanitation, 312–313, 482
Football, 452, 453, 454
Fourteenth Amendment, 461
Fraud, 141–142
  advertising medical services and, 413
  failure to disclose a risk as, 150, 153
  mail and wire, under RICO, 137–138, 268
  medical research and, 206–208
  medical students and residents and, 251
  Medicare/Medicaid laws covering, 128, 132–134
Free speech rights, 385
Future earning capacity, 41–42

General denial, 21
Genetic counseling, 390–400
  abortion views and, 392–393
  choice of father and, 399–400
  consent in, 393
  critical points about, 390
  ethical questions in, 393–399
  genetic history in, 396–397
  screening in, 395–396
  time limitations in, 398–399
  torts and, 390–393
Ghost surgery, 532–533
Good faith decisions, peer review of, 278–279
Good Samaritan laws, 496, 498
Group health insurance, 47
Growth hormone deficiency, 443
Group health insurance, 469

Guardianship, 165–167, 169
  emergency and, 166–167
  establishing, 165–166
  informed consent and, 147, 441
  release of medical records and, 103
Gunshot wounds, 296

Handicapped persons
  communicable diseases and, 336
  school doctor and, 459
Harvard Medical Practice Study, 8, 79–80
Health and Human Services Department. *See* Department of Health and Human Services (HHS)
Health Care Finance Administration (HCFA), 14, 216
Health Care Quality Improvement Act of 1986, 259, 265, 268, 271–282
  bias issues in, 280
  critical points about 271
  good-faith decisions under, 278–279
  potential adverse impacts of, 279–280
  requirements of, 271–278
Health departments, 308–309, 312–313
Health maintenance organizations (HMOs), 121, 259
  alternative dispute resolution (ADR) and, 27
  closed-panel, 119
  contractual arrangements between physicians and, 119
  incentive plans under, 138–139
  market factors in choice of, 130
  physician-patient relationship in, 114, 119
  protocols in, 223
Health officer, and disease control, 304, 305, 313
Hearsay rule, 34, 98
Hepatitis B (HBV), 316, 325, 335, 339, 341, 464
Herd immunity, 433
HHS. *See* Department of Health and Human Services (HHS)
High school athletics, 453–454
High-technology medicine, 507–520
  anesthesia and, 527–529
  critical points about, 507
  informed consent and, 148–149
  life support under, 175
  malpractice and, 84–85
  medicalization of reproduction and, 349, 350
Hippocratic Oath, 175
HIV infection. *See* Human immunodeficiency virus (HIV) infection
HMOs. *See* Health maintenance organizations (HMOs)
Home deliveries, 421–422
Homosexuals, discrimination against, 329

Hospitals
  abortion, sterilization, and contraception counseling and, 370–371
  charitable immunity of, 74
  consultations within, 242–244
  delegation of authority by physician and, 218–219
  disease control in, 311–312, 342
  emergency room staffing in, 500–501
  guardianship authority and, 165, 166
  liability of physician for employees of, 74–75
  life support system termination and, 176, 183–184, 185
  medical malpractice and, 81
  medical records in, 102, 104–109
  obstetric care in, 413, 421
  ownership by physicians of, 131
  parental consent for minor care and, 166, 169, 170, 171
  patient dumping practices and, 67, 237, 501
  peer review duty of, 259, 261–262, 276–277, 281
  physician's legal relationship with, 5, 119
  power of attorney to consent to medical care and, 162–163
  prison doctor and, 464
  referrals to, 237, 239
  refusal of care by patient and, 182
  staff privileges in, 239, 260, 263, 267
  surgical assistants in, 524–525
Human growth hormone, 443, 454
Human immunodeficiency virus (HIV) infection, 301, 315, 339, 371
  children with, 356, 357
  contraception counseling and, 322, 368, 376–377
  disease control for, 321–328, 406–407
  fear of, 320, 343–344
  immunosuppression and, 333
  medical duties regarding, 328–330
  obstetric care and, 420–421
  prisoner doctor and, 463–464
  reasonable accommodation, 344–345
  risks posed by, 320–321, 343–345
  school doctor and, 458, 459
  screening for, 327, 344, 407
  testing for, 324–325, 329–330, 372
  warning third parties regarding, 308, 309, 310
  workplace infection with, 335, 340, 343–345
  See also Acquired immunodeficiency syndrome (AIDS)
Husbands
  as artificial insemination donor, 405
  power of attorney to consent to medical care and, 163–164
  reproductive counseling for wives and, 371, 405, 417

Hydration, termination of. *See* Life support system termination

ICD-9, 52
Immunization, 309, 432–438, 458
  consent for, 434–435
  disease control programs with, 302–303, 333
  medical exemptions for, 435–436
  political factors in, 432–433
  prison doctor and, 464
  reportable events following, 437–438
  Vaccine Compensation Act on, 436–438
Immunosuppression, 333–334, 340–341, 342–343, 435
Implants
  contraception with, 375–376
  medical records for, 100–101
Inadvertent abandonment, 123
Incentive plans, 124, 128, 268
Independent contractor physician
  occupational medicine and, 467, 468–469, 484
  prisons and, 464–465
Indirect economic damages, 44–45
Induction of labor, 422, 423
Infectious disease, 318. *See also* Disease control
Information theory, 511–512
Informed consent, 7, 148–157
  abortion and, 386
  alternative treatments and, 152
  artificial insemination and, 405
  cesarean section and, 423, 424
  conflicts of interest on, 131
  consultations and referrals with, 232
  contraception and, 373, 376, 379
  critical points about, 145
  disease control reporting and, 305, 309
  documentation of, 157–160
  emergency care exception to, 146–147
  forms for, 157, 158–159
  genetic counseling and, 393
  HIV testing and, 329–330
  illiterate patients and, 159
  immunizations and, 434–435
  as individual liberty issue, 149–150
  knowable and unknowable risks and, 154
  legally mandated treatment and, 147
  legal standards for, 150–151
  medical records on, 105, 158
  medically unnecessary procedures an, 155–156
  medical research and, 192, 197–200, 204–206
  medical value of, 156
  non-English speakers and translation in, 158–159
  obstetric care with, 417, 426
  oral, 159–160
  paternalism of physician and, 149
  patient's expectations and, 156–157
  physician-patient relationship and, 4, 51
  reproductive care and, 371
  school doctor and, 457, 459
  sports and injuries and, 453
  sterilization and, 379, 380, 381–382
  surgery and, 530–533
  surrogacy contract and, 364
  teaching programs and, 256, 257
  therapeutic exception to, 147–148
  voluntariness of, 154–155
  withheld information and, 148, 149
Injunction, 13
Insider trading, 209
Institutional review boards (IRBs), 193, 195–197
Institutional practice, 451–465
  consultations within, 242–244
  critical points for, 451
  physician's legal relationship with, 5
  proxy consent for, 169
  referrals to, 237
  school doctor and, 455–460
  teams and, 452–455
  See also Hospitals; Prisons; Teaching institutions; *and specific institutions*
Insurance companies
  abandonment of patient and, 122–123
  attorney fees and, 16, 58
  collateral source rule and, 46–47
  college students and, 460
  damages payment by, 47, 48
  fraud and abuse settlement coverage by, 136
  HIV testing and, 329
  incentive schemes from, 124, 128
  malpractice data from, 80–81
  obstetric care and, 422, 423
  pediatric care and, 444
  physician-patient relationship and contracts with, 119
  referrals and, 237
  rehabilitation expenses and, 43
  service of process receipt and, 19–20
  subrogation provision and, 47
  See also Malpractice insurance companies; Third-party payers
Intensive care medicine, 176, 186, 218, 244
Intentional abandonment, 122
Intentional torts, 67, 74
Internal Revenue Service (IRS), 14, 72–73
International classification of disease, revision 9 (ICD-9), 52, 293
International codes on medical research, 190–193
Interrogatories, 29, 30
Intoxication, reporting of, 296–297, 463
Intrauterine devices (IUDs), 373, 375

In vitro fertilization (IVF)
  embryo custody after divorce and, 358–360
  unmarried couples and, 404
  See also Fertility treatment
Invoking the rule, 23
Isolation, in disease control, 301, 311–312
IUDs, 373, 375

Joint Commission on Accreditation of Healthcare Organizations (JCAHO), 35, 98, 104–109, 261, 281
Joint research agreements, 189
Joint ventures. *See* Business ventures
Judgment in trial, 25–26
Judges, role of, 6
Justice Department, 134, 140

Kaposi's sarcoma, 316, 317
Kidnapping, and adoption, 356

Labor
  emergency care during, 504
  fetal monitors during, 508, 509–510
  induction of, 422, 423
Laboratories
  ownership by physicians of, 131–132
  protocols for, 225
  research in. *See* Medical research
Laser surgery, 531
Law
  difference between finding and making, 6
  origins of, 5–7
  professional paradigm for, 3
  types of, 10–14
  See also Federal laws; Medicare/Medicaid laws; State laws; *and specific laws*
Law audit, 60–62
Law enforcement reporting, 295–296
Lawyers. *See* Attorneys
Legal education, 56–57
Legal privilege, 37
Legal records, and discovery, 37
Legal standards, 64–77
  critical points about, 64
  importance of, 76–77
  product liability and, 75–76
  proving malpractice in, 64–75
Legal system, 3–14
  appellate process in, 6–7
  critical points about, 3
  federal court system and, 8–9
  litigation bias in, 7
  relationships within, 4–5
  role of judges in, 6
  sovereignty determination in, 9–10
  state court system and, 9
Legitimacy
  assumption of, 351–352
  determination of, 349, 353, 399

Letter of termination, 125
Levonorgestrel implants, 375–376
Liability
  communicable diseases and, 334–335
  disease reporting and, 309
  emergency care and, 498
  hospital employees and, 74
  hospital ownership and, 131
  referrals and, 238–23
  vicarious, 72
Libel, 264
Licensing
  adoption and, 351
  delegation of authority by physician and, 216, 217
  disease control reporting and, 301, 308
  emergency care and, 497–498
  laws regulating, 73
  medical device users and, 529
  nurses and, 73, 218
  peer review and, 265
  physician extenders (PEs) and, 73, 227
  reproductive medicine counseling and, 369
  residents and, 251–252, 255
  rights of physician under, 129–130
Life support system termination
  clear-and-convincing-evidence standard in, 178, 179
  Cruzan case and, 177–182, 185–187
  duty to counsel in, 181–182
  ethical issues regarding, 174–177
  families and, 7, 176, 180, 186–187
  hospitals and, 176
  judicial intervention in, 13, 184–185
  legal aspects of, 7
  patient's wishes in, 179, 181, 183–184, 187
  persistent vegetative state and, 180
  physician's advisory role in, 51
  right to, 174
  society's interests in, 176–177
  See also Refusal of medical care
Limited-code orders, 519
Limited engagement doctrine, 51–52
Litigation, 15–28
  alternative dispute resolution (ADR) instead of, 26–28
  cost of, 15–18, 40
  critical points about, 15
  discovery in, 29
  emotional impact of, 15, 62
  informed consent requirements and, 153
  legal system bias toward, 3, 7
  making a claim in, 19–20
  medical records in, 96
  peer review and, 263
  privileged communication under, 36–38
  See also Court system; Trial
Living will
  critical care unit (CCU) and, 518

emergency rooms and, 504–505
proxy consent using, 163, 179, 181, 183
Locality rule, 69–70
Lost earnings, 41–42, 46
Lump sum damage payments, 47–48

Maintenance organizations. *See* Health maintenance organizations (HMOs)
Malpractice
  alternative dispute resolution (ADR) in, 26, 27–28
  anesthesia and, 79, 522, 525, 526, 527
  artificial insemination and, 404
  breach of contract and, 65, 71–72
  buying insurance for, 93
  changing nature of coverage for, 90–91
  court system and, 9, 12
  crisis in, 79–94
  critical points about, 79
  damage awards in, 13
  defensive medicine and, 84–86
  delegation of authority and, 216
  disease control reporting and, 301, 308
  duty of physician in, 65, 237
  emergency care and, 504
  insurance company data in, 80–81
  litigation bias and, 7
  myths of, 81–84
  obstetric care and, 82, 88–89, 412, 415
  occupational medicine and, 468
  prison doctor and, 460
  proving, 64–75
  referrals and, 237
  research problems in, 79–80
  sexual assault and, 68, 132
  specialty focus and, 86
Malpractice insurance companies, 86–93
  alternative dispute resolution (ADR) and, 27–28
  buying insurance from, 93
  changing nature of coverage and, 90–91
  claims-made policy from, 90
  competition and, 89–90
  conflicts of interest of, 91
  damages paid by, 23
  laboratory ownership by physician and, 132
  medical research and, 189
  occupational medicine and, 468
  rates set by, 83, 87–88, 445
  regulation of, 86–87, 89–90
  reserves of, 87–88
  sexual assault claims paid by, 68
  tail coverage from, 90, 93
  teaching programs and, 254
  tort reform and, 83–84
  trial costs and, 24, 59
  trial representation provided by, 91–93
  underwriting standards and, 88–89
Malpractice litigation, 22
  adoption and, 356

  attorney conflict of interest in, 59
  attorney fees in, 53, 57, 59
  conflicts of interest in, 91
  costs of, 24, 40
  damage awards in, 23, 42, 44, 45, 46, 92
  depositions in, 30
  discovery in, 29, 36
  emotional distress claims in, 45
  expert witnesses in, 21–22, 69
  independent representation in, 91–93
  medical expenses in, 44
  medical records in, 96
  patient's expectations and, 156
  pediatric care and, 444, 445
  peer review of settlements of, 274–276
  preexisting illness and, 42
  prima facie case in, 20, 64–65
  punitive damages in, 46
  risk of being sued in, 81
Managed care plans, 138, 218–219, 239, 263. *See also* Health maintenance organizations (HMOs); Preferred provider organizations (PPOs)
Marketing, and obstetric care, 412–413
Market share
  choice of provider and, 130–131
  peer review and, 266–267
Marriage
  abortion, sterilization, and contraception decisions and, 371
  domestic violence reporting in, 296
  fertility treatment and, 404
  genetic counseling and, 400
  sterilization of partner in, 380
  See also Husbands; Wives
Master-servant relationship, 72
Material nonpublic information, 208
Material safety data sheet (MSDS), 492–493
Maternal serum alpha-fetoprotein (MSAFP), 395–396, 414
Measles, 303
Mediation, 27
Medicaid. *See* Medicare/Medicaid laws; Medicare/Medicaid programs
Medical businesses. *See* Business ventures
Medical care standard. *See* Standard of care
Medical devices, and product liability, 75–76
Medical education, 56
Medical expenses, in calculation of damages, 42, 43–44
Medical insurance. *See* Insurance companies; Malpractice insurance companies
Medical malpractice. *See* Malpractice
Medical practice
  as a business, 128–129
  legal relationships in, 4
  models of, 121

562　Index

Medical practice—*Continued*
peer review and, 260
protocols in, 223
quality assurance program for, 229–230
regulation of, 217. *See also* Regulations
teaching programs and, 254–257
Medical records, 95–110
alterations for, 95, 99–100
basic information in, 95–96, 98
consistency of, 99
contraception counseling for minors and, 378–379
critical care unit (CCU) and, 509
critical points about, 95
as defensible record, 96–97
destruction of, 101–102
development and growth of child on, 439–440
discovery process before trial and, 30, 31, 32, 33
disease control reporting and, 307
historical perspective on, 97
HIV testing and, 329
hospital records as, 104–109
informal consultations documented in, 118
informed consent documented in, 105, 158, 162
as legal document, 95–96
legal requirements covering, 35–36, 98–99
maintaining, 98–102
malpractice litigation and, 96–97
of minors, 103, 162, 168, 378–379
obstetric care and, 415–416
occupational health and, 485–486, 487–492
off-chart records as, 102–103
office records as, 97–104
pediatric care and, 432, 438–440
peer review and, 282
police access to, 297–298
preemployment medical examination and, 476, 477
primary uses for, 97
protection of, 100, 491–492
readability of, 99
refusal of care documented in, 182
release of, 95, 103–104, 488–489
retention of, 100–101, 477
selling or transfer of, 104, 124
statutory requirements affecting, 101
subpoena of, 33
telephone calls documented in, 116, 118, 441
termination of care documented in, 124–126
Medical research, 82, 189–210
children and, 204–206
contracts covering, 13
controversial nature of, 189

critical points about, 189
disease registries and, 295
fraud and misconduct in, 206–208
HHS regulation on, 193–207
informed consent for, 192, 197–200, 205–206
institutional review boards (IRBs) and, 195–197
international codes covering, 190–193
malpractice data from, 79–80
NSF regulations on, 207–208
ownership of data from, 210
pregnant women and, 200–204
prisoners and, 196, 202–204, 463
security law on, 208–210
Medical schools, 56, 208, 209. *See also* Teaching institutions
Medical staff committees, 259, 261–262
Medical students, 252–253
abortion, sterilization, and contraception training of, 369–370
fraud and, 251
legal status of, 253
patient introduction to, 250
supervision of, 249, 255–256
Medicare/Medicaid laws, 9
business-as-usual approach to, 135–136
fraud and abuse under, 128, 132–134
Health Care Finance Administration (HCFA) regulations and, 14
obstetric care under, 421
politics of prosecution in, 136–137
safe harbor regulations and, 134–135
Medicare/Medicaid programs, 8
life support under, 175
medical records retention under, 101
reimbursements under, 137
teaching programs and, 254
Medicine, professional paradigm for, 3
Mental impairment
HIV infection and, 344–345
reproductive care and, 371
sterilization and, 368, 380
Midwife
classes of, 245
consultations and referrals with, 232, 244–246
delegation of authority to, 218
Mini-trials, 27
Minors
abortion, birth control, and pregnancy information for, 170, 171, 187, 377–379, 386, 395
communicable disease treatment for, 170, 171
consent issues for, 147, 162, 167–171, 441
emancipated, 171
family circumstances and decision making regarding, 168–169
guardianship for, 169

Index   563

institutional practice and, 451
legal status of, 168, 171
obstetric care for, 417
parental conflict regarding, 169–170
parents' legal rights over decisions regarding, 167–168
proxy consent for, 168
release of medical records and, 103
statutory right to treat, 170–171
sterilization of, 368, 380
substance and drug abuse treatment for, 170, 171
See also Children, treatment of
Model Penal Code, 139
Monetary damages. *See* Damages
Mothers
addiction of, 354
adoption and, 355
artificial insemination and, 351
diseases of, 420
embryo donors and, 354
fathers and medical decisions of, 351
surrogacy contracts and, 358, 361–365
See also Obstetric care; Pregnancy
Motion for production, 32

National Institute for Occupational Safety and Health (NIOSH), 486, 492
National Practitioner Databank, 80, 271
National Science Foundation (NSF), and medical research, 207–208
Natural family planning, 376
Nature of risk, with communicable diseases, 340
Neglect of child, 171, 432, 442
Negligence
causation and, 72
preventive law audit for, 60
prima facie case of, 20
product liability and, 75, 76
res ipsa loquitur doctrine and, 66
Negligence per se, 66–67, 308
Neural tube defects, screening for, 395–396, 414
Neuromuscular development, 440
No-code orders, 519
Nonphysician personnel
referrals to, 236–237
sports staff and, 454
See also Physician-employee relationship *and specific types of employees*
Nuremberg Code, 190–191, 192
Nuremberg Doctrine, 146, 148, 175
Nurse-anesthetists, 222, 526–527, 531
Nurse-midwives, 245
Nurse-practitioners, 218
Nurses
attending physician and, 74–75
critical care unit (CCU) and, 517
delegation of authority to, 218–219
licensing of, 73, 218

medical records and, 97, 102
physician's legal relationship with, 4
public health and, 312
school doctor and, 455, 457
surgery and, 524
teaching institutions and, 253–254
Nursing care plan, 228
Nursing diagnosis, 228–229
Nutrition, termination of. *See* Life support system termination

Obstetric care, 412–428
behavioral risks in pregnancy and, 424–427
birth-injured infant and, 427–428
birth plan in, 416–419
critical points about, 412
evaluation of mother's medical condition in, 419–421
home deliveries and, 421–422
malpractice and, 82, 88–89, 412, 415
marketing of, 412–413
medical interventions in, 422–424
refusal to treat by, 119
structured approach to, 413–416
surrogate parenthood and, 408–409
zero-defects management in, 414
Occupational medicine, 451, 467–482
Americans with Disabilities Act (ADA) and, 474–482
critical points about, 467, 484
legal and ethical problems in, 467–469
material safety data sheet (MSDS) in, 492–493
medical record information and, 485–486, 487–492
physician-patient relationship in, 469–474
preemployment medical examination and, 471, 476–479
release from work certification in, 472–473
return to work certification and, 471–472
trade secrets and, 493–494
worker's compensation and, 481–482
Occupational Safety and Health Administration (OSHA), 484–494
communicable diseases in the workplace and, 341
critical points about, 484
medical records retention and, 101, 485–486, 491–492
occupational medicine and, 468, 472, 484–494
Office, medical records, 97–104
Office of the Inspector General (OIG), Department of Health and Human Services, 134, 136, 137
Operating room, surgeon's authority in, 75

564 Index

Oral contraceptives
  HIV infection and, 322
  informed consent for, 373
  legally mandated warnings on, 373–375
  privacy on decisions on, 371
  religious beliefs and use of, 220
  See also Contraception
Oral deposition, 31–32
Oral informed consent, 159–160
Orders
  critical care unit (CCU) and, 518–519
  delegation of authority with, 221–223
  direct, 222–223
  limited, 519
  medical records and, 102, 106–107
  medical students and writing of, 253
  no-code, 519
  preprinted, 222
  public health, 290
  standing, 218, 222
OSHA. See Occupational Safety and Health Administration (OSHA)
Ostensible agency, 456
Ownership
  of hospitals, 131
  of laboratories, 131–132
  of research data, 210

Pain, damage awards for, 42, 44–45
Pan American Health Organization, 305
Paramedical personnel, 4–5, 499–500
Parental rights, 349–365
  adoption and, 355–356
  assumption of legitimacy in, 351–352
  baby-selling and, 356
  child abuse and, 442
  critical points about, 349
  immunization programs and, 434
  legal aspects of, 350–358
  legitimacy determination and, 349, 353
  medical treatment of children and, 168–169, 354–355
  surrogacy and, 358–365, 407–409
  termination of, 353–355
  unfitness and, 354
Parents
  child abuse and, 295–296
  college health programs and, 460
  conflict between children and, 170
  conflict over treatment decisions by, 169–170
  contraception counseling for minors and, 378–379, 386
  custody arrangements and, 168–169
  drug abuse treatment and, 171
  guardianships and, 165, 166, 169
  proxy consent for care from, 169
  refusal of medical care for child by, 166, 167
  sports and injuries and, 453–454
  suspicion of child abuse and, 169
  See also Surrogate parenthood
Parker v. Brown immunity, 267
Partner notification, 326
Paternity
  assuming legitimacy of children and, 352–353
  determination of, 349, 353, 399
  genetic counseling and, 399
Pathologists, 117, 243–244, 428. See also Specialists
Patient dumping, 67, 237, 501
Patient education, and HIV infection, 321–322, 326
Patients, 111–211
  ability to pay fees by, 118–119, 122–123, 249, 257, 444
  as consumers, 81–81, 156
  physician right to refuse, 114, 118–119
  See also Physician-patient relationship
Patient Self-Determination Act of 1990, 181
Patient's rights movement, 4
Pediatric care, 432–445
  child abuse seen in, 441–443
  consent in, 441
  critical points about, 432
  immunizations and, 432–438
  interests of child versus parents in, 443–444
  malpractice litigation and, 444
  records in, 438–440
  school doctor and, 455
  statutes of limitations in, 444–445
  telephone calls in, 440–441
  unique legal aspects of, 432
Peer review, 259–269
  bias issues in, 280
  critical points about, 259, 271
  definition of, 259
  documenting, 281–282
  Health Care Quality Improvement Act on, 268, 271–282
  historical context for, 259–260
  hospital medical staff committees and, 261–262
  legal climate for, 262–268
  RICO litigation covering, 140–141, 268
  standard of care and, 76
  standards for conducting, 272–273
Performance enhancement drugs, 454–455
Per se violation of antitrust law, 266
Personal injury litigation, 42
Personal knowledge test for business records, 35, 98
Physician assistants, 4, 73
Physician-employee relationship
  borrowed-servant doctrine in, 74
  captain-of-the-ship doctrine in, 75
  contracts and, 13

control in, 73
employment criteria set out in, 74
as legal relationship, 4
method of payment and, 72–73
scope of employment and, 73–75
vicarious liability and, 72
Physician extenders (PEs)
delegation of authority to, 215, 220
documentation of work of, 229
drug prescription by, 219
licensing of, 73
nursing diagnosis and, 228–229
supervision of, 217, 227–228
use of term, 215
Physician fees, 129
patient inability to pay, 118–119, 122–123
Physician-patient relationship, 113–126
abandonment of patient in, 122–123, 257
abortion, sterilization, and contraception counseling and, 369–370
attorney-client relationship different from, 50–51
backup coverage and, 122, 123
consultations and, 239–240
criminal activity and, 11
critical points about, 113
disease control and, 304–305
duty of physician in, 65, 113, 119–120, 123, 142
emergency care and, 119
establishment of, 113–120
expectation of continued treatment in, 121–122
fiduciary relationship in, 128, 129–131
follow-up on missed appointments in, 123, 125–126
independent medical judgment in, 114–118
informal consultations and, 118
informed consent and, 145, 186, 187
as legal relationship, 4, 113
occupational medicine and, 469–474
paternalistic aspect of, 51
pediatric care and, 442–443
privileged information in, 36–37
referrals in, 121
refusal of care and, 174
romantic attachments in, 132
specialists and, 117–118, 120–121
surgery and, 522–523
teaching programs and, 256
telephone calls and, 115–116, 440
terminal illness and, 187
termination of patient in, 122–126
termination of physician in, 124
treatment recommendations and, 114, 115–116
walk-in patients and, 116–117
Physician-player relationship, 452–453

Physician-prisoner relationship, 461
Physician's orders. *See* Orders
Placenta analysis, 427, 428
Plagues, 303, 318
Pleading, 20–21
Pneumocytis carinii pneumonia, 317, 342
Police, and reporting, 295–296
Polio, 301, 302
Political factors
abortion and, 383
immunization programs and, 432–433
Medicare/Medicaid law prosecution and, 136–137
Power of attorney, 162–163, 459
Practice. *See* Medical practice
Predicate act, 137
Preembryos, custody of, 358–360, 403. *See also* Fertility treatment
Preemployment medical examination, 471, 476–479
Preferred provider organizations (PPOs), 259
incentive plans under, 138–139
market factors in choice of, 130
peer review in, 140, 141
physician-patient relationship and contracts in, 120
Pregnancy
divorce during, 355
duty to counsel in, 394–395
emergency care and, 504
high-risk, 426
medical research during, 200–204
midwifes and, 244–246
minors and information on, 171
past-term, 423
refusal of care during, 184, 421, 422
risk analysis in, 417–418
self-destructive behavior during, 426–427
testing for, 419–420
work-place acquired infection and, 334–335, 341
work-place discrimination against, 48–481
See also Fertility treatment; Obstetric care
Prenatal care
diagnostic procedures during, 398
screening programs in, 413–414
structure medical records in, 97
See also Genetic counseling; Obstetric care
Preponderance of evidence standard, 10
Prescription practices
development and hormonal techniques and, 455
licensure and rights under, 129, 130
medical students and, 253
performance enhancement in sports and, 454–455

Prescription practices—*Continued*
  state regulation of, 131, 219
  telephone calls and, 115
  treatment of family members and, 131
Preventive law audit, 60–62
Prima facie case, 20, 36, 64–65
Prisons
  adequacy of care in, 461
  disease control in, 464
  emergency care in, 463
  medical research in, 196, 202–204, 463
  physician in, 451, 460–465
  privacy and medical information in, 298
  public health and, 463–464
Privacy of patient
  abortion and, 383–384
  consultations and, 234
  contraception, sterilization, and abortion decisions and, 368, 371
  disease control and, 304, 308, 310, 343
  genetic counseling and, 395
  police access to records and, 298
  prison doctor and, 461
  public health and, 290
  sexual history taking and, 372
Private attorney general laws, 264
Private placement adoption, 350, 356
Privileged information, 36–38
Privileges, hospital staff, 239, 260, 263, 267
Procedural due process, 265–266
Process server, 19
Product liability, 75–76, 436, 528–529
Professional review organizations (PROs), 259
Proof, standard of, 11
Protocols
  critical care unit (CCU) and, 515
  delegation of authority with, 220–221, 223–227
  medical students and writing of, 253
  nursing staff and, 218
  sample text for, 224–227
  telephone calls in pediatric care and, 441
  use of term, 223
Proxy consent, 162–165, 168, 170, 441
Psychiatrists
  medical records and, 103
  physician-patient relationship for, 11
  sexual relationships between patients and, 132
Public health, 287–298
  AIDS and, 315–330
  communicable diseases in the workplace and, 332–345
  critical points about, 287
  disease control and, 301–313
  historical overview of, 287–289
  law enforcement reporting and, 295–298

  legal standards for, 289–291
  prison doctor and, 463–464
  reasonable-belief standard in, 290
  school doctor and, 455, 458–459
  state and physician and, 4
  vital statistics in, 291–295
Public health laws, 7
  coercive measures for disease control under, 309
  mandated treatment under, 147, 310–311
  prison doctor and, 464
  reporting under. *See* Reporting laws
Public Health Service (PHS), 189, 206–207, 381
Public policy
  informed consent and, 155
  surrogacy and, 363–364, 407–408
Pulse oximetry, 508, 510
Punitive damages, 45–46, 153

Quality assurance programs, 76, 229–230, 254
Quarantine
  disease control with, 301, 309, 311–312
  HIV infection and, 326–328
  precedents for, 7, 287
  public health and, 287

Racketeering Influenced Corrupt Organizations Act (RICO), 137–141
  business failure under, 141
  incentive plans under, 138–139
  mail and wire fraud under, 137–138
  patterns of racketeering under, 140
  peer review under, 140–141, 264, 268
  prosecution of claim under, 140–141
Racketeering laws, 9, 128
Radiologists, 117, 242–243. *See also* Specialists
Reasonable-belief standard, and public health, 290
Reasonable-person standard, and informed consent, 151–152
Record keeping
  adoption and, 356–358
  consultations and, 241–242
  preventive law audit of, 60
  statutory requirements affecting, 101
  See also Business records; Legal records; Medical records
Red Book, American Academy of Pediatrics, 435
Referrals, 235–239
  consultations differentiated from, 232
  continuing care and, 238
  critical points about, 232
  duty of physician regarding, 236–237
  to institutions, 237–238
  liability for, 238–239

Medicare/Medicaid regulations covering, 134–135
to nonphysician, 236–237
obstetric care and, 413
occupational medicine and, 469, 471
patient refusal of, 238–239
physician refusal of, 239
protocols for, 226–227
school doctor and, 458
specialists and, 120, 121, 235, 236
Refusal of medical care
by adult, 166
blood transfusions and, 443
by parent for child, 166, 443–444
by physician, 119, 256–257
pregnancy and, 184, 421, 422
prisoners and, 461–463
referrals and, 238–239
religious grounds for, 443
right to, 174
teaching institution and, 250
termination of life-support cases and, 184–185
See also Life support system termination
Registries
adoption records, 358
communicable diseases, 295
toxic effects of chemical substances, 486
Regular course of business test for business records, 34–35, 98
Regulations
administrative law and, 14
courts enforcing, 14
delegation of authority under, 216, 217
federal and state laws covering, 8
licenses under, 73
malpractice insurance business and, 86–87, 89–90
medical research and, 193–208
prison care and, 460–461
See also Medicare/Medicaid laws
Rehabilitation, and damage awards, 43
Rehabilitation Act, 336, 344, 475
Reissuance, 87
Relationships in law, 4–5, 113
Release from work certification, 472–473
Release of medical records
authorization for, 103–104
occupational medicine and, 488–489
refusal of, 103
Religious beliefs
abortion, sterilization, and contraception counseling and, 369–370, 384, 394
care for minors and, 166–167, 443
faith healers and, 219–220
immunization programs and, 434
refusal of medical care and, 167, 184
Remitted judgment, 26
Reporting laws

child abuse and neglect and, 169, 242, 295–296, 432, 441–442
consultation and, 242
disease control and, 171, 290, 295, 301, 304, 305–308, 458, 461, 464
HIV infection and, 325
immunization programs and, 436–437
law enforcement and, 295–296
malpractice data from, 80
midwives and, 245–246
peer review of settlements, 274–276
substance abuse and, 427
violent injuries and, 296
Reports, consultation, 242, 243
Reproduction
balancing physician's and patients' rights in, 369–370
ethical dilemmas in, 368–371
medicalization of, 349
parental rights and, 350
sexual history taking and, 371–372
surrogacy and, 358
See also Artificial insemination (AI); Embryo transplantation; Fertility treatment; In vitro fertilization
Requests for admissions, 29, 30
Requests for production, 32
Research. See Medical research
Reserves, in malpractice insurance, 87–88
Residents, 249, 251–252
critical care unit (CCU) and, 518
death certificates and, 294
emergency room staffing by, 500
fraud and, 251
licensing of, 251, 252, 255
Res ipsa loquitur doctrine, 66
Respectable minority rule, 65–66
Respondeat superior, 72
Restatement of Torts, 75
Return to work certification, 471–472
Review of court judgment, 26
Review, peer. See Peer review
Rhythm method, 376
RICO. See Racketeering Influenced Corrupt Organizations Act (RICO)
Rights
to choose medical care, 145–146, 175, 249–250, 392
to choose physician, 234, 250
to counsel, 11–12
of licensed physician, 129–130
of parents to refuse care for children, 166, 167–168
to refuse treatment, 123, 147, 167
Risks
birth-injured infants and, 417, 427–428
communicable diseases in the workplace and, 336, 337, 338, 340
contraception and pregnancy and, 373
duration of, 340

Risks—*Continued*
  factors influencing patient's tolerance of, 157
  genetic counseling for, 391–392
  HIV infection and, 320–321, 343–345, 377
  informed consent regarding, 147–148, 149, 150, 154
  knowable and unknowable, 154
  nature of, 338
  pregnancy and, 417–418, 426
  preventive law audit for, 60–62
  teaching programs and management of, 254, 255
  withheld information concerning, 148
Rubella, 302, 420
RU 486 pill, 387

Safe harbor regulations, 134–135, 136, 142
Scheduling system, 123
School doctor, 455–460
  college students and, 459–460
  comprehensive care and, 460
  consent and, 457, 459
  duty to patient in, 459
  handicapped children and, 459
  medicines at, 457–458
  public health and, 458–459
  school clinics and, 456
  screening programs in, 458
School nurse, 455, 457
Screening
  artificial insemination and, 406
  emergency rooms and, 501–502
  HIV infection and, 327, 344, 407
  neural tube defects and, 395–396, 414
  neuromuscular development on, 440
  obstetric care with, 413–414
  preemployment medical examination and, 478–479
  prison doctor and, 464
  school doctor and, 458
  tuberculosis and, 340, 341–342
Security law, and medical research, 189, 20–210
Service of process, 19
Severity of communicable diseases, 340
Sex education, 321
Sexual abuse, reporting of, 296
Sexual assault by physician, 68
Sexual history, taking of, 371–372
Sexually transmitted diseases (STDs), 339
  contraception counseling and, 376–377
  risk for, 378
Sherman Antitrust Act, 262, 266
Sickle cell trait, 406
Significant risk of substantial harm, 336, 337
Slander, 264

Smallpox, 289, 310
Social Security Administration, 14
Society
  physician's role defined in, 4
  life support system termination and, 176–177, 185
Special education programs, 459
Specialists
  emergency care and, 499
  expert witness qualifications and, 69
  informed consent and, 151
  locality rule and, 70
  malpractice litigation and, 86
  physician-patient relationship and, 117–118, 120
  referrals to, 120, 121, 235, 236
  technology-oriented medicine and, 84
Sperm banks, 405, 406
Spontaneous abortions, 402
Sports medicine, 452. *See also* Team doctor
Staff. *See* Physician-employee relationship *and specific types of employees*
Standard of care, 65–71
  competition and, 77
  critical care unit (CCU) and, 514
  distinctions among schools concerning, 69
  establishing, 68–71
  expert witness and, 66, 70–71, 76, 83
  intentional torts and, 67
  legal definition of, 65–66
  locality rule on, 69–70
  malpractice insurance and, 89
  negligence per se and, 66–67
  patient examinations and, 68
  res ipsa loquitur doctrine and, 66
  sexual assault by physician and, 68
  surgery and, 523
Standing orders, 218, 222
State, physician's relationship with, 4
State agencies, 14
State court system, 9
  administrative regulations enforced in, 14
  appellate process in, 6, 9
  definition of death by, 180
  malpractice data from, 80
  medical malpractice in, 9
  sovereignty of, 9–10
State laws
  ability to pay and right to care under, 249–250
  abortion and, 368, 392–393
  adoption and, 349, 350–351, 355, 356, 357
  artificial insemination in, 403, 404
  authority for medical decision making under, 73
  autopsies under, 295
  caps on lawyers' fees under, 17

collateral source rule and, 47
commercial bribery and incentive plans under, 139
communicable disease plan under, 341
definition of death under, 180, 294
delegation of authority and, 216, 217, 220
emancipated minor under, 171
emergency care under, 67, 166, 170, 497–498
faith healers under, 219
fertility treatment and, 403
HIV infection and, 325, 326–327
immunization programs and, 434, 458
informed consent under, 151–152, 153, 186
legitimacy determination in, 349, 353
licensing under, 227, 497–498
life support system termination and, 177, 181
locality rule in, 70
malpractice insurance under, 86, 87–88, 89
medical care for minors under, 166, 169, 170–171
medical practice under, 217
medical records under, 101, 104
midwives under, 244, 245
occupational medicine and, 468
origins of, 5–6
parental rights and, 350, 354
peer review under, 263–264
physician-patient relationship in, 4
power of attorney to consent to medical care under, 163, 164
prescription regulation under, 131, 219, 454
public health authority under, 289–290, 309
refusal of care under, 183
regulation of medical practice under, 8
religious beliefs and medical care under, 166
reporting under. *See* Reporting laws
sports and athletics under, 453
status of physicians created by, 4
substance abuse and, 427
trial judgments under, 26
vital health statistics under, 291 293, 357
worker's compensation in, 473–474
State taxes, 72–73
Sterilization, 368, 379–383
federal law requirements on, 381–383
informed consent for, 379, 380, 381–382
minors and mentally impaired patients and, 368, 380
Steroids, and sports, 454
Stock fraud, and medical research, 189, 20–210

Strict liability, 75
Structured settlement of damage awards, 48
Students. *See* College students; Medical students; School doctor
Subjects in medical research
children as, 195
definition of, 194
HHS regulations covering, 193–206
See also Medical research
Subpoena, 32–33
Subpoena duces tecum, 29, 33
Subrogation agreement, 47
Substance abuse
medical records of treatment of, 101
minors and, 170, 171
preemployment medical examination and, 478–479
pregnancy and, 425, 427
testing and reporting of, 297
Substantive due process, 265
Substituted consent
definition of, 174
drawbacks of, 186–187
Supervision, 129
consultation and, 242
of physician extenders (PEs), 217, 227–228
physician-physician legal relationship in, 5
school doctor and, 455–456
sports and athletics and, 454
teaching institutions and, 249, 251, 253, 255–256
Supreme Court, 6, 138, 163, 171, 329, 368, 369, 434, 462
abortion and, 141, 368, 383, 385, 386, 387, 392
federal court system and, 8–9
disabilities legislation and, 336, 338, 340, 342
parental rights and, 352, 354
peer review and, 260, 266–267, 267–268
public health and, 288, 289–290, 291
right to counsel and, 11, 12
terminal illness and treatment and, 174, 177, 179–180, 185, 187
Supreme courts, state, 9
Surgery, 522–525
anesthesiologists and, 530–533
consent for, 530–533
critical points about, 522
experimental treatments with, 531–532
operating room team and, 75
standards for, 523–525
Surgical assistants, 524–525
Surrogate parenthood, 358–365
American College of Obstetrics and Gynecology (ACOG) on, 407–409
Baby M case and, 361–365

Surrogate parenthood—*Continued*
  consent and, 162
  divorce and preembryos in, 358–360
  parental rights and, 349
Syphilis, 318, 319, 320, 420

Tail insurance coverage, 90, 93
Take nothing judgment, 25–26
Taxation, and method of employee payment, 72–73
Tay-Sachs disease, 397
Teaching institutions, 249–257
  conflicts between legal norms and medical practice in, 254–257
  critical points about, 249
  faculty physicians in, 250–251
  medical students, residents, and fellows in, 251–254
  patients' rights and, 249–251
  personal knowledge test for medical records and, 35
  physician-student relationship in, 256–257
  supervision in, 249, 251, 255–256
  teaching protocols in, 224
Team doctor, 452–455
  children as athletes and, 453–454, 458
  performance enhancement and, 454–455
  physician-play relationship in, 452–453
  role of, 452
Technology-oriented medicine. *See* High-technology medicine
Telephone calls
  pediatric care and, 440–441
  physician-patient relationship and, 115
  treatment recommendations and, 115–116, 118
Temporary injunction, 13
Terminal illnesses
  autonomy of patients with, 187
  refusal to accept treatment for, 167
  withheld information about, 149
Termination of life support system. *See* Life support system termination
Testimony
  expert witnesses and, 21–22
  laboratory ownership by physician and, 131–132
  at trial, 23
Testing
  artificial insemination and, 406
  consultations for evaluation of, 233, 234, 240–241, 242–243
  defensive medicine against malpractice and, 85–86
  delegation of authority to evaluate, 221
  disease control and, 305, 309–310
  for drug use, 192–193, 297, 298
  genetic counseling with, 393, 395–396, 398
  HIV infection and, 324–325, 357, 372
  incentive plans and conflicts in, 138–139
  intoxication and, 296–296
  multiple test panels used in, 85–86
  occupational medicine and, 471
  paternity and, 353
  performance enhancement drugs and, 455
  for pregnancy, 419–420
  specialist evaluation and, 117
  window period in, 326
Third-party payers
  abortion, sterilization, and contraception counseling and, 370–371
  consultations and, 234, 239
  life support system termination and, 176, 186
  peer review and, 259
  physician-patient relationship and, 4
  teaching programs and, 255, 257
  See also Malpractice insurance companies
Timely entry test for business records, 35–36, 98
Tortious interference, 264
Torts, 10, 11, 45, 75, 516
  alternative dispute resolution (ADR) for, 26
  damages in, 40
  genetic counseling and, 390–393
  intentional, 67, 74
  midwives and, 246
  need for reform of, 83–84
  workplace infection and, 335
Tracking system for medical records, 100–101
Trade secrets, 493–494
Training
  abortion, sterilization, and contraception counseling and, 369–370
  damage awards and need for, 43
  midwives and, 244, 245
  occupational medicine and, 468
  right to practice medicine and, 129
Transcription of patient notes, 35, 99
Transmission of communicable diseases, 338–339, 340–341
Treatment decisions
  alternative treatments in, 152
  court-mandated, 147, 298, 310–311
  fraud regulations covering, 153
  incentive plans and conflicts in, 138–139
  paternalism of physician and, 149
  patient's right to refuse recommendations in, 123
  by physician of own family, 131
  physician's advisory role in, 51
  protocols for, 225–226
  telephone calls and, 115–116, 440–441

withheld information concerning, 148, 149
   See also Life support system termination; Refusal of medical care
Triage, and critical care unit (CCU), 515–516
Trial (court), 22–25
   adversarial aspect of, 18–19
   attacking defendant or plaintiff in, 24
   costs of, 24–25
   cross-examination in, 33–36
   delays and progress of, 22, 25
   discovery before, 29
   focus on people in, 23–24
   judgment rendered in, 25–26
   pleading in, 20–21
   preparing for, 18–22, 25, 65
   procedures after, 25–26
   surviving, 25
   witnesses in, 21–22
Trials, in drug testing, 193
Tuberculosis, 301, 311, 315
   carriers of, 309, 310
   drug-resistant, 7, 291, 312, 334
   HIV infection risks in, 343–345
   prison doctor and, 463, 464
   screening for, 340, 341–342
   workplace infection with, 335, 336, 340, 342
Twins, and fertility treatment, 402–403
Typhoid, 303–304, 309, 326, 334

Underwriting, in malpractice insurance, 88–89
Unfitness of parents, 354
Universities
   medical research in, 189, 208–210
   student health programs in, 459–460
Urine testing for drugs, 455

Vaccine Compensation Act, 432, 436–438
Vaccinations
   public health and, 289
   smallpox and, 289
Vasectomy, 380. *See also* Sterilization
Venereal disease, 319
   college students and, 460
   of minors, 171
   reporting of, 171
   treatment of, 171, 298

Vicarious liability, 72
Videotape deposition, 31
Violent injuries, reporting of, 296
Vital statistics, 291–295
Volunteers, and school doctor, 455, 456

Wages, damages and lost, 41–42, 46
Waiver
   college health programs and, 460
   informed consent requirements and, 153
   of parental rights in adoption, 355
   worker's compensation claim with, 470
Wards, 165, 206. *See also* Guardianship
Washington Manual of Medical Therapeutics, 224
Weight loss clinics, 153
Western blot test, 325
Wire fraud, 137–138, 268
Witnesses, 21–22
   cross-examination of, 33–36
   establishing qualifications of, 22
   hearsay rule and, 34
   informed consent documented by, 160
   invoking the rule and, 23
   See also Expert witnesses
Wives
   abortion, sterilization, and contraception decisions and, 371
   power of attorney to consent to medical care and, 163–164
Women, sexual history taking with, 371–372
Worker's compensation insurance, 73
   confidentiality in, 470
   disabled workers and, 334, 481–482
   occupational medicine physician and, 468, 473–474
   subrogation provision in, 47
Workplace
   communicable diseases in, 332–334
   HIV infection risks in, 343–345
   immunosuppressed workers and, 342–343
   screening tests in, 341–342, 344
   transmission modes in, 338–339, 340–341
World Health Organization, 304, 435
World Medical Association, 190, 191–192
Wrongful birth action, 391
Wrongful life claim, 391